You'll Be Able To...

- ☑ Educate yourself before you buy
- ☑ Understand software upgrades
- ☑ Get familiar with the parts of your computer
- ☑ Learn about drivers
- ☑ Create a backup disk
- ☑ Open up your computer safely
- ☑ Evaluate how much RAM you have, and how much you need
- ☑ Install a new CPU
- ☑ Install a new hard drive step by step
- ☑ Configure the BIOS
- ☑ Install a disk drive
- ☑ Install an internal tape drive
- ☑ Install a high-capacity storage device
- ☑ Install a CD-ROM drive
- ☑ Install a DVD-ROM drive
- ☑ Install a sound card
- ☑ Install a new graphics card
- ☑ Install a new monitor
- ☑ Install an internal or an external modem
- ☑ Choose and install a keyboard
- ☑ Learn about your options with input devices
- ☑ Learn about infrared technology
- ☑ Use voice-recognition software
- ☑ Install a printer
- ☑ Install a parallel port or SCSI-interface scanner
- ☑ Learn about ports
- ☑ Install a SCSI adapter, an I/O port, or a USB port
- ☑ Judge the need for a new motherboard
- ☑ Install a motherboard step by step
- ☑ Install a new power supply
- ☑ Decide what to upgrade on your portable computer
- ☑ Understand the nuts and bolts of networks
- ☑ Build your own PC
- ☑ Try out DVD technology
- ☑ Find the best compression utility
- ☑ Upgrade your operating system
- ☑ Dual-boot operating systems
- ☑ Troubleshoot all your new components
- ☑ Use helpful tips on all your new components

PC UPGRADING & MAINTENANCE

NO EXPERIENCE REQUIRED

PC UPGRADING & MAINTENANCE

NO EXPERIENCE REQUIRED™

SECOND EDITION

Smart Computing

San Francisco • Paris • Düsseldorf • Soest • London

Associate Publisher: Gary Masters
Contracts and Licensing Manager: Kristine O'Callaghan
Acquisitions & Developmental Editor: Gary Masters
Editor: Davina Baum
Book Designers: Patrick Dintino, Catalin Dulfu, Maureen Forys, Robin Kibby
Electronic Publishing Specialist: Maureen Forys, Happenstance Type-O-Rama
Production Coordinator: Blythe Woolston
Indexer: Matthew Spence
Cover Designer: Design Site
Cover Illustrator/Photographer: Design Site

Library of Congress Card Number: 98-83176
ISBN: 0-7821-2471-2

Manufactured in the United States of America

10 9 8 7 6 5 4 3 2 1

Contents at a Glance

Table of Contents

Introduction

Personal computers are a peculiar type of appliance. They have few moving parts, so they last a long time. But product development in computers is so rapid, the minute you buy your PC it starts to fall behind the technology curve.

The weird juxtaposition of longevity and light-speed obsolescence creates a problem for some computer owners: The system you buy today may not do everything you want it to do next year. Although the computer works just as well as it always did, technologically speaking, the rest of the world has passed it by.

At least it can seem that way. Actually, unless you have some compelling need to process information a bit faster, or do something via software that you couldn't do before, there's no reason to play a continual game of catch-up with your computer. You can keep on chugging away with your current PC until something new comes along that you really can't live without.

At that point, you'll have two choices:

- You can buy a new system with all the latest bells and whistles.
- You can upgrade—or add new capabilities to—your current PC.

Most people don't want to spend $2,000 every year buying a new computer, and that explains the popularity of upgrading. Adding a component or two to your computer is a relatively inexpensive way to greatly extend its useful life. Luckily, upgrading most components on a PC is not that difficult. It does help, though, if you have a knowledgeable friend available who can lend a hand.

That's where we come in. *PC Upgrading & Maintenance: No Experience Required* will take you step-by-step through the process of upgrading virtually every component on your computer. We explain the benefits of particular upgrades, how difficult they are, how long they take, what they cost, and which tools you'll need. We even walk you step-by-step through the upgrading process.

This book covers software upgrades as well, so if you're looking for some tips about upgrading applications, or want to know how to install a new operating system, you'll find it here. For those people who would like to get more out of their computers without having to worry about adding new hardware, we introduce some software alternatives to adding hardware.

All the material in this book is presented in an easy-to-read, plain-English style. Even if you're a fairly inexperienced computer user who has never "popped the top" off a PC, you'll be able to understand and follow along as we walk you through the upgrade process.

What Will You Learn from This Book?

This book aims to get you comfortable getting down and dirty with your computer. We will teach you how to understand the needs of your computer and judge what is best for you; that is, what will fit your budget *and* maximize the use of your computer. *PC Upgrading & Maintenance: No Experience Required* will guide you through a safe and effective installation of new hardware and software, including expanding performance with more RAM, or new hard drives, CPUs, and disk drives, bringing your computer into the latest technology via multimedia, video, modems, and operating systems, as well as going through the more prosaic everyday maintenance that every computer—like every car—needs in order to last longer.

Skill 1 will get you situated, and start you thinking about what's right for you, and how to go about getting what you need. Skill 2 will go more in depth on this issue and will get you familiar with the tools available to you in figuring out the capabilities of your system. A computer is an electrical appliance, however advanced. Safety is a big issue in any installation, and Skill 3 addresses it in a clear and easy-to-understand manner. Skill 3 will also show you how to back up your system, a handy thing if anything goes wrong! Skill 4 gets into the meat of the matter; the upgrading begins, with Random Access Memory. Skills 5, 6, and 7 continue in this manner, addressing the installation of CPUs, hard drives, and disk drives, all aimed at getting you the most efficient and fastest computer for your buck. We also cover high-capacity storage devices. Skills 8 and 9 get into the fun stuff: multimedia. These skills will ready your computer for the sights and sounds of the latest software. Skill 10 will delve into the other big topic of the day: the Internet. Installing a modem is the first step!

The next few skills will focus on the external stuff that will complement the technology booting up inside. Skill 11 will deal with keyboards, mice, and other input devices. Printers are covered in Skill 12, and Skill 13 deals with scanners. Skill 14 will make sure that you have all the right places to plug in your new hardware. Next, we'll get into the nitty-gritty. That aging PC can get a real boost with a new motherboard/processor upgrade; Skill 15 will equip you with the knowledge and proficiency you need. Skill 16 will guide you through installation of a new power supply. Skill 17 will focus on upgrading your PC Card for that laptop of yours. Skill 18 will move to the bigger picture, with instructions on how to set up an Ethernet network. Skill 19 will look into the viability and ease of actually building your own PC.

Skill 20 will go into how you can maximize the hard drive space that you do have. With all the space and speed that you will have, what next but Skill 21, in which you will learn what it takes to upgrade or change operating systems, as well as other software. Skill 22 will look at upgrading your BIOS for true cutting-edge performance.

Skill 23 will look at all the problems that typically arise, and the best way to deal with them. Finally, Skill 24 will cover all those little tips and tricks that the experts have discovered in their technical journeys. As you read, you'll see along the way many references to companies that can provide you with the hardware and software that we're talking about; in the appendix, you'll find a quick reference and an easy way to contact many of the biggest and best-known companies around.

Conventions Used in This Book

Here are some items that you will see nestled in these skills:

- When we ask you to type a word or a phrase, we'll put the word or phrase in **bold** font.
- New terminology can sometimes be confusing—particularly when you don't know that it's new. For this reason, we'll use *italics* to signal the first appearance of an important word or phrase.

These are some other elements that you will become familiar with:

NOTE NOTE NOTE NOTE NOTE NOTE NOTE NOTE NOTE NOTE NOTE NOTE NOTE NOTE NOTE

This is a Note. It provides a piece of additional information about a topic.

TIP TIP TIP TIP TIP TIP TIP TIP TIP TIP TIP TIP TIP TIP TIP TIP TIP TIP TIP TIP TIP TIP TIP TIP TIP

This is a Tip, which is intended to be a shortcut or a trick that helps you be more productive.

WARNING WARNING WARNING WARNING WARNING WARNING WARNING WARNING

This is a Warning. It indicates a condition or an action that could be potentially harmful to your work or your computer.

This Is a Sidebar

Occasionally, we'll discuss a topic that requires more space than a note. If putting the discussion into the main body of the text would disrupt the flow, we'll present it to you in a sidebar that looks like this.

Ready, Set...

No experience is required, but motivation and curiosity are. Upgrading your PC can increase your productivity at home and at the office (as well as letting you play the latest 3-D game). We hope this book helps you extend the useful life of your computer. Let's go!

SKILL 1

Getting Started

- Educating yourself before you buy
- Getting familiar with what you can upgrade
- Understanding software upgrades

A recent ad on a university electronic bulletin board repeated a sad story often told. "Free computer equipment," it said, letting readers know they could take whatever they wanted out of a particular hallway before it was picked up as garbage the next morning.

Such is the fate of countless old machines. It is estimated that some 15 million computers are disposed of each year in the United States by either dumping them in the trash, sending them to specialty recycling firms, or simply relegating them to the Storage Room of No Return. Fighting to keep up with the steady march of computer technology makes for an impossible battle. Yesterday's expensive electronic marvel is today's heap of slow-moving, cursed-at trash.

Nothing changes the inevitable life cycle of a computer in a significant way, but users can stave off the day of reckoning through upgrading. Replacing certain old components of a system with up-to-date counterparts is a way to give trusty old systems a second wind. Depending upon a user's specific needs, upgrading can be a much less expensive method to take advantage of the newest technology than purchasing an entire new system.

Bigger hard drives, extra random access memory (RAM), better video adapters, even new motherboards or central processing units (CPUs) can be installed by the average user. The process isn't always painless, but many people might be surprised about how big a difference a relatively easy operation can make in a tired computer's performance.

On the other hand, running an old machine better, stronger, and faster than it was before comes at a price. They don't give away those upgrading parts, and occasionally the most well-planned foray into system improvement brings on hours of frustration as new components struggle to be accepted by old components. There are choices to be made along the way to upgrading nirvana, and sometimes it is hard to know the best route until taking a few steps down the wrong path.

To Upgrade or Not to Upgrade

The shiny new computer parts in all those newspaper and magazine ads look tempting, but upgrading is not for everyone. Only you can decide if the advantages of a particular upgrade are worth the time and money that goes into making it work.

Even the oldest computers may not require upgrades if they meet your needs. That old 286 IBM PS/2 still makes a good basic word processor, for instance, and many people might say the formula for typing hasn't improved enough to warrant spending money to change. Buying something new will add a lot of gizmos, but chances are none of them will make you think better or write more lyrically. Just because something "better" is available doesn't necessarily mean the old machines are suddenly worthless.

Newer components, however, might allow your computer to perform tasks you didn't realize could be so easy. Better graphics, more storage space for data and software, substantially faster operation, and fancy sound playback are just a few of the reasons many people consider upgrading. Updated hardware might be necessary to keep up with multimedia software, stay compatible with friends and business associates, or to navigate the Internet at a reasonable speed.

Assessing Your Needs

The current market for new computers makes upgrading a more difficult choice than it once was. Prices for decent machines have fallen from the $2,000 neighborhood to $1,000 and even lower. Often, these sub-$1,000 PCs lack the bells and whistles of their more expensive brethren, but even relatively stripped-down models might be better than older computers with upgraded parts. While it once made financial sense to spend hundreds of dollars for upgrade parts rather than thousands of dollars for a new computer, the calculus today is different. It doesn't take long before an upgrade bill starts to approach new computer prices.

What this means is that upgrading makes the most sense for users who have specific needs their computers are not fulfilling. Usually, one or two upgrades will do the trick in such cases. For older computers that have all-around deficiencies, upgrading is a bigger chore and doesn't often compare favorably to simply getting a new computer.

The solution to the problem lies in knowing exactly where to spend upgrading resources and when to stop. One upgrade can easily lead to others. Programs that run thanks to your speedy new CD-ROM, for instance, can churn pretty slowly without some additional RAM. Many users confront this slippery slope of ever-increasing upgrade daydreams.

Set a Goal

It may be best to choose a realistic, limited goal and then explore the various alternatives to reach it. One idea for owners of older systems might be to review hardware requirements listed on boxes of software they want to run and compare them to the components they already have. If the price tag for making the necessary upgrades starts to get scary, forget the *a la carte* menu and take a look at new systems.

Another factor to consider is how much the old machine might be worth if it were sold to help buy a new model. These days, it is difficult to sell anything less than a Pentium-based computer, but you just never know what a classified ad might bring. Almost certainly a complete system will fetch a better price than selling parts as you upgrade piece by piece. Another reason for keeping the old system intact is to have a spare; even new computers aren't as reliable as their price tags indicate.

Technical Skills

This process of determining whether an upgrade is necessary should be the only barrier to actually trying it. Lack of technical expertise shouldn't stop people from upgrading if they believe their computing experience will benefit. Being handy with a lot of tools is not a requirement; a screwdriver generally is about as fancy as an upgrading job gets. The physical task itself is not difficult.

What can take up time and tax patience is convincing old components to be neighborly with the new arrivals. Some tasks, such as plugging in some new RAM, requires almost no finagling at all. Other jobs can whip up some hassles depending upon the age of your computer and the mix of components already installed.

The worst problems are those that can't be predicted. Certain brands of some hardware sometimes just don't get along with other kinds of hardware of other brands. Many of these conflicts have been solved in the Windows 95 era thanks to Plug-and-Play technology, but the rare nightmare can happen.

Explore Your Options

A horror story or two shouldn't discourage someone from the attempt. These tales should encourage smart shopping. Any would-be computer mechanic should buy components from stores that agree to refund money in the event of intractable problems.

This is especially important for those planning on taking the mail-order route. Check into companies a little before committing yourself. Try to steer clear of

operations that seem to offer prices too good to be true. Paying by credit card affords the greatest level of protection when dealing with distant merchants.

When finding out about the company, also find out about its products. Books such as this one can help you decide whether a particular component will work with your machine, but don't forget to look at your user manuals, as well. For some of the most specific information, try Internet newsgroups. Newsgroups are a vital source of opinions and true-life stories detailing what works, how to get around things that don't work, and what you can forget about trying. A good way to find particular newsgroups or particular postings is the DejaNews search engine Web site (`http://www.dejanews.com`).

Another great resource is the World Wide Web. Besides the must-see official hardware-developer sites, there are a host of pages created by average users detailing their upgrading experiences. The Net is full of information to help make difficult choices regarding motherboards, central processing units (CPUs), video cards, and more. Use your favorite search engine to explore your options.

Out with the Old

Once you have the necessary research complete, dive in. Just about everything inside a computer case can be swapped out for something newer and better. The question is whether the operation is worth the cost. What follows is an overview of the major types of upgrades you might consider. For more information about particular types of parts, turn to the corresponding installation chapters.

Motherboards

Exchanging an old motherboard for a newer version is about the closest you can come to buying a new computer without paying new-computer prices. The *motherboard*, which is the main circuit board of the system, is where all other components meet electronically and share information. Replacing a motherboard can substantially improve a system's overall speed and allow the use of newer CPUs and additional memory.

Motherboards are not the easiest upgrade because changing one means basically taking apart the whole computer. This probably isn't the first upgrade project a new user should tackle, but for users relatively confident in their skills, it can be a good way to salvage an investment in expensive expansion cards and other hardware when upgrading to a new category of PC. Putting in a new Pentium II motherboard, for instance, will give users access to the fastest new CPUs and likely provide support for the emerging Universal Serial Bus (USB) standard, as well.

Motherboards require even more research and advice-gathering than the average component. All of them look pretty much the same and trumpet equal features, but there actually is a difference in quality among the various brands. Cheaper models might be the product of a new company trying to build its business, or they might be cheaply made and prone to crack.

In general, the motherboard mavens say, you pay for what you get in this category. In other words, motherboards can be expensive. Buying a new motherboard also will likely require the purchase of a new CPU, pushing the cost even higher. At some point, it might be cheaper just to buy a new computer and keep your old one as a spare.

NOTE NOTE NOTE NOTE NOTE NOTE NOTE NOTE NOTE NOTE NOTE NOTE NOTE NOTE NOTE

Dip into Skill 15 for more information on installing motherboards.

CPUs

As the computer's main brain, the *CPU* (central processing unit) is important in determining how fast a machine runs and for which tasks it is suitable. Installing a CPU is actually quite easy, especially now that most computers include zero-insertion force (ZIF) CPU sockets. Usually, it is a matter of snapping one chip out and snapping in the new one.

Computers are generally classified by which type of CPU they contain. Finding out what kind of CPU you are using right now can give you a pretty good idea about your various upgrading options. For instance, old machines based upon the Intel 80386 standard—386 for short—are just about used up. If that 386 doesn't work for you as is, you should forget about pouring money into it and consider new machines.

Closer to the realm of real upgrading options are systems based upon Intel's 486DX chip. With a healthy supply of RAM, a 486 can explore the Internet, run Windows 95, and support most business software, such as word processors and spreadsheets. The 486, however, is outclassed by Pentium-based machines when it comes to multimedia operations. It still is possible to buy special CPU upgrades to transform a 486-class system into something like a Pentium, but without a new motherboard as well, such a computer will never reach true Pentium performance.

Users who have a Pentium PC but want something faster are in prime upgrading territory. With prices for Pentium chips coming down, it can be economical to replace base Pentium chips (133 megahertz [MHz] and slower) with newer, zippier Pentium chips. Depending upon your motherboard, it might be possible to just plug in a new Pentium 200MHz chip with MMX technology. If your investigation shows that isn't an easy possibility, Intel offers a line of OverDrive MMX Pentium chips designed to bring the fastest speeds to older motherboards.

WARNING WARNING WARNING WARNING WARNING WARNING WARNING WARNING

The latest popular CPU, Intel's Pentium II, will not fit on a standard Pentium motherboard. If you want to upgrade all the way, it will be necessary to buy both parts.

Another choice is to skip Intel altogether and go with a competing chip from AMD or Cyrix. Once also-rans, the AMD and Cyrix processors today offer a viable alternative to the Intel monopoly at lower prices. This is another decision, however, that should be made only after reading up on the options. All CPUs have certain weaknesses and strengths, so it makes sense to match up your needs with some test results. Check the Web for more information. A good place to start is `http://www.versalogic.com/WhitePaper/ChooseyourCPU.htm`.

Before buying any CPU, make sure your motherboard will support it. Motherboards might have different socket shapes, different voltages, clock speeds, and other variables that can harm the new CPU if set improperly. It is best to read through computer instruction manuals and manufacturer Web pages carefully to make sure a new chip is compatible with your motherboard. If you can find knowledgeable salespeople (not an easy job) ask them.

NOTE NOTE NOTE NOTE NOTE NOTE NOTE NOTE NOTE NOTE NOTE NOTE NOTE NOTE NOTE

Installing CPUs is covered in Skill 5.

Memory

Electronic memory includes RAM, cache memory, and special memory for video and sound hardware. Depending upon which software you run and how you use it, adding memory of any type can improve performance.

Memory upgrades usually are simple affairs that involve pushing modules into slots. Given the price of memory these days (about $50 for 16 megabytes [MB]) this is probably the most cost-effective upgrade a user can make.

There isn't much more to say about memory. The bottom line, basically, is to buy some.

NOTE NOTE NOTE NOTE NOTE NOTE NOTE NOTE NOTE NOTE NOTE NOTE NOTE NOTE NOTE

RAM installation is covered in Skill 4.

Expansion Slot Components

Expansion slots are the home of a wide variety of user-upgradable components such as video cards, sound cards, and internal modems. Some types of peripherals that work outside the computer, such as scanners, might include an expansion slot adapter that must be installed before everything will work.

There are several types of expansion slots found on motherboards of different ages. Today's standard is the *Peripheral Component Interconnect* (PCI) local bus. However, many motherboards include a few slots based on an older, slower standard such as ISA (*Industry Standard Architecture*) or EISA (*Extended ISA*). Cards designed for ISA slots will also fit in EISA slots, but they won't fit in PCI slots. Many older components are built for ISA or EISA while newer cards generally fit in PCI slots.

TIP TIP TIP TIP TIP TIP TIP TIP TIP TIP TIP TIP TIP TIP TIP TIP TIP TIP TIP TIP TIP TIP TIP TIP TIP

It pays to know how many slots of each type your computer has before shopping for a new component. Installing an ISA video card on a computer with a free PCI slot will slow performance unnecessarily. Buy PCI cards when possible.

The most common residents of expansion slot real estate are video cards, sound cards, and modems, although some machines might have certain components, especially video adapters, built directly into the motherboard. In most cases, however, these three buddies will be lined up together. Many users come to the conclusion that one or all of these crucial components might need to be traded in for something newer.

Video Cards

Video cards come in a bewildering array of styles with wide-ranging capability levels. As graphical displays have become increasingly important to modern

multimedia software, the video card has risen to a place of prominence under the computer's hood. Which kind of video card purrs in there can significantly affect overall computing speed—less so for programs such as word processors, more so for eye-massaging games.

Upgraders will want to take a look at the different accelerated three-dimensional (3D) video cards. Some of the newest Pentium II motherboards include an *Accelerated Graphics Port* (AGP), a new kind of connector for specialized 3D video cards. AGP is only meant for video and is not a general PCI replacement.

Sound cards come in a couple of varieties. The word to look for when upgrading is wavetable. *Wavetable* cards have memory that stores tiny snippets of actual instrument recordings. These recordings are manipulated to sound different notes for music playback that actually sounds like real musical instruments. If you have PCI slots available, a PCI wavetable card is the best bet.

NOTE NOTE NOTE NOTE NOTE NOTE NOTE NOTE NOTE NOTE NOTE NOTE NOTE NOTE NOTE

See Skill 9 for video card installation and more on AGP.

Modems

Many modems are external models, but if you have never upgraded your original equipment modem, it likely lies inside the machine. Just because your present modem is internal or external doesn't mean you have to stick with that type when you upgrade. If you have sufficient expansion slots and don't want another piece of equipment on your desk, get an internal modem. If you value the convenience of a modem you can easily turn off, or if you are simply mesmerized by small blinking lights, pick up an external modem.

Either way, the most important modem factor is speed. Two speeds are generally available, 33.6Kbps and 56Kbps. Now that the V.90 standard for 56Kbps has finally been adopted, the faster modems will likely banish slower models from the market. Unfortunately, not all ISPs support the faster modem yet, but that too will change.

NOTE NOTE NOTE NOTE NOTE NOTE NOTE NOTE NOTE NOTE NOTE NOTE NOTE NOTE NOTE

Skill 10 will walk you through installing a modem.

I/O Cards

Aside from video, sound, and modem cards, other expansion cards you might see or consider adding include input/output (I/O) cards and specialty devices. Windows 98 includes new support for TV tuner cards, for example, which allow users to watch television on their computer screens.

Installing an expansion card is not difficult. The case will have to come off, which can be a pain on some models, but usually doesn't entail too much swearing. After that, it's just a matter of pushing the card into an empty slot.

NOTE NOTE NOTE NOTE NOTE NOTE NOTE NOTE NOTE NOTE NOTE NOTE NOTE NOTE NOTE

Check out Skill 14 for more on I/O cards.

Drive Bay Components

These parts fit in the front of the computer where devices such as CD-ROM drives and disk drives reside. Devices that fit in drive bays include hard drives, 3.5-inch and 5.25-inch disk and tape drives, CD-ROM and DVD-ROM drives, internal Zip drives, and other removable storage media devices. Users who want to add more storage space or install a way to read particular storage media will probably be spending some time in the drive bay.

Drive bay upgrades generally are not difficult. The most limiting factor is space. Some desktop computers may only have one or two upgradable drive bays, and those might already be full of existing components. Users in such cases must decide whether they can swap an old part for something new or try to find an external version of the component. Tower cases usually have extra drive bay space.

CD-ROM Drives

The most popular drive bay upgrade is the CD-ROM (*compact disk read-only memory*) drive. Users who don't already have a CD-ROM drive may find them necessary in today's software market where a lot of software is starting to be found only on that medium.

Users who have an older CD-ROM drive might want to upgrade to the newer, speedier models. The classic two-speed (2×) drive is blown away by today's 24-speed (24×) and faster monsters. If you like to play CD-ROM–based games

or frequently use CD-ROM multimedia reference software, a faster drive can make the experience much more enjoyable.

NOTE NOTE NOTE NOTE NOTE NOTE NOTE NOTE NOTE NOTE NOTE NOTE NOTE NOTE NOTE

CD-ROM installation is detailed in Skill 8.

DVD-ROM Drives

Looming at the sidelines is the DVD-ROM (*digital video disk read-only memory*) drive, a CD-ROM–like component that promises to become a popular upgrade in the near future. The new DVD standard crams substantially more information on normal-sized compact disks, allowing uses such as digitized, full-length movies or simply replacing software that once filled multiple CD-ROM sets with a single DVD.

The DVD advantage will likely propel many computer owners to try upgrading. DVD shouldn't cause space problems because the drives are backward-compatible with CD-ROM discs. That means users can just replace that old CD-ROM drive with a new DVD-ROM drive without losing their investment in CD-ROMs.

NOTE NOTE NOTE NOTE NOTE NOTE NOTE NOTE NOTE NOTE NOTE NOTE NOTE NOTE NOTE

You can get on the DVD bandwagon simply by delving into Skill 8.

Zip Drives

Another drive bay upgrade growing in popularity are the "super-floppy" alternatives to disks. The most famous is Iomega's Zip drive, which can hold 100MB of information on a disk-like medium. Similar choices based on competing standards are popping up in the marketplace. With DVD-ROMs set to remain read-only for the time being, the Zip drive and its competitors offer the ease of convenience of disks without their absurdly small size limitation.

For users low on drive bay territory, many of these components are available as external peripherals.

NOTE NOTE NOTE NOTE NOTE NOTE NOTE NOTE NOTE NOTE NOTE NOTE NOTE NOTE NOTE

Storage devices—including Zip drives—are covered in Skill 7.

External Peripherals

The easiest upgrade of all is adding an external peripheral, which is as simple as plugging something into the back of the computer. External modems are a popular option, for instance. There are also external versions of devices that are normally internal, such as CD-ROM drives and hard drives. Although they generally cost more than their internal counterparts, external components are fantastically easy to set up.

Choosing external over internal comes down to weighing space, money, and simplicity. Although internal upgrades often are much simpler than they sound, a few can baffle even an experienced computer user. The extra money invested in external components can be thought of as an insurance policy virtually guaranteeing nothing too horrible will happen. The problem with external peripherals, however, is that they take up desk space. Plus, only so many of them can be plugged into the back of your computer. Where do you have the most extra room: the back of the computer or the drive bays?

With many external devices, of course, you don't have a choice. Monitors, printers, scanners, speakers, and input devices all plug into the back of the machine somehow. As long as you can find a place for them to go, the actual upgrading itself is a snap.

Upgrading Case Studies: Realistic Improvements for Your PC

Rather than attempting to upgrade the oldest computers to today's standards, the following case studies focus on realistic upgrades that owners might actually want to ponder.

Case Study 1: The 486

Intel's 486 central processing unit (CPU) is far from today's state of the art, but with a few modifications, a 486-based machine can still run fast enough to suit a wide variety of needs.

Typical machine 66MHz 486DX2, 8MB of RAM, 400MB hard drive, two-speed (2×) CD-ROM drive, 14.4Kbps modem.

Possible goal You're not interested in the fanciest games, but it would be great to run up-to-date software and Windows 95, and surf the Internet in style.

continued

Upgrade solutions Where do we start? This older machine is a good candidate for mainstream uses, but building it up to meet all of today's standards would be more expensive than buying a sub-$1000 Pentium-based machine.

The first thing to do is buy some RAM. The 8MB in this machine just isn't enough to run Windows 95 at anything faster than paint-drying speed. It's likely there are two single inline memory module (SIMM) sockets, each filled with 4MB. You might as well forget about those. Empty out the small SIMMs and fill those spaces with two 16MB SIMMs for about $80–$100.

Next, see whether a 56Kbps modem makes sense in your area. In most cases, local ISPs can handle the extra speed. This will run about $100, but for people who spend a lot of time on the Net, the investment is well worth it.

Things start to get a little tougher beyond these two obvious upgrades. Sure, a person could concentrate on specific components to fill specific needs. More storage could be dropped in with a bigger hard drive or removable media such as a Zip drive; significantly speedier CD-ROM drives don't cost that much these days. On the other hand, when you start spending all this money, you begin to approach the realm of new-computer prices.

Case Study 2: Low-End Pentium

When you bought it, this early Pentium PC was the fastest thing going. Today, it seems to barely deserve the Pentium name.

Typical machine 90MHz Pentium CPU, 16MB of RAM, 800MB hard drive, 4× CD-ROM, 28.8Kbps modem.

Possible goal Your computer doesn't seem that old, and you think there must be some way to bring this investment up to today's standards.

Upgrade solutions Depending upon how much you want to spend, this machine can be upgraded all the way to today's top standards.

continued ➧

The first move would be to upgrade the CPU and memory. Because this machine is a 75MHz or faster Pentium, an Evergreen MxPro MMX processor upgrade (about $210) or similar products from Intel can boost performance noticeably. Team up the new processor with another 16MB of memory, and you will have a system that can run the latest software at something much closer to its potential.

For added multimedia muscle, you can toss in a new video card or updated sound card. Heavy Internet use demands a new modem. That CD-ROM drive looks kind of slow now with all those new parts humming...maybe a DVD-ROM drive instead?

As you can see, the shopping list starts to grow. To avoid spending the price of a new computer, concentrate on just those components that will benefit the type of software you run. The CPU and memory upgrades make sense for a slower Pentium and will speed up almost every program.

Case Study 3: Mid-Level Pentium

Your computer still seems to run most programs fine, but sometimes you wonder if you are missing anything with all those Pentium II PCs on the computer store shelves.

Typical machine 200MHz Pentium CPU, 16MB of RAM, 1.2GB hard drive, 8× CD-ROM, 33.6Kbps modem.

Possible goal Making this computer match your specific needs should be as easy as adding one or two components.

Upgrade solutions A Pentium with a 200MHz CPU is still a good system by almost any standard. A little tweaking will let this pup run with the big dogs.

With memory as cheap as it is these days, it never hurts to jump up to 32MB or even more. From there, it depends upon your tastes and the way you use the system. An MMX OverDrive upgrade isn't worth the price because the CPU is already decent: MMX capability alone just doesn't provide that much gain. A person could go hog wild and install a new Pentium II motherboard, but that is a rather expensive option.

continued ➧

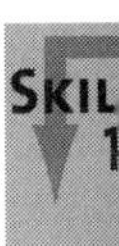

The best course would be to aim for specific needs. Heavy graphics users will find that a new 3D video card brings the screen alive. Audiophiles will hear the difference a PCI wavetable sound card can make. To keep up with the march of technology, a DVD-ROM drive might be a good investment, and for goodness sake, get a 56Kbps modem if you use the Internet for more than checking e-mail.

The price on this one can range from just the memory investment all the way up to new-computer prices, so just set your sights on a couple of items.

Operating Systems

One last major type of upgrade involves changing a computer's software rather than hardware.

The operating system (OS) is the software foundation for a computer. The OS provides an interface for users to interact with their machines to manipulate files, open programs, and share data among programs. The OS is always running in the background, allowing other software to work with the computer's hardware.

Various versions of DOS, a text-based OS, were the mainstay for older PCs and can still be found alive and kicking here and there. Windows, the first popular graphical user interface for IBM-compatible PCs, provided a more intuitive way to navigate.

Windows 3.*x* users may be able to upgrade to Windows 95 or Windows 98 depending upon just how much RAM and processor power is available. Windows 98 features built-in Internet browsing abilities that make navigating the Net and local files similar processes. Just be prepared to give up some disk space and try to have at least 32MB of RAM.

NOTE NOTE NOTE NOTE NOTE NOTE NOTE NOTE NOTE NOTE NOTE NOTE NOTE NOTE NOTE

Upgrades to operating systems are covered in Skill 22.

Smart Software Upgrades

Computer company ads scream at you to get the newest, fastest, and most full-featured software available. But in the world of computers, the best doesn't necessarily mean the latest and greatest system. Finding programs that suit you and your needs is what makes your computer system a useful tool rather than an overpriced, rarely used gadget.

But determining what's best is not an easy chore. When you own a computer, you will sooner or later need to make decisions about upgrading its software. These decisions can be a tough call. Some people avoid the issue altogether, using their tried-and-true software because they're wary of trying anything new. Others are human guinea pigs, trying out unproven software as soon as it hits the market.

The smart computer user, however, assesses his or her needs carefully and considers all aspects of upgrades, including operating systems, new software products, cost, and more.

Lay the Foundation

Before you consider upgrading your software, first consider upgrading your hardware. This might seem like an odd recommendation, but if you don't have the proper hardware foundation, your software enhancements might be wasted. You don't want to buy software that is too powerful for or is under-utilized by your computer. If you're using your computer primarily for household tasks, you'll have very different needs, for example, from someone who is telecommuting.

So before you run out and buy the latest software, consider some hardware upgrades as well.

A Newer OS Is (Usually) Best

Because newer operating systems (OSs) can run more and better software than older OSs, upgrading your operating system can increase your other software options. When deciding among operating systems for PCs, you should first ask yourself what you plan to use your system for. If sending text-based e-mail is the only thing you use your computer for, and you've been happily plugging away on your Windows 3.*x* machine, an OS upgrade probably is not necessary.

But say, for example, you are a Windows 95 devotee, and your work requires you to perform office-type applications. You may want to upgrade to a Windows NT Workstation machine because that operating system is targeted more toward

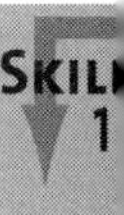

business. And, for example, if you are planning to acquire new software for a growing home-based business and your computer runs on Windows 95, you can save time in the future by upgrading to Windows 98 now, so you don't have to upgrade the software to make it compatible with Windows 98 later.

While some of the upgrade decision is based upon your system needs and your own comfort level in learning new operating systems, part of the upgrade choice depends upon the operating system itself. New operating systems are notoriously full of *bugs* (flaws in the program) when they first hit the market.

Another important consideration is the cost of an operating system upgrade. If you're upgrading from Windows 95 to Windows 98, the upgrade will probably sell for about $100. That price may be worth it. If, for example, you want to upgrade to Windows NT 4, and if you have an earlier version of Windows NT, it will cost you less than $150. But the upgrade won't work on machines that don't have Windows NT already installed, meaning you will have to pay more than twice that amount to upgrade from a Windows 95 machine.

Hidden costs are also important to consider. You might have to spend time training yourself or employees on a new operating system. If you install an operating system incorrectly and it crashes, you could lose days of productivity. Find out whether the new operating system can coexist peacefully with your old one. If so, you might consider installing the new operating system in a separate directory on your hard drive.

Needs Assessment

After your hardware and operating system are up to snuff, you are ready to improve the quality of your software. Software upgrades can give you needed features, speed up your work, and make your work easier. But before you upgrade your software, you should first determine what you need.

How can you determine what you need? Ask yourself the following questions:

- **Am I using the software now?** It's tempting to pick up the latest copy of Microsoft Internet Explorer or Netscape Communicator, but if you rarely go on the Web, you don't want to spend time installing and training yourself on a piece of software you rarely use, even if it is free.
- **Does the upgrade fix my current problems?** If the answer is no, then upgrading makes no sense. On the other hand, if you're encountering a little glitch, you may find it makes more sense for you to download a patch rather than invest in a whole new piece of software.

- **Does the upgrade have new features I need, and do I need them now?** Upgrading can be very expensive. You can save yourself lots of money and time if you upgrade, say, every other version rather than upgrading every version.
- **Will I need help with an upgraded version?** As we mentioned before, software upgrades tend to have problems with bugs, and you should check into the quality of the technical support the company provides. If you don't have the time or energy to figure out how to use an upgraded version's features, it may just sit on the shelf.
- **Can I afford an upgrade?** If the new features will make it easier and quicker for you to perform tasks, the upgrade could be extremely cost-effective.

After you've looked at your needs, it's time to gather information about the software. The Internet is a valuable tool. The software manufacturer's Web site often has press releases and links to product reviews. Internet newsgroups carry on long discussions about new features, bugs, and more. Plus, Internet mailing lists allow you to ask all sorts of questions.

Along with the Internet, you may find help from local computer user groups around the country.

The Meaning of Version Numbers

Have you ever looked at software versions and wondered what all those numbers stood for? Software is inconsistent when it comes to version numbers, but manufacturers tend to follow general rules. Here's a handy reference guide.

No version number If you have a piece of software—we'll call it "Generic Software"—with no version number, it's probably the product's first release. As common sense should tell you, the first time the product is released, it is likely not to have a version number, and games often lack version numbers. The program also might be called "Generic Software 1.0."

continued

Major version number, minor version number, patch level (or update) version number If you have just picked up a copy of "Generic Software 2.1.3," the first digit, 2, stands for the major version of the software. This means the software has undergone a major revision from version 1.0. The program will have new features and has undergone a major rewrite in its code. The program might have a new interface, added functionality, and greater speed.

The second digit, 1 in our example, stands for the minor version number. This number represents new features of the product, but most likely the software has not undergone significant rewriting of its code. For example, a company may add database support to a product and then release a new minor version of that product.

The third digit, 3 in our example, is called the "patch level" or "update" version number. Companies generally release a product with a new patch number when customers have complained about bugs in the program. The software manufacturer adds a patch level version number when it wants to quickly get the fix version onto the market, but it is not yet ready to release a new major or minor version.

Beta versions Sometimes you will see a software release with a letter in the version number. Most of the time, that letter will be a *b*, which stands for a *beta* (or trial) version of a new product or updated release. Companies don't always make their beta versions available to the general public. Often, they will open up a beta trial to a limited number of customers. Beta versions may be available only as downloads from the Internet to the general public (you won't find them sold in software stores). A beta version will almost always be in the form "3.0.b" or "2.b" and not "3.1.0.b" because software companies won't perform beta tests on an insignificant patch-level change.

Installation Tips

When you're ready to upgrade your software, it's important to keep in mind that a smooth installation can save you numerous headaches later.

David Krieger, president of Mr. Software Computer Consultants in South Orange, New Jersey, has compiled a checklist of things to consider and do before and during a software upgrade installation.

Back up your system. Before installing new software, you should make backup copies of everything on your current system, including all your system files (such as your CONFIG.SYS and AUTOEXEC.BAT files). Backup applies to more than the current system; software manufacturers usually allow you to make a backup copy of the software upgrade. If you can back up the upgrade, do so, although this is becoming less common as many upgrades are either released on CD-ROM or available on the Web for download as many times as you would like.

Test the upgrade. Do you have a computer you aren't using? It's a good idea to test a new piece of software on a secondary computer. If you're installing this upgrade on your home system, this may not be feasible, but if you're doing so at work, ask your co-workers or employer for a test computer.

Make it easy on yourself. When installing an upgrade, you're probably installing on top of a path name that has already been created. Set your path names directly to a name you'll remember so you can go back in and work with them later.

Ben Nguyen, Vice President of B&B Office Solutions in Mobile, Alabama, offers the following tips for installing software.

Install software with installation wizards. Windows 95/98 and Windows NT have an easy-to-use installation program, accessible via the Start menu. Using the installation wizard will ensure the program is compatible with your operating system; if you don't use the wizard, you may have conflicts later.

Always use a virus program. Even though you have installed the program before, the upgrade will have new code, and a virus program can protect you against unwanted code sneaking into your system. This is especially important if you download the upgrade from a Web site that is not the manufacturer's own or that you cannot verify as reputable.

REGISTERING SOFTWARE

When you buy new software, the last thing you want to do is fill out the product's registration card. But it's important to register all software, even upgrades, and you may even be required to do so if you're downloading the upgrade from the manufacturer's site on the World Wide Web.

The registration process may be more palatable, however, if you know the benefits you're receiving. Many companies offer technical support to registered users only, a logical move on their part when you consider the size of the market for pirated software. Also, software registration forms often ask you which type of computers you own, and registration responses might prompt manufacturers to consider enhancements, such as creating versions for other operating systems.

And what if your upgrade has a bug? If the manufacturer has your name and address, it can mail you important information on how to avoid and fix the bug.

Of course, the benefits of registration work both ways. Companies know that repeat customers are a good source of revenue, and the database they can compile from the registration information allows them to send you and others special fliers and facts about other products they make. But watch out for companies that sell their mailing lists. If you want to avoid receiving an avalanche of unwanted mail, include a request in writing when you register that your name not be sold.

Cost Considerations

When it comes to buying software, remember the cost of programs is usually about the same no matter which vendor you purchase it from. Therefore, we recommend you buy products from companies you trust. You may save money up front by going through a non-certified distributor, but if it goes out of business, you might be stuck without support.

Unfortunately, upgrades can be expensive, and one way to save yourself some money is to upgrade with every other release rather than every new release. This situation is changing, though, thanks to widespread use of the Internet. Companies often put free versions of new releases or beta versions on their Web sites, and you may save money by acquiring the latest, albeit widely untested, upgrade.

One last tip: If you buy your upgrade in a package, don't forget to check the box. Many companies offer rebates on the front of their boxes, but after you've paid for the upgrade, it's up to you to take advantage of them.

Time to Decide

There are two big questions to ask before charging into an upgrade: First, will this improvement enhance the machine in a way that will serve present needs and needs in the foreseeable future? Second, will the upgrade cost significantly less than the price of a new system? If you can look in the mirror and answer yes to both of those questions, an upgrade may be the way to go.

For users who plan to buy a new computer at some point down the road but just can't bear to give up on the old investment, remember there comes a point where upgrading just doesn't make sense anymore. Adding a component or two is fine, but it may not be wise to go overboard on parts that won't be useful when the new machine finally does arrive.

For instance, buying a new sound card can improve your listening experience now, but anything you buy will likely be outdone by the sound card that becomes standard in the new computer you're thinking of getting in six months. Unless the eventual goal is to have two machines, it makes more sense to buy unusual components that aren't likely to be included with a new machine so you can move them to the new computers when it arrives.

Some users end up replacing entire systems over time, piece by piece. This sort of extensive upgrading isn't the most efficient way to acquire an up-to-date machine, but it does tend to spread out the payments for people who are electronically inclined but don't want to shell out the bucks all at once.

When a new computer seems years down the road, and it is possible to identify a specific need today, upgrading may make sense. With extra memory or maybe a new CPU, the world can seem new again. Just remember to keep an eye on the bottom line.

Are You Experienced?

Now you can...

- ☑ determine the best time to upgrade
- ☑ assess what you need to upgrade and what you can comfortably keep
- ☑ understand the balance between keeping old hardware and adding new hardware
- ☑ make smart choices about what kind of software you need

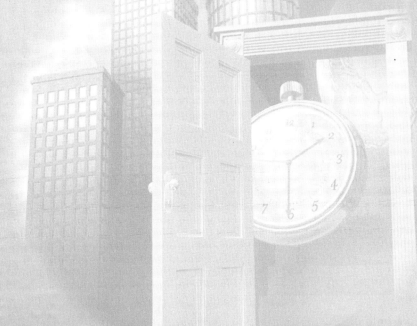

SKILL 2

Learning about Your Computer

- Getting familiar with the parts of your computer
- Figuring out what's inside with MSD
- Using Device Manager to peek inside

Upgrading is serious business, so it's important to ascertain which hardware is already on your system before you begin. There are several ways to find the names and specifications of each PC part. You can unplug the system, remove the cover, and take a good look. That's the hard way; too many parts are tiny, hard to identify, or placed under something bigger and sight-obscuring.

Another way is to look at the computer's manual. This method isn't completely foolproof. Manufacturers often list several different system setups in the same manual, and you may not be able to identify which system you have just from the manual.

The most efficient way is to use the manual in conjunction with a program such as the Windows utility Microsoft Diagnostic or add-on third-party software (see the "Alternatives to MSD" sidebar).

Exploring the Parts

Have you ever wished your computer were like a giant PEZ dispenser so you could flip the top open and see all the goodies inside? To satisfy your curiosity, we've lifted the top off our computer and described its major parts. Figure 2.1 illustrates the movement of information.

- A sound card is an expansion card that lets a computer produce sound. Examples of practical uses for sound capabilities include games, music applications, and interactive educational software.
- The expansion card is a circuit board that slides into an expansion slot. Use it to add features, such as sound or a modem, to your computer.
- An expansion slot is an opening on the motherboard into which a board or card can be placed, expanding the capability of the computer.
- The motherboard (also called a system board or circuit board) is the most important part of the system. Acting as the foundation of a computer, the motherboard supplies all of the electrical connections among various components of the computer, including the CPU, ROM, and RAM.
- The central processing unit (CPU) is the actual brain of a computer. It is responsible for processing instructions and carrying out users' commands. Other parts of the computer serve the microprocessor, enabling it to do its job.

3 When the M reaches the microprocessor, the microprocessor translates the keystroke into information your monitor can understand. The microprocessor passes the signal on to the video adapter card, a circuit board that controls your monitor. The video card then passes the information along to the monitor, where the image is placed on the screen through a combination of blue, green, and red dots. Each red, blue, and green dot is known as a pixel.

4 What happens when you want to save that information? When you open the File menu and select the Save option, the software gets involved. The letters on-screen go to a buffer, and the software, which is temporarily stored in RAM, grabs the data in order to save it. The request then travels to the microprocessor, where the data is processed and passed to the hard drive. Inside the hard drive, a read/write head magnetically stores the information on platters, which look like miniature records.

5 All this happens at lightning-fast speed. The more powerful your hardware components, the faster data appears on-screen and files are saved.

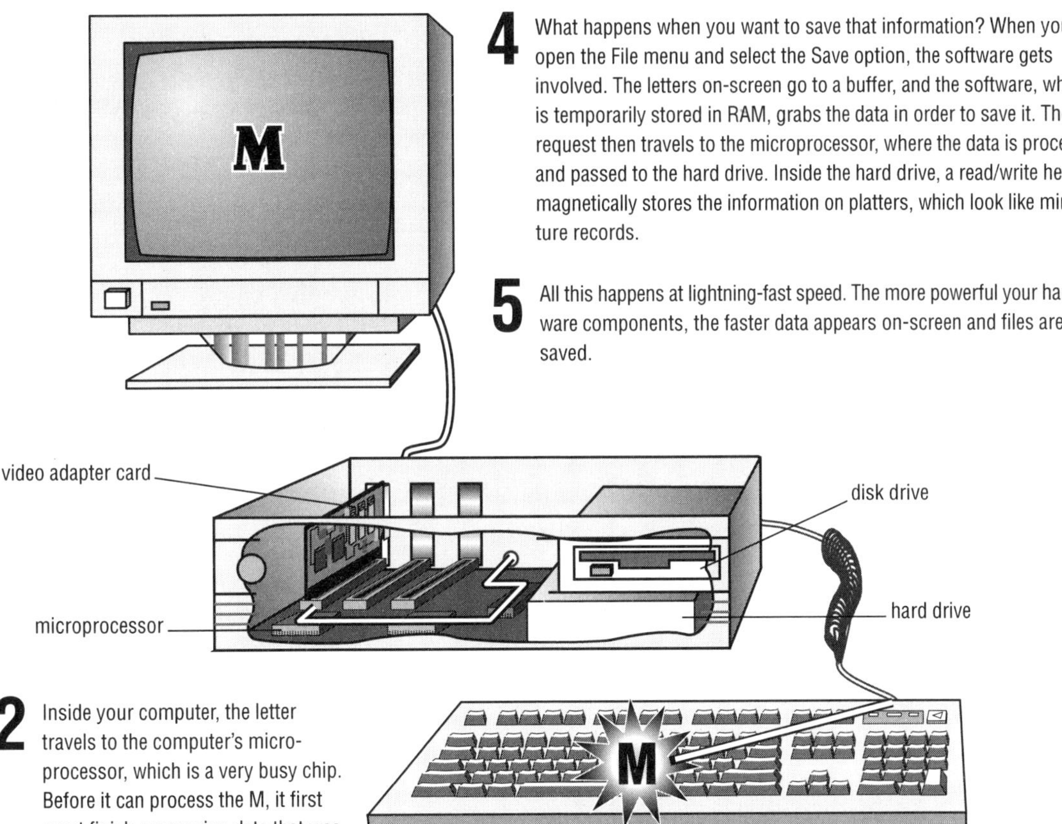

2 Inside your computer, the letter travels to the computer's microprocessor, which is a very busy chip. Before it can process the M, it first must finish processing data that was requested earlier. Thus, the M first travels to a RAM buffer, which is like a waiting room for information. The M shouldn't have to wait too long; keystrokes are assigned one of the highest processing priorities in your computer.

1 Let's start when you press the M key on the keyboard. When you depress the key, your keyboard uses its own microprocessor to pick up the signal and translate it into a language your system understands. The signal is transmitted to the PC via a cable that connects to a port on the back of the computer.

FIGURE 2.1: A schematic of how information travels inside your computer

- Read-only memory (ROM) contains the commands your computer needs to activate itself. Instructions in ROM let the computer start when the power is turned on, and, unlike RAM, its contents are retained even when the power is off.
- RAM (random access memory) determines how many projects can fit on your desktop at one time. When you run a program, it is loaded from your hard drive into RAM. Ultimately, the more RAM you have, the more programs and files you can have open at once. Remember to save any work you intend to keep on a hard drive or disk because whatever is in RAM gets erased when the computer is turned off.
- RAM chips, the physical components that contain the memory, are grouped in rows called SIMMs (or *single in-line memory modules*). These modules are small bars, usually containing eight or nine memory chips. When you want to add more memory to your computer, just plug in one or more SIMMs. A memory chip is the integrated circuit that actually contains the RAM.
- The power supply is the vehicle through which electricity is regulated and sent to the various components of a computer.
- A CD-ROM drive reads information from CD-ROMs, the high-capacity medium used for most multimedia software.
- The disk drive reads and writes information on disks that usually hold 360,000 characters to 1,440,000 characters. Because you can remove disks from the drive and replace them with others, a disk drive can let you access a virtually unlimited collection of data.
- While RAM acts as your desktop, a hard drive (or hard disk or fixed disk) acts as a computer's file cabinet. A hard drive, though more expensive than a disk, allows the most rapid access to your programs and data and can store millions (and even billions) of characters.

Microsoft Diagnostic

Both DOS and early versions of Windows come with a much-maligned little program called *Microsoft Diagnostic* (MSD). MSD is a resident-utility program which was new to DOS 6 and Windows 3.1.

NOTE NOTE NOTE NOTE NOTE NOTE NOTE NOTE NOTE NOTE NOTE NOTE NOTE NOTE NOTE

Windows 95/98 users may want to skip down to the "Device Manager" section.

Windows 3.*x* and DOS

MSD was initially created for use by Microsoft technicians and beta support staff so they would have a complete picture of customers' systems. Despite this humble beginning, MSD is also a good resource for the end user. It helps detect installed hardware and can compile this information for you in a separate file.

MSD comes with several built-in command-line switches typical of a DOS-type program. The best use of MSD is to detect all the functional hardware on your PC. This is also the main drawback to using MSD; only functional software will be detected, so if there's a driver problem or the device simply isn't working, MSD won't tell you about it.

Still, for our hardware-inventory purposes, MSD does the trick.

Starting MSD

For the best results, it's absolutely vital that MSD be run directly from DOS. This is true even though Windows 3.*x* offers a DOS prompt window. Running MSD from within Windows can result in inaccurate information that won't serve you well when you're getting ready to invest hard-earned cash in upgrades.

Going directly to the regular DOS prompt for Windows 3.*x* users means exiting Windows. Once in DOS, you should see the C:\> prompt. Type **msd** at the prompt. The Microsoft Diagnostic screen appears to inform you it is examining your system. This could take a few seconds or nearly a minute depending upon the speed of your computer.

System Summary

When MSD finishes its examination, the System Summary Screen appears. This screen contains three menu items (File, Utilities, and Help) as well as several blocks of information, including Computer, Memory, Video, Network, OS Version, Mouse, Other Adapters, Disk Drives, LPT Ports, COM Ports, IRQ Status, TSR Programs, and Device Drivers. Some versions also include a Windows block. (See Figure 2.2.) Each block contains a screen of its own, which can be accessed by pressing the block's highlighted letter.

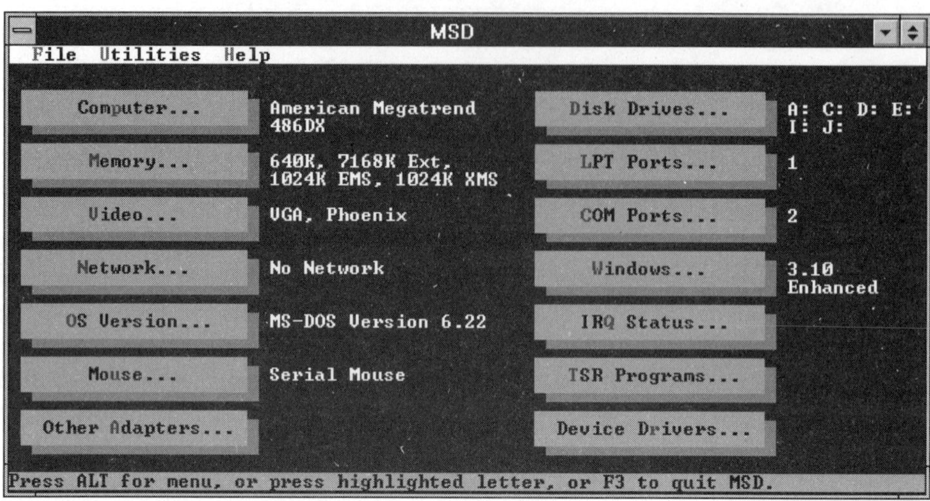

FIGURE 2.2: You can learn about your computer's components and capabilities from the main menu of Microsoft Diagnostics.

Computer To the right of this block are two lines. The top line lists the type of ROM (read-only memory), followed by the BIOS (Basic Input/Output System) manufacturer's name. Often, the information is the same for both items. The second line lists the PC's processor type. Pressing the **P** key brings up the Computer information screen, listing all kinds of information from the name of the computer to keyboard specifications.

Memory On the main screen, several numbers are shown: the PC's amount of conventional RAM (random access memory), extended memory, and any available memory. Press **M** to get a more complete picture.

Video Not surprisingly, this screen lists the PC's video capabilities.

Network If you're not part of a network system, the words No Network appear on the main screen to the right of this block. If you are, press **N** and the name of the network pops up.

OS Version OS stands for operating system. The name says it all.

Mouse Wondering which kind of mouse you're using? Find that titillating tidbit here. Its IRQ (interrupt request) address is found here, as well.

Other Adapters This section displays facts about game adapters, such as joysticks, should you have one installed on your system.

Disk Drives This block contains disk drive information. Pressing **D** will give you a list of all drives, their letters, type, free space, and total size.

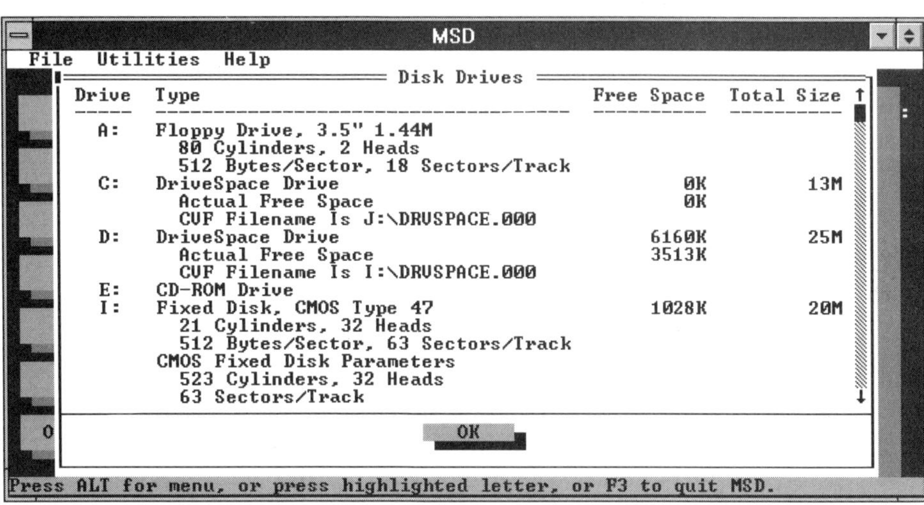

LPT Ports On the main screen is a number showing how many LPT (line printer terminal) ports MSD has located on your PC. The LPT screen gives you the base I/O (input/output) address of the port, as well as different status data.

COM Ports Again, the number on the main screen indicates the number of COM (communications) ports detected. Pressing **C** brings up the COM Ports screen with port addresses, baud rates, and other communications information.

Windows The current version of Windows in use is displayed on the main screen. If you delve further, you'll see the technical information and Windows directory path.

IRQ Status Pressing **Q** displays one of the most useful screens in MSD. It lists in order IRQ numbers 0 through 15 and each number's corresponding hardware. Each device is described, and its hexadecimal address is displayed. This is particularly handy when installing new hardware; knowing which IRQs are free will save you a headache or two.

TSR Programs Here, the *terminate-and-stay-resident* (TSR) programs are outlined. TSRs are DOS programs that remain in memory for quick access, even when they're not running.

Device Drivers If you're interested in viewing all the device drivers on your system, take a peek in this section. Device drivers are programs that let hardware communicate with the computer.

Reporting Options

A great reason to use MSD is to get a reference sheet of your hardware configurations. You can write them all down from the screen, which is both tedious and time-consuming, or you can print a report.

The simplest way to print a report is found under the File menu. Choose Print Report, and the Report Information screen appears. Here, you can select the report information you need, as well as a printer port. To choose different bits of information, use the Tab key to move the cursor down the screen. Press the Spacebar to select or deselect the individual items. An X in the checkbox identifies that item as part of the report.

It's also possible to put an X in the first box, Report All, which then reports all information contained in MSD. Unless you want to wade through oodles of CONFIG.SYS, AUTOEXEC.BAT, and initialization (.INI) files data, it's best to choose just the items you want.

After you've selected the needed information, choose a printer port and press Enter to continue. Next up is the Customer Information screen, which prompts you to personalize the report with your name, address, and other vital statistics. Again, the Tab key moves you from prompt to prompt. You don't have to enter anything in this screen to continue with the report. If you're ready to print, just press Enter.

Now prepare to wait. The report might be long, depending upon how many doodads your PC contains. If you don't feel like waiting, save the report as a file instead. To do this, you'll have to go back to the Report Information screen and tab down to the Print To section. The last option is File: [Report.MSD . . .]. There, you can enter the drive name and filename of where you would like to save the report.

Windows 95

Microsoft vacillates with MSD in its Windows 95 operating system. Essentially, the company excluded MSD in favor of the new Device Manager. Device Manager is an integral part of Windows 98, as well.

Microsoft, however, didn't completely get rid of MSD in Windows 95. A newer version, MSD 2.13, was shipped with the Windows 95 installation CD-ROM, but wasn't part of the automatic installation. MSD wasn't included anywhere, automatic or not, on the 14-disk version of Windows 95. And users of the OSR2 may not have received a copy as part of their operating system package.

MSD is old; there's no doubt about it. And Microsoft hasn't updated it to report on Windows 95's Registry or any of the newer OS enhancements. Despite this, it's still useful for diagnosing IRQ and identifying basic hardware in Windows 95. CD-ROM owners can find MSD.EXE in the \OTHER\MSD folder on the Windows 95 CD-ROM. It's not a bad idea to locate it and copy it to a bootable disk.

Alternatives to MSD

For users who find Microsoft Diagnostic (MSD) a little too primitive or who are afraid of delving into DOS, third-party utilities can save the day. There are many popular troubleshooting diagnostic programs on the market that include tools to identify and report system components.

One of the best-known is Symantec's Norton Utilities, a comprehensive collection of troubleshooting tricks and maintenance utilities. Symantec makes several software packages to meet a variety of needs. The company's best choices for folks seeking system information are Norton Utilities 8 for DOS/Windows 3.*x* and Norton Utilities 3 for Windows 95. Both have data-protection programs, as well as software for testing essential system components and ironing out potential interrupt request (IRQ) conflicts before hardware installation. Check out `http://www.symantec.com/us.index.html` for the details on all their products.

Giving Norton a run for its money is Nuts & Bolts, a Network Associates troubleshooting utility. This suite of tools also includes hardware diagnostic and reporting tools and can give your PC a tune-up. Overall, this utility package resembles Norton Utilities, but is gaining a reputation all its own. Go to `http://www.nai.com` for the details.

continued ➧

For those seeking simplicity, Cybermedia's First Aid 98 could be the utility that meets your needs. First Aid 98 has a terrific interface; users need only click the corresponding icon to test a specific component or peripheral, and there are options to check all at one time. While First Aid's primary purpose is to resolve software troubles, it also packs a set of hardware diagnostic tools and tune-up tricks. If you're a novice in the utility arena, this package won't intimidate you. For more information, go to `http://www.cybermedia.com`.

For those users who want less automation than First Aid 98, but less complexity than Norton, Touchstone's CheckIt 5 could be the answer. Although it doesn't include a disaster-recovery program like the other packages mentioned, it does offer tools for testing hardware components. Its easy-to-use hardware diagnostics utility accurately reports on IRQs and other system resources. CheckIt can be checked out at `http://www.touchstonesoftware.com`.

Device Manager

The newer hardware identification system in Windows 95 is the *Device Manager*. To access it from the Start menu, select Settings, then Control Panel, then double-click the System icon. From the Device Manager tab, users can view hardware by type or by connection. When hardware is viewed by type, each device is listed with an icon. Any devices with additional information or more than one device under that heading are displayed with a plus (+) sign. Clicking the plus sign shows the entire hierarchical list of hardware connected to that device. Clicking the Disk Drives plus sign, for example, might reveal a generic IDE drive, a disk drive, and a Zip drive, if these drives are installed. Figure 2.3 shows an example of the Device Manager tab, viewed by type.

When viewing hardware devices by connection, the components are listed under the hardware to which they are connected. The same plus sign system applies here, too. This is a more confusing list, so if you're trying to figure out which hardware is installed and any other details, stick to viewing by type; the icons keep everything clearly organized.

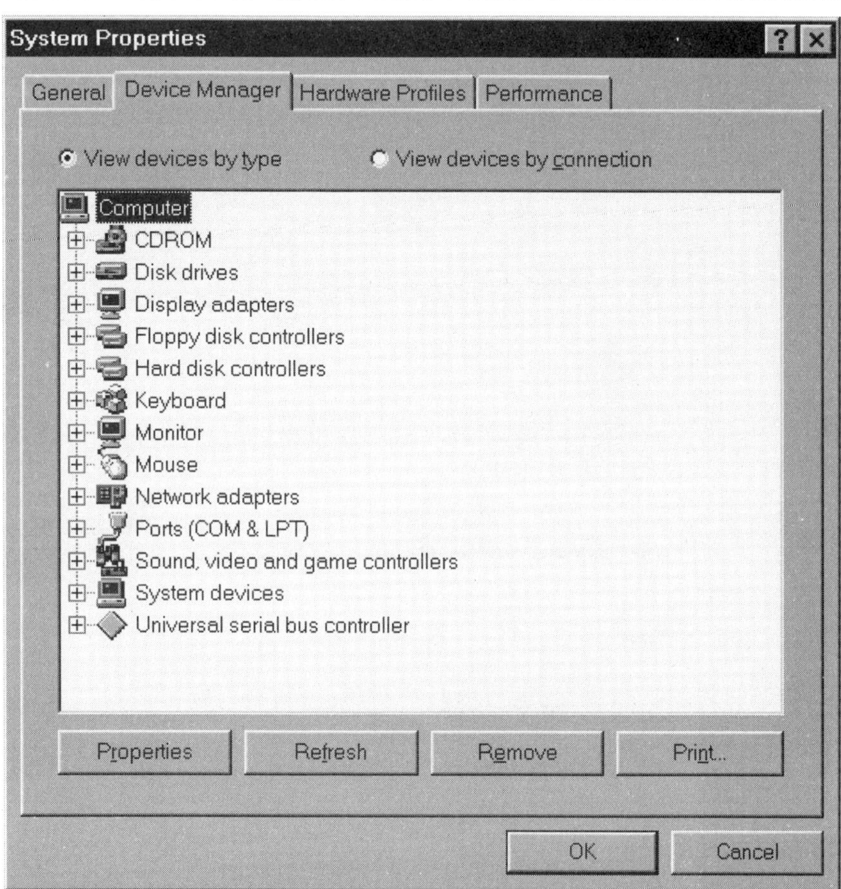

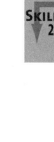

FIGURE 2.3: Explore your system resources through Device Manager in Windows 95.

Regardless of which way you view Device Manager, it's simple to see the properties of any component by double-clicking its icon. In this window, you'll see the device type, manufacturer, and hardware version. Device Manager also indicates here whether or not the device is working properly, and if not, what might be wrong.

At the top of the Device Manager hierarchical list is Computer. Double-click this icon to see useful overall system properties. In the View Resources tab, you can list all devices according to IRQ. This is a great way to see which settings are being used by which hardware. Like MSD, Device Manager lists the IRQs in order from IRQ 0 to 15.

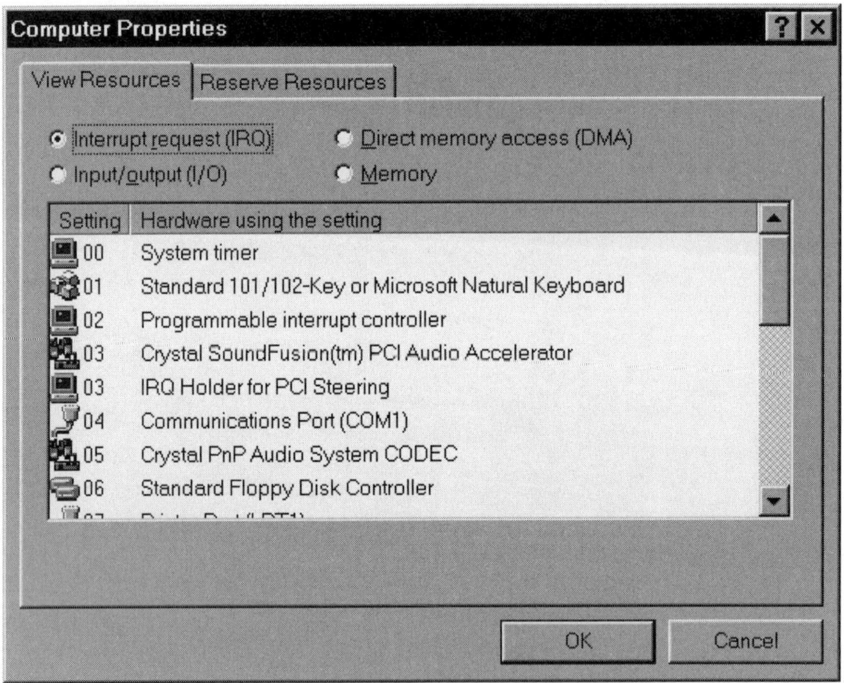

For general information about the central processing unit (CPU) your system has, turn to the first tab in the System applet titled, appropriately, General. Windows 95 lists on this tab the operating system in use, the type of CPU installed, and the total amount of RAM installed. This is the easy way to determine this information, all of which is essential to making the correct upgrade choices.

Printing Reports

As with MSD, it's a good idea to make a hard copy of the computer specifications for future reference. To do this in Device Manager, begin by pressing the Print button at the bottom of the Device Manager window. A Print dialog box pops up that lists the default printer, and offers you three report options: System Summary, Selected Class or Device, and All Devices and System Summary.

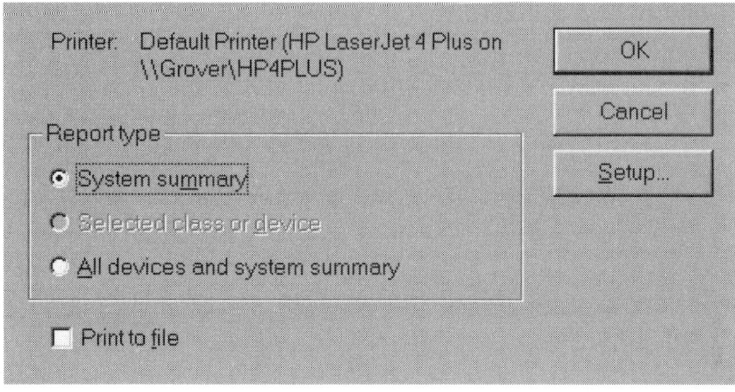

- Choosing System Summary prints out a plethora of information, including bus type, BIOS and CPU details, and summaries for IRQ usage, I/O port usage, upper memory usage, DMA Channel usage, memory, and disk drives.
- Printing a Selected Class or Device report requires you to click one class or device, such as disk drives or monitor. It prints a brief report naming the devices in that class along with any resources they use.
- The All Devices and System Summary report fills more than a few pages; the amount of information depends upon how much is on your system. It includes all the sections printed in the System Summary report, but also adds the details of each class and subsequent device. This is a terrific resource you should update each time you add a new device.

If you don't want to spend the time or the paper on the report, save it to file, and put it on a disk for safe keeping. Go to the Printer dialog box again, place a check in the Print to File box and enter a file name, folder, and drive where you want the file saved.

With system information and your manual in hand, you'll be able to choose and purchase new components for your upgrade. Microsoft Diagnostic, Device Manager, and third-party utilities let you know what you have so you can decide what you need.

Are You Experienced?

Now you can...

- ☑ identify the parts of your computer
- ☑ use MSD to see what you've got inside your computer
- ☑ use Device Manager to see what you've got inside your computer

SKILL 3

Taking Precautions Before You Begin

- Learning about drivers
- Understanding the importance of backups
- Creating a backup disk
- Opening up your computer safely

Almost since the dawn of personal computing, users have considered the PC as a product that could be upgraded numerous times over its life. In some cases, upgrading allowed users to incrementally improve their computers and keep relatively current in computing capabilities. Back in the days when computers often cost several thousand dollars, upgrading was an excellent way to extend a PC's usefulness.

Times are changing, however. Continually falling computer prices are forcing users to re-evaluate the value of upgrading.

Fortunately, there are still many cost-effective options that allow users to maintain their investment in their computers. We take a look at some of these options, recommending particularly good values that can improve the way you compute while counseling against upgrades that offer more of an ego boost than performance benefits. But before we do that, let's look at some basic upgrading truths that can save you trouble later.

The Limits of Upgrading

Just as there comes a time to retire a beloved car from everyday use, there comes a time when a computer has outlived its usefulness. Older PCs can certainly still be used as useful tools for word processing and other applications, but when a computer no longer keeps up with the software and hardware you want to use, it is to your advantage to save for a new system instead of pumping more money into your old one.

If you want more enjoyment from an older system, consider investing in a better printer, modem, monitor, or keyboard. But don't try to squeeze performance from a rock by putting new processors and hard drives into an old computer. Even with the upgrades that are possible, your system still won't be able perform the tasks and run the programs that most new computers can.

Upgrading shouldn't—and won't—be an ordeal if you use common sense at every step. First, always follow the instructions of the upgrading kit or new component. Second, before opening your computer for any reason, you should always perform a complete system backup of both your personal files and your system information. Finally, if you ever feel yourself getting in over your head, consult an expert. The small investment you make to have your computer serviced will ensure your computer will work and that you will have someone to repair the computer if it should not work.

TIP

The key to successful hardware upgrades is to buy and install permanent improvements that you can use on your next computer. These upgrades include monitors, mice, and keyboards. When you upgrade internal components, think of it only as a short-term solution; to keep current in this rapidly changing industry, you'll probably need a new computer in the next three years anyway.

Upgrading under Different OSs

How you upgrade your computer and which hardware you can add depends a great deal upon which operating system is installed on your computer. Fortunately, there are ways to make installing your new hardware as simple as possible when using Microsoft's DOS, Windows 3.*x*, or Windows 95/98 operating systems. We'll describe some of these methods and share tips designed to simplify your upgrading experience.

Driver Primer

Keep in mind that DOS, Windows 3.*x*, and Windows 95/98, differ in the way they handle *device drivers*, which are the programs that allow hardware to communicate with a computer. DOS loads some types of drivers from the AUTOEXEC.BAT and CONFIG.SYS files; these drivers then run continuously in memory. Typically, these drivers are installed from a disk. The second type of driver—particularly those for modems and printers—is contained in the DOS programs themselves and must be separately configured.

In Windows 3.*x*, some drivers are loaded from the AUTOEXEC.BAT and CONFIG.SYS files. However, some drivers—most notably for printers—are designed especially for Windows 3.*x* and can be used by all Windows programs.

Windows 95/98, on the other hand, doesn't use the AUTOEXEC.BAT and CONFIG.SYS files for much of anything. Instead, all drivers are automatically loaded when a computer is booted through Windows 95/98 hidden system files. Drivers are usable by all Windows programs.

NOTE

CONFIG.SYS is a text file that specifies the drivers and system parameters in MS-DOS–based systems. AUTOEXEC.BAT is a batch file that executes several commands related to computer startup.

Editing System Files

Because Windows 3.*x* and DOS use your CONFIG.SYS and AUTOEXEC.BAT files, you may need to edit these key system files.

There are several reasons why you would need to tinker with these files. A common reason is to add or delete references to drivers. You may need to temporarily disable a driver that's causing your computer to run improperly; you can disable a line in either of these files by adding the command REM before it. (This is often referred to as *remming out* a line. You can reactivate the line by removing the REM from the front of the line.)

Also, you sometimes will need to change miscellaneous configuration settings in your CONFIG.SYS and AUTOEXEC.BAT files. Of course, it should go without saying that you should not make changes in your AUTOEXEC.BAT and CONFIG.SYS without first making a hard copy (or printed version) of the files so you can restore the settings later if need be.

Editing System Files in DOS If you need to edit your CONFIG.SYS or AUTOEXEC.BAT files, you can use the Edit application included with versions of DOS 5 and newer. At a DOS prompt (C:\>), type **edit** then the name of the file you want to edit. For example:

edit autoexec.bat

Edit is easy to use, particularly if you've ever used Windows (see Figure 3.1). You can move through the screen with your arrow keys and edit text like you would with a word processor. To use the functions—such as Save and Exit—on the menu bar, simply press the Alt key on your keyboard. You can then navigate through the menus with the arrow keys. To use a function, highlight it and press Enter; to return to editing without selecting a function, press Alt again.

WARNING

Don't try using the Edlin feature supplied in DOS before version 5 unless you have an expert nearby walking you through it.

```
File  Edit  Search  View  Options  Help
c:\config.sys

FILES=20
BUFFERS=20
DEVICE=C:\WINDOWS\HIMEM.SYS /TESTMEM:OFF
DOS=HIGH,UMB
DEVICEHIGH=C:\WINDOWS\SETVER.EXE
REM DEVICEHIGH=C:\CDDRV\TOSCDROM.SYS /D:TOSCD001

rem  SystemSoft CardWorks(TM)
rem SystemSoft CardWorks(TM) PCMCIA drivers:
device=C:\CARDWORK\SSTPIC95.EXE /SKT:2
device=C:\CARDWORK\CS.EXE /POLL:1
device=C:\CARDWORK\CSALLOC.EXE
device=C:\CARDWORK\CARDID.EXE

Commands for manipulating files
```

FIGURE 3.1: Using DOS' Edit utility, available in version 5.0 and newer, is the best way to add and remove items to CONFIG.SYS and AUTOEXEC.BAT files.

Editing System Files in Windows 3.*x* and Windows 95 Both Windows 3.*x* and Windows 95 include a helpful configuration-file editor called Sysedit (Figure 3.2). To use it in Windows 3.*x*, select File from the Program Manager menu bar then select Run. In the window that appears, type **sysedit** and click OK. The System Configuration Editor window will appear. To use it in Windows 95, select Run from the Start menu. In the window that appears, type **sysedit** and click OK.

In the interior windows, you will see the major configuration files that Windows (and DOS) uses. From here, Sysedit is like a word processor; you can move through the windows editing the files. When you're done editing, select Save from the File menu.

Adding Drivers

If you need to add a driver (which you should do only if your documentation tells you how to do so), you can use the Edit and Sysedit tools. You're generally better off if you add new drivers at the end of your CONFIG.SYS and your AUTOEXEC .BAT files. Add new drivers in the order your documentation tells you to add them.

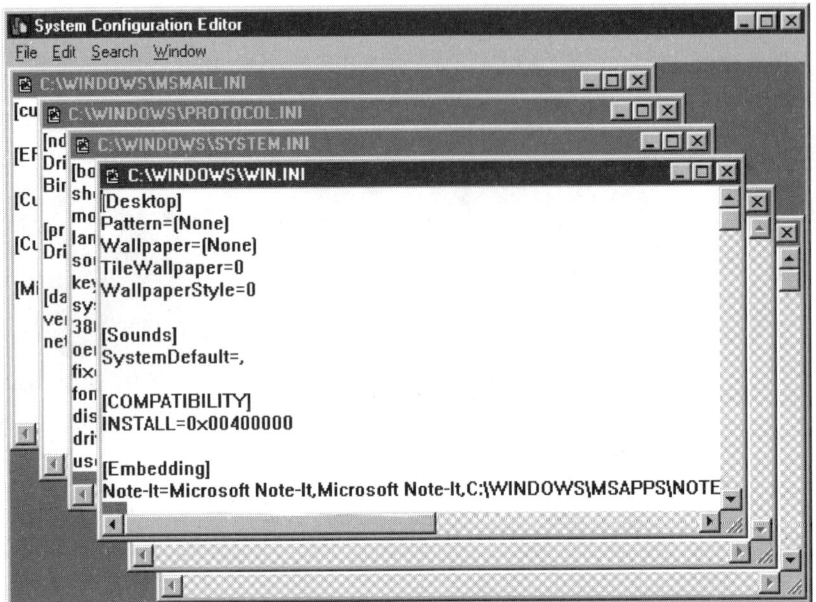

FIGURE 3.2: Yet another reason to upgrade to Windows 95; Sysedit gives you even more flexibility when editing your system files.

Using MemMaker

After making any changes to your AUTOEXEC.BAT and CONFIG.SYS files, we recommend running DOS' MemMaker to optimize your PC's memory. MemMaker forces your hardware drivers to use *upper memory* instead of *conventional memory*, which is the workspace given to DOS and applications and the data they handle. DOS runs faster when MemMaker is allowed to force programs into upper memory and out of the way of DOS activity in conventional memory.

MemMaker comes with MS-DOS 6 and newer; it can be run on any computer with a 386, 486, Pentium-class, or Pentium II-class processor. If you're using a memory optimizer such as Quarterdeck's *QEMM*, you should refer to that software's documentation to see if you should use MemMaker.

WARNING WARNING WARNING WARNING WARNING WARNING WARNING WARNING

Don't ever run MemMaker on a Windows 95/98 computer.

You can run MemMaker in two ways. The easiest way to is to type the following at a DOS prompt:

memmaker /batch

This command forces MemMaker to run on its own, using all the default settings. This doesn't give you the best optimization, but it will prevent you from making a key mistake.

Your second option is to run MemMaker manually. This gives you the most control over the process, but it might also force you to make choices you don't feel qualified to make.

1. To run MemMaker manually, type **memmaker** at a C:\> prompt. You'll then see the welcome screen. MemMaker will ask if you want to continue. Press Enter to allow MemMaker to run.

NOTE

When you're given a choice, MemMaker allows you to cycle through the choices by pressing the Spacebar on your keyboard.

2. MemMaker then asks whether you would like to run Express or Custom setup. Because Express setup allows good memory optimization without allowing users to mess up internal settings, you should choose Express setup. Press Enter to continue.
3. The next question is whether you want to use EMS (Expanded Memory Specification) memory, which is a DOS method of using memory above 640KB. Unless you have a reason for not using it (such as you have been told explicitly that you should not use it or know that none of your applications uses Expanded Memory), you should run EMS. Make your choice, and press Enter to continue.
4. MemMaker then warns you it must restart the computer to continue. Press Enter. After MemMaker restarts your computer, MemMaker then tells you it must reboot yet again. Press Enter to continue.
5. While the PC reboots, watch your screen carefully for any errors. Then, after the reboot, MemMaker will ask you whether there were any problems while the computer was booting up. Answer the question based on your observations and then press Enter. (If there were errors, MemMaker will allow you to undo the changes that it made.)

Let's assume there weren't any errors, and you answered that the computer was working fine and pressed Enter. MemMaker will then produce a report on how it optimized memory. The statistic you'll want to concentrate on is conventional memory. If you have less conventional memory available after running MemMaker than before, you'll want to revert to your original settings by pressing Esc and then pressing Enter. If you have more conventional memory after running MemMaker, you'll want to keep your settings by pressing Enter. In either case, after you make your selection, MemMaker will make any final changes and then close.

Judging Your Resources

After your hardware is installed, its driver will use hardware resources to communicate to the rest of your PC. While you don't need to know exactly how these resources operate, you do need to know that having multiple devices assigned to the same resource is a primary cause of hardware troubles. Think of resources as phone lines that communicate with the computer. If more than one component is trying to use the same line, the lines will cross and the computer will fail to function correctly.

The three types of hardware resources you'll run into most often are IRQs, DMAs, and I/O addresses. *IRQ* (Interrupt Request Line) numbers are channels by which computer components ask the microprocessor for attention. *DMA* (Direct Memory Access) numbers represent channels by which hardware ships information directly to random access memory (RAM) without having to go through the processor first. Accessing memory in this way is much faster than going through the processor. *I/O* (input/output) addresses represent yet another way for a component to ship memory back and forth to the rest of the PC.

NOTE NOTE NOTE NOTE NOTE NOTE NOTE NOTE NOTE NOTE NOTE NOTE NOTE NOTE NOTE

Not all hardware will be assigned all (or any) of these three resources types. For example, printers and mice are plugged into ports, which are assigned their own resources; therefore, the ports have the resources, not the hardware plugged into them.

DOS, Windows 3.*x*, and Windows 95 all use resource settings. But while Windows 95/98 gives you a great degree of flexibility in assigning these resources, Windows 3.*x* and DOS require these resources to be set on the hardware devices themselves via *jumpers* (small connectors on hardware whose position determines configuration settings) or switches. Sometimes, these settings must be configured within the drivers themselves.

Make a List, Check It Twice

The best way to keep these resources under control is to create a list of resources currently in use by hardware components. These lists include IRQ and DMA numbers in use and often include I/O addresses. Once you have this inventory, you should never be in doubt about which resources you can use when installing new hardware.

Windows 3.*x* and DOS Unfortunately, neither Windows 3.*x* nor DOS comes with good tools to help users create resource inventories. The main included tool, Microsoft Diagnostics (MSD), is useful, but only in a limited manner. (For more information about MSD, see Skill 2.) Of course, you can always take your computer apart and comb through your documentation and figure out which resources are in use at any time. This will entail studying jumper configurations and combing through your system files, which is not a very practical exercise unless you are enamored with looking at your PC's parts.

Your best bet for creating a resource inventory is a third-party utility. There are many fine utility packages on the market that allow users to make inventories and have powerful tools for troubleshooting. For example, Symantec's Norton Utilities 8 for Windows and DOS and Norton Utilities 3 for Windows 95 are valuable for any user. If you're a more sophisticated user, take a look at Watergate Software's PC-Doctor, which is designed for computer professionals and true power users.

Windows 95/98 It is easy to create a resource inventory with the Computer Properties window within Windows 95/98.

1. Select Settings from the Start menu.
2. Select the Control Panel, double-click the System icon, then click the Device Manager tab.
3. Highlight the Computer icon at the top of the list, then click the Properties button. This will present you a window listing the different resources in use. You can change your view by selecting the different radio buttons at the top of the window. Make notes on which resources are in use, and you will have your inventory.

Troubleshooting Hardware Problems

If you run into problems after installing hardware, you should check a few things first. Did you follow your documentation's installation instructions? Is the device plugged in properly? If the device is a card, is it seated in its slot correctly? Are the settings in Windows' Control Panel correct (if applicable)? If none of these things is the culprit, read on for advice regarding particular operating systems.

NOTE

Skill 23 covers troubleshooting extensively.

DOS and Windows 3.*x*

Be sure to check your inventory, as described above, to ensure you don't have a resource conflict. Check your documentation and your device to make sure the jumpers and switches (if applicable) are set correctly. Also, check your documentation: You may have to tweak settings within your AUTOEXEC.BAT and CONFIG.SYS files.

Windows 95

To check your drivers and resources, open the Settings menu from the Start button. Then select Control Panel and double-click the System icon. Select the Device Manager tab. Figure 3.3 shows the View Resources tab of the Device Manager.

If there are any problems with your hardware, Windows will flag the listings with an icon of an exclamation mark inside a yellow sign. Generally, the best way to fix a problem is to use the Troubleshooter; unfortunately, many users don't even know about it.

1. To open the Troubleshooter, select the Help feature from the Start button menu.
2. Click the Contents tab then double-click the Troubleshooting listing.
3. In the list that appears, find your problem, then double-click the appropriate listing. For example, if you believe you're having a hardware conflict, you would select that listing then follow the directions in the dialog boxes that appear.

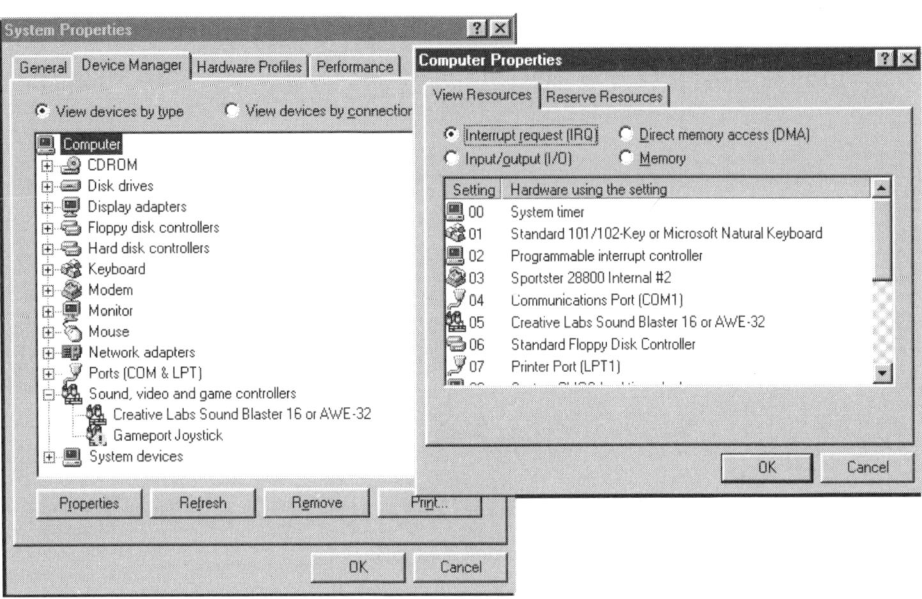

FIGURE 3.3: Windows 95 includes hardware troubleshooting capabilities, unlike Windows 3.*x* and DOS.

To do troubleshooting on your own, find your device as listed on the Device Manager. If you can't find your driver, double-click the listing that describes its type. For example, if you're looking for a CD-ROM drive listing, double-click the CD-ROM listing. Also, be sure to check under the Unknown devices category; your hardware may be lurking there. If your device isn't listed, then it is likely it does not have the driver and you need to install it as described in your documentation.

Once you find the listing that corresponds to your device, double-click that listing to open the device's Properties window. First, check the Driver tab. If the driver is missing or incorrect, click the Change Driver button to correct the driver. Follow the directions from there; you'll need the disks that came with your hardware.

If the Driver tab checks out, check out the Resources tab, which will tell you which resources are in use. Check out the pane at the bottom. If the resources are correct, it will say so. If they are incorrect, you'll need to change them.

1. First, uncheck the Use Automatic Settings box if it is checked.
2. Click the problem Resource listing; you'll know which one it is by the information at the bottom of the window.

3. Click the Change Setting button. This will open a box where you can scan through possible new settings by using arrow buttons.
4. When Windows tells you that you have found an unused setting, click OK to change the setting.
5. When you're done with the Windows, click OK to save your changes and Cancel to close the window without saving them.

The Panic Button

Once you've tried the steps above and exhausted the options listed in your documentation, it's time to call your hardware manufacturer for technical support. There may be a problem that they can easily diagnose, or the hardware may be defective.

Prevent Upgrading Woes with Backups

When you start digging around in your computer, there's always the chance—however remote—that you might mess something up and lose all your data. That's why it's important to back up your data before you perform an upgrade. Most hardware upgrades go smoothly, but "most" doesn't mean "all." Problems can range from minor annoyances to catastrophic computer lockups and destroyed data. Creating bootable disks and system backups lets you quickly recover if the upgrading process veers off course. Without these backups in hand, upgrade problems can quickly turn into a computer catastrophe; with a properly backed-up system, there are few problems from which you can't smoothly recover.

Regardless of whether your computer is running DOS, Windows 3.*x*, Windows 95, or Windows 98, you need to create an emergency *bootable disk*—also called a *system disk* or a *startup disk*. The disk will contain the system files needed to start a computer when it cannot boot up from the hard drive. You insert it into a disk drive before turning on the computer so the computer will understand it needs to search for the system files from the disk rather than the hard drive.

Creating a System Disk

It's possible to remove most of the risk involved in upgrading by completing a few quick steps before you start the process of upgrading. Creating a system disk, backing up important data, and performing several precautionary routines before opening the computer all protect your system against potential catastrophe.

Under normal circumstances, the computer finds data, called *system files*, on your computer's hard drive. During an upgrade, the system files are changed to account for the new hardware or software that has been added to the computer system. Most of the time, these changes don't cause any problems. But once in a while, the computer can't make sense of the changes, and as a result, it becomes inoperable. That's when a system disk comes in handy.

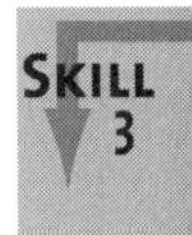

When you need to use it, insert the system disk in the disk drive before the computer is *booted up* (turned on). The computer automatically locates the files on the disk and launches the operating system. Then you can fix the problem—usually that means calling technical support—and resume normal computing operations.

Creating a system disk is simply a matter of transferring some files from your hard drive to a 3.5-inch disk. In DOS and Windows 3.*x*, the process is easy. In Windows 95 and Windows 98, it's even easier. All you need is a blank disk.

First Things First: Housecleaning

Before you do any of that, however, we recommend running CHKDSK (in DOS 6.1 or older) or ScanDisk (in DOS 6.2 or newer and Windows) to clean up your hard drive. You should be running these utilities on a regular basis, but it's an especially good idea to run them before performing an upgrade. After all, you don't want a glitch on your hard drive wreaking havoc with your new software and hardware.

To run CHKDSK in DOS 6.1 or older, simply type **chkdsk** at the C:\> prompt. Similarly, to run ScanDisk in DOS 6.2 or newer, type **scandisk** at the C:\> prompt. Users of Windows 3.*x* should run ScanDisk or CHKDSK from within DOS.

To run ScanDisk in Windows 98 and Windows 95, click the Start button and choose Programs. Open Accessories, select System Tools, and click ScanDisk. In the resulting window, click the OK button. When ScanDisk is finished, click Close to return to the desktop.

Now you're ready to proceed with the other pre-upgrade procedures.

Backups to Make Before Upgrading

You have a few options when creating a bootable disk. One type is often called a "clean" bootable disk and is designed to force a system to run in a simplified mode so the user can perform troubleshooting tasks. But the type we discuss below will get your computer running as close to normal as possible. You can use it during a failed upgrade to troubleshoot your computer if it can't access startup routines from its hard drive or when the routines on the hard drive aren't running properly.

You may not know the functions of all the files we discuss, but having these files on a bootable disk could be crucial when working with a technical support person and will save you lots of time when trying to recover your system.

DOS and Windows 3.*x*

Windows users should exit to the DOS prompt. Insert a disk in the disk drive and type **format a: /s** at the DOS prompt (where "a" is the drive letter assigned to the disk drive). This command formats the disk and copies the COMMAND.COM, IO.SYS (or IBMBIO.COM), and MSDOS.SYS (or IBMDOS.COM) files to the disk. When the process is complete, DOS will prompt you for a volume label. Enter a name, such as BootDisk, or leave it blank; then press Enter.

To copy the remaining system files to the disk, type the following commands at the DOS prompt, pressing Enter after each line.

```
copy c:\autoexec.bat a:
copy c:\config.sys a:
copy c:\dos\fdisk.exe a:
copy c:\dos\format.com a:
```

Windows users should execute the following commands as well, pressing Enter after each line.

```
copy c:\windows\win.ini a:
copy c:\windows\system.ini a:
```

In these examples, "c" refers to the drive letter assigned to the hard drive and "a" refers to the drive letter assigned to the disk drive.

TIP

Microsoft also recommends you copy .INI, .GRP, .DAT, and .PWL files from C:\WINDOWS. The files are not crucial to the computer's bootup routine, but they are worth having copies.

Copying these system files will get your computer up and running, but you should consider copying other files to your bootable disk. The best way to do determine which files to copy is to examine your CONFIG.SYS and AUTOEXEC.BAT files, particularly when their lines involve parts or device drivers stuffed into their own directories and folders on the hard drive. For example, your CONFIG.SYS file probably has lines such as these:

```
DEVICE=C:\WINDOWS\HIMEM.SYS
DEVICE=C:\WINDOWS\EMM386.EXE NOEMS
```

That means when you boot up your computer, it will look in the C:\WINDOWS directory for the crucial startup files HIMEM.SYS and EMM386.EXE. That will work fine if these files can be found on your hard drive (C:) as expected, but to allow your bootable disk to run on its own, it's best to copy files directly to it, and then use a text editor to change the lines to read as follows:


```
DEVICE=A:\HIMEM.SYS
DEVICE=A:\EMM386.EXE NOEMS
```

And, for example, suppose your CONFIG.SYS file has a line that reads: DEVICE= C:\SOUNDSW\CDSETUP.SYS, meaning that your computer will search your C: drive in the \SOUNDSW directory for a file called CDSETUP.SYS. If you needed this file, you would copy CDSETUP.SYS to the bootable disk, too, and, as above, correct the line in the CONFIG.SYS file. Not copying this file probably won't crash your computer, but it might keep something from working right.

NOTE NOTE NOTE NOTE NOTE NOTE NOTE NOTE NOTE NOTE NOTE NOTE NOTE NOTE NOTE

Windows 3.*x* users can format and create a system disk from within File Manager, as well. Just open File Manager's Disk menu, select the Format Disk or Make a System Disk command, and follow the on-screen prompts. This is one instance where it's actually quicker and easier to use DOS, however, and we recommend users employ the DOS method if it's available.

Here are some other files that probably need to be copied to your bootable disk:

- SQY55.SYS
- SSTBIO.SYS
- SSTDRIVE.SYS
- AH1544.SYS
- ILIM386.SYS
- ASPI4DOS.SYS

- SCSIHA.SYS
- SCSIDSK.EXE
- SKYDRVI.SYS
- ATDOSXL.SYSNONSTD.SYS
- DMDRVR.BIN
- SSTOR.SYS
- HARDRIVE.SYS
- EDVR.SYS
- FIXT_DRV.SYS
- LDRIVE.SYS
- ENHDISK.SYS

You also will want to copy these disk compressor files:

- STACKER.COM
- SSWAP.COM
- SSTOR.EXE
- DEVSWAP.COM
- XTRADRIV.SYS

TIP

We strongly suggest copying the following utilities from the C:\DOS directory to your disk: FORMAT.COM, SYS.COM, FDISK.EXE, ATTRIB.EXE, SCANDISK.EXE, CHKDSK.EXE, and MSCDEX.EXE.

Windows 95 and Windows 98

Creating a system disk in Windows 95 and Windows 98 is as easy as opening Control Panel, selecting the Add/Remove Programs icon, clicking the Startup Disk tag in the Add/Remove Programs Properties window, and clicking the Create Disk button. Just put a disk in the disk drive before clicking the Create Disk button. You may receive an error message asking you to insert the appropriate installation disk in the CD-ROM drive. Insert the disk and click OK to continue.

An on-screen dialog box tracks the progress of the process. When the creation process is complete, the Add/Remove Programs Properties window will appear on-screen again. Click the OK or Cancel button at the bottom of the window to return to the desktop.

A Windows 95 or Windows 98 bootable disk automatically includes many, but not all, the files we suggested for DOS and Windows 3.*x*. It's a good idea to check your bootable disk for the files it contains and then manually copy any other files you need to the disk. And if you can fit them on a mass storage drive such as a Zip disk, it's a great idea to make backups of crucial Registry files, such as SYSTEM.DAT and USER.DAT.

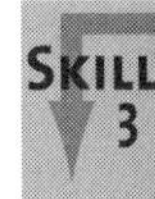

TIP TIP TIP TIP TIP TIP TIP TIP TIP TIP TIP TIP TIP TIP TIP TIP TIP TIP TIP TIP TIP TIP TIP TIP TIP TIP

When you've finished the process of creating a system disk, regardless of which operating system you used to create it, label the disk clearly and store it in a safe place.

It's also a good idea to add the line `PROMPT=BOOTED FROM FLOPPY $P$G` to your AUTOEXEC.BAT file. This will create a DOS prompt that reminds you the system has been booted from disk and shouldn't be considered fully operational.

Windows 95 and Windows 98 users will find that it's crucial to copy the MSCDEX.EXE and any special CD-ROM drivers to their boot disk. (DOS and Windows 3.*x* users also might find it useful.) Often, such CD-ROM drivers such as MSCDEX.EXE are essential to force a CD-ROM drive to run when the operating system isn't starting normally. SBIDE.SYS, TIMCD.SYS, and ASPI8CD.SYS are names of other common CD-ROM drivers, but the names are as varied as brands of CD-ROM drives.

To find your CD-ROM driver regardless of its brand, look in your `CONFIG.SYS` file for a line that reads `/D:MSCD001` or something similar. That's your cue the name of the driver you need is listed on that line. The actual entire line would read something such as `DEVICE=C:\SBCD\SBIDE.SYS /d:MSCD001`. In this example, the driver is the file SBIDE.SYS that's located in the C:\SBCD folder.

NOTE NOTE NOTE NOTE NOTE NOTE NOTE NOTE NOTE NOTE NOTE NOTE NOTE NOTE NOTE

With DOS and Windows 3.*x*, this approach always works because DOS and Windows 3.*x* *always* have lines in AUTOEXEC.BAT and CONFIG.SYS activating the CD-ROM drive. This driver is more difficult to find in Windows 95 and Windows 98 because these operating systems, once running, can work without such drivers and might not be referenced in the CONFIG.SYS file. If not, contact the maker of your CD-ROM drive for the information or, if your system is up, download the driver from your CD-ROM drive maker's site on the World Wide Web.

Testing Your Bootable Disk

Always test a bootable disk *before* you need it! Put the disk in the disk drive and restart the computer. If the computer starts more or less normally (or at least takes you to a DOS prompt) your boot disk is operational.

NOTE NOTE NOTE NOTE NOTE NOTE NOTE NOTE NOTE NOTE NOTE NOTE NOTE NOTE NOTE

If your hard drive has large device driver software such as Disk Manager or EZ-Drive, don't be surprised if your bootable disk doesn't allow you to access your hard drive. These utilities allow pre-1994 computers to use drives larger than 528MB, and pre-1996 computers to use drives larger than 2GB. Making a bootable disk that will work properly with them may require special procedures. Contact the device driver manufacturer for directions.

In Windows 95, the bootable disk won't fully restart the operating system, but the screen should read Starting Windows 95... and it will take you to a DOS screen. If you type **ver** and press Enter, you should see a message similar to Windows 95 [version 4.00.950]. And if you type **c:** and press Enter, you should be able to access your hard drive. If you can't, something's wrong.

Backup Software

Besides creating disks to get your system up and running in an emergency, a key tenet of safe computing is to make a full backup of all files on your system. A full backup is more than a bunch of files you've copied onto disks or Zip disks, It's a procedure that reproduces the entire contents, operating system, directory folder structure, and all that crucial configuration work and drivers needed to make your system work right.

Although we recommend using third-party backup or disk-cloning software (see the "Outside Backup Help" sidebar, below), you can use your operating system's built-in backup software in a pinch. In DOS, the utility Msbackup can be launched by typing **msbackup** at a DOS prompt. The utility is shown in Figure 3.4.

In Windows 3.*x*, you'll often find a utility called MWBACKUP.EXE. If you don't find an icon for activating it in Program Manager, you can use File Manager to find it in C:\DOS and then double-click it to start it. Unfortunately, both these backup utilities are limited because they can only back up to disks, which is impractical unless you have only 20MB to 30MB to back up.

FIGURE 3.4: It isn't pretty and your options are limited, but DOS' Msbackup utility can work in a pinch to back up your system.

In Windows 95 and Windows 98, you will find a backup program under the Start menu by selecting Programs, then Accessories, then System Tools. If it's not there, go to the Start menu, then select Settings ➢ Control Panel ➢ Add/Remove Programs, then install it from the Windows Setup tab. Then highlight Accessories and press the Details button to install it. (See Figure 3.5.)

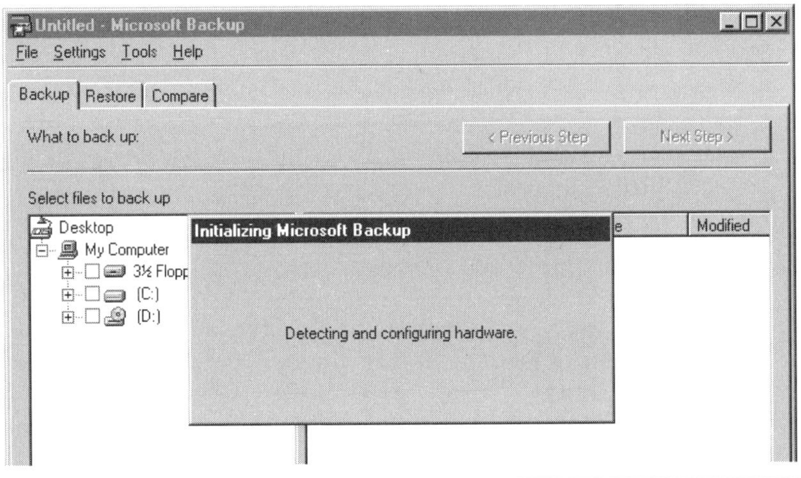

FIGURE 3.5: Windows 98 has a capable backup utility, but third-party backup software is still your best bet.

Windows 98's backup utility, produced by Seagate Software (`http://www.seagatesoftware.com`), is better than Windows 95's. Unfortunately, like Windows 95's backup program and unlike Seagate's retail version, it still can't create its own bootable disk, even though its help screens (at least in beta versions) give specific instructions for doing so.

Most backup software offers a mode called "verify," which double-checks during the backup process that what's recorded on the backup matches what's on the computer. It's a good idea to use the verify mode, run two backups, or both.

Remember to keep a copy of your backup software outside the computer. If your whole hard drive gets trashed, it will take your backup program down with it. After a total crash (or after installing an empty new hard drive) you would have to reinstall Windows before you could reinstall the backup program, if your backup program runs from Windows, before even starting to use your precious backup tapes or disks. So, you have to reinstall your operating system before you can reinstall your operating system! The problem is especially bad in Windows 95 and Windows 98. You also will have to get your CD-ROM drive running before you can even reinstall Windows. So, if you're running Windows 95 or Windows 98, we suggest getting backup software that makes its own disaster recovery disk.

TIP TIP TIP TIP TIP TIP TIP TIP TIP TIP TIP TIP TIP TIP TIP TIP TIP TIP TIP TIP TIP TIP TIP TIP TIP

At each step of your upgrade, run another backup. If, for example, your multimedia kit installation has your CD-ROM drive successfully running but not your sound card, perform a backup. If you don't, attempts to get the sound card working could set you further back. We suggest you run partial backups, not full backups, during an upgrade.

In your backup software, look for a mode called "differential" or something similar. It's the upgrader's most useful backup tool. Differential backs up your complete system without performing full backups. Obviously, you must run one full backup before the differential backup will work. But once you've got your full backup, a differential backup is a fast way to keep your backups current. Don't confuse differential with "incremental" backups, which don't work as well.

After a Windows 95 or Windows 98 system is installed and running, avoid using Windows 3.*x* or DOS backup software to restore old files to the system; the old software doesn't understand the Windows 95 system of long filenames and can create havoc.

Bootable disks and full system backups are your best prevention against upgrading nightmares. The backup process might seem like a pain at times, but the time and trouble you invest is nothing compared to the problems caused if you don't properly back up your computer.

TIP TIP TIP TIP TIP TIP TIP TIP TIP TIP TIP TIP TIP TIP TIP TIP TIP TIP TIP TIP TIP TIP TIP TIP TIP TIP TIP

When the backup process is complete, clearly label the disks or disks and mark the date on them, then store them in a safe place. If you later find a need to restore the backed up data to the hard drive, retrieve the disks or disks and use your backup utility's Restore command.

OUTSIDE BACKUP HELP

Microsoft's operating systems come with backup programs, but you're better off with some of the third-party backup utilities on the market.

NovaStor's NovaBack (`http://www.novastor.com`), Seagate's Backup Exec (`http://www.seagatesoftware.com`), and Computer Associates International's Cheyenne Backup (`http://www.cheyenne.com`) are all polished backup utilities, and each makes its own self-booting, one-step disaster-recovery disk. And these programs offer more backup options than Windows' built-in utilities.

Some of the best backup software is called *disk-cloning software*. It's often designed to quickly copy the entire contents of a hard drive or a partition onto another hard drive, Zip or Jaz disks, or even tape by using its own bootable disk. This type of software doesn't even need an installed operating system; typically, it can even back up disks containing several different operating systems.

These programs run up to 10 times faster than ordinary backup software. Disk-cloning utilities can be particularly useful if your upgrade involves installing a new or second hard drive because they can directly back up disk to disk, often saving time and hassles by bypassing tape, Zip or Jaz disks, or other removable media.

PowerQuest's DriveCopy copies one drive to another within one computer and automatically resizes partitions to fit a larger hard drive. And PowerQuest's Drive Image does everything DriveCopy does and is more of a true backup in that it backs to removable media and can even restore individual files.

continued ➧

Like Drive Image, Innovative Software's GHOST (`http://www.ghostsoft.com`) is pitched to folks supporting multiple computers. But don't ignore it if you only have one computer. Ghost's working downloadable demonstration version is free. The catch? It stops working at the end of the calendar month.

Although designed to handle many disk-swapping chores, Ontrack's disk utility, Disk Manager for Windows (`http://www.ontrack.com`) includes FileCopy, which does much the same painless disk-to-disk backup that DriveCopy does. Seagate's similar DiscWizard (`http://www.seagate.com/discwiz.shtml`) is free, but only with Seagate's retail hard drives and requires at least one Seagate drive in the system or it won't run. Also consider Quarterdeck's RealHelp (`http://www.quarterdeck.com`). Although not a normal backup program, it's designed specifically to record and back up all software upgrade changes you make and provide a seamless one-button escape if things go sour.

Opening the PC

The difficult part is complete. Creating a system disk and backing up data is the most time-consuming portion of the pre-upgrade process. Now it's just a matter of unplugging the computer and removing the cover.

Close any open applications, shut down your computer's operating system, and turn the computer off. Unplug the computer's power cable from the wall socket; do the same for any peripherals, such as printers, scanners, monitors, etc., that are connected to the computer. It may be helpful to unplug the peripherals from the computer, as well. Pay attention to where each peripheral connects to the PC, labeling each corresponding port and cable if necessary.

TIP

Colored tape works especially well for keeping track of corresponding ports and cables.

Next, clean off your desk or move your computer to a room where you have plenty of room to spread out the installation manuals, the new hardware, and your tools. We recommend performing the installation in a well-lighted, uncarpeted room, such as a kitchen or workroom.

It's especially important to avoid carpeted rooms if you can. Carpet is a problem for two reasons. First of all, it's tough to find screws when they fall in the carpet. Second and more importantly, carpet is a prime conductor of static electricity.

Static electricity, which causes those nasty shocks you get from touching a metal doorknob in a carpeted room, can damage a computer's fragile circuits and chips. For this reason, leave your new components in their antistatic bags until you're ready to insert them. Also, ground yourself by touching the computer's metal frame before you touch any of your computer's innards. Finally, even if you're working in an uncarpeted room and have grounded yourself repeatedly, it's a good idea to keep fingers and tools away from the computer's intricate circuitry.

The act of removing the computer's cover (which also may be referred to as the computer's case) is different for every make and model of computer. Some computer covers slide off; others are held in place by screws. A few computers even employ locking devices that require you to use special tools or keys to remove their covers. Check your user's manual for the exact removal procedure you should follow for your PC.

Don't be afraid to apply some force when removing the cover, but you shouldn't have to strain. If you feel the cover bending or hear anything crack, stop immediately and double-check the user's manual or contact the manufacturer to learn the correct way of removing the cover.

Before you use your screwdriver—and check to see whether you need a Phillips or a flat-head screwdriver before you take a trip to your toolkit—make sure you know which screws hold the cover on. As a rule, don't remove any screws that aren't located along the edge of the cover. *Never* remove any screws near your computer's fan, AC connection, or ports. (See Figure 3.6.)

When you remove a screw, remember where you put it so you can re-insert it when you're done with the upgrade. We recommend using a small bowl or cup to hold your screws while you work so you don't accidentally knock them on the floor or lose them among the installation tools.

After you've removed it, put the cover out of the way. Read the instruction manual completely before beginning the installation. This may save you some time in the long run and will help you understand the installation procedure before you have a chance to mess things up.

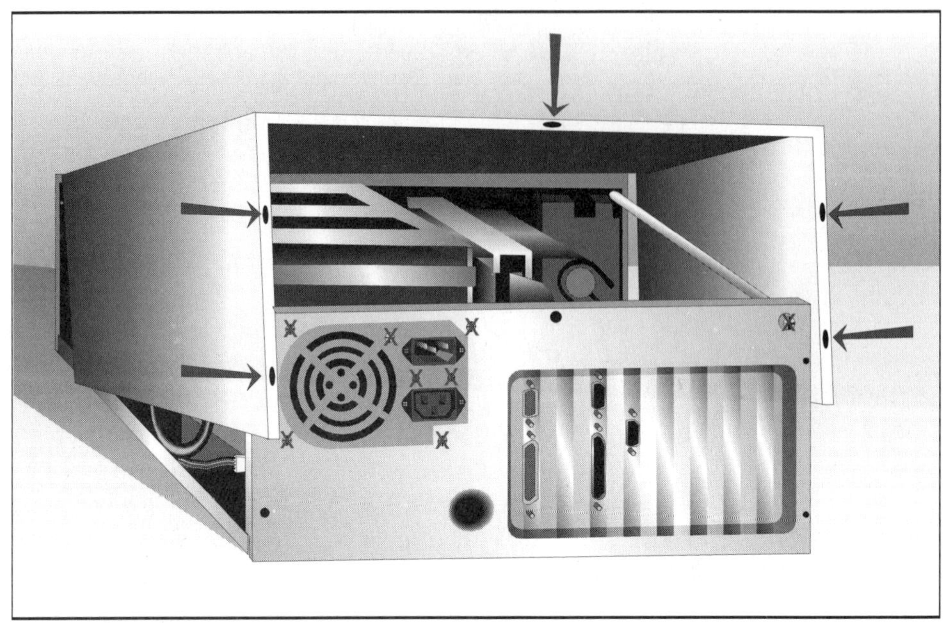

FIGURE 3.6: Remove the appropriate screws carefully.

Finally, ground yourself one more time by touching the computer's frame. Take a deep breath, and dig in.

Are You Experienced?

Now you can...

- ☑ edit system files
- ☑ troubleshoot backup problems
- ☑ make a backup disk
- ☑ choose backup software
- ☑ open up your computer

SKILL 4

Installing Random Access Memory

- Understanding your upgrade options with RAM
- Learning about the different kinds of memory modules and RAM
- Evaluating how much RAM you have and how much you need
- Locating the SIMM sockets on the motherboard
- Removing and replacing RAM

When it comes to computers, there's no such thing as too much memory. Random access memory (RAM) gives the machine room to maneuver. It defines performance more than any other subsystem, with the exception of the central processing unit (CPU). Thus it's no surprise that a computer with a Pentium processor running at 100MHz and 32MB of RAM outperforms a 133MHz Pentium computer with only 8MB of RAM.

RAM is also one of the cheapest and easiest upgrades you can make. With memory as cheap as it is (less than $5 per megabyte), it's foolish *not* to stock up on RAM to ensure faster PC performance.

What You Need to Know

Tools: Phillips screwdriver

Time: 10 to 30 minutes if slots are exposed and easy to get to

Cost: 16MB approximately $100

32MB approximately $199

64MB approximately $399

Skill Level: Easy to Intermediate

Benefits: Provides increased speed and a general performance boost

All the RAM You Can Get

The amount of memory installed in a computer determines the number and size of the applications your computer can handle. It also determines the size of the largest data file. When you direct your computer to launch an application, the operating system copies the program from the hard drive or diskette into memory, where it executes application instructions and processes data. Therefore, it's logical that the more RAM your computer has (without exceeding the maximum allowable configuration), the faster it will work.

In the days before Microsoft Windows, personal computers functioned quite well on less than 1MB of RAM. When the popular DOS character-based computing environment gave way to the graphical 16-bit operating system known as Windows, memory requirements increased dramatically. While users could run Windows 3.1 on a 386-based system with only 2MB or 4MB of memory, the system experienced noticeable performance improvements with 8MB.

Today, Windows 95 needs at least 16MB of RAM just to run. The peripherals attached to your system also affect memory requirements. For example, large-screen monitors require more memory to display graphics than smaller screens. Add to this the demands of memory-intensive word processors, spreadsheets, database managers, desktop publishers, and Internet browsers, and you can understand why memory-hungry 32-bit operating environments such as Windows 95 and Windows NT run much better with 32MB to 64MB of RAM, respectively. You also will find that systems used for graphic arts, publishing, or multimedia run faster with at least 64MB of RAM. You can expect memory requirements to increase as software and operating system developers add new features.

Hard Drive Access

Today's computers come with large hard drives; storage capacities range from 500MB to more than 8GB. They tend to work similar to a filing cabinet; just as you don't climb inside a filing cabinet to work, your computer can't really work inside your hard drive. When you tell the computer to launch an application or open a document, it retrieves information from hard drive storage and places a copy of it (or a copy of just the portions it needs) into RAM. As a result, the more memory you have, the more applications and files you can work with at one time.

When several programs are open simultaneously, the operating system must swap between them, which means the hard drive has to be accessed frequently. RAM allows programs to be accessed from memory rather than the hard drive. Because memory access is faster than drive access, swap time decreases and performance improves when plenty of RAM is available.

There is no doubt that performance suffers on memory-challenged systems: Actions execute slowly, and pop-up messages advise that you can't run a program, create a large file, or print one document while working in another. These error alerts are "out of memory" messages. Your computer is telling you it doesn't have enough RAM to do what you want. It is not a question of storage; you can have lots of hard drive space and still be short on memory. If you frequently run out of memory while working, it may be time to buy and install some more.

Types of Memory

To simplify installation and conserve space inside the computer, memory manufacturers mount several RAM chips on the surface of a tiny printed plastic circuit board or card called a *memory module*. Each card has a gold or tin/lead contact that inserts into a special socket on the motherboard. Instead of plugging in large amounts of memory one chip at a time, you simply insert one or two memory modules, each containing eight RAM chips.

Long and Short Term Memory

A computer can store information on its hard drive, or it can place it in memory on integrated circuits known as chips. Memory comes in a couple of forms; volatile and non-volatile. Memory is considered *volatile* (temporary or short-term) if the storage area in the semiconductor holding the data clears out whenever you reset or turn off your computer. However, memory is *non-volatile* (permanent or long-term) if the storage area continues to retain data when power is turned off.

When a computer runs out of short-term memory, it can store information on the hard drive, but this degrades system performance. On the other hand, if the computer loads an application into memory rather than accessing it from the hard drive, you can get more work done in less time because you don't have to wait for the system to respond to your commands or complete requested tasks.

Volatile integrated circuits are typically identified as RAM because a computer can read data from or write data to these chips in any order. Non-volatile circuits devoted to memory storage include *read-only memory* (ROM), a kind of memory that can be read but not written to; *programmable read-only memory* (PROM), a type of ROM that cannot be reprogrammed once data has been written to it with a hardware device known as a PROM programmer; and *erasable programmable read-only memory* (EPROM), a memory chip that is programmed after manufacture, but can be reprogrammed only if the chip is exposed to ultraviolet light when its protective top cover is removed.

Memory Modules

Some computers require *single in-line memory modules* (SIMMs). Other computers require *dual in-line memory modules*, known as DIMMs. Older 386- and 486-based computers use 30-pin SIMMs, while some 486- and Pentium-based computers use 72-pin SIMMs. Newer Pentium machines may use 168-pin DIMMs. The 30-, 72-, and 168-pin modules are of different lengths, but they all take up very little horizontal surface area on the motherboard. To find out how many pins are in a module, simply look for a stenciled pin number on one side of the module.

SIMMs differ from DIMMs in terms of how their pins are wired. The pins on either side of a SIMM are electrically joined (see Figure 4.1 for an illustration of a SIMM socket), while the lead pins on either side of a DIMM are electrically independent, allowing for faster data access. The pins on a module allow information to pass between RAM chips and the CPU.

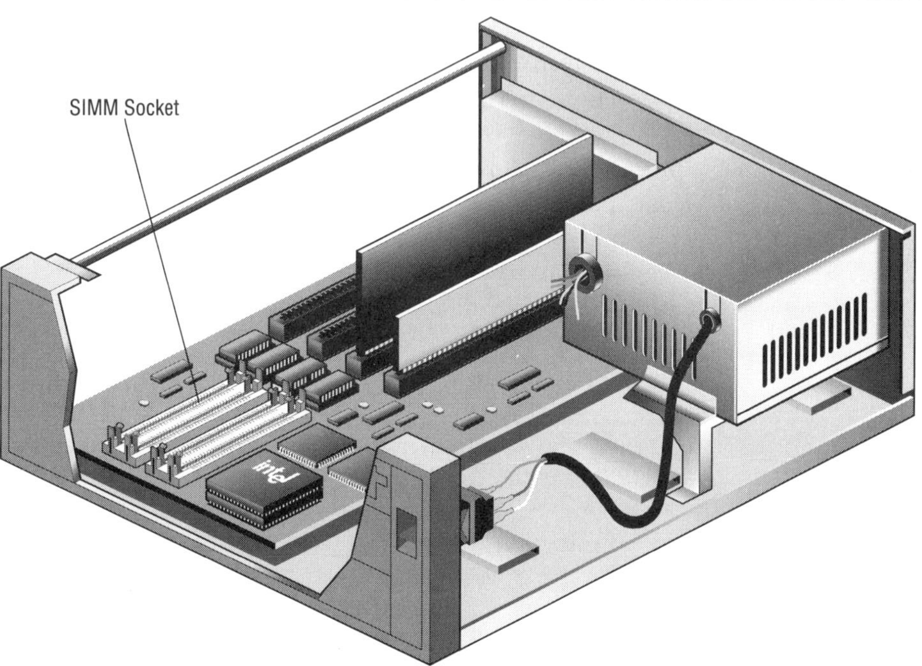

FIGURE 4.1: The SIMM sockets are usually long, white parallel channels, and the pins of the SIMM are joined.

RAM Chips

There are several kinds of RAM chips. Popular types include *dynamic RAM* (DRAM), *static RAM* (SRAM), *Extended Data Output* (EDO) *RAM*, and *synchronous DRAM* (SDRAM).

- DRAM chips are less expensive than SRAM chips, because they have more simplistic circuitry. They also are slower (with access speeds of 60ns or more), because they store information in chips containing *capacitors* (battery-like components able to hold an electrical charge), which must be continuously refreshed. When a DRAM chip is being refreshed, it cannot be read by the processor.
- SRAM does not need to be continuously recharged. It can store only about one-fourth of the information of a comparable DRAM chip, but because it has an access speed of 15ns to 30ns, it runs much faster. SRAM is typically used in a RAM *cache* (a special area of memory that stores the contents of frequently accessed data and their locations), in order to pass it directly to the CPU.
- EDO RAM is a kind of DRAM. It improves system performance by allowing for faster read times than any DRAM of comparable speed. With EDO, information from a previous read cycle is made available to the CPU while the next memory read cycle is about to begin. By allowing your system to start the next read cycle more quickly, it increases performance from 5 percent to 20 percent, depending on the computer.

NOTE NOTE NOTE NOTE NOTE NOTE NOTE NOTE NOTE NOTE NOTE NOTE NOTE NOTE NOTE

Not all computers can take advantage of EDO RAM. If you have a Pentium system board with an Intel Triton, Opti Viper, or VLSI chip set, you have an EDO-compatible system. To see for yourself, turn on your computer and note the Basic Input/Output System (BIOS) version number that displays. If you see the extension BS0T, BR0T, CS1T or CS0T, then you can use EDO.

- SDRAM is RAM that is synchronized to the system clock controlling the CPU. It boasts data retrieval times up to 25 percent faster than EDO RAM because it eliminates wait states, utilizes several memory banks simultaneously, and offers support for a "burst" mode that addresses an entire block of data rather than just one piece.

Finding How Much RAM You Have and How Much You Need

You can tell how much RAM your PC has when it powers on. Just keep your eyes on the welcome screen. After the system runs a memory test, but before reaching the C:\> prompt or launching Windows, it displays a tag line with the total amount of installed memory (measured in kilobytes).

Once in Windows 95/98 or Windows NT, you can tell how much RAM you have installed by clicking the System Control Panel and reading the RAM information that is displayed on the General tab in the System Properties dialog box. Windows 3.*x* users can check system resources by opening the About Program Manager dialog box. DOS and Windows users can type **MEM** and press Enter at the C:\> prompt to obtain the current RAM count.

Which RAM Is Right for You?

Before adding more RAM, determine what kind of RAM your computer needs. You'll find this information on the original invoice or packing slip. It may read *4 × 4MB 70NS, No Parity Memory*. This means that you have 16MB of 70 nanosecond non-parity memory, inserted in four separate memory banks, with every bank containing 4MB of RAM.

Or, you might see something such as *48MB SDRAM, 2 DIMMs*, which means you have 48MB of SDRAM, distributed in two DIMM modules, each containing 24MB of SDRAM. (*Parity* refers to the method most 386- and 486-based machines use to check memory for data integrity. Parity memory adds a single bit to each byte of data. This bit then checks for errors in the byte's other 8 bits. If you install *non-parity* SIMMs in a system that needs parity SIMMs, it will not function properly.)

If your system is more than 4 years old, you'll most likely need 30-pin, 70ns fast-page mode (FPM) SIMMs. These are shorter than 72-pin SIMM modules and are used in most older Industry Standard Architecture (ISA) systems. If your system is less than 4 years old, it may use 72-pin non-parity SIMMs. Most systems with Pentium processors also use non-parity chips, while current system boards are likely to use 168-pin DIMMs.

Call your computer manufacturer to determine your system's RAM specifics. Questions you should ask include:

- Does your system take SIMMs or DIMMs?
- How many memory module sockets are there in your computer?

- How are your current SIMMs or DIMMs configured?
- What is the maximum RAM configuration your system permits?
- What kind of RAM is installed? Is it FPM, EDO, SDRAM, or something else?
- Is it buffered or unbuffered? Buffered DIMMs have a centered notch. The notch on unbuffered DIMMs is off to the right.
- Must RAM be installed in pairs? In other words, if you want to add 32MB of RAM, can you insert just one 32MB SIMM or DIMM into an empty socket or must you purchase two 16MB SIMMs?

NOTE NOTE NOTE NOTE NOTE NOTE NOTE NOTE NOTE NOTE NOTE NOTE NOTE NOTE NOTE

Pentium systems typically require memory to be installed in pairs.

- What are the voltage requirements for the new SIMMs or DIMMs? Typically, an unbuffered DIMM is rated at a 5-volt operating voltage, while a buffered DIMM is rated at 3.3 volts.
- What speed chips must you buy? For example, a Gateway P5-90 with an installed Intel P54C (Plato) motherboard requires SIMMs rated at 70ns. It may be OK to add faster chips, but not slower. The faster the chip, the lower its ns rating. Thus, 60ns chips are faster than 70ns chips.

Finally, ask if there's any other information you should know. Technical support folks should be able to tell you if there is anything specific to look out for when adding RAM to your system.

Shopping for RAM

RAM is a commodity; once you know what your system needs, shop around. Keep in mind, however, not all memory is created equal. For example, you can put EDO and FPM RAM in the same system as long as two different types aren't paired together. Stick with EDO if you have a choice. Don't mix parity and non-parity, and don't mix speeds.

Don't sacrifice quality to save a few dollars; purchase RAM from a company that will stand behind its products. Troublesome memory isn't worth the aggravation and downtime.

If you're looking for a reputable vendor, try Kingston Technology (`http://www.kingston.com`), currently the world's largest memory module manufacturer. Kingston may charge more for its memory modules than others, because it designs modules to be system-specific: You know they will be a perfect match for your computer. Also, Kingston memory modules come with a lifetime warranty, plus toll-free technical support to walk you through the installation process or troubleshoot any problems you may encounter.

New Jersey–based PNY Technologies Inc. (`http://www.pny.com`) is another reputable memory module manufacturer offering a lifetime warranty on its modules. However, due to the market shortage of 70ns chips, PNY modules use 60ns RAM chips. While it may be possible to install 60ns chips in a slot rated for 70ns, check with your computer manufacturer to confirm your computer can handle the speed bump.

How Much Do You Need?

Before you make a purchase, make sure you know how much RAM you need to buy. If sockets are limited, you may have to remove an installed SIMM or DIMM to make room. For example, because memory in a Dell Dimension XPS M200s can be increased to a maximum of 64MB and the system board features only two DIMM sockets, a system that contains 48MB of RAM is configured with a 32MB DIMM and a 16MB DIMM. To increase system RAM to a maximum of 64MB, you must remove the 16MB DIMM and replace it with a 32MB DIMM.

Ready to Install

Once you've gathered all of the tools you are going to need, it's time to roll up your sleeves and get down to business.

1. First and foremost, make sure that you have read Skill 3, and have backed up your system.
2. Turn off and unplug the computer and all peripherals.
3. Remove the computer cover (store any cover-mounting screws in a cup or tray for safe-keeping). Do not use a power-driven screwdriver.

4. Before removing the new memory module from its antistatic package or touching any components inside the computer, ground yourself by touching a metal surface.

5. Remember to handle the memory module by its ends, without applying any excessive pressure.

Installing a SIMM

The steps described below provide a general approach to installing a 72-pin SIMM (see Figure 4.2). Not all installations are alike, so refer to you computer's reference manual for specific instructions. If you feel nervous about proceeding, call the computer manufacturer's tech support line for assistance.

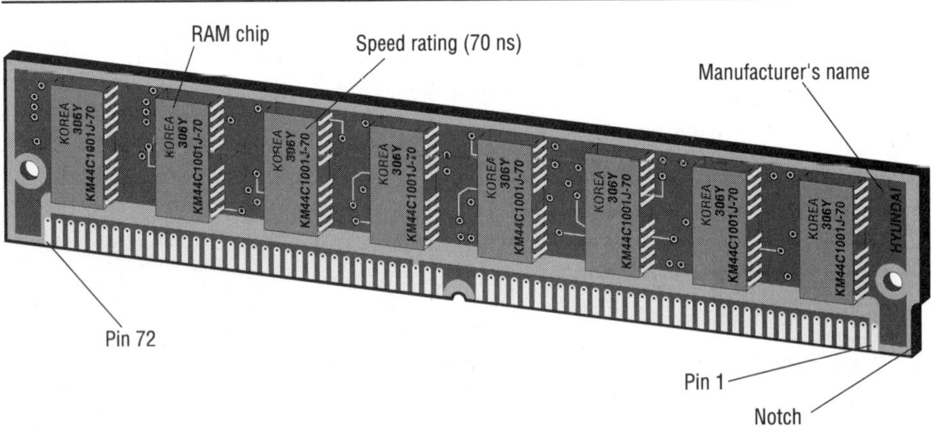

FIGURE 4.2: A typical 4MB 72-pin SIMM

1. If you have 72-pin SIMMs, there should be 2- or 4.25-inch white, tan, or black sockets with metal or plastic clips on the end. These are the SIMM sockets.

2. If you must remove a memory module in order to upgrade, wait at least 5 seconds after turning off the computer before removing the module. Gently pull out the metal or plastic socket clamps to release the SIMM from the socket. Tilt the module towards the front of the socket and gently lift it out.

3. Line up the new SIMM's center cutout with the middle plastic tap in the socket.

4. Insert the SIMM into the socket, starting the module at about a 45 degree angle. Make sure the SIMM aligns the same way as the other modules currently installed. Using both hands, place your index fingers on the corners of the module, and push it up to a 60 degree angle. Continue pivoting the SIMM upward toward the back of the socket. When the module is between 60 and 90 degrees, it will push the clamps outward as it passes them. The clamps lock into place behind the module when the SIMM is at a 90 degree angle (see Figure 4.3).

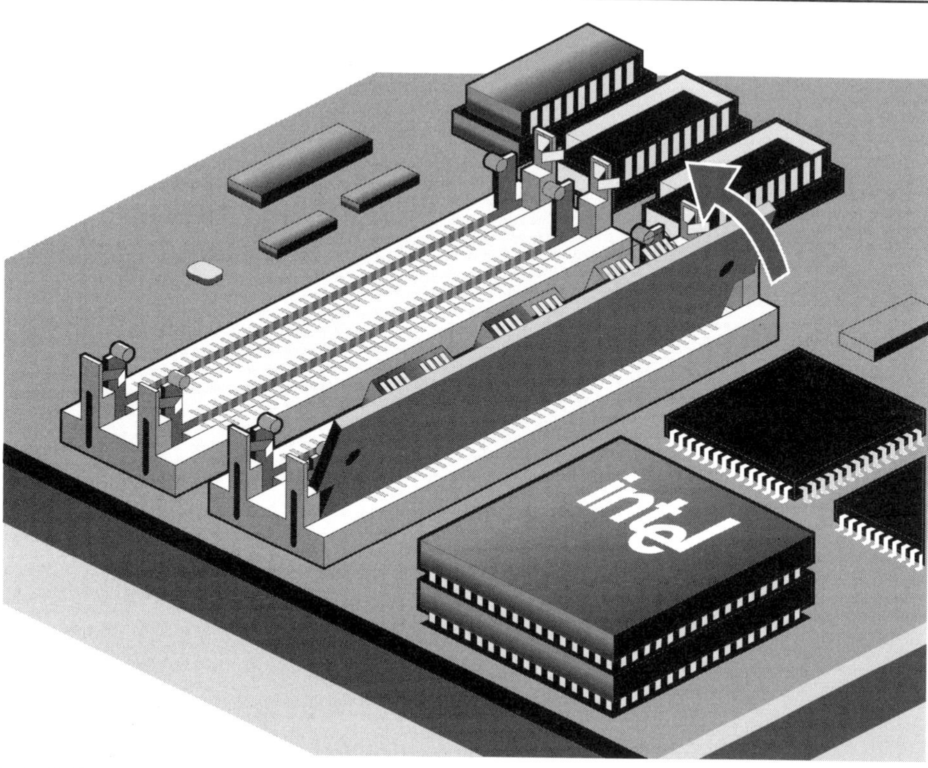

FIGURE 4.3: SIMMs are installed at an angle, then snapped into the metal clipholders.

Installing a DIMM

To perform a DIMM memory upgrade, follow the instructions outlined above for work inside the computer and refer to the installation instructions in the computer's user manual. You also can follow the general steps outlined below. Consult your computer manufacturer's tech support line for step-by-step assistance.

1. If you must remove a memory module before upgrading, wait at least 5 seconds after turning off the computer before removing the module.
2. Carefully press down on the ejector tab at each end of the DIMM socket to pop the DIMM out of the socket.
3. To install a new DIMM, orient the module with its socket, aligning the ends of the DIMM with the pair of guides at each end of the DIMM socket.
4. Hold the DIMM by its top edges. Insert one end, then the other, into the socket; pressing the ends, one side at a time, until the module is fully seated. Do not insert the DIMM by pressing on its center.
5. Snap each ejector tab over the top of the DIMM at each end of the module.

Testing the New Memory

To make sure you've done everything correctly, follow these steps:

1. Replace the computer cover and reconnect it to its power source. Turn on the computer.
2. Watch the welcome screen to verify that the memory you've just installed now figures into the memory total that displays on-screen after the computer runs its memory test.
3. If everything checks out, continue working as you would normally. If the memory total is incorrect, turn off the computer once the startup completes. A blank screen may result if memory is installed incorrectly or if the wrong memory is installed.
4. Disconnect the computer from the power source. Remove the cover and make sure the installed modules are correctly seated in their sockets. Make adjustments if necessary and then repeat step 1.
5. Press Del+F1, or whatever keys are necessary to enter the computer's Setup program. Once in Setup, the computer should automatically input the right

memory settings. Verify that Setup's Extended Memory category reflects the newly installed RAM total. Save the settings and exit to reboot with the new configuration.

6. If the memory test still doesn't acknowledge the newly installed RAM, you may have a bad memory module. Call the manufacturer.

Once everything is working correctly, you should find that your applications run faster, and your computer performs better.

Are You Experienced?

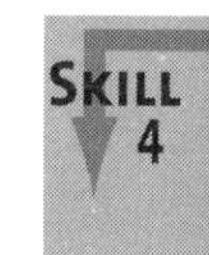

Now you can...

- ☑ evaluate the types of RAM and memory modules
- ☑ find out how much RAM you have
- ☑ shop around for RAM
- ☑ install RAM into your computer
- ☑ test your installation

SKILL 5

Installing a CPU

- Weighing the benefits of upgrading your CPU
- Learning the components of a CPU
- Understanding the differences in CPU architecture
- Installing a new CPU

Your computer's *central processing unit* (CPU) is the most important part of any computer. It's the brains of the outfit: the chip that transfers data throughout your PC. The CPU, often called the processor, also determines the speed at which your computer processes data.

The CPU is the brain of your computer, responsible for routing and performing each and every task. As you may guess, upgrading this little chip can have a big influence on how quickly your system runs and what it can run.

What You Need to Know

Tools: Screwdriver, your computer's or motherboard's manual, chip extraction tool (included in upgrade kit if needed)

Time: 15 to 45 minutes

Cost: $100 to $300

Skill Level: Intermediate to Difficult

Benefits: Improves your computer's processing speed, allowing it to run more advanced programs more quickly

Considering an Upgrade

Be careful when you consider upgrading your CPU. With computer prices continually falling, you're often better off saving your money for a new computer with components that are far faster than your present setup. When you upgrade a processor, you also must often upgrade your memory and hard drive to eliminate information bottlenecks, which are slow data-transmission areas that limit the computer's speed.

Another problem with upgrading processors is that, unlike many kinds of upgrades, processors are not interchangeable. You can take any printer or modem and use them on most newer computers, but you cannot do the same with a processor. CPUs have different voltage requirements and fit into different types of slots. Intel offers upgrade kits, such as its Pentium OverDrive upgrades (see the "Put That Old Chip into Overdrive" sidebar), to allow you to safely navigate these technical differences. Remember, *never* just replace one processor with another.

PUT THAT OLD CHIP INTO OVERDRIVE

Although it's not the first upgrade that you should consider, upgrading a CPU can be effective if you can do it for less than $200.

If you want to upgrade your processor, don't just pop a new processor onto your motherboard. Instead you'll need to use a kit, such as the OverDrive processor upgrade kit from Intel, the leading manufacturer of PC processors. As the name implies, you get more with a kit than just the processor; you get a processor housed in a specially designed casing that allows it to work with an older computer.

First, the kit will regulate the power coming into your processor; voltage requirements of processors are continually changing and the kit needs to perform this regulatory function to prevent from blowing out the processor. Second, the kit's processor itself usually must be specially designed to allow it to work correctly with an older computer. Also, it may include a special fan to cool the new processor. (Because of these requirements, you need to find a processor that works with your computer. Not all upgrade kits fit all computers. Ask your local computer store for more information.) Your best bet to find a processor upgrade kit is to look at a local computer store.

If you have a pre-486 chip, you're probably out of luck; you're far better off to look for a new computer than to waste time looking for an upgrade. While Intel is no longer pushing 486 upgrades, you may be able to find a good deal from one of the lesser-known manufacturers such as AMD (`http://www.amd.com`) or Evergreen Technologies (`http://www.evertech.com`). As for cost, you can expect to pay about $100 to upgrade a 486 processor. You may be able to get an even better deal if you find a store closing out these kits.

If you're looking to upgrade a Pentium-class processor, expect to spend about $250 for a high-end Pentium with MMX running at 200MHz. To upgrade to a lower-speed Pentium, such as a 166MHz Pentium with MMX, you can expect to pay about $200.

continued

Here is the latest line of Intel OverDrive processors, listing the original processor and the processor option(s) that will work with that system.

Original Processor	New Processor
Pentium 75MHz	Pentium 150MHz with MMX
Pentium 90MHz	Pentium 180MHz with MMX
Pentium 100MHz	Pentium 166MHz or 200MHz with MMX
Pentium 120MHz	Pentium 180MHz with MMX
Pentium 150MHz	Pentium 180MHz with MMX
Pentium 166MHz	Pentium 200MHz with MMX

Remember to consult with your computer store before upgrading because you need to make sure you're getting the right processor for your system. Better yet, have a professional install your new CPU.

If you choose to upgrade your processor, you probably won't be able to unless your computer has at least a 486 CPU. If your computer has an 8088, 8086, 286, or 386 CPU, forget about upgrading; you won't be able to find decent processors to replace your present model. If you have a 486, you have some options available, even though Intel seems to have stopped pushing these upgrades.

If you have a Pentium-based PC that's faster than 75MHz, you can perform decent upgrades on your system with an OverDrive upgrade. Incremental leaps in processor speed are not worth the money; aim for doubling your clock speed when you perform this type of upgrade.

But microprocessor upgrades aren't for every computer. Performance enhancements vary greatly. Some microprocessors can't be upgraded, and others just aren't worth it. The good news is, if your computer can handle a faster CPU, it's easier than you might think to do the actual installation. In fact, the hardest part is finding out whether your computer can be upgraded, and then getting your hands on the correct unit.

A Brief History of CPU Architecture

Much of the confusion about upgrading CPUs has to do with their changing architecture. For many years, IBM-compatible microprocessors, in a market ruled by Intel, marched along in an orderly fashion: the 286 family, then the 386, then the 486. Each family of processors was more advanced, with a faster array of clock speeds.

The numbering sequence was thrown off in 1993, when Intel introduced its Pentium family to replace the 486 processor, and then again in 1997 when Intel added MMX technology to the Pentium chip to enhance its multimedia capabilities.

Nevertheless, the processor remained in a familiar form: a small, flat chip inserted into a socket on the *motherboard*, the main circuit board to which all electrical components are attached. Some CPUs fit into different-sized sockets ("Socket 5" and "Socket 7" are two common sizes), but the idea of upgrading was the same: You popped out one chip, then put in another.

Then came Intel's Pentium II, which basically merged the capabilities of the home-geared MMX chips and the business-geared Pentium Pros. If you've asked about swapping out your existing CPU for a Pentium II and have been puzzled by the response, a simple glance at both processors would answer your question. Instead of a square microprocessor chip, the Pentium II is a larger cartridge, more specifically, a *Single Edge Contact* (SEC) that consists of the processor and its *cache* (an area where frequently accessed data and machine instructions are stored), packed into plastic and metal. This cartridge is inserted into a special slot on the motherboard.

The design change is fundamental enough that although you may be able to upgrade your existing MMX-based Pentium chip to something faster, it won't be called a Pentium II unless you get a new motherboard or new computer.

Terms to Remember

Every PC processor has two major characteristics: the *generation* and the *clock speed*. A new generation of computer occurs when significant improvements are made to a class of CPUs. Generations often are referred to in numbers. The oldest PC processors are the 8086 and the 8088, followed by the 286, the 386, and the 486. This numerical progression was

continued

interrupted by chip-maker Intel when the company introduced its Pentium processors, the equivalent of the 586. Since then, Intel has introduced the Pentium Pro (686) chip, the Pentium with MMX Technology, and most recently, the Pentium II, which is the fastest of this class of processors. Of course, the other processor makers, led by Cyrix and AMD, continue to release processors with numerical names reminiscent of the Intel line of processors.

Clock speed is the relative measure of the processor's speed and is measured in megahertz (MHz). Clock speed of a processor is only one factor in a computer's performance and should never be taken as an absolute measure of a system's speed, even though some people like to compare clock speed numbers like they compare horsepower in cars. The thing to remember is this: If—and only if all other things are equal—you take two computers of the same generation from the same manufacturer, the one with the higher clock speed will be faster. Clock speed comparisons are only meaningful when you compare two chips of the same generation and manufacturer. For example, you cannot compare the clock speeds of a 486 running at 75MHz and a Pentium running at 150MHz and say the Pentium is twice as fast.

Can You Upgrade?

Here's what your upgrade options boil down to, depending of course on whether your specific system is upgradeable:

- If you have an MMX-based computer and you want it to run faster, you're too far ahead in the CPU race to have any options, aside from replacing the whole motherboard. If you're itching to upgrade *something*, you're probably better off turning your attention to the amount of RAM. (See Skill 4.) Then, sit back and content yourself with fond memories of the day you became the first on your block to bring home MMX.

- If you have a Pentium-based machine *without* MMX, the news is better. Chip upgrade companies sell kits, often based on microprocessors made by Intel's rival AMD, to users who want richer multimedia experiences. Intel also has a line of OverDrive processors specifically for upgrading to MMX.
- If you have a 486-based machine, you won't be able to upgrade to MMX, but you can hook yourself up with a more advanced chip. Intel has discontinued its OverDrive line for this generation of processors, but other companies are still serving users looking to breathe life into older machines.
- If you're still hanging onto a 386-based machine or older, however, you're essentially out of luck. These upgrade kits are difficult to find. And even if you do manage to get your hands on an old one, you may find it's not worth the money in the long run. Your computer still won't be able to run most of the software you see in stores, unless you upgrade lots of other things—and by then you may as well buy a new computer.

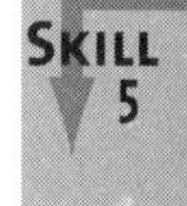

Investigating Upgrade Kits

Most of the microprocessors on the market are sold by Intel, AMD, and Cyrix, but Intel is the only chip manufacturer that offers upgrades directly. This is where the chip upgrade kits we've mentioned come in.

These more complete kits help you sort out all the "ifs" of the upgrade process—from figuring out whether the upgrade is compatible, to providing you with the tools and parts you need (aside from a small screwdriver), to walking you through the installation process and providing a technical support number.

If you want to upgrade, you can start by contacting either Intel (`http://www.intel.com`) or a company that sells upgrade kits, such as Evergreen Technologies (`http://www.evertech.com`), Kingston Technology (`http://www.kingston.com`), or Trinity Works (`http://www.trinityworks.com`). Also, you can contact your computer's manufacturer or inquire at the store where you bought your computer.

Delving into the Details

You may see CPUs advertised in computer circulars and think that you can just go buy any new chip, take it home, and install it. If only it were that simple. We don't recommend that the average home user attempt a chip upgrade without an upgrade module of some sort or professional help.

CPU Components

You *could*, in theory, buy and install a new processor on your own, but there are more subtle issues that need to be resolved when you upgrade a CPU. This is true despite the fact that chip upgrade kits make you feel as if swapping chips is all there is to CPU upgrading. In reality, depending on your system, any number of related items may come into play.

First of all, the new chip simply may not fit. Upgrade kits will accommodate for this and may even come with some kind of a socket extender to make up for the difference.

Cooling Systems

The cooling system may consist of a *heat sink* and/or fan. A heat sink is a device, usually made of metal, that absorbs and dissipates the heat generated by all the electrical currents coursing through a microprocessor. Heat sinks are often a grid-like pattern of metal fins that actually take up more space than the chip itself (see Figure 5.1). Some chips come with heat sinks attached to their tops by epoxy, while others come as a separate part and must be attached to the chip, usually with an adhesive backing.

FIGURE 5.1: A heat sink for a CPU

In addition, the design of components in some computers is such that the regular air flow through the computer (generated by the computer's main fan) is enough to dissipate the heat and keep the chip cool—this sort of design is called *passive heat sink*. But other manufacturers mount a fan on the chip's heat sink to move air through the fins, and such systems are called *active heat sinks*. This fan may be powered through the chip or separately.

If either the old or new processor has a separately-powered fan, unattaching or attaching it adds a step to the upgrading process. The chip upgrade kit helps you sort out the details and makes sure the CPU has the right type of cooling system.

BIOS

Another consideration is that you may need to upgrade your *Basic Input/Output System* (BIOS). The BIOS is a combination of hardware and software built into the read-only memory (ROM) of most computers. It controls the startup processes and other basic functions. Without the correct BIOS, your system may not be able to recognize a new microprocessor.

Some upgrade kits include a disk with the BIOS upgrade, and you basically just run the program. If the kit doesn't include a BIOS upgrade and your computer needs one, the upgrade kit should at least help you find the right place to call. (For more information, see Skill 23.)

Voltage

Finally, there are important issues of voltage to consider. Oftentimes, when manufacturers improve processors, the required voltage changes. For example, one may run at 5 volts, and another at 3.3 volts. If you replace one with the other, the computer may work fine for a while, but eventually the new processor will burn up. Some kind of a *voltage regulator* is required to change the old voltage into one the new chip can handle. Chip upgrades have this built in, so you should never have to think about it.

Types of Sockets

Most likely, particularly on a Pentium-based computer, the processor is in a *zero-insertion force* (ZIF) socket. With a ZIF socket, a tension arm—or possibly an overhead bar or retaining screw—holds the microprocessor in place.

Your existing CPU may, however, be in a *low-insertion force* (LIF) socket, formerly known as a standard socket, with no handle. If so, the upgrade kit should include a chip removal tool, similar to a miniature crowbar, for removing the chip. Some experts recommend having a technician perform this type of extraction, however, members of our own staff with no previous experience replacing microprocessors have performed such upgrades with no difficulty. Nevertheless, be aware that there is more risk of damaging the computer with this type of socket. If you are uncomfortable, consider having an expert perform the upgrade. See Figure 5.2 for an example of each of these types of sockets.

In rare cases, you may find that the CPU is soldered to the board, or *surface-mounted*. Whereas a socketed CPU's sides are flush with the sides of the socket, a surface-mounted CPU has fine wires radiating from it to the board.

WARNING WARNING WARNING WARNING WARNING WARNING WARNING WARNING

Never attempt to move a surface-mounted CPU.

FIGURE 5.2: The LIF socket versus the ZIF socket

Types of Upgrades

The type of CPU upgrade kit you'll want depends upon the type and speed of the computer you want to upgrade. CPU upgrades fall into three categories: piggyback upgrades, daughtercard upgrades, and chip-for-chip upgrades. *Piggyback upgrades* are performed by stacking a new processor on top of the old one. *Daughtercard upgrades*, sometimes called card replacements or board replacements, involve installing a small board with a CPU chip attached. However, most of the upgrades sold today are *chip-for-chip upgrades*.

Chip-for-Chip Upgrades

This type of upgrade involves taking out the old chip and putting in the new one. A variation of this occurs in some computers with special (pre-Pentium) OverDrive sockets. Instead of removing the original microprocessor, the OverDrive processor pops into the extra OverDrive socket on the motherboard.

Most chip upgrades are incredibly simple, if all goes as it should. However, if you aren't comfortable doing the upgrade by yourself, you have other options. A local "screwdriver shop"—the kind that builds and repairs computers—can take care of the upgrade for you. Also, retail stores where you buy computer equipment may have upgrade centers. Some corporations have technical teams that do upgrades, and even if you're doing an upgrade at home, you might be able to convince someone to help you.

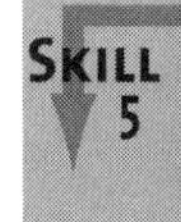

Installing the CPU

Once you have the kit, the installation should be quite simple. But because *should* is such a slippery term, we must offer a caveat. There may be variations between our instructions and the situation with your specific machine and upgrade kit.

WARNING WARNING WARNING WARNING WARNING WARNING WARNING WARNING

Always use the directions from your upgrade kit over our generalized ones, and have technical support numbers handy.

1. Run the utilities disk, if included. Chip upgrades often come with some kind of a diagnostics disk to check the BIOS compatibility, review system information, and make sure everything is working correctly before the upgrade. If your kit has such a disk, run it. At this point, you may need to upgrade the BIOS; follow the on-screen instructions or the ones that came with your chip kit.

2. Be sure that you have backed up your system. See Skill 3 for the details.
3. Locate the microprocessor. Its location varies from computer to computer, but it will be a square chip on the motherboard that looks a lot like your new chip, perhaps with a fan or heat sink on top.

NOTE NOTE NOTE NOTE NOTE NOTE NOTE NOTE NOTE NOTE NOTE NOTE NOTE NOTE NOTE

You may need to remove some hardware, such as an adapter card or drive bay, to get at the microprocessor. If so, proceed carefully, and keep track of where each piece goes and how it's installed. This way, you'll be able to put everything back together correctly when you're done.

4. Determine how the current processor is in its place. (See "Types of Sockets," above.)

NOTE NOTE NOTE NOTE NOTE NOTE NOTE NOTE NOTE NOTE NOTE NOTE NOTE NOTE NOTE

If you're installing a pre-MMX OverDrive chip to upgrade a 486 to a Pentium, look for an OverDrive socket—an empty socket next to your current processor. If you find one, skip ahead to step 8. If the chip is soldered to the board and you don't see an empty socket, the CPU is not upgradeable.

5. Next, take a look at how the CPU is aligned on the board. You may find what's called a *Pin 1 corner*, indicated by a notched corner, beveled edge, missing or extra pin, or distinguishing mark such as a dot, arrow, or half circle—some marking that makes one corner different from the three others. This will help you determine which direction the new chip should face. If you see such a corner, make note of which one it is before you remove the chip.
6. Remove the CPU from the socket. If your old microprocessor has a fan, disconnect it from the power source by unplugging it. Also, some heat sinks are held down with clips that need to be unfastened. A special tool may be included, but basically you'll need to press down on the retaining clip tab, then unlatch the clip (see Figure 5.3).

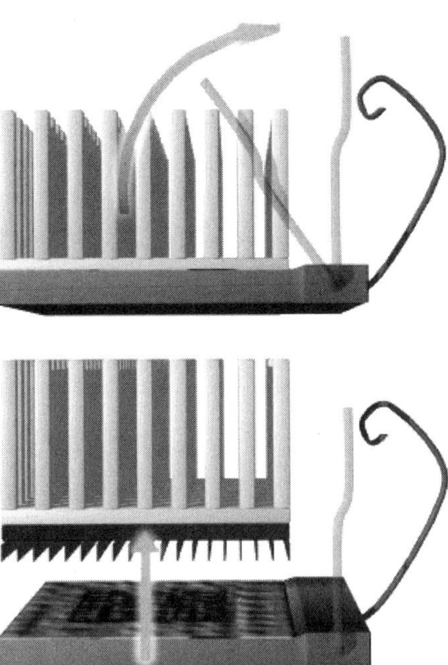

FIGURE 5.3: Unlatch the clip to remove the CPU from its socket.

If your CPU has a ZIF socket Most ZIF-socketed chips are held in place with a tension arm. When this arm is released, the chip pops out. No force is required to remove or install the chip, so be careful not to force anything.

If the chip is held down with a tension arm, without touching other parts of the computer, carefully lift the arm slightly to the side and then up until it's at a 90-degree angle to the motherboard. If you can't reach the bar with your finger because the microprocessor is tucked into a corner, you may need to use a screwdriver.

If the CPU is held down by a retaining screw rather than a tension arm, rotate the screw. If it's held down by an overhead bar, lift the bar up and over the chip. You should feel the chip lightly release from the motherboard.

Remove the chip and put it someplace safe, being careful not to touch its delicate connector pins. Eventually, you may want to store the old chip in the package the new chip came in.

If your CPU has a LIF socket Carefully pry the chip up, using the tool provided. Be sure you are only removing the chip itself, and not attempting to pry the actual socket. If you raise one side up too much more than the other sides, you may bend the pins on the bottom of the chip. Gently loosen each side of the chip, one side at a time, until you can remove the CPU with your fingers. Eventually, you can store the old chip in the new one's package.

7. Set jumpers and bus speed, if necessary. The *jumpers* are small metal pins that have plastic blocks covering some of them; moving the plastic blocks changes the settings of a hardware device. The *bus speed* has to do with the megahertz the chip runs at. The instructions for the chip upgrade kit will tell you if you need to adjust these switches. You may need to consult the system or motherboard manual. Be sure to write down any old settings before you change them, and store them with the old chip.
8. Install the new CPU. Pick up your new chip by the sides. First, determine which way the chip fits. If you noted a Pin 1 corner, look for the identifying corner on the new chip. Otherwise, look at the pattern of the pins on the bottom of the chip and the holes in the socket (see Figure 5.4). On most systems, the chip and socket both have a pin or hole that appears to be missing on one corner; this allows you to position the chip correctly.

FIGURE 5.4: Align the holes in the socket with the pins on the chip.

WARNING WARNING WARNING WARNING WARNING WARNING WARNING WARNING

Before attempting to put the chip into the socket, verify that you have the pins correctly aligned. Sometimes, chips fit into the sockets more than one way; misaligning the chip can do major damage to both the computer and the chip.

If your CPU has a ZIF socket Make sure the socket is unlocked and in a fully open position, or you could damage the pins. Place the new CPU in the socket. If it's aligned correctly, it should fit snugly, but should not need to be forced into position. Then, close the socket, probably by pressing down the tension arm.

NOTE NOTE NOTE NOTE NOTE NOTE NOTE NOTE NOTE NOTE NOTE NOTE NOTE NOTE NOTE

Some types of ZIF sockets require a *socket extender* to accommodate for differences between the chips—for example, if you're installing a 169-pin chip into a 168-pin socket. If so, your chip kit's upgrade guide should tell you how to proceed.

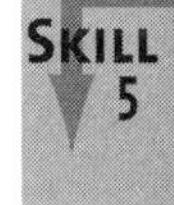

If your CPU has a LIF socket Installing a new microprocessor in a LIF socket requires some pressure, but the wrong kind of pressure can damage the pins or the cooling system. With the chip correctly aligned, press it into the socket with firm, even pressure from above, being careful not to press down in the middle of the fan. You will be able to feel and hear the processor snap into place.

9. Attach the new fan, if needed. Some fans, such as the one on Intel's Over-Drive chip that upgrades a Pentium to MMX, are powered directly through the CPU. However, other fans need to be hooked up to a power source.
10. If your fan has a power cord, find an unused power cable and plug in the fan. If all the power cords inside your computer are occupied, the fan's cord can be plugged into the middle of a cord that's in use. Temporarily disconnect a power cord from a device, such as a CD-ROM drive. Plug the fan cord into the free end of the power cord, then connect the cord's other end to the device it was originally connected to.
11. Test the new CPU. At this point, you can plug all the cords and cables back in and fire up the machine. If you run into problems—common ones are no power, an unstable system, a computer that won't boot, or a blank machine—go over the instructions again. Did you put everything back together? Is

everything plugged in? If you've triple-checked everything and the computer still isn't running properly, it may be time to contact technical support. Most likely, though, the computer will start up just fine. Make sure the fan is spinning, if there is one. If the kit came with a disk, you may need to run it again to check the new system performance.

12. Finish up. When everything is working, turn off the computer again and install any related items that may have come with the kit, such as a separate heat sink or plastic shroud. Then put the computer back together. Afterwards, you can just sit back and enjoy the improved speed and performance. The CPU is such an important part of the computer that you may feel as if you have a whole new system.

Are You Experienced?

Now you can...

- ☑ **evaluate the necessity of a new CPU**
- ☑ **consider differences in CPU architecture**
- ☑ **distinguish between a ZIF socket and a LIF socket**
- ☑ **install a new CPU**

SKILL 6

Installing a Hard Drive

- Choosing a new hard drive
- Installing the drive step by step
- Configuring the BIOS
- Partitioning and formatting the drive
- Installing a second hard drive

Let's get straight to the point. Replacing a hard drive is one of the most difficult upgrades you can attempt. It involves a complex hardware installation and a complex software installation. Plus it carries some pretty hefty risks, not the least of which are total data loss and system failure.

Nevertheless, replacing the hard drive is one upgrade that can significantly extend the functional life of an older model PC. For example, your computer's 66MHz 486 processor may have more than enough power to handle your processing needs. Unfortunately, that 528MB hard drive may not have the capacity to accommodate Windows 95/98, Microsoft Office, Quicken, and your Internet software.

What You Need To Know

Tools: Phillips screwdriver, needle-nosed pliers, paper and pencil

Time: Two hours minimum (probably much more)

Cost: $100 and up, depending on the capacity of the hard drive

Skill Level: Difficult

Benefits: Increases on-board storage capacity

Evaluate Your Need

Don't assume you have to upgrade your hard drive if you're experiencing a data crunch, though. An array of new storage alternatives, such as the Iomega Zip and Jaz drives, the SyQuest SparQ drive, and the drives that conform to the LS-120 technology, gives users various options for handling a dearth of byte-space. (See Skill 7 for more on storage options.)

Similarly, a storage crunch is the perfect opportunity to evaluate your computing situation. You may realize your hard drive has plenty of space once you get rid of all those applications you don't really need.

But these options won't solve everybody's storage dilemma, and many users find they must choose between buying a new computer or upgrading the hard drive. Considering there's probably a $1,700 difference (give or take a few hundred dollars) between the two options, it's easy to see why many users choose to perform a hard drive upgrade.

Examine What You Have

Before you buy a hard drive, you need to examine your system to determine what type of hard drive it can support. Failing to do so before you buy the drive may cost you a trip to the store or additional postage to return the drive later.

BIOS Barriers

The typical hard drive sold today has a capacity of anywhere between 2.1 and 8.4GB. This creates a problem for users who have computers that were built before July 1994.

Due to limitations in their Basic Input/Output Systems (BIOS: software that controls the startup processes of a PC), many of these older computers can't support hard drives that have capacities greater than 528MB. In the computer industry, where everything has an official name, this is referred to as the *528MB Problem*.

Users who have these older PCs should purchase a hard drive that has a capacity of less than 528MB. Check out a retailer of old and refurbished computers, such as Computer Renaissance, to find these smaller hard drives.

Operating System Barriers

Another limitation that may restrict your hard drive selection is the *8.4GB Barrier*. The DOS operating system cannot support drives that have a total capacity greater than 8.4GB. If you run DOS, Windows 3.*x* or older, or an upgrade version of Windows 95 (one that was installed over DOS), you shouldn't purchase a drive with a capacity that exceeds 8.4GB.

The full version of Windows 95 (one that was installed on a clean hard drive) and Windows 98 support drives with capacities greater than 8.4GB. If you want to add a hard drive that exceeds an 8.4GB capacity, you must upgrade to a full version of Windows 95 or Windows 98.

Drive Interface Barriers

The interface is the connection between the drive and the PC. There are two drive interfaces in popular usage today: Integrated Drive Electronics (IDE) and Small Computer Systems Interface (SCSI).

An IDE drive has its *controller* (a device that manages the flow of information between a computer and a peripheral) integrated into the drive, which allows the drive to connect directly to the motherboard instead of connecting via an expansion card. This makes it less expensive to produce IDE drives, and for that reason, they have come to dominate the desktop market. An estimated 105 million IDE drives were shipped in 1997 alone.

SCSI drives tend to have higher data transfer rates than IDE drives and are better than IDE drives at insuring the integrity of the stored data. A SCSI port also can accommodate as many as seven peripherals at a time, and SCSI allows for multitasking of *input/output devices* (I/O devices: any device that accepts or transmits data, such as a printer or keyboard).

Although it seems as if SCSI drives tend to have every advantage over IDE drives, the truth is that their advantages are negligible on typical stand-alone desktop systems. SCSI drives tend to be found predominantly on servers and network computers. Unless you're replacing the hard drive on a network computer, you'll probably want to get an IDE drive. The IDE drive will be slightly easier to install and will cost less than the SCSI drive.

Drive Bay Availability Barriers

Most hard drives are 3.5 inches wide. Older hard drives may be 5.25 inches wide. Before you purchase a new hard drive, check the size of the old drive so you know what will fit into its place.

A 3.5-inch drive can be equipped with special mounting brackets to fit inside a 5.25-inch *drive bay* (the area within a computer specially designed to accommodate a drive). A 5.25-inch drive, on the other hand, cannot be restructured to fit into a 3.5-inch drive bay. Most of the hard drives sold today are of the 3.5-inch variety.

Install the Drive

Once you've determined what type of drive your system can support, it's time to make the purchase and perform the upgrade. We installed a Maxtor Diamond-Max 2880 hard drive with a capacity of 11.52GB and an IDE interface. Because our test computer was built in 1997 and runs Windows 95, we knew it could support this drive.

Every computer system is unique, so your installation may differ slightly from ours (see Figure 6.1 for an example). The type of computer you have (desktop vs. tower model), the type of hardware you have installed in the PC, and the computer's software configuration all affect the installation process. Use our guide to assist you in the upgrade, but defer to the drive's installation manual if you encounter a contradiction between the two.

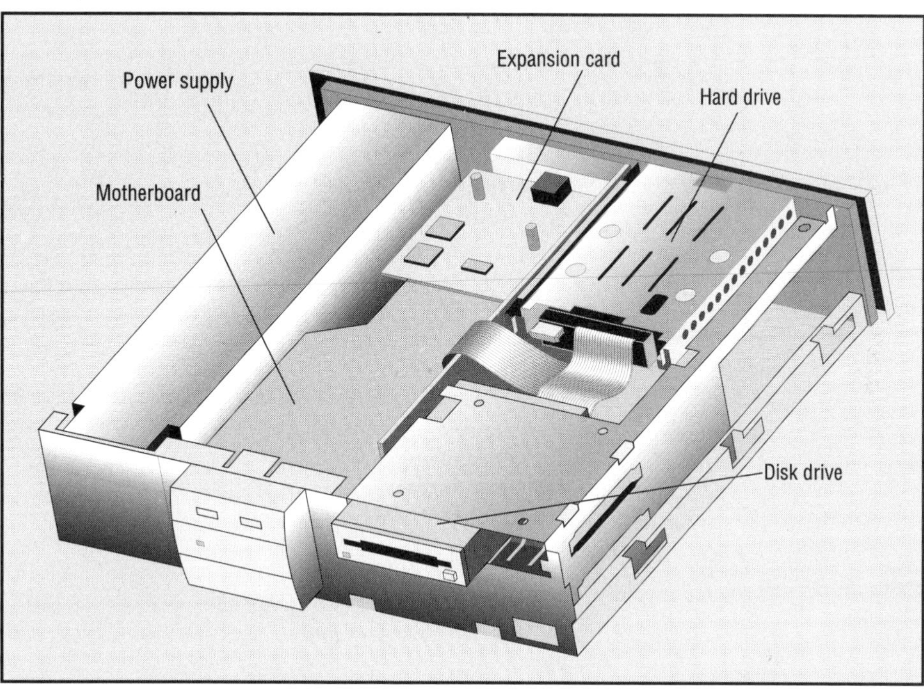

FIGURE 6.1: All computers have the same basic components.

Removing the Old Drive

Now, you're ready to begin.

1. Read the instructions on pre-installation in Skill 3. It is very important that you back up your data before replacing your current hard drive. Otherwise, you *will* lose access to all the data stored on it. Also, read the installation instructions entirely before you start the upgrade.

2. If the new drive has been stored in extremely hot or cold temperatures, let it reach room temperature before you install it. Also, leave the drive in its protective packaging until you're ready to install it. You don't want dust, static electricity, or an accidental bump to damage the drive before you have a chance to use it.

3. Locate your current hard drive inside your PC. It is a thin metal box, approximately 1 inch thick, 3.5 or 5.25 inches wide, and 6 inches long. It may be mounted near the other drive bays, near the power source, or anywhere on the computer's frame. Your computer's user manual may include a system diagram detailing its exact location.

4. Check how the hard drive is positioned in the computer; you must install the new drive in the exact same position. For example, if your current hard drive is positioned horizontally with the label facing up and the cables extending from the back, you must install the new drive in a horizontal position with the label facing up and the cable connectors facing the back.

TIP TIP TIP TIP TIP TIP TIP TIP TIP TIP TIP TIP TIP TIP TIP TIP TIP TIP TIP TIP TIP TIP TIP TIP

You may have to remove expansion cards and disconnect cables attached to other devices in order to remove your old drive and fit the new drive into your PC. Take note of anything you remove or disconnect so you can get your system put together correctly when you've finished installing the hard drive.

5. If the hard drive you are replacing is the only drive in your system or if it is the primary drive in the system, it is referred to as the *master* drive. If the hard drive you are replacing is the secondary drive in your computer, it is referred to as the *slave* drive. You must know whether the drive is the master or slave drive in order to complete the installation.

NOTE NOTE NOTE NOTE NOTE NOTE NOTE NOTE NOTE NOTE NOTE NOTE NOTE NOTE NOTE

For this installation, we assume you are replacing your system's master hard drive. If you are adding a second hard drive or replacing the slave drive, you should refer to the "Installing a Second Hard Drive" section.

6. Your current hard drive should have a flat, gray ribbon cable and a multicolored power cable extending from the back of it. The ribbon cable, which is called the *data cable*, carries data to and from the hard drive. The data cable may have multiple connectors attached to it, and the connectors may be attached to other devices as well as the hard drive.

7. Disconnect the ribbon cable and the power cable from the back of your current hard drive. Grip the connectors between your fingers or use the needlenose pliers to remove them. You should be able to remove the connectors without exerting much effort. If a connector seems stuck in the drive, you can rock it back and forth to remove it from the drive.

8. Keep track of which cables you removed from the drive because you'll plug those cables into the new drive. Use a piece of tape to mark the cables as you remove them. Don't disconnect the cables from the computer or from any other devices to which they are connected unless you have to do so in order to remove the drive.

9. Remove the screws that hold the drive in place (Figure 6.2). You may need to hold the drive with one hand as you remove the last two screws to keep it from crashing onto the motherboard. Keep track of the screws as you remove them. You may need them when you install the new drive.

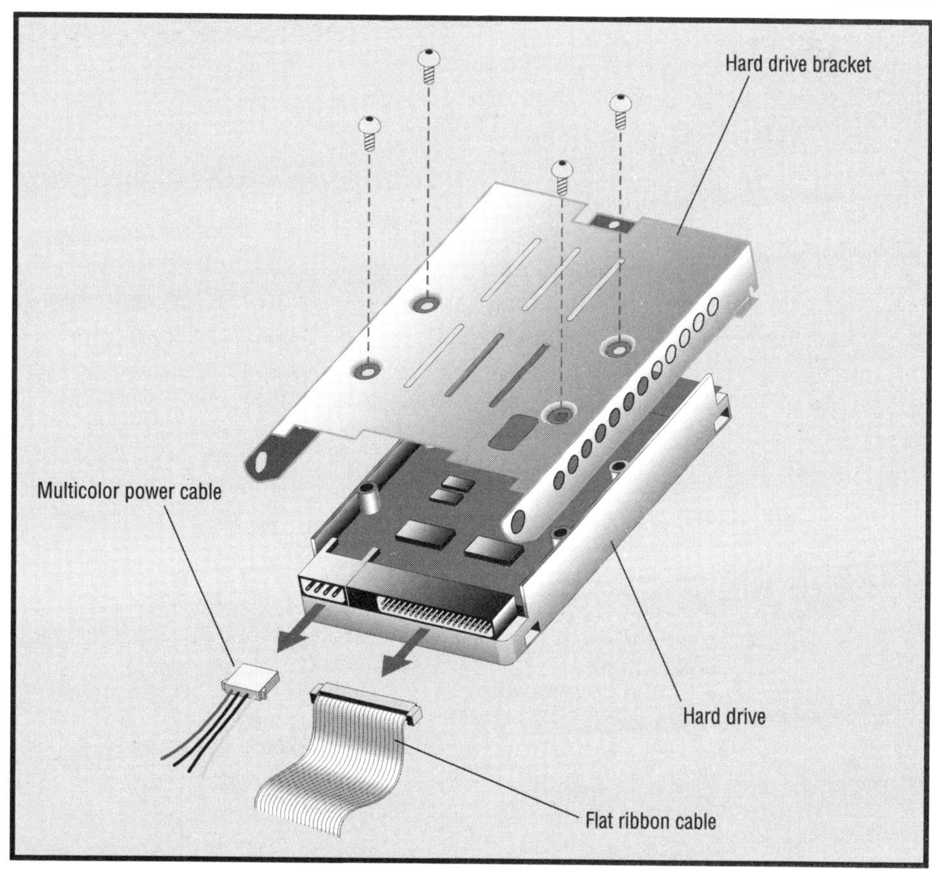

FIGURE 6.2: Removing the screws on the bracket frees the hard drive.

10. After you've removed the screws (there should be between four and eight), gently slide the drive out of the bay. If it doesn't slide out easily, there must be a cable or screw holding it in place. Carefully extricate anything that is hampering the drive's removal, then try to remove it again.

TIP TIP TIP TIP TIP TIP TIP TIP TIP TIP TIP TIP TIP TIP TIP TIP TIP TIP TIP TIP TIP TIP TIP TIP TIP

Once you have removed the old drive from your PC, treat it with care. It contains all your old data, and it's much easier and less expensive to retrieve data from your old drive if it's in good shape than if it has been damaged. The drive also may come in handy if you encounter any difficulties with your new hard drive. If you have to remove the new drive and send it back to the manufacturer, you can put the old drive back into your PC until a replacement arrives.

Installing the New Drive

Once you've removed the old drive, you're ready to put the new one in.

1. Ground yourself by touching the computer's frame, then remove the new drive from its protective packaging. Handle the drive by its edges, and be careful not to touch the fragile circuitry on top of the drive. Write down the information listed on the drive's label. The information you should record includes the drive's model number and the number of cylinders, heads, and sectors on the drive.

2. See how the drive will fit inside the computer. If it's too small, you'll need to attach mounting brackets to the drive before you can install it. To obtain mounting brackets for your new drive, contact the drive's manufacturer.

TIP TIP TIP TIP TIP TIP TIP TIP TIP TIP TIP TIP TIP TIP TIP TIP TIP TIP TIP TIP TIP TIP TIP TIP TIP

Save the drive's protective packaging. You can pack your old drive in it when you're done.

3. Position the drive for installation. Remember, it must be installed in the same position as the old drive. Use the screws that held the old drive in place to attach the new drive to the computer frame. Make sure the drive is held securely in place but don't attach the screws too tightly. Overtightening the screws can bend the frame of the hard drive.

4. Reconnect the data cable and the power cable. Make sure you're using the same cables you removed from the old hard drive (unless you replaced the

old cables with new ones). The power cable connector has notched corners and fits into its socket in only one way. The data cable also connects to the drive in only one way, but the proper fit may not be as obvious.

5. Connecting the data cable should be easy if the cable connector has an upraised tab in the middle of it. Just match the tab to the notch in the drive's receptor, then insert the connector.
6. If the connector doesn't have an upraised tab, however, you'll have to align the colored strip, which runs along one edge of the data cable, with Pin 1 on the drive's receptor. Pin 1, which is the bottom-right pin (or upper-left pin, depending on how you look at it) on the receptor, usually is designated by a tiny "1" printed next to it. If you're not sure how the data cable attaches to the receptor, check the installation manual for details.
7. Don't force either cable connection, but make sure they are snug and secure. A loose connection is all it takes for a drive to malfunction.
8. Make sure the cables aren't pressing awkwardly on any other components inside the PC and check that you didn't accidentally disconnect any cables while installing the hard drive. When you're sure everything is in its proper order, replace the computer's cover. Connect the external peripherals to the computer and plug the computer into the wall.
9. Insert the system disk in the disk drive. If you received a bootable disk with your new hard drive, insert it in the disk drive instead. Our drive came with a bootable disk, so we inserted it in the disk drive. Don't turn on the PC until you've read the instructions for the rest of the installation.

Prepare the Drive for Use

The rest of the installation consists of three steps: configuring the BIOS to recognize the drive, partitioning the drive, and formatting the partitions.

Configuring the BIOS

You started the process of configuring the BIOS in Step 9, above, when you inserted the system disk or bootable disk in the disk drive. The system disk allows you to access the BIOS when you turn on your PC. But before you do that, you should understand the two methods of configuring the BIOS.

The first method involves the software that came with the drive. If your new hard drive comes with BIOS configuration software, use it. This software usually configures your BIOS, partitions the drive, and formats the partitions automatically. Just follow the on-screen instructions and read the installation guide. Contact the drive manufacturer if you encounter any difficulties.

Although this is the easiest method of BIOS configuration, it's not available to all users. Hard drives with capacities of less than 528MB are unable to use most of these applications, and many newer computers have configuration software built into their BIOSs and don't need these third-party applications. Read the instruction manual that came with your new drive to determine if it includes BIOS configuration software, then read the computer's user manual to see if it supports this software.

If it doesn't, as was the case with the hard drive we installed, you must configure the BIOS manually. This is the second BIOS configuration method and is a bit more complex than method number one.

1. With the system disk or bootable disk inserted in the disk drive, turn your computer on. Immediately look for instructions for entering the BIOS Setup. Usually, you'll see on-screen messages, such as Press F2 to Enter Setup or F1 = Setup, telling you how to do it. Press the indicated key as soon as you can. If you don't press it quickly enough, you'll have to turn off the computer and start over.

2. Locate the hard drive setup area and follow the on-screen instructions for entering this area. If you have a newer computer, the computer may have detected the new drive automatically or it may give you the option of using an autodetection feature. If this is available, use it.

3. Once the drive has been detected and the relevant information has been imported to the BIOS Setup, check the settings to make sure they're correct. You do that by comparing the settings in the BIOS Setup to the settings you wrote down in step 1, above. If you notice a discrepancy and need to change the information, follow the on-screen instructions for making a change.

4. If your BIOS doesn't offer an autodetection feature, you must enter the information manually. Refer to the drive's documentation or the list you made in step 1, above, for most of the information. Because this is the master drive, enter the settings in the Primary Master area. If your computer's

BIOS Setup doesn't include such an area, check the user manual or contact the manufacturer to determine where you should enter the settings.

5. After you've entered the information correctly, save it and exit the BIOS setup. Restart your computer.

Partitioning the Drive

A partition is an area on your hard drive that is treated as a separate storage area. Each partition is assigned a unique identifying drive letter. As with the BIOS configuration, you can partition the drive using the software that came with the drive or using the FDISK utility on your system disk.

NOTE

Due to limitations imposed by most operating systems, including DOS and Windows 95, your drive may be limited to partition sizes of less than 2.1GB. Unless your computer's operating system uses a 32-bit file allocation table (FAT32), you will have to create partition sizes smaller than 2.1GB.

When you run the partitioning software, you'll know whether your new drive is functioning properly. If you try to partition the drive and receive an error message, you'll have to retrace your steps to see where the installation went astray.

As with the BIOS configuration, there are two methods of partitioning the hard drive. The first method involves the software that came with your drive. Just follow the on-screen instructions and enter any requested information. Write down the size of each partition and its assigned drive letter when you're done.

The second method of partitioning the drive involves the FDISK utility, which should be stored on the system disk. Although FDISK is a DOS utility, it is fairly easy to understand.

1. Type **fdisk** at the A:\> prompt to start the utility.
2. You need to create an active partition. This is the area of the drive that contains your operating system and will bear the drive letter C. To create this partition, choose the Create a DOS Partition or Logical DOS Drive option from the on-screen menu. In the resulting menu, select the Create Primary DOS Partition option.
3. Specify the size of the partition in megabytes or as a percentage. Make sure you use the percent sign (%) if you want the partition to be a percentage of

the entire drive size. For example, to create a 500MB partition, enter **500**. To create a single partition for the entire drive, enter **100%**.

4. After you've entered the size of the primary partition, return to the main menu and select the Set Active Partition option. Follow the on-screen instructions to set the drive active.
5. Next, you need to create any additional partitions. From the main menu, choose the Create A DOS Partition Or Logical DOS Drive option from the on-screen menu. But this time, select the Create Extended DOS Partition option from the resulting menu. Specify the size of this partition, but don't set it active.

At this point, FDISK will prompt you to create a logical drive or drives. You can create as many as 23 logical drives. We suggest you don't create that many, however, as it could get quite confusing for you later on. Follow the on-screen instructions for creating the logical partitions.

Formatting the Partitions

This should be the easiest part of the installation process. You'll start by formatting the primary active partition, otherwise known as the C: drive. Make sure the system disk is in the disk drive and type **format c: /s** at the A:\> prompt. When the format is complete, remove the system disk from the disk drive and restart the PC. If the computer starts properly, the format was a success and your C: drive is up and running.

Format the remaining partitions using the same process as above, except specify the drive letter of the partition to be formatted, and don't type the /S parameter. For example, to format your F: drive, simply type **format f:** at the C:\> prompt. To format the G: drive, simply type **format g:** at the C:\> prompt. You don't need to restart the PC between each format.

TIP TIP TIP TIP TIP TIP TIP TIP TIP TIP TIP TIP TIP TIP TIP TIP TIP TIP TIP TIP TIP TIP TIP TIP TIP

Any problems you encounter during the formatting portion of the installation are probably caused by the BIOS. Contact your computer manufacturer for assistance. You may only need a copy of the latest BIOS.

Now, you can install your operating system or reinstall the system backup you created before you began this whole upgrade ordeal. Expect to spend some time getting your programs and data files up and running again.

Installing a Second Hard Drive

In the old days of personal computing, users who wanted to increase the storage capacity of their computers had only one option: Get a new hard drive. But instead of replacing the original hard drive with a newer model, many users chose to keep their original hard drives and add second drives to their systems. It didn't seem economical to throw away a hard drive that worked fine just because it was a bit small. And besides, two is always better than one, right?

Well, things have changed, and high-capacity removable storage devices are all the rage today. These devices, which include the Jaz, SparQ, and SuperDisk drives, offer large storage capacities, fast data access, and portable storage media. These drives aren't much more expensive than hard drives and they can be of more practical value than an extra hard drive. Consequently, an increasing number of users are upgrading their PCs to include one of these drives and fewer users are opting to install second hard drives. (You can explore your options with regard to high-capacity storage in Skill 7.)

Why Install Another?

In many situations a second hard drive isn't just a viable solution, it's the best solution. A second hard drive is the best way to run two operating systems on one PC. It's also the best way to ensure against data loss; after all, you can't lose your data when it never leaves your PC. And it's still true that two is better than one. If you're going to add a new hard drive, you may as well keep the old one in there.

Of course, it can be difficult to add a second hard drive. But if you have a newer PC, it's no more difficult than installing any internal storage device. Just read the installation instructions carefully before you start the upgrade and keep the technical support telephone numbers close at hand.

Installing the Drive

Installing a hard drive—or any internal storage device, for that matter—is not child's play. It requires knowledge of your PC, understanding of the way everything fits together, and confidence that you're taking the right steps to complete the process.

Except for a few small differences, installing a second hard drive is virtually identical to installing a first, so you should read the preceding sections in this skill. You should certainly also read the instruction manual that came with the drive. These sources will help you get a better grasp of what's going on and what's coming up when you're performing the upgrade.

Your first task is to read Skill 3, paying special attention to the sections on creating a system disk and backing up your data. You should back up your computer system any time you plan to poke around in it. Otherwise, you run the risk of losing all your data.

Then, after the cover is removed, look inside the PC to decide where you want to put the drive. The best place to put it is right next to the other hard drive. You may have to move things around inside your PC in order to install the drive. Remove any expansion cards and unplug any cables that get in the way of the hard drive's new home. Fortunately, you shouldn't have to remove any major system components to install a second hard drive. Just take notes while you remove the expansion cards and cables so that you remember how to put them back in.

Accommodating the IDE/EIDE

The most difficult part of the installation involves configuring the drive to accommodate your computer's Integrated Drive Electronics (IDE) and Enhanced IDE (EIDE) settings. This is also the most important part of the installation. If you get this wrong, you'll have to start over.

The easiest way to configure the drive's EIDE/IDE settings is to call your computer's manufacturer and tell a support technician that you want help determining two things: your computer's EIDE/IDE configuration and the jumper settings for all your EIDE/IDE peripherals. Follow the directions provided by the support technician. When you're done, skip ahead to the next section. If you can't call your computer's manufacturer for technical support, you'll have to determine the EIDE/IDE settings yourself. Follow steps 1 through 6, below.

1. Open your computer and locate its EIDE/IDE controller ports. The ports are approximately 2 inches long, located on the motherboard, and situated immediately next to one another. In most personal computers, they connect to your hard drive or CD-ROM drive via a *ribbon cable* (a thin, wide cable with 40-pin connectors at either end, and perhaps an additional connector or two in the middle).

NOTE

Older model PCs may have only one EIDE/IDE port. If your PC has only one EIDE/IDE port and you have a CD-ROM drive and a hard drive, you may have to purchase and install an EIDE controller card.

2. Examine the EIDE/IDE ports and the ribbon cables connected to them. Follow the cables to determine which devices are connected to each cable and how many empty connections are available on each cable. A typical computer, with a hard drive and a CD-ROM drive, will have two EIDE/IDE ports. One port will connect to the hard drive; one port will connect to the CD-ROM drive. Each cable probably has an empty connector on it.

TIP TIP TIP TIP TIP TIP TIP TIP TIP TIP TIP TIP TIP TIP TIP TIP TIP TIP TIP TIP TIP TIP TIP TIP TIP

If a port is connected to only one device and the ribbon cable has no empty connectors, you may need to purchase a new 40-pin ribbon cable. We recommend purchasing a three-connector ribbon cable.

3. The port connected to your hard drive is the primary EIDE/IDE port. The other port is the secondary EIDE/IDE port. If you're installing a second hard drive, it's usually best to connect it to the primary EIDE/IDE port. If you're installing some other type of storage device, it's usually best to connect it to the secondary EIDE/IDE port. It really doesn't matter which one you choose, though, as long as you configure it correctly. Decide whether you want to connect the drive to the primary or secondary port and write down your decision on a piece of paper.

4. Next, determine whether the drive will be in the master or slave position. If you're adding the drive to an empty port, it will be the master device on the port. If you're adding the drive to a port that already is connected to an EIDE/IDE device, the new drive will be the slave device. Write down the drive's position on your piece of paper.
5. Now look at what you wrote down and refer to the drive's installation manual to determine how you should set the drive's *jumper*. The jumper, a piece of black plastic positioned over two metal pins, is located on the back of the drive. Most drives are preset to the master position. To change the setting, slide the plastic jumper off the jumper pins and slide it back on the pins in its new position, as dictated by the installation manual.
6. Before you proceed to the rest of the drive installation, make sure the jumper settings are compatible with the jumper settings for your existing EIDE/IDE devices. Refer to the user manuals of these devices to determine their jumper settings.

You may need to reconfigure the jumper settings for some or all of your other EIDE/IDE devices at this time. Follow the same procedure you used to set the jumper on the new drive to set the jumpers on the other drives. Write down the EIDE/IDE configuration for all your drives. You'll need it during the software installation.

Proceeding with the Installation

Now you're ready to proceed with the hardware portion of the drive installation. Basically, this involves mounting the drive to the computer frame and connecting the data and power cables to the drive. Refer to steps 1 through 9 in the "Installing a New Drive" section, above, for a more detailed description of the process.

Because this may be the second drive connected to an EIDE/IDE port, you may have to use the second connector on a ribbon cable. Make sure you mount the drive close to the drive with which it will share the cable, then connect the cable to the second connector on the cable.

Don't force the connection, but make sure it is snug and secure. A loose connection is all it takes for the drive to malfunction. Also, double-check the cable's other connections to make sure they didn't jiggle loose during the drive installation.

When the drive is securely mounted and all the relevant cables are connected to it, reinstall any expansion cards and plug in any cables you had to remove in order to position the new drive inside the computer. Then make sure all the cables are tucked neatly inside the computer, double-check all the cable connections, and put the cover back on the PC.

Follow the steps outlined in the "Prepare the Drive for Use" section, above, to configure the BIOS, partition the drive, and format the partitions. Or, if installation software came with the drive, follow the on-screen instructions and the instructions included in the drive's installation guide.

NOTE

If you've configured your new drive to have multiple partitions and your old drive is already configured for multiple partitions, you could run into some interesting situations when the computer assigns drive letters. You may have to check the File Manager in Windows 3.*x*, or My Computer in Windows 95 and Windows 98, to determine if or how the drive letters have changed. If you have additional drives, such as a CD-ROM drive, a Jaz drive, and an LS-120 drive, attached to your PC, you'll also have to determine if or how their drive letters have changed. You may have to reinstall the software for these drives so your computer will recognize the drives again. Contact the manufacturer of your new hard drive if you need help.

The Fun Begins

Now is the time to copy anything you want to the new drive. Take things slowly at first and don't be too hasty to delete anything. This could be an easy drag-and-drop exercise or a total configuration nightmare, depending on how the applications and data files react to the move.

Are You Experienced?

Now you can...

- ☑ **make an informed choice of a new hard drive**
- ☑ **open up your computer and install a new drive**
- ☑ **configure and format the drive so it's ready to go**
- ☑ **install a second hard drive**

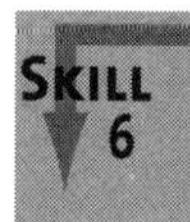

SKILL 7

Installing Disk and High-Capacity Drives

- Differentiating between storage devices
- Installing a disk drive
- Installing an internal tape drive
- Installing a high-capacity storage device

You may be thinking "Hey! This is supposed to be an *upgrading* book. Why should I read about 3.5-inch disk drives?" Patience, my friend.

We aren't saying that 3.5-inch drives are going to be around forever. They won't. Many new high-end computers, such as those with Pentium II processors, already carry the drives that will probably replace the disk drives. These PCs include Zip or DVD-ROM drives. Compact Disc-Recordable (CD-R) and LS-120 drives are also starting to filter into the marketplace. These new drives are intruding on the 3.5-inch drive's turf because one disk for one of these high-capacity drives can store more information than a stack of 3.5-inch disks.

But these peripherals are only now making their way into the mainstream. They probably won't match the 3.5-inch drive's popularity for a few more years. Clearly the 3.5-inch disk drive is going to be around for a while, even though its glory days are fading. This skill will cover both sides of the spectrum: the tried-and-true disk drives and the newer high-capacity drives. Along the way we'll also pass through internal tape drive territory. You choose which you need.

Installing a Disk Drive

The near-universal availability of 3.5-inch drives helps keep them alive (see Figure 7.1). The 3.5-inch drives are clearly practical. There's still no cheaper way to physically transfer or back up files. You could send the information on a Zip disk if your friend or co-worker has a Zip drive, but the disks cost about $10 each. And you know if you hand that Zip disk to your co-worker, you'll never see it again. Besides, it's not worth sacrificing an entire 100MB disk for 1MB of files.

On the other hand, nearly everyone who has a computer has a 3.5-inch disk drive. And the disks practically fall from the sky like raindrops. You can pick up a couple of loads for about the same price as a can of soda and a big sandwich. Who cares if your friend uses the disk as a coaster? It only cost 60 cents.

We're not telling you to forget buying a high-volume storage peripheral. They clobber 3.5-inch disks at tasks such as large-scale backups, transporting entire sets of programs, and storing large graphics or multimedia files. But clearly, if you have a few hundred kilobytes of files you need to hand off to someone or shuttle between PCs, these disks are a great option.

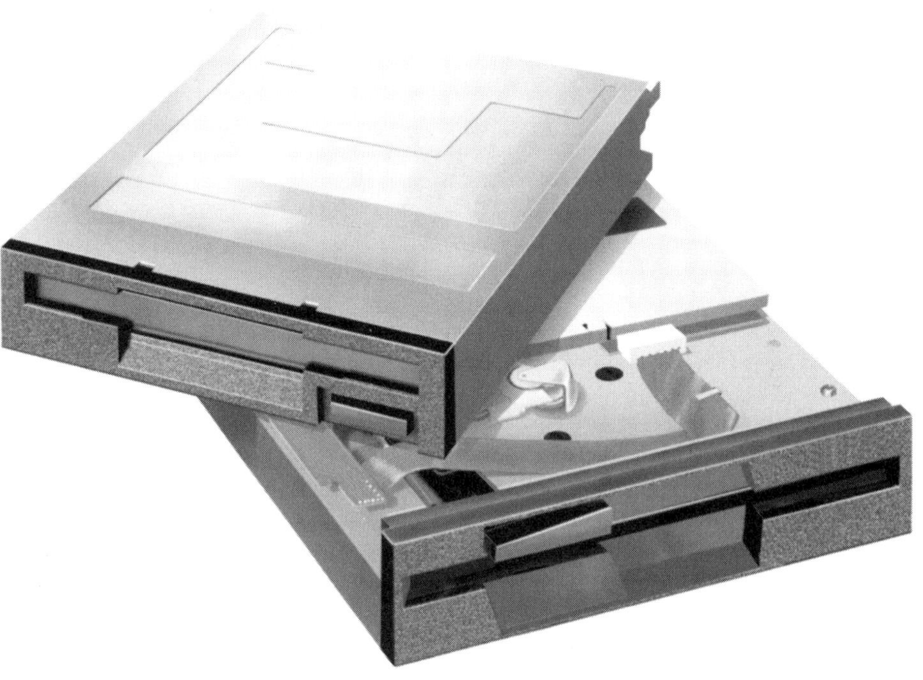

FIGURE 7.1: Unlike some other computer components, the basic design of disk drives has not changed in years.

Disk drives tend to be pretty reliable, but they do break down. Perhaps your 3-year-old tried to toast a Pop-Tart in your 3.5-inch disk drive and, well, it just hasn't been the same since. Or, you may want to add another disk drive to your machine to simplify copying between two disks. In any case, if your disk drive stops working or you simply want to add another one, upgrading is worth the effort.

You can find a 3.5-inch disk drive for less than $50, and the installation is easy. But don't expect to find one at your local Best Buy or CompUSA. Try a local second-hand computer store. If that fails, you can find one on the Internet. Try visiting ICS at `http://www.ics-driveshop.com` or M. Farris & Associates at `http://www.mfarris.com/index.html`.

What You Need to Know

Tools: Screwdriver

Time: 15 to 30 minutes

Cost: $20–$75 for a 3.5-inch internal disk drive

Skill Level: Easy

Benefits: Cheap storage solution, portable and practical

Removing a Disk Drive

Removing an old disk drive and installing a new one should be a fairly painless process, but it's more involved than simply popping a card into an expansion slot inside the computer's case.

1. The first step is to turn off your computer. Then, remove the computer's cover and ground yourself by touching the metal frame of the computer. Read the instructions in Skill 3 if you need a refresher or if you haven't backed up your system.
2. If you're replacing your current 3.5-inch disk drive, locate it inside your computer. It should be inside a metal bracket and will be attached to two cables. One is the ribbon cable (gray with a red stripe along the edge), which transfers data from the drive to the motherboard. The other cable, the power source, connects the drive to your power supply. The power source cable will consist of several wires attached to a white connector at one end. Disconnect both cables from the drive.
3. You'll probably find that it's easier to detach the entire bracket from the computer case and then remove the disk drive. Trying to remove the drive without removing the bracket can be complicated. There's little room to maneuver around in there. So loosen the screws holding the bracket to the case. You should be able to pull out the bracket, and anything attached to it, without trouble (see Figure 7.2).
4. Release the drive from the bracket. After removing the screws, slide the drive out of the bracket.

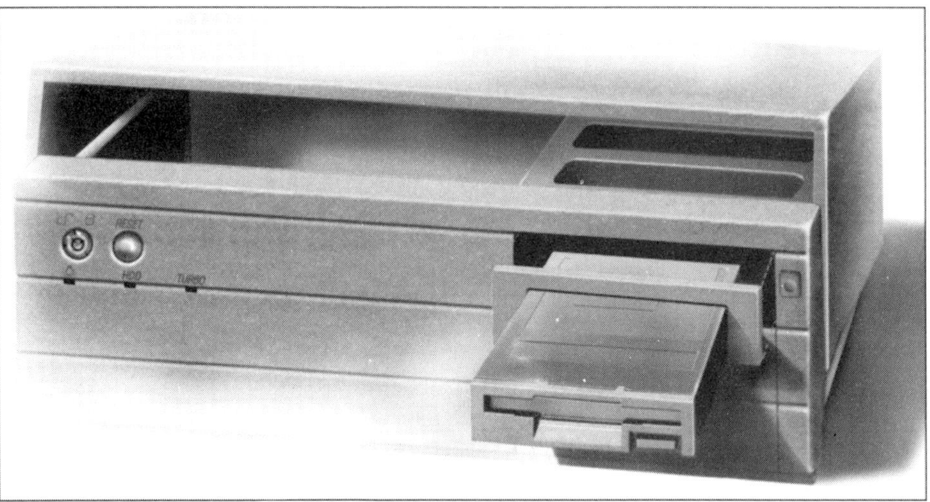

FIGURE 7.2: The disk drive resides in a metal box in the computer.

Installing a New Disk Drive

Out with the old, in with the new. Follow these steps to install your new drive.

NOTE NOTE NOTE NOTE NOTE NOTE NOTE NOTE NOTE NOTE NOTE NOTE NOTE NOTE NOTE

If you're adding a second disk drive, and you install it in a 5.25-inch drive bay, make sure you get a face plate adapter for the drive. You'll need to pop the adapter in the drive bay so the disk drive will fit securely. Remove the face plate for the 5.25-inch drive bay, insert the adapter, and continue with the following instructions.

1. Insert the new drive into the bracket. There will be several holes in each side of the disk drive. Line these up with the holes in the bracket, so the new drive is in the same position as the previous drive. If you misalign the drive, it may stick out too far or not far enough. Attach the drive to the bracket with the screws.

2. Before you reattach the bracket to the computer case, you'll want to connect the cables to the drive. It's easier to do it now than to wait until the bracket is reattached. Plug the ribbon cable into the connection on the back of the

new drive. You'll notice that the ribbon cable has a stripe along one side. Line the red stripe up with the left bottom pin (Pin 1) on the drive's connector. Now attach the power supply cable to the power supply connection on the back of the drive.

3. Once the cables are securely in place, it's time to reattach the bracket. Make sure the disk drive fits properly in its slot as you move the bracket into position. If the drive sticks out too far or not far enough, pull out the bracket, and adjust the position of the drive. Screw the bracket into place, and double-check the cables to make sure their attachment is secure.
4. Put the lid back on the computer and start it up.

The physical part of the installation is complete, but now you must make sure your computer is ready to use the drive. Your computer's BIOS is in charge of that task. You'll have to enter the Setup screen to check the BIOS settings for your disk drive. You can do this when you first start your computer. Usually, this involves pressing the F1 or F2 key. Look for a phrase such as Press *x* Key If You Want To Run Setup, where *x* is the key or key combination you use to access Setup.

If you're replacing a disk drive, you'll probably find that the following settings are already in place, so your computer should be able to use the new drive without changing them. Still, you should check the settings, just to make sure.

1. Enter the Setup screen. Somewhere in there (hopefully on the first screen), you'll see a section that lets you change your disk options. Open that section and make sure Disk A: is set to 1.44MB 3.5-inch. A: is generally the default drive letter for disk drives, so you'll want to use that for the installed drive.

WARNING WARNING WARNING WARNING WARNING WARNING WARNING WARNING

If the drive you are installing is a second disk drive, this letter should be assigned a drive letter that it not already being used by another drive.

2. Now make sure your computer will read the A: drive before it reads the hard drive (C:) during startup. Check it under Boot Options. You always want your computer to check the A: drive first. If some kind of hard drive malfunction prevents your computer from starting up, you can pop a bootable disk in the A: drive to boot the system and correct the problem.

3. After you check the settings and make any necessary changes, save the settings and exit the Setup screen. Your computer will finish starting up, and you'll be ready to use the new drive.

There are many portable storage options these days, but you should stick with a classic, at least for now. You'll want your computer to be able to read and write to 1.44MB disks, even if you use another storage solution for backups. There are simply too many of those old disks still floating around to give up on them.

Installing an Internal Tape Drive

With the recent release of a whole gamut of high-capacity, portable storage alternatives, it may seem as if tape drives were a thing of the past.

The truth is that for the average computer user, they probably are. Tape drives are excruciatingly slow because they access data serially instead of directly. These drives record data on tape, not disks. When you want to access data from a tape cartridge, the drive has to forward or rewind through all the data that precedes or follows it.

Because they're so slow, they're not much good for anything other than data backups. Tape drives aren't multifunctional enough to satisfy average computer users who want to get the most from their PCs. And they cost just as much as the other storage alternatives, so they're not a real bargain.

But tape drives haven't gone the way of the 5.25-inch disk drive, either. Among the business markets, tape drives are still in wide use today. Used almost exclusively for data archiving, tape drives are running in full force every night, backing up irreplaceable data in tens of thousands of businesses around the world.

WHAT YOU NEED TO KNOW

Tools: Phillips screwdriver, needle-nosed pliers or tweezers

Time: 30 minutes

Cost: $150 and up, depending on the model

Skill Level: Easy

Benefits: Gain the ability to perform large backups

The Benefits of Internal Tape Drives

It's their ability to hold so much data that makes tape drives invaluable to businesses. Tape cartridges have storage capacities that are much larger than any of the new storage alternatives. For example, the tape drive we installed, the Iomega Ditto Max Professional, could hold as much as 10GB of data on a single cartridge.

For any business that needs to back up more than 2GB of data on a regular basis, a tape drive is a perfect solution. Both internal and external models are available. External drives are the easiest to install; plug a cable into a parallel port, and it's ready to archive. Internal models, on the other hand, are less expensive, consume less desk space, and provide faster service.

Installing an internal tape drive is one of the easiest and most risk-free upgrades you can perform as long as you have room for it. Every internal tape drive installation is unique, and the steps for installing your tape drive may differ slightly from the steps we took to install our drive. Use our guide as a complement to the installation manual that came with your tape drive.

Installing the Tape Drive

Follow these steps to install your tape drive.

1. Read Skill 3 to prepare for the installation.
2. Some users choose to install accelerator cards along with their tape drives. An accelerator card, such as the Iomega Ditto Dash, decreases the time it takes to write data to a tape cartridge and may be a valuable investment for a business that needs to back up a lot of data in a short amount of time.

NOTE NOTE NOTE NOTE NOTE NOTE NOTE NOTE NOTE NOTE NOTE NOTE NOTE NOTE NOTE

We chose not to install an accelerator card with our tape drive. If you decide to install one, you should do so before you install the tape drive. Follow the instructions listed in the accelerator card's installation manual or contact the card's manufacturer for assistance.

3. Look inside your computer to find an available 3.5- or 5.25-inch drive bay to accommodate the tape drive. The drive bay can be positioned either horizontally or vertically, but it must have an opening to the front of the computer. It also must accommodate the size of the drive. For example, you can fit either a 5.25- or a 3.5-inch drive into a 5.25-inch drive bay, but you cannot fit a 5.25-inch drive into a 3.5-inch bay.

NOTE NOTE NOTE NOTE NOTE NOTE NOTE NOTE NOTE NOTE NOTE NOTE NOTE NOTE NOTE

If all the drive bays are occupied, you'll have to remove a drive to make room for the tape drive or you'll have to exchange your internal tape drive for an external model.

4. Once you have located an available drive bay, you need to remove the plastic panel, called a drive bay cover, that protects the mouth of the drive bay (see Figure 7.3). On some computers, there is a metal panel situated behind the drive bay cover. It needs to be removed, as well. Usually, you can remove both panels by inserting your hand through the drive bay and pushing through to the outside. Be careful not to disconnect any cables or jostle any drives already installed in your computer. Remember where you put the panels in case you ever decide to remove the drive and need to cover the mouth of the drive bay again.

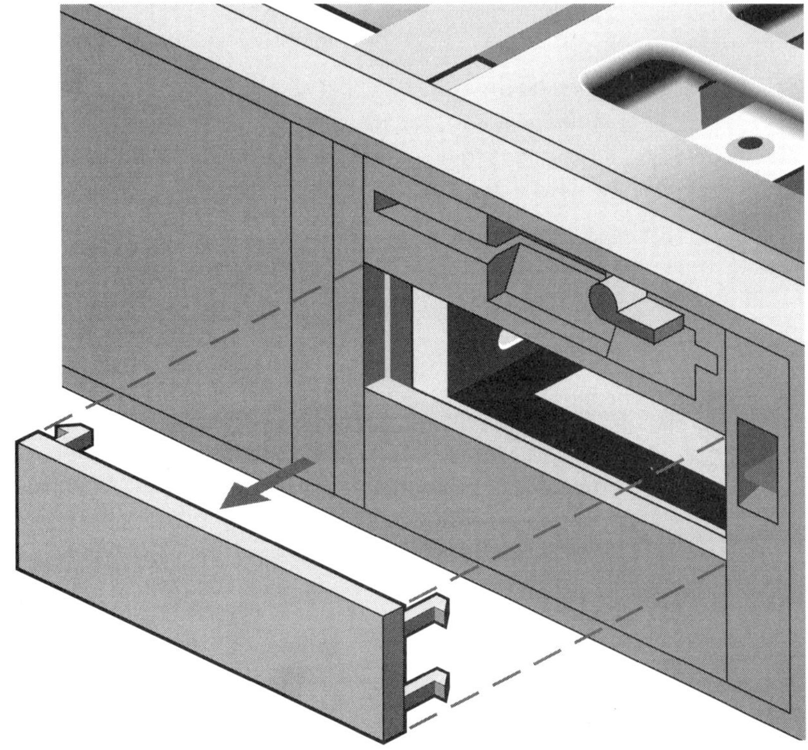

FIGURE 7.3: Remove the plastic cover to access the drive bay.

WARNING WARNING WARNING WARNING WARNING WARNING WARNING WARNING

If you encounter any difficulties while removing the panels, refer to the computer's user manual for instructions on how to do so.

5. If you're installing a 3.5-inch drive into a 5.25-inch drive bay, you need to attach mounting brackets to the drive. A mounting set, which usually consists of two metal rails and a faceplate that has a slot in it, may be included with the drive. If it isn't, contact the manufacturer to obtain a mounting set.
6. Use the included screws to attach the metal rails to either side of the drive. The screws are usually quite tiny, and you might need to use a pair of needle-nosed pliers or tweezers to hold the screws in place while you tighten them. Tighten the screws until they're secure, but don't overtighten them. Overtightening can damage the drive.
7. The faceplate should snap into the mouth of the drive bay. Be gentle attaching the faceplate so you don't crack it. Refer to the installation instructions included with the mounting set for the exact mounting instructions.
8. Insert the drive into the drive bay. Be careful not to disconnect the cables inside the computer when you're inserting the drive. If you attached mounting brackets to the drive, be especially careful as you guide the drive into the drive bay. You don't want to bend or break the mounting brackets.
9. Now is the time to attach the cables to the drive (Figure 7.4). First, attach a power cable. This cable, which consists of four multicolored wires attached to a plastic plug, may connect directly to the drive or it may connect to the drive via an adapter cord.

NOTE NOTE NOTE NOTE NOTE NOTE NOTE NOTE NOTE NOTE NOTE NOTE NOTE NOTE NOTE

Consult your installation manual to determine whether you need to use an adapter cord. If you do, an adapter cord should have been included with the tape drive. If an adapter cord wasn't included with the tape drive, contact the manufacturer to obtain one.

10. Next, you'll attach the 40-pin ribbon cable, which is also called the *data cable*, to the drive. Depending on the way the drive connects to your PC, there are three options for performing this part of the installation.
    - The first and easiest way is to connect the drive to the disk drive controller, which is located on the motherboard. Locate the data cable

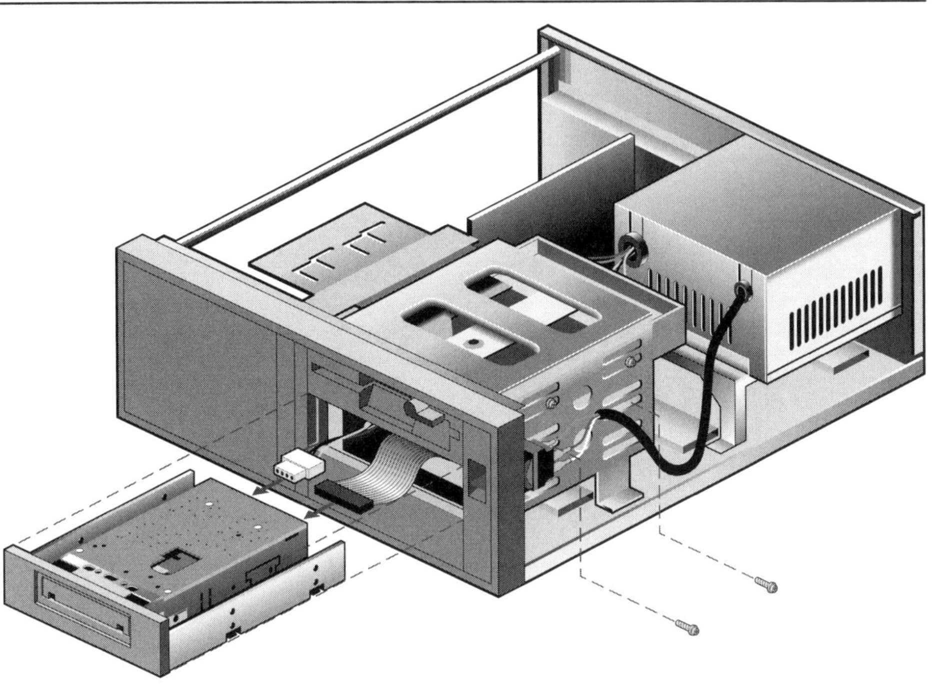

FIGURE 7.4: Attach the cables as shown.

that connects the disk drive to the motherboard. If it contains an extra connector, you may be able to connect this extra connector to your tape drive. Consult the drive's installation manual to determine if this is a viable option.

- The second way, which is almost as easy, involves using the ribbon cable that came with your tape drive. Remove the disk drive's data cable from the controller, then connect the tape drive's data cable to the disk drive controller. Finally, plug the disk drive's data cable into the pass-through connector on the tape drive's data cable. Again, consult the installation manual to determine if this is a viable option.
- The third way to connect the data cable to the PC involves connecting the tape drive to an accelerator card instead of the disk drive controller. Follow the installation instructions included with your accelerator card to learn the exact connection procedures.

Regardless of which method you use to connect the tape drive to the computer, you need to be careful when connecting the data cable to the drive and PC. Because it carries data between the PC and the tape drive, it's imperative that the cable is connected correctly in both locations (see Figure 7.5).

11. If the cable connector has an upraised tab in the middle of it, just match the tab to the notch in the receptor. Then insert the connector.

12. If the connector doesn't have an upraised tab, you'll have to align the colored strip, which runs along one edge of the data cable, with Pin 1 on the receptor. Pin 1, which is the bottom-right pin (or upper-left pin, depending on how you look at it) on the receptor, usually is designated by a tiny "1" printed next to it. If you're not sure how the data cable attaches to the receptor, check the installation manual for details.

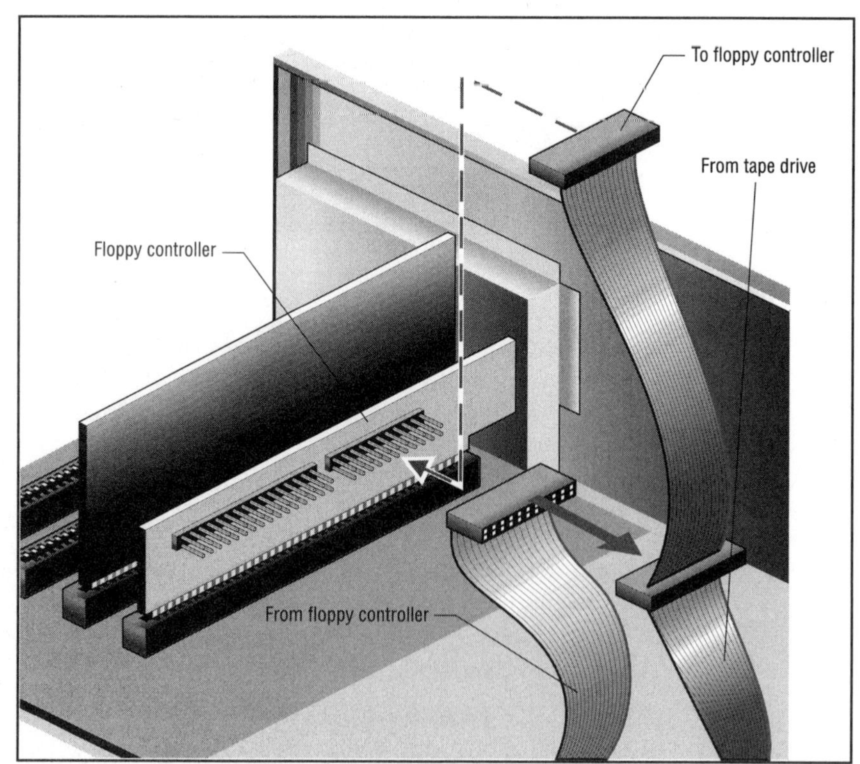

FIGURE 7.5: Connecting the cables

13. You probably won't have much room in which to work when you're attaching the cables. Needle-nosed pliers might make the job a little easier. Be careful not to jostle any other cables loose when you're inserting the data cable. Also, don't force the connections, but make sure they're snug and secure. A loose connection is all it takes for a drive to malfunction.
14. Secure the drive to the computer frame. Align the holes in the drive or align the mounting brackets to the holes in the computer frame, then insert the screws. The screws are tiny, so you might need to use those needle-nosed pliers or tweezers again.
15. Double-check the drive to make sure it's securely in place. Also check that you didn't accidentally knock any of the surrounding cables out of place during the installation of the drive. Put the cover back on the computer and plug it in. Turn the computer on and wait for the operating system to load.

Setting Up Your Drive Software

It's time to install the software.

1. Insert the setup disk in the disk drive and activate the setup according to the directions in the instruction manual. Follow the on-screen instructions for installing the device driver or use the Windows 95/98 Add New Hardware wizard.
2. The setup software will assign a drive letter to the tape drive. Check File Manager in Windows 3.1 or My Computer in Windows 95/98 to make sure the computer recognizes the drive. You should see an icon corresponding to the newly assigned drive letter. Insert a tape cartridge in the drive to see if the drive recognizes its storage medium.

The tape drive should come with backup software. This software allows you to designate the files you want to back up on a regular basis. After installing the software, run the backup application right away. That way you'll know it works and you'll have taken the first step in creating a regular backup routine. After all, that's why you purchased the tape drive.

Installing High-Capacity Storage Devices

In the past, choosing a data storage option was a matter of choosing between two extremes. Option number one was the immovable, high-capacity hard drive. Option number two was the transportable, small-capacity disk drive.

Now, thanks to advancements in storage technology, users have a third option that combines the flexibility of a disk with the high capacity of a hard drive. These drives, including those produced by Iomega and SyQuest, as well as those that conform to the LS-120 storage technology, offer users the chance to choose storage solutions that meet their individual needs.

We decided to install an Iomega Jaz drive, a SyQuest SparQ drive, and a Hi-Val SuperDisk drive. Of these three, the Jaz drive is the most complex device to install, so that's where we'll focus our attention.

What You Need to Know

Tools: Phillips screwdriver and tweezers or needle-nosed pliers

Time: Two hours

Cost: $279.95 for the Jaz drive; $99.95 for the Jaz Jet SCSI PCI card; $199.95 (suggested retail price) for the SparQ drive; $129.95 (suggested retail price) for the SuperDisk

Skill Level: Intermediate to difficult

Benefits: Combines the portability of a disk with the performance of a hard drive

The Jaz Drive

Iomega is perhaps the most popular manufacturer of high-capacity, transportable storage devices. The company's Jaz drives use storage media that are small enough to fit in your shirt pocket, fast enough to run multimedia applications, and capacious enough to support a full backup of most hard drives.

A Jaz drive is a *Small Computer System Interface* (SCSI; pronounced *skuzzy*) device. SCSI refers to the way a peripheral connects with a computer. It allows for superfast data transfer rates and is most often used with scanners, CD-ROM drives, and hard drives. But SCSI devices require SCSI connections, and not all computers have SCSI connections. Our computer didn't, so we needed to add one. We added a Jaz Jet SCSI Peripheral Component Interconnect (PCI) card.

In addition to adding a SCSI connection, your computer has to be trained to recognize and communicate with the SCSI device. And this is what can give you—and your computer—a headache. Because of the potential problems that could be caused when you add a SCSI device, we recommend that you clean up your system a bit before you install a Jaz drive. Run ScanDisk to ensure that your hard drive is ready to accept new software. Back up your important files so you don't lose them in case a problem arises.

NOTE

Iomega claims the Jaz drive will work with a 386-based system and DOS 4.0, but we don't recommend trying to force such a low-end system to support such a high-end peripheral. You'll have better luck with the installation and with drive performance if your computer has a Pentium processor or newer and runs a 32-bit operating system, such as Windows 95/98 or Windows NT.

With the formalities out of the way, we're ready for the installation. If your computer runs DOS, Windows 3.*x*, or Windows 95/98, then skip ahead to the "Installing the SCSI Card" section. If your computer runs Windows NT 3.51 or newer, read the following section.

Windows NT Users

If your computer runs Windows NT 3.51 or newer, you need to install the software *before* you install the SCSI card. Turn the computer on and wait for the operating system to load. Insert the installation disk that came with the SCSI card into your disk drive. Follow the directions that correspond to your version of Windows NT.

NT 3.51 Follow along with these steps.

1. Open the Main group, then double-click the Windows NT Setup icon.
2. In the resulting window, open the Options menu, then choose the Add/Remove SCSI Adapter option. Click Add.
3. In the list of adapters, select Other.

4. When you're asked for the location of the adapters, type **a:\Win.nt** (where a: is the drive letter of the drive where the installation disk is inserted). Click OK.
5. From the resulting list of adapters, select the Jaz Jet PCI option and click OK.
6. Click the Install button. Windows NT will install the drivers automatically.
7. After the installation is finished, shut down the operating system and turn off the computer.
8. Proceed to "Installing the SCSI Card," below.

NT 4.0 Follow along with these steps.

1. Click the Start button, select the Settings option, then open the Control Panel.
2. Choose the SCSI Adapters option.
3. Click the Drivers tab and click the Add button.
4. Click the Have Disk button.
5. Select the A:\Win.NT setting. If the installation disk is not in your A: drive, highlight the drive where it is located. Click OK.
6. From the list of Iomega adapters, choose the Jaz Jet PCI option. Click Next.
7. At the next screen, click OK and Windows NT will install the necessary drivers.
8. After the installation is complete, click OK. Shut down the operating system and turn off the computer.
9. Proceed to "Installing the SCSI Card," below.

Installing the SCSI Card

Before installing a SCSI card, make sure your computer doesn't have a SCSI connection already. The computer's documentation should indicate if it does. If the documentation confuses you, call the computer's manufacturer and ask for help. If the computer already has a SCSI connection, skip to the "Installing the Jaz Drive" section below.

1. Turn your computer off, unplug it, and remove the computer's cover. The step-by-step instructions in Skill 3 tell you how. We recommend performing

the installation in an uncarpeted room. Carpet increases the risk of picking up static electricity and makes it difficult to find dropped screws.

2. Locate an available PCI expansion slot inside your computer. The expansion slots are built onto the motherboard, and there's usually a row of them. Some of the slots have two sockets and some have just one. A PCI slot has just one socket, approximately 3 inches long.
3. Remove the screw that holds the corresponding slot cover in place and slide the slot cover out of its position. Set the screw and slot cover aside, but keep track of the screw; you'll need it later.
4. Remove the SCSI card from the box. Before you remove it from the static-free bag, ground yourself by touching a metal screw on the computer. Then remove the card from the bag. Be careful to touch only the sides of the card. You don't want to damage the fragile circuitry.
5. Line up the card's connector (it looks like a strip of vertical metal pins) with the designated PCI slot and insert the card into the slot. You may have to rock it gently back and forth to get it into the slot. You should hear a click when the card finally locks into place, and the metal plate on the edge of the card should fit neatly into the area formerly occupied by the slot cover.
6. Use the screw that held the slot cover in place to fasten the card to the frame of the computer. Tighten the screw until the card is secure.
7. Make sure the card is securely in place. Also, check that you didn't knock any of the surrounding expansion cards out of place during the installation.
8. If your computer runs Windows NT, you can skip ahead to "Installing the Jaz Drive," below, because you've already loaded the device drivers. If your computer runs DOS, Windows 3.*x*, or Windows 95/98, however, you still need to install the drivers. Put the cover back on the computer and plug it in.

NOTE

Although you can install the Jaz drive at this point, we recommend waiting to install the drive until the drivers for the SCSI card are loaded on the computer.

9. Turn the computer on. After the operating system has loaded, insert the Jaz Jet Install disk into the disk drive. Refer to the instructions below that pertain to your operating system.

NOTE NOTE NOTE NOTE NOTE NOTE NOTE NOTE NOTE NOTE NOTE NOTE NOTE NOTE NOTE

The procedure for installing software varies for each computer, depending on the hardware and software configuration of the system. Our instructions are based on the installation procedures for a typical computer setup. Always defer to the software installation wizard for the exact steps you should follow.

Windows 95/98 After the operating system has loaded, you'll see a pop-up message indicating that new hardware has been found on your system. This is the easiest way to install the SCSI software; basically, you just follow the on-screen directions.

When you see a message asking for the location of the drivers, choose the Driver From Disk Provided By Hardware Manufacturer option and click OK. In the Install From Disk window, make sure the A: drive (where A: is the drive letter of the drive where the installation disk is inserted) is indicated in the Copy Manufacturer's Files From dialog box. Click OK.

As Windows 95 installs the drivers, your system may appear to lock up temporarily. Things should return to normal after the drivers are loaded. If the computer locks up for more than 20 minutes, however, then you'll need to restart your computer.

Windows 3.1 and DOS You need to run the software installation from the DOS prompt, so exit Windows if necessary. At the DOS prompt, type **a:\install** (where a: is the drive letter of the drive where the installation disk is inserted). Press Enter. During the installation, you'll be asked to choose Express or Custom installation. Select the Express Install option.

After the installation, choose the Reboot option. This shuts down and restarts your computer. After the computer restarts, you may receive some error messages because the Jaz drive isn't installed yet. Ignore these messages.

Installing the Jaz Drive

Now you're ready for the real installation.

1. Make sure the computer has a SCSI connection. If you just installed a SCSI card, you know it does. Otherwise, check the computer's documentation or call the computer's manufacturer to find out for certain.

2. Turn the computer off, unplug it, and remove the cover. See Skill 3 for more information about preparing for an internal installation.

3. Look inside your computer to find an available 3.5- or 5.25-inch drive bay to accommodate the Jaz drive. The bay can be positioned horizontally or vertically. There should be a plastic panel, called a drive bay cover, protecting the mouth of the drive bay. Behind this plastic panel may be a metal, clip-out panel. These panels need to be removed. Usually this can be done by inserting your hand through the drive bay and pushing through to the outside. Be careful not to disconnect any cables or jostle any drives already installed in your computer. Keep the panels in a safe place in case you ever decide to remove the drive and need to cover the mouth of the drive bay again.

NOTE

If you're inserting the drive into a 3.5-inch drive bay, skip to step 7. If you're inserting the drive into a 5.25-inch drive bay, go to step 4.

4. The drive needs to be mounted to mounting brackets so it can fit inside the 5.25-inch bay. A mounting set, consisting of left and right rails, a plastic faceplate, and four screws, is included with the drive. Connect the rails to the faceplate by snapping the plastic tabs of the faceplate into the slots on the metal rails. Make sure the connection is tight and secure.

5. Slide the drive between the two rails and press it against the faceplate. The face of the drive should fit into the slot in the faceplate. Along the bottom edges of the drive are four tiny holes. Four small posts in the rails fit into these holes. It may take some force to get the posts into the holes. Be gentle; you don't want to damage the drive.

6. Use the screws to fasten the drive to the rails. The screws are quite tiny, and you might need to use some needle-nosed pliers or tweezers to hold the screws in place while you tighten them. Tighten the screws until they're secure, but don't overtighten them. Also, use only the screws included with the kit. Overtightening and long screws can damage the fragile circuitry inside the drive.

7. Attach the data cable to the drive. This cable carries the data between the drive and the computer, so it's imperative that the cable is connected correctly to the drive. Fortunately, the cable fits only one way. Fit the upraised tab on the cable connector into the notch of the receptor on the drive. The connection should be tight and secure. Don't force the connection; if you meet with heavy resistance, pull out the cable, realign it, and push it in again.

8. Insert the drive into the drive bay. You'll have to thread the data cable through the drive bay before inserting the drive. Be careful not to disconnect other cables inside the computer when you're inserting the drive.
9. Connect the data cable to the computer's internal SCSI receptor. If you inserted the Jaz Jet PCI SCSI card, which is designed specifically for use with the Jaz drive, the cable connects only one way. Insert the upraised tab on the cable connector to the notch on the receptor.
10. If the receptor doesn't have a notch, you'll have to align the colored strip, which runs along one edge of the data cable, with Pin 1 on the receptor. Pin 1, which is the bottom-right pin (or upper-left pin, depending on how you look at it) on the receptor, usually is designated by a tiny "1" printed next to it. If you're not sure how the data cable attaches to the receptor, check the user manual or contact the manufacturer.
11. Attach an internal power cord to the drive. The power cord usually consists of four colored wires and a plastic plug, which attaches to a four-pronged socket on the drive. The plug attaches to the socket only one way. It should slide in easily, and if you meet resistance, remove the plug and realign the connection before trying again.
12. Use the remaining four screws that came with the drive to secure the drive to the computer frame. The screws are tiny, so you might need to use those needle-nosed pliers or tweezers again. Tighten the screws until they're secure. Don't overtighten the screws; you can damage the drive that way. Also, use only the screws included with the kit; longer screws can damage the drive's fragile circuitry.

NOTE NOTE NOTE NOTE NOTE NOTE NOTE NOTE NOTE NOTE NOTE NOTE NOTE NOTE NOTE

If your computer is a desktop model, you should be able to insert two screws in each side. If your computer is a tower model, you might have to insert all four screws in one side.

13. Double-check the drive to make sure it's securely in place. Also, check that you didn't accidentally knock any of the surrounding cables out of place during the installation of the drive. Put the cover back on the computer and plug it in. Turn the computer on and wait for the operating system to load. If your computer runs Windows 95/98, a pop-up message, indicating the system has detected new hardware, may appear on-screen. You can ignore this message.

14. Check to see if the drive is active by inserting the included Jaz Tools disk into the Jaz drive. It may take some force to insert it completely. The orange light on the drive should flash and you should hear a faint hum when the disk is inserted correctly. When the light stops flashing, the drive is ready for use. If the light never flashes, the drive probably wasn't installed correctly; go back to Step 7 and make sure the cables are inserted correctly.
15. A pair of installation disks come with the drive. Disk 1 is for systems that run DOS, Windows 3.*x*, and Windows 95/98; Disk 2 is for systems that run Windows NT. Insert the appropriate installation disk for your computer into the disk drive.

If your computer runs DOS, skip ahead to the DOS section. If your computer runs Windows 3.*x*, Windows 95/98, or Windows NT, refer to the instructions below that pertain to your operating system.

After activating the installation, a blue setup screen should appear. Follow the on-screen instructions to complete the installation.

If you have questions or encounter problems during the software installation, consult the online manual. It's located on the Jaz Install Disk 1 disk. Open File Manager (for Windows 3.*x* and Windows NT 3.51) or My Computer (for Windows 95/98 and Windows NT), open the A: drive (where A: is the drive letter of the drive where the installation disk is inserted), and double-click the MANUAL.EXE file.

Windows 95/98 Open the Start menu, select Settings, choose Control Panel, and double-click the Add/Remove Programs icon. On the Install/Uninstall page, click the Install button. In the Install Program From Floppy Disk/CD-ROM window, click Next. Windows 95/98 will locate the SETUP.EXE file and begin the installation.

Windows NT In Windows NT 3.51, open the File menu of Program Manager, then select Run. In Windows NT 4.0, open the Start menu and select the Run option. Either way, type **a:\setupnt.exe** in the Run dialog box (where a: is the drive letter of the drive where the installation disk is inserted). Click OK. This activates the installation.

Windows 3.*x* In the Program Manager, open the File menu and choose the Run command. Type **a:\setup.exe** (where a: is the drive letter of the drive where the installation disk is inserted), then click OK. This activates the installation.

DOS Installation is a three-part process in DOS. First, at the DOS prompt, type **a:\guest.exe** (where a: is the drive letter of the drive where the installation disk is inserted). This portion of the installation assigns a drive letter to the Jaz drive. Take note of this letter.

After this portion of the setup is complete, type **e:\dosstuff\install.exe** (where e: is the drive letter of the Jaz drive) at the DOS prompt. When the installation screen appears, use the Tab key to select the Express option. Follow the on-screen instructions to complete the installation.

After this portion of the installation is complete, type **e:\dosstuff\reclaim.exe** (where e: is the drive letter of the Jaz drive) at the DOS prompt. This portion of the installation gives you the ability to save data to the Jaz Tools disk.

If you have more questions or encounter problems during the software installation, consult the online manual by typing **a:\manual.exe** (where a: is the drive letter of the drive where the installation disk is inserted) at the DOS prompt.

The SparQ Drive

SyQuest's SparQ, a 1GB storage device, is similar to the Jaz drive. It seems lighter and a little less robust than the Jaz drive, but it is a bit easier to install in your PC. For one thing, the 3.5-inch drive comes premounted in the brackets for a 5.25-inch drive bay. To remove the brackets, just twist a few screws.

The trickiest part of a SparQ drive installation is configuring the drive to accommodate your computer's Integrated Drive Electronics (IDE) and Enhanced IDE (EIDE) settings. Refer the instructions in Skill 6 on installing a second hard drive for details on configuring the EIDE/IDE settings.

To mount the drive, follow the steps in the "Installing the Jaz Drive" section, above. Once it's mounted, double-check the drive to make sure it's securely in place. Also, check that you didn't accidentally knock any of the surrounding cables out of place during the installation of the drive. Put the cover back on the computer and plug it in.

Before you turn on your PC, insert the SparQ Starter cartridge into the SparQ drive, then turn on the PC. The light on the drive should blink when you turn on the computer; if it doesn't, shut down the PC and double-check your power cable connection.

Insert the installation disk and follow the on-screen instructions and the SparQ users guide for help with the software installation. Refer to the "Installing the Jaz Drive" section, above, for additional help.

The LS-120 Drive

The Hi-Val SuperDisk drive is just one of the many drives that adhere to the LS-120 technology. LS-120 drives are unique among these high-capacity portable storage devices because they are compatible with standard 3.5-inch disk drives. In other words, they can read data from and write data to just about any 3.5-inch disk, whether it has a capacity of 120MB, 1.44MB, 1.2MB, or 720KB. Consequently, you can replace your computer's disk drive with the SuperDisk drive if you want.

The SuperDisk drive installation is almost identical to that of the SparQ drive. Refer to the "The SparQ Drive" section, above, for more details. One noticeable difference between the two is that the Hi-Val SuperDisk drive's jumper comes preset in the slave position, whereas the SparQ drive's jumper comes preset in the master position. Use the installation disk included with the SuperDisk drive to complete the software portion of the installation.

Ready to Store

That's it. The drive should be up and running. You're now equipped to back up your hard drive, store large multimedia files, or do whatever you need to do with an infinite supply of portable storage space.

Are You Experienced?

Now you can...

- ☑ install a disk drive
- ☑ install an internal tape drive
- ☑ install a high-capacity storage device

SKILL 8

Installing Multimedia

- Looking into multimedia kits
- Installing a CD-ROM
- Installing a DVD-ROM
- Installing a sound card

In the pre-PC days, keeping up with the neighbors was easy. If the Joneses bought a new car with a sun roof, you bought a new convertible. If the Smiths bought a 19-inch TV, you bought a 21-inch TV. If the Kings bought a new lawnmower, you hired their son to mow your lawn.

But in the world of computing, keeping up with the latest technology is tougher than mowing your own lawn. It often seems today's exciting new technology is passé by next week. As a result, it's now difficult to keep up with the latest computer toys.

When it comes to multimedia computing, with older computers, you could add or upgrade your multimedia components fairly easily with a multimedia kit. It contained all the components you needed, including software, a CD-ROM drive, a sound card, and speakers. A few included joysticks or video cards.

But with newer computers, the upgrade isn't quite as clear cut. Shelves in computer stores that used to be filled with multimedia kits now contain more individual components than kits. More DVD-ROM drives now occupy shelves where CD-ROM drives once stood alone. This skill will cover all you need to know about the competing technologies and their peripherals.

The Evolution of Multimedia Kits

If you want to upgrade your computer's multimedia capabilities, what's your best option? When is it best to upgrade a single component versus using a multimedia kit? We'll discuss what's available in multimedia kits and some of the changes the multimedia hardware industry is experiencing.

Multimedia Components

To achieve a multimedia experience, you need several components. *Multimedia* is a difficult term to define, but it refers to any type of computing that involves a combination of video, graphics, audio, images, and text. Multimedia software uses these components to enhance the information it provides. Multimedia hardware gives your computer the ability to properly present multimedia software.

Here are the hardware components that allow you to gain the most from multimedia software.

CD-ROM and DVD-ROM Drives

Because multimedia software can require hundreds of megabytes of file-storage space, CD-ROMs and DVD-ROMs are invaluable storage media. Without the introduction of CD-ROM several years ago, multimedia computing certainly wouldn't have developed as quickly as it did. CD-ROM drives have graduated from a hardware component that users wanted for multimedia capabilities to a hardware component users must have for basic computing tasks as well as multimedia. Nearly all new software is shipped on CD-ROMs rather than on multiple disks.

A disk can hold 1.44MB of data, while a CD-ROM disk can hold 650MB of data, which is about 450 times more data than a disk. DVD-ROM disks can hold about 17GB of data, which is about 25 times more than CD-ROM disks.

To play these disks , you need a CD-ROM drive or a DVD-ROM drive. (For more information on the two types of drives, see the "DVD-ROM versus CD-ROM" sidebar.) The faster these drives spin the disks, the faster information is transferred from the disks to your computer's random access memory (RAM). The speed of CD-ROM drives has increased tremendously in the past couple of years.

DVD-ROM drives, which are the newest technology, can read both CD-ROMs and DVD-ROMs. A 1× DVD-ROM drive is almost equal in speed to a 10× CD-ROM drive.

DVD-ROM VERSUS CD-ROM

When considering a multimedia upgrade, are you better off choosing a DVD-ROM kit or a CD-ROM kit? We'll look at both types of technologies and the current benefits and drawbacks of each one.

DVD, short for *digital video disk*, is a type of storage technology designed to eventually replace compact disks (CDs), video tape, video-game cartridges, and CD-ROM disks. DVD video, often shortened to DVD, is designed for home-entertainment use, whereas DVD disks are placed in a DVD player and shown on a television. DVD-ROM is a read-only computing format, similar to CD-ROM.

DVD-ROM disks and CD-ROM disks look similar physically, but actual similarities are few. A DVD-ROM disk can hold about 25 times more information than a CD-ROM disk, making it an ideal storage medium for applications

continued

and games requiring more than one CD-ROM disk. DVD-ROM also is ideal for storing large video and audio streams. For example, an entire movie can be stored on a DVD disk, with plenty of storage space to spare. (Media is a term used for computer storage material such as floppy disks, compact disks, and tapes—devices on which information can be stored. Medium is the singular form of this term.)

As with computing CD-ROMs, DVD-ROM currently is a read-only medium. And, as with CDs, DVD for computing will become available as recordable and rewriteable media that can be written to once or multiple times.

DVD-ROM drives can read CD-ROMs, but CD-ROM drives and CD audio players can't read DVD-ROM disks. Not all DVD-ROM drives can read all compact disk-recordable (CD-R) and compact disk-rewriteable (CD-RW) media; if you need to read these disks, make sure you purchase a DVD-ROM drive containing this ability.

Because of DVD-ROM's advantages over and backward-compatibility with CD-ROM, DVD-ROM is expected to eventually replace CD-ROM as a computing storage format. Many hardware manufacturers eventually plan to stop making CD-ROM drives in favor of DVD-ROM drives. Computer manufacturers are including DVD-ROM drives on many newer computers.

Current DVD-ROM drives are slightly slower than the fastest CD-ROM drives. For example, a 2× DVD-ROM drive is about equal in speed to a 20× CD-ROM drive. However, as DVD-ROM becomes more popular and more widely installed, its speed should surpass the fastest CD-ROM drives.

So, should you purchase a DVD-ROM upgrade kit now? DVD-ROM isn't ready to put CD-ROM drives on the flea-market shelves just yet, says Edward Meadows, executive vice president of sales and marketing for Hi-Val Inc., a leading manufacturer of multimedia kits. Until more software titles use DVD-ROM, Meadows says, DVD-ROM's hold on the market probably will continue to advance slowly.

InfoTech, a leading computer industry market research firm, estimates that only about 500 DVD-ROM software titles will be available by the end of 1998. However, InfoTech estimates that 80,000 DVD-ROM software titles will be available by 2005.

continued

Meadows says the price range influence of DVD-ROM will be another key to determining its ability to control the market. Currently, a computer containing a DVD-ROM drive will cost $75–$150 more than a computer containing a CD-ROM drive (when all other components are similar).

"Does the end user want to pay another $100 to have a DVD unit?" Meadows asks.

On the other hand, Meadows recognizes that the influence of DVD-ROM provides an ability to change how users perceive computer multimedia, in much the same way CD-ROM revolutionized multimedia several years ago. For example, DVD-ROM users could interact with a movie playing on their computer by clicking an image of an actor and following a link to the actor's World Wide Web site.

"We want to differentiate DVD-ROM between the computer player and the movie player," Meadows says. "There needs to be more you can do (on the computer), otherwise, why have it?"

Another issue that will affect the DVD-ROM market is the popularity of Windows 98. Support for DVD-ROM is included with Microsoft's newest operating system; such support isn't included with Windows 95.

Glenn Ochsenreiter, vice president of marketing and membership at the Software Publishers Association, says many software publishers are waiting to see how Windows 98 fares before deciding whether to expend resources on DVD-ROM software. Software publishers realize that if most Windows 95 users fail to upgrade to Windows 98, they could experience compatibility problems with DVD-ROM software and hardware, and therefore, may not be as enthusiastic about the DVD format.

"Many publishers are waiting for Windows 98 to be in wide use, others are already moving forward," Ochsenreiter says. "The majority have held back, looking for a stable platform. Software companies are beginning to move forward (with DVD-ready software), but those software publishers who are going into this (direction) recognize today the market is small, but it has the capability to grow."

Sound Cards

The computer's sound card is an expansion card that allows it to reproduce audio clips. The newest sound cards can provide three-dimensional (3-D) positional sound, which is designed to make it seem as though sounds are originating from various positions around you.

Newer sound cards contain their own processing chips, allowing the computer's microprocessor to take care of other processing concerns, thereby enhancing the overall multimedia experience.

Speakers

Speakers for computing continue to improve, reproducing a sound quality that's similar to stereo speakers. Top-of-the-line speakers, however, often are fairly expensive. Most people will receive the audio performance they want from smaller, average speakers. Then again, even the latest and greatest sound card won't produce earth-shattering audio when paired with small, low-quality speakers. If audio is a key component of your multimedia or gaming experience, high-quality speakers are as important as a high-quality sound card.

TIP

In some computing environments, such as a busy, noisy office, you may want to opt for headphones instead of speakers. Speakers for computing are made differently than speakers for a stereo. Stereo speakers can't be used with a computer.

Microphones

If you want to record your own audio clips, a microphone is a must-have multimedia component. Microphones will continue to grow in importance if and when voice-recognition programs become popular. Multimedia kits will soon be available containing voice-recognition software, music-editing software, microphones, headphones, and compact disk-recordable (CD-R) drives, allowing users to create their own audio CD-R disks.

Video Cards and Monitors

As larger video clips and complex graphics continue to become a greater aspect of multimedia through DVD-ROM, you'll need a high-quality video card and a high-quality monitor to display them. Video cards often contain their own processors, allowing them to reproduce graphics and video quickly.

While video cards and monitors are key to multimedia performance, they're rarely included in multimedia kits because of their high price tags.

What Will Your Kit Include?

Multimedia kits in today's market are more simplistic than they were a few years ago. In the past, multimedia kits typically contained a sound card, speakers, a microphone, a CD-ROM drive, a joystick, and dozens of programs. Today's kits usually are limited to a CD-ROM drive, a sound card, and a few programs. Some kits also contain speakers and a microphone.

The average price of a CD-ROM multimedia kit is $150–$200. DVD-ROM multimedia kits cost about $250. Kits that contain additional hardware, such as a video card or high-quality speakers, or additional software will cost more.

As people become more comfortable with their computers, they're more apt to swap out a single multimedia component versus purchasing a multimedia kit.

With the massive changes occurring in the multimedia marketplace, the Software Publisher's Association (SPA) has decided to abandon its Multimedia PC (MPC) specifications in favor of concentrating on DVD-ROM-compatibility issues (see the "MPC Yields to DVD" sidebar). In the past, a user could make sure a multimedia kit would meet basic multimedia guidelines if the kit contained a "MPC-compatible" logo. But, because the latest MPC specifications were released two years ago, they aren't useful for consumers to follow anymore.

MPC Yields to DVD

In the computing industry, longevity is an unknown entity. If any aspect of computing stays current for a full year, it seems like forever. Two or three years seems like an eternity.

How about seven years? An impossibility. But that's how long the Multimedia PC Working Group was able to keep its Multimedia PC (MPC) specifications current before they began to fade into the background earlier this year. The MPC specifications, introduced in 1991, have given consumers, software programmers, and multimedia hardware manufacturers guidelines for providing an enjoyable multimedia experience.

The MPC logo appeared on hardware that met the minimum specifications set by the Multimedia PC Working Group, which operated under the

continued

SPA. Three versions of MPC specifications were introduced in the past seven years. But Glenn Ochsenreiter, vice president of marketing and membership at SPA and a representative who has served as liaison for the Multimedia PC Working Group, says there will not be a MPC4.

Instead, the SPA is turning its attention to the DVD-ROM Initiative. As computers containing DVD-ROM capabilities become more available, the SPA is hoping to develop basic standards for software programmers and hardware manufacturers to follow concerning DVD-ROM.

The DVD-ROM Initiative will attempt to introduce DVD-ROM applications to the market, to promote confidence among developers in DVD-ROM, and to allow participating companies to cooperate on DVD-ROM issues. (For more about the DVD-ROM Initiative, visit `http://www.spa.org/dvd/default.htm` on the Web.)

"From the SPA's point of view, there will be a significant installed base of DVD-capable computers starting now and moving to major proportions in the next year," Ochsenreiter says. "It'll be a great move forward for software publishers and for consumers. It makes sense for us to smooth the transition."

And where does that leave MPC? The specifications, which have survived improvements in computing from 386 machines to Pentiums and have seen the average hard drive increase 18 times in storage space, will fade into the background. Newer computers and software have advanced so quickly in the past couple of years that MPC3 no longer qualifies as a minimum standard for multimedia, even though it was just released in 1996.

"DVD has such an area of its own, it made more sense to focus on DVD," Ochsenreiter says. Furthermore, Ochsenreiter advises, the process used to create the MPC and keep it current will transfer well to the DVD-ROM Initiative.

"When (the MPC specifications) first came together, the purpose was to create an awareness of CD-ROM and set those standards so customers would make sure they received compatible equipment and an experience that wouldn't disappoint them," Ochsenreiter says. "There's a similar set of issues now with DVD."

Should I Upgrade Now?

Even with the changes occurring in the multimedia industry, the basic rule for determining whether you should upgrade hasn't changed: If the software packages you want to use commonly require faster and newer components than your computer has, it's probably time for an upgrade.

You may want to choose a multimedia kit if you need more than one component or if you need an overall system boost. If your computer is a couple of years old and you've never upgraded any of the hardware, a multimedia kit probably will serve your needs. Multimedia kits combine more than one piece of hardware and cost less than buying multiple pieces of hardware individually.

In some instances, though, you may be better off upgrading a single component. For example, if you're noticing audio-related system errors or poor-sounding audio, it may be time to trade in your sound card, even though your CD-ROM drive may still be performing well.

It's likely that as DVD-ROM becomes more popular and more accessible to the average user, multimedia kits will make a comeback, offering an upgrade from CD-ROM drives to DVD-ROM drives.

Because of the high amount of processing power required, current DVD-ROM kits usually contain a DVD-ROM drive and a DVD-ROM expansion card that contains its own processing chip, which increases the kits' cost. Ochsenreiter says DVD-ROM drives in upcoming years will be able to use the computer's processor, allowing them to come down in price. A typical DVD-ROM kit in the future probably will consist of a DVD-ROM drive and a video card or an audio card.

DVD-ROM looks like the next great breakthrough for multimedia content and storage technology. DVD-ROM proponents expect it will have a shelf life at least as long as CD-ROM did. Hopefully they're right; users could use some stability in multimedia innovations. It's tough enough keeping up with all the neighbors' latest purchases the way it is.

CD-ROM Installation

If you think your computer's performance could use the boost of a faster CD-ROM drive, don't let the thought of opening your computer case and installing it discourage you from making this simple upgrade. Installing a new CD-ROM drive is one of the easiest improvements you can make to your computer. The important thing to ask yourself before upgrading is, "Do I really *need* to upgrade?"

What You Need to Know

Tools: Phillips screwdriver (user guides will indicate other tools needed, if any)

Time: 15 to 30 minutes

Cost: Multimedia kits - $100 to $350, CD-ROM drive - $50 to $300

Skill Level: Easy

Benefits: Higher data transfer rates, faster access speeds, digital audio output, and less work for the microprocessor

Assessing Your Needs

Fortunately, the answer to that question is fairly straightforward. Because of the large storage capacity of compact disks (CDs)—approximately 650MB of data, or the capacity of roughly 450 1.44MB disks—you'll definitely want to add a CD-ROM drive to your computer if it doesn't already have one. Software packages are getting bigger and bigger, making installation from disks a lengthy process, if it's even an option.

If your computer already has a CD-ROM drive, there are several symptoms it may be displaying which will tell you if an upgrade is in order. A classic symptom is visible when loading CD-ROM software. An undue amount of time spent waiting for your computer to churn through the installation of a game or office suite is a sure sign that you may benefit from a faster drive.

Slow *access time* (the length of time required for a computer to process a data request and retrieve data from the drive) is another symptom that's especially noticeable to avid game players. Today's games tend to be quite graphics-intensive; they may include motion video and/or they may be *multipart* (meaning they skip between different parts of the disk). CD-ROM drives that are slow to access data will leave you waiting as your computer awkwardly stumbles and pauses its way through programs. If this sounds familiar you, it may be time to upgrade.

Buying Considerations

Once you've determined that your computer qualifies for a new CD-ROM drive, it's time to start investigating the options. The two main considerations you should look into are speed and placement.

Speed

You're probably familiar with the "×" number (16×, 24×, etc.) assigned to the varying speeds of drives, but you may not understand how that number is derived. To give you a frame of reference, the first CD-ROM drives transferred data from the disk to the computer at a rate of 150 kilobytes per second (kbps), which was expressed as 1× and known as single speed. The *transfer rates* have now reached speeds of 5,100kbps, an increase of 34 times. The × number, whether it's 2×, 4×, or 34×, represents the speed increase in relation to the original, single-speed drive.

It's also important to have an idea of what kind of performance boost you can expect from varying drive speeds. Data burned onto the outer rings of the disk spins by faster than does data burned onto the inner rings. Thus, even though a drive may claim, for example, to be a 24× drive, it won't necessarily read data at that speed all the time.

CD-ROM drives will usually perform at or near their rated speed for such tasks as installing software, but if you typically play games, search databases, or in any way pull data haphazardly from the disk, speeds will fluctuate considerably. You can expect a 24× drive to actually read data at speeds anywhere from 12× to 24×, depending on what you are doing or where the data happens to be burned on the disk.

The bottom line is that if you intend to run programs from the CD-ROM drive rather than install them on the hard drive, you'll want to purchase one of the faster drives available. However, if you only occasionally access applications from the CD-ROM drive, a mid-range speed will suffice.

Positioning

Besides choosing your speed, you also will face the decision of whether to get an external or internal drive. External drives are easier to install because you don't need to remove the computer case. They also can easily be switched from one computer to another. However, external drives usually use a *Small Computer System Interface* (SCSI) rather than an *Integrated Drive Electronics* (IDE) interface or an *Enhanced Integrated Drive Electronics* (EIDE) interface to connect to the motherboard.

SCSI interfaces are found on many of today's PCs. It is a much faster interface than either the IDE or the EIDE, but a CD-ROM drive that plugs into a SCSI port on the back of the computer will usually cost $100 to $200 more, discouraging many people from going that route.

Most internal CD-ROM drives use an IDE interface. Many motherboards include built-in support for IDE devices, while others require a separate IDE adapter to be plugged into an expansion slot. The updated version of IDE is EIDE, which can shuttle data to and from the drive three to four times faster than the IDE standard and can support larger storage devices. Most newer PCs have EIDE slots on the motherboard.

Installation

Before launching into the installation, there are a few housekeeping chores that must be taken care of first. You'll want to round up all the tools you're going to need. This includes a Phillips screwdriver and any other tools specified in the manufacturer's instructions. Also, read through the instructions that came with the drive. Check to see how much hard drive space is required by the new CD-ROM drive. The amount of free space required by your drive probably won't pose a problem, but it's always best to check before you start the installation process. If you are working on a non-Pentium machine, skip down to "Non-Pentium Installation," below.

NOTE NOTE NOTE NOTE NOTE NOTE NOTE NOTE NOTE NOTE NOTE NOTE NOTE NOTE NOTE

Because PCs and CD-ROM drives differ from brand to brand, the following instructions and illustrations may differ slightly from what you see inside your computer (see Figure 8.1). Although they will give you a good place to start, you will want to follow the instructions that came with the upgrade kit you purchased.

1. First, read Skill 3 for pre-installation preparations. Remember to unplug the computer, and always be sure to ground yourself by touching a metal surface before touching any of the components inside. This will prevent any electrical damage to the computer's delicate circuitry.

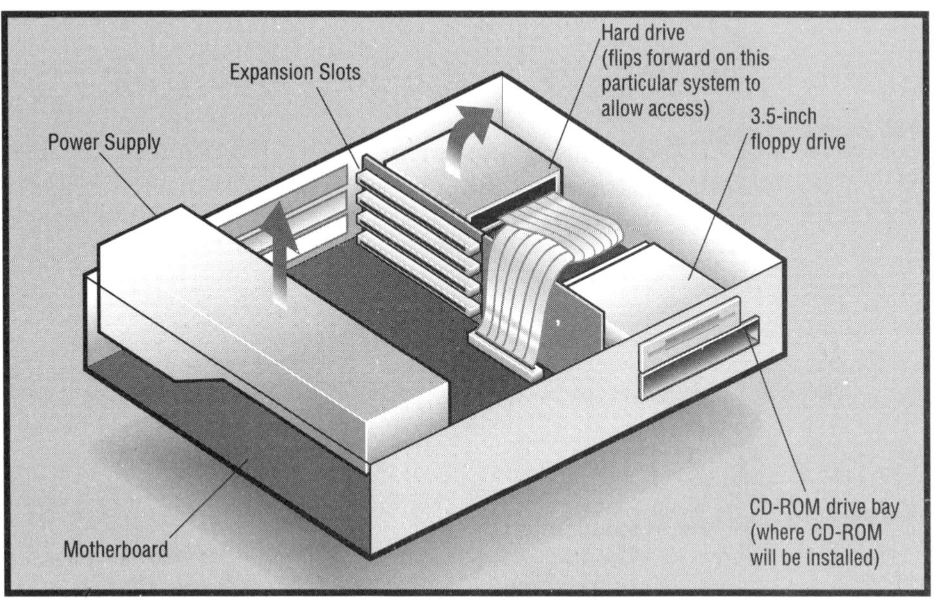

FIGURE 8.1: This is one example of a computer's configuration (the location of computer components varies from computer to computer).

2. Look carefully at the back of the new drive you are going to install. There are three cables that connect the drive to the computer. The first is the power cable that comes from the computer's power supply. Then, there's the interface ribbon cable that connects to an IDE, or EIDE, slot on the motherboard. Finally, there's the audio cable, connecting the CD-ROM drive to the sound card. You will want to take note of where each of these cables plugs into the new drive before jumping into the installation process.

3. While you're looking at the back of the CD-ROM drive, it's always a good idea to check the *jumper settings*. Besides the three cable connectors on the drive, you'll notice a small cluster of pins, otherwise known as jumpers. There should be a little plastic cap, called a *jumper drive select*, strategically covering a particular set of pins. Check your instruction manual to see what the jumper setting should be for the drive, and then make sure that the jumper drive select is in the proper position. In most cases you won't have to adjust the jumper settings, but if you do, it's better to find out sooner than later (Figure 8.2).

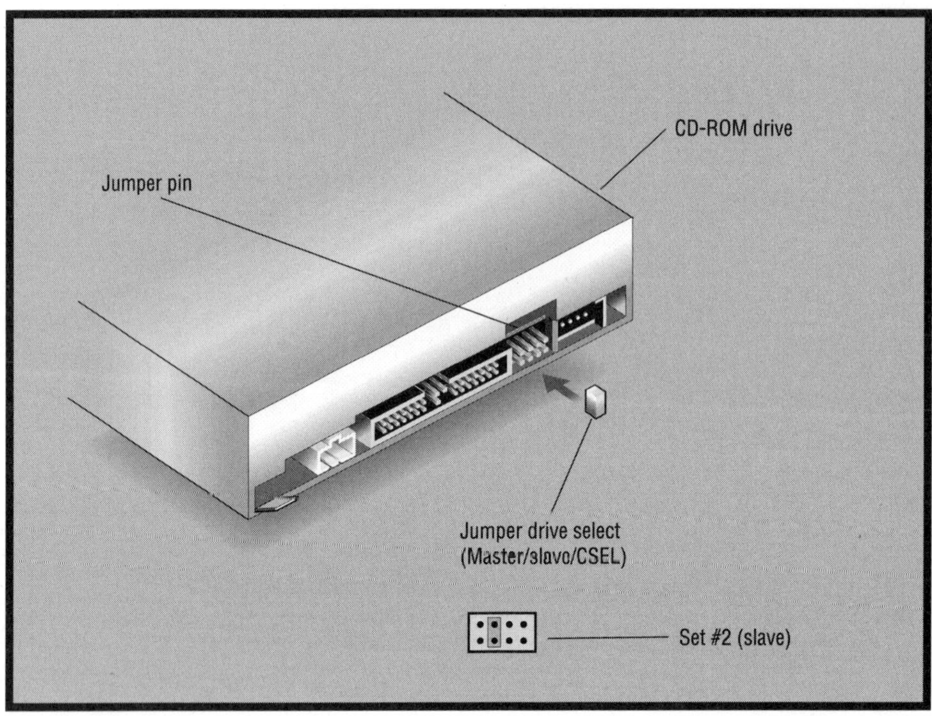

FIGURE 8.2: The jumpers on the back of the drive are usually set by the manufacturer.

4. Most likely, you're replacing an old CD-ROM drive with a new one. Your first step is going to be removing the old drive to make room for the new one. Simply loosen the screws on either side of the old drive, then carefully unplug the cables from the back of the drive. Remove the power cable first.

5. If you purchased the new drive as part of a multimedia kit, it probably came with a new sound card, as well as a new audio cable. That means you will need to not only unplug the old audio cable from the old drive, but you'll also need to follow that cable to where it connects to the old sound card. Unplug it from the sound card and use your screwdriver to loosen the screws that hold the card in place. Then, carefully pull it out of the slot. We'll cover how to install your new sound card in the "Installing a Sound Card" section, below.

6. If you purchased a CD-ROM drive by itself, it most likely came with a new audio cable. You will still need to use your old sound card, so don't remove it. Unplug the old cable from the old drive and from the sound card. Take note of where the cable attached to the sound card because you'll plug the new audio cable into that same connector.
7. Finally, remove the interface ribbon cable. Don't worry if you feel like you have to pull hard on the cable; it may require a gentle tug to unplug it from the old drive. Follow the interface cable to where it connects to the computer and unplug it there, as well.
8. You are now free to swap the old CD-ROM drive out for the new one. Carefully slide the old drive out of the 5.25-inch drive bay, then, slide the new drive into the vacated space (Figure 8.3). Insert the screws and tighten them until the drive is firmly in place.

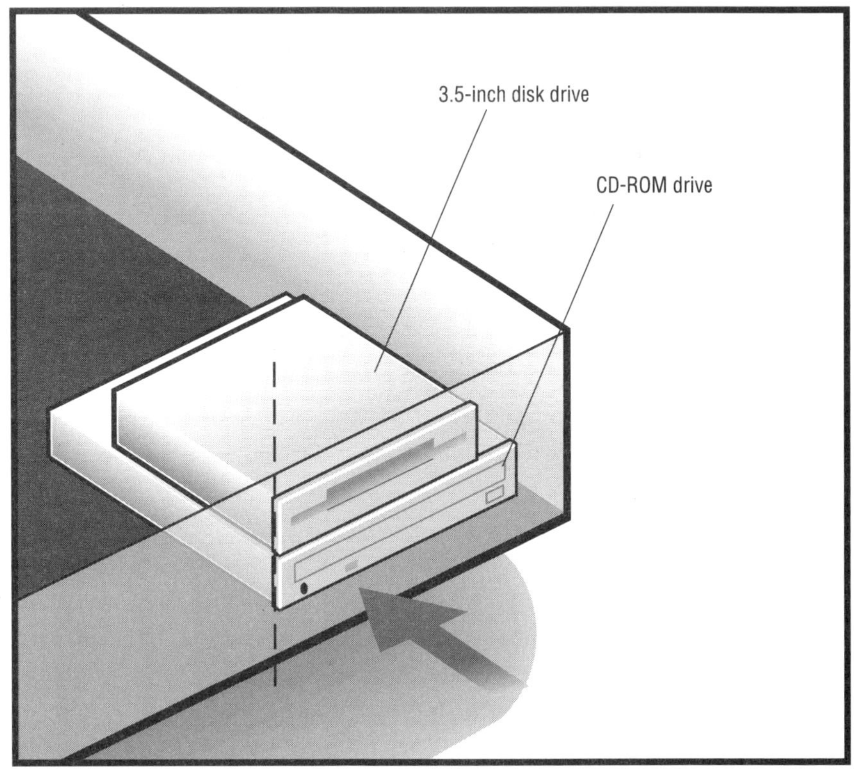

FIGURE 8.3: Slide the CD-ROM drive so that it's flush and aligned with the floppy drive.

9. Next comes the task of re-attaching the three cables you unplugged from the old drive. The first step is to find the power supply cable that you unplugged from the old drive; plug it into the power connector on the new drive (Figure 8.4).

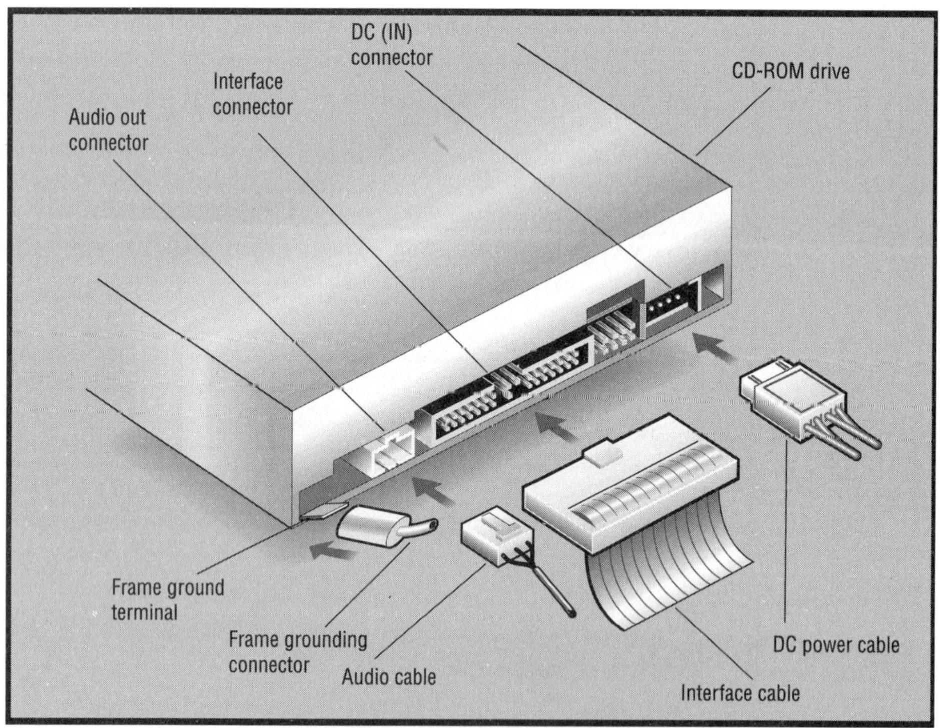

FIGURE 8.4: The CD-ROM won't be of much use unless it's connected.

10. The new drive should come with a new interface ribbon cable. Plug one end of this cable into the back of the CD-ROM drive, then, plug the other end into the IDE or EIDE slot on the motherboard where the old cable was connected.

11. Next, you'll need to locate the audio cable that came with the new drive. This cable plugs into the Audio Out connector at the back of the CD-ROM drive. If you purchased a multimedia kit that included a new sound card, you'll need to carefully insert the new card (using a back and forth rocking motion) into the same slot the old sound card occupied. Using your screwdriver,

secure the card firmly into place. Connect the audio cable from the CD-ROM drive to the connector on the sound card, following the manufacturer's directions.

12. If you purchased only the CD-ROM drive, run the new audio cable from the back of the drive to the connector on the old sound card; the same connector you pulled the old cable out of.

These steps make up the typical installation process for the average Pentium-based computer. However, if you're trying to install a CD-ROM drive in a 486-based machine that didn't already have a CD-ROM drive, the procedure may be a bit different. Again, don't forget to read Skill 3 for pre-installation preparations. Also, remember to unplug the computer and ground yourself by touching a metal surface before touching any of the components inside the computer case.

Non-Pentium Installation

If you are working on a non-Pentium machine, follow these steps.

WARNING WARNING WARNING WARNING WARNING WARNING WARNING WARNING

Be aware, however, that a 12× drive is the fastest speed that a 486-based computer can handle. You can install a faster CD-ROM drive if you want, but the processor will only allow it to read data at a maximum speed of 12×.

1. The first step is to find a location for the new drive. After removing the computer cover, locate an empty 5.25-inch drive bay. Remove the plastic drive bay cover; it will easily snap in and out of place. Then, slide the new drive into the drive bay and screw it into place.

2. You will have the same three cables that connect the CD-ROM drive to the computer as mentioned in the instructions above. First, locate the cables that come from the power supply. There should be an extra one for you to plug into the power cable connector on the new drive.

3. Plug the new audio cable that came with the CD-ROM drive into the back of the drive and the old sound card. If you purchased a multimedia kit that included a sound card, you'll need to remove the old sound card. Insert the new card into the vacated slot, screw it down, and plug the audio cable into it as specified in the manufacturer's instructions.

4. The major difference between a Pentium machine and a non-Pentium machine is that you probably won't have an IDE or EIDE slot on the motherboard to plug the interface cable into. If your computer lacks a spot for the interface cable, you will need to install a special interface card into one of the open expansion slots. Most manufacturers don't ship this special interface card with their drives anymore, but if you need one, you can request it from the drive's manufacturer.
5. To install the interface card, remove the metal cover from an empty expansion slot on the back of your computer. Insert the interface card into a vacant ISA slot on the motherboard. Tighten the screws holding the card into place, then connect the interface cable to the appropriate slot on the interface card.

NOTE

***Industry Standard Architecture* (ISA) expansion slots have more connectors, letting them transmit 16 bits of data at a time. This is the most common expansion slot variety and still appears in new PCs, though usually alongside other slots, such as *Peripheral Component Interconnect* (PCI). PCI slots are faster than ISA slots and have become today's standard.**

Installing Drivers

After you have finished the hardware work inside the PC, replace the computer's lid, plug in the computer, and boot up the system. If you are running Windows 95, a dialog box should appear on-screen. That's the computer's way of telling you that it has found the new CD-ROM drive. You may be prompted to insert the disk that came with the new drive to install new device drivers in order for your computer to be able to communicate with the new hardware. In most cases, though, it should recognize the drive automatically and add it.

If you are running Windows 3.*x*, you'll boot up to a DOS prompt. Insert the disk, and type **a:\install** (where a: is the letter of your disk drive). Proceed, following the on-screen instructions. These may vary from one manufacturer to another, but the process is simple.

If, after completing all the steps, your new drive does not work, check to make sure all the cables are firmly connected in the appropriate places. You may need to reinstall the drivers.

CD-ROM drives are an easy upgrade; once you've completed the process, you'll wonder why you didn't do it sooner!

DVD-ROM Installation

DVD, or digital versatile (or video) disk, is often seen as the next big thing in computing *and* home entertainment, and the technology behind it could usurp both compact disks and video cassettes. With upgrade kits now limboing in under the $300 mark, the drives are becoming a real option—especially since they play not only DVDs, but also audio compact disks (CDs), CD-ROMs, and sometimes CD-recordables, while providing a link to television sets. Still, the drives aren't for everyone, and installing one yourself is not a task to be taken lightly.

A DVD disk is the same size as a CD, and the drive looks like a CD-ROM drive. But DVDs can store more than 25 times the information of a conventional CD: 4.7GB on a single-sided, single-layer disk, or up to 17GB on a double-sided, double-layered disk—more than the hard drives on most PCs.

So much elbow-room can lead to spectacular results. Imagine watching a movie with multiple sets of subtitles and soundtracks, various choices of camera angles, crisp zooming and slow motion, letterbox or standard television viewing sizes, and background information about any of the actors or actresses. Or picture your favorite video game fitting onto one disk, rather than five. The advanced technology of DVD makes other things possible as well, such as a parental lockout feature to prevent adult disks from being played.

What You Need to Know

Tools: Screwdriver, computer manuals

Time: 120 minutes or more

Cost: $150–$600 or more

Skill Level: Difficult

Benefits: Ability to play DVD-ROMs, which pack in lots of information and video, while still playing CDs and CD-ROMs

Wading through the Competition

As good as the technology sounds for consumers, though, a tangle of issues has made DVD's long-term role more than a little unclear, mainly because of rival technology *Digital Video Express* (Divx), owned primarily by Circuit City.

This type of DVD disk will require users to have a special Divx drive. Users would purchase Divx disks that could be played for 48 hours from the time it's inserted into the player and registered via a dial-up connection. If users want to play the disk after that, or play it on another Divx drive, they'll have to pay again or purchase permanent rights. Because current DVD players will not be able to access Divx disks, but Divx drives will be able to read regular DVDs, this technology makes things murky.

Nevertheless, DVD titles continue to trickle into the software and movie aisles, and the drives are increasingly coveted by gamers and movie buffs alike. For only a few hundred dollars, a home user can install a DVD-ROM drive and decoder card into a PC, then hook the computer to the television. Hi-Val Inc. even sells DVD kits that promise to transmit signals up to 300 feet for a wireless PC-to-TV connection.

Chances are you already know in your gut whether a DVD-ROM drive is right for you. If you want one, you have to have one; if you don't care, you may as well wait and see what happens with the technology. Prices will certainly continue to drop. For example, the price of Creative Labs' award-winning Encore Dxr2 DVD upgrade kit recently dropped from $379 to $299, only half a year after the kit was introduced. This price matches (to the dollar) that of Diamond Multimedia System's comparable MC20 upgrade kit.

The only gray area of upgrading might be for those who are considering upgrading CD-ROM drives and aren't sure whether to purchase CD-ROM or DVD-ROM. Second-generation DVD-ROM drives are roughly equivalent to 20× CD-ROM drives. (Unlike the first generation drives, they also can read CD-recordable and CD-rewriteable disks.)

Assuming your machine can support the DVD-ROM drive, your purchase is probably best left up to money and patience. CD-ROM drives are getting cheaper, too, and DVD-RAM drives are just starting to appear on the horizon.

Think about how much you want DVD technology *now*, and how long you'll be hanging onto the system you're upgrading. See what titles are available. (For movie availability, check NetFlix at `http://www.netflix.com`.) If you decide you'd really like to play DVDs on your computer and television, the upgrade kits are definitely worth looking into.

System Requirements

System requirements vary, but count on having at least a Pentium running at 100MHz or 166MHz, 16MB of random access memory (RAM), Windows 95, and a good sound card with decent speakers. You could install a DVD-ROM drive on a lesser machine, but the technology would go to waste. You'll also need an open 5.25-inch drive bay (the space, accessed from the front panel of a computer, reserved for drives), and a VGA monitor.

Finally, all the DVD-ROM drives we've seen require an Integrated Drive Electronics (IDE) controller, which a Pentium-level machine should have. Some CD-ROM drives, particularly external ones, use a Small Computer Systems Interface (SCSI) connector hooked up to an expansion card instead.

In addition, many kits come with a *decoder card* that allows the computer to read MPEG-1 and MPEG-2—widely used video compression standards—and, probably, Dolby Digital AC-3 surround sound. To install this card, you'll need an open Peripheral Component Interconnect (PCI) expansion slot. If the kit doesn't include a decoder card, you may need to buy one separately.

A good upgrade kit should have all the cables you need, as well as technical support numbers, detailed instructions, a warranty, and a few DVD titles. When you bring it home, familiarize yourself with its components and read all the instructions. As always, if our generalized instructions vary from the ones you received for your specific computer and DVD drive, follow the specific ones.

Installation

Think about whether you want to replace your CD-ROM drive or add on the new drive. If you're installing a slower first-generation DVD-ROM drive, hang onto the existing CD-ROM drive for faster access to CD-ROMs and the ability to read CD-recordable and CD-rewriteable disks. If you're installing a second-generation DVD drive, however, it's up to you. You may want to keep the old drive just for playing CDs. It doesn't really matter as far as the installation: Removing the CD-ROM drive takes extra time, but it may make the DVD-ROM drive installation quicker.

When you're ready, set aside plenty of time. Although the drive and card could conceivably be installed in less than two hours, if you run into any snags at all, you could be looking at a day-long project. When you're powered with the patience, technical manuals, and time, start the installation.

Depending on the upgrade kit's instructions, you may need to check the Windows 95 version before you do anything else. To do so, go to the Windows 95

Start menu and select Settings, then Control Panel. Double-click the System icon. The General tab includes System information, including the version.

1. Read and follow the instructions in Skill 3.
2. Install the decoder card, if included. First find a free PCI expansion slot on the motherboard, and then touch a grounded surface. Remove the metal plate and screw from the expansion slot, keeping track of the screw. Take the decoder card out of its antistatic bag and press it firmly into place, without forcing it. Secure it with the screw.
3. If you're replacing the CD-ROM drive, remove the screws that hold it in place and slide it out. Unplug the cables from it, although you can leave the cables in the machine in the meantime to help guide you.
4. If you're adding the DVD-ROM drive, pop out the cover panels from the bay where the new drive is going. Take the drive out of its antistatic bag, and then, from the front of the computer, slide the drive part way in to make sure it fits. If it does, put the DVD-ROM drive in place. Your computer may require mounting rails, which will not be included in the upgrade kit. Consult your system manual for more details if mounting rails are required.
5. Attach the cables to the DVD-ROM drive. Find an unused power cable and plug it into the drive. The power supply is usually in one of the corners of the computer's case; several cords extend from it. Plug in the audio cable included in the upgrade kit.
6. Next, locate the interface cable that came with the upgrade kit. IDE or Enhanced IDE (EIDE) cables are standard for connecting CD-ROM drives, hard drives, and tape drives. They're wide and flat with a colored stripe running down one side, and you can tell which side the colored stripe goes on by looking at the outlet you're plugging it into—the colored stripe lines up with the Pin 1 side. An interface cable should fit snugly into its connector but not need to be forced. Plug the interface cable into the DVD-ROM drive.
7. Connect the DVD-ROM drive to the motherboard. When you attach the drive, you'll need to check the jumper setting, determined by a group of metal pins on the back of the drive, partially covered by a small piece of plastic or rubber. The DVD-ROM drive will be either the master or slave, depending on the configuration needed. These names imply the relationships between the drives: The slave drive runs through the master.

8. To determine how a drive is set, look at the letters that appear above the pins: CS, SL, and MA. Don't worry about the CS (*Cable Select*), setting; the ones you'll deal with are SL (*slave*), and MA (*master*). To move a jumper, carefully remove the piece of plastic with your fingertips, then slide it over the pins underneath the letters for the desired configuration. The plastic should slide on and off easily.
9. Next, find the IDE or EIDE connectors on the motherboard after consulting your computer manual. There should be two: the *primary* connector for the hard drive, and the *secondary* one that probably houses the CD-ROM drive. The DVD-ROM drive needs to attach to one of those. If you've removed the CD-ROM drive, unplug and remove the cable that had been hooked up to the CD-ROM drive, and plug the DVD-ROM drive cable into that connector. The colored stripe should be aligned with Pin 1 and the drive set as master.
10. If the secondary IDE connector is already open, your CD-ROM drive is probably connected to a SCSI connector, a hardware interface that allows peripheral devices to be attached via an interface card. Plug the DVD-ROM drive into the open IDE connector, with the colored stripe aligned with Pin 1, and set the new drive as master.
11. If you want to keep your CD-ROM drive, you may run the DVD-ROM drive through either connector, but running it through the CD-ROM drive connector (called *daisy-chaining*) may not be recommended for Windows 95 versions. Consult the upgrade kit's manual for recommendations.

    Through the CD-ROM drive Configure the DVD-ROM drive as the master drive and the CD-ROM drive as the slave. You may need to remove the screws holding the CD-ROM drive in place, then pull it part way out, to reach the jumpers. Completely remove the interface cable connecting the CD-ROM drive to the motherboard. Connect the middle part of the DVD-ROM's interface cable to the CD-ROM drive, and the end of the cable to the secondary connector on the motherboard where the CD-ROM drive had been attached. Be sure the colored edges face the correct direction, lined up with Pin 1 on the connector.

    Through the hard drive Set the jumpers so that the DVD-ROM drive is the slave; the hard drive should already be the master.

WARNING WARNING WARNING WARNING WARNING WARNING WARNING WARNING

You should always back up the hard drive before doing any kind of installation, and be sure not to ever skip the backup when you do anything to your hard drive!

12. Remove the interface cable that connects the hard drive to the motherboard. Now, connect the middle of the DVD-ROM's interface cable to the hard drive, then connect the end of the cable to the primary connector where the hard drive had been attached. Make sure the colored edges face the correct way.
13. Secure the DVD-ROM drive. If cables are in the way, gently move them aside. Slide the drive into place until it is flush with the case and you can see the holes for the securing screws. Fasten the drive in place with the screws provided. If you loosened one of the other drives, secure it.

TIP TIP TIP TIP TIP TIP TIP TIP TIP TIP TIP TIP TIP TIP TIP TIP TIP TIP TIP TIP TIP TIP TIP TIP TIP

Before you do anything else, confirm that everything is still connected. In fact, if the drive doesn't work correctly after the installation and you have to troubleshoot, these connections are the first thing to check—and the most likely things to be problematic. The CD-ROM drive and DVD-ROM drive should each have firm interface and power connections, plus audio cables. In particular, make sure the disk drive, now probably sandwiched in the middle, is still connected.

14. Connect everything else. The hookups required will depend on your system. If the upgrade kit did not include a decoder card, the DVD audio cable should plug directly into the sound card.
15. If your upgrade kit did include a decoder card, the audio cables from both the CD-ROM drive and the DVD-ROM drive plug into the Audio In connectors on the card, and an audio connector cable will run from the decoder card to the sound card. Also, a short connector cable may be included for the outside of your computer case, to connect the decoder card to the VGA card, where your monitor had been plugged in; the monitor now should plug into the back of the encoder card. Another cord may be included for plugging the card into a television set.

16. Install the driver. Put everything back together, then power up the machine. Even if Windows 95/98 recognizes the new drive, you may need to install special drivers provided with the kit. Use the disk included.
17. Install the software. The DVD software, which will include a player along the same lines as Windows 95/98's CD Player, may come on a DVD. Otherwise, it will probably be on a CD-ROM, so you can still test out your new drive.
18. Press the eject button, and place the disk in the unit, being careful not to touch the DVD on either side. The drive may have anchor tabs for holding disks in place, in case the drive is installed vertically. The software may make some adjustments to your video output, or you may need to tweak it yourself.

Once everything is set up, though, you should be blown away by the quality of the DVDs, whether in software or movie form. But most of all, you should be impressed with yourself for taking care of the upgrade.

Sound Card Installation

Users of early computers expected—and got—little from their machines in the way of sound. Computers were lucky to emit more than one kind of beep. Like everything else in PCs, however, that's changed.

Sound is now an essential element in multimedia computing. It's even possible to set up your PC's sound to rival that of your home stereo and do more than listen to your favorite tunes or hear the thunder of engines in the latest games. If you have a microphone attached to your computer, you can record sounds or special effects and save them on your hard drive. The Internet increasingly makes use of audio in applications from radio broadcasts to sound effects.

Sound cards aren't just for play, however. A sound card and its software make up the key components in a home recording studio where you can record, edit, and mix music. You also can incorporate sound into business applications, giving them that added bit of flavor.

But you won't be able to do any of those things without a sound card. This circuit board inside the PC stores and processes sound in your computer. It's one of those wonderful pieces of hardware that makes your computer fun.

What You Need to Know

Tools: Screwdriver

Time: 10 to 15 minutes

Cost: $20–$160

Skill Level: Easy

Benefits: Much better, more realistic sound; faster processing with a PCI sound card frees up system resources; more sounds at one time

Catching Up with the Times

The key buying considerations for sound cards are in a transition period due to changes in two main areas. First, sound cards are shifting from Industry Standard Architecture (ISA) buses to Peripheral Component Interface (PCI) buses. (Buses transfer data among a PC's internal components.) The standards that guarantee your sound card will work properly with different software are also changing.

The shift in sound cards from the ISA bus to the PCI bus is a welcome change. PCI buses transfer data faster than ISA buses, and PCI-bus sound cards rely on the PC's central processing unit (CPU) less than ISA sound cards. ISA cards need the CPU to intervene every time your application wants to play a sound, according to Creative Lab's Micah Stroud, audio products marketing manager for the Americas. That's not the case with PCI cards. "Because [PCI] is actually its own bus controller, the card can assume full responsibility for that." This may provide better performance from games and other applications that use audio.

Sound cards that use PCI also can take advantage of the new sound application programming interfaces (APIs) developed by Microsoft. Specifically designed for Windows 95 and 98, these two new standards, DirectSound and DirectSound3D, will be the standard in Windows applications. The DirectSound/DirectSound3D standards require more legwork from the sound card. Because older sound cards rely heavily on the CPU, they will be unable to take full advantage of the power of these new standards. Newer sound cards, however, can take advantage of the new standards and process audio on the sound card itself, rather than relying on the CPU. This efficient audio processing frees your CPU to focus more of its attention on other tasks.

The main standard for ISA sound cards has been the widely supported SoundBlaster standard. But this standard cannot be applied to PCI cards because of differences in operation between the PCI and ISA buses. The SoundBlaster standard will be around for a while yet because the vast majority of sound cards presently in use, not to mention nearly every game for the past several years, relies on it.

Another long-running, widely supported standard is still in the running. Musical Instrument Digital Interface (General MIDI) is basically a predefined "bank" of 128 specific sounds, or voices. Stroud says this standard is used for music recording and playback. The problem with General MIDI, however, is each brand of sound card implements General MIDI a little bit differently, which means sound quality can vary from card to card. Kettle drums may sound great on your system, but less realistic on someone else's.

It'll be a few years before the old SoundBlaster and General MIDI standards are phased out, so when you're shopping for a new card, find a PCI sound card that supports all three standards. At the very least, make sure it supports DirectSound/DirectSound 3D. Some new sound cards that support DirectSound even work in conjunction with your current sound card to maintain compatibility with older applications. The drawback of this is you have two sound cards taking up space inside your computer.

What to Look For

Finding a PCI card that supports all three major standards is your first priority when looking for a new sound card, but you'll run into a lot of other terms when shopping.

Wavetable Synthesis

You'll probably find that most sound cards provide wavetable synthesis. This means the sounds stored on the sound card are actual recordings of real instruments. This differs from the old FM synthesis, in which the sound card tries to approximate the sound of various voices by attempting to reproduce their frequencies. FM synthesis tends to sound artificial, so you definitely want a wavetable card. Don't fall for the super-low prices of FM sound cards.

If you already have an FM sound card and want the quality of wavetable synthesis without spending the extra bucks for a new high-end sound card, consider a software upgrade. Creative Labs offers a SoundBlaster Upgrade Pack for $29.95 that will give your SoundBlaster 16 FM card wavetable sound. You can order and download the software from SoundBlaster's Web site at `http://www.soundblaster.com/sound/wave-up`.

If you look around shops that sell used computer parts, you may come across a wavetable daughterboard. This device snaps on to an FM card and upgrades the sound to wavetable synthesis. Before buying, make sure the daughterboard is compatible with your present card. If you know your existing sound card and the daughterboard are both SoundBlaster-compatible, everything should work.

These options will give you wavetable sound, but you wouldn't have to spend much more to get a basic card with wavetable synthesis. You'll have to decide whether upgrading your present card is worth the small savings.

Signal-to-Noise Ratio

You'll appreciate the better sound of a wavetable card, but a few other specifications give you an idea of how good the sound will be. One of these is the signal-to-noise ratio, which refers to the "cleanness" of the sound. The higher the signal-to-noise ratio, the less static, or random noise, you'll hear in the background. The signal-to-noise ratio should be at least 85 decibels, and many sound cards have a signal-to-noise ratio that exceeds 90 decibels.

Sampling Rate

If you plan to record sounds, as well as play them, pay close attention to the sampling rate, which is the number of times per second a sound is recorded. The higher the sampling rate, the higher the sound quality. Rates range from about 5KHz to 48KHz or higher, although few of us can hear a difference in sounds recorded at frequencies above 35KHz, Stroud says. Sounds recorded at higher rates sound awesome, but they require more disk space when you save them.

3-D Effects and Polyphony

Space is another key development in today's sound cards—not disk space, physical space. Sound card makers commonly tout three-dimensional (3-D) audio, which is geared almost entirely toward gamers. Instead of playing a game in two-dimensional (2-D) stereo sound, you get a full 3-D aural effect. If someone's running up behind you, you will hear that person behind you. It's an interesting effect quickly finding its way into sound cards, as well as computer gamers' hearts.

Three-dimensional features affect where you hear sound, but how much sound you hear is determined by a sound card's polyphony, which is the number of sounds, or voices, your sound card can play at once. Typical new sound cards can play 32 voices simultaneously although you may find one that can play 64 voices. Cards with higher polyphony cost a little more, of course, so you must decide whether the extra sound is worth the extra bucks. You certainly don't need it to enjoy high-quality audio, but audiophiles may want to consider it.

Memory

Die-hard music lovers should consider a sound card that can accept more memory. Most sound cards come with 1MB to 4MB of memory, but you can find cards that can handle considerably more, up to 24MB. This can boost sound quality by letting you hear more sounds recorded at higher sampling rates. Higher sampling rates mean higher quality sound, remember? This gives the voices on your sound card a greater range of expression, which can bring out the subtleties in music.

Peripherals

You'll probably notice when shopping that almost all sound cards include a joystick port. Sound cards tend to be designed with gamers in mind. The cards also will have several inputs and outputs for speakers and other external audio devices. If you want to put together a high-end PC sound system, you should make sure the sound card will support four speakers, instead of the usual two.

Installation

Now that you're armed with the knowledge to pick out a good sound card, it's time to install it. Read Skill 3 before proceeding. Where and how you install your sound card will depend on what kind of sound card you buy. We'll cover the fundamentals, but be sure to refer to the sound card manufacturer's instructions for specifics on how to install your card. Figure 8.5 shows a typical sound card.

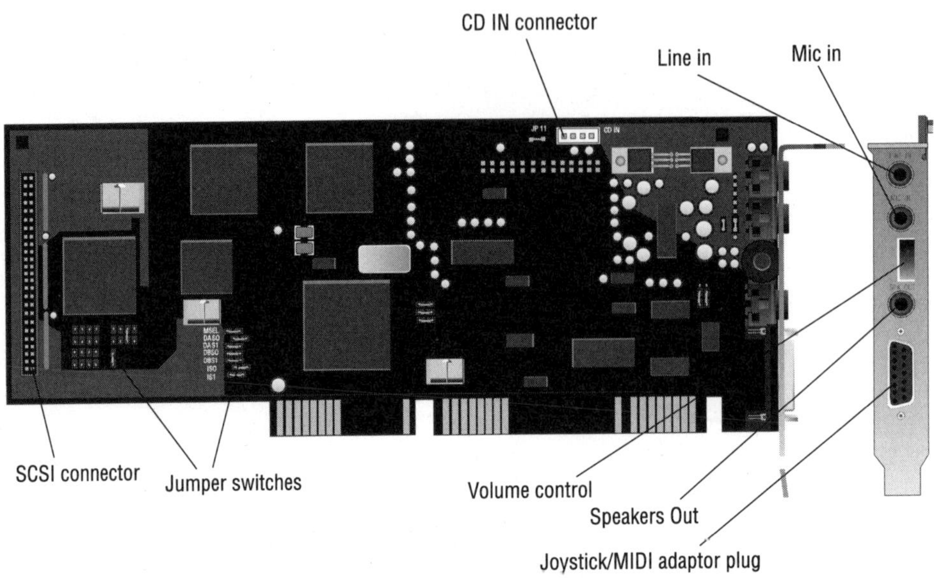

FIGURE 8.5: It should be clear how to connect your sound card to the CD-ROM drive.

1. First, shut down your computer and remove its cover. As always, ground yourself by touching the metal part of your computer's frame before touching any expansion cards. This will prevent them from suffering damage by static electricity.
2. If you don't plan to use your new sound card with your existing card, remove the screw holding the old card in the case, then remove the card by gently pulling it from its slot. (You may have to rock it back and forth a little.)
3. Next, disconnect the cable that runs from your old sound card to your CD-ROM drive. If you plan to use your new sound card with your old card, just disconnect the cable from the old sound card to the CD-ROM drive.
4. Now it's time to install the new card. If you purchased an ISA sound card, you'll need to install it in an open ISA slot, which will be a long black one. If you purchased a PCI sound card, which we recommend, it will go in a PCI slot, which is shorter and a white or ivory color. Remove the metal bracket from the back of your computer that coincides with the slot in which you will install the sound card. Save the screw so you can use it to secure the

new sound card once it's installed. Place the sound card in the appropriate slot and push down on both ends of the card (Figure 8.6). You may have to rock it back and forth a little to coax it into place. Once it snaps into place, secure it with the screw.

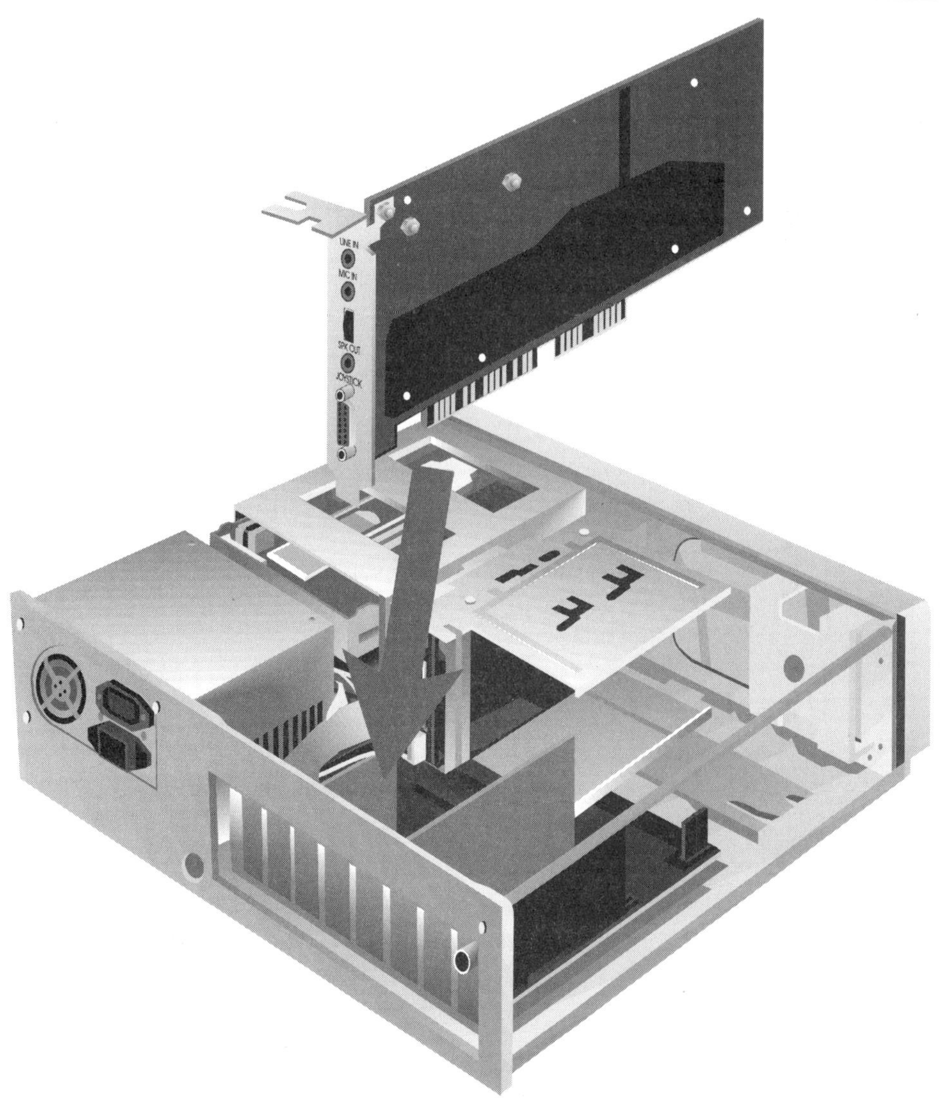

FIGURE 8.6: The board you are installing will fit into one of the slots at the back of the computer.

5. Connect the cable from the CD-ROM drive to the new sound card. The connector on the sound card should be labeled CD.
6. If you're using your new sound card in conjunction with your old one, you'll have to connect them. Your manufacturer's instructions will tell you how.
7. Once you complete these steps, replace your computer's cover and connect your speakers and joystick to the new sound card.
8. After installing the hardware, you'll need to install the software device drivers (software that controls a hardware component) and any additional software that came with your sound card. Generally, the software will include an audio playback and recording utility, and maybe some games, depending on which sound card bundle you buy. The audio and recording utility should be an improvement over Window's Sound Recorder and CD Player. The games are hit and miss. If you happen to like the games included in the bundle, consider it a bonus. Restart your computer and follow the manufacturer's instructions for installing the drivers and additional software.

Once that's done, it's time to pull out your favorite tunes or your favorite game, slip on the headphones, and disappear into another dimension of sound.

Are You Experienced?

Now you can...

- ☑ choose between a CD-ROM and a DVD-ROM
- ☑ install a CD-ROM
- ☑ install a DVD-ROM
- ☑ install a sound card

SKILL 9

Installing Monitors and Graphics Cards

- Evaluating the need for a new monitor or graphics card
- Shopping around for the best deal
- Installing a new graphics card
- Upgrading the RAM of your graphics card
- Installing a new monitor

When we think about our computers, we often think about the display first. Yes, we know the case or tower that houses the actual computer is the brain of the machine, but the display is what we interact with most of the time. Working with a quality display makes the computing experience much more enjoyable. And it's certainly easier on the eyes to work with a larger, faster display.

Your monitor is only half of the display; the dumber half, actually. The real brains of the display operation lie in the *graphics card* (known interchangeably as a *video card*). The graphics card is inserted into a slot on your computer's motherboard. It then speaks to the monitor about what the computer is asking it to do. The graphics card determines how fast graphics display, how crisp they look, how many colors can be used, and much more. You can have the world's best and most expensive monitor, but without a graphics card capable of bringing out the best in it, you might as well have the world's cheapest monitor.

You may have all the video you need. Or, you may only need a small change, such as adding some video memory or a new card, which can pay big dividends in how your monitor performs. And there comes a time when a small screen just isn't enough. We're going to look at how to upgrade a monitor and/or graphics card and who would benefit from an upgrade. We'll discuss these benefits and the particulars of making the purchase and upgrade.

What You Need to Know

Tools: Screwdriver

Time: 20–30 minutes

Cost: Monitor prices depend on size, $300–$1,800; Graphics card, $100–$450; Video RAM prices fluctuate but average $50–$100

Skill Level: Easy

Benefits: Superior resolution, more colors, crisper and faster display, possibly 3-D graphics; a top priority for gamers and users who work intensely with graphics (CAD, animation, graphic design); a help to those who spend a lot of time on the Web

What Does Upgrading Get Me?

So who would benefit from upgrading their monitor and/or graphics card? There are three groups of computer users who would gain the most:

Gamers If you're seriously into computer gaming, you'll want the best video setup you can afford. In fact, part of the vast improvement in computer video has been the result of gamers demanding better graphics in their never-ending quest to immerse themselves completely in the gaming environment. Gamers will want a video card that is capable of 3-D, fast graphics, with at least 4MB of memory on the card. One of the latest graphics capabilities, 3-D makes the display far more lifelike with textures that seem more real.

Heavy graphics users Those whose work includes graphics, especially rendering, computer-aided design (CAD), and animation, definitely will want a large monitor and a video card capable of supporting it. It's a matter of productivity, and the money spent to upgrade to a first-rate display eventually will pay for itself in the ability to be creative without constantly waiting on the display to refresh or redraw. You'll want the largest monitor you can afford, either a 19- or 21-inch display, and a fast graphics card with 4MB of memory.

Web surfers If you are on the Web a lot, you'll also gain by improving your display. While the real culprit in slow Web surfing is bandwidth (the speed of your modem or other connection to the Net), upgrading your video card can help speed things up a bit. Additional video memory can be a help in any graphical environment such as the Web.

If you're feeling cramped on a 14- or 15-inch display, consider this: Going from a 15-inch to a 17-inch monitor gives you about 30 percent more display area. Going from a 15-inch to a 21-inch gives you 50 percent more on-screen real estate. Windows 95/98 suddenly makes a lot more sense when you can open several windows without overlapping them or peering through an electron microscope to see each window.

How Much for All of These Goodies?

So let's cut to the chase: What can you expect to pay? Table 9.1 offers average costs of computer monitors, and, as you can see, the prices have a wide range. However, it's not always true that more money will get you a better monitor. We'll discuss how to choose a monitor later in this skill.

TABLE 9.1: New Computer Monitor Prices, by Size

Size	Price
15″	$300–$600
17″	$500–$800
19″	$700–$1,200
21″	$1,200–$1,800

NOTE NOTE NOTE NOTE NOTE NOTE NOTE NOTE NOTE NOTE NOTE NOTE NOTE NOTE NOTE

Before you decide to buy a larger monitor, make sure your desk can support its extra weight: 21-inch monitors, for instance, can weigh as much as 70 pounds. They definitely can't be placed on top of a computer case as can smaller monitors.

Video cards average between $100 and $450, although you'll find cards above and below that range. Again, a higher cost doesn't necessarily mean a better card, and it certainly doesn't mean one that is right for your computer system.

When it comes to purchasing, the first step is to find out what sort of video card your computer and monitor will support. If you're going to buy a new monitor with the card, you'll still need to know what kind of card your computer will accept. It's best to decide upon the video card first.

Before you can upgrade, you need to know what kind of video card is presently in your computer. Check the documentation for the computer, monitor, and video card to find out what sort of video card you have, what bus the computer will support (see the next section), and how much memory is currently on your video card.

Graphics Cards

To power your monitor, you'll need a decent graphics card. Look for models with at least 2MB of memory, although 4MB and 8MB are better for those users who enjoy entertainment software such as games or do a lot of graphics work. Another option is to add memory to your existing graphics card, which can greatly improve the speed and resolution of your graphics adapter. Many graphics cards allow this kind of upgrade; check your documentation for more information about how to do this.

Choosing the Right Card

There are three considerations when buying a video card:

- A compatible bus
- Memory
- Speed

When you're looking to upgrade your graphics card, your choice is probably between the VESA local bus (VL-bus) cards and the Peripheral Component Interconnect (PCI) bus cards. Of the two, the PCI bus cards are generally better. Check your computer's documentation to see which kinds of slots you have, and then you'll probably have to open your computer to see which slots are still open and which are occupied by cards. The latest graphics card standard is Accelerated Graphics Port (AGP). If your computer can run an AGP card, this is your best option.

Game players and graphics programs users should consider an upgrade to a 3-D accelerator card, which allows better depictions of three-dimensional (3-D) images. Although many 3-D accelerators are designed to work in conjunction with a 2-D graphics card, there is a new generation of graphics accelerator that incorporates both 2-D and 3-D into a single card. Below, we'll refer to accelerator cards that perform both 2-D and 3-D tasks as *integrated cards*.

When upgrading from a 2-D card, the choice between separate cards and an integrated card depends upon several factors. First, as with any upgrade, make sure you have space for an additional card to handle 3-D. If you don't have the space, consider replacing your 2-D card with an integrated card, which will perform both

2-D and 3-D functions but will take up only one spot. Second, determine if your present card is compatible with newer 3-D cards. Third, consider the speed of your present card; if it is a 2-D VL-bus card, and you have a PCI port available, you should consider replacing your old adapter with an integrated PCI card, which should give you a sizable improvement in performance. Also, look for a card with a minimum of 4MB of on-board memory; 8MB is quickly becoming the standard and offers even better performance.

When buying a 3-D card, remember games must be specially optimized for different types of cards. If you're not careful, you could end up with a card that doesn't work with your favorite games. The best way to deal with this issue is to follow the leaders. Of the first generation of graphics cards, the most popular and most supported cards are those equipped with the Voodoo chip set by 3Dfx Interactive. If you're looking for a next-generation card, and don't want to wait to see which one the market anoints as champion, look at cards running the new Voodoo 2 chip set, also by 3Dfx Interactive. Based upon its predecessor's success, Voodoo 2 has a great shot to take over the graphics market.

Considering Bus Type

You need a video card that is compatible with your computer's *bus*. A bus is the electrical connection linking the internal sections of a computer, such as the central processing unit, expansion cards, and other peripherals such as keyboards and other input devices. The different types of buses have different types of slots on the motherboard, so they require peripherals that accommodate the same standard.

There are three main bus types in use today:

- Industry Standard Architecture (ISA)
- Peripheral Components Interconnect (PCI)
- Accelerated Graphics Port (AGP)

Your computer probably has a combination of ISA and PCI slots. PCI is the preferred video bus because it is much faster and more advanced than the older ISA standard. Check your computer documentation for specifics. Make sure you have a free slot for the new video card. For instance, if you currently have an older system that uses an ISA video card, and you want to upgrade to a PCI card, make sure you have a PCI slot available. Most likely, though, you'll be taking a card out of the ISA slot and replacing it with a PCI card in an unused PCI slot.

If your computer has the latest standard, an AGP bus, you've probably just bought your computer and won't benefit from upgrading the video card: Your AGP card is state-of-the-art. You eventually may add memory or buy a premium AGP card, or you may have kept an older smaller monitor despite AGP's powerful capabilities. When you're ready to splurge on that larger monitor, make sure it can take advantage of everything AGP has to offer.

When you know which type of bus you have, you're better able to select a video card that is compatible with that bus.

Considering Speed and Memory

Video card speed measurements require sophisticated benchmarking equipment. Our advice is to sift through magazines and Web sites that feature benchmarked comparisons of video cards. Information that is two to six months old already is outdated, so find the latest articles you can. This is not the time to dig through a magazine's archives on its Web site; you want recent information. Take a careful look at what they say about speed, performance, and supported features (such as 3-D and the ability to take advantage of MMX, if you have a Pentium chip that supports MMX).

In terms of memory, more is certainly better if your monitor and video card can support it. However, using a 4MB video card with a 15-inch monitor may be overkill. Video memory controls resolution and the number of colors, not the speed of the card. An overall rule of thumb: Get at least 2MB of video memory unless you're using a larger monitor, then start with 4MB of memory. Look for a video card with room for additional memory as your needs change or if you want to upgrade your monitor in the future.

Monitors

The following items are the most important when choosing a monitor. Even if you don't test out a monitor thoroughly, as we suggest below, you'll want to make sure of the following:

- Buy a monitor that meets the Super Video Graphics Array (SVGA) standard. You may hear about color/graphics adapter (CGA), video graphics array (VGA) and others, but these are older standards. If you're reading this chapter, it's possible you're upgrading from one of these standards to SVGA.

- Look for a monitor with dot pitch of .28 *dot pitch* or lower. Dot pitch is the distance, measured in millimeters, between *pixels* on a monitor (a pixel is the smallest part of an image that a computer printer or display can control). In this case, the lower the number, the better the resolution. Do not go higher than .28; it's not worth whatever small amount you might save.
- Take note of the *refresh rate*, sometimes called the scan rate, which is measured in Hertz (Hz). (The refresh rate is simply the number of times per minute that a computer screen image is renewed.) In this case, the higher the number, the better the scan rate. We recommend you don't settle for anything less than 60 Hz, and we prefer monitors that are 70 Hz and more.
- Make sure your monitor is non-interlaced. Some of the older models are interlaced, and that can cause display to flicker a lot.
- Remember that the size of the monitor is not the actual viewable area of the monitor. A 17-inch monitor can have a viewable size of anywhere from 15.8 to 16.2 inches. That extra space can make a difference.

With the above in mind, the best monitor is the one that looks best to you. Go to a store that has a wide range of manufacturers and types of monitors. A monitor is a major investment that costs a chunk of change; don't be rushed or put off by a salesperson who is too busy to help you. If the monitors you have in mind all meet the above criteria, and all look good to you, try some of the tests below. Keep in mind, though, that the monitor you see in the store may be hooked up to a video card that isn't worthy of it, so you may not see the monitor at its best. When in doubt, read the comparisons and benchmarks in the computer trade papers and online. Don't forget to find out about the return policy whether you buy in a retail store or via mail-order.

Here are some testing tips:

- Look at Windows 95/98 on the monitor. Move icons around, resize some windows, start some programs. How's the focus? Are the colors crisp and true? Does the display fade out toward the edges or corners?
- Using a graphics program, draw a circle. Check to make sure it's not distorted into an oval shape.
- Load a word processor. Type a sentence or two, then change it to a font size of 8 points or smaller. Can you still read the text? Is it crisp or fuzzy?

- Turn the brightness control up and down slowly while looking at the corners of the screen. Notice any changes? Do images or corners swell, bloom, bend, or bulge?
- Check bright text against a black background, first in the center and then at the corners of the screen. Make sure all the letters are readable, especially letters that can easily blur such as a lowercase *e*.
- Look at white lines against a black background. Are they really white or do they have bands of color in them?
- Create solid blocks of reds, blues, and greens. Make sure they stay true to color throughout the block. Resize the block several times, and pay attention to the trueness of the color.
- Display a white screen. Make sure the brightness of the white is consistent, that there are no clouded blotches or gray areas.
- Take a few steps back from the monitor. Stand at least as far back as you'll be working from it. Is it clear, bright, crisp, sharp, and flicker-free?

Installation

Before you install your new video card, add video memory, or install a new monitor, make sure you have the accompanying documentation handy. Also take note of the manufacturer or computer vendor's support information: phone numbers, Web sites, and fax-back services.

See Skill 3 for more information on what you should do before beginning the installation. Read through it carefully if you are not experienced working with computer hardware to avoid harming yourself or any of the components in your system. Make sure you have everything you need close at hand.

TIP TIP TIP TIP TIP TIP TIP TIP TIP TIP TIP TIP TIP TIP TIP TIP TIP TIP TIP TIP TIP TIP TIP TIP TIP

It's OK if you have a magnetic screwdriver, in fact, that will help. The tiny amount of magnetism that's in the screwdriver won't interfere with your computer's functioning.

Installing a New Graphics Card

Replacing a video card isn't hard at all. You'll need a screwdriver, the video card, the disk that should come with the card (it contains the software drivers that help the computer recognize the card), and about 20–30 minutes. It's usually helpful to have a flashlight to use while working inside your computer case.

NOTE

Leave the video card in its plastic pouch, which protects it from static that can hurt the card, until you're ready to put the card into the computer.

1. Unplug the monitor connected to the back of your computer. It's connected to the video card you're about to replace.
2. Turn the computer off and unplug it from the power outlet on the wall or the surge protector. Remove the case and ground yourself.
3. Unscrew the old card from the back slot. Make sure you keep track of the screws. We like to use small paper cups to hold computer hardware screws while working under the hood.
4. Remove the old card. You may need to rock it back and forth gently to dislodge it from the bus slot (see Figure 9.1).
5. Find the compatible slot for the new card. If you're moving from an ISA video card to a PCI card, make sure you have a free PCI slot. (You likely did this before you started the upgrade process.)
6. Install the new card by firmly pressing it into place. You may have to "rock" it into place (see Figure 9.2). Tighten the screws holding the card into the slot.
7. Put the case back on the computer.
8. Plug the monitor into the video card.
9. Plug the monitor and computer back into the power outlet.
10. Install the software drivers on the disk that came with the graphics card. If your video card is Plug-and-Play compliant, it's possible Windows 95/98 already will have recognized the card.

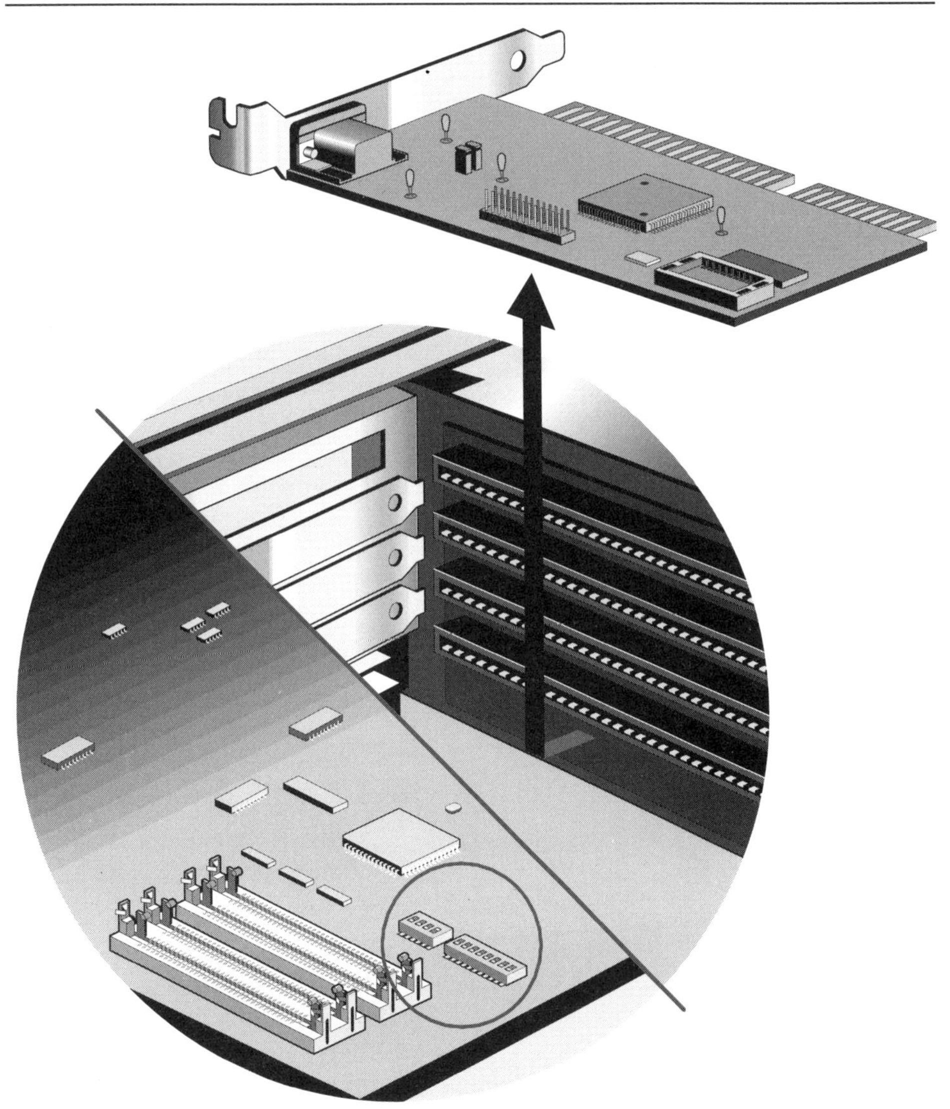

FIGURE 9.1: The graphics card must be removed from the expansion slot.

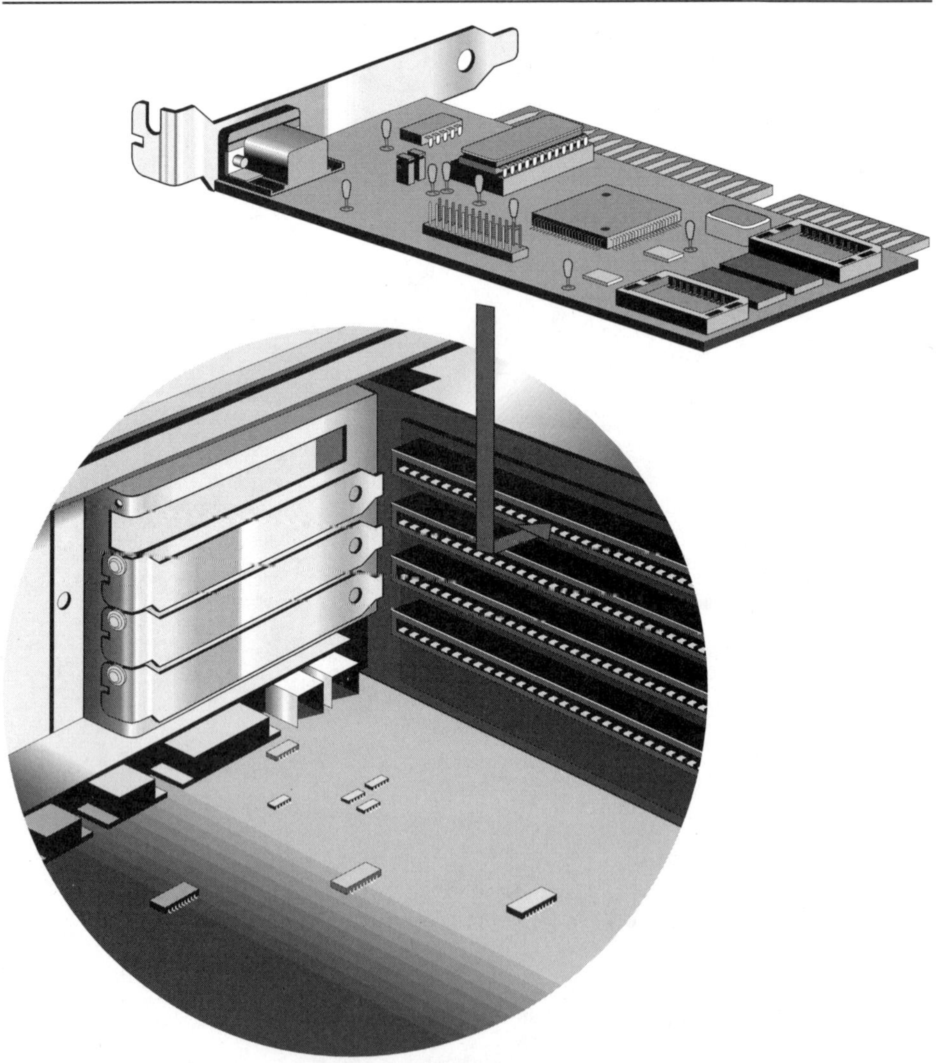

FIGURE 9.2: The new card is inserted into the vacant slot.

Upgrading Your Video Card's RAM

Upgrading video RAM is painless and takes no more than 10 or 15 minutes. You'll spend more time deciding if the upgrade is worthwhile. If you have 1MB of video memory on an older machine and don't do much with graphics, you're probably fine. To deal with the graphical environment of Windows, 2MB of memory is preferred. And, if you're a gamer or have intense graphic needs for design programs, you'll need all the video memory you can afford.

In terms of upgrading, your most likely scenario will be:

- You have 1MB on a 2MB card, and are adding another megabyte.
- You have 2MB on a 4MB card, and are adding another two megabytes.
- You have 4MB on a card that will let you add more memory, anywhere from another 4 to 8 megabytes and possibly more.

Remember, adding more memory to your video card will not make graphics run faster. It will improve the resolution and increase the number of colors you can display.

NOTE NOTE NOTE NOTE NOTE NOTE NOTE NOTE NOTE NOTE NOTE NOTE NOTE NOTE NOTE

Do not remove the memory chips from their protective bag until you are ready to put them on the card.

1. See Skill 3 for information regarding steps to take before starting the upgrade procedure.
2. Turn the computer off and unplug it from the power outlet on the wall or the surge protector. Remove the case and ground yourself.
3. Remove the video card from its slot.
4. Lay the card on a flat, secure surface.
5. Take the memory chips out of their protective bag.
6. Each of the memory chips has a small dot in one corner. Each memory socket has one beveled corner. Match the chip's dotted corner with the beveled corner on the socket. Make sure the pins on the memory chip line up with the grooves on the socket. If everything lines up, press the chip into

the socket (Figure 9.3). The chip should be pressed in firmly but not hammered in. Make sure it's secure by turning the card upside down—the memory chip should remain in the card. Repeat for each memory chip.

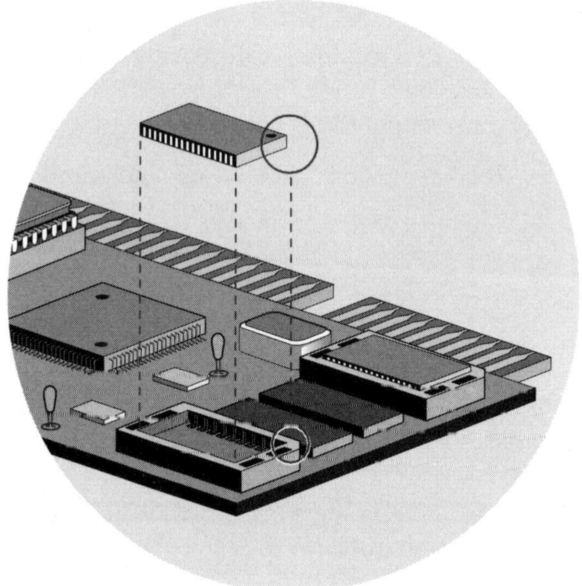

FIGURE 9.3: The RAM chip must line up precisely with the socket.

7. Replace the card in the machine. Close the case, connect the cables, and start the machine. As the machine starts, you'll notice the new memory amount. If you don't see the amount that you should now have, repeat this installation. If you still have a problem, you may have bad memory chips. In that case, call the manufacturer or retailer for support.

Installing a New Monitor

Assuming you've installed your card, installing your new monitor is even easier:

1. Turn off and unplug the current monitor. Turn off the power to the computer and unplug it from the power outlet on the wall or from the surge protector. Disconnect the old monitor from the back of the PC and set it aside carefully.

2. Unpack the new monitor. Take a good, long look at it to ensure it's in pristine condition. Make sure all the correct power and video cables are there. Keep the box! If you need to return the monitor, you'll need the box. If you move to another location, nothing works to protect your monitor like the box in which it came.

3. Place the new monitor on your desk or table. Do not put a larger monitor on your computer case as you might have put a smaller one. Larger monitors are too heavy.

4. Plug the monitor's video cable into the video card in the back of the computer; then connect the power cable.

5. Turn on the computer and the monitor.

6. Install the software drivers included on the accompanying disk. If your monitor is Plug-and-Play compliant, it's possible Windows 95/98 will recognize it. Follow the prompts.

7. Adjust the resolution and other factors by going to the Control Panel and selecting Display. Go to the Settings tab (you can play with the settings in the other tabs later). For the color palette, try to select the True Bit combinations. On the Desktop Area control, select the resolution your video card and monitor will support. For a 17-inch monitor, you can use at least the 800 × 600 setting. A 21-inch can go for settings of 1024 × 768 or 1280 × 1024 (see Figure 9.4). You may prefer something different. Adjust other settings to suit. (You can get to Display Properties from the Control Panel or by double-clicking anywhere on the Windows desktop.)

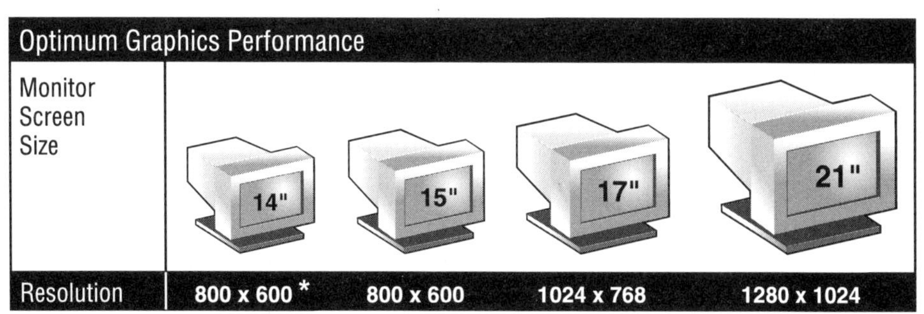

FIGURE 9.4: The best resolution varies depending on the size of the monitor.

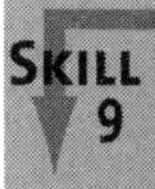

Are You Experienced?

Now you can...

- ☑ decide what kind of graphics card and monitor suits you best
- ☑ install a new graphics card
- ☑ upgrade the RAM on your graphics card
- ☑ install a new monitor

SKILL 10

Installing a Modem

- Choosing the right modem
- Installing an internal modem
- Installing an external modem

If you own a computer and a modem and have access to a local Internet service provider (ISP), the entire world is only a few clicks away. The phenomenal growth of the Internet over the past few years has given us access to nearly everything imaginable, from academic resources to shopping for gourmet food. The Internet is also becoming more sophisticated as it grows up. Once upon a time, graphics and sound were unheard of on the Net. Now, they're commonplace.

But a persistent flaw comes as a result of the Internet's tremendous popularity: It is simply too slow. There are many reasons why you may end up staring blankly at your computer screen while a World Wide Web site loads itself at a glacial pace. Paul Kraska, product marketing manager at Multi-Tech, a popular modem manufacturer, offers a few examples. "If your ISP has a tremendous amount of traffic," he says, "and the servers are old technology, you could experience delay there." Kraska also points out that your processor could be the culprit. He says the more powerful your processor, the quicker data can be handled at your end, which will speed up your Web surfing experience.

The Internet itself could be slowing you down, too, due to congestion. Taking a speedy modem onto a crowded Internet, Kraska says, is "like trying to drive a Porsche in a traffic jam." Of course, many Internet users hardly notice high-volume traffic days because they're plodding along with slow modems that hamper every online journey. If you're still trying to squeeze by with a 28.8 or 14.4 kilobits per second (Kbps) modem, a faster model should be your first step to getting around the Web more easily.

What You Need to Know

Tools: Phillips screwdriver

Time: 5–15 minutes

Cost: \$50–\$200

Skill Level: Easy

Benefits: Faster Internet access; quicker download times; universally supported standardized modem

Choosing the Right Modem for You

Modems come in all sorts of flavors these days, with the main distinction being internal or external versions. There is no difference in online performance between internal and external modems, but they do have some unique traits. External modems are easier to install, but they cost a little more, and you must buy an extra serial cable to attach the modem to your computer. External modems also must be plugged into a power outlet. You may not have enough room to plug in an external modem if you already have a monitor, computer, scanner, printer, and who knows what else plugged into your wall socket.

Internal modems are a little less expensive, take up no space on your desktop, and don't require you to purchase any extra cables. These circuit boards draw power from the computer, so they require no separate outlet. You must open the computer to install it, however, which some users may find a little intimidating. Also, internal modems must be installed in an Industry Standard Architecture (ISA) slot inside the PC. You probably have an empty ISA slot available in your computer, but if you have already installed several other peripherals, you may find it's getting a little crowded in there. If that is the case, you may want an external modem.

The 56K Problem

The last few years have seen the growth in popularity of 56Kbps (or just 56K) modems, but modem manufacturers' boasts that these speedy modems lived up to their names turned out to be misleading. Federal Communications Commission (FCC) regulations limit the amount of data transferred over normal phone lines to 53Kbps. Furthermore, due to the myriad of things that can affect an Internet connection, most consumers still weren't cruising along at even 50Kbps. One can usually get connected around 40Kbps with this type of modem, however, which is still fast enough to see an improvement over older models.

A major issue kept consumers from embracing this new technology wholeheartedly: Two incompatible 56K modem standards were competing in the industry. One was the x2 standard developed by U.S. Robotics, now owned by 3Com. The other was the K56Flex, developed jointly by Rockwell and Lucent. Because the two were incompatible, and most ISPs offered only one standard, consumers needed to be sure they were buying the 56K modem supported by their ISP. If you bought a K56Flex modem, and your ISP supported x2, switching ISPs may have become necessary.

Fortunately, a solution has been found. 3Com and Lucent agreed to develop one universal standard for modems. The International Telecommunications Union (ITU-T), which approves standards in the modem industry, ratified the new standard, which was initially called *v.pcm* (*pulse code modulation*). The new standard, named *V.90* by the ITU-T, will let all 56Kbps modems work together. It also removes the misleading 56K label from the name. Now that the standard is formally approved, modem manufacturers will make the software code for the new standard available to their consumers.

If you already own a 56K modem, you should be able to upgrade to the new standard for free, or for a nominal fee, depending on the manufacturer. To upgrade from 56K to V.90, you'll have to go to your modem manufacturer's Web site and download the new drivers (software instructions that tell your computer how to use a peripheral, such as a modem). Once the installation of the new drivers is complete, your 56K modem will become a V.90 modem, and you won't have to worry about having the "right" modem anymore.

56K Modem Differences

3Com's x2 and Rockwell's K56flex standards for 56Kbps modems have been competing against each other for some time. Many observers have seen relatively little difference between the two standards—until now.

Some industry reports indicate modems using the K56flex standard do not maintain their high-speed capabilities when upgraded to the upcoming V.90 standard. By contrast, the x2 modems could be successfully upgraded to V.90 without losing their performance.

What does this mean for the consumer? First, you can have faith that Rockwell, which produced the K56flex architecture, is working to resolve the problem. Second, the manufacturers that produced the modems will probably ensure the modems will be upgraded or will offer some kind of rebate. In the final analysis, however, users must watch out for their own interests. In this case, it looks as though x2-based modems are the best choice until the V.90 standard takes hold.

One last note before you rush out to the store. If you have a 33.6Kbps modem, you may be able to upgrade it to a 56Kbps modem at a good price. Some modem manufacturers, such as 3Com, let you download software from their Web sites that turns your 33.6Kbps modem into a 56Kbps modem. (3Com charges about $60 for the upgrade.) Once that's done, you can upgrade from a 56Kbps modem to the new V.90 standard. Check your modem manufacturer's Web site to see if you can upgrade your 33.6Kbps modem to a 56Kbps and then a V.90 modem. You will probably save a little money by upgrading this way.

Installation

Now that you've decided which kind of modem you want, it's time to upgrade. The following instructions should work for most, if not all modems. You should consult the instructions, however, that came with your modem.

WARNING WARNING WARNING WARNING WARNING WARNING WARNING WARNING

Heed this warning: Using a modem over digital phone lines could damage the modem. Before you begin, find out what type of lines you have. Home users shouldn't have to worry, but many offices use digital phone lines, so make sure you're running your modem through an analog phone line.

External Modems

External modems are small boxes you connect to your computer with a serial cable. You will have to buy the serial cable separately, but you should be able to find one for less than $10. You will probably need a 25-pin male to 9-pin female serial cable, although you might need a 25-pin male to 25-pin female serial cable. Consult your modem's instructions to find out exactly which serial cable you need.

1. Before you install any components on your computer, be sure to shut it off. Also, shut off any other devices attached to your computer, such as a printer or scanner. (For more information, read Skill 3.) Connect one end of the serial cable to your modem (the 25-pin male end) and the other end to a serial port on the back of your computer. Look for a 9- or 25-pin port labeled Com, Modem, or Serial. Do not try to plug the serial cable into a port labeled Parallel, LPT, Game, or Aux. Plug the serial cable into the appropriate port.

2. Now, plug one end of a phone cord into the modem and the other end into a wall phone jack. You've probably noticed your modem has two phone jacks. That's so you can run another phone cord between your modem and a phone, if you want. The two jacks should be labeled so you can tell which is which. Next, you'll plug one end of the AC adapter into the modem, and the other end into the socket. That takes care of the physical installation. Now it's time to set up your new modem to work with your computer.
3. Turn on your PC and your external modem. If you're using Windows 95, and the modem you purchased follows the Plug-and-Play standard, you may see a New Hardware Found screen. This will make installation even easier. The software will automatically install itself or will ask you to install the disk containing the software needed for the installation.
4. If you do not see the New Hardware Found screen, install the software that came with your modem, according to the manufacturer's instructions. Once the software installation is complete, you'll want to make sure your modem is set up properly. Open the Control Panel in Windows 95 by clicking Start ➢ Settings ➢ Control Panel. Double-click the Modems icon. Your new modem should be listed and highlighted; if it isn't, click it. The highlighted modem is the one your computer will use. Check details of the modem setup by clicking the Properties button. You can remove your old modem by highlighting it and clicking the Remove button.

In Windows 3.*x*, you can check your modem settings in the Terminal program. Double-click Accessories in Program Manager and then double-click Terminal. Click Settings at the top of the Menu bar. In this menu you can set the phone number for your ISP and check other information about your modem such as the port it's using.

Here's one more thing you should check. Open the Dial-Up Networking window by clicking Start ➢ Programs ➢ Accessories ➢ Dial-Up Networking. Then right-click the icon representing your Internet connection and click Properties. You should see a drop-down list box at the bottom of this dialog box, labeled Connect Using. If your modem does not appear in this box, click the down arrow and highlight your modem. Now, try to dial in to your ISP. Your new modem should be ready to go.

NOTE NOTE NOTE NOTE NOTE NOTE NOTE NOTE NOTE NOTE NOTE NOTE NOTE NOTE NOTE

Your ISP will probably have a different phone number for 56K access. Contact your ISP for more information.

Internal Modems

Installing an internal modem requires a little more work, but it may be worth it, due to their lower price. If your computer does not support Plug and Play, you may have to set the jumpers (small switches) on your modem. Do this before you try to install it. The jumpers on a modem card are two series of small pins at the base of the card, with black connectors attached to them (Figure 10.1). The position of the connectors determines the Com and Port settings for that modem. See the instructions that came with your modem for the proper jumper settings.

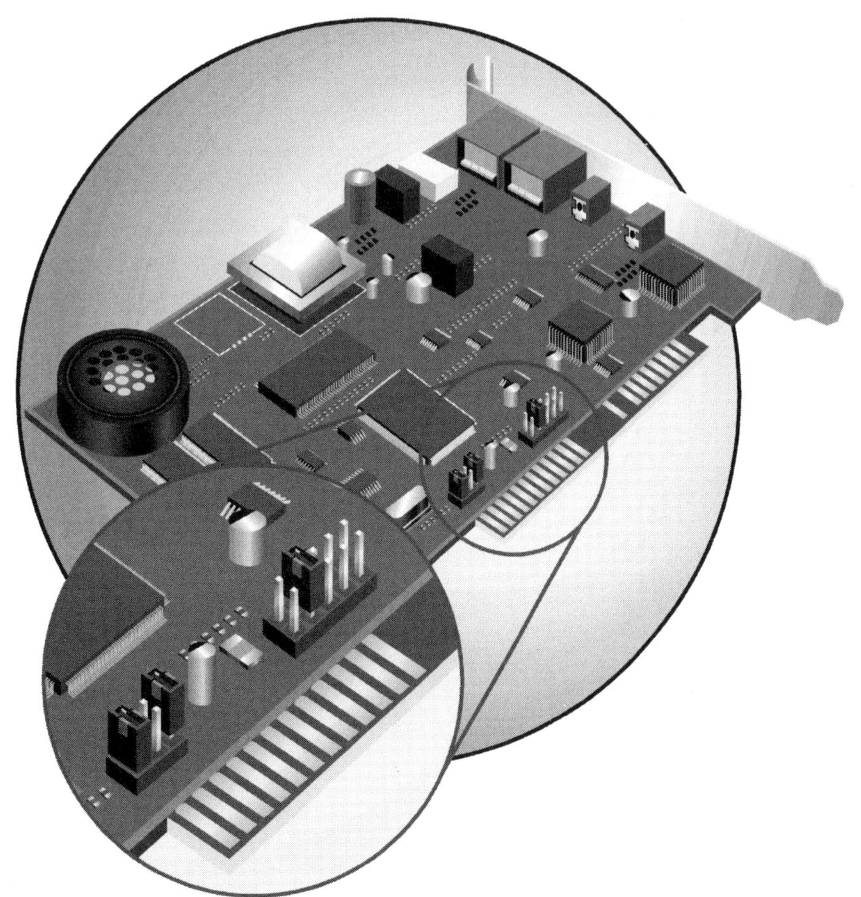

FIGURE 10.1: If you install an internal modem that is not Plug-and-Play compliant, you may have to set the jumpers on the modem card.

If your computer supports Plug and Play, you shouldn't need to worry about the jumper settings. In fact, you'll probably only have to remove the connectors. Your computer will take care of the Com and Port settings automatically. If the modem you purchased is Plug-and-Play compliant, there should be no jumpers on the modem card.

1. Shut off your computer and remove its case. Inside, you should see several long black slots, some of which may have circuit boards inserted into them. These are the ISA slots we mentioned earlier, the ones into which you will insert the modem. Don't confuse these with Peripheral Connect Interface (PCI) slots, which are the short white ones. Ground yourself by touching the metal part of your computer's case. This will prevent you from accidentally sending a potentially harmful charge of static electricity through your modem card.
2. Now remove one of the protective metal strips in the back of the computer's case, in front of the slot you want to use. Save the screw for later. Now, hold the card at either end, and gently but firmly push the modem card into the ISA slot. You may have to rock it back and forth before it snaps into the slot (Figure 10.2). Now tighten the screws holding the card in place.

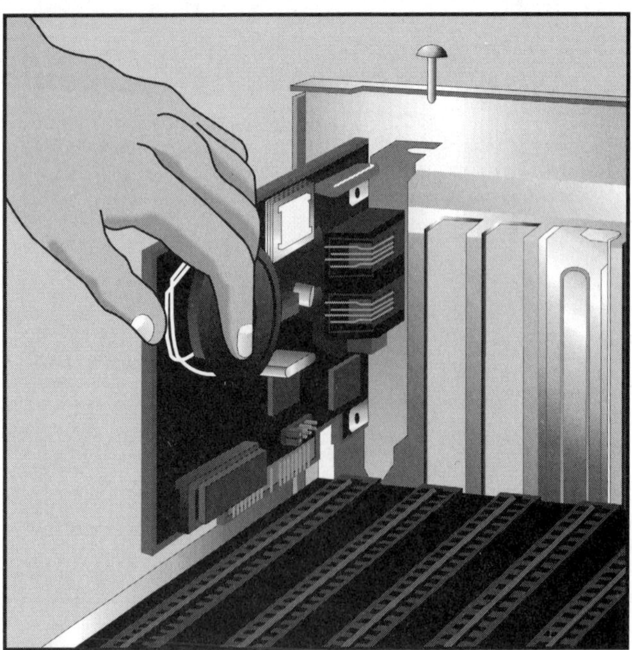

FIGURE 10.2: The modem card should slide into the slot.

3. All that's left at this point is to plug one end of a phone cord into the modem and the other end into a wall phone jack, just as you would with an external modem (Figure 10.3). Restart your computer and install the software that came with your modem. If your computer supports Plug and Play, you may see the New Hardware Found message. The computer will install your modem automatically. Otherwise, follow the instructions that came with your modem. Again, you'll want to be sure to double-check your new modem's settings in the Control Panel and in the Dial-Up Networking window. The process is exactly the same as for an external modem, so refer to those instructions earlier in this skill.

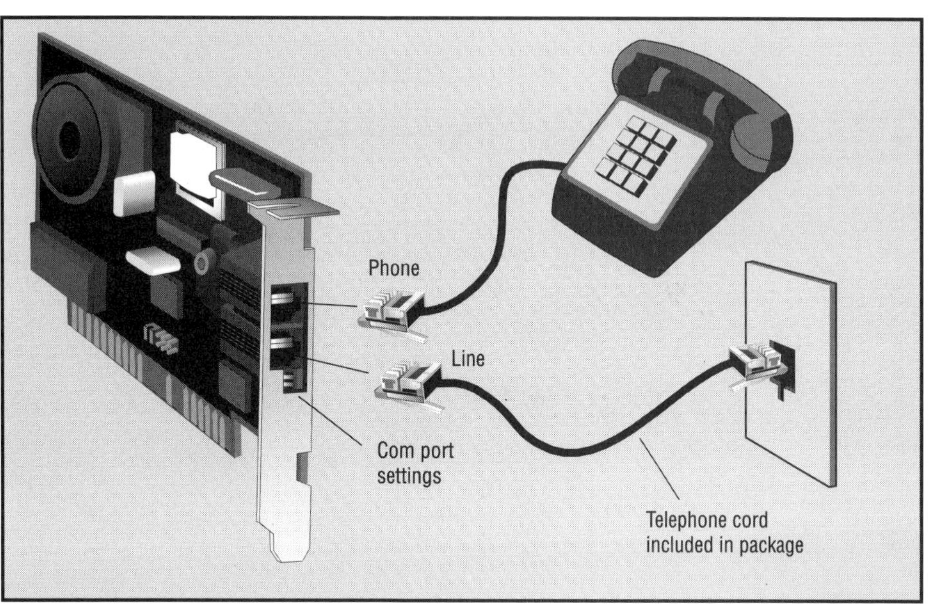

FIGURE 10.3: The phone line is plugged into a jack on the modem card.

If you're not using a 56Kbps modem, you really should consider getting one. The price is right, the new standards are on the way, and faster Internet access means you won't have that glazed-over look on your face so often when you're surfing the Web. If you're going to spend time on the Internet, spend it doing something, instead of waiting.

Are You Experienced?

Now you can...

- ☑ pick an internal or external modem
- ☑ navigate the 56K waters
- ☑ install an external modem
- ☑ install an internal modem

SKILL 11

Installing Keyboards, Joysticks, and Mice

- Choosing and installing a keyboard
- Learning about your options with input devices
- Adding a joystick
- Learning about infrared technology
- Using voice-recognition software

Many computer users never consider upgrading their keyboards or mice because they don't realize that these items can dramatically improve their computing through better *ergonomic* design. (Ergonomics is the study of how people interact with their work environment.) Installing a newer mouse and keyboard can mean a reduction in repetitive stress injuries such as carpal tunnel syndrome. Mice and keyboards designed with good ergonomics mean you can use your keyboard and mouse longer—and more safely.

Upgrading your keyboard and mouse is easy. Just make sure your computer has the appropriate port. Most modern computers have PS/2 ports (6-pin ports designed particularly for mice), which frees up a serial port for other peripherals. Keyboards come with either 5-pin or 6-pin ports. This shouldn't limit your choices in devices; you can generally buy adapters that let you use any keyboard or mouse with your computer.

Installing Your Keyboard

A keyboard is an essential part of your computer system. A standard no-frills keyboard was most likely included with your computer, but the basic keyboard has evolved into a variety of designs and functions you may find beneficial.

If you frequently use a keyboard, you run the risk of developing carpal tunnel syndrome and other conditions associated with repetitive tasks. Ergonomic keyboards are designed to alleviate such injuries by making the keyboard more comfortable to use. What's comfortable for one person may not be for another, so there are a variety of ergonomic keyboards available. Options include contoured wrist rests, keys set at an incline, and split keyboards that position your hands at different angles.

Wading through the Options

Keyboard upgrade options don't stop with ergonomic concerns. You have a wide range of upgrade choices. If you're using Windows 95, for example, you can add a keyboard specifically designed for that operating system. Windows 95 keyboards add three keys to the standard 101-key layout. These extra keys function as shortcuts to the Start menu and the right-click pop-up menus. While not necessary, the extra keys offer the convenience of issuing commands without moving your hands from the keyboard.

If you have kids, chances are they like to spend time on your computer. Several keyboards on the market are geared toward the younger set; these keyboards offer durability, eye-catching colors, and larger keys. Some, such as kidBoard from kid-Board Inc., use color-coded keys for numbers and letters to help children learn letter and number placement. There are even keyboards for toddlers, such as the ComfyKeyboard Activity Center by Comfy Inc. and Kidtech's My First Keyboard, if you want to give your kids an early start. Many of these keyboards include interactive children's software to help kids get acclimated to the world of computers.

Multimedia keyboards include speakers and microphones. Others have touch pads, trackballs, or other input devices built into them. A cordless keyboard offers a greater range of movement. Windows 98 brought with it keyboards that take advantage of the Universal Serial Bus (USB) port rather than the standard keyboard port.

Once you've purchased a new keyboard, you need to install it. The installation process is relatively easy.

1. Close any open applications and turn off your computer.
2. You don't need to take the computer's cover off for this installation because the keyboard port is on the back of your computer. Your old keyboard should be plugged into it. If not, most systems have a keyboard icon by the port to identify it. Remove your old keyboard by pulling its connector from the keyboard port.
3. Check to see which kind of keyboard port you have. The 6-pin PS/2 port is a small round port with six holes in it. The 5-pin DIN port (also referred to as an IBM AT port) is larger and has five holes (Figure 11.1).

NOTE NOTE NOTE NOTE NOTE NOTE NOTE NOTE NOTE NOTE NOTE NOTE NOTE NOTE NOTE

These first three steps will be the same for any keyboard you install. The following steps will vary.

4. Now look at the connector at the end of your new keyboard's cable to see if it matches the port on your computer. If your port and connector don't match, most keyboards come packaged with an adapter to make them fit together, or you can buy one. If you need to use an adapter, plug the end of your connector into the corresponding end of the adapter and plug the adapter into your keyboard port. If the adapter is already connected to your keyboard cable and you don't need it, simply pull it off and connect your keyboard to the port. When plugging the connector into the port, carefully line up the pins to the holes before pushing in the connector.

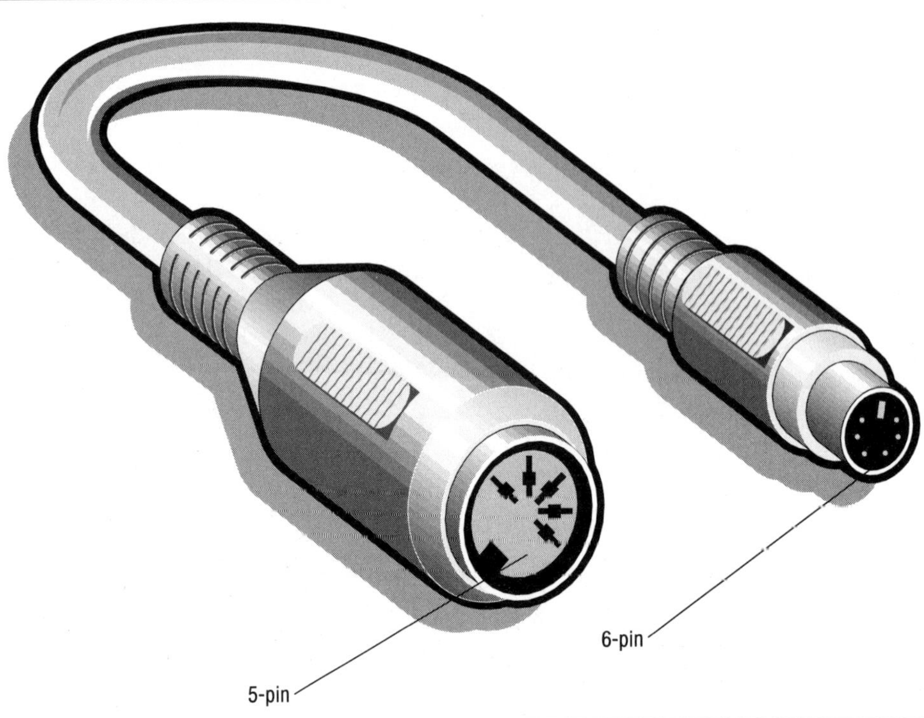

FIGURE 11.1: Some keyboard installations will require an adapter.

5. After connecting the keyboard, turn on your computer. Most keyboards will use the software driver already on your system and will be recognized when you turn the system on. Windows 95/98's Plug-and-Play technology will detect new hardware and load the necessary driver or prompt you if one is needed. If your keyboard requires driver installation, the software and instructions will be included with the keyboard or may be on your Windows 95/98 installation disks.

6. In Windows 3.*x*, driver installation generally requires inserting the installation disk into the drive, opening up the Program Manager File menu, selecting Run, typing a command such as **a:install** or **a:setup**, and selecting OK. In Windows 95/98, insert the installation disk, click Start and select Run. Type **a:install** or **a:setup** (the specific command will be included with your keyboard software), select OK and follow the prompts as they appear on-screen.

No matter which operating system you have, you will need to restart your computer after installing the software for the new settings to take effect. Some installation programs will automatically restart your computer; others will prompt you to do so at the appropriate time.

Multipurpose Keyboards

Keyboards are evolving into peripherals that have many uses, such as housing speakers and microphone. Many include a touch pad, trackball, or other input device. The installation of a multipurpose keyboard probably will take a few more steps to enable all of its functions.

Installation will vary, but the first three steps described above will be the same. The steps you follow next will depend upon the specific keyboard and the features it provides. For example, the following installation is for a ConcertMaster Multimedia Keyboard that includes speakers, a microphone, and a headphone.

1. Follow steps 1–3, above.
2. The cord for the multimedia keyboard splits into four thinner cords: a connector that plugs into the keyboard port, with an adapter (if needed) for the proper connection; a microphone plug; a speaker plug; and a power connector that attaches to the AC adapter included with the keyboard. The end of each cord is marked with an icon to identify its use.
3. Determine if you need the adapter, then plug the keyboard connector into the keyboard port. Plug the speaker plug into the Speaker Out jack and the microphone plug into the Mic In jack on your sound card (Figure 11.2). If you already have a set of speakers plugged into your sound card, remove its speaker and microphone connections first. Plug the AC adapter plug into the jack on the keyboard's power connector and then plug the AC adapter into an electrical outlet.
4. When all the connections are made, turn on your computer. Turn the keyboard's power switch to Speakers or Microphone. To operate the keyboard without audio capabilities, leave the power switch in the Off position.
5. External headphones or speakers can be connected using the microphone jack on the right-hand side of the keyboard. An external microphone can be connected to the adjacent microphone jack. If you are using a headphone with attached microphone, use both keyboard jacks to connect the headset. Multimedia keyboards will have different sound controls, such as a volume control or mute button to control audio functions, or you can use the sound software installed on your system.

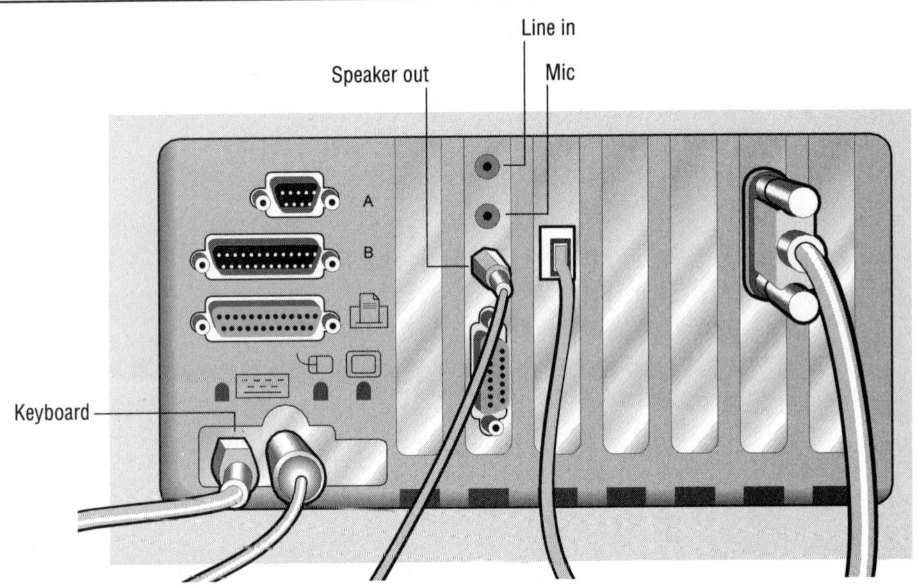

FIGURE 11.2: The three round ports on the back of the computer should be clearly labeled.

Other multipurpose keyboards, such as the Wave Keyboard 2 by Cirque, might use a mouse port. In addition to having a split keyboard for ergonomic comfort, this keyboard includes a touch pad. Its installation steps are as follows.

1. Follow steps 1–3, above.
2. The keyboard cord splits into two thinner cords: a PS/2 connector that plugs into the keyboard port and a serial connector that plugs the touch pad into the mouse port. (If you already have a mouse or other input device plugged into your mouse port, you will need to remove it.) Check to see if your ports match the keyboard's connectors. If not, use the supplied adapters. If both your keyboard and mouse ports are PS/2 ports, they will look the same, but they will be identified with an icon or description. Be careful not to switch the cables.
3. When the connections are made, turn on your computer. The keyboard and its touch pad will work without installing any extra software, but if you want to enable extra options such as extra cursor control and customized shortcuts, you will need to install the Cirque software driver.

Cordless Keyboards

If you don't like being tethered to your desktop, a cordless keyboard might be what you need. Using infrared or radio frequency (RF) technology, cordless keyboards can communicate with your computer without a physical connection.

A cordless keyboard that uses RF technology, such as Logitech's Cordless Desktop, emits radio frequencies as a way of communicating with your computer. This requires the connection of a receiver that will pick up the RF signals and transmit them to the computer. An infrared keyboard operates similar to your TV remote and also will require the installation of a receiver. Installing the receiver will be similar to installing a keyboard with a touch pad; there will be one cord that connects to the keyboard port and another that connects to the mouse port. You will need to install the software that comes with the keyboard and insert batteries, typically AA.

Finishing Touches

To adjust your keyboard's repeat rates and sensitivity, click Start ➢ Settings ➢ Control Panel and double-click the Keyboard icon. Select the Speed tab and make any necessary adjustments to the length of time it takes for a key to repeat and the rate at which it repeats.

If your keyboard fails to respond or responds erratically, make sure its connections are secure. If you are using a cordless keyboard, check its batteries to make sure the receiver is positioned properly.

WARNING WARNING WARNING WARNING WARNING WARNING WARNING WARNING

If you suspect your keyboard's internal circuitry is damaged, do not attempt to repair it yourself. Contact the keyboard's manufacturer or local computer repair technician, or replace the keyboard.

Installing Mice and Other Input Devices

Your computer system undoubtedly came equipped with a basic mouse. However, you may not find it very comfortable to use. A different-shaped mouse or an alternative input device such as a trackball, touch pad, or digital pen might work better for you. Another reason to upgrade is to take advantage of extra features, such as scrolling and programmable mouse buttons.

An input device is any peripheral you use to enter information into your computer. Keyboards are one kind of input device, but this section will deal with smaller devices such as trackballs and touch pads. Note that in some cases, touch pads, trackballs, and pointing sticks are built into keyboards and are not installed as a separate device.

Upgrade Options

You have a growing number of choices when it comes to purchasing input devices. A *mouse* is the most familiar device for most users. The long tail and round shape of a standard mouse vaguely resembles the furry rodent of the same name, but there also are cordless mice, and mice that come in a variety of shapes. You can buy novelty mice shaped like footballs or cars, pen-shaped mice, and even a foot-controlled mouse.

As the mouse is moved along a flat surface, a ball in the bottom of the device rolls with it. The cursor position on the screen is related to the position of the rolling ball. The mouse also has at least two buttons that let you interact with a graphical user interface (GUI), such as Windows. To select an item such as a menu option, you press the left button. The right button is used for special functions, and in Windows 95/98 it activates drop-down menus.

Early mice were simple point-and-click devices, but they are becoming increasingly sophisticated. Many include programmable buttons so you can assign different responses to customize the mouse for your system and needs. Some mice include scroll wheels that allow you to scroll through documents and screen displays without using scroll bars. In addition to better navigational control, mice are being designed for ergonomic comfort to relieve stress injuries caused by frequent use.

Trackballs are proving to be a popular second choice as an input device. They look a bit like a mouse turned upside down, with a roller ball on the top instead of the bottom. Rather than moving the trackball around a flat surface as you would a mouse, it remains stationary while you use your fingers and thumb to move the roller ball on top. Trackballs include two or more buttons; generally, a thumb button functions like the left button on a mouse, with other buttons serving as the right button and other programmable functions. These devices come in a wide range of ergonomic designs.

Touch pads have been gaining popularity, particularly as technology has increased their accuracy and ease of use. You operate a touch pad by moving your finger across a touch-sensitive pad. The movement of your finger directs the cursor on

the screen. To click something on the screen, tap your finger instead of pressing a button. Tap twice to double-click, and tap twice and drag to click and drag.

Digital pens are similar to touch pads, except you move a cordless digital pen instead of your finger across a writing tablet. Usually, the operation involves pressing the pen's tip against the tablet surface to perform left-mouse functions. A switch on the barrel of the pen activates right-mouse button functions.

Pointing sticks are often found on laptop computers and look like a very small joystick. However, instead of gripping the stick with your whole hand, a pointing stick is operated with your finger. By pushing or pulling with your finger, you move the stick in the direction you want the on-screen cursor to go. A pointing stick usually is accompanied by two buttons that function like mouse buttons.

There are other input devices, such as light pens, that are used in contact with the computer screen, and remote control pointers that help navigate through electronic presentations. Some multipurpose devices are appearing on the market, such as keyboards that contain a trackball or touch pad, and joysticks that also function as mice. In addition, there are input devices designed for children, with larger buttons and roller balls to make it easier for small hands to manipulate the device.

Mouse/Trackball Installation

The installation of a mouse or trackball is relatively easy. The installation steps for your particular device may vary from those described below. Refer to the instruction manual that came with your input device for specific installation steps.

1. Close any open applications and turn off your computer.
2. Taking the cover off your computer is unnecessary for the installation process. Locate the port on the back of your computer that you will be using for the mouse or trackball. If your old device is still plugged into a port, remove it by loosening its thumbscrews and pulling its connector from the port.

NOTE NOTE NOTE NOTE NOTE NOTE NOTE NOTE NOTE NOTE NOTE NOTE NOTE NOTE NOTE

Most mice and trackballs come with an adapter that lets you connect them to either a PS/2 port or a serial port (see Figure 11.3). PS/2 ports are small and round; the connectors that fit into them are round with six pins. Serial ports are trapezoidal and usually have 9 pins although older ones have 25. Adapters are available to plug 9-pin serial devices into older 25-pin ports and are sometimes included with the input device.

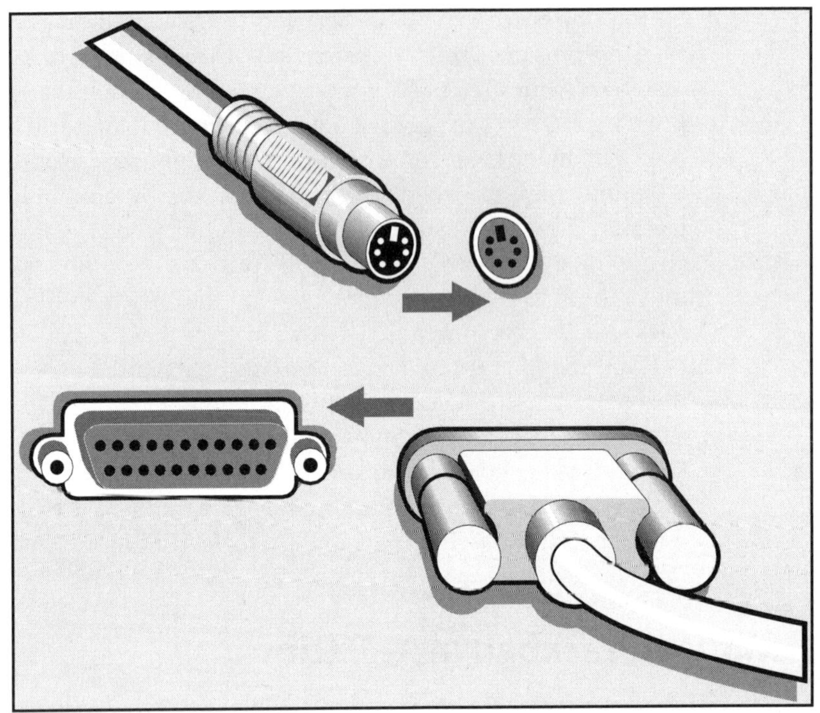

FIGURE 11.3: Most input devices connect to either a PS/2 port (above) or a serial port (below).

3. Look at the connector on the end of the mouse or trackball you are installing. If you need to use an adapter, plug the end of your connector into the corresponding end of the adapter and plug the adapter into the port. Tighten the thumbscrews to hold the connector firmly in place.
4. When connecting to the port, carefully line up the pins to the holes before pushing in the connector. Note that the connector will only fit into the port one way. Most connectors have a flat side or an arrow to help guide you. Don't force a connector in if it doesn't seem to fit. Instead, look to see if you have it upside down, and check to see if the connector and port are compatible.

5. After plugging the device into the port, turn on your computer. Because both Windows 3.*x* and Windows 95/98 include standard drivers (programs that allow input devices to communicate with your computer), a simple mouse or trackball will be readily recognized when your system is turned on. Windows 95/98's Plug-and-Play technology will detect new hardware and load the necessary driver or prompt you if one is needed.

More complex input devices, such as those with programmable buttons and scroll wheels, come with their own software. For example, Microsoft's IntelliMouse Trackball's functions will work fine without any additional software, but you must install its IntelliPoint software to enable the wheel and wheel button. Similarly, the Kensington Internet Mouse must have MouseWorks software installed for its auto-scroll functions to work. If your mouse or trackball requires the installation of a driver or other control programs, the software and instructions will be included with the device.

In Windows 3.*x*, software installation generally requires inserting the installation disk into the drive, opening up the Program Manager File menu, selecting Run, typing a command such as **a:install** or **a:setup**, and selecting OK.

In Windows 95/98, insert the installation disk, click Start, and select Run. Type **a:install** or **a:setup** (the specific command will be included with your keyboard software), select OK, and follow the prompts on-screen.

No matter which operating system you have, you will need to restart your computer after installing the software for the new settings to take effect. Some installation programs will automatically restart your computer; others will prompt you to do so at the appropriate time.

Double-Tasking

If you share your PC with a left-handed user, have children who use a different device, or you just get tired of using the same mouse all the time, you can double up on your input device choices. Attaching one device to your serial port and one to your PS/2 port lets you switch between trackball and mouse or left- and right-handed devices without unplugging and replugging. Both devices need to support the same drivers, or you'll have to switch drivers when switching devices. To change drivers, go to Control Panel and double-click Mouse, then click the General tab. Click the Change button, and select the appropriate mouse and driver.

Touch Pad Installation

Installing a touch pad will be similar to installing a mouse or trackball. The following instructions are for a Cirque Power Cat touch pad; installation steps for other touch pads may vary, so be sure to follow the instructions that came with your input device. The Power Cat is only available for Windows 95.

1. Close all applications and turn off your computer.
2. Locate the port on the back of your computer. The touch pad can be plugged into either a PS/2 or serial port. If your old device is still plugged into the port, remove it by loosening its thumbscrews and pulling its connector from the port.
3. Attach the provided adapter, if necessary. Plug the touch pad into the port and tighten the thumbscrews.
4. Turn the computer on and start Windows 95/98.
5. The touch pad should work with the existing drivers on your system. If you see a "New Hardware Found" dialog box after booting your computer, select Cancel and proceed with installing the software that came with the touch pad. If the touch pad works without installing the software, you still may want to install it to take advantage of its advanced features, such as using the signature pen.
6. Insert the software disk into the drive. Click Start, select Run, and type **a:setup**, and select OK. Follow the prompts as they appear to install the software, and reboot your system when you are done.

After installing the hardware and software, click Start ➢ Settings ➢ Control Panel, and double-click the Mouse icon. Tap the different tabs to configure tapping pressure, pointer movement, scrolling, and other options. Double-click the signature icon in the Toolbar to open the Signature Capture program. Use that program to create and save signatures and/or notes with the pen included with the touch pad.

Adjusting Software Settings

You might need to make some adjustments to software settings to make your input device work the way you prefer. Fine-tuning your input device will make it easier and more convenient to use. For example, you can adjust a mouse for left-handed use, change to larger mouse pointers that are easier to see, or change

the double-click speed. Some changes can be made through Control Panel. Other programs come bundled with the input devices or are available as shareware or in retail outlets.

Left-handed users In the Windows 95/98 Control Panel, double-click Mouse to display the Mouse Properties box. The Buttons tab lets lefties switch buttons on the mouse by choosing Left-handed in the button configuration box (Figure 11.4). When the buttons are switched, the right mouse button (under your index finger) becomes the primary button used to "click" and the left-mouse button becomes the secondary button. Remember when instructions say to "right-click" you will actually be left-clicking.

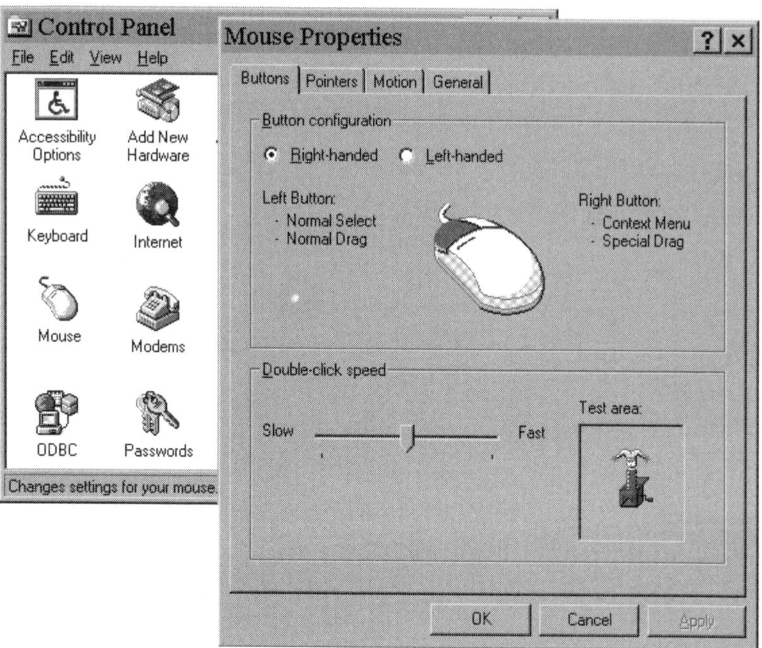

FIGURE 11.4: You can customize your mouse using Windows software settings.

Double-click speed At the bottom of the Buttons tab is an adjustment area for your double-click speed. By setting it slower or faster, you will change the amount of time that can pass between clicks of your primary mouse button when you are double-clicking an object. If you are an inexperienced mouse user or are having difficulty getting double-click to work, try moving the slider to the left to lengthen the interval needed between clicks. Use the test area in the dialog box to test the double-click speed. If the jack-in-the-box appears or disappears, your double-click action has been recognized.

Cursor movement To adjust the speed at which your cursor moves on the screen, click the Motion tab. Use the slider to make the movement slower or faster. Adding a trail makes your cursor look like several arrows in a row when you drag it across the screen. This makes it easier to see, particularly on LCD screens. To enable this option, select Show Pointer Trails and use the slider to adjust the length of the trail.

Pointers As you work on your computer, the pointer shape provides a visual clue about what the system is doing or what action you can perform next. It might appear as an hourglass, a pointer, crosshairs, or other design and can be stationary or animated. Click the Pointers tab to change the design scheme of the pointer, and then select a pointer scheme from the drop-down list to display the pointers associated with that scheme. To change a pointer's appearance, select Browse and double-click the file name of a different pointer.

When you click Browse, a list of available Windows cursors should appear. If they do not, click Add/Remove Programs in the Control Panel and select the Windows Setup tab. Then click Accessories ➢ Details to see if a checkmark appears next to Mouse Pointers. If not, select it and double-click to add the files. These cursor schemes include large and extra large cursors for easier viewing. Animated cursors will have a file extension of .ANI, static cursors will have one of .CUR. Many shareware and retail programs are available that provide a wide variety of pointers.

Use Your Keyboard as a Mouse

Windows 95/98 comes with options designed to make it more accessible to users with physical impairments although they are useful to anyone. One option, MouseKeys, lets you use your numeric keypad to move the mouse pointer. This is a convenient feature if you're recovering from a repetitive stress injury or if you have a notebook computer on which you don't want to install a mouse.

To access these features, double-click the Accessibility Options icon in the Control Panel. If this component is not available, click Add/Remove Programs in the Control Panel, select the Windows Setup tab, click Accessibility Options, and click OK to install. To enable MouseKeys, click the Mouse tab in the Accessibility Options dialog box and check the Use MouseKeys box.

Installing a Joystick

A simple game such as Solitaire can be played using the keyboard, but if you want to enjoy fast-action, arcade-like games, you'll need a joystick. Most systems don't come with a joystick, so you'll probably need to purchase and install one.

Even if you already have a joystick, you may want to upgrade to take advantage of new features. Joysticks are no longer the primitive devices they were years ago when we were content with a simple stick and trigger. They now include multiple and programmable buttons, hat switches (thumb-controlled mechanisms that allow you to change your point of view), trim controls (which allow you to center your joystick and fine-tune your positions), spin-control knobs, and throttles.

Digital technology and features such as force feedback, which lets you feel those jolts and recoils, add to the realism of today's games. In addition, new cordless joysticks offer more freedom of movement.

Many other gaming devices are available, such as gamepads, flight yokes, rudder pedals, throttles, and racing steering wheels. Your purchase decision will depend upon the type of games you want to play and whether you are a casual or competitive game player.

We installed a CH Products Gamestick, Techmedia's wireless 3DZonemaster, and a CH Products Gamecard3. While these instructions apply to most other similar devices, they may differ slightly for the particular one you select. Be sure to read the installation instructions that come with your gaming device.

Game Cards

A game card is not essential for playing games or using a joystick, but it makes it possible for multiple players, and can enhance the speed and response of the joystick. Because only one game port can be active, you will need to disable or remove the other game port on your system.

NOTE

The procedure for disabling or removing a game port varies, depending upon the manufacturer. If the steps below do not work, consult your computer's or sound card's documentation, or contact the manufacturer's technical support department for assistance.

In Windows 95/98:

1. Click Start, select Settings, then Control Panel. Double-click the System icon and select the Device Manager tab.

2. Click the icon for Sound, Video, and Game Controllers. Find your joystick driver in the list and double-click it.
3. In the Properties window, select the General tab. At the bottom of the window is a box labeled Usage. If you are using an earlier version of Windows 95, deselect the check box by clicking it. In later versions of Windows 95/98, select the Disable option and deselect the Exists In All Hardware Profiles option. If you are not using Plug-and-Play hardware, you might have to remove the device from the Device Manager list by selecting it, clicking Remove, and then physically removing the device from your computer.

In Windows 3.*x*:

1. Double-click the Main program group, double-click the Control Panel icon, and then double-click the Drivers icon. The Drivers window will display all available drivers.
2. Locate the joystick driver. Double-click it to see if it gives you an option to disable it. If not, click the Remove button to remove the driver. If it is a Windows system driver, it will only be removed from the list but will remain on your hard drive. If it was a driver you installed yourself, be sure you have the disk that you originally installed it from.

After disabling or removing any game ports, you are ready to install the game card.

1. Close all open applications and turn off your computer. Make sure all power to your system is off. Remember to unplug the computer, and always be sure to ground yourself by touching a metal surface before touching any of the components inside. This will prevent any electrical damage to the computer's delicate circuitry. (For more information about pre-installation preparations, read Skill 3.)
2. Remove the cover from the computer and identify an open expansion slot. If necessary, remove the corresponding plate at the rear of the case.
3. Remove the game card from its protective packaging. Plug the card into the slot; gently, but firmly pushing the contacts into place. The ports should be exposed through the slots in the rear of the case. Secure the card with the bracket-retaining screw.
4. Replace the computer cover and plug your joystick into the "A" port.
5. Turn your computer on and check for operation. You may need to install a driver or other software that came with the card and/or joystick.

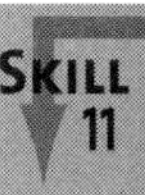

TIP TIP TIP TIP TIP TIP TIP TIP TIP TIP TIP TIP TIP TIP TIP TIP TIP TIP TIP TIP TIP TIP TIP TIP TIP TIP TIP

If you have difficulty installing or configuring your joystick or game card, consult the troubleshooting section of the instructions that your game hardware came with it. When trying to solve a joystick problem, general suggestions are often not enough. The source of your difficulty could be your particular device, the driver or utility program you are using, the game you are trying to play, or your system itself. All major joystick manufacturers offer technical support and have useful information on their Web sites that will get you back in the game.

Hardware Installation

A joystick connects to your PC's game port, which is a port built into virtually every system and is included on many sound cards.

1. Close all applications and turn off your computer. It is not necessary to remove the PC's cover, unless you are also installing a game card. For more information, see the "Game Cards" section.
2. Locate the game port on the back of your computer. It is a 15-pin port and might be labeled. If you are using a game card that has two ports, use the one labeled "A." Plug the joystick connector into the port and tighten any thumbscrews (Figure 11.5).
3. Turn the computer back on and proceed with installing the software.

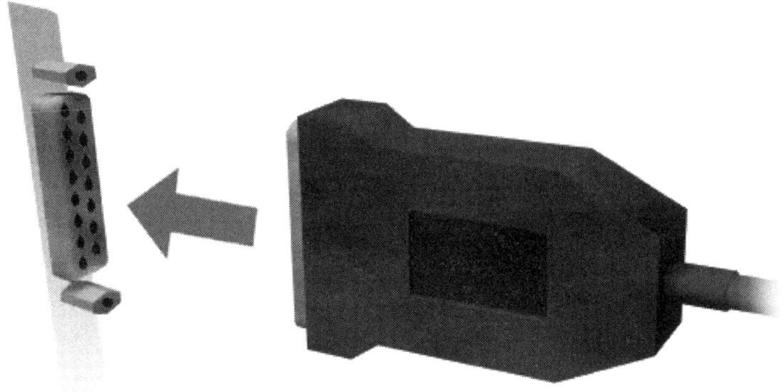

FIGURE 11.5: The 15-pin joystick cord plugs into the matching port on the game card.

Software Installation

Once the joystick is connected, you'll need to install the driver, which is a program that lets a hardware device and computer communicate. Many joysticks will be compatible with the drivers included with Windows 95/98 and will be functional when you turn your computer back on. More sophisticated joysticks with multiple programmable buttons will require the installation of software to activate and control those features. The software should be packaged with the joystick. Many manufacturers also include joystick utilities and demo games on their installation disk or CD.

To install the software in Windows 95/98:

1. Insert the installation disk or CD-ROM into the appropriate drive.
2. Click Start and select Run.
3. In the prompt box, you will type a command such as **a:setup** or **a:install**. The instructions that came with the software will tell you the exact command to type. Click OK and continue to follow the instructions to complete the installation.

In Windows 3.*x*:

1. Insert the installation disk or CD-ROM into the appropriate drive.
2. From the Program Manager, click File, then Run.
3. In the command line, type the installation command the software documentation provides. Click OK and continue to follow the instructions to complete the installation.

After installing on either system, reboot the computer to activate the new driver. If you installed an analog joystick, you will need to calibrate it after installing the hardware and software (digital joysticks do not need calibration). If you have a joystick with programmable buttons, you can also customize the use and response of the joystick. Custom options will vary, so you will need to consult the documentation that came with your joystick.

Calibration

Calibration is a process used to configure the mechanical and electrical alignment of the joystick. Calibration options are included in most games and may be

included with the joystick's installation software. In Windows 95/98, you can calibrate using the Control Panel. The steps are as follows.

1. In earlier versions of Windows 95, double-click the Joystick icon in the Control Panel. Under Current Joystick, select the appropriate number (usually Joystick 1). Select the appropriate Joystick Configuration and click Calibration.
2. In later versions of Windows 95 and 98, double-click the Game Controllers icon in the Control Panel. Click the General tab, select the appropriate game controller, and click Properties. Then, click Calibration.
3. Carefully follow each step of the on-screen instructions for calibrating your joystick.

Depending upon the game you will be playing, you might have to follow another calibration routine provided with the game. This tells the software which values your joystick uses for specific locations and what the extreme positions are for each axis. The software can then make calculations based upon these positions to determine where the joystick is located at any time.

Each game will have its own routine. You might be asked to move your joystick from side to side, forward and backward, from corner to corner, or rotate in a full circle. Take it slow when calibrating. Read and follow the instructions that came with the game; some are very specific as to which buttons you must press, and in what order.

Wireless Joysticks

Although most joysticks come with a long cord, you might enjoy the freedom offered by a wireless joystick, such as Techmedia's 3DZonemaster. Best described as a cross between a Star Trek phaser, Orca the killer whale, and a banana, this ultrasonic positioning device (UPD) also can be used as a mouse and a remote control for non-gaming applications.

Installation of the 3DZonemaster requires the placement of a frame unit on the top of your monitor. The connector on the frame unit's cord is then plugged into serial port COM1 or COM2. After connecting the hardware, you must install software to configure and customize the joystick. An instruction manual is provided to step you through the installation process.

Once installed, the Joystick Control Center allows you to customize joystick options for specific games and save them for future use. The Remote Control Center lets you configure buttons for non-gaming applications. The device has an on/off switch under its nose and can be used in conjunction with another mouse. Because it is a digital device, it does not require any calibration. However, because it is wireless and baseless, the center point must be redefined throughout game play using the Centering button.

The Infrared Advantage

The term "wireless" somehow sounds incredibly high-tech and, in some ways, unattainable. It's like watching an old Star Trek episode as a child and hearing "Beam me up, Scotty," then watching in amazement as some unknown futuristic technology produces incredible results.

But infrared, the technology that allows the wireless "beaming" of data from one device to another, is far from high-tech. In fact, you don't have to go far to find examples of infrared around your own home. How about that remote control you use every night to channel surf?

What Is Infrared?

Technically speaking, *infrared* is a band of electromagnetic waves slightly below the frequency of visible light (see Figure 11.6). Infrared devices place data within electromagnetic waves like a television signal, except these waves move as a straight beam towards a device that can accept and process it. As long as the two devices maintain a direct line of sight, the beam can continue to quickly shuttle information between the devices.

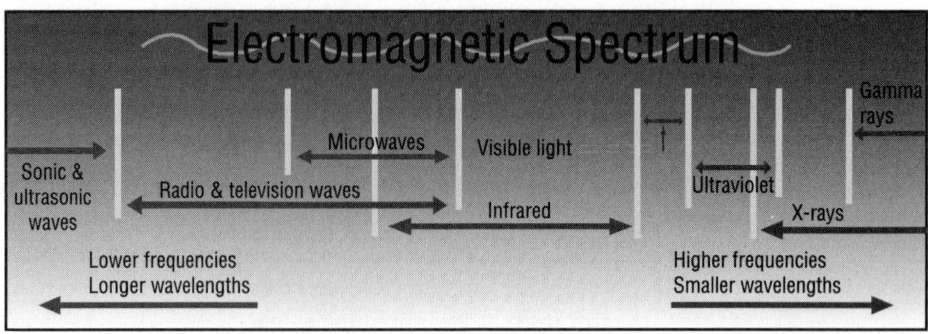

FIGURE 11.6: Infrared is part of the electromagnetic spectrum that can't be seen.

To try and combat any pitfalls surrounding infrared technology, the Infrared Data Association (IrDA), a consortium of more than 160 computer, peripheral, and telecommunications vendors, was formed. The IrDA is dedicated to developing a universal set of standards throughout the infrared industry for the purpose of compatibility and quality. You can learn more about the IrDA on the Web at `http://www.irda.org`.

Common Infrared Uses

According to John LaRoche, executive director of the IrDA, there are between 50 and 60 million devices equipped with infrared in use today, and most of those are portable computers whose owners aren't even completely aware of infrared's capabilities. Here are some ways to put that unused infrared port to use:

- Transferring data to your desktop computer
- Printing directly to an infrared-equipped printer (there is only a handful of these today, including models from Hewlett-Packard and Minolta)
- Logging onto a local-area network (LAN)

Because most desktop computers and printers lack infrared ports, there are numerous solutions for retrofitting them to support the infrared capabilities found in portable devices. The most popular external infrared devices come from Extended Systems (`http://www.extendsys.com`). Its line of JetEye products include the JetEye PC ($99), which attaches to a standard serial port and works just like a standard serial device. The JetEye Printer ($179) adds similar capabilities to your printer. A line of JetEye Net products enable users to equip their LAN (Ethernet or Token-Ring) with a wireless LAN connection as well as with printing capabilities.

Another source for similar external infrared devices is ACTiSYS (`http://www.actisys.com`). Both ACTiSYS and Extended Systems have desktop and printer infrared devices that support the older IrDA standard (version 1.0) with a 115.2Kbps data rate. Extended Systems' JetEye Net products, on the other hand, already include the implementation of the Fast Infrared standard. They have a 4Mbps data throughput and support popular network operating systems such as Novell NetWare, Transmission Control Protocol/Internet Protocol (TCP/IP), Windows NT, and IBM LAN Manager/LAN Server.

Infrared Use in Portables

Infrared has been filtering into the computer industry for several years now. In fact, if you're a portable PC owner, you probably have infrared support built into your machine without even being aware of it. Even though you may not have realized the existence of your infrared port, when you're ready to use it, it's reassuring to find the small, red window mounted on the rear of your portable PC with the rest of the ports.

Portable PC manufacturers have been including infrared ports in their machines for more than three years now because it had become one of those features, like a CD-ROM drive or Pentium microprocessor, that had been added to many buyers' checklists of "must-have" functions.

This can be attributed to the idea that portable computers should be unencumbered by wires, regardless of whether users are in or out of the office. Happily for portable manufacturers, adding infrared is incredibly inexpensive—under a buck in most cases. In that spirit, infrared ports were readily added to notebooks to enable printing to infrared-equipped printers, logging onto an infrared-based local-area network (LAN), and swapping data with a desktop PC.

Unfortunately, desktop manufacturers haven't followed suit with universal infrared support and, instead, those who want to "beam" data from a portable (or other infrared-equipped device) to a desktop PC have to purchase add-on infrared products.

On the other end of the spectrum, handheld computer users have definitely motivated the personal digital assistant (PDA) industry by being exuberant about utilizing the infrared ports on their tiny computers.

Anyone who uses two computing devices, say a desktop and a portable, can attest that keeping data up-to-date on both machines is a relative nightmare. Even with file synchronization programs, such as Windows 95's Briefcase feature or Traveling Software's *LapLink*, the process is still tedious. There's always a lot of fumbling with cables and wires. Now, think about performing that same process with a handheld device and your desktop. Doesn't sound fun, does it? Finally, infrared has infiltrated the world of computing by establishing a tangible reason for its existence—to transfer data.

Drawbacks to Infrared

A drawback of infrared is its lack of sophistication. For example, infrared requires a point-to-point connection that can be made only with an unobstructed infrared beam. That means devices must be lined up in a direct light of sight to be able to exchange data. If not, the result could be signal distortion or signal loss. This is often a problem for users with crowded desks or crammed office environments.

Similarly, try to connect from too great a distance (the IrDA standard says more than 3 feet), and you're out of luck. In addition, infrared that is dubbed as Fast

Infrared by the IrDA can transfer data at up to 4Mbps, although the much slower 115.2Kbps is still more common in many devices. As a result, most infrared transfers are still performed at the lowest common speed available. Still, if infrared is right for you, these problems are only minor obstacles, and the infrared convenience factor will win out.

A Little History

The IrDA standards got their first stamp of approval in late 1995 when it was announced that Windows 95 would include support for IrDA-compliant devices. IrDA had assumed Microsoft's support would help speed the technology's acceptance and make it easy for PC users to take advantage of all that infrared has to offer.

Unfortunately, this has not been the case. There were numerous drawbacks to the Windows 95 support, including lack of cross-platform support. The Windows 95 drivers only supported Windows 95–to–Windows 95 communication, so those using other operating systems (including other Windows environments) had to go elsewhere for support.

Then came Windows CE, the version of Windows that runs on handheld PCs. With the original Windows CE, Microsoft again was thinking of platform-to-platform support that would only allow data transfer from one Windows CE device to another. The more current version of Windows CE offers cross-platform support, as do Windows 98 and Windows NT.

When working in Windows 95, infrared is fairly easy to use. Once the appropriate drivers are installed, a taskbar icon will let you know when your infrared-enabled devices are in range, when they have made a connection, and when data is being transferred.

If you require cross-platform support, you also can check out Intellisync software from Puma Technologies (`http://www.pumatech.com`). Intellisync (or Tranxit as it was known in early versions) is loaded on virtually every portable computer with an infrared port. Plus, it already supports Fast Infrared, a speed that the Windows 95 driver does not support.

Intellisync was built around the concept of wireless data transfer and Puma has been quick to stay ahead of the crowd in terms of file synchronization support for common portable applications. It supports a wide range of applications including Microsoft's Outlook and Schedule+, Lotus' Organizer 97, Symantec's ACT!, Goldmine Software's Goldmine and more, as well as a wide range of devices, such as the PalmPilot and Palm III from 3Com.

The Future of Infrared

Even if you don't have a portable or handheld computer equipped with infrared, there may be other reasons to add infrared capabilities to your desktop computer. The future will see more infrared-equipped devices, including digital cameras, pagers, and smart phones. Why fumble with a cable to download those vacation photos when you can easily "beam" them to your desktop or printer? Though current standards for sending pictures directly to a printer from a digital camera are not in place, you can expect a such products to be available soon.

Then there are the soon-to-be-announced smart cellular phones being promoted by companies such as NEC, Nokia, Qualcomm, and AT&T. These mobile phones promise to give users access to all sorts of wireless communication, including infrared for beaming business card data and calendar information. Pagers may offer similar features soon.

In the beginning, infrared ports were showing up in portable PCs without device drivers to support them—not to mention without any other devices to transfer data to. Therefore, the ports sat dormant, awaiting an awakening that is really only happening today.

You could say infrared technology was ahead of its time. Infrared was fashioned with mobility in mind and only now is mobility becoming *truly* attainable with extremely lightweight notebook PCs, handheld computers, and other devices. Infrared promises to become an important player in the wireless world of our future.

Voice-Recognition Software

Imagine yourself leaning back in a comfortable chair (or, if you prefer, pacing the room), dictating into a microphone and then seeing your words appear on-screen. Just a few more words of dictation, and now you're surfing the Web or sending e-mail.

The mission of voice and speech recognition software is to turn that fantasy into reality. Voice-recognition applications transform spoken words into either typed text or into a command function (such as saving a file or navigating a menu).

The Evolution of Voice-Recognition Technology

Even though voice-recognition technology has been used in mainframes, minicomputers, and in large corporate systems for more than 20 years, it hasn't been much of an option to the average PC user.

Until recently, dictation software worked in only one way, using a method called *discrete voice recognition*. To make a discrete voice, the user must pause between each word spoken. This. Is. A. Frustrating. Way. To. Talk. In fact, some discrete voice recognition users start losing their voice because of the strain.

Another general drawback to these first-generation systems is that the voice-recognition software didn't work with existing programs. As a result, the user had to dictate with the voice recognition software and then cut and paste the dictated text into another application.

To be fair, discrete voice-recognition works well in mouse-replacement (or command) applications because you're mostly using one-word orders anyway, such as "File. Save. Exit."

Continuous Speech Recognition

A breakthrough in voice technology, a process called *continuous speech recognition*, has changed everything. The user can now speak normally—saving the users' vocal chords and raising the dictation speed levels.

Continuous speech-recognition software is available via two options. First, as a standalone program that also voice-enables one or more existing programs (for example, it lets you dictate within Microsoft Word), and as an included component in a specific application. An example of this is in Lotus Development's SmartSuite, Millennium Edition, where all the programs are already voice-enabled.

An Imperfect Art

Not surprisingly, continuous speech-recognition software also primed the voice-recognition technology market. New products are appearing every day, and prices are plummeting. So, everyone should run out and get it, right? Maybe not. Anyone who has been using computers for longer than a few minutes knows that there is always a reality gap between a salesman's implications and how things really work.

There is no doubt, however, that we are witnessing the dawn of a new age in voice recognition. Or, as recently typed by one voice-recognition program, we are witnessing the "Don Avenue H invoice recognition." And there you have voice recognition's enduring weakness—what you speak, won't always be what you get. Although all systems predict you'll enjoy dictation accuracy approaching 100 percent, that is only after at least a month of daily word and speech-pattern training.

The second reality jolt is that the computing power needed for any continuous speech recognition program—especially random access memory (RAM)—is voracious. Minimum system requirements for these programs, on average, are a 166MHz Pentium computer with a CD-ROM drive, 16MB of RAM available exclusively to the continuous speech-recognition program (in addition to what Windows and your other software is using), 20–60MB of hard drive space, a 16-bit SoundBlaster-compatible sound card (built-in sound chipsets are sometimes problematic), and a desktop or headset microphone.

Given the hardware expense, the tedious training, and the guarantee that the system will never work 100 percent all the time, why bother? The answer is that even with its flaws, this technology can save you time and pain in the long run. Only you, however, can plug in the numbers to determine if a cost/benefit analysis for your situation comes out thumbs-up or thumbs-down.

Cost and Benefit Factors

Since voice recognition's primary function is usually dictation, you must first ask yourself how much actual keyboarding you're doing every day and then be brutally honest about your typing speed. (Download a shareware typing program and test yourself, if need be.)

Here are some numbers for you to crunch. The best dictation speed you can hope for from a voice-recognition system—and you should check the documentation of the system you intend to buy because some are lower—is about 160 words per minute. Although excellent typists can operate at 140 words per minute, most people who bill themselves as professional typists are actually in the 100-120 words-per-minute range. Any typing speed at less than 45 words per minute isn't worth counting unless you're enrolled in Typing 101.

If your keyboarding skills are in that Typing 101 classification, you'd clearly benefit from voice recognition technology because, even when factoring in the time needed for error correction, you'd still be way ahead of the game. On the other hand, if your typing is at the professional speed level, voice recognition probably won't speed up your data entry in the overall scheme of things—even if you ignore the training time.

Voice recognition might, however, help in another arena. Specifically, if all that speedy typing is causing pain in your wrists and you are having nightmares about carpal tunnel syndrome, voice-recognition software can give your tendons a needed break. Even if you don't use it all the time, simply switching between voice recognition software and keyboarding will reduce the strain on your wrists.

Even if voice recognition technology won't improve data entry speeds, don't forget the other aspect of voice recognition—command functions. Voice-recognition programs can also replace or supplement mouse duties in virtually any application. Using your voice to file, save, or launch a program may save you a lot of mouse-clicking. And, of course, anyone with physical challenges who finds using a mouse a lot harder than it was meant to be needs little convincing to give voice-recognition software a chance in the command arena.

Going Shopping

Assuming voice-recognition technology might be in your future, your shopping list will include the continuous-speech recognition software of your choice, a microphone, and whatever you must purchase to bring your hardware up to (at least) the minimum requirements recommended.

If you don't have a microphone, you'll be happy to learn that they often come packaged with speech-recognition software. Also, if you have a microphone built into your computer (in the monitor or keyboard, for example), it won't qualify for the job of dictation, but it should be OK for command functions.

If you must buy a microphone, a headset is the best choice because it's impossible to turn away from the microphone or accidentally move in or out of its range. The top-of-the-line headsets promise higher accuracy, but decent headsets don't have to be expensive.

Andrea Electronics (`http://www.andreaelectronics.com`) makes headsets that use their own active voice-reduction technology. Another company, VXI (`http://www.vxicorp.com`) specializes in headsets for call centers and telephony systems. If you use your computer to transmit voice (like a phone call) over the Internet, then you may want to spend more and get a higher-rated headset. If you don't have a standard sound card, make sure the headset you're buying is compatible with the sound card you have—usually a list comes with the card.

Software Choices

The leading players in voice-recognition technology are Dragon Systems (`http://www.dragonsystems.com`), IBM (`http://www.software.ibm.com/is/voicetype`), and Lernout & Hauspie (`http://www.lhs.com`), who acquired another voice recognition company named Kurzweil Applied Intelligence (`http://www.lhs.com/kurzweil`). Although new voice products are being introduced at an amazing pace, virtually all are made using licensed technology from one of the four mentioned here.

Dragon Systems' Dragon NaturallySpeaking continuous speech products are, arguably, the best of the best. Dragon NaturallySpeaking comes in three versions. The Personal version works only in its own word processor and contact with other applications is through primitive cut-and-paste methods only.

The Preferred edition has a 230,000-word vocabulary (30,000 active) and can make voice macros, read text, play back your dictation, and work with virtually any Windows application.

The Deluxe edition allows you to set a larger active vocabulary and comes with more development tools. The Preferred edition is a good bet and can be found for about $180 or less. Dragon Systems claims a top dictation speed of 160 words per minute.

IBM's ViaVoice line comes in two levels, the top-of-the line ViaVoice Gold (about $150) and ViaVoice ($99). Both ViaVoice products claim to work at up to 125 words per minute and will integrate with Word 97 (version 8). The Gold level also works with Word versions 6c and 7, plus virtually any Windows 95/98 application.

ViaVoice Gold's features are roughly comparable to Dragon NaturallySpeaking, Preferred edition. The less expensive ViaVoice (without the Gold) has one major drawback; you must use the mouse to make corrections, instead of voice. Also, it will not accept vocabulary modules (more about these in a moment), so you can't expand it.

Kurzweil AI's lower-price VoicePad, VoicePlus, and VoicePro product line uses discrete voice technology (the pause-between-words process) and has a limited vocabulary. VoicePro, the high-end product, has a retail price of $70 and works with a number of major Windows 95 and Windows 3.*x* applications. It also uses a technology called *continuous digit recognizer* that makes the process of entering numbers into a spreadsheet a lot easier.

Kurzweil AI has just introduced a product called VoiceCommands that works exclusively with Word 97 (version 7 or 8). VoiceCommands ($60 retail) is not, however, a text dictation system. VoiceCommands replaces arcane Word menu, editing, and formatting procedures with natural English voice commands.

Kurzweil AI provides evaluation copies of all their products from its Web site. Go to `http://www.lhs.com/kurzweil/pcapps` and click the product you want to try. When you land on that product's page, you'll see the option to download in the left margin. (You can also get a copy of VoiceCommands from Microsoft's Try This! Web page at `http://www.microsoft.com/magazine/tryit/free.htm`).

IMSI (`http://www.imsisoft.com`) brings us another pair of inexpensive applications—with a twist. VoiceDirect, Standard edition ($40), and VoiceDirect, Professional edition ($60), are powered by the older discrete voice technology of Dragon

Systems' DragonDictate and both work with Windows 3.*x* and Windows 95/98. In addition, they both have a healthy 120,000-word total vocabulary (30,000 active).

The Standard edition works only with Word and Corel WordPerfect while the Professional edition can handle virtually any Windows application. Here's the twist—users have the option to upgrade the word processing portion of both versions to the newer and improved technology of continuous-speech recognition.

Finally, VoiSys International (`http://www.voisys.com`) offers free trials, downloadable from its Web site, on two interesting command-only products, Voice Power for Internet Browsing (for Netscape Navigator and Microsoft Internet Explorer 3.*x* and earlier), and Voice Power for PowerPoint. VoiSys has a third product you cannot download, Voice Power for Windows, that voice-enables Windows 95 and Windows NT 4.0 commands.

One additional curve to consider is that most dictation applications can be expanded with industry-specific vocabulary modules. Check out your add-on options first before making a final decision.

You may also want to check in with voice and speech-recognition dealers who represent all (or most) of the available products. These dealers often market their own command and voice macros and can discuss customization alternatives. Several such dealers include 21st Century Eloquence (`http://voicerecognition.com`), Metroplex Voice Computing, which is primarily a DragonSystems reseller (`http://www.metroplexvoice.com`), and Voice Recognition Systems (`http://www.talktoyourcomputer.com`).

What to Look For

The general benchmarks to keep in mind while shopping for dictation software is how well the product can be integrated with applications that are important to you, the size of the vocabulary, the ability to add more words (either via modules or user entry), speed (words per minute), easy corrections, and accuracy (you may never achieve the numbers documented, but higher benchmarks give you a fighting chance). And, finally, remember that both continuous-speech recognition and discrete voice-recognition technologies are currently available. Make sure you've checked the software box carefully to get the one you want.

Once you've made your decision and acquired the software of your dreams, the next step is installation. Voice recognition applications require an extended setup process. Expect to spend up to an hour during this initial phase as the software automatically tests your microphone and then listens to you talk, and talk, and talk.

Perform the setup in the same physical environment that you intend to use regularly with your voice-recognition software. Session-to-session uniformity, in regards to microphone placement (close, but not so close that it picks up your breathing), the volume and tone of your voice, enunciation, and ambient (background) noise, all help minimize errors.

Training

Once the introduction is over, you'll be allowed to use the software and begin the heavy training that continues for several weeks. For example, when an error crops up as you dictate, you should correct it on the spot and, if necessary (or possible), record the word so the program can learn the difference between what it did and what you wanted. Allowing errors to slip unfortunately reinforces the error in the so-called mind of the voice-recognition program.

Nevertheless, no matter how much training you go through, there are some obstacles—like the difference between *Don* and *dawn* or *there* and *they're*—that will always be a struggle.

Please remember, as you work through the initial training period, you're also learning a new way to work—verbally—an approach that will feel uncomfortable just because it's new. Give yourself some slack as you figure out how to make the process work best for you.

If you're just using your voice for commands-only purposes or as a mouse-replacement system, you'll need very little, if any, training. This is because the application uses a limited vocabulary of commands.

Voice and speech recognition technology is bound to become the dominant interface for computers because, quite simply, it's already the dominant interface for people. In fact, Nicholas Negroponte, founder and director of the famous MIT Media Lab, predicts that eventually the power of voice will become the common interface for everything from toasters to telephones.

Are You Experienced?

Now you can...

- ☑ **install a new keyboard**
- ☑ **choose which kind of input device is best for you**
- ☑ **find and install the right joystick**
- ☑ **take advantage of infrared technology**
- ☑ **explore voice-recognition technology**

SKILL 12

Installing a Printer

- Installing a printer with DOS
- Installing a printer with Windows 3.*x*
- Installing a printer with Windows 95/98

Printers have advanced far beyond the days of pale, thin dot-matrix output. These days, consumers can afford inkjet printers that produce excellent color output or personal laser printers that produce near-professional-quality text.

WHAT YOU NEED TO KNOW

Tools: No special tools needed

Time: 5 minutes

Cost: $150–$500

Skill Level: Easy

Benefits: Produces hard copies of data

A Few Simple Rules

If you feel left out by the boom in printing, don't worry: Upgrading a printer is a simple process if you simply follow instructions and a keep a few common sense rules in mind.

- First, always turn off your computer and printer before connecting the printer to the computer. This will prevent the possibility of damage to both units.
- Second, before starting the installation process, make sure you have the correct kind of cable on hand. Don't assume cable is included with the printer because most of the time it isn't.
- Last, follow the printer's documentation. That documentation is prepared by the hardware manufacturer with your best interests in mind, so always follow the instructions.

Making the Connection

After bringing your new printer home, the first step is to clear a place for it. Give yourself enough room to get inside the printer when necessary, and allow several inches of ventilation space wherever there are air vents. Obviously, you'll also want to place your computer close enough to the computer for the cable to reach.

When your computer is in a good place, consult the printer's documentation on how to prepare it for installation. Generally, this is a straightforward process that entails plugging the printer into the computer, connecting the power cord, and installing the new ink or toner cartridge. However, the place where users most often run into difficulty is in the removal of all the packing material. Refer to your documentation to find and remove all the packing tape and little pieces of plastic designed to protect the printer during shipping. You'll also need to assemble the paper tray if it is packed separately.

Be sure to check your computer's documentation to ensure you are connecting the printer to the correct port. You'll need to know to which port you've connected the printer later in the installation. Although most newer computers have clearly marked ports, some older computers were not so well designed. Also, although most parallel ports (a faster port that transmits data in a double, or parallel, stream) have 15 pins and most serial ports (a slower port than parallel because it only transmits data in a single stream) have nine pins, you cannot necessarily assume all 15-pin outlets are parallel ports. Some older computers have serial ports that look amazingly like parallel ports.

Refer to the documentation for the correct time and procedure for installing the ink or toner cartridge. Generally, it involves turning off your computer, then opening the cabinet. From there, remove the old cartridge, insert the new one, and close up the printer. This procedure varies from printer to printer and often involves loosening a latch or lever. Don't improvise your way through this; use the documentation.

Calling All Drivers

Once your printer is set up physically and connected to your computer, plug in and turn on both the computer and printer. (Refer to your documentation for instructions on how to turn the printer on; some newer printers don't even have power switches.)

At this point, you can install printer drivers, which are miniprograms that allow hardware peripherals to communicate with a computer. Without these drivers, your printer will not function correctly—or at all. Below we look at installing drivers in DOS, Windows 3.*x*, and Windows 95/98.

Driving a Classic

With a DOS system, the first thing you'll want to do is run any installation programs that came with the printer. If your printer didn't come with disks, refer to the documentation to make sure it doesn't need any. Follow the instructions in the documentation to run the program. Usually, you will run it from the disk drive, so you will type **a:** at the prompt, and then press Enter. Then, type the name of the program, which generally is called something such as **Install**, and press Enter.

Second, you will have to configure each program that will use the printer. This procedure varies, so check your application's documentation. If your printer is not listed, try a generic printer driver listed. Another option is to use a common printer driver such as an Epson or Hewlett-Packard driver to see if you can tweak your printer into acting like this common printer. This often is called *emulation mode* because your computer is acting like another printer. With a little experimentation, you may be able to find a driver that works; of course, it is always best to use a specially designed driver.

Windows 3.*x* at the Wheel

With Windows 3.*x*, you can add a printer driver once and all your Windows programs will work with it, which is a great improvement over DOS.

To install a printer driver in Windows 3.*x*, go to Program Manager, double-click the Main group, then double-click the Control Panel icon. In the Control Panel, double-click the Printers icon.

1. You now will see the Printers dialog box. To add a printer, simply click the Add button; this will expand the Printers window to include a list of printers. Look through this list and, if your printer is listed, highlight it and click the Install button. You then will be prompted to put one of the Windows 3.*x* installation disks in your drive; Windows will install the printer driver from its own stash of drivers.

2. If your driver is not listed, highlight the Unlisted or Updated Printer listing and click the Install button. In this case, Windows will prompt you to insert your driver disk.

3. If you don't have a driver, check with the store or your printer's manufacturer to see if one is available. Also, you can check the Internet for a new driver. You also can use the generic driver named in the list of printer drivers, but this is never the best option.

4. After installing the printer driver, highlight your newly listed printer in the Printer window and click the Connect button. This will allow you to make sure the printer settings are correct. You want to make sure your port is correct. If you're using a parallel port printer, you will select LPT1, LPT2, or LPT3—whatever the port is named. If you're using a serial printer, you will select one of the serial ports: COM1, COM2, COM3, or COM4. Check your computer's documentation to make sure you know which port your printer is plugged into. Save the settings, and click OK to return to the Printers window.

5. Now, click Setup to configure the printer's special functions, including its fonts and graphics. Refer to your printer's documentation to ensure your settings are configured properly.

6. If you have multiple printers installed, you'll want to set one as the default printer, which is the printer that Windows will use unless you tell it otherwise. Highlight a printer in the installed drivers list, then click the Set As Default button.

Riding Shotgun in Windows 95/98

Windows 95/98 has made installing printer drivers much easier than in DOS and Windows 3.*x*. The best way to install printers in Windows 95/98 is to use the Add Printer Wizard. Not just a pretty interface, the wizard allows you to install a printer quickly and painlessly.

Even though the Add Printer Wizard usually is the best way to install a printer, some manufacturers have elected not to use the wizard for their installation. If your printer documentation tells you to use a particular installation program rather than the Add Printer Wizard, do as it says. Hewlett-Packard often has its own installation programs to make it easier to install its printers' special features and management tools.

If the manufacturer demands you use their installation, always read the installation instructions on your printer software before attempting to install. However, if the installation wizard is used, then the instructions below should easily see you through the process.

1. The first step is to open the Printers folder. Click the Start button, select the Settings menu, then select the Printers folder. You also can get to the Printers

folder by double-clicking the My Computer icon, then double-clicking the Printers icon.

2. Next, double-click the Add Printer icon. The first window that appears tells you this wizard will install your printer, so click the Next button at the bottom of the box. If Windows 95/98's network capabilities are enabled, you will get a box that prompts you to choose Local or Network installation. Local means your printer is attached directly to your computer; Network means your printer is attached to a network and is not directly attached to your computer by a cord. Select the type of installation and click Next.

NOTE

If you select Network, you'll be prompted to give the path to your printer, or you can browse through the Network Neighborhood to find it. The path is the printer's address on the network—it's easier to browse for it than to type in the complete path name. Just look for the name of the computer to which the printer is attached.

3. Once you've made these decisions, you will see the driver-selection screen. If you have a driver disk from the manufacturer, click the Have Disk button. Windows then will ask you which drive the disk is in. Usually, you will enter **A:/** or **D:/** in the box because you will be installing from a disk or a CD-ROM, and these are the most common letters for those drives, respectively. After inserting the disk in the appropriate drive and making sure the appropriate drive letter is indicated in the box, click Browse.

4. In the Browse window, Windows will keep you updated as you come across drivers in your browsing. Manufacturers usually put the drivers in the root directory or in a clearly marked folder. (If you have a problem, check your printer's documentation. If you are unable to find the driver on the disk, you can use another disk, or click Cancel to return to the previous screen.) Windows 95 will find your drivers and list them so you can choose the right one. Make sure you select the one that exactly matches your printer type (e.g., don't select 5M when you should be selecting 5MP). Simply highlight your printer's name and click Next.

5. If you don't have a disk, click the printer manufacturer's name in the left pane in the box where most users click Have Disk. Once you do, the right

pane will give you a list of all the drivers for printers made by that manufacturer. Find your printer, highlight it, and click Next.

6. Now you'll be able to select your printer port (as long as you aren't doing a network installation). Typically, as mentioned above, newer printers connect to the parallel port. Generally, this means you'll be using the LPT1 port because most computers only have the one parallel port. Of course, if you're using a serial port, indicate which COM port you're using. If you don't know which port your printer is using, consult your computer's documentation. Don't click the Configure Port button unless you use DOS programs that don't print without special configuration. If you use those DOS programs, click the button and make sure the box next to Spool MS-DOS Print Jobs is unchecked, then click OK.

7. Once you have the correct port selected, click Next. This will allow you to name the printer (unless you're doing a network installation). We recommend keeping the name Windows suggests. This also is the box where you may be asked whether this new printer is going to be your default printer. If Windows asks, click the Yes radio button if you want the printer to be your main printer, and click No if you don't. Then click Next to continue.

8. In the next box, you have the option of printing a test page. This is a good idea, so click Yes, then click Next to continue. You may be prompted to insert your Windows 95/98 CD-ROM or disk, and you may have to tell Windows 95/98 where the disk is. Generally, you'll be entering **D:\win95** at this prompt. Once Windows 95/98 knows where the driver is, it will copy the drivers over and finish up the installation. You then will see a new printer icon in the Printers folder.

9. Right-click the printer icon in the Printer folders to see the basic printer controls. The most important is the Set As Default option, which designates your printer as the one Windows 95/98 will use unless you tell it otherwise.

Printing Forever

If you ever get into trouble installing a new printer, consult the printer's documentation or call technical support. Just use common sense, follow the directions, and you should have many years of printing with your newest computer component.

Are You Experienced?

Now you can...

- ☑ install a printer under the DOS platform
- ☑ install a printer on the Windows 3.*x* platform
- ☑ install a printer on the Windows 95/98 platform

SKILL 13

Installing a Scanner

- Installing parallel port scanner
- Installing a SCSI-interface scanner
- Making sure the scanner works with the TWAIN driver

The scanner is the tool that has made the virtual world of the computer screen more lifelike by adding photographs to on-screen and computer-printed documents. The rise of the World Wide Web and the fusion of photography and digital imaging have led to a massive increase in the popularity of scanners and a big drop in prices. Before you take the plunge, make sure you know what you'll need to buy and how you install it to get the most from your new graphics tool.

What You'll Need to Know

Tools: A screwdriver (have both a flat-head and Phillips available)

Time: 1–2 hours

Cost: $100–$1,800

Skill Level: Intermediate

Benefits: Ability to convert drawings and photos into computer graphics; ability to convert printed text into word processing files

How Scanners Work

Regardless of the type of scanner you choose, the fundamental operation of all scanners is similar. Scanners convert the original document into digitized form and allow the resulting file to be edited by graphics programs (usually included with the scanner). Flatbed and sheet-fed scanners also may be used with page-recognition software, which performs optical character recognition (OCR) on the text and, in some cases, also transfers fonts and layout to a text file (see Figure 13.1). Some scanners come with page-recognition software, but it also can be added later.

Virtually all scanners use a small program called a TWAIN driver to perform the actual scanning operation. *TWAIN* (which means *Technology Without an Interesting Name*) allows graphics and OCR programs to control the scanner and bring in the scanned image without the need for the scanning program to save it first. This also means the same scanner can be used by many different graphics and page-recognition programs. All these programs need is the ability to acquire a TWAIN image.

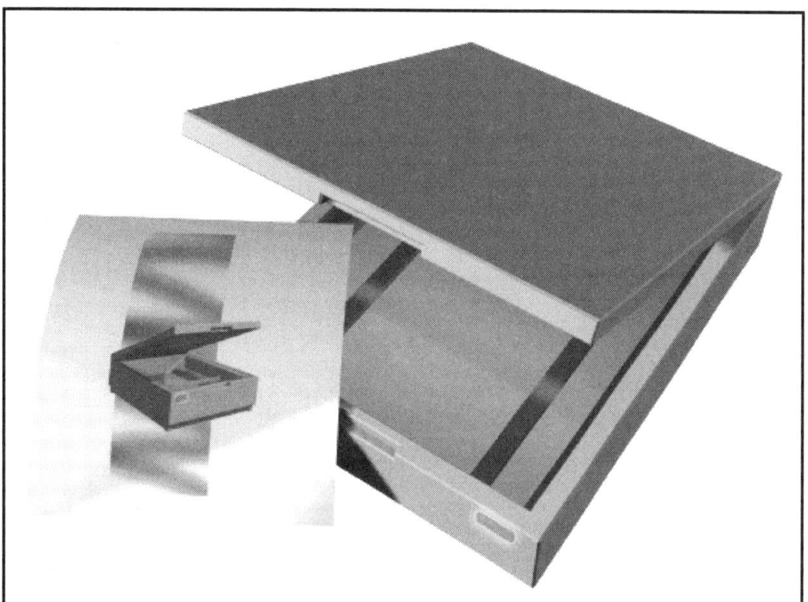

FIGURE 13.1: A typical flatbed scanner

Installation

With the demise of handheld scanners and their proprietary interface cards, you'll find there are two basic ways to attach a scanner to your system: the computer's parallel port, and a Small Computer System Interface (SCSI) card, which is usually an add-on.

Most sheet-fed and all-in-one combination units use the parallel (or printer) port. This virtually eliminates the need to open the computer, but it isn't always a painless procedure. If you're already using your parallel port for a printer and a second device (such as a Zip drive, tape backup, or CD-ROM), you'll need to remove the other device when you want to scan something.

Low-cost flatbed scanners also use the parallel port, but more expensive scanners use SCSI interface cards. SCSI cards also can be used to connect to many other devices simultaneously, but setup can be tricky.

A third option will become more common in the near future: Universal Serial Bus (USB) peripherals can be daisy-chained to the small square USB ports found on most computers since late 1996. However, as driver and device support develop, this is still a "someday" option.

Installing a Parallel Port Scanner

Before you begin, make sure you've done the following.

1. Check the scanner's documentation to determine if a special parallel port setting such as enhanced parallel port (EPP), extended capabilities port (ECP), or EPP/ECP is required or recommended for scanner operation. These settings are high-speed bidirectional options that allow the scanner to send data at top speed back to the computer. Once you determine if such a port setting is necessary, you need to see if your parallel port is already configured for the required mode.
2. If your port is built into the computer's system port, start up the computer and enter the Basic Input/Output System (BIOS) setup screen. On most computers, you'll see a message on startup telling you which key(s) to press to enter the computer's BIOS setup program. If the parallel port isn't listed on the opening screen, you'll probably find it listed with other peripherals. Switch to the screen listing peripheral options, reset the port settings if necessary, save the changes to the BIOS setup, and after the computer reboots, you'll be ready to continue.
3. On a few computers, you'll find the parallel port is part of a multi–Input/Output card that also may contain serial (COM) and game ports, among others. Check the board's settings to see if it will be suitable for scanning, and adjust the settings if necessary. Most boards with a parallel port are adjusted with small plastic jumper blocks, which are moved across pins to make and change settings.

Connecting the Scanner

Follow these steps to connect your new scanner.

1. Turn off the computer and printer, and disconnect the parallel printer cable from the printer port. The printer (LPT) port is a 25-pin port with holes (a so-called "female" port; see Figure 13.2).
2. Attach the data cable to the scanner. If the scanner can be used with either a SCSI or parallel port connection, select the correct port.

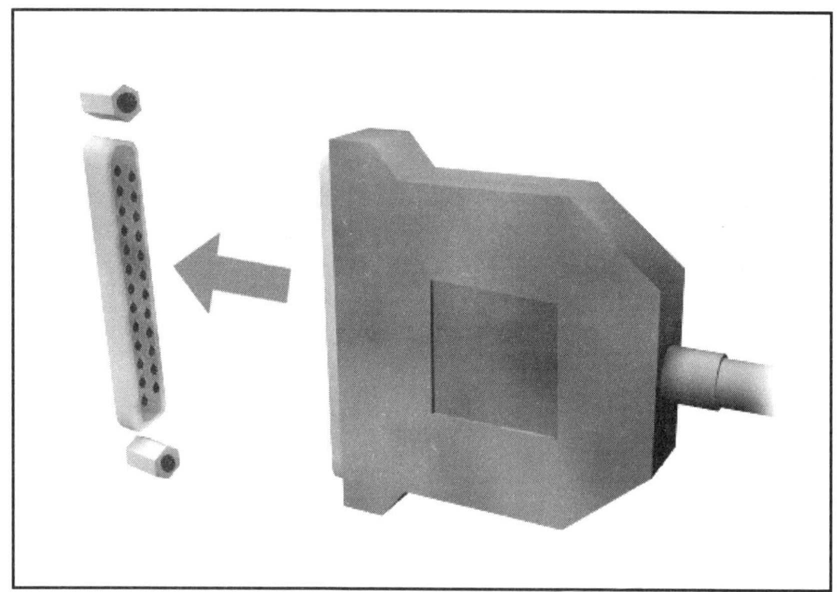

FIGURE 13.2: The 25-pin LPT port is where the scanner is attached.

3. Connect the data cable from the scanner to the printer port.
4. Connect the printer cable (formerly plugged directly into the computer) into the pass-through connector on the scanner. This will allow both scanning and printing with the same port.
5. Before proceeding, check the documentation for the scanner software. Any of these options are possible:
   - You may need to install the scanner software before you have the computer detect the scanner. In this case, leave the scanner and printer turned off until the software is installed.
   - The scanner may be detected (either by the Plug-and-Play feature in Windows 95/98 or by the Add New Hardware Wizard), and you will insert the correct disk or CD-ROM as directed.

   The scanner may be detected, but you will skip installing the drivers at that time and install them later.
6. Turn on the scanner, then turn on the printer and the computer.

Once the computer is turned on, the sequence of events varies according to the type of computer and version of Windows you're using.

With Windows 95/98 and a Plug-and-Play BIOS, the computer may detect the scanner as Windows starts. The screen will display an Installing Unknown Device message, and then the message changes to list your scanner. If this is the first time you've installed your scanner, you'll be prompted to insert the setup disk or CD-ROM so the drivers can be read and installed.

During this installation process, the TWAIN driver also may be installed, or you may need to do this manually.

Once the scanner is installed, check Windows 95/98's Device Manager to see if it shows as an installed device. It may be listed in the scanner category or sometimes as an unknown device.

Installing a SCSI-Interface Scanner

Before you begin, see if you already have a suitable SCSI card installed in your computer. SCSI is becoming increasingly popular because a true SCSI card can run up to seven devices at a time by daisy chaining the devices. Typical devices that use SCSI cards include most CD-R (recordable CD) drives, some high-performance CD-ROM drives (including multiplatter changers), and a few high-capacity tape backups.

If you're running Windows 95/98, open the System Properties icon in the Control Panel and click the Device Manager tab. If you see a device category called SCSI controllers, open it and see what is listed. If you see only Iomega Parallel Port Zip Interface, this is the driver used by the parallel port Zip drive and is not suitable. Look for an interface card from vendors such as Adaptec. If you find one listed, you may be able to use it for your scanner, as well.

Adding the SCSI Card in Windows 95/98

If you've followed any of the installation instructions elsewhere in this book, these steps will be a piece of cake.

1. Check the Device Manager and double-click the Computer icon at the top of the list of devices. Compare the list of available settings for interrupt request lines (IRQs), direct memory access (DMA), input/output (I/O) port, and memory addresses to the SCSI card's available settings. If your computer and SCSI card supports Plug and Play, you should be able to install it quickly. You may need to flip a small switch on the SCSI card to enable Plug and Play.

2. Shut down the computer, and turn it off.

3. Open your computer and look for an empty slot of the same type as your SCSI card. Most SCSI cards shipped with scanners are called ISA cards and fit into a slot with two connectors. Remove the screw that holds the slot cover in place, and slide your SCSI card into place (Figure 13.3). Carefully line up the connector with the slot, and push it into place. Fasten the card bracket to the system with the screw you removed earlier.

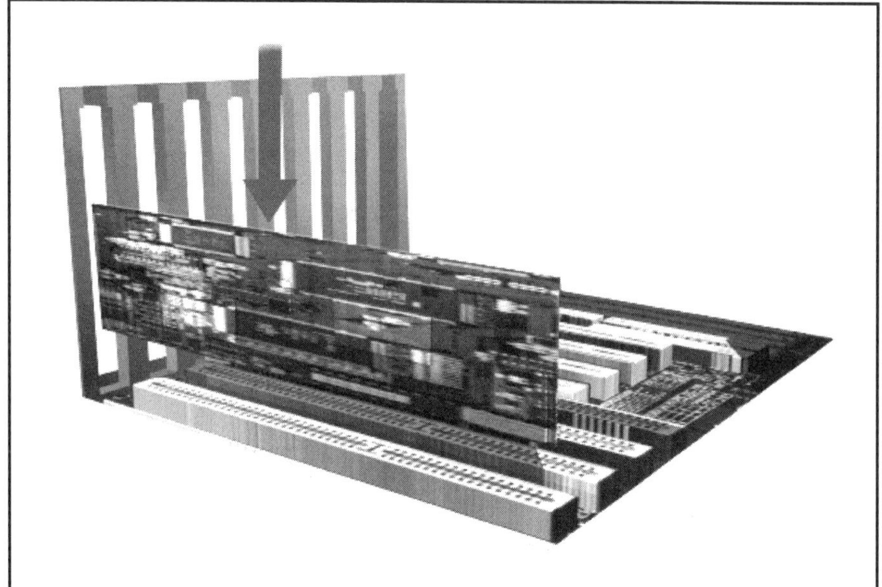

FIGURE 13.3: The SCSI card slides into the open slot.

4. Turn on the computer, and see if the card is detected by Windows 95/98. If it is, insert the driver disks or CD-ROM as directed to complete the installation. If not, run the Add New Hardware Wizard to detect and install the SCSI card.

You'll know you've succeeded when the SCSI card is listed as a SCSI controller in the Windows 95/98 Device Manager. Make sure you don't see a yellow "!" symbol next to the card. This indicates a problem. Follow the directions on-screen to determine what to do to solve the problem. You may need to install new drivers or change hardware settings.

Attaching Your Scanner to the SCSI Card

First, turn off the computer and make sure the scanner also is turned off.

1. If you're using a SCSI card that came with your scanner, attach one end of the supplied cable to the card bracket and the other end to the scanner. There are a variety of SCSI connectors, so if one end of the cable won't fit the card, look at the other end.
2. Because even the simplest SCSI connection actually is a "network on your desk," you'll need to assign a logical unit number (LUN) to your scanner. Look for a rotary knob or a sliding switch on the scanner's rear (near the SCSI cable) that's numbered zero through seven. Choose a number between one and six. If you choose an LUN that's already in use, your scanner won't work.
3. Each end of the SCSI bus must also be terminated so the signals will properly run between devices. Because all SCSI devices can be daisy chained, you should see a second SCSI connector beside the one you're using at the rear of the scanner. Some scanners require you to attach an external terminator (which looks like a SCSI connector without a cable) to the second connector. Others use an on/off switch. If this is the only SCSI device you have, you'll need to terminate the signals at the scanner with one of these methods.
4. If you're adding a scanner to a system that already has a SCSI card in use, you'll need to attach the scanner to the end of the daisy-chain of devices.
5. If the cable that came with the scanner won't attach to the empty SCSI port on the back of your other SCSI device, you will need to buy a new cable. Note the required connectors and buy a suitable cable. These cables cost $20–$50.
6. You'll also need to disable the termination on the last SCSI device and turn on the termination at the scanner (if it's now the last device). Check the LUNs already in use to make sure the scanner is set to an unused number. If you're using an Adaptec card, a program called SCSI Interrogator may already be installed on your computer. Run this program to see which LUNs are in use, and which ones are free.
7. Turn on the scanner and other SCSI devices before you turn on the computer. To allow all devices to work, wait about five seconds before you turn on the computer. Watch to see if your scanner is detected, and follow the instructions shipped with the scanner to complete the installation of the driver software.

Getting Your Scanner TWAINed

Once your scanner is attached and its drivers are loaded, you'll still need to follow a few more steps to make sure it's working properly. If you haven't yet installed the TWAIN scanning software supplied with the scanner, do it now.

1. Once the software is installed, look for the scanner's program group and test the scanning software directly. Although you'll normally access the scanner through a full-featured graphics program, it's best to try to run it alone first.

2. Some scanners come with a test sheet containing a black-and-white photo, a color photo, a grid, and colored bars. This test sheet is designed to help you check your scanner's performance and set the colors properly.
3. Insert the test sheet face-down into the scanner, or slide in any photo if you didn't get a test sheet, and run the scanning software. With most programs, you can *prescan* or *preview*, which does a quick low-resolution scan. Try it.
4. If you get a distorted image, check the image type. Most scanners require you to select the type of picture you're scanning. For the test sheet or a color print, select Color Print. For text, select Line Art or OCR.
5. Once you get a good preview scan, select an area and scan at various settings. You should see an enlarged image on-screen. Save the scan to disk.
6. Once you've determined that the scanner is working, close the scanning software.
7. If you have a graphics program already installed that you're comfortable using, open it and look in the File menu for an option called Import or TWAIN. Select the scanner from the Select Source option, and then select Acquire Image. The scanner software should start, allowing you to scan without leaving your graphics program. After you've scanned an image, close the scanner software, and your scan should now appear in the graphics program's editing window.
8. If you don't have a suitable graphics program installed, most scanners come with an easy-to-use image editor you can install instead. Set it up and test it as listed above. If your scanner has OCR/page-recognition software included, install it and test it. Good OCR can save a lot of retyping.

Are You Experienced?

Now you can...

☑ install a brand new scanner

☑ calibrate your scanner to work with your system

☑ make sure that your scanner is TWAIN-compliant

SKILL 14

Installing Ports and Expansion Slots

- Learning about ports
- Installing a SCSI adapter
- Installing an I/O port
- Installing a USB port

You can hook up all kinds of hard drives, tape backup machines, scanners, and printers to your PC. In fact, so many useful things are out there that can connect to a computer, you may find you don't have enough places to plug them in.

This is particularly true of devices that connect to your computer through a parallel or serial *port*. (A port allows access in and out of the computer for cables.) Most computers have a couple of extra parallel and serial ports available when you buy them. All it takes, however, to find yourself running short on ports is one game pad and one printer.

Fortunately, a variety of ways are available to solve this problem. We'll show you three options that will let you add those extra devices.

SCSI to the Rescue

The first solution is a *Small Computer System Interface* (SCSI, pronounced scuzzy) host adapter. This card lets you add up to 15 internal and external SCSI devices to your computer. The number of devices you can add depends on the SCSI host adapter you buy.

When talking about SCSIs, you may hear references to SCSI-2. SCSI-2 is simply a standard for SCSI devices such as scanners, hard drives, and tape backup drives. SCSI allows for faster data transfer rates among devices, and supports a wider array of devices than the original SCSI standard. The newest standard (also the most expensive) is the SCSI-3, which is faster than SCSI-2, and lets you connect an even greater number of devices to your computer.

What You Need to Know

Tools: Screwdriver

Time: 5 to 15 minutes

Cost: $60 to $170

Skill Level: Intermediate

Benefits: Adding a SCSI host adapter, a USB port, or extra parallel and serial ports increases the number of peripherals you can connect to your computer.

NOTE NOTE NOTE NOTE NOTE NOTE NOTE NOTE NOTE NOTE NOTE NOTE NOTE NOTE NOTE

Because SCSI-3 devices are more expensive than SCSI-2 devices, most home users should stick with SCSI-2 for now.

Some SCSI-2 devices offer higher performance than the typical SCSI-2 devices. For example, Fast SCSI devices are just that—faster. They transfer data at faster speeds than normal SCSI-2 devices, up to 10 megabits per second (Mbps). Ultra SCSI devices are faster yet; they can transfer data up to 20Mbps. The most popular types of Fast and Ultra SCSI devices are hard drives.

When you connect SCSI devices to a host adapter card, you create a SCSI bus, which is the electronic pathway between the host adapter and the SCSI devices. Data from your SCSI devices travels through this pathway to the host adapter card, and then to your computer's processor. The SCSI bus includes both internal and external devices.

SCSI devices are pretty common. If there's a particular type of device you're interested in, such as a Zip drive or a scanner, there's probably a SCSI version of that device. The most popular types of SCSI devices are memory-related devices, such as hard drives, tape drives, removable storage drives, and compact disc, read-only memory (CD-ROM) drives. That's because SCSI host adapters transfer data quickly. On the downside, SCSI devices tend to cost more than non-SCSI versions and can be a little more difficult to set up.

When you set up SCSI devices to your computer, you don't connect all of them directly to the host adapter. External devices are daisy-chained together. (A daisy-chain is a set of hardware components connected to each other in a series.) The devices are connected via special SCSI cables that should come with your external SCSI device.

The internal devices are connected to a ribbon cable, which is then connected to the host adapter. The ribbon cable will have a few connectors on it for the internal devices. If you buy a SCSI host adapter card, it should include a ribbon cable. It is possible, however, that the ribbon cable won't have enough connectors for all the internal SCSI devices in your computer. If that's the case, you'll need to buy a ribbon cable that has a connector for each device.

Installing a SCSI Device

Installing a SCSI host adapter card and connecting SCSI devices to it isn't very difficult. However, before beginning the installation process, read Skill 3.

1. First, remove the cover of your computer. Locate an empty PCI slot on your computer's motherboard. Peripheral Component Interconnect (PCI) slots

are the short white or ivory slots (not the longer black Industry Standard Architecture [ISA] slots). Remove the metal cover strip on the back of the computer that lines up with that slot (Figure 14.1). (Save the screw, because you'll need it in a minute.) Touch the metal frame of your computer to ground yourself before touching the host adapter card.

2. Now, insert the host adapter card into the PCI slot, gently rocking it back and forth until it clicks into place (Figure 14.2), and then replace the screw you removed earlier.
3. Now it's time to connect your SCSI card to your SCSI devices. First, make sure the last connected device at either end of the SCSI bus is terminated. That means the electrical resistors must be installed or activated to make sure the bus transfers data reliably. For internal devices, this usually means flipping a switch or setting a jumper on the device. Consult the device's documentation for how to do this. The terminated internal device should be the device connected farthest from the host adapter card on the ribbon cable. Do not terminate the other devices on the ribbon cable.

Terminating an external device usually consists of inserting a plug into the second SCSI port of the device. The plug should be included with the device. Again, check the device's documentation on how to do this. And again, the terminated device will be the last one in the chain. If you are using internal and external SCSI devices, don't terminate the host adapter because it's in the middle of the bus. If, however, you are using only internal or only external devices, you must terminate the host adapter card because it's at one end of the bus.

NOTE NOTE NOTE NOTE NOTE NOTE NOTE NOTE NOTE NOTE NOTE NOTE NOTE NOTE NOTE

Here's another thing to keep in mind when you are setting up the SCSI bus. The physical length of the bus (the cables) must not exceed 6 meters (a little less than 20 feet). If you are using any Fast SCSI devices, the physical length of the bus cannot exceed 3 meters (just less than 10 feet). This shouldn't be a problem in most cases, however.

To plug in an external SCSI device, attach one end of the cable that came with the device to the port on the back of the device. There should be two ports, so make sure you plug in to the right one. Then attach the other end of the cable to the external port of the host adapter card, on the back of the computer.

To plug in internal SCSI devices, attach a connector on the ribbon cable to the connection on the device. Then, attach one end of the ribbon cable to the connector on the host adapter card (Figure 14.3).

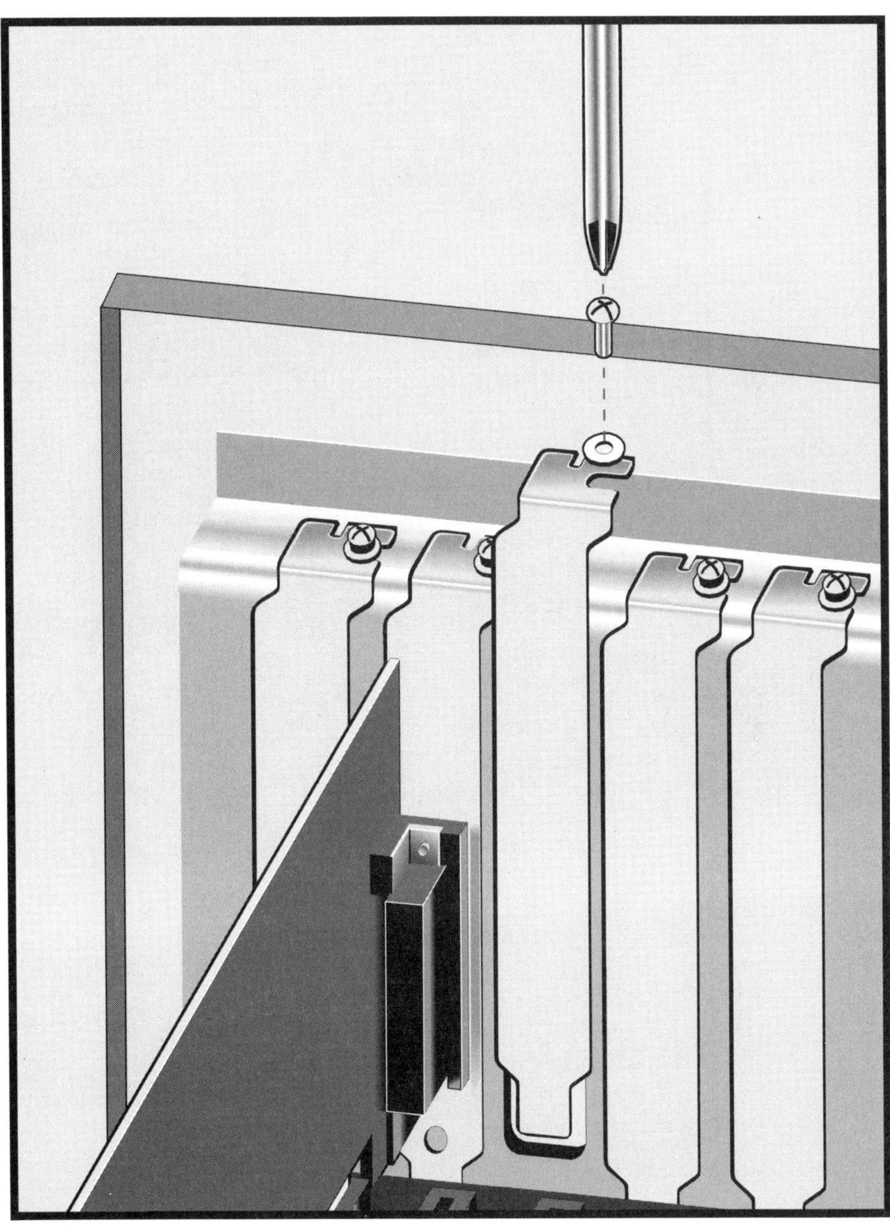

FIGURE 14.1: You'll need to remove the screws that keep the slot covers in place.

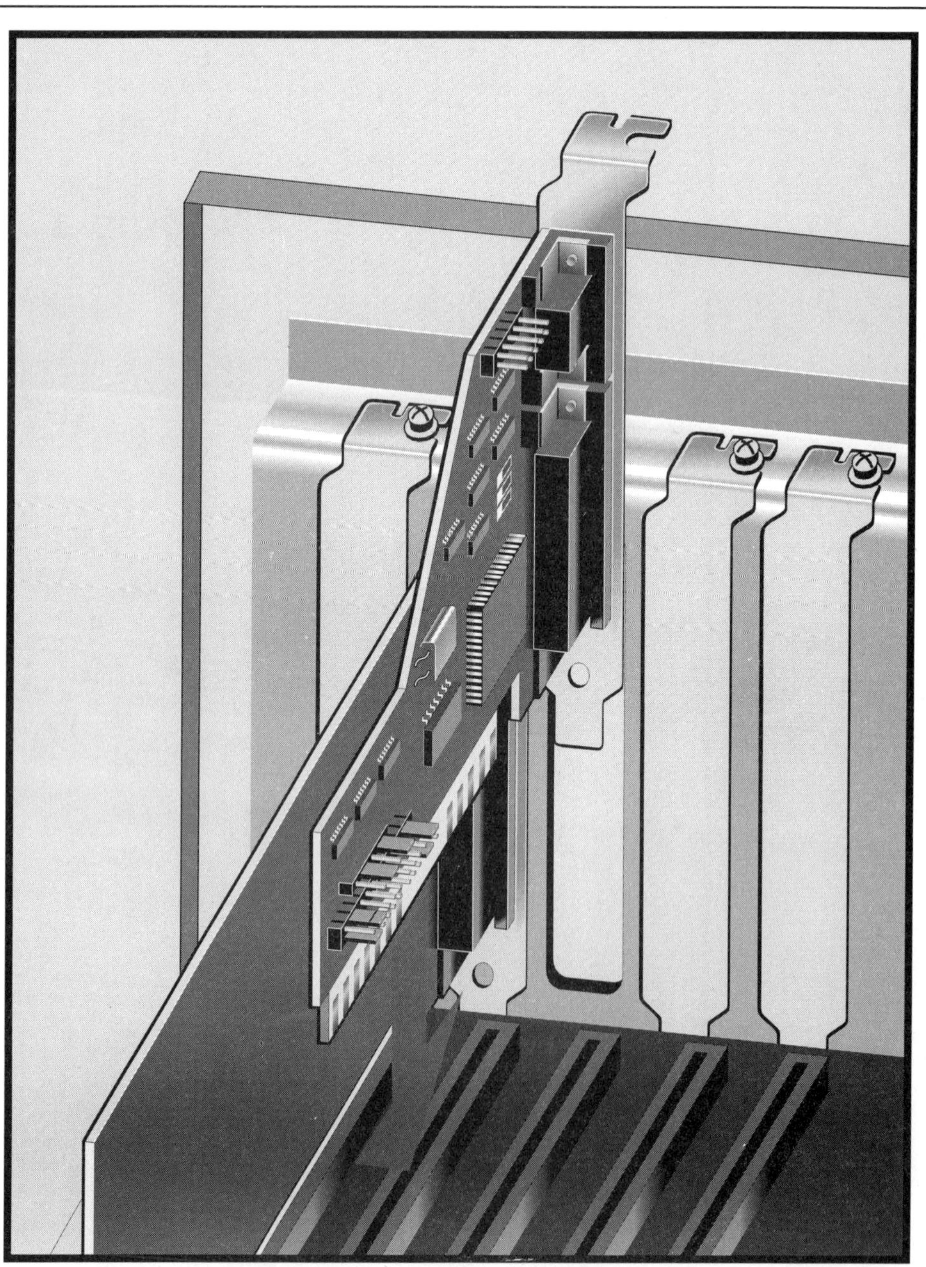

FIGURE 14.2: The expansion card slides into place.

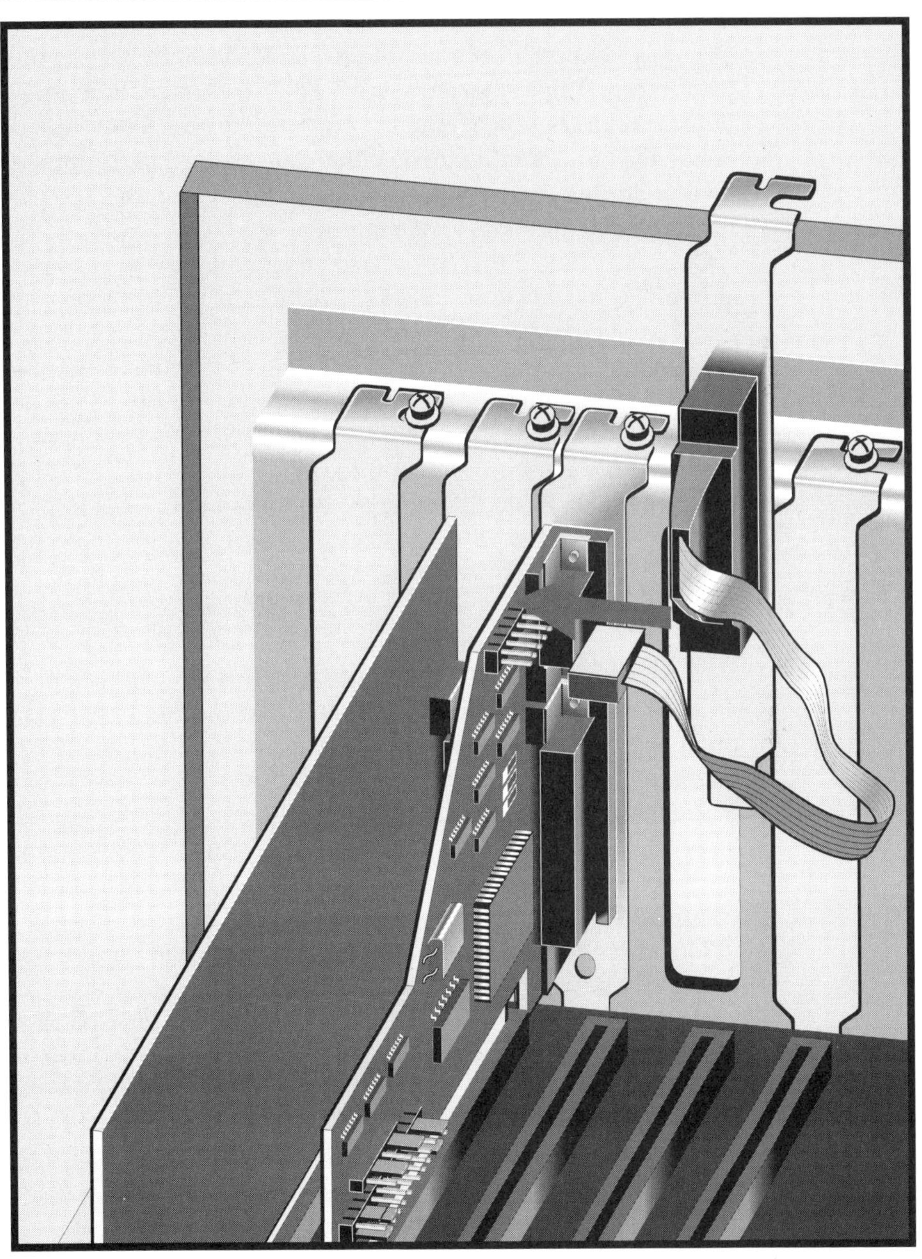

FIGURE 14.3: The interface cable runs from the port to a plug on the card.

Assigning IDs

Once you connect all of your internal and external devices, you need to assign the ID numbers. You can assign seven ID numbers, zero through six, to your devices. It doesn't matter which number you assign to which device, as long as you don't assign the same number to more than one. Setting an ID number for a device may involve adding or removing jumpers on the device, changing a switch setting, or turning a dial to choose an ID number.

One way to avoid this hassle is to buy a host adapter card and peripherals that support *SCSI Configured AutoMatically* (SCAM). SCAM is an extension of the Plug-and-Play standard developed a few years ago. If you have a SCSI host adapter card and devices that support SCAM, you can set the ID numbers via software, rather than fumbling around with the hardware itself. This is definitely the way to go because it makes the setup process easier. Most newer SCSI host adapter cards and devices should let you configure the devices with software, rather than tampering with the hardware directly.

Serial Solutions

SCSI devices are great, but that's not the end of your options if you want to expand your computer's capabilities. You can add serial and parallel ports to your computer by adding an *Input/Output (I/O) expansion card*. Serial ports transfer data 1 bit at a time, and are used primarily for devices such as your computer's mouse or modem. They are sometimes referred to as *communications* (COM) ports. Parallel ports transfer data eight bits at a time and are used primarily for printers or scanners. They are sometimes referred to as *line printer terminal* (LPT) ports. Your computer should already have at least two COM ports and one LPT port open.

You have several types of I/O cards from which to choose. You can buy one with one serial port and one parallel port, for example, or two serial and two parallel ports or more. When you are shopping for an I/O expansion card you should look for two things. First, if you are buying an I/O card with a serial port, make sure it has a 16650 Universal Asynchronous Receiver-Transmitter (UART) chip. A UART chip is designed to work with your modem. Many I/O serial cards have a 16550 UART chip, which will work with 28.8 kilobits per second (Kbps) modems. If you have a 56Kbps or V.90 modem, however, you'll want the 16650 UART chip. The 16650 UART chip can handle the faster modem speeds.

If you're a Windows 95/98 user, you also should try to get an I/O card that supports the Plug-and-Play standard. This will make installing the card much easier. Basically, all you'll have to do is install the card, install the drivers, and any software that came with the card, and you're set. If you don't get a Plug-and-Play card, however, you'll have to enter the nether regions of changing interrupt request line (IRQ) settings, which can be a big headache in Windows 95/98.

Installing the card itself is similar to installing the SCSI card discussed above. Open your computer, find an open ISA slot (the long black ones), unscrew the metal covering for that slot, and insert the card in the slot, gently rocking it back and forth until it snaps into place.

Once that's done, put the lid back on, fire up your computer, and install any device drivers or software that came with the card.

Trouble-Free USB

Installing extra serial and parallel ports will let you add extra external peripherals to your computer, but there's a better way if you're a Windows 95/98 user. Many, if not all, new PCs come with *Universal Serial Bus* (USB) ports. USB ports have several advantages over their serial and parallel counterparts. First, you won't have to configure a new USB peripheral when you install it. USB automatically configures it for you. You also don't have to restart your computer when you install a USB peripheral, thanks to a feature called hot-swapping. Hot-swapping means you can attach or detach a peripheral, and the computer will detect the change. It'll automatically make any necessary configuration changes, and you don't have to do a thing.

Furthermore, you can attach 63 peripherals to a single USB port! You do this by daisy-chaining the peripherals together, much like external SCSI devices. Most computers come with two USB ports, allowing you to connect up to 127 peripherals to your computer (they sneak an extra peripheral in there somewhere).

You can buy an expansion card that will let you add a USB port to a system that doesn't have one. However, there aren't that many on the market right now because new systems don't need them, and the demand for USB ports isn't very high. Also, you have to be a Windows 95/98 user. Windows 3.*x* and DOS users are out of luck. Furthermore, if you are using Windows 95/98, you have to have the right version. Version B supports USB while version A doesn't. If you don't have USB ports on your computer already, you probably have version A. That doesn't mean you can't install a USB card on your system, however. If you buy a USB expansion card, it should come with the necessary drivers and software updates you'll need to make it work on your system.

Installing a USB card is identical to installing a SCSI host adapter card. Open your computer, find the PCI slot, insert the card in the slot, and close the computer. Then you fire up your system, install the software, and start plugging in those peripherals.

You need plenty of flexibility if you want to take advantage of all the cool gadgets available for your computer. Follow these upgrade options to give your computer the room it needs. See Figure 14.4 for a view of all three types of port.

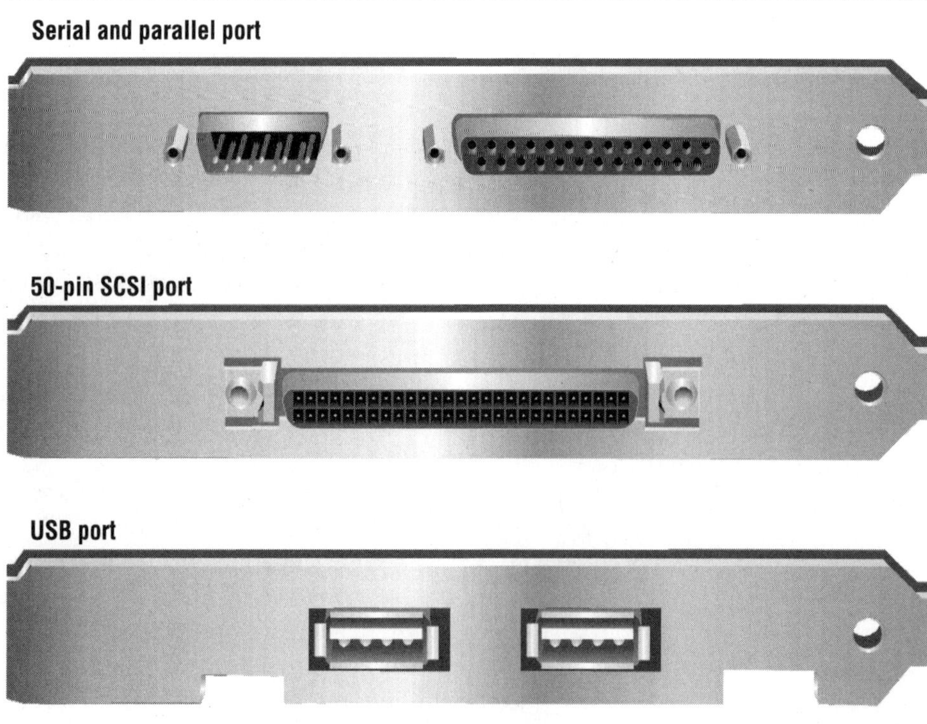

FIGURE 14.4: Any of these ports will allow you to expand your possibilities.

Are You Experienced?

Now you can...

- ☑ choose the right port or expansion card for your needs
- ☑ install a SCSI card
- ☑ install an I/O card
- ☑ install a USB port

SKILL 15

Installing a Motherboard

- Judging the need for a new motherboard
- Evaluating which components can be upgraded
- Installing a motherboard step by step
- Testing your new motherboard

Replacing the motherboard on your personal computer is one of the more challenging upgrades you can undertake, but it also will be one of the most rewarding, in terms of computing performance and personal satisfaction.

A *motherboard* consists of the circuitry that connects the computer's microprocessor (the "brains" of the PC) to devices such as the hard drive, CD-ROM drive, random access memory (RAM), and the video controller (which converts data into the signals viewed on your PC's monitor). A new motherboard lets the microprocessor communicate more quickly with these devices, which dramatically speeds up your computer.

With the possible exception of upgrading the microprocessor, no other upgrade will have as much impact on your PC's performance. And, because many motherboards are sold with new microprocessors already installed, replacing the motherboard can give your PC a double-barreled performance boost.

What You Need to Know

Tools: Phillips screwdriver, needle-nosed pliers, paper, pen, and patience (and possibly a hexdriver and utility knife)

Time: Minimum of one hour

Cost: Anywhere from $90 to $500 depending on the features built into the new motherboard and whether it comes with a new microprocessor installed. Local retailers may base their prices on trading in your old motherboard and single inline memory modules (SIMMs).

Skill Level: Difficult

Benefits: Expect dramatic improvements in data transfer rates, especially in the amount of time it takes to start large programs or open files from your disk drive. However, improved performance may require buying a new hard disk drive controller, video controller, or sound card.

Motherboard Math: When It Pays to Upgrade

Replacing the motherboard in your computer offers many performance advantages and is one of the most cost-effective upgrades you can make, but it's not for everyone.

Depending on the new motherboard, you can stand to gain:

Faster data transfer between your microprocessor and components You can trade in your old motherboard's 16-bit wide ISA expansion slots, which are capable of transferring data in 16-bit bursts at a maximum rate of 8MB per second for PCI expansion slots capable of transmitting data in 32-bit bursts at rates of 132MB per second.

TIP

Moving to a PCI controller will have the greatest impact on loading information from a hard drive or CD-ROM drive, especially large files such as databases, desktop publishing files, or audio files. In addition, many new motherboards are compatible with the new universal serial bus (USB) technology, which can move data even faster than PCI.

Access to larger hard drive Some older PCs can't recognize hard drives with more than 500MB of memory. Installing a new motherboard will let you replace your present hard drive or add a second hard drive with more capacity.

Access to more RAM If your old motherboard has only two sockets for single in-line memory modules (SIMMs), look for a motherboard with four SIMM sockets or more.

Flash BIOS If your PC is particularly old, its motherboard uses preprogrammed chips to store the Basic Input/Output System (BIOS; see Figure 15.1). To update the BIOS to work with new technology (such as larger hard drives or Plug-and-Play peripherals), you had to replace the BIOS chip. New motherboards use a *Flash BIOS*, which can be upgraded with software as technology advances.

Access to the Pentium II class microprocessors If you want to upgrade your present PC with one of Intel's new Pentium II microprocessors, you'll need an entirely new motherboard with a long, narrow Socket One design socket. (The original Pentium chips required a square Socket Seven design socket.)

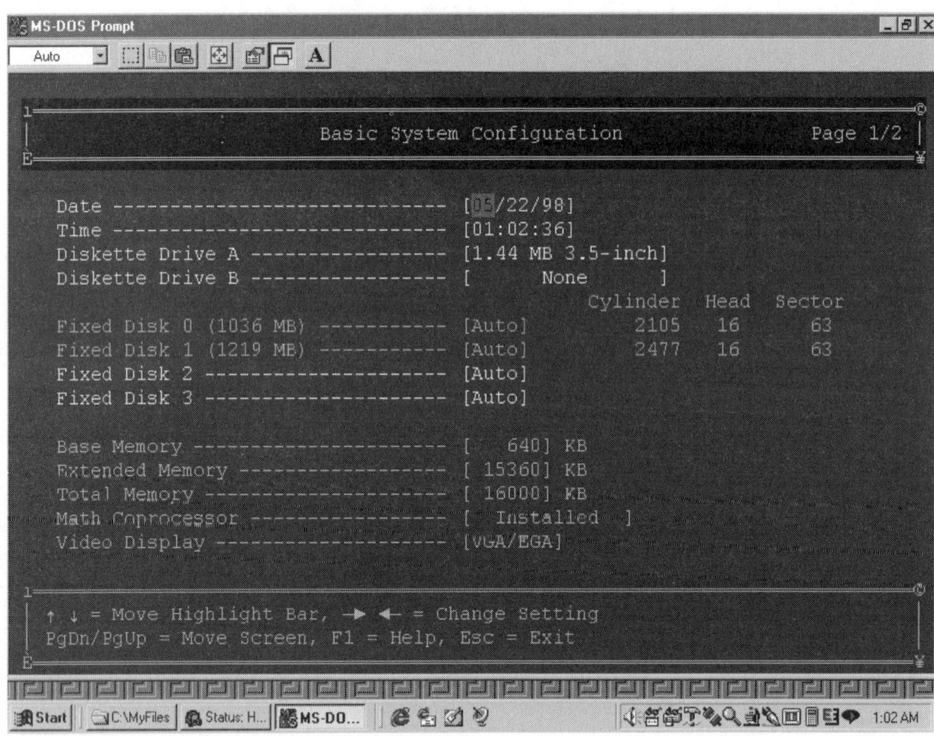

FIGURE 15.1: A computer's BIOS utility, which can be launched during logon or from DOS, provides the technical information you need to install a new motherboard.

Most manufacturers sell new motherboards with pre-installed microprocessors so you can upgrade both with the same operation. And these motherboard–microprocessor combinations cost relatively little more than either alone. For example, you can buy a motherboard without a microprocessor for as little as $90 or a motherboard and a 166MHz Intel Pentium MMX processor for $199 online.

The Downside

Motherboard upgrades make the most sense when you are happy with the performance of most of your present PC's equipment, such as the video controller, audio card, disk controller, and hard drive. A new motherboard improves the rate at which data travels from these devices to your microprocessor.

Shopping for a New Board

If you're looking for a whole new motherboard, you'll have some decisions to make; there are more boards on the market than you can shake a stick at.

Motherboards come with different socket shapes, voltages, clock speeds, and other variables. Research your present board's specifications so you know what will fit in your computer case and which hardware you want to reuse. Compatibility is essential.

Next, decide on a chip; not all CPUs fit all motherboards. With that decision made, concentrate on quality because the old adage of "you get what you pay for" rings true here. If you see one priced too good to be true, it's probably neither good nor true.

Buy a motherboard from a manufacturer that has an online presence. The World Wide Web is the best way to get the latest Flash BIOS (Basic Input/Output System) update as well as at-your-fingertips information about your motherboard. But don't rely solely on the Net. You should never buy a motherboard that doesn't come with a detailed manual. Messing with jumper settings without a manual is like playing Russian roulette with your PC.

Consider, too, how many Peripheral Component Interconnect (PCI) and Industry Standard Architecture (ISA) slots the motherboard has. The more the better. The same is true for the number of single in-line memory module (SIMM) and dual in-line memory modules (DIMM) banks. Be sure your new board supports both. Look for one that supports 32MB and larger SIMM modules so you'll have more room to upgrade that in the future.

Plug-and-Play support is a must. Buying a motherboard with support for Universal Serial Bus (USB) makes sense, too, because USB is the new standard for installing peripherals.

After you have a short list of choices, go online. Read Web pages devoted to hardware reviews. Check into newsgroups, too. Make use of other people's pain: Some people may be suffering from the same upgrade blues as you. Weed out the whiners and concentrate on the folks who seem sincere. They could help you avoid some pitfalls and make better choices.

If you're not satisfied with the performance of these devices, though, it makes little sense to upgrade the motherboard. For example, if you're using a 16-bit ISA disk controller, you won't gain any performance by installing it in a 32-bit PCI slot. Ditto for 8- and 16-bit video cards.

Besides, are you really taking advantage of your present PC's motherboard? If your PC is only one or two years old, odds are excellent that it has one or two PCI slots in the expansion bus. You may be able to cut the time it takes to load files by installing a PCI-compatible disk drive controller in one of the slots. You may improve video performance by installing a PCI-compatible video controller in another. And they're a lot simpler to install than a new motherboard.

The cost-effectiveness of a motherboard upgrade drops dramatically if your present motherboard uses built-in circuitry to control video, audio, or the disk drives. Many PCs sold for home or small business were designed with built-in controllers to hold down costs.

If you have one of these all-onboard motherboards, upgrading to a new motherboard will mean buying a whole slew of new controllers: a video controller for your monitor, audio card for your speakers, fax/modem, and hard drive controller. At $50 for a disk controller, $200 for a three-dimensional video controller, $150 for an audio card and so on, pretty soon we're talking real money.

When you reach that point, it's time to consider purchasing an entirely new computer.

When to Upgrade

You certainly don't want to spend as much on upgrading as you could spend buying a whole new system. It's essential you evaluate the upgrade's cost before jumping into the fray. The cost to upgrade a 386, for example, would far outweigh the benefits. It's ridiculous to spend several hundred dollars to get nowhere near the machine you could buy new for $1,000.

If your 486 treats you right, however, and you just want to boost its performance, upgrading some of the components on the motherboard is a viable option. Just be sure to weigh the options. Will one new component be enough to provide the boost you need, or will you need to upgrade two or three? Keep in mind that for a lot of people, a little RAM can go a long way.

Whatever your needs, consider your options and make informed decisions. And by all means, make use of that PC manual.

The Preliminaries

The motherboard, also known as the *system board* or *main board*, is a green board embedded with circuits that connect transistors, sockets, slots, and integrated circuits (or *chips*). It is attached to the computer case with screws and stand-off posts.

Finding Your Way around the Motherboard

The microprocessor, single in-line memory modules (SIMMs, or RAM chips), expansion cards (such as internal fax/modems), keyboard, and mouse all plug into sockets or slots on the motherboard (see Figure 15.2). Some motherboards use built-in circuits to control the disk drive and hard drive, and others use built-in circuitry to convert data into the images displayed on the computer's monitor. This is particularly true of budget PCs sold for home and small-business use.

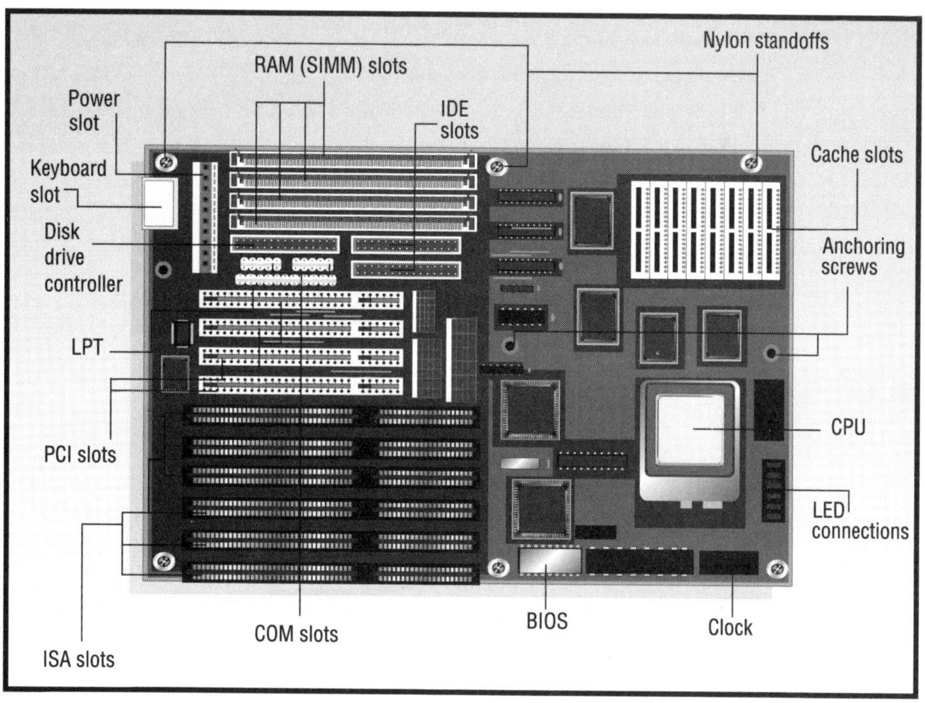

FIGURE 15.2: It's a good idea to become familiar with the different parts of a motherboard before beginning installation.

Most PCs don't use these onboard controllers. Instead, special circuit boards called *expansion boards* or *expansion cards* that you insert into the motherboard's expansion bus perform these functions. Usually, you can tell by opening your case whether these circuits are built into the motherboard or onto expansion cards. If not, consult your PC's owner's manual.

Ribbon cables (flat, wide cables) and wires attach the motherboard to other devices attached to the case, including the power supply (which converts 110-volt alternating current into lower-voltage direct current used by the PC), disk drives, and a small speaker. Some carry data and some supply power.

Except in the oldest IBM PCs and IBM XT computers, the motherboard will fall into one of three basic categories: an AT-style motherboard, a baby AT motherboard, or an ATX motherboard. Each type offers a seemingly endless variety of options ranging from the number and type of expansion slots (Industry Standard Architecture [ISA], Peripheral Component Interconnect [PCI], Video Electronics Standards Association [VESA], etc.), the type of Basic Input/Output System (BIOS) chips, and even the type of microprocessor socket.

New motherboards feature either a Socket Seven or Socket One design. The Socket Seven design is a small, white square perforated with holes designed to accept the pin connectors in the bottom of a conventional Pentium-class microprocessor. The newer Socket One design is a long, narrow socket that rises from the motherboard and accepts the Intel Pentium II microprocessor (which is approximately the size and shape of a candy bar). You can choose a motherboard with Socket Seven or Socket One, but you won't find both on the same motherboard.

Replaceable Parts

We take a look at the hardware components that connect to the motherboard and your upgrading options.

CPU

If the motherboard is the computer's backbone, the *CPU*, also known as the microprocessor or processor, is its brain. The CPU processes information and sends data to the appropriate hardware destinations.

Two numbers are used to classify microprocessors: type and speed. Types of processors developed by processor giant Intel include 386, 486, Pentium, Pentium Pro, and Pentium II. Speed is measured in megahertz. For example, a Pentium 166 is shorthand for a Pentium chip running at 166 megahertz (MHz).

Upgrading CPU speed while staying with the same type of chip is simple thanks to *zero-insertion force* (ZIF) CPU sockets; usually the old CPU easily snaps out and the new one snaps in with no force used by the installer. Users with older Pentium PCs, for instance, might be able to drop in a new Pentium 200MHz MMX processor for a faster and more powerful system.

Going from one type of processor to another is more difficult. Unfortunately, you can't just plug a Pentium chip into a 486-based motherboard. Intel has made things even more difficult for people wanting to upgrade to a Pentium II processor by redesigning the chip as a long narrow piece instead of the standard square chip. Because of this, if you want a Pentium II, you'll need a whole new motherboard or a whole new computer. The same is true of the Pentium Pro.

If your motherboard won't accept even standard Pentium chips, you might want to take a look at Intel's line of OverDrive Pentium chips. These CPUs are designed to bring today's speeds to older motherboards. Unfortunately, anything older than a 486 clocking at 50MHz is out of luck. The latest Pentium OverDrive chips add MMX technology in addition to increasing speed, but these are only available for Pentium sockets. Another choice is to skip Intel altogether and go with a competing chip from AMD or Cyrix (see the "More Than Intel Inside" sidebar).

Before you add any new processor to the board, you'll need to iron out voltage issues. As processors improve, they are designed to use less power. This fact can lead to ugly results if you try to replace a CPU that's been running on five volts with a newer one that uses only 3.3 volts with no compensation for the difference. Resolving this problem can be easy if the new CPU replacement comes equipped with a voltage regulator.

More Than Intel Inside

AMD (Advanced Micro Devices) and Cyrix were at one time considered cheap Intel knockoffs. Today, these once poor cousins offer an economical alternative to Intel without scrimping on performance.

Both brands consistently perform well against Intel. The best thing about these non-Intel chips is users often can achieve Pentium II performance without throwing out their whole motherboard. In contrast to Intel's redesign of the Pentium II chip, AMD and Cyrix still offer chips designed for the zero-insertion force (ZIF) Socket Seven chip socket, making it possible for consumers with adequately supported older boards to upgrade to Pentium II performance levels.

continued

One problem with comparing Intel and AMD or Cyrix chips is that in some ways you're comparing apples to oranges. AMD and Cyrix both use a different performance architecture than Intel, so chips that appear equal in terms of speed-measure numbers such as clock speed may be nothing alike.

The best way to solve this comparison glitch is to look at CPU *benchmark tests*. These tests use systems that are identical in every way except for the CPU and perform a scripted set of applications on each one, noting the performance differences. With benchmark tests, you can see that faster clock speed doesn't necessarily indicate a faster computer.

Use the benchmark ratings to make decisions based on your needs and upgrading plans. Using something other than Intel inside can be daunting, so be sure you've done your homework and make an informed decision.

RAM

Often, the easiest component to upgrade on the motherboard is memory. *Random access memory* (RAM) is memory that acts as temporary storage and is read from and written to by the CPU and hardware peripherals. RAM affects your PC's performance and reliability. Newer applications require more memory than older programs, so RAM is increasingly important. Thankfully, memory is easy to upgrade.

Most motherboards include slots for adding memory. RAM upgrades usually involve little more than pushing the new modules into these slots. Typically, RAM comes in the form of *single in-line memory modules* (SIMMs), but there are other types, as well. *Dual in-line memory modules* (DIMMs) have a different pin configuration than SIMMs and won't fit into the motherboard's SIMM slots. *Extended Data Out RAM* (EDO RAM) comes in a SIMM package, but it may not be compatible with some motherboards, particularly on 486-class computers. To find out which types of RAM work in your system, check your computer manual or call the manufacturer.

Cache

Cache is a bank of high-speed memory set aside for frequently-accessed data. Many microprocessors have small built-in memory areas called *Level 1* (L1) caches. These caches generally cannot be upgraded.

The larger secondary or *Level 2* (L2) cache is external to the microprocessor and may be upgraded. L2 cache is present in almost all Pentium-class computers and usually is made up of *static RAM* (SRAM). SRAM is much faster than plain-old RAM and certainly more expensive. Intel integrates SRAM memory into the chip packaging of both the Pentium Pro and Pentium II CPUs. This optimizes performance, but denies the user a simple upgrade. Replacing the entire CPU (or the CPU module in the Pentium II) is the only way to increase L2 cache size for these systems.

Some manufacturers solder the L2 cache directly to the motherboard. This doesn't make it impossible to upgrade, but it isn't something we would recommend you do yourself. Other manufacturers use socketed, edge-connected modules that plug into the motherboard like RAM.

Because L2 cache comes in a few varieties, sizes, and speeds, you should again turn to your trusty manual to decide what is right for your system.

BIOS

Another essential part of the motherboard is the *BIOS*. Although some refer to BIOS as software, it's actually a kind of *firmware*, instructions encoded directly in hardware circuitry. It performs many background tasks, such as testing components to see if they are functioning properly when you start up your computer. When you see lights flashing on your disk drives or on the keyboard immediately after you power up, that's the BIOS doing its daily routine. When finished with this inventory ritual, the BIOS loads the operating system.

BIOS comes in two forms: flash and nonflash. Most computer systems sold in the past couple of years use flash BIOS, which is easy to upgrade. Users just visit the manufacturer or vendor site on the World Wide Web, download updated software, and then follow the installation instructions.

Nonflash BIOS isn't as easy to upgrade; you must remove the old BIOS chip and replace it. To find out the make and version of your BIOS, you'll need the BIOS information that briefly appears at the top of the screen during startup. Without bionic eyes, however, you'll need some help writing the information down. To get to the BIOS utility, check your manual for instructions.

System Clock

This is the motherboard's watch. The quartz crystal clock coordinates all timing applications and keeps everything moving at an even clip. Should it ever fail to operate properly, you should take it to a professional for repair. If that becomes too costly, chuck it for a whole new motherboard.

The system clock should not be confused with the time and date clock you view on the desktop. This CMOS clock (also located on the motherboard) keeps track of this time while the computer is off. This clock is maintained through the motherboard's CMOS (complementary metal-oxide semiconductor) battery. Unlike the system clock, this battery can be replaced easily if it isn't soldered to the motherboard; pull the old one out and snap in the new one. For more details, check the computer's manual.

Graphics and Sound

Sound and video cards typically slip into motherboard expansion slots, and upgrading to the latest three-dimensional (3-D) video and wavetable audio standards means pulling the old switcheroo.

Expansion slots are not necessarily alike. Determine the type of bus your computer uses before choosing a new card. A bus is the electronic connection through which a computer transfers information. Today's standards are the Peripheral Component Interconnect (PCI) bus and the Universal Serial Bus (USB). Still, many motherboards contain slots for older standards such as Industry Standard Architecture (ISA) and Extended ISA (EISA). That dog-eared manual should come in handy when making this determination, too.

Ports

Adding more ports to your system lets you add more plug-in peripherals. Special expansion cards plug into the motherboard and extend the additional ports out the back of the computer. These add-ons are called serial and parallel ports. *Serial* refers to communication ports that connect to peripherals, such as modems, that transfer data one bit at a time. *Parallel* ports typically are used to connect to devices, such as printers, that transfer data over more than one wire at a time.

A Small Computer System Interface (SCSI) host adapter allows you to add SCSI-supported peripherals. The host adapter usually fits into a PCI slot and has two attachments. One is a ribbon cable that hooks to internal devices; the other is a special SCSI cable. Through this external cable, you'll be able to *daisy chain* devices together, which means you can plug a peripheral into the host adapter, then plug a second peripheral into the first one, and so on. In doing so, you will have created a SCSI bus that acts as an electronic pathway between the adapter and the SCSI devices.

The sticky part of adding additional ports is dealing with address problems and interrupt request lines (IRQs). Every installed device has an IRQ address that determines its order in requesting actions from the computer. Conflicts arise when different devices are assigned the same IRQ address and try to use it simultaneously. Keep in mind that if you add new ports, you'll need to know which IRQ addresses are already assigned so you can avoid this traffic jam. Using expansion cards that support Plug-and-Play technology is one way to avoid this mess.

Exploring Your Options

Ironically, your motherboard choices are limited only by the computer's lowest technology component: the case itself. Both the AT motherboard and the baby AT motherboard (which simply is a more compact version of the original AT) can fit in one type of case. The newer ATX motherboard, however, requires an entirely different case design. You'll also have to make certain the case has enough openings in the back for all of the slots in your new motherboard's expansion bus.

NOTE NOTE NOTE NOTE NOTE NOTE NOTE NOTE NOTE NOTE NOTE NOTE NOTE NOTE NOTE

If your new motherboard has a mouse socket built into it, make sure your old case has a hole for the mouse socket. If not, you'll need to drill a hole or cut one with a hacksaw before installing the new motherboard.

Fortunately, AT, baby AT, and ATX motherboards are built to an industry standard that defines the exact location of expansion slots, keyboard sockets, etc. That means most computer cases have holes in the right places for sockets, stand-off posts, bolts, and so on.

Unfortunately, though, a handful of computer manufacturers deviate from these standards. Instead of building the expansion slots directly onto the motherboard, for example, they use a second *daughterboard* (sometimes called a *riser*) to hold the expansion slots. Before you attempt to replace your motherboard, make sure your present computer doesn't use one of these nonstandard designs. (Your best bet: Tell the motherboard sales rep the manufacturer and model of the PC you're upgrading.)

Installation

Replacing a motherboard requires the usual tools: a Phillips screwdriver and a pair of needle-nosed pliers. If your computer case uses special hex nuts, you may need a special hexdriver to open it. A razor knife or utility knife also may come in handy, as will your PC's owner's manual and any documentation that came with the new motherboard.

The three most important tools you'll need are a pen, paper, and patience. Replacing a motherboard takes at least an hour; much longer if you need to call a technical support line.

Recording CMOS Information

Before you do anything, make a record of information stored on your present motherboard's *complementary metal-oxide semiconductor (CMOS)* chip. The CMOS tells the computer what kind of hardware is installed (such as the microprocessor and hard drives) and how to communicate with it, information that may have to be programmed into the new motherboard's CMOS.

Your computer will display the CMOS information on-screen when you press a specific key or key combination while the PC is booting up. Sometimes, the PC will display a message such as "Press Delete to display CMOS information."

With some PCs, you'll need to press the F1 key when turning it on. With others, you'll type Ctrl+Alt+Enter or Ctrl+Alt+Esc at the C:\> prompt. If none of these works, consult your owner's manual index under CMOS.

Record *everything* in the CMOS display. Even if you don't understand what it means, the computer does. And you may need it with the new motherboard.

Step by Step

Once you've got the CMOS information, you're ready to begin.

1. Unplug everything from the computer: power cords, keyboard and mouse cables, the monitor cable, Zip drives, etc.
2. Before you open the computer case, discharge any static electricity that you may have built up. (Touch a doorknob, the metal part of a desk, anything to ground yourself and discharge the electricity.) Even the smallest spark of static electricity can fry a circuit and ruin a board.
3. Once the case is open, make a rough sketch of the PC's inner workings. Now start to disconnect the wires and cables that connect the myriad of components to the motherboard. You will find three types of wires in the motherboard: wires that supply power, wires that transfer data, and wires that turn indicator lights on and off.
    - Power wires will run from the power supply to the motherboard, disk drive, and some expansion cards in the expansion bus, such

as the disk drive controller. Not all devices draw power from the power supply. Some, such as the video controller, will take all the power they need from the expansion slot socket. If your computer uses a small fan to keep the microprocessor from overheating, a small power lead will run from the motherboard to the fan.

- Data transfer wires connect the disk drives to the motherboard.
- Wires connect some devices inside the computer to indicator lights on the exterior of the computer. For example, a wire leading from the drive controller indicates when the hard drive is downloading data to the microprocessor. Another indicator wire shows whether the PC is turned on.

4. Every time you disconnect a wire or a cable, make a note on your sketch. Each note should include:
    - The location of the motherboard connector or expansion board to which the cable or wire was attached. With the exception of the larger connectors for the ribbon cables, there should be a small mark on the motherboard. Some will be labeled plainly, such as Pwr LED for the connector that leads to the power light on the front of the case or Spkr for the connector to the internal speaker. Some will use more cryptic labels, such as J7.
    - Any marking on the cable or wire plug, such as Spkr or Pwr LED.
    - The color and number of the wires for each connector.

NOTE NOTE NOTE NOTE NOTE NOTE NOTE NOTE NOTE NOTE NOTE NOTE NOTE NOTE NOTE

This information will help you when you are reconnecting the wires and cables to the proper plugs after you install the motherboard.

5. Now, remove any expansion cards from the old motherboard's expansion bus (Figure 15.3). Unscrew the plate that holds the expansion cards to the back of the PC case, then lift them up and out of their sockets. Be careful with these cards; you will almost certainly need them for the new motherboard.
6. You also can reuse the old motherboard's SIMMs in the new motherboard. To remove a SIMM, release the spring that holds it in place, then tilt it back from its upright position and slide it out of the socket.

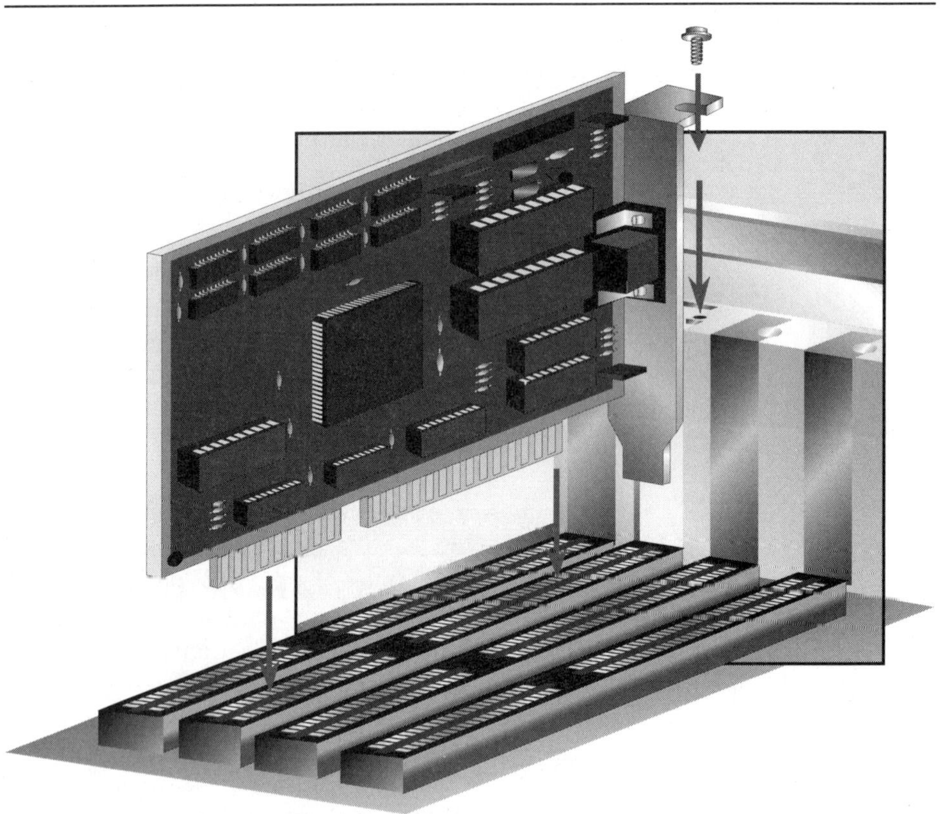

FIGURE 15.3: Expansion cards must be handled carefully.

7. Most likely, you'll also need to remove the power supply, a hard drive, a disk drive, a CD-ROM drive, or any combination of these devices before you can remove the motherboard. Be careful, especially with the hard drive. You'll definitely want to reuse it with the new motherboard.

8. Find the bolts that hold the motherboard to the case. There will only be two or three. Now you're ready to remove the motherboard. This is a bit tricky. Although screws hold the motherboard firmly to the case, small stand-off posts or *spacers* keep the motherboard from touching the case and creating electrical short circuits. The posts fit in a hole-and-slot socket in the case, so you have to *slide* the motherboard out of the slot before you can *lift* the posts out of the hole (Figure 15.4).

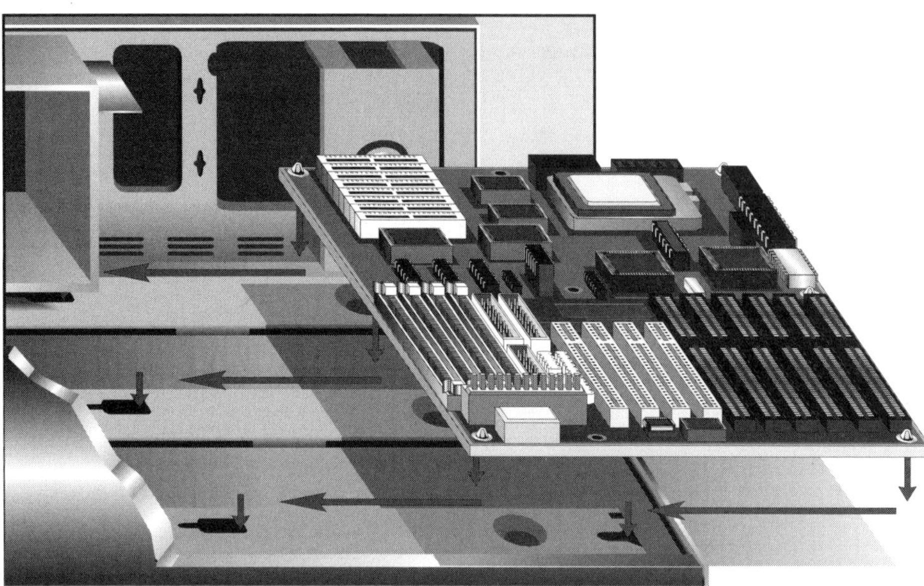

FIGURE 15.4: With the screws out, it's time to remove the motherboard.

9. Small plastic tabs keep the stand-off posts from slipping out of the holes in the motherboard. Once you have the motherboard out of the case, use needle-nosed pliers to depress the tabs on the posts, then pull the posts through the bottom of the motherboard. (Be careful. The bottom of the motherboard has lots of small sharp wire ends that can cut your fingertips.)
10. Before installing the stand-off posts on the new motherboard, test fit the motherboard by lowering it into the case to see where the holes for the spacers and the screws line up. Check how the expansion slots and mouse and keyboard sockets line up with openings in the case, too.

Don't be concerned if the new board is smaller than the previous motherboard (particularly if you've moved from an AT to a baby AT-style motherboard). As long as all of the holes and sockets on the new motherboard line up with appropriate holes in the case, you're in good shape.

Reassembly and Reconfiguration

You're half way there.

1. Look over your new motherboard and make a rough sketch of the connectors and sockets that will connect it to your hard drive, power supply, etc. It will be a lot easier to read the small type on the motherboard now than after you've installed it in the case. If your motherboard came with a schematic (a diagram showing the connectors and sockets), compare it to the motherboard now.
2. You're ready to install the new motherboard. Insert the new microprocessor in the motherboard and install the SIMMs (Figure 15.5).

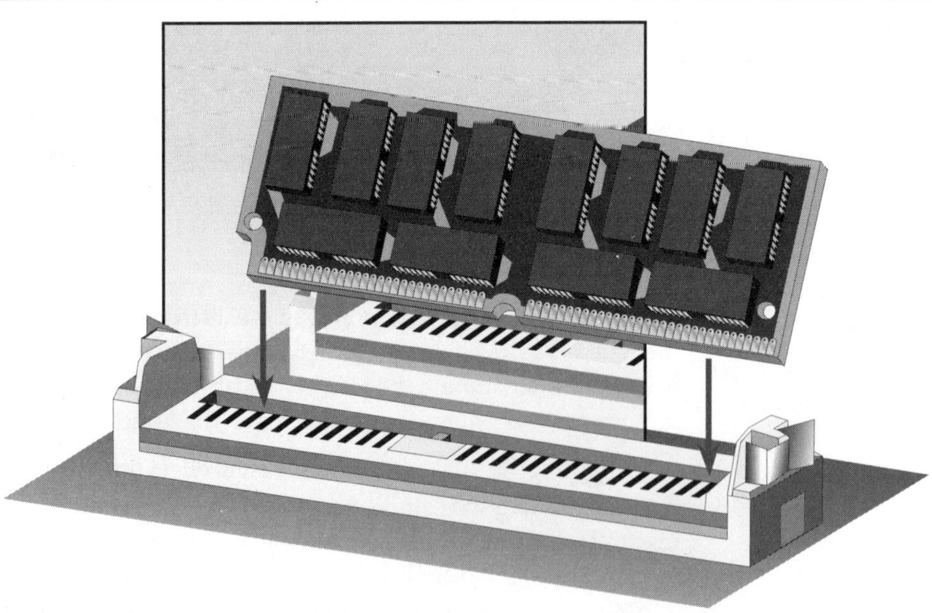

FIGURE 15.5: Slide the SIMM into its slot at a 45-degree angle.

3. Insert the stand-off posts by pushing them up through the bottom of the motherboard until the plastic clips snap into place. Lower the motherboard into the case so the posts fit into the appropriate mounting holes, then slide the board until the spacers are snug in the slots. Screw the motherboard in place.

4. Replace the power supply, hard drive, and any other components that you removed from the case to take out the motherboard.
5. Reattach the wires and cables to the motherboard. Use the notes you made during disassembly to identify the wires and cables, then insert them into the appropriate connectors on the motherboard.

NOTE

Don't be surprised if you have a few wires with no sockets, especially if you have a three- or four-year–old computer case. Older PCs had a *turbo* switch that could be used to speed up the motherboard's internal clock and had two sets of wires: one connecting the switch to the motherboard and another connecting the motherboard to a *light-emitting diode* (LED, indicator light) to show whether the turbo function was turned on. New PCs automatically operate at the fastest clock speed, so these sets of wires aren't accounted for on new motherboards. Just tie them in a knot so they won't touch the motherboard and push them out of the way.

6. Your new motherboard may be equipped with built-in circuits that control communications to the disk drives, monitors, and external speakers. What you do next depends on whether you want to use these built-in "controllers" or use controllers that plug in to the expansion bus.
   - If you use the built-in controllers, life is easy. Install the ribbon cable attached to the disk drives to the disk drive controller socket on the motherboard. Plug the monitor cable and speaker wires to the sockets on the back of the computer case. That's it; they're installed.
   - If you don't use these built-in controllers, life is a bit more difficult. Start by inserting the controller cards into sockets (slots) on the new motherboard's expansion bus. Screw the metal plate at the rear of the controller card into the case. (This simply keeps it from wiggling around and coming loose.)
7. You're not done yet. The CMOS chip on your new motherboard expects to use the built-in controllers. If the hard drives, etc., are not plugged into the onboard controller, CMOS won't know where to find them and will act as if they don't exist.

That means you'll need to disable these devices, then reinstruct the CMOS where to find them. To disable the onboard controllers, consult the technical documents that came with the new motherboard. If the documentation doesn't provide the information you need, it's time to call the technical support number for the motherboard manufacturer.

Sometimes, disabling a controller may require moving tiny jumpers (which connect two or more wires to complete a circuit) or flipping dual in-line package (DIP) switches. But with today's motherboards, it's unlikely you'll ever touch a jumper or a DIP switch. It's more likely that you'll reconfigure the motherboard using the CMOS when you boot up the PC for the first time.

If your new motherboard doesn't have built-in controllers, simply re-install your old controller cards. Remember to connect wires from the power supply to the controller cards.

Getting Connected

Refer frequently to the notes you made during the disassembly process. For example, inserting a ribbon cable backward in its socket will prevent the computer from communicating with the disk drives. That will prevent the computer from booting.

1. Two physically identical cables connect the power supply to side-by-side sockets in the motherboard. Refer to your notes and the color patterns of the cable to insert them in the proper order.
2. The sockets at the ends of the wires on your computer may need some trimming to fit the sockets on the new motherboard. For example, some PCs use a tongue and groove design for the power supply plug and socket. If the old power supply plug has tongues, but the new motherboard power socket doesn't have grooves, you'll need to very carefully trim the tongues off of the connector. A razor knife, such as a utility knife or Exacto knife, will probably do the job on the plastic connector.
3. Occasionally, the plug on the end of a wire won't fit in the space provided for it on the new motherboard. You may be able use the razor knife to trim the plug if—and only if—a four-wire plug was used on a two-wire line. You can trim away the excess plastic as long as you don't expose the wires or metal connectors.

If this makes you skittish, contact the motherboard manufacturer's technical support line.

Test Flying Your New Motherboard

Once you've re-installed all of the devices and completed all of the necessary internal connections, insert the cables connecting the PC to the keyboard, mouse, and monitor. (To keep things simple and uncluttered, don't plug in any optional devices such as speakers, Zip drives, or modems just yet.) Attach the power cables and turn on the PC. Leave the case off the computer just in case things don't work perfectly at first.

The new motherboard will automatically run a *power on self test* (POST) to look for all of the devices the CMOS tells it should be attached. Because this is the first time the motherboard has been turned on, it almost certainly won't recognize all of the hardware. When this happens, the computer will instruct you to enter the CMOS setup program. Remember the CMOS notes that you made before you removed the old motherboard? This is where they come in.

Go through the new CMOS menu item by item. Where the CMOS doesn't list a device that was listed on your old motherboard's CMOS, insert the appropriate information. Generally, you will use the keyboard's arrow keys to move through the CMOS menu and change the selection. In only a few instances should you actually have to type in information.

You may encounter a situation where the new motherboard's CMOS simply won't offer menu options that match the devices attached to your computer. One good example is a really old hard drive. If that happens, choose the "AUTO" or "AUTOMATIC" option in that menu. With any kind of luck at all, the new, sophisticated motherboard will configure itself to work with the device.

Trial, Error, and Success

There will be a certain amount of trial and error before you get the computer working exactly the way it used to. But don't stop there. Now is the time to start experimenting with the performance capabilities of the new motherboard. With faster access to your hard drives, for instance, you may decide to reduce that amount of hard drive memory that you set aside to cache information. You might install a new fax/modem that takes advantage of the new motherboard's faster universal serial bus (USB) or PCI expansion slots. You may enable video and audio functions that once dragged your computer's performance down to a snail's pace.

Go ahead and experiment. After changing the motherboard, you can do almost anything.

Are You Experienced?

Now you can...

- ☑ evaluate the pros and cons of an upgrade
- ☑ understand which parts of your computer can be upgraded
- ☑ install a new motherboard
- ☑ test your new motherboard

SKILL 16

Installing a Power Supply

- Evaluating your need for a new power supply
- Understanding how power supplies work
- Installing a new power supply

Power supplies never need any kind of fuel, unlike your car, a 727, or a commuter train's locomotive. Why not? What we call a *power supply* actually is a power converter because it converts potentially lethal 110-115 or 220-230 volt alternating current (AC) into low-voltage direct current (DC). Traditionally, power supplies for desktop computers have provided two DC voltage levels: 5 volt for powering memory and other computer chip power supplies, including the central processing unit (CPU), and 12 volt for powering disk drives and other motors.

The process of converting AC to DC current and reducing its voltage creates a lot of heat, and this is why normal power supplies feature an onboard fan. The fan dissipates heat generated by the AC-DC conversion process, and motors and chip power supplies on the motherboard.

What You Need to Know

Tools: Flat-head and Phillips screwdrivers

Time: 45 minutes

Cost: $50–$75

Skill Level: Intermediate

Benefits: More reliable system performance, ability to add more drives and cards reliably, and longer system life

Power supplies are the invisible heart of the computer. While everyone wants to know what processor your new PC boasts, few people care about the power supply until it fails. When a power supply fails, though, this obscure component will be noticed.

Knowing When It's Time for a Change

A failing power supply provides several clues that should be heeded before it stops working completely. Spontaneous rebooting is an important symptom. The power supply has a single orange cable that runs to the motherboard. This carries the *power good* signal, and its rated level is 5 volts. If the power supply sends a significant undercurrent (2.4 volts or less) or a slight overcurrent (more than 5.2 volts DC) to this line, the computer will reboot without warning, and all unsaved files are lost.

A second major symptom is a noisy fan. The fan is integral to the power supply, and worn-out bearings indicate it's time to replace the power supply. If the fan stops turning, this also can indicate a fan failure. Because dangerously (even fatally) high levels of current remain in the coils of the power supply's voltage converter, you should never open the power supply and try to replace a fan. If the fan is dead, get a new power supply.

Another indication of a possible power supply problem is an overheating computer. Signs of overheating include system lockups after the computer has reached operating temperature, and a too-hot-to-touch power supply enclosure. Overheating can result from an excessive wattage load on the power supply. Each drive, chip, and motor in your system uses some of the total wattage rating of your power supply. If your power supply has a rating of at least 200 watts, it is large enough to drive your system and all normal internal devices.

Check All the Possibilities

Before you assume an overheating power supply means it's time for a replacement, make sure you have a properly cooled system. Verify all slot covers are in place along the back side of the case. Make sure the power supply air intakes are clean, and the power supply fan is clean and turns properly. Clean the air intakes on the computer case, and avoid blocking them with items such as sticky notes, books, etc.

The most obvious sign of a power supply failure is if you turn the system on and nothing happens. If that occurs, check the plug, the cord, the surge protector, and the circuit. If they are OK but there's no power getting to your system, check the voltage selector switch. In North America, it should be set to 110/115 volts. If it's set to 220/230 volts, the computer will not start up. Next, check to see if your computer has a replaceable fuse. If there's no fuse, or you've replaced it, you need to look for short circuits or incorrect voltage levels inside the computer.

A short circuit can be caused by any metal-to-metal contact over a powered circuit. Look for loose screws, loose cards touching each other, and broken or badly worn power supply connectors. If your system uses Y-splitters to turn a single power cable into a dual power feed, keep in mind bad connections where the two cables come together also can cause a short. Remove any Y-splitters before you assume the power supply is bad.

Check voltage levels with a multimeter. To do so, set the multimeter to read DC voltage. Take the black probe and hold it firmly on the power supply case (not the grill or any exposed area). Select an unused ISA expansion slot (PCI slots are shorter and have narrower connectors) and look at the left side of the slot (the side away from the power supply). Firmly push the red probe against the connectors listed in Table 16.1 and see if the readings fall within the listed limits.

TABLE 16.1: Connector Voltage

Connector	Rated	Minimum	Maximum
B3 (B1 is at rear of motherboard)	+5 volts	+4.8 volts	+5.2 volts
B5	–5 volts	–4.5 volts	–5.4 volts
B9	+12 volts	+11.5 volts	+12.6 volts
B7	–12 volts	–10.8 volts	–12.9 volts

If any of these readings are incorrect, turn off the computer. Remove all expansion cards and try the readings again. If you now get good readings, replace each card and redo the readings until you insert a card that causes the readings to fail. If your readings are still bad with all cards removed, replace the power supply.

Power Supply Types

As with many other computer technologies, there is no such thing as *the* power supply. Instead, there are various types from which you need to select the correct version.

If your computer is from a major manufacturer, call the company or check its Web site for prices. You may discover the cost is substantially higher than a third-party unit, but you may not have a choice. If your system uses a proprietary case design, it may require a special power supply, as well. You may not be able to buy a higher wattage-rated unit either. But, before you assume you're locked into a high-priced unit from the computer maker, check with power-supply specialists.

There may be a customized unit available with the features and pricing you'll like. Check these Web sites for more information:

- `http://www.pcpowercooling.com`
- `http://www.power-on.com`
- `http://www.jdr.com`
- `http://www.amtrade.com`

Opening It Up

If your computer uses a standard desktop or tower case, you have more choices and more homework to do before buying a new unit. You'll need a screwdriver or hexdriver to open the computer's case. Once you've opened the case, look for red, yellow, and black wires running from the disk drives and the motherboard. At the other end, you'll find the power supply.

Most computers today have a push-button on/off switch that has an extension cable to the actual power supply. Or, it may have an on/off switch directly on the side of the power supply case. Either way, measure the width, height, and depth of the unit and look at the rear of the computer, where the power supply attaches to the case. Your new power supply must have the same dimensions, mounting holes, and switch type to be a suitable replacement.

Typically, you'll find a data sheet on the top of the power supply, listing its voltage requirements and wattage rating. Your new unit should have at least the same wattage rating, and if you plan to use most of the expansion slots and drive bays, a higher-rated unit would be desirable to provide plenty of power for additional devices.

Check the power leads of your existing power supply unit. Chances are your present unit is using Y-splitters to provide power for all internal drives. If the splitter wires and connections aren't loose or frayed, they can be removed and used on the new power supply.

Finally, look at the power supply connection to the motherboard. Most computers manufactured before 1997 use two six-wire connectors to attach to a 12-wire motherboard power connector. If your computer uses a 20-wire connector (two rows of 10 connectors) you need an ATX power supply, which uses the extra connectors to provide the 3.5-volt level used by newer processors and automatic power-down features.

Armed with this information, you can purchase your new power supply and start the upgrade procedure.

Upgrading a Power Supply

To get started, turn off the computer, remove the cover and locate the power supply. Now you're ready to begin.

1. Note the location of the power supply and how it is mounted. Typically, four screws attach the back of the power supply to the computer case's back wall, and one or two screws attach the bottom edge of the power supply to a retaining shelf inside the case (see Figure 16.1). The screws that hold the power supply on the back of the unit are around the edges of the power supply. Many power supplies have a pair of screws flanking the voltage adjustment switch. Don't remove these at any time.

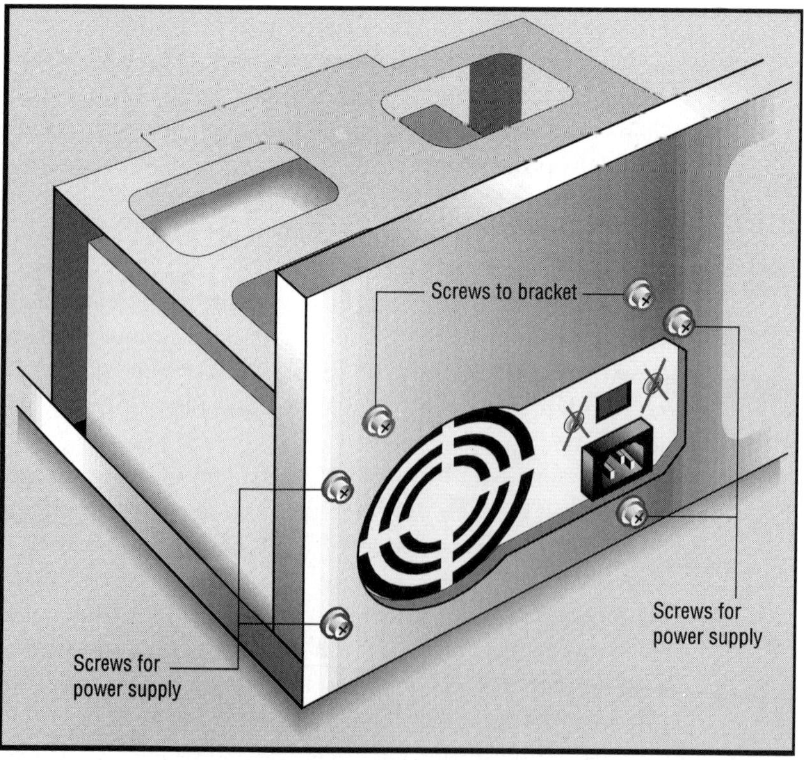

FIGURE 16.1: The power supply is usually at the back of the computer on the right side.

NOTE NOTE NOTE NOTE NOTE NOTE NOTE NOTE NOTE NOTE NOTE NOTE NOTE NOTE NOTE

On some systems, there also may be a bracket holding the power supply in place. Loosen the screws and carefully remove the bracket.

2. Carefully move the ribbon cables for drives and ports away from the power supply leads.
3. Before removing the power connectors from the motherboard, note the orientation of the cables. The six-pin connector with an orange cable is usually marked P8, and the other one is P9. The new power supply will be attached to the motherboard in the same way. The black wires of P8 and P9 will need to be placed together when the new power supply is connected to the motherboard.
4. Trace the power connectors that go to the disk drives back to the power supply. You may discover some drives are getting power from a Y-splitter cable. In this case, you'd remove the power connector from the Y-splitter and leave the splitter connected to the drives. Disconnect the power connectors that run from the motherboard from disk drives and the motherboard. Note which drives use a large four-wire connector (a "Molex") and which use the small four-wire connector. Pull on the connectors, not the wires, to remove them from the drives and motherboard. See Figure 16.2.

5. If your CPU chip has a fan on top, most of these use a patch cable that attaches to a large four-wire drive connector and provides a pass-through to provide power to a drive. Be very careful when you remove these. We suggest removing the power connector from the drive and then removing the fan's patch cable from the power supply's power connector (not the CPU).
6. On power supplies with a cable-mounted switch, you'll need to detach this cable from the computer's case. Typically, you'll find two screws holding a metal bracket in place to secure the power supply switch and cable at the front of the computer (Figures 16.3 and 16.4). The wire bundle that connects the switch to the power supply usually has a separate wire that connects the power supply to the computer's chassis as a ground. Disconnect the ground wire, loosen the screws holding the bracket, and release the power switch cord. Save the screws and mounting hardware.

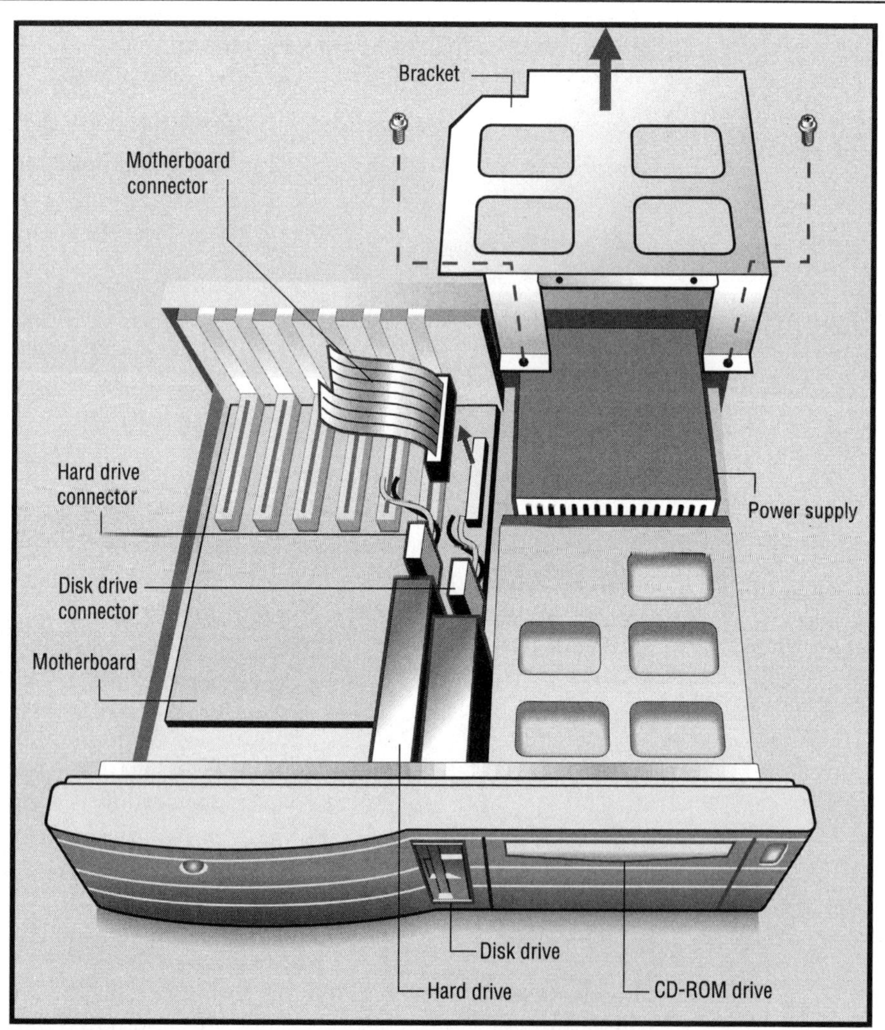

FIGURE 16.2: The main components will be disconnected from the power supply.

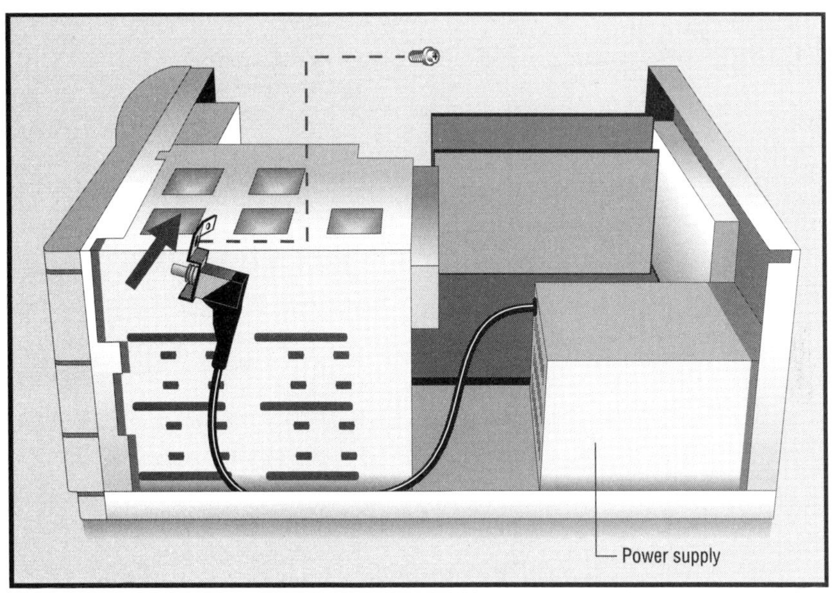

FIGURE 16.3: The on/off cable is detached from the computer's case.

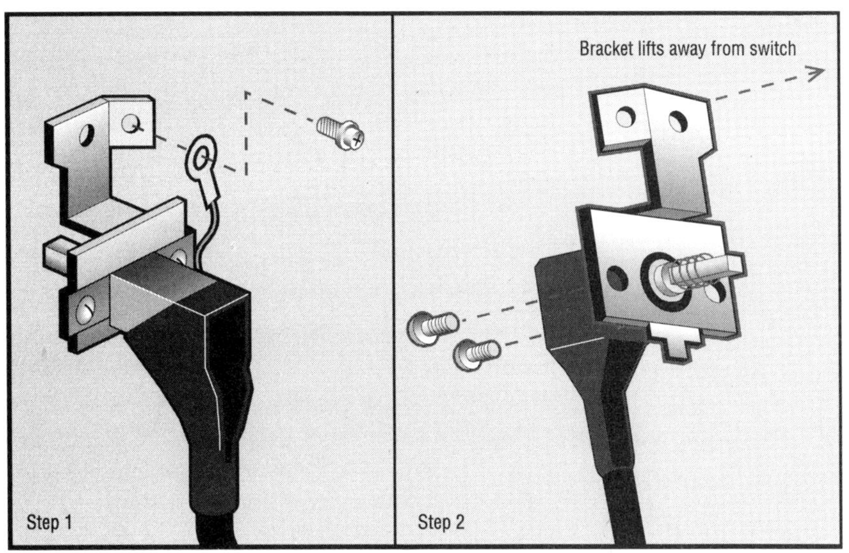

FIGURE 16.4: Remove the screws to release the power switch cord.

7. Cut any plastic cable ties that hold power or switch cables in place. On some systems, these may be bundled with excess lengths of data cables. Be careful not to damage any power or data cables.
8. Once all cables have been disconnected or cut loose from the system, you can safely remove the power supply from the case.
9. Place the power supply you've removed from your system and compare it to the replacement you've purchased. Before you install the new unit, make sure the mounting holes line up and the new unit has enough drive power connectors for the drives your system contains. Also, double-check the motherboard power connectors. The AT-style uses a 12-wire or dual six-wire connector, and the new ATX style uses a 20-wire connector.
10. Place the new power supply into the computer's power supply bay. Line up the four screw holes in the power supply casing with the corresponding holes in the computer case (Figure 16.5). Gently insert the screws into these holes to attach the power supply to the computer's case.
11. Before you tighten the screws at the back of the computer case, make sure the power supply mounting holes inside the case line up with the corresponding screw holes. Insert screws and tighten firmly.
12. If your power supply is held in place by a bracket, replace it and attach it with the appropriate screws.
13. Once the power supply is attached to the inside of the case, finish tightening the screws at the rear of the case.
14. Attach the new power supply's switch to the bracket, and reattach the bracket with power supply cable/switch to its original position. Locate the ground wire in the switch's wire bundle and reattach it to the same screw hole the old ground wire used.
15. Attach the power connectors from the power supply to the drives or to the power splitters that you left connected to the disk drives. Attach the pass-through connector to the CPU fan to a power connector, and then attach the other end to a drive (if necessary). Check to see if you are stretching any power cables because stretched cables can fail. To avoid stretching, either buy a single-cable extension or a Y-splitter cable that provides extra length. Attach either one to the power connectors that are too short.

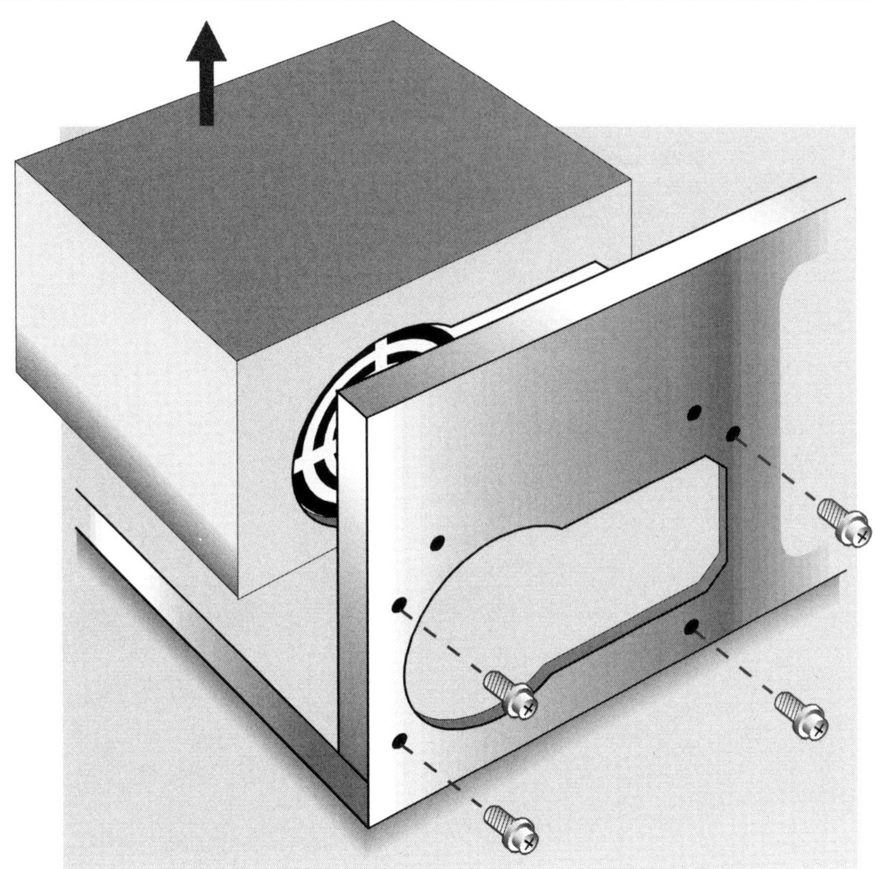

FIGURE 16.5: Replace the screws to secure the power supply.

16. Reroute ribbon data cables around the new power supply's cables. Keep both power and data cables away from the edges of the case because closing the case can damage them.

17. Before you close the case, turn on the computer while you can see the power supply fan. Is it turning? Does the hard drive spin up? Is the fan on the CPU turning? Does the computer start? If all are true, then you can shut down the computer after it finishes booting and replace the computer case.

Are You Experienced?

Now you can...

- ☑ evaluate whether you need a new power supply
- ☑ survey different types of power supplies on the market
- ☑ install a new power supply

SKILL 17

Upgrading Your Portable PC

- Deciding what to upgrade on your portable computer
- Understanding how PC Cards work
- Using the many types of PC Cards

Your portable PC may have seemed packed with features when you bought it three years ago, but now it's sorely lacking in just about every way. Should you toss the machine you paid nearly $3,000 for or consider upgrading your system? We'll help you answer this question.

Considering Your Options

Unlike desktop computers that come apart like a stack of Legos to be reconfigured when the next processor hits the market, portable PCs are, shall we say, slightly less flexible. You can't just can run down to the nearest computer superstore and pick up an extra hard drive, more RAM, or an upgraded processor to pop into your machine. Instead, each portable PC has expansion options of its own, a fact you'll quickly discover when you embark upon answering your upgrade questions.

Older Can Be Better

Although it might be hard to believe, the older your laptop is, the more upgrade options you're likely to have. That's because the length of time a machine has been on the market correlates to the time third-party vendors have had to develop the upgrade options. Similarly, the more popular a machine, the more likely you'll find the upgrades you desire. A no-name portable PC purchased three years ago from a company that has long since gone out of business is not likely to give you much leeway for upgrading. In this case, it's better to buy new and count your blessings that your notebook lasted this long without needing any serious "out-of-warranty" repairs.

Don't overlook that in today's competitive computer market, entry-level machines from major manufacturers, such as Toshiba and Hitachi, can go for as little as $1,699 and come equipped with plenty of power, including 166MHz Pentium MMX central processing units (CPUs), 2GB hard drives, 16MB of RAM, and 16× CD-ROM drives. Now, this may not be the power you're used to from your desktop (you'll still have to pay top dollar—about $3,500—for that luxury) but it's something to consider when debating whether or not to upgrade that old portable.

When (and What) to Upgrade

There are many instances when it makes sense to invest in an upgrade for your portable PC, especially when it comes to storage and memory.

RAM

If you're considering adding extra memory (RAM) to your portable PC, then by all means do so. This is the easiest and most effective upgrade you can make. Either seek out extra RAM from your portable PC's manufacturer or contact a third-party company such as McGlen Micro (`http://www.mcglen.com`) where you'll find an entire list of old and new portable computers and their additional RAM options.

Though your portable PC's manual will probably lead you through a step-by-step process for upgrading memory, if you are nervous about the procedure it's a good idea to visit a local computer store and pay the labor charge for installing it. (For more about how to install RAM, see Skill 4.)

Hard Drive

Upgrading your computer's hard drive might sound daunting, but it is not necessarily impossible. You have many options, including upgrading your portable's internal hard drive or adding an external storage device. The more convenient choice for most users is to upgrade the internal hard drive. However, unless you have a relatively popular machine (i.e., IBM, Toshiba, NEC, Digital), you could have tough time finding these devices.

A company called Apricorn (`http://www.apricorn.com`) offers a device called the Universal EZ-GIG Notebook Hard Drive Upgrade Kit. The EZ-GIG, available in 1.4GB, 2.1GB, and 3.1GB configurations, is said to work with almost any portable PC and can be installed by users. The EZ-GIG comes with a kit to transfer your old data to your new drive. Apricorn also has a large selection of replacement hard drives available.

EasyBundle from CMS Peripherals (`http://www.cmsperipheralsinc.com`) is available for most major portables from AST, Compaq, Dell, Hewlett-Packard, IBM, NEC, and Toshiba. EasyBundle comes in 1.4GB, 2GB, and 3.1GB sizes.

If these solutions don't appeal to you, there's always the option of an external drive connected via the parallel port, SCSI port or PC Card slot. If your notebook has a standard Personal Computer Memory Card International Association (PCMCIA) slot that supports either one Type III card or two Type II cards, you'll be able to use a PC Card–based hard drive.

External drives have a couple drawbacks here: You won't have room for an additional PC Card (such as a modem or network card) and the space available in these cards is somewhat limited. On the plus side, PC Card hard drives are extremely durable, and they can be easily used in any machine that supports a Type III card. One company offering PC Card hard drives is Eiger. For more about Eiger products, see the MobilePlanet Web site at `http://www.mplanet.com`.

Unless your notebook PC is extremely old, it's likely to support an external storage system such as the popular Zip drive from Iomega (`http://www.iomega.com`). This device will give you the ability to move 100MB of data. Just plug the drive into your notebook's parallel port, and you're in business.

If your notebook PC has a removable CD-ROM and disk drive, you may be able to use Iomega's Notebook Zip, which fits into the multipurpose bay slots of Toshiba, Compaq, IBM, and Hewlett-Packard notebook PCs. With a Zip drive installed in your machine, you won't have to labor with cables and connectors. For information about Notebook Zip drives, visit the Iomega Web site. To purchase the drive, contact an Iomega reseller such as CNF.

You also can go the traditional route with a standard external hard drive that attaches via a parallel, SCSI, or PC Card port. This allows you to transfer your data to any machine you desire at the expense of a lack of portability, as most external hard drives require a power supply.

Battery

You wouldn't trade your car in because its ashtray was full, so don't toss your portable PC because your battery no longer works. This component is probably the most likely to be replaced during the lifetime of your portable PC. You shouldn't expect your battery's lifetime to be more than three or four years. If you've owned your portable PC for a couple of years, you've probably noticed your battery pack is dying quicker each time you boot up your PC.

Unless your machine is extremely dated, you shouldn't have too much trouble finding a new battery for it. You may even get lucky and be able to upgrade from the older nickel-metal hydride (NiMH) batteries to the newer lithium-ion (Li-ion) ones, which gives you more battery life per square inch. AccessMicro (`http://www.accessmicro.com`) has a good selection of batteries for portable PCs.

PC Card Slot Add-Ons

PCMCIA card slots are the most universal input device a notebook can have. If your portable is equipped with one, you'll be able to add all sorts of hardware, including a hard drive.

Typical PC Card devices include modems (internal modems can be upgraded) and adapters for connecting to a network. This slot can make a seemingly obsolete portable more youthful by adding multimedia capabilities, including a CD-ROM drive (about $400 for an 8× CD-ROM drive with sound) and 16-bit audio. You also can add a joystick for heavy-duty game playing.

Docking Station

To give your notebook a little more flexibility when it sits on your desk, consider buying a docking station. A docking station replicates your notebook's present ports while perhaps adding some additional functionality, such as extra PC Card slots and Industry Standard Architecture (ISA) card slots, for example.

Typically, your notebook will need a dedicated expansion port to plug into a docking station although there are a few universal docking stations. CNF (`http://www.cnfinc.com`) offers a product called Digitari that adds four ISA card slots, two half-height peripheral bays, one parallel port, one serial port, two PS/2 ports, two speakers, and a microphone. Future models will include integrated Zip drives and CardBus technology.

Online Portable Upgrading Sources

Here are some handy sites on the World Wide Web where you can find information about upgrading portable computers:

Apricorn

Apricorn specializes in portable computing storage products.

`http://www.apricorn.com`

CMS Peripherals Inc.

CMS Peripherals specializes in data storage and offers hard drive upgrades and data transfer products.

`http://www.cmsperipheralsinc.com`

continued

CNF

CNF Inc. offers a wide array of products to enhance your portable.

`http://www.cnfinc.com`

Components Direct

This company bills itself as "the affordable upgrade solution for mobile computer users."

`http://componentsdirect.com`

McGlen Micro

This online store has more than 40,000 products, including memory, hard drives, external add-ons, batteries, and more.

`http://www.mcglen.com`

MobilePlanet

Mobile Planet has paper- and Web-based catalogs for all your portable computing needs.

`http://www.mobileplanet.com`

Notebook Upgrades

This Canadian-based company specializing in upgrading portable PCs.

`http://www.notebookupgrades.com`

Upgrades Inc.

This company specializes in upgrading notebook processors.

`http://upgradesinc.com`

When Not to Upgrade

There are times when upgrading your notebook will be too costly to bother with. Though it's worth spending a few hundred dollars to keep your original $3,000 investment in working order, it doesn't make much sense to throw bad money after good by upgrading costly components in a machine that has otherwise seen its day.

Display

If you're suffering from a poor portable display, your options are limited. Perhaps you opted for the passive-matrix (or dual-scan) screen over the more eye-pleasing active-matrix display for cost reasons. Or, worse yet, maybe your active-matrix display suffers serious pixel outages.

With an active-matrix display, pixels are made up of three dots (red, blue, and green) and if pixels go bad, the result can be a disturbing burst of color on a portion of the display. In this case, you're not likely to find much solace from your portable PC's manufacturer because your warranty probably expired before something like this occurs. Replacing a portable PC's crummy display is too expensive. Instead, you should either purchase a new-and-improved portable computer or an external monitor to use with your computer.

Processor

There are quite a few companies out there that are willing to upgrade your portable PC's processor. In the past, this type of upgrade would have been impossible, but with today's technology, it's feasible. Whether it's prudent is a whole other issue.

This is another area where you'll have more luck with an upgrade if you have a more popular machine. Corporate Upgrades (`http://upgradesinc.com`) is one company offering CPU upgrades. Most CPU upgrades offered here were for the AMD 133MHz and 150MHz 5x86 CPU. If your portable still sports an old 486DX processor from Intel, you'll want to look into this upgrade option, as it promises to make your machine four times faster.

This process is not for the faint-hearted, as the technique involves removing the soldered CPU using a specially designed hot jet tool that shoots hot air (up to 700 degrees) over the pins, without destroying the CPU and the surrounding chips on the motherboard. Once the original CPU is safely removed, a new and more powerful CPU is inserted and resoldered. You won't be performing this upgrade at home, of course, so you'll have to live without your machine while it visits Corporate Upgrades' shop for its operation.

The other bonus of upgrading your portable's processor is that your old basic input/output system (BIOS) chip also is replaced, letting you avoid any potential Year 2000 problems your old BIOS chip or clock chip might have experienced.

A Worn-Out Machine

If your notebook PC is three or four years old, it might be time to throw in the towel. If your machine didn't come with a PCMCIA slot or a CD-ROM drive, you're likely to feel as if you're living in the Dark Ages of computing. Just about every program comes on a CD-ROM nowadays, so unless you opt for an external PC Card-based CD-ROM drive (which means you had better have an available PC Card slot), you'll be hard-pressed to find good uses for your notebook PC.

If your computer is beat up from too much wear and tear, you'll probably want to consider a new model. If, for example, your notebook's keyboard has had coffee spilled on it one too many times, or the keys have been destroyed by aggressive typing, you can plug in an external keyboard while sitting at your desk, but your portable PC is no longer portable.

Portable PCs can be upgraded, but like all other upgrade issues you will read about in this magazine, the key is knowing when to add components to boost your portable PC's performance and capabilities and when to abandon ship and buy a new computer.

New Uses for Old Portables

If upgrading your notebook doesn't seem reasonable, here are some ideas of what you can do with that old portable.

Use it as a dedicated fax machine. Using an old notebook PC only for sending and receiving faxes will let you keep your old notebook plugged in at home while your new notebook is with you. You won't miss any more incoming faxes.

Create a two-computer network. Your old portable still has some life in it, so there's no reason to dump it and its resources now. Instead, create a mini-network between your old portable PC and your new one so you can access your old portable's hard drive for storage.

Donate it. One man's trash is another's treasure, so why not donate that old portable PC and accept a tax write-off? There are thousands of charities that can use your castoff portable PC. Just poke around sites on the World Wide Web to find an accepting party (`http://www.guidestar.org` and `http://www.charitynet.org` are good places to start when looking for valid charitable organizations). Or, you can give it to your child's school or to a grateful family member.

PC Cards

PC Cards are ideal for portable computers because portable PCs are small and aren't as easily upgradable as a desktop computer. You can't easily swap an expansion card or replace a disk drive inside a portable computer case because the hardware components in a portable are designed to conform to an exact position. It's also difficult to gain access to those components because the interior of the portable's case has minimal space for maneuvering.

Nevertheless, upgrading a portable computer is extremely easy. Nearly every portable computer is equipped with a *PC Card reader* that allows you to add hardware devices ranging from a modem to a hard drive to a serial port. A PC Card reader looks like a disk drive, but it's not as wide.

PC Cards, which are about the size of credit cards, can be swapped in and out of the PC Card reader (also called a PC Card adapter, a PC Card drive, or a PC Card slot), allowing you unlimited access to different hardware components, usually with Plug-and-Play ease.

We'll discuss the various PC Cards available and their costs. We'll also discuss some changes in the PC Card industry.

The Portability Advantage

PC Cards have become an indispensable component for portable computer users and for Windows CE handheld computer users. It's the upgrade you can take with you anywhere.

For example, you could personalize your presentations for several businesses, no matter how large the files are, by placing each one on a different flash memory PC Card. And, because PC Cards are so small, you can travel with several of them without adding much weight to your portable computer setup. Think of your PC Card collection like your automobile's emergency travel kit. You certainly won't need every type of PC Card every day, but you'll be glad to have a modem at your fingertips from time to time.

PC Cards are also referred to as PCMCIA Cards. The PCMCIA, or Personal Computer Memory Card International Association, oversees the standards for the PC Card industry, setting guidelines for companies that are members of the association to follow. PC Cards are the actual hardware devices that follow the PCMCIA guidelines. (For more information about the PCMCIA, see `http://www.pc-card.com` on the Web.)

PC Card Types

PC Cards are manufactured in three thicknesses. *Type I* cards are 3.3mm thick and represent the original PC Card technology. *Type II* cards are 5mm thick, and *Type III* cards are 10.5mm thick. See Figure 17.1.

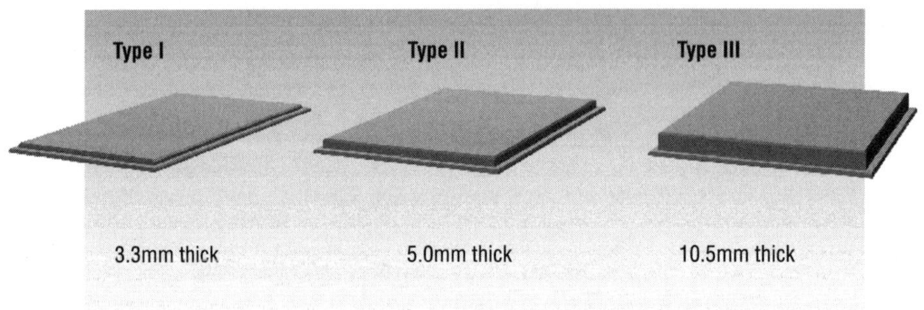

FIGURE 17.1: The three types of PC Cards vary in thickness.

Because all three types of PC Cards contain 68 pins that connect to a slot inside the PC Card reader, all newer PC Card readers can recognize and communicate with any of the three types of PC Cards. The thickness is in the center of the card, not on the edges.

Most PC Card readers contain two slots stacked on top of each other in a single opening. This allows you to insert two Type I or Type II cards, or one Type III card. (If you use a Type III card, one slot will connect to the card's pins, and the other slot will be blocked from use because of the card's thickness.)

A PC Card reader containing three slots will have an opening slightly higher than the thickness of a Type III PC Card. Some PC Card readers contain four or more slots stacked on top of one another, allowing for a wider opening and the insertion of additional PC Cards simultaneously.

Older PC Card readers may not contain an opening tall enough to accommodate a Type III card, but you can purchase an adapter that plugs into the PC Card reader slot and allows Type III connections outside the opening.

PC Card readers work in tandem with software to recognize and communicate with the PC Cards as they're inserted into the slots. PC Cards can be removed and added as you're working, a process called *hot swapping*. The PC Card software recognizes when you do any hot swapping and adjusts the computer's hardware setup accordingly. Some PC Cards need you to install device driver software before they'll work properly.

A new type of smaller PC Card is usually one-fourth to one-half of the size of a regular PC Card. These flash memory cards typically are used with digital cameras or in certain industrial settings. They can be read by regular PC Card readers after they are inserted into an adapter that is the size of a typical PC Card. Two different technological standards exist for these smaller cards, which are called Miniature Cards by Intel and its allies and are called Compact PC Cards by another group. The two types of cards are not interchangeable.

How Do I Use Them?

PC Cards are extremely versatile. Nearly any hardware component you want to add to your portable computer can be added through a PC Card. Some components, such as a hard drive or flash memory, are contained within the PC Card, while other components, such as a CD-ROM drive, simply connect to the portable computer through a PC Card and a cable.

Fax/Modem

One of the most popular types of PC Cards are fax/modems allowing 56Kbps connection speeds. The cost from $175–$225. A year ago, you probably would've paid close to this price for just a 33.6Kbps PC Card fax/modem. Cellular fax/modems will cost $25–$50 more than an analog fax/modem. If you want to save money, you probably can find a 14.4Kbps PC Card fax/modem for about $25.

Flash Memory

Flash memory is another popular PC Card. It's available in two types, linear memory and Advanced Technology Attachment (ATA) flash memory. (*Flash memory* is a read/write data storage method in which the PC Card doesn't lose its data when the card's power source is removed. Flash memory can be transferred from the card to a hard drive very quickly, which is one of its advantages.)

With *linear memory*, instructions to access the data in memory must come from the operating system, while with *ATA flash memory*, instructions for accessing the data are contained on the card, similar to a typical hard drive. Digital cameras use flash memory to save the photos you take. Depending upon the type of photos and their resolution, 4MB of memory can store about 25 photos, and 40MB can store about 275 photos.

Both linear and ATA flash memory have plunged in price by almost 50 percent in the past year. Prices for both types of memory are fairly similar. You'll pay $75–$100 for a 4MB card, $150–$175 for a 16MB card, $350–$500 for a 40MB card, and $750–$1,000 for an 85MB card. Cards containing other memory amounts are available, too.

Hard Drives

Some PC Cards contain a hard drive inside the PC Card, while others allow you to connect an external drive through the PC Card slot. For hard drives inside the PC Card, you'll pay $300–$350 for a 170MB drive and $550–$600 for a 520MB drive. The PC Card/external hard drive combination gives you much more storage room than the PC Card hard drive, but the external hard drives aren't as easy to carry. You'll pay $375–$425 for a 1.4GB PC Card/external hard drive setup and $750–$800 for a 3.2GB setup.

LAN Adapter

You can connect to your company's Ethernet or Token Ring network through a local-area network (LAN) PC Card. Most people will want to purchase a 10Mbps and 100Mbps combination card because it currently costs almost the same as just a 10Mbps card, about $125–$175.

Wireless LAN adapters are available with a wide range of costs ($400–$1,000). You also can purchase a combination LAN and modem card, allowing you to dial into your company's network while traveling. A combination LAN card with a 56Kbps modem will cost $350–$450.

Multimedia

Through PC Cards, you can add nearly any aspect of multimedia, ranging from an external CD-ROM drive to a joystick to audio computer speakers. You can purchase a 20× external CD-ROM/PC Card combination for $350–$450, or a game port PC Card, allowing you to add a joystick, for $50–$75. Video and audio components can be added for $200–$400.

SCSI Adapter

You can add serial ports to your computer for hardware accessories such as scanners with a Small Computer System Interface (SCSI) adapter PC Card. You'll pay about $150 to add one SCSI device and about $500 to add four SCSI devices.

Miscellaneous Needs

Dozens of other computing needs can be filled with a PC Card. For example, you can purchase a combination PC Card and pager to receive and track pager messages on your portable computer for about $30 a month. Some areas of the country, however, aren't yet equipped to handle the necessary paging frequency.

Some PC Cards can turn your portable computer into a bar code reader for about $400. Other PC Cards can help you set up a global positioning system in your automobile or in an agricultural setting for about $500.

PC Cards and Your Desktop

PC Cards are the key to providing your portable or handheld computer with unlimited power and hardware options. So it's natural to wonder when PC Cards will migrate in droves to the desktop platform. Rest assured, many people have been wondering the same thing for most of the 1990s, and they're still wondering.

For whatever reason, PC Card readers for the desktop haven't really caught on in the home-user and general-business computing markets. In most cases, PC Card readers are installed on desktop computers in industrial and agricultural settings for use with robotics or manufacturing technology. Companies also use PC cards to transfer image files from a digital camera to a desktop PC.

PC Cards also appeal to users who need to exchange information readily between desktop and portable computers. And other users find PC Cards valuable as a removable data storage option in a high-security environment or to replace disks as a primary removable storage medium.

Average desktop users haven't felt a need to use PC Cards in part because many PC Card components are standard fare on desktop computers. For example, flash memory cards are one of the more popular types of PC Cards in use for portable computers. But desktop users usually prefer a Zip drive for fast, large, removable storage options. And hardware components inside desktop computers are much easier to upgrade than the components inside portable computers.

In addition, even though PC Card readers are available for desktop PCs, rarely are they included on the typical computer you'll buy locally. They're sometimes included on computers made for special industrial uses. For the most part, however, if you want to add a PC Card reader to your desktop computer, you'll have to purchase one as an upgrade component and install it, just as you would with an additional disk drive. (For more information, refer to the "PC Card Reader Installation" sidebar.)

PC Card Reader Installation

Installing a PC Card reader is fairly simple. It's similar to installing a CD-ROM drive or a disk drive. We'll provide with some general instructions. Read through these instructions for installing an internal PC Card reader before beginning the hardware installation.

1. First, figure out where you want to install the hardware. Most computers have an empty bay near the disk drive or the CD-ROM drive to house the PC Card reader. Computers have both 5.25- and 3.5-inch bays. Most PC Card readers will fit correctly in a 3.5-inch bay; in the larger bay, you'll need to use a bracket, which should be included with the PC Card reader hardware. If needed, attach the reader to the bracket now.
2. Turn off your computer and monitor and unplug the computer. Take off the computer cover. Usually a piece of plastic is covering the empty bay slot; you'll need to remove this plastic piece. (Your computer's manual should provide these instructions.) Set aside the cover for now.

   Remember, before you do anything with your computer's internal components, be sure to ground yourself by touching the computer cover's metal frame. Static electricity can damage a computer's fragile circuits and chips.
3. Attach the PC Card reader to the ribbon cable connector by following the PC Card reader's enclosed instructions before sliding the reader into the empty bay. Remember to thread the cable properly so it can be connected to the expansion card. Because the inside of your computer is fairly crowded with components, take care to avoid knocking any other cables loose.
4. Adjust the PC Card reader (and bracket, if needed) so it fits snugly into the opening. You should be able to easily screw the reader to the computer's frame; don't force a screw into place if it doesn't line up properly.

continued

5. Next, insert the PC Card reader's expansion card into an empty expansion slot. Again, be sure to ground yourself before taking the expansion card out of its static-resistant packaging. You'll probably have to unscrew a metal plate on the computer frame before you can install the expansion card. (Save the screw to attach your expansion card to the computer's frame.) You also may need to remove a plastic cover on the computer's cover to gain access to the expansion card once the computer's cover is reattached.
6. The expansion card will fit tightly into the expansion slot. You may find it easier to install the card by first inserting a corner of the card and then rocking the card into place. It should fit into the slot far enough so only a small area of the gold pin connectors are visible. Take care not to damage the card. Touch only the edges of the card and don't force it into the slot.
7. The card's metal plate should line up properly with the slot in the computer's frame. Attach the expansion card's metal plate to the computer's frame with the screw you removed earlier.
8. Attach the ribbon cable connector to the expansion card. If you don't have much room to maneuver around your other expansion cards, it might be easier to connect the cable to the card before inserting it.
9. Now replace the computer's cover. (If your cover is difficult to remove and replace, you may not want to replace it until you've tested the PC Card reader and installed any software drivers.)
10. Reattach the computer's power cables and turn it on. With Windows 95 or Windows 98, the PC Card reader should automatically be detected. You may need to insert your Windows 95 or Windows 98 installation CD-ROM for any needed files.
11. In addition, you may need to insert any disks included with the PC Card reader that contain its device drivers, especially if you're using Windows 3.*x* or DOS. Follow the documentation included with your PC Card reader for any special instructions needed to install drivers and software. The PC Card reader now should be ready to accept PC Cards.

On the other hand, if you have individual reasons why you want to install a PC Card reader on your desktop computer, finding a PC Card reader won't be a problem. Several companies manufacture PC Card readers designed for usage on the desktop. Most are intended to fit in an empty disk bay on the front of the computer, while others can be accessed from the back of the computer. A few are external units. Most internal PC Card readers designed for the desktop cost $125–$175; external readers cost closer to $200.

Here are some of the leading manufacturers of PC Card readers:

- Adtron, `http://www.adtron.com`
- Greystone Peripherals, `http://www.grystone.com`
- Magic RAM, `http://www.magicram.com`
- Quatech, `http://www.quatech.com`
- SCM Microsystems, `http://www.scmmicro.com`
- Simple Technology, `http://www.simpletech.com`
- Spyrus, `http://www.spyrus.com`

PC Cards do their part by fulfilling a niche in the computing industry. Even various desktop users can take advantage of the portability and convenience offered by PC Cards. More importantly, if you are a user whose life revolves around mobile computing, no matter which type of hardware you want to add to your portable or handheld computer, a PC Card probably can handle your request.

And, just like other computing hardware, PC Cards continue to plummet in price while still offering additional power and the latest in computing technology, which makes their upgrade benefits even more appealing. So if you are a mobile computing connoisseur, don't leave the office without your PC Cards; they're as indispensable as ever.

Are You Experienced?

Now you can...

- ☑ **make upgrading decisions that make sense**
- ☑ **upgrade parts of your portable PC**
- ☑ **understand how PC Cards work and what they can do for your laptop**

SKILL 18

Setting Up an Ethernet Network

- Understanding the nuts and bolts of networks
- Learning about different kinds of cables
- Investigating the kinds of servers available to you
- Deciding when to upgrade

If you've used a computer in a business or educational environment, you've undoubtedly used a PC connected to an Ethernet network, and you've experienced the benefits of working with networked computers. You probably were happy to have access to the network to make your work easier.

But now you're the business owner, and you have to decide whether to set up and maintain a network. You know it's a good idea, but you don't know whether you have the resources to set up a network that will meet your business needs. We'll give you some advice concerning networks and networking upgrade options. If you haven't looked at networks for few years, you'll find the networking industry has undergone several major changes, and we'll discuss them, too. One aspect of networking that hasn't changed is that Ethernet networks remain the standard worldwide for networking. A few other options, such as token-ring, are still in use, but they're rarely found.

Ethernet provides dozens of hardware options that affect the network's speed and power. Deciding among these options is the key to determining whether you need a network upgrade, as well as the key to making sure your network meets the needs of your users with minimal hassles, whether you're starting a network from scratch or upgrading your existing network. We'll discuss your networking options and help you determine whether an upgrade will improve your network's performance.

Getting to Know Networks

Somewhat surprisingly, only about one in four small businesses with multiple computers uses a local-area network (LAN). Rather than Ethernet, other small businesses move files from computer to computer on disk; a process called *sneaker-net* by networking companies.

"In the past, we were really talking about networks that couldn't go fast enough, so people were walking their files across the room because it was faster," says Ken Haase, director of product marketing for Farallon, which is a division of Netopia. "Sneaker-net (remains) more widespread than you'd imagine."

Not surprisingly, companies that provide networking services are starry-eyed about the possibilities for sales to network-challenged offices.

"There's a huge opportunity in this marketplace, given the number of people who feel comfortable with their computers and want to connect them," says Brad Romney, who works with Intel's small-business networking options.

Many small-business owners understandably are nervous about starting a network from scratch, not knowing exactly how much networking power they need. So how do you avoid purchasing more power than you need and wasting money? And, if you have an existing network, how do you know when it's time to upgrade? Small businesses need to do plenty of planning before choosing network components. In general, you'll need faster, more expensive components if you have a lot of users or if you use large files.

Evaluating Your Network Needs

One sign that definitely indicates you need to upgrade your network is a slowdown in overall performance. Several factors can cause a slowdown. For example, if you add several new users, the traffic on the network will increase, which will ultimately slow the overall performance of the network. If you add a new network service (such as Internet access) without adding hardware, you'll slow down the network, as well. Or, if you upgrade a commonly used application, chances are the new version is going to require more processing power and will create larger data files, causing another concern for network slowdown.

Client/Server Versus Peer-to-Peer Networks

When choosing an Ethernet setup, you will have two choices: client/server or peer-to-peer. In a *peer-to-peer network*, each computer on the network is connected to all of the others in a ring topology or a bus topology. A *ring topology* is a network layout where each component is connected back to back and forms a closed loop, whereas a *bus topology* is where all computers and servers in the network layout are connected to a single main cable.

In this type of a setup, each network user can access files and hardware devices, such as a modem or CD-ROM drive, installed on the other network computers. While those devices are being accessed, the overall performance of the computer hosting the hardware device slows down.

Whether peer-to-peer will work for you depends on the type of networking you need. If you're working with small files and only require networking for some file sharing, in-house e-mail, and call messaging, peer-to-peer is a workable option that's easy to set up and manage because Windows 95 and Windows 98 support it.

As your network grows in number of users and the type of work they're doing, you probably will want to migrate from a peer-to-peer network to a client/server network. A *client/server network* is a more flexible network option, but it's also more expensive and more difficult to set up. A client/server network requires a *star topology*, which is a network layout where each component on the network is connected to a central piece of hardware, called a hub.

Some small businesses may choose to only share larger files or printing options through a server, while keeping a peer-to-peer network in place for other networking needs. Servers are similar in many ways to a typical desktop computer, but they feature a few key differences. Desktop computers are designed to be user friendly for a single user, but because servers aren't run directly by individual network users, they don't need to waste resources by providing an easy-to-use interface. Instead, they're designed to transfer, manage, and receive data as quickly as possible. When compared to desktop PCs, servers usually use faster (and sometimes multiple) microprocessors, use multiple network interface cards, feature improved reliability options, and offer several backup options.

When is it time to upgrade from a peer-to-peer network to a client/server network? If you answer yes to the following questions, it may be time for your network to consider the upgrade.

- Do users need unlimited access to a large common file, such as a database?
- Have you added several users and increased your computing workload in recent months?
- Do you want to provide Internet access to your employees?
- Do you want to make sales and provide customer information through the World Wide Web?

Server Types

In the typical client/server network, servers allow users to share resources also connected to the network, such as printers or Internet connections. Servers provide particular types of services for the network users. We'll discuss the various functions servers provide, starting with one of the fastest-growing functions—Internet servers.

Internet Servers

Internet servers provide all users on your network with a fast, reliable connection to the Internet, usually through an ISDN connection. (Internet servers sometimes are called ISDN servers.) Instead of tying up valuable telephone lines with separate

Internet connections from each workstation, you can have each workstation connect to the Internet through the network's Internet server.

For most small businesses, providing employees with an Internet connection is extremely important. Through the Internet, employees can stay in contact with customers through e-mail, they can showcase and market products through the business Web page, as well as take orders online, research products from competing companies, and stay informed with the latest industry news.

Romney says the desire for improved and easy Internet connection has led many small businesses to finally choose to install a network. When individual workstations each have their own Internet access account, costs increase dramatically. If you try and save money by having only a couple of Internet accounts, users are frustrated by an inability to make connections when their co-workers are using the Internet.

"It's causing people to understand the need for networking," Romney says. "People are rushing to the Internet. First they get one user connection by a phone line. They get frustrated sharing the one connection, so they get a second and a third and a fourth, and then they attach everybody's PC, and costs skyrocket. It makes sense to share a single modem and a single connection."

Many companies are offering all-in-one Internet servers for small businesses that feature Internet access for all workstations, Internet e-mail accounts, business Web pages, and security features. Varying speeds of Internet connections are available. Most of all, though, the all-in-one packages are designed to be easy to use.

"When you can share a single Internet connection with a single Internet service provider account, and you're getting good performance, you start to look more like a big business," Romney says. "We need to make these services very easy. Small businesses often are reluctant (about the Internet). That's sort of a daunting project. But if reaching the Internet is easy (through the network), then that can cause them to be more at ease with other services on their networks."

Some small businesses with a limited need for Internet access could survive with an Internet connection on a peer-to-peer network. However, the host's workstation would run frustratingly slow whenever an Internet connection was occurring.

CD-ROM Servers

A *CD-ROM server* provides network users with access to multiple CD-ROM drives without the need for all of the traditional hardware contained in a PC. In many networks, CD-ROM servers aren't used. But if your network users need constant access to certain CD-ROMs, a CD-ROM server is a helpful and affordable option.

On a peer-to-peer network, all users have access to the CD-ROM drives on other computers connected to the network. This can be a problem, though, if someone removes the CD-ROM other people want.

Database Servers

A *database server* is dedicated to processing requests made by network users concerning particular database files. For example, a user might request names of all customer in the database who have made a purchase in the past two weeks. The database server will process the request, sending only the requested data to the user.

Many client/server networks contain database servers because it frees the processors in network computers and file servers for performing other tasks. This is especially advantageous for networks using large complex databases.

Fax Servers

A *fax server* can take care of automatic facsimile transmissions made by network users and it can free up phone lines, a benefit similar to that which is provided by Internet servers. Instead of each network user sending faxes through individual phone lines connected to their computers, network users will send each of their fax requests through the network to the fax server. The faxes then are transmitted through dedicated modems connected to the fax server.

Incoming and outgoing faxes can be managed by communications software. You simply need to determine how many phone lines to dedicate to the fax server. By limiting the number of phone lines that can send faxes, you'll keep more phone lines free for incoming customer calls.

Faxing through a peer-to-peer network is possible, but it can be frustrating. If people on the peer-to-peer network send several faxes at a time, the computer hosting the fax modem can become easily bogged down.

File Servers

Sharing files is the most common type of usage on a network. Nearly every client/server network will have a *file server*, which allows users to share files and applications.

The most common use for a file server is to allow workstation users to access a commonly used data file, such as a database containing customer information, or any file that requires every user to have access to the same information. Network administrators can determine whether each user would have read-only or read/write access to the shared file.

Another common use for a file server is to store software applications needed by most users on the network. For example, if your employees all use Microsoft's PowerPoint to create presentations, your network administrator might want to place the company's copy of PowerPoint on a file server, giving all network users access to the program at any time, with a site license. The program may run a little slower off a file server than it would directly from a workstation, but using a server with a fast hard drive and plenty of random access memory (RAM) will minimize any delays.

Another advantage to running applications from a file server is that the network administrator only needs to update one copy of the program when changes are made, rather than updating dozens of copies stored on individual workstation hard drives.

Whenever using a file server, it's extremely important to back up the data on the server at regular, scheduled intervals. Choose a server with either a tape backup or a compact disc-recordable (CD-R) drive to make the backup chore easier.

For peer-to-peer networks, file sharing is the reason for setting up such a network. With a peer-to-peer network, all users have access to files on the hard drives of other users. However, file sharing could become a problem on a peer-to-peer network if you have a couple of large data files that several network users often need.

Print Servers

A *print server* works similarly to a fax server, managing all of the requests for print jobs from the network's users. In most cases, a print server isn't a full-fledged PC; instead, print servers contain only a processor and connections to the printer and to the network. This makes print servers extremely affordable and commonplace in client/server networks. At other times, a file server can double as a print server.

On a peer-to-peer network, however, one PC would be connected to a printer. During lengthy print jobs, that PC will bog down, so it's recommended that print jobs on a peer-to-peer network be limited to times when the computer controlling the printer is idle.

LAN Servers

As you can see from these descriptions, servers not only perform different tasks, but they also are available in varying levels of computing power. You can connect dozens of *LAN servers* to expand your network. LAN servers are the most popular types of servers because they feature enough power for most average networks and because they're the least expensive option.

Some simple LAN servers, such as a print server, can cost as little as $500. Typical LAN servers cost $2,000–$3,000, similar in cost to high-end desktop PCs. More expensive choices include *superservers*, which use multiple processors and high input/output speeds; and *mainframes*, which offer almost unfathomable speed and processing power. However, superservers cost up to $100,000 and mainframes often cost millions of dollars, making LAN servers the typical hardware choice.

Other Network Components

Several other components are key to creating the perfect network.

Operating system Several operating systems are available for varying sizes of networks. For small networks and peer-to-peer networks, Windows 95 and Windows 98 will satisfy your needs. For larger client/server networks, you may want to use Unix, OS/2 Warp Server, Windows NT Server, or NetWare. Each operating system provides varying levels of security, depending on your network needs.

Network interface cards The network interface card is an expansion card installed in each workstation and server on the network. The card contains connectors for network cabling and serves as the liaison for sending requests and receiving data through the network.

TIP TIP TIP TIP TIP TIP TIP TIP TIP TIP TIP TIP TIP TIP TIP TIP TIP TIP TIP TIP TIP TIP TIP TIP TIP

Intel's Romney suggests purchasing a network card that supports both original Ethernet and Fast Ethernet, making upgrades easier. He says the cost for a dual network card is only a few dollars more than for a card that supports only original Ethernet. Network cards cost about $50–$100. (*Fast Ethernet* is a networking technology that supports a performance up to 100Mbps. It can move data 10 times faster than the original 10Mbps Ethernet.)

Hubs The hub is a must-have component for a client/server network and costs $100–$300. All workstations and servers are connected to the hub, rather than being connected directly to each other. The data passes through the hub to the intended workstation or server. Individual hubs are limited to the number of connectors they have (usually 8 or 16), but you can connect several hubs to increase the size of the network.

If you're using twisted-pair or fiber-optic cabling, you must use a hub because those types of cables allow only two connections. Use of hubs in a star topology makes the network extremely reliable because a networking error on one length of cable only affects the workstation or server at the end of the cable. It won't take down the entire network.

Switches A switch helps split a large network into smaller subnetworks by replacing the hub. With proper planning, the subnetworks can work faster than a single large network because data from the one subnetwork won't clog the cable serving other subnetworks.

Workstations are grouped into subnetworks based on the types of applications and files they use, or based on their physical location. Workstations from one subnetwork can still transmit data to workstations on another subnetwork whenever needed. A switch probably will cost $500–$1,000.

Repeaters A repeater is a piece of hardware that boosts the network signal, allowing it to surpass the maximum set length for a segment of cable. A repeater basically hooks together two or more segments of cable. Repeaters aren't needed on the average network, but, if you're trying to connect users who aren't close together or if you're setting up a *wide-area network* (WAN), which is the connection of two or more LANs, you probably will need a repeater.

TIP TIP TIP TIP TIP TIP TIP TIP TIP TIP TIP TIP TIP TIP TIP TIP TIP TIP TIP TIP TIP TIP TIP TIP

It's best not to use more than three repeaters in a row; if you have to use more, your signal reliability will be better if you're using fiber-optic cable or a router. Repeaters sometimes are combined with hubs, and they usually cost $200–$500.

Routers A router is used with large networks and with WANs. Routers vary greatly in price, starting at about $500 for simple hardware units. More complex units cost $2,000 and more. The router provides a method of transmitting network data over long distances, similar to a repeater, but it is designed to help make sure the data arrives in the correct place, whether that is your workstation or the mainframe. The router can move data around busy areas of the network.

Routers used with a WAN often use a dedicated, high-speed phone line to transmit their data to remote locations on the network. To save money rather than getting a dedicated line, some routers work with software called a firewall to transmit data across the Internet to remote offices on the WAN.

NOTE NOTE NOTE NOTE NOTE NOTE NOTE NOTE NOTE NOTE NOTE NOTE NOTE NOTE NOTE

The *firewall* allows you to transmit your data across the Internet while preventing other Internet users from gaining unauthorized access to your network's data.

Some less-sophisticated routers allow you to connect to a remote office using a generic voice phone line. The data won't move as quickly, but it will be less expensive than a dedicated line.

To Ethernet or Ether Not

Because of the cost and the work required to set up and maintain a network, it isn't going to fit in with every business. But recent changes in networking, including improvements in the reliability of networking and in overall speed, have made it a much more viable option than it was a few years ago.

Networking still can be somewhat expensive, but the advantages of allowing your users to share resources and hardware will help a network pay for itself eventually. The reliability of twisted-pair cabling has made networks nearly failure-proof. Fast Ethernet can handle transfers of nearly any file type and size smoothly. There is one drawback, though. You'll have to find another method of exercising after you abandon your daily walk from computer to computer on your sneaker-net.

Ethernet Cabling Options

Choosing the correct type of cable is important when creating or upgrading an Ethernet network. The network cabling controls the speed at which the data is transmitted. It also can control the stability of the network's performance.

Coaxial and *twisted-pair* cables are similar in cost, around $30–$40 for 100 feet. Fiber-optic cable, however, is extremely expensive, around $350–$500 for 100 feet.

Ethernet Terms to Know

Backbone The connection between hubs and servers in a client/server network.

Bandwidth The maximum amount of data a network cable can carry, measured in bits per second (bps). Ethernet cable carries 10Mbps, Fast Ethernet carries 100Mbps, and Gigabit Ethernet carries 1,000Mbps, or 1Gbps.

Baseband The method of sending signals used by an Ethernet network, where electrical signals or light pulses are used to represent data. In a 10Base-T Ethernet cable, the *Base* represents *baseband.*

Bus topology A network layout where all computers and servers in the network are connected to a single main cable. This is used most often with coaxial cable and in older Ethernet network layouts.

Client In a client/server network, a client represents a user's computer. Also known as a workstation, it uses resources provided by a server on the network.

Coaxial cable A type of network cable, often shorted to *coax*. It's rarely used with new Ethernet networks.

Fast Ethernet Networking technology that supports a performance up to 100Mbps. It can move data 10 times faster than the original 10Mbps Ethernet.

Gigabit Ethernet Network technology that supports up to 1Gbps (1,000Mbps) performance. It can move data 10 times faster than Fast Ethernet, but development and standardization of Gigabit Ethernet is still ongoing. It is, and will mostly be used, as a backbone for larger networks. It rarely will be used for connections to clients.

Local-area network (LAN) The LAN connects a group of computers and servers, allowing them to share files and common hardware.

Node An individual component of the network, this can be a workstation or a server.

continued

Peer-to-peer network A type of network system in which servers aren't used. Each computer in the network is connected to the others, and each network user can use resources from the other computers on the network.

Ring topology A network layout where each component is connected back to back and forms a closed loop.

Server A node that allows access from the user PCs on the network. Servers usually are devoted to a single task, such as providing file sharing, printing, or Internet connections.

Star topology A network layout where each component on the network is connected to a central piece of hardware, called a hub.

Wide-area network (WAN) The connection of two or more LANs, usually through high-speed, dedicated telephone lines or through the Internet.

Workgroup Usually a subnetwork of the LAN, the workgroup consists of a group of workstations, servers, and other network devices that usually share common resources. Workgroups usually consist of users in a common location or who perform a similar type of work. Various workgroups can be connected together by switches to create a company's overall LAN.

Workstation A user's computer that is connected to the network. It's the client in a client/server network system.

When choosing cabling, you can mix and match on the network. For example, some network engineers choose to use faster, more expensive cabling to connect the servers and the hubs on the network, allowing them to move data through the backbone more quickly. In this same example, slower, less-expensive cabling is then used to transfer the data to the workstations.

We will discuss three types of Ethernet cabling and the considerations of each.

Twisted-Pair Cables

Twisted-pair cabling is the most popular type of cabling used in Ethernet networks today. Twisted pair, also called 10Base-T or 100Base-T, is most often available in

Category 5 cable. Category 5 can be used with either original Ethernet or Fast Ethernet. Most new networks use Category 5 twisted-pair cable, which uses four pairs of twisted-pair wires.

Twisted pair provides many networking advantages, including the ability to upgrade from Ethernet to Fast Ethernet without changing the cabling. In addition, it provides more reliability in network performance and easy connections using hardware similar to a telephone jack (RJ-11 and RJ-45 connectors). Most newer network cards only contain twisted-pair jacks.

Twisted pair requires a star topology, in which each node on the network must be connected to a hub. This type of layout requires a longer length of cable than does a bus topology, but it's more stable in performance. When one segment of cable fails or is disconnected, it only affects the workstation to which it's connected. In a bus topology using coaxial cable, however, a malfunctioning or disconnected cable can take down the whole network.

NOTE NOTE NOTE NOTE NOTE NOTE NOTE NOTE NOTE NOTE NOTE NOTE NOTE NOTE NOTE

Refer to the "Ethernet Terms to Know" sidebar for the full definitions of each type of topology.

"(Twisted-pair cable) is a fail-safe operation," says Intel's Brad Romney, "Each workstation has its own connection to the hub. Someone can't step on the cable and take down the whole network (as with coax). Lots of things can go wrong with coax connections."

A drawback to twisted-pair cable can be cost. With twisted pair, you'll need to purchase hubs. Coaxial cable connections can be made with inexpensive parts.

Finally, twisted pair is limited to 328 feet of cabling without the use of a repeater, which boosts a fading network signal. However, very few network layouts require a length of cable more than a few dozen feet.

Companies that use twisted-pair cabling for their networks often will use *wiring closets* to house the hubs and servers. The cables will run under the floor or in the ceiling from the workstations into the closets (that often are shared with telephone lines).

Coaxial Cables

In many older networks, coaxial cable is still in use, but it's rarely used to install a new network. Coaxial cable looks like the cabling used for cable television or to connect a VCR to a television, with a single wire protruding from the center of the flexible cable.

Two types of coaxial cable are used with Ethernet, 10Base-2 and 10Base-5. 10Base-5, or Thick Ethernet, is the original cabling used with Ethernet, but it is rarely found in a network today. Thick Ethernet can be used over long distances, about 1,640 feet. Thin Ethernet, or 10Base-2, is the type of coaxial cable most often in use today, although industry experts estimate Thin Ethernet is installed in new networks only about 5 percent of the time.

When using coaxial cable, each component of the network is connected in a bus topology fashion. Each end of the cable must be capped with a terminator. Connections are made from the network components to the main cable through T-connectors.

Thin Ethernet has some major drawbacks. Because of its linear layout, any malfunction or disconnection along the network will cause the entire network to crash, so Thin Ethernet is nowhere near as stable as twisted-pair cabling. Also, Thin Ethernet cable segments are limited to 30 users and about 607 feet.

Many new network cards don't contain connectors for coaxial cable, meaning you may have to purchase a custom card, which can cost $5–$15 extra. Thin Ethernet also is limited to a speed of 10Mbps. However, for a small network in a small area, Thin Ethernet may work well.

Fiber Optic Cables

Fiber optic cabling is the fastest, and most expensive, type of cabling available. Because of its expense, very few networks use fiber optic over the entire network; instead, some networks use fiber optic to connect their hubs and servers and then use twisted pair to connect the hubs and the workstations.

Fiber optic cable can handle the speeds of original Ethernet, Fast Ethernet, and Gigabit Ethernet; no other type of cable can handle Gigabit Ethernet (1,000Mbps). But fiber-optic cable's high expense will keep Gigabit Ethernet out of reach for nearly all small-business networks for a while.

NOTE NOTE NOTE NOTE NOTE NOTE NOTE NOTE NOTE NOTE NOTE NOTE NOTE NOTE NOTE

Fiber optic achieves its great speed by sending data as pulses of light, rather than as electrical signals, which twisted pair and coaxial cables use.

Fiber optic is similar to twisted pair in needing a star topology layout and the use of hubs. Up to 2,000 feet of cable segments are allowed, making fiber optic ideal for connecting subnetworks located far away from each other.

The Path to Upgrading

Most businesses follow similar paths when creating a computer network, based on the number of users and the type of work they do. If you're considering upgrading your network, you probably will be upgrading from one of the following scenarios.

The smallest companies may look like this:

- Fewer than 10 employees
- Using peer-to-peer networking
- Original 10Mbps Ethernet connections
- Probably using coaxial cabling
- Shares a few small data files (less than 1MB)

The best time to upgrade would be when user machines are bogged down from network requests.

Smaller companies follow this outline:

- Up to 20 employees
- Probably stretching the limit of peer-to-peer
- May have a small client/server network in place or may be combining client/server with peer-to-peer
- Original 10Mbps Ethernet connections
- Shares several small data files

It is most likely time to upgrade when you begin using more complex data files or when the reliability of coaxial cable isn't good enough.

A small company will be similar to the following:

- Up to 50 employees
- Has outgrown peer-to-peer
- Should have client/server network in place
- Probably using Fast Ethernet as backbone between hubs and servers, probably using mixture of Fast Ethernet and original Ethernet to workstations

- Probably using twisted-pair cabling
- Often shares small data files and some larger data files (1MB–10MB)
- Probably uses one file server and a print server
- Might use large multimedia files

This company will want to upgrade when it needs additional dedicated servers for Internet access or database management, or when multimedia files or large database files start dragging down the network's performance.

A large company will look like this:

- Up to 100 employees
- Client/server network in place, probably using switches and subnetworks to speed network performance
- Probably using Fast Ethernet throughout the network
- Shares large mixture of file types and sizes
- Using more than one file server and a few dedicated servers
- Might use video and complex graphics files

When management of several local-area network (LAN) servers becomes too unwieldy, or when adding several new users or services bogs down the network, it is probably a good time to upgrade.

The next step up looks like this:

- Unlimited number of employees
- Client/server network in place, probably using switches and subnetworks to speed network performance
- Using Fast Ethernet throughout the network, possibly using Gigabit Ethernet as backbone between hubs and servers
- Shares large mixture of file types and sizes
- Using several powerful file servers and several other dedicated servers; may have a superserver

A logical time to upgrade would be when trying to connect remote offices to the network or when network speed is extremely important.

Finally, the largest companies consist of the following:

- Unlimited number of employees
- Client/server network in place; probably using subnetworks, and possibly using wide-area network (WAN)
- Using Gigabit Ethernet as backbone between hubs and servers, probably using mixture of Gigabit Ethernet and Fast Ethernet to workstations
- Using mixture of fiber-optic and twisted-pair cabling
- Shares large mixture of file types and sizes
- Using several powerful file servers and several other dedicated servers; probably has at least one superserver or mainframe

An upgrade is appropriate for this type of company whenever additional top-of-the-line, new technology is available.

Are You Experienced?

Now you can...

- ☑ **understand what makes a network function**
- ☑ **distinguish among the different types of networks**
- ☑ **figure out whether Ethernet is right for you and your company**

SKILL 19

Building a PC

- Considering the benefits of building your own PC
- Evaluating your needs and selecting components
- Assembling the computer
- Testing the results
- Installing the mouse, modem, and CD-ROM drive

"I think I would like to build my own computer."

Not so long ago, a statement like that from the average computer user might have brought questioning stares from co-workers, worried glances from loved ones, and quips about flying pork. But talk of building a computer isn't always the delusional ranting of a PC user gone mad. It really is possible, even if you aren't a computer genius.

Building a computer, once the territory of only hard-core computer enthusiasts, has become accessible to the masses. Improved technology, intense competition among manufacturers, and a growing population of computer users who aren't afraid of their machines have made building a computer a viable alternative to buying one off the shelf or through the mail. And when you come right down to it, who better to create your dream machine than the person who plans to use it?

In this skill we discuss the reasons a normally sane person might endeavor to build a computer. We also take a look at what you'll need to build your masterpiece and how much it will cost you.

Reasons for Building Your Own

Anyone who has successfully built their own computer can usually rattle off a mile-long list of reasons why it is better to build your own than to buy one at the nearest computer-chain megastore. Then again, if you talk to somebody who has tried and failed or who has never opened up their computer, they can probably argue a pretty convincing case for buying a manufactured model.

Most people decide to build their own computer mainly because they can put it together exactly as they want it, it is easier to repair, and it makes future upgrades a breeze, says Gregg Roseberry, manager of InfoLinc Computer Systems & Solutions in Lincoln, Nebraska. The store sells a wide range of computer components and builds custom computers for those who like the "build your own" concept but are afraid to take the plunge.

The real beauty of building your own computer is that you pick out exactly what you want, and you don't have to pay for features you don't need. For example, if you have no desire to join the millions of people herded onto the Internet each year by online companies and Internet service providers, you can leave out the modem. Or maybe you do want to visit the World Wide Web, but you want to wait until the prices on the faster modems drop down a bit. When you build your own, you make the call.

Another reason you might opt for building your own machine is that, when something breaks down, you are in a much better position to fix it. You put it all together and know where everything is. If you know the problem is with the video card, you can go directly to that card and decide what to do. If you still have a warranty on it, you probably can get it repaired, or get a new one, for free. If not, you can choose from the wide range of video cards available, spend as much as you see fit, then install the new one. You can complete the whole process within a day—if you can get a video card locally—and move on with your life.

According to Roseberry, repairs aren't always that simple when it comes to a computer manufactured by a name-brand company and sold off the shelf. For starters, you probably wouldn't dare try fixing it yourself, especially if it is still under warranty. Unfortunately, you probably can't simply take your machine back to the chain store where you bought it. Most often, the store will tell you to contact the manufacturer or the local shop "authorized" by that manufacturer to work on the PC. Once you've finally found the right people, you may find out that the video card—like most of your computer's components—is proprietary, which means you must replace it with a part from the same company. That doesn't sound too bad until you find out the card could cost quite a bit more than your average video card or is nearly impossible to find.

Even worse than that, many manufactured computers have components such as the video card built into the motherboard. The motherboard is the heart of the computer and houses the central processing unit (CPU), which is the brain of the operation. If you have a motherboard with a dead video card, you may have to replace the whole package, and that isn't going to be cheap. (For more detailed information on motherboards see Skill 15.)

Whatever the final scenario, you could end up losing your computer for days, weeks, or even months as you ship it off to the manufacturer, your local shop waits for the right parts, or you start over with a new motherboard.

Out with the Old...

Another reason to build your own computer is that it will give you a great deal of flexibility when it comes time to upgrade in a few years. Yes, even with your souped-up ultra machine, you'll have to add memory or more disk space to keep up with the constantly evolving software out there.

With your custom-built computer, upgrading is as simple as replacing a bad part. You take out the old stuff, put in the new stuff, and away you go.

Unfortunately, again, it isn't that simple with most manufactured machines. As with repairs, when you upgrade, you may face the high prices of proprietary parts and the liabilities of components built directly onto the motherboard.

According to Roseberry, the built-in components can do more than hinder an upgrade; they can make it nearly impossible if the computer maker hasn't created a way to work around these parts. In some situations, the best you can hope to do is salvage your drives and a few other items and start over.

"Their idea of an upgrade is usually 'buy a new computer,' " Roseberry says.

Dollars and Sense

In recent years, if users opted to build their own computers, they could expect to save some serious money. But with competition for the computer buyer's dollar increasing all the time, many new computer systems are selling at incredibly low prices.

Today's average first-time computer builder will probably spend about the same amount of money to build a computer as they would to buy a comparable one off the shelf. A custom-built computer from a store such as InfoLinc usually will cost about 10 percent more because of labor charges and added support.

We should point out that this non-scientific cost comparison comes from figuring in the cost of using good components from established manufacturers. If you buy a bunch of no-name brands from fly-by-night companies, you probably can build a pretty cheap machine and save some money. That's fine until things start to go bad and you find these companies are no longer in operation. It can be pretty difficult to get a non-existent company to honor its one-year warranty on your hard drive.

Our price comparison also hasn't accounted for the possibility that you might have some components already available to you. If you have an old keyboard or disk drive that does everything you need it to do and it is compatible with your new components, then use it. Or maybe you have a friend who wants to sell some components off her old machine. Maybe you can use them and save a few dollars.

Before giving our final plug for building your own computer, we'll mention one other option apart from doing it yourself or buying a PC off the shelf. You can always order a system from a mail-order company.

Buying a complete computer system through most mail-order companies is something of a cross between building your own and buying off the shelf. Most mail-order companies build their machines like a custom computer, with few proprietary parts. This makes them easy to repair and upgrade. The bad news is that if you aren't careful, you might find yourself repairing and upgrading often because you bought a computer loaded with low-quality parts. A cheap purchase price can cost you more money in the long run. If you do go with a mail-order package, stick with a company that will tell you exactly what goes into each machine. Make sure you are getting exactly what you want, and read the fine print in those magazine ads.

Convinced Yet?

We believe that building your own computer can be the right way to go. Anyone who has some experience with installing computer hardware or working with electronics, and who has a healthy store of self-confidence, should be able to pull this off. Even so, it might be a good idea to find a friend or relative who knows their way around a motherboard *before* you get started.

If you're a little nervous about taking the lid off the computer you have now, or the concepts of a hard drive and a disk drive are still a little fuzzy, you might not be ready to tackle this. Don't feel bad; the big computer companies still love you.

Shopping Around

Once you choose to build, you face another set of decisions. The first involves determining what components you need and want in your machine and how much you are willing to spend for the whole package.

The best place to start your list is with a set of minimums. Set the bottom limits of what you will accept in terms of components and their performance. Then set a budget. As you begin to compare prices, you may decide that you can afford a larger hard drive or a better monitor, and you can make those adjustments before you buy.

Once you're ready to buy, you must decide whether to purchase your equipment from your local computer store or through a mail-order company. Each approach has its advantages.

When you buy components from a local store, you will probably pay a higher price. In exchange for the extra money, however, you can expect more personal service and greater accountability should anything go wrong with the part. If your video card stops working a month after you install it, it's much easier to take it out and run it over to the local store than to send it off to a company halfway across the country. And it is almost always easier to get the results you want when you can talk to someone in person instead of on the phone.

The greatest advantage to buying from a mail-order company will be a lower price, and it can be a substantial savings. While dealing with a salesperson or customer service representative over the phone and through the mail can be a hassle, a reputable company will do its best to take care of any problems you encounter. The key to a successful mail-order experience is to ask around and find out who your friends and coworkers have had the best luck with, then ask plenty of questions—including the cost of shipping and handling—when you get ready to place your order. If the salespeople on the phone are rude or act as if you are taking too much of their time, take your business elsewhere.

NOTE NOTE NOTE NOTE NOTE NOTE NOTE NOTE NOTE NOTE NOTE NOTE NOTE NOTE NOTE

Wherever you decide to buy, make sure you know exactly what you are getting and beware of any company that has prices that look too good to be true.

Regardless of whether you choose a local store or mail order, try to buy the majority of your components (especially your motherboard, CPU, and memory) from the same company. This can help cut down on compatibility problems later. Some companies will even install the CPU and memory chips on the motherboard for you, which can save you some time and frustration. Also, buying most of your equipment from one place can save you shipping costs on mail orders, and it's easier to keep track of where to call if there is a problem.

We decided to use a mail-order company: Computer Craft Inc. in St. Petersburg, Florida. They carried a good selection, had very competitive prices, and the salesperson we talked to was very knowledgeable and courteous. They impressed us.

The prices listed in Table 19.1 give an idea of the cost of putting together a fairly standard computer. These prices were current at the time of this writing but like the prices of all computer components they are subject to rapid—and unpredictable—change.

TABLE 19.1: The Cost of Building Your Own Computer

Item	Price
Motherboard, pipeline cache, and Pentium processor	$302
16MB RAM	$160
Monitor and video card	$374
Hard drive	$209
CD-ROM kit with sound card and speakers	$219
28.8Kbps modem	$119

TABLE 19.1: The Cost of Building Your Own Computer *(continued)*

Item	Price
Disk drive	$22
Case and power supply	$65
Mouse and keyboard	$24
Shipping and handling	$58
Total Cost	**$1,552**

The Basics

There are some components that you simply cannot build a computer without. We'll discuss the necessities first and the fun stuff later.

CPU and Motherboard

We don't recommend skimping on these two items because if they fail, you're out of luck. Spend your money on quality, and you won't be sorry. For us, quality means buying an Intel Pentium CPU.

NOTE NOTE NOTE NOTE NOTE NOTE NOTE NOTE NOTE NOTE NOTE NOTE NOTE NOTE NOTE

Anything less than a Pentium will be obsolete before you even get your new system booted up.

Stick with an Intel motherboard as well to ensure quality and complete compatibility. We like the peripheral component interconnect (PCI) bus over the rest because it gives you the speed you need and full Plug-and-Play capabilities. While you should avoid a board that has too many built-in items, we like the ones with the integrated drive electronics (IDE) interface.

TIP TIP TIP TIP TIP TIP TIP TIP TIP TIP TIP TIP TIP TIP TIP TIP TIP TIP TIP TIP TIP TIP TIP TIP TIP

You don't want to get stuck with a board with a built-in video or sound card. It might make your life a bit easier now, but you'll probably regret it in the future.

We opted for the Intel 100MHz Pentium CPU on an Intel Triton Pentium 75-133MHz PCI motherboard. The board includes an IDE interface, 256KB pipeline cache, fan, flash BIOS, three PCI slots, and four industry standard architecture (ISA) slots. There are faster CPU/motherboard pairs out there, but this unit seemed like a good price/speed combination for our needs. We can always upgrade down the road. The cost of the CPU and motherboard combination was $366.

Memory

You can't run a motherboard without random access memory (RAM), and the more you have, the better. If you don't plan to run Windows 95/98 or much of the software that is coming out now, you probably can get by with only 8MB of RAM. However, we suggest at least 16MB.

RAM comes in the form of single inline memory modules (SIMMs), which you can purchase in many different configurations. Your motherboard should have at least four slots for SIMMs, so if you want 16MB, you can buy four SIMMs with 4MB each, two with 8MB each, or even one with all 16MB.

NOTE NOTE NOTE NOTE NOTE NOTE NOTE NOTE NOTE NOTE NOTE NOTE NOTE NOTE NOTE

If you plan to use only one SIMM, make sure your motherboard will run off a single SIMM; some require pairs.

When you buy your SIMMs, make sure they have the same number of contacts (usually 72) as your motherboard. Since you will probably want to add memory in the future, choose a configuration that leaves your options—and at least two slots—open. Also, most SIMMs come in speeds of 60 nanoseconds (ns), 70ns, or 80ns. The lower the number, the faster the SIMM and the better your RAM performance.

We opted for a 16MB package at 60ns. We purchased two Texas Instruments 8MB, 72-pin SIMMs for a total cost of $250. In addition, the folks at Computer Craft installed the RAM—along with the CPU—on the motherboard for us and ran a test to make sure everything worked before they shipped it. Not all companies will do this; we recommend you find one that will.

Hard Drive

When it comes to choosing a hard drive, size is important. Not very long ago, a 340MB hard drive was considered huge. But the newest software continues to demand more room, and the drives just continue to get bigger. We recommend at least a 1GB hard drive with an access speed of 11 milliseconds (ms) or lower. Make sure you get one with an IDE interface if that is what you have on your motherboard.

NOTE

Don't go cheap on the hard drive; it is too important. Stick with the big names such as Western Digital and Seagate. And remember: You just can't have too much hard drive.

We chose the Caviar 21200 from Western Digital. It is an extended IDE hard drive with 1.2GB of storage and an 11ms access speed. The total cost was $249.

Disk Drive

Disk drives are cheap, even the good ones. Unless you are looking for a special drive that can run both 3.5- and 5.25-inch disks, you should be able to find a 3.5-inch wide, 1.44MB drive with an IDE interface for relatively little cash.

We picked a Mitsumi 1.44MB drive for $25.

Monitor and Video Card

Monitors can be a tricky proposition, since what sounds good on paper doesn't always look good in person. Also, postage can be pretty high for shipping a monitor. In the interest of quality and cost control, consider trying to find one locally, even if you are buying most of your components by mail order. Either way, when you buy a video card to operate the monitor, make sure the two are compatible. Again, it is probably best to buy both from the same dealer and ask to make sure the two work well together.

We recommend a 15-inch, noninterlaced, SVGA monitor with digital control and a dot pitch of .28mm or less. Monitor manufacturers measure screen sizes diagonally, so a 14-inch screen doesn't really have all that much space. A 15-inch screen is better, while a 17-inch screen is excellent.

The best test of a monitor is for you to examine it in person, view it with both text and graphics on the screen, and consider what kinds of programs you will be viewing. Then just decide what looks the best and what you can afford.

Don't bother to buy a good monitor if you plan to use a poor video card. Make sure your card is at least 64-bit and that it has 1MB or 2MB of RAM. You should also consider whether you want a card with *Motion Picture Experts Group* (MPEG) capabilities. MPEG is a video compression format that makes it easier for your computer to show full-motion video. It comes in software or hardware versions, and we recommend the software version because the hardware could limit your ability to upgrade later.

We chose a 15-inch Samtron SC-528UXL monitor with .28mm dot pitch and digital control for $329. Computer Craft offered a package deal with the monitor that included a 64-bit Video-57P card with 1MB (upgradeable) of RAM and software MPEG capabilities for $85.

Case and Power Supply

You can buy either a desktop or tower case. Most come with a power supply already installed. Be sure you buy one with enough bays to let you expand your system in the future. Before you buy, be sure to ask if you also receive all the interior carriage parts you need. Cases are another item that can be pretty expensive to ship, so ask about cost before you order by mail.

We purchased a Pro Case brand mid-tower with seven bays that included a power supply and everything else we needed on the inside. The cost was $65.

Keyboard and Mouse

You can spend a little or a lot for these items. If you want a high-quality keyboard, you can spend upwards of $80, while a cheap brand can run you as little as $15. The same applies to the mouse. Since the low-end products are so cheap, you can buy them now and help keep down your initial cost. You always can go back and buy a better keyboard later; that way, you will have a spare in case one of them has a run-in with a can of soda.

We went with a no-name keyboard for $16 and a low-end mouse from Genius for $8.

The Fun Stuff

Let's continue our shopping spree by purchasing some items that cannot strictly be classified as essential but that add a lot to a computer in terms of enjoyment.

Multimedia

Most computer users today wouldn't dream of buying a new computer without multimedia capabilities. When it comes to putting multimedia into your own computer, you have a number of choices. One way is to buy the CD-ROM drive, sound card, and speakers separately. That way, you can spend as much money on each item as you want. The second option is to buy a kit that contains everything you need. While buying separate pieces allows you more flexibility, buying a kit can help guarantee compatibility between the components (plus you usually get a stack of CD-ROM software titles). We don't recommend buying anything less than a 4× (quad-speed) CD-ROM drive.

We chose a kit from Creative Labs called the SoundBlaster Value CD 4×. The kit contains a 4× CD-ROM player with an IDE interface, 600KB per second transfer rate, and a 250ms access rate. The sound card is a 16-bit SoundBlaster that is upgradeable to wavetable synthesis. The speakers are decent, but nothing too fancy. We obtained our kit from A+ Computer in Sterling Heights, Michigan, for $199.

Modem

If you decide you want a modem as part of your computer setup, your first decision is whether to buy an internal or external version. An internal version slides into one of the slots on your motherboard like the other cards listed earlier. An external modem has its own case and plugs into one of your computer's ports. The advantages of an internal modem include less clutter on your desktop, a free computer port, and a lower overall cost. The benefits of an external modem include easy installation and removal and the ability to see what the modem is doing through its set of blinking external lights.

Once you have decided on internal or external, you have to pick the speed. The faster the modem, the less time you have to wait for Internet connections and data transfers. The modems most commonly sold transmit data at 33.6 kilobits per second (Kbps). The next lowest transmits at 28.8Kbps.

In the interest of price, we picked a 28.8Kbps internal fax/modem from Rockwell. Its price was $127 from Computer Craft.

There are a number of other items that some people will decide they don't need, at least not right away, while others will insist they can't live without them. The biggest item in this category is probably a printer. If you plan to use your new computer primarily for word processing, you'll probably want a printer from day one. If you plan to use your new machine mostly for Internet access, you can probably do without. A tape backup is another must for some people. If you can't afford the losses that can occur if your computer crashes, you should install a tape backup drive when you build the computer. If a crash doesn't mean the end of your world, you can probably wait.

NOTE

The chance to decide what is or isn't important is one of the most exciting things about building your own computer. You decide what goes in, what stays out, and what can wait until later. And you decide just how much you want to spend on each part.

The total cost of equipment ordered for our computer was $1,777, including shipping and handling. We should point out that this doesn't include any software, which you normally find in relative abundance in most store-bought computer packages.

Putting Together the PC

Now that we've gathered all the components, all we have to do is build the computer.

The Motherboard

The first order of business is the motherboard. When we removed our motherboard from its protective bag, it was pretty much ready to go. That's the beauty of purchasing most of your components from one store. We had the people at Computer Craft, Inc. (where we bought most of our equipment) install our Pentium CPU and fan, pipeline cache, and random access memory (RAM) onto the motherboard. They took care of all the necessary jumper settings and made sure that everything worked before it left their shop. You can do this all yourself, but if you can find a good store to do it for you, we highly recommend it.

If you insist on buying these parts separately, however, installing them on the motherboard is the first thing you need to do. If your motherboard came with a protective sponge mat stuck to its underside, leave it there when you set in down at your workspace. Otherwise, make a bed of newspapers to set it on to protect the underside of the board as you work. When you do handle the board, make sure you hold it by the edges and try not to disturb any of the chips or electronic gizmos that populate the interior of the board. Check the documentation for your CPU and motherboard and find out whether you need to set any jumpers to accommodate your components. Once you have done that, you can install the brains of the operation.

Installing the CPU

Installing a CPU isn't difficult, but if you do it incorrectly, the whole project is a bust. First, determine whether your CPU has a cooling fan (Pentium CPUs require their own fan) and whether you need to attach it. The CPU fan requires a power supply to operate, so don't forget to plug it in later when you are connecting power supply cables to your drives. Once you get the fan mounted, examine the CPU socket on your motherboard and determine whether it is a zero-insertion force (ZIF) socket with a lever attached or a low-insertion force (LIF) socket with no lever.

To install your CPU in a ZIF socket, lift the lever to about a 90-degree angle, align the pin number one on your CPU with the pin number one designation on the socket, put the CPU down into the socket, and lower the lever down alongside it. You should see the CPU lock into place. If your socket is of the LIF variety, again you need to align the two pin number one markings, then push the CPU down into the socket until it is seated securely.

Sliding in the RAM

To install your RAM SIMMs, you first must find the correct sockets on the motherboard. Your motherboard's documentation should show you where the RAM sockets are and how to line up the SIMMs correctly. Different sockets accept SIMMs differently, so be sure to read your documentation.

Most of the time, you can simply slide the SIMM in at about a 45-degree angle, then pop it up into a vertical position (see Figure 19.1). There should be a post or clamp at each end of the socket to hold the SIMM in place. Once the SIMM is in place, it should not move around. If it does, you need to try again.

Pipeline Cache

The pipeline memory module should have a designated socket that accepts the module with little effort. Check your documentation and follow the instructions there.

Port Connections

While you are working on the motherboard, you might as well take a moment to plug in the two COM port cables and the parallel port cable. See your documentation to find where the connections are on the motherboard and make sure you

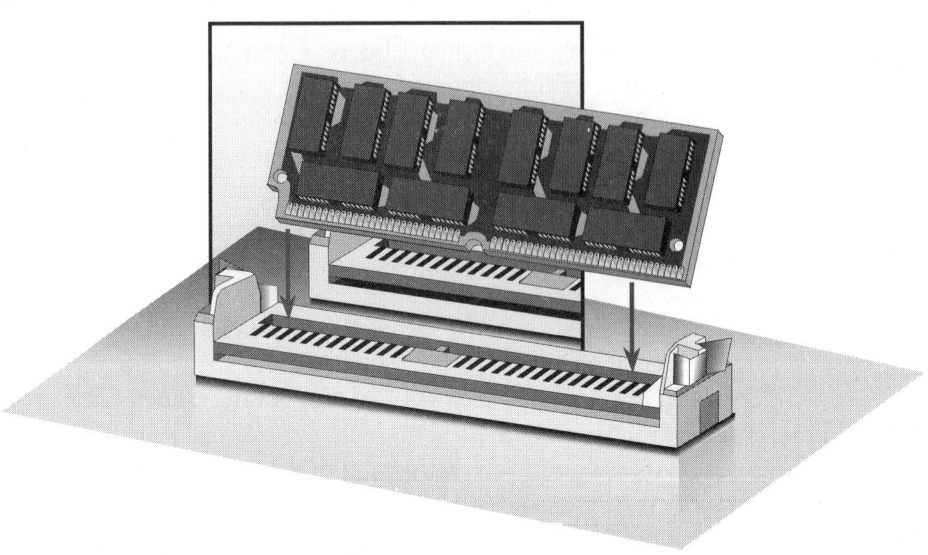

FIGURE 19.1: Most SIMMs slide into the socket at an angle and then pop up to sit vertically.

line up the colored edge of the ribbon with the number one pin on each connection. After you have the cables installed, set the actual ports and their metal brackets off to the side of your motherboard. Never set anything on top of your motherboard.

Once you have all the essentials loaded onto your motherboard, you need to connect it to the power supply. To do this, you must remove the case lid and set the case with the open side of the internal framework facing toward you. In the tangle of colored wires extending from the power supply box at the back of the case, there should be two white, flat connectors (they're usually labeled P8 and P9) with six multicolored cables each. This is the link between your motherboard and the power supply. Find the 12-pin power supply connector on your motherboard and insert the two sets of connectors with the double black wires side by side in the middle.

WARNING WARNING WARNING WARNING WARNING WARNING WARNING WARNING

It's very important that you connect the power correctly or you can damage your new motherboard. Make sure there are four black wires in a row in the center when you finish.

The Essential Drives

Now that your motherboard is mostly ready to go, you need to give it something to work with. First on our list of components is the disk drive.

Disk Drive

To identify the ribbon cable used for the disk drive, look for a cable that splits into three parts; the middle strand has a twist in it. Connect the cable to the back of the disk drive, making sure that you line up the colored edge of the ribbon with pin number one. Though you might have to look hard to see the pin number marking, it's there. Be sure to push the connector in all the way. Now run the cable to the IDE interface on your motherboard (check your documentation if you can't find it) and connect it. Be sure to line up the colored edge of the ribbon with pin number one.

The disk drive needs power, so go back to your power supply box at the back of your case. Grab one of the standard power supply lines (it should have two plastic connectors, a big one and a little one) and run it to the back of your disk drive. The drive should take the smaller of the two connectors, and it should only accept it one way. Be sure to seat the power connector fully on the disk drive pins and set the drive down on the table off to the side of the motherboard.

Hard Drive

Next on our list is the hard drive, which is installed almost exactly the same way as the disk drive. Find your second ribbon cable (the one without a split) and attach it to the drive, making sure the colored edge of the cable lines up with the number one pin, on both the drive and the IDE interface on your motherboard (see Figure 19.2). Be sure to push both ends of the cable in all the way.

When you're ready to plug in a power supply cable, remember the CPU cooling fan we talked about earlier and insert its power cable between the cable from the power supply box and your hard drive. (The power supply cable connects to the fan cable, which connects to the hard drive.) Be sure to seat the cable firmly onto the pins on the drive.

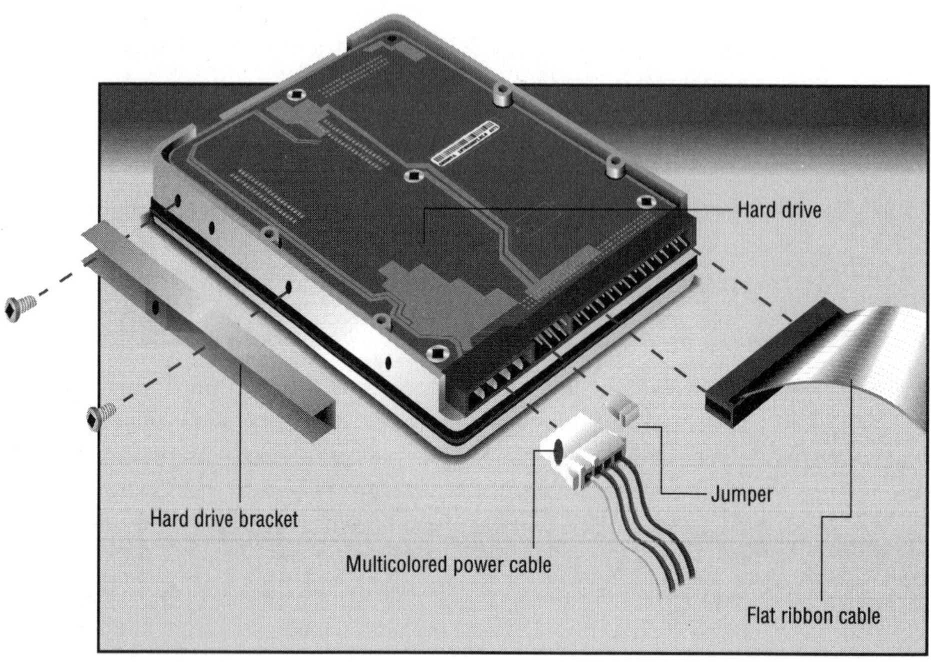

FIGURE 19.2: Most computer cases require some type of hard drive bracket to secure the drive in the bay.

Monitor and Video Card

If everything is going as planned, you should now have a basic functional computer. But to test that theory, we have to see what the computer is doing. To do that, we must get the monitor and the video card operating.

To install your video card, pick an appropriate slot on your motherboard (check your documentation if you're unsure which to use). Line up the card so the metal bracket that houses the monitor port on the card hangs off the side of the motherboard. Gently but firmly push the card into the slot. Be sure to push the card all the way in, then connect the cable from the monitor to the port.

Test Run

It's almost time to give your new computer a test run. But first, find the keyboard connector on your motherboard (a short round connector located on one of the corners) and plug in the keyboard. Next, look at the diagram for your case and find out how to connect the power switch on the front of your computer to the power supply at the back of the case. There should be a long, thick, black cable that runs out of the power supply. On the end of that cable should be four smaller colored cables. Your documentation should show which prongs each of those four cables connects to behind the power button. Now plug the power cords into the back of your case and monitor and the surge suppressor, cross your fingers, and push the power button.

You should hear the power kick on and your system begin to operate as the hard drive and fan start spinning. You also should see information appear on your monitor. So far so good.

Now press the setup key on your keyboard. Different motherboards assign this function to different keys, so check your documentation (or possibly the screen in front of you) to see which one applies to you. Ours was the Delete key. Pressing the correct key should cause some type of setup screen to appear.

Configuration

When you arrive at the system setup screen, you should have some type of menu. Choose the Standard CMOS Setup (or your version of it) option and type in the time and date, the disk drive type (1.44MB), and the video type (VGA or SVGA).

If you're using an old hard drive and you know all of the drive's vital statistics, you can type them in here. If you have a new hard drive, follow the instructions in your documentation on how to run the autodetection utility.

TIP TIP TIP TIP TIP TIP TIP TIP TIP TIP TIP TIP TIP TIP TIP TIP TIP TIP TIP TIP TIP TIP TIP TIP

Hard drives can be tricky beasts, but if you have new equipment, it shouldn't be that difficult. Just be sure to read all about your hard drive before you get started.

Return to the main menu and work your way through the rest of the categories, reading everything carefully and making changes only where you need to. If you

are unsure about a category or listing, leave it at the default setting. You can always come back and change it later.

Save and exit the setup screen, and turn off your computer. Now it's time to install your operating system.

The Big OS

As we mentioned before, we recommend Windows 95/98 for your new machine. We admit Microsoft's baby is far from perfect, but most new applications are written for Windows 95/98, and the operating system can help make your hardware installations easier. Some users are staunch OS/2 Warp supporters, but IBM's operating system has a vastly smaller marketplace following.

Since we don't have a CD-ROM drive installed yet, we used the disk version of Windows 95/98 to install the operating system on our machine.

NOTE NOTE NOTE NOTE NOTE NOTE NOTE NOTE NOTE NOTE NOTE NOTE NOTE NOTE NOTE

This process takes some time, so as you wait for the signal to insert one disk after another into your disk drive, occupy yourself with some necessary tasks. These include separating and identifying the various types of screws included with your case and brushing up on your knowledge of Windows 95/98 hardware installation tactics.

Once you have Windows 95/98 up and running to your satisfaction, close out of the operating system; shut off the PC; unplug the power cords, monitor, and keyboard; and prepare to transplant your computer's guts to inside the case where they belong.

The Case

If you are careful, you can move your motherboard and drives into the case without having to unplug anything.

The first thing you need to install is the motherboard itself. In a tower case, the motherboard rests on the left side of the case, inside the internal frame but behind the framework for the drive bays. Insert the pegs into the appropriate holes in the back of your motherboard. Carefully slide the motherboard in and up into the appropriate position (see Figure 19.3) with the keyboard connector and monitor connector on your video card in line with the openings in the back of the case. Be careful not to unplug your drives or to dislodge your video card.

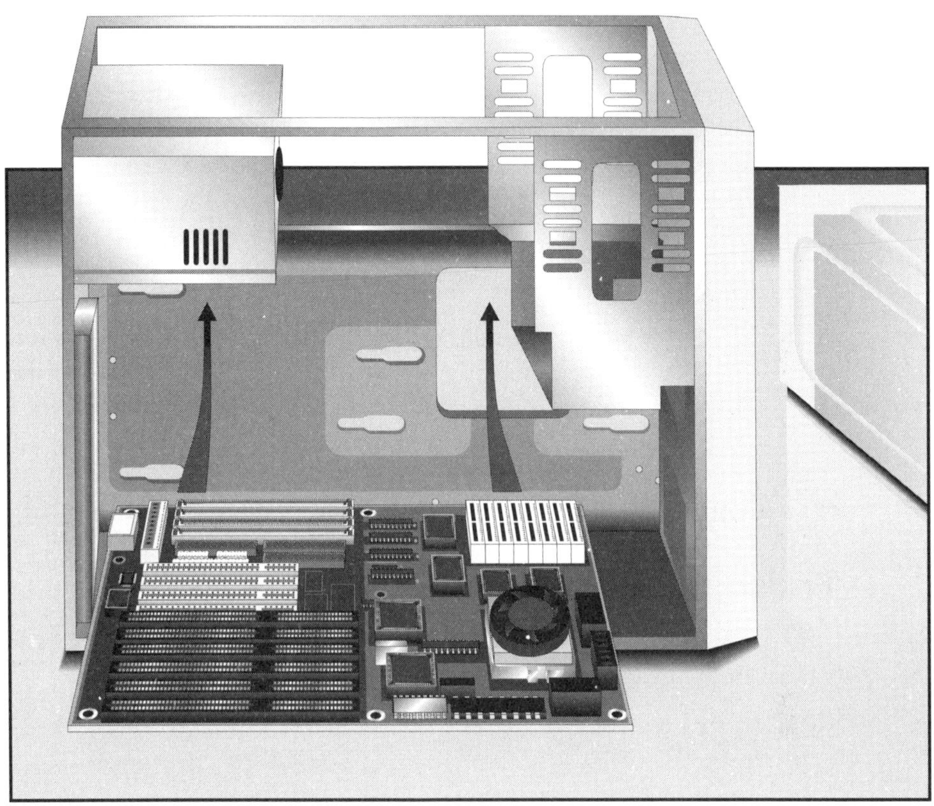

FIGURE 19.3: The motherboard will slide into place.

Gently insert the pegs into the slide holes in the back of the internal frame, being sure to keep the bottom of the motherboard from actually touching metal. Find the aligned screw holes in the motherboard and the frame and secure the motherboard, being careful not to tighten the screws too much. Attach the metal bracket on the video card to the back of the case using the appropriate screw. Now attach the serial port and parallel port brackets to the back as well.

Once you have the motherboard in place, you can take a moment to attach the wires that lead from the case's front display to the motherboard. These are the wires that make the reset button work and the hard drive light flicker, among other things. Consult your case and motherboard documents to find out which wires go where.

Once you have completed this monumentally tiny task—the connectors are really small—move your hard drive into the bottom 3.5-inch drive bay. You may have to attach a metal extender to one side of the drive (most cases include them) to make it fit properly in the bay. Then simply slide the drive into place and secure it using the appropriate screws. Take a moment to make sure the plastic cover is in place on the front of the case to protect the hard drive.

Installing the disk drive involves essentially the same procedure. When you get ready to slide the drive into place, be sure to remove the plastic cover on the case and mount the front of the drive flush with the front of the case. Secure the drive to the internal frame.

Once you have the motherboard and drives in the case, we recommend plugging the power cords, monitor, and keyboard back in to the surge suppressor and making sure it all works. If you did knock something loose, now is the time to find out, before you start putting in more boards and drives. Once you've determined that everything is working (or have taken steps to make it so), unplug the power cord again and get busy with the last few items on your list.

Finishing the Job

There are a few more details that need to be taken care of before your computer is fully up and running.

Mouse

The next order of business should probably be your mouse, since it will make the rest of your installation tasks a bit easier. If you installed Windows 95/98 as your operating system, its Plug-and-Play capabilities should make mouse installation pretty easy. Shut down your computer and plug your mouse into the serial port. Now restart your computer. When we did this, Windows 95/98 realized that we had added a mouse to the mix and asked whether we wanted to install it. Hopefully, you'll have the same luck we did, and the installation will be as easy as following the instructions on the screen.

If Windows 95/98 doesn't detect the new mouse during the bootup, use the arrow keys to select the My Computer icon. Select the Control Panel icon. Then select the Add New Hardware icon and follow the instructions there for detecting a new piece of hardware. If Windows 95/98 doesn't detect the new hardware, follow the instructions on the screen to manually install your mouse.

NOTE NOTE NOTE NOTE NOTE NOTE NOTE NOTE NOTE NOTE NOTE NOTE NOTE NOTE NOTE

If you continue to have problems, consult your Windows 95/98 documentation or the instructions included with your mouse.

Once you have your mouse up and running, you can move on to your modem.

Modem

Installing an internal modem is pretty simple. Shut down your system, unplug everything, and find an open slot on your motherboard. Insert the modem card in the same manner that you did the video card, using steady force to push it in all the way. Then secure the bracket to the back of the case using the appropriate screw.

Again, follow the procedure for detecting new hardware. If all goes well, Windows 95/98 will make this job an easy one. Then simply install your modem's software following the instructions in your documentation.

CD-ROM Drive

We expected the CD-ROM drive installation to be among the more difficult parts of our project, but it proved to be as simple as the rest. That probably had a lot to do with the fact that we bought a kit. We purchased a Creative Labs SoundBlaster Value CD 4× kit from A+ Computer and avoided the possible pitfalls of piecing together a separate CD-ROM drive and sound card. In the Creative Labs kit, the CD-ROM drive operated off the sound card through a ribbon cable and an audio cord.

Connect the ribbon cable and audio cord to the SoundBlaster card and insert the card in a slot in your motherboard. Make sure the metal bracket with your speaker and joystick ports lines up with an opening in the back of the case. Secure the bracket with the appropriate screw. Then attach the ribbon cable and audio cord to the back of the CD-ROM drive. Install the CD-ROM drive in one of your 5.25-inch bays and secure it to the internal frame. Now connect a power supply cable to the drive.

Plug your power cables back into the wall outlet and restart your computer. Windows 95 should detect your new card and drive. Follow the procedures onscreen and install the necessary device drivers and other software. Once you have the CD-ROM drive running, and the speakers plugged in and working, turn off your machine one last time.

Tuck all cables and cords neatly into the interior of the case. Slide the lid back on, replace the screws at the back of the case, and you're finished.

Start up your new machine, sit back, and admire your work. You now have a one-of-a-kind computer that should be easier to upgrade and repair than any manufactured model. You didn't have to buy anything you didn't want, and you didn't have to settle for somebody else's idea of a dream machine. And you did it all by yourself.

Are You Experienced?

Now you can...

- ☑ **decide whether building a PC is really for you**
- ☑ **evaluate your needs and the cost, and select the best components for the job**
- ☑ **put together your computer**
- ☑ **configure, test, and troubleshoot your computer**
- ☑ **install the mouse, modem, and CD-ROM drive**

SKILL 20

Increasing Space on Your Hard Drive

- Evaluating your storage options
- Looking into the future with DVD technology
- Find the best compression utility

Computer data has turned into a steadily growing monster, seeking computer resources to devour. It wants more processing power from your microprocessor. It wants communications outlets so it can travel more quickly to more computers. And it most certainly wants more storage space so it can grow bigger and bigger.

Less than 10 years ago, about 40MB of storage was all most users would ever need. Now one gigabyte seems laughable. Unfortunately, there's no way to stop the data demon. Over time, programs will require more space for installation. Multimedia features with huge video and sound files will become more prevalent. Online services will continue to offer worlds of data to access and acquire. The best you can do is arm yourself appropriately.

Before you add storage devices to your computer, our advice is to first examine your needs. Do you want to run more applications? Do you want to make a backup copy of your data? Or do you need to save big video files? And which of these storage options we've discussed can best store that type of data at the most affordable prices? Once you've determined your needs, then you will know which storage alternative is the best to contain your data demon. You may be interested in file compression; we'll cover that too.

Storage Options

Various storage alternatives offer several choices for saving data, and they aren't just for backing up data. You could do any of the following to increase storage:

- Install a second hard drive
- Add a Zip drive or a SparQ drive
- Install a drive that allows you to save data to CD-ROMs

Because of their different capacities, prices, and methods for storing data, the drives are best-suited for different uses. Some drives can store up to 100MB on a disk, while others can pack more than 1GB on a cartridge.

The most affordable options start at about $99, but others can cost more than $1,000 for drives that put several gigabytes of data on a disk. And while a tape drive is better suited for making a second copy of your data, a compact disc-recordable (CD-R) drive is ideal for saving data you want to pass along to other users.

Our goal is to introduce you to the storage options available for average consumers. We will show you how the drives store data, how much they cost, and which type of storage they're best at. We also discuss the degree of difficulty when it comes to installation. Then you can decide which option best fits your needs.

Installing a Second Hard Drive

To fight the storage shortage, you could go right to the heart of the matter, or to the heart of the computer, that is, and add another hard drive. Or, you could replace your current hard drive with an even bigger hard drive of more than 10GB of storage space.

A second hard drive definitely has its strong points. None of the other options can come close to accessing data as quickly as an internal hard drive, making it great for storing programs. Therefore, it's probably your best candidate if you want to run more programs on your computer. Plus, you can save all sorts of files, from multimedia presentations to World Wide Web pages, on a new hard drive. The types of data you can put on a hard drive are endless.

Weighing the Benefits

The storage capacity of a second hard drive, however, is not endless. If you buy a 5GB hard drive, you only get 5GB of storage space. If you buy a storage alternative that use removable disks, the capacity is only as limited as the number of disks you can afford to plug into them.

NOTE NOTE NOTE NOTE NOTE NOTE NOTE NOTE NOTE NOTE NOTE NOTE NOTE NOTE NOTE

Installing a hard drive is also no walk in the park. We found it to be a little more difficult than installing any of the other drives. For more information about installing hard drives, see Skill 6.

First, you need to determine if your hard drive adapter card can support a hard drive that's larger than 1GB. (This is probably in your computer or hard drive documentation.) If the new drive will replace the old one, you need to know exactly how much storage capacity is necessary for your operating system, software, and other personal computing preferences.

Prices for hard drives are the best they have ever been. For example, you can get a Fireball EL 5.1GB drive by Quantum (`http://www.quantum.com`) for about $199 or a Quantum Bigfoot TX 12GB drive for about $399. Seagate (`http://www.seagate.com`) offers its Medalist 6531 with a 6.5GB storage capacity for $226 as well as its 10240 with a 10.4GB capacity for $379.

When you look at the price per megabyte of storage, a new hard drive seems very appealing compared to other options. It only seems appealing, however, until you consider that the cost of adding just one more megabyte of storage to your computer is the cost of buying yet another, bigger hard drive.

Installing a Second Floppy

One way to combat that expense is to add a drive that lets you remove the medium when it's full and replace it cheaply and easily. (*Media* is a term used for computer storage material such as disks, compact discs, and tapes; devices on which information can be stored. *Medium* is the singular form of this term.)

A line of very affordable drives has been available for a couple of years, allowing you to save about 100MB to 200MB per disk. Because these disks have bigger capacities than regular disks, you can save multimedia files on them that won't fit on a 1.44MB disk. Removable drives also can kill two data problems with one disk, so to speak, because they also can back up data from the hard drive.

These drives are somewhat easier to install. Most come in two versions, an external version that connects to the computer's parallel port or an internal *Small Computer System Interface* (SCSI) version. (SCSI is a type of computer interface that allows the computer to work with peripherals and networks.)

The parallel port versions usually require you to plug in the drive and install some hardware to get up and running.

SCSI drives, on the other hand, require more work and are often less expensive than the external versions. If your computer doesn't have a SCSI connection inside, you will need to add an expansion card and set up the system to work with the SCSI interface, which can cause some hassles. But because the unit is internal and doesn't have to send information through a cable, it might access data faster than the external unit.

Zip Drives

One of the most popular choices of the "big floppy" lineup is the Iomega Zip drive. These lovely purple drives can save up to 100MB on a thin disk, and the company hopes one day that its drives may become the new replacement for the old disk drive. Iomega (`http://www.iomega.com`) announced in December 1997 that it had shipped more than 11 million Zip drives. They can be found already installed in some personal computers on the market.

Zip disks save data magnetically, similar to regular disks. Zip drives, however, can store significantly more data per disk because the medium inside the Zip disk is bigger than the medium inside a regular disk. Also, the read/write head inside a Zip drive can save and access data from a disk more efficiently than a regular disk's read/write head.

Because the Zip drive can save up to 100MB on each disk, it can easily store sizable graphics files, Web pages, and all sorts of things you don't want to clutter up your hard drive. It can even help to make a backup copy of important files.

Although Zip drives can't access data as fast as a hard drive, Zip drives can do it quickly enough to store and run programs from Zip disks. However you wouldn't want to store programs you use often or those that rely on speed to operate, such as graphics-intensive games or educational software.

The Zip drive's price tag is one reason it is so popular. The internal version costs $99 and the external drive sells for $149. And the disks are inexpensive too, costing about $12.95 a piece. It's a minor upfront investment that can help average consumers get a handle on all those data demons.

The Zip drive also is available in another form, the ZipPlus. The ZipPlus drive ($199) is bundled with a bunch of software packages and includes Autodetect technology that can sense if the drive is working with a PC or Macintosh computer. This is great if you want to use the drive on two computers, perhaps if you have a PC at work and a Macintosh at home.

Iomega also recently announced a $99 *ATAPI*, or *AT Attachment Packet Interface*, version that was designed to work with sub-$1,000 computers. (ATAPI is the specification for the popular *Integrated Drive Electronics* [IDE], interface that ordinarily connects CD-ROM drives and tape drives to a PC.)

LS-120 Drives

Zip's big competition is from drives using LS-120, or *laser-servo*, technology. This technology developed by Compaq, 3M, Matsushita-Kotobuki Electronics, and O.R. Technology packs 120MB on a disk that looks almost identical to an ordinary disk. In fact, LS-120 drives also can read from and store information onto ordinary disks (but only up to the 1.44MB they are formatted to handle).

Laser-servo technology can place more data on a disk because it uses a combination of magnetic and optical means to manipulate the data. An optical sensor positions the read/write head in the drive over the data tracks very precisely, and then the data is stored magnetically, just as in an ordinary disk.

Imation is a company making a big push to popularize the LS-120 drives (see Figure 20.1). Under its SuperDrive label, Imation (`http://www.imation.com`) sells the external drives for $149.99.

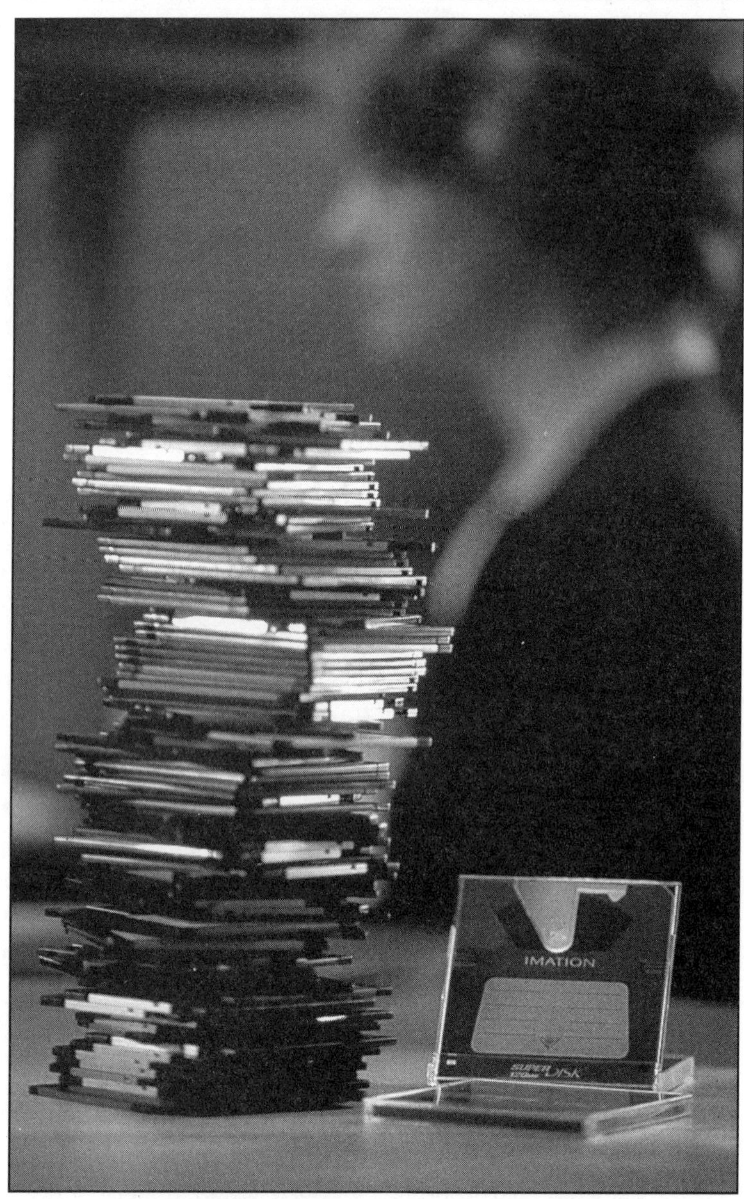

FIGURE 20.1: It takes 83 1.44MB disks to store as much information as one 120MB SuperDisk from Imation.

The 120MB disks from Imation (known as SuperDisks) sell for about $49.99 in a three-pack, which is about $17 a piece. Special encryption disks are also available to work with the SuperDrives. Priced at about $65 for a three-pack, these disks include an encryption program so you can protect private files and place a password on them so other users can't read them.

Other Options

Two other options available in the same entry-level range are the EZFlyer by SyQuest (`http://www.syquest.com`), which can store 230MB per cartridge, and the Avatar Shark drive, which can store 250MB per disk.

The EZFlyer drives sell for about $149, and cartridges are available for about $24.99 each. The EZFlyer operates a little differently than other removable disk drives, placing all the same heads, motors, media, and electronics used in regular hard drives in the SyQuest cartridges.

The Shark by Avatar (`http://www.goavatar.com`) sells for about $199, and the 250MB HARDiskette media sells for about $39 each. Avatar also has a Shark drive designed for portable systems that can be powered directly through the portable computer and doesn't require an additional power outlet, like other portable drives do.

The Removable Hard Drive

Perhaps the data monster in your computer eats up storage in bytes bigger than 100MB or 200MB increments. Perhaps you want to capture and save full-screen video. In that case, you will want to move up to a drive that's similar to a removable hard drive, saving more than 1GB of information per disk. These drives are ideal for video, photo albums, backing up hard drives, and storing huge databases. And because these "hard drives" are removable, you just pop them out when they get full and stick in another one.

Again, most of these bigger drives are available as parallel port or SCSI options. So whichever option you choose will determine how long and difficult your installation time will be, as well as how quickly the drive will access the data.

Looking at Your Choices

Both Iomega and SyQuest make drives that use hard drive–like cartridges. Iomega offers the Jaz drive, which can store up to 1GB of information per disk.

The drives sell for about $299.95 for an internal model and $399.95 for an external model. The disks sell for about $89.95 each.

Iomega also recently introduced a 2GB Jaz model that sells for about $549 for an internal unit and $649 for an external unit, with disks selling for about $149 each when purchased in a three-pack. The 2GB models are also backward-compatible with the 1GB models, meaning that you can read and write 1GB of information from the 1GB Jaz disks when you plug them into a new 2GB Jaz drive.

SyQuest offers removable hard drive choices including a new SparQ model for about $199 that can store 1GB of information on a $33 cartridge. The cheap price makes the SparQ an extremely attractive choice for any user who generates a lot of data. SyQuest also continues to offer its 1.5GB SyJet drive for about $299 for the internal model and $399 for the external. SyJet cartridges cost about $79.

And weighing in at a whopping 4.7GB, SyQuest plans to unveil the Quest drive by the end of this year, although pricing for the drives and media aren't yet available. So far, you can't get that much storage capacity in a removable drive unless you are willing to shell out extra money for a drive used by professionals, which would cost you $1,000 or more.

Installing a Compact Disk Drive

Of course, not all storage options save information magnetically. *Compact disc-recordable* (CD-R) and *compact disc-rewriteable* (CD-RW) drives store information optically. Data is stored on these discs with lasers that burn the data onto their shiny surfaces. CD-R and CD-RW discs look just like regular CD-ROMs (compact disc read-only memory), and you can play them in regular CD-ROM drives. That's the advantage for this kind of data storage.

As far as installing and operating both the CD-R and CD-RW drives, some are external parallel port units while others are internal and require SCSI setups. You may be able to drag and drop files to copy them to discs, but most drives include software that allows you to catalog, categorize, and manage the information you store on discs.

CD-R Drives

You can use CD-Rs to transfer big files from your hard drive or make backup copies of data. They are better used for information you want to pass along to other users. Place your own applications, multimedia advertisements, or training programs on the CD-Rs, and you can distribute them to be used by anyone with a CD-ROM drive.

NOTE NOTE NOTE NOTE NOTE NOTE NOTE NOTE NOTE NOTE NOTE NOTE NOTE NOTE NOTE

Although you can access data from these discs in ordinary CD-ROM drives, it doesn't mean that CD-R and CD-RW drives can operate at the same speeds as ordinary CD-ROM drives. You have to give up a little speed to gain the ability to record. For example, while you can find CD-ROM drives today that operate at ten-speed (10×) to 32×, a really fast CD-R drive might read data at 12× and record it at only 4×.

Of the two optical storage methods, CD-R drives have been around longer. (It was introduced in 1995.) The CD-R technology uses special gold CDs that have a blue-green dye polymer. To store information, a laser inside the drive burns unreflected areas and reflected areas making the ons and offs, or 0s and 1s, of digital data.

CD-R discs can be played in CD-R drives, CD-ROM drives, and CD-RW drives. You can store about 650MB of information on these discs. Once you store information on the disc, however, it's there for good. You can't rewrite the information.

CD-RW Drives

Which leads us to CD-RW. This is a newer technology, introduced in 1997, that you might also hear referred to as *compact disc-erasable* (CD-E) technology. Instead of changing dyes, *phase change* technology alters the material on the disc from a reflective state to an opaque state, creating the ons and offs of digital data.

The new technology also can be rewritten. You can go back and re-record information over the top of old information. And CD-RW is extremely adaptable. You can read from CD-RW discs in CD-RW, CD-R, and CD-ROM drives. You also can record to both CD-RW and CD-R discs in a CD-RW drive.

Paying the Price

The price depends upon the speed of the drive you want. Smart and Friendly's (`http://www.smartandfriendly.com`) CD-R 2006 can write at 2× and read at 6× for $350 for an internal unit. A faster unit from Smart and Friendly, the CD-R Speedwriter Deluxe, can write at 4× and read at 12× and costs about $549. CD-R discs are extremely inexpensive. They can be found in packs of five for about $5.

CD-RW drives are usually priced at about $100 or more for a comparable drive. For example, Smart and Friendly's CD-RW 426 Deluxe, which can write to CD-RW discs at 2×, CD-R discs at 4×, and read at 6×, costs about $600 for an internal unit. The CD-RW media costs about $18 to $22 per disc.

Although CD-RW seems to have the edge over CD-R drives, most users will likely find that CD-R drives are good enough for their needs, says Mary Bourdon, principal analyst at the Dataquest market research firm. CD-RW drives are still struggling to find the "killer app," she says. Most users don't need a drive that can rewrite data to a disc. They're using their CD-R drives to store their applications or marketing materials for distribution.

Installing a Tape Drive

Perhaps you aren't looking for a storage option that lets you manage files, create your own programs, or put together multimedia scrapbooks. If all you want is some type of medium that can make a backup copy of your data, a tape drive could be the way to go. Small businesses that want to make secondary copies of important company information periodically may find that the tape drive is the most efficient way to keep their data safe.

Instead of using disks with magnetic platters inside, like most of the other magnetic media we've discussed, tape drives save data on magnetic tape reels, somewhat similar to audiocassettes. But this causes one drawback: Instead of instantly jumping a read/write head to the location your data is stored, the tape drive has to reel through the tape until it comes to the location your data is located. This takes significantly more time to retrieve and replace data. It took us more than an hour to back up 200MB of data. Therefore, the tape drive is not designed for primary data storage.

Tape drives can come in all sorts of prices and capacities, but most consumers will be interested in drives that use minicartridges, which are about the size of a deck of cards, but can store several hundred megabytes or several gigabytes on a single cassette.

Again, tape drives are available as external parallel port units or internal units that normally fit in ordinary drive bays and connect to the same connectors as ordinary disk drives. You can't necessarily drag and drop files into your tape drive. Most drives include special software to help you manage which files should be copied.

This software also makes it easier to schedule backups of your data. You can even choose to copy only new information, so you don't have to repeat the same data on the tape over and over for each copy you make.

Prices of tape drives keep falling, making them quite inexpensive. For example, Iomega's Ditto Max tape drive sells for about $199 and can store from 3GB to 7GB of compressed information on minicartridges. The minicartridges are priced at $20 for 3GB and $30 for 7GB.

What's in Store

While the old data demon keeps growing, so does the storage selection. *Digital Video Disc* (DVD) drives can be found bundled in many new systems, but usually they're in read-only memory (ROM) form. You can't record with these drives, but it won't take long for more advanced drives to become available that make recording possible.

Rewriteable DVD

Rewriteable DVD drives are expected to enter the marketplace soon, with prices that are fairly attractive. Unfortunately, the Rewriteable DVD category of drives is a little confusing; there are currently more than five formats in the works.

The format that will probably make it to the market first is *DVD-RAM*. DVD-RAM discs are capable of holding 2.6GB per side. The DVD Forum also approved the format. Panasonic, Toshiba, and Hitachi have recently produced DVD-RAM drives, which need cartridges to house the double-sided discs.

Sony and Philips split from the DVD-RAM group late last year to continue with their own format, *DVD+RW*, according to Bourdon. This standard allows users to store 3GB of data on a one-sided DVD disc, and it doesn't require a cartridge to house the disc. These drives, however, probably won't be available until the beginning of 1999, she says. In addition, Pioneer is continuing with its own version, *DVD-R/W*, which can store 3.95GB per side.

Time will tell which format has the advantage. DVD-RAM drives will be available first, and to their advantage, DVD-RAM discs can be used interchangeably with any DVD-RAM drives by a number of manufacturers. The developers of the other DVD formats can't really say that their discs can be used in other manufacturer's DVD drives.

When the drives become available, they will probably be priced starting at $700, with the discs costing just less than $50, Bourdon estimates.

Even more storage options may develop. For example, Sony is working on a 200MB disk drive that the company hopes will replace the 1.44MB disk drive. The *HiFD*, or *High Floppy Disk*, technology will also be backward-compatible with 3.5-inch disks, as well.

It'll Cost You...

Table 20.1 maps out the cost of various storage alternatives. Most drives include at least one free disk or cartridge with the drive. Prices for the DVD-RAM drive and media are anticipated estimates.

TABLE 20.1: Drive Options and Their Costs

Drive	Cost for at Least 1GB of Storage	Cost to Add 1MB of Storage
Quantum Fireball EL 5.1GB	$199 for the 5.1GB drive	$199 for another drive; price per megabyte: $.04
Iomega Zip (internal)	$215.55 (for the drive and one free disk, plus nine disks)	$12.95 for another 100MB disk; price per megabyte: $.13
Imation SuperDrive (external)	$235.99 (for the drive and one free disk, plus eight disks)	$17 for another 120MB cartridge; price per megabyte: $.14
SyQuest EZFlyer	$248.96 (for the drive and one free cartridge, plus four cartridges)	$25 for another 230MB cartridge; price per megabyte: $.11
Avatar Shark	$316 (for the drive and one free cartridge, plus three cartridges)	$39 for another 250MB cartridge; price per megabyte: $.16
Iomega Jaz 1GB (internal)	$299.95 (for the drive and one free cartridge)	$89.95 for another 1GB cartridge; price per megabyte: $.09
Iomega Jaz 2GB (internal)	$549 (for the drive and one free cartridge)	$149 for another 2GB cartridge; price per megabyte: $.07
SyQuest SparQ	$199 (for the drive and one free cartridge)	$33 for another 1GB cartridge; price per megabyte: $.03
SyQuest SyJet (internal)	$299 (for the drive and one free cartridge)	$79 for another 1.5GB cartridge; price per megabyte: $.05
Smart and Friendly CD-R 2006 (internal)	$351 (for the drive and one free disc, plus one disc)	$1 for another 650MB disc; price per megabyte: $.002

TABLE 20.1: Drive Options and Their Costs *(continued)*

Drive	Cost for at Least 1GB of Storage	Cost to Add 1MB of Storage
Smart and Friendly CD-RW 426 Deluxe (internal)	$618 (for the drive and one free disc, plus one disc)	$18 for another 650MB disc; price per megabyte: $.03
Iomega Ditto Max (tape drive)	$199 (for the drive and one free minicartridge)	$20 for another 3GB cartridge; price per megabyte: $.007
DVD-RAM	$700 (for the drive and one free disc)	$50 for another 2.6GB disc; price per megabyte: $.02

Storage Pros and Cons

You'll find Table 20.2 useful for at-a-glance reference.

TABLE 20.2: Storage Pros and Cons

Storage Option	Pros	Cons
Second Hard Drive	Cheap cost per megabyte Fastest option for accessing programs	More difficult to install Once you use all the storage, it's gone
Big Disk Drive (Zip, LS-120, Shark)	Cheap startup cost Can clear unnecessary and little-used programs from the hard drive	Drives are proprietary, disks only work in specific drives Cost is higher per megabyte Some drives also use 1.44MB disks
Removable Drive (Jaz, SparQ, SyJet)	Best for large graphic and video storage Can clear unnecessary and little-used programs from the hard drive	Drives are proprietary, disks only work in specific drives
CD-Recordable	Best for storing your own programs or promotional material for distribution Great cost per megabyte	Once you store data on a disk, you can't store over it

TABLE 20.2: Storage Pros and Cons *(continued)*

Storage Option	Pros	Cons
CD-Rewriteable	Good option for storing your own programs or promotional material for distribution Can re-record data on disc	Significantly more expensive than CD-R
Tape Drive	Bundled software offers the best options for making and retrieving backups Slow to save data	Slow recovery of data Best cost per megabyte

File and Hard Drive Compression

Hard drives with the capacity of four, seven, or even nine gigabytes may at first seem like the lap of storage luxury, but hard drives, like hall closets, eventually run out of space.

Some user attempts at avoiding the inevitable include using Add/Remove Programs in the Control Panel of Windows 95/98 to uninstall any unused software. Frequently, however, Add/Remove doesn't list every application you've installed. In addition, running this applet doesn't guarantee that all files and folders associated with a program will be removed.

You will find it easier to reclaim valuable hard drive resources by working with more robust uninstall programs such as Symantec's Norton Uninstall Deluxe or CyberMedia's Uninstaller Deluxe. These programs examine your hard drive to identify and remove any unnecessary programs and files, including duplicates, Registry orphans, redundant dynamic-link library (.DLL) and initialization (.INI) files, Internet cookies, and obsolete leftovers in cache, temporary, and history folders.

How Compression Works

While compression techniques vary from one program or strategy to another, the idea behind each one is the same. Every file or drive compression utility uses special algorithms to create a smaller file from a larger one. The compressed file contains the same information as its source. It can be decompressed to recreate the larger file, either by demand or on-the-fly. By allowing you to store a scrunched up file instead of a larger one, you conserve storage space on a drive.

To reduce files to their minimum, all compression programs squeeze out redundancy and remove unused portions from existing data. In text-based files, this may refer to repeated characters or blank spaces. In graphic files, it may be colors and blank spaces.

Bit map (.BMP), Tagged Image File format (.TIF), and Paint (.PCX) files may shrink as much as 95%, because every bit is compressed, even blank spaces. Joint Photographic Experts Group (.JPG) files can be compressed very well because the format itself includes color compression. You'll probably get good compression results with spreadsheet worksheets, database files, ASCII text, and word processing documents. Software applications (such as files that have an .EXE extension), on the other hand, shrink very little when compressed.

Once a file has been compressed by any technique, running it through another compression program rarely gains additional space. And, due to some file header information, a fully compressed file could grow larger by a few bytes if compressed by a second compression program.

File Compression Utilities

Budget-strapped consumers worried about their computer's diminishing storage space also can avoid spending hundreds of dollars on a new hard drive by reducing the overall size of existing data. There are basically two kinds of compression programs. File compression utilities such as Luckman Interactive's MicroHelp Zip, Nico Mak's WinZip, or PKWARE's PKZIP (see Figure 20.2) free up storage space by paring down existing files to about half their original size.

Similarly, Kiss Software's DoubleZip 97 (a utility which backs up your data to removable storage media), features a built-in compression scheme that stuffs about twice as much data as usual onto Zip-, SyQuest-, and Jaz-compatible disks. As a result, a conventional 100MB Zip disk, for example, ends up holding nearly 200MB of information.

File compression utilities give you control over which files to compress. They shrink only the files or groups of files you choose. Generally, they also allow you to combine compressed versions of several files into a single *archive* so you can manage them as a unit. Archiving is very convenient for sending files via modem over the Internet because it takes less time to upload or download an archive than its individual parts.

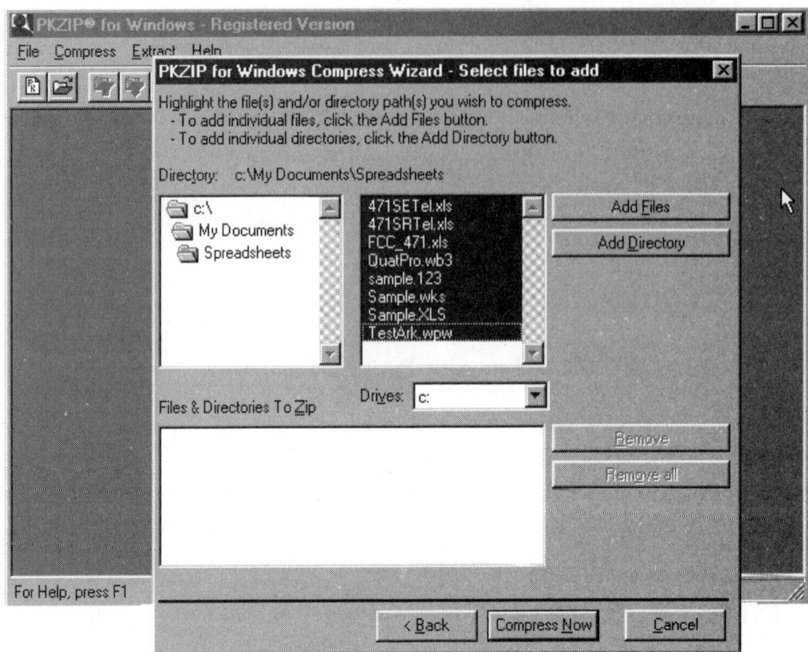

FIGURE 20.2: File compression utilities such as PKWare's PKZIP free up storage space by paring down existing files to about half their original size.

These utilities also provide a simple solution for users wanting to compress only certain files. However, the process is completely manual. You must consciously decide to compress or decompress selected files. And, if you try to read a compressed file before decompressing, it looks like gibberish.

Drive Compression Utilities

Drive compression utilities, such as the DriveSpace program built into some Microsoft operating systems, serve as a convenient alternative. Like their file compression counterparts, they free up storage space by paring down existing files to about half of their original size. However, they double the current storage capacity by building compression and decompression strategies into the operating system. Each file is automatically compressed when saved to the hard drive and is automatically decompressed when accessed or read from the drive.

Users may find drive compression more convenient than file compression because its activities require little (if any) intervention. But since your computer must compress, decompress, and recompress every file you use, you may notice a performance slowdown when an application reads data from a compressed drive.

DriveSpace 2

DriveSpace 2 is a free compression utility that Microsoft bundles with Windows 95. The "2" is meant to distinguish it from the 16-bit DriveSpace compression tool that came with MS-DOS 6.22.

DriveSpace 2 works with hard drives and removable media such as disks. It features a graphical interface and a 32-bit device driver. Users should not experience any problems installing Windows 95 (and the DriveSpace 2 compression utility) on a system compressed with DoubleSpace or previous versions of DriveSpace.

You can access DriveSpace 2 from the Start menu by choosing Programs ➢ Accessories ➢ System Tools ➢ DriveSpace. DriveSpace 2 supports file cluster sizes as large as 8KB, limiting the size of a compressed volume file (.CVF) to 512MB.

When you compress an entire drive with DriveSpace 2, all files and programs on the compressed drive are actually stored in a single hidden .CVF file, which resides on an uncompressed host drive containing some free space and system files. A DriveSpace 2 compressed drive is no longer a *real* hard disk drive, even though it may appear to be and Windows may treat it as such.

For example, if you decide to compress your hard drive, the compression utility will assign it another drive letter, such as H. Drive H serves as an uncompressed host for drive C. DriveSpace compresses the data on drive C and stores the information as a .CVF file on drive H. While the file on drive H is displayed as if it were in drive C on-screen, it will have more free space than it did before compression.

When you mount a compressed volume, the files it contains become accessible. You can work with each of them as you would with any uncompressed file. (A volume is referring to situations where a hard drive is partitioned into several drives, each of which is known as a volume.)

By default, DriveSpace 2 automatically mounts all compressed drives. A Settings command (within the Advanced menu) lets you turn off the automatic mounting feature, although it doesn't make much sense to deactivate it. DriveSpace 2 can mount compressed volumes in the foreground or background. Background operation enables you to continue working in another application. However, when it compresses (or decompresses) a drive, you cannot use the computer. And, you can't leave the computer to compress or decompress on its own because you must answer on-screen questions to complete the job.

Decompressing Time This process can take hours, depending on the amount of hard drive data, the speed of your processor, and the speed of the hard drive. First, DriveSpace 2 checks for drive errors, then it restarts your computer in a special operating mode. Next, it defragments the drive. Finally, it compresses, defragments the hard drive again, and then restarts your computer.

It took DriveSpace 2 exactly one hour and 47 minutes to compress an AST Adventure 75MHz Pentium system with an 812MB Integrated Drive Electronics (IDE) hard drive. Compression yielded 144.65MB of free space on the compressed drive and 527.9MB of free space on the host drive. Selecting Change Ratio from the Advanced menu tells you the current ratio at which data is compressed. The test system logged in at 1.5:1.

Decompressing the drive and removing the DriveSpace 2 driver took one hour and 28 minutes. Built-in data security ensures that if the compression process is interrupted by a power outage, DriveSpace 2 will continue where it left off, without losing any data once power is restored. In case of a potential mishap, it asks you to back up your files before actually compressing the drive, using a link to the backup utility supplied with Windows 95.

Disks compressed with DriveSpace 2 are unreadable on systems that do not have DriveSpace or DoubleSpace installed. To compress a 1.44MB disk, it must contain at least 512KB of free space. It took DriveSpace 24 minutes to compress files on a 1.44MB disk with 911KB of free space before compression. Decompression took three minutes. If your disk is too full when it is compressed, you might have to drag some compressed files to the Recycle Bin before DriveSpace 2 will restore the disk to its original condition.

NOTE

The Windows 95 user manual contains virtually no DriveSpace 2 printed documentation. For operating instructions, you must consult online help, accessed from the DriveSpace Help menu.

DriveSpace 3

DriveSpace 2 is not as powerful as DriveSpace 3, the drive compression utility bundled with Microsoft Plus!, a collection of Windows 95 enhancements. DriveSpace 3 features higher compression rates (up to a maximum of 2GB per compressed volume), three levels of compression, and more compression options. DriveSpace 3 also sports a 32-bit architecture and can achieve higher compression rates than DriveSpace 2 because it handles file cluster sizes as large as 32KB.

When you install DriveSpace 3, it replaces DriveSpace 2. A 3 in the DriveSpace icon (see DRVSPACE.EXE in the WINDOWS folder) lets you know which version of the compression technology is currently installed.

Be sure to install DriveSpace 3 with the System Agent option. System Agent runs the Plus! Compression Agent to shrink your files even more (according to settings that you specify). The Compression Agent kicks into action when your computer is on, but not in use, or at specified times according to settings that you designate. The Compression Agent may be paused or stopped during operation without affecting data it has already compressed.

You can access DriveSpace 3 from the Start menu by choosing Programs ➢ Accessories ➢ System Tools ➢ DriveSpace. DriveSpace 3's interface, pull-down menus, and dialog boxes are similar to DriveSpace 2 (see Figure 20.3).

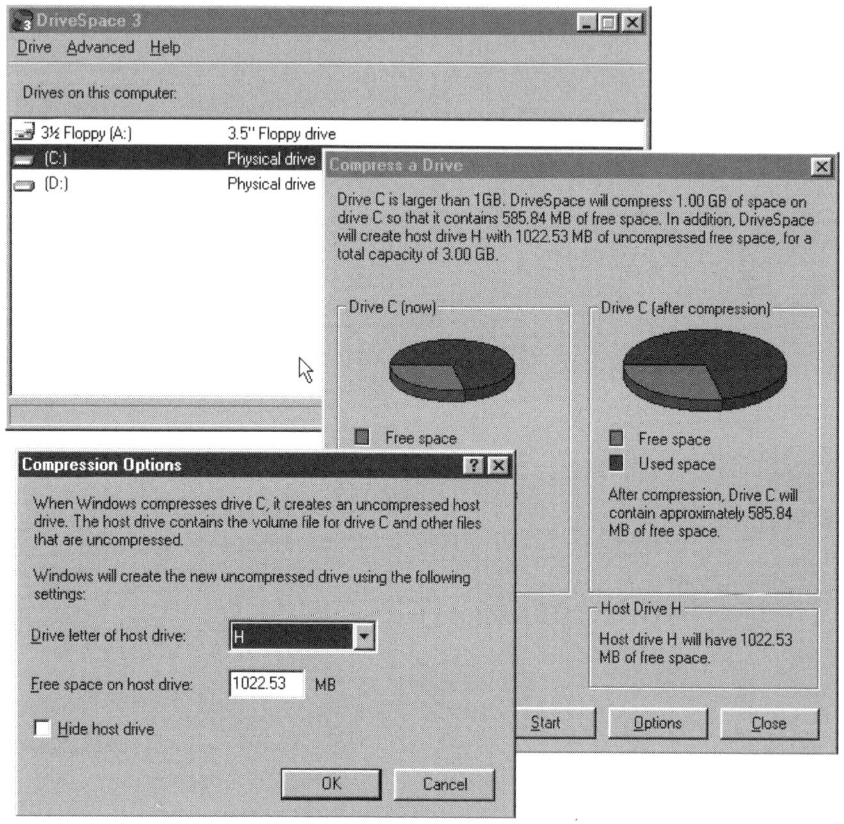

FIGURE 20.3: Microsoft's DriveSpace 3 features compression rates of up to a maximum of two gigabytes per compressed volume with three levels of compression.

Before compressing your hard drive, DriveSpace 3 prompts you to update your Windows 95 Startup drive just in case there's a compression mishap. If your drive is already compressed with DriveSpace 2 or DoubleSpace, you don't have to decompress the hard drive before upgrading to DriveSpace 3. Just right-click the drive icon of the drive you want to upgrade, select the Compression tab from the Properties option, then click Upgrade Now. This Compression tab also gives you convenient access to several DriveSpace 3 compression options.

Like DriveSpace 2, DriveSpace 3 lets you determine the amount of free space that will reside on the uncompressed host drive. You also can choose from three DriveSpace 3 levels of compression: Standard, HiPack (offering compression rates 10 to 20 percent better than Standard rates), and UltraPack (offering the highest compression rate). If you choose Standard or HiPack, files in a compressed hard drive compress and decompress on-the-fly as you work with them or save them.

UltraPack files seem to open more slowly. Perhaps it's because compressed data are more tightly packed. The only way to compress files using UltraPack is to run the Compression Agent. There's also a No Compression option, which directs Windows to save files in uncompressed format if you have the appropriate amount of drive space. A Fine-Tuning Plus! option lets you readjust the balance between compression speed and the space a compressed file takes.

Decompressing Time It took DriveSpace 3 one hour and 34 minutes (running the Standard compression option) to shrink the 812MB test drive containing 401MB of used space and 411MB of free space. Compression resulted in a C drive with 1.09GB of free space (an effective gain of 709.81MB of space), plus a host drive of 10MB of free space. The compression ratio for Standard compressed files logged in at 1.6:1. It took one hour and 25 minutes to restore the hard drive to its normal uncompressed state.

To test the gain in space by choosing another compression setting, we directed DriveSpace 3 to compress the test drive a second time. After the drive was compressed, we directed the DriveSpace 3 Compression Agent to UltraPack files not used within the last 30 days and to HiPack the remaining files. It took Compression Agent three hours and 45 minutes to do the work. The same drive experienced an additional space gain of 53.8MB for files compressed with UltraPack and 4.58MB for files compressed with HiPack. Total gain by running the Compression Agent: 58.38MB with a compression ratio of 1.82:1.

It took DriveSpace 3 about four minutes to compress files on a 1.44MB disk with 912KB of free space before compression. The disk had 1.94MB of free space after compression, for a total gain of 1.05MB. The compression ratio equaled 1.3 to 1. Decompression took three minutes, 26 seconds.

NOTE NOTE NOTE NOTE NOTE NOTE NOTE NOTE NOTE NOTE NOTE NOTE NOTE NOTE NOTE

The printed documentation for DriveSpace 3 in the Microsoft Plus! manual is limited to seven pages. You're better off consulting online help to learn more about program features.

Compression Warnings

When you use compression to make changes to your hard drive, you put your data at risk. If the compressed file or application cannot be restored exactly as it was originally, down to the last byte, it won't open or run. So here are a few words of advice. Make a full uncompressed backup of your data files before compressing them. Don't use another utility to compress a file or drive that's already compressed. Don't delete or tamper with hidden Drvspace files.

If you want to change operating systems, make sure the new one supports your old compression scheme and is smart enough to update it. Create an emergency rescue disk with a drive recovery utility such as CyberMedia's First Aid 98, Symantec's Norton Utilities, or Network Associates' Nuts & Bolts so that if you can't start your computer from the compressed drive, you still have a backup plan.

Are You Experienced?

Now you can...

☑ **evaluate your storage options and choose the best one for you**

☑ **look into the future with DVD**

☑ **manage your file compression**

SKILL 21

Upgrading Software

- Finding the right software on the Internet
- Knowing what to avoid
- Upgrading your operating system
- Dual-booting operating systems

Remember back in the old days when, to upgrade your computer system, you had to trudge to the computer store…three miles each way…barefoot…in the snow?

OK, so maybe your effort didn't rival your parents' school days, but as old-timers will tell you (or as you may know yourself), upgrading your PC used to mean multiple trips to the store or multiple phone calls to a software or hardware manufacturer—or both. With the rapid growth of the online world, this has changed. Now, you can get a complete update, try a new demonstration version, and fix a bug in your program, all without stepping out of your home or office.

Cool new software isn't the only thing you can get online; you'll also find upgrades for operating systems on the Net. You can find them in a store too, of course. This skill will also go into how to upgrade most any kind of operating system.

Find the Software You Need on the Internet

The Internet is a handy tool for those who want and need software upgrades. You can download the latest edition of your favorite software. You can try out new features without paying for an entire program. And you can choose from a wealth of information online. Here's a look at how to use the Internet efficiently to upgrade your software.

Why Should You Upgrade Your Software?

First, let's take a look at what you'll find on the World Wide Web. When it comes to software upgrades, the Web is a boon to both software manufacturers and consumers.

Suppose you run a small business from home and have discovered a fabulous accounting package. You've used it for two years and can't imagine working without it. It helps you track payroll information, keep tabs on your receivables, and perform a variety of other necessary tasks.

But now your business is growing, and the current version of your software isn't sufficient for handling all your employees' data. Coincidentally, a new version of this accounting package has been released, and the new version is much more *scaleable* (able to process a greater number of entries). In addition, it likely has some other features that you can take advantage of, such as an improved interface.

Rather than buying a whole new package, you can go on the Internet and acquire the latest version. Most software manufacturers make updated editions of their content available on the Web—and for good reason. Think of the cost savings companies can achieve by not footing the bill for packaging costs, mailing fees, etc. There also are marketing benefits; software companies can track how many customers are updating old software and how many customers are buying the software for the first time. Companies also can encourage registration by forcing users to register for the update before they download it. To take advantage of online updates, you just locate the software (more on that in a minute), download it, install it, and you're ready to go.

Trying Out Something New

Another important use of the Internet in upgrading is adding new programs that enhance an entire system's functionality. Many companies offer demonstration versions of their software that you can try out to see if it can enhance your computing experience. Demonstration versions of software (often called *demos*) can show you improvements you can make to your system without requiring you to invest a lot of money in software you may not need.

Hundreds of companies offer trial versions of software, often with either time restraints (the most common is a 30-day time limit) or limited functionality (you get added features by buying a different version). Some software companies even let you download the complete version of the software, and after the month-long trial is over and the software *locks* itself, you can fill out a Web form or call in or fax your credit card number, and the company will then send you a *key* that lets you remove the lock.

Fixing Problems

Demos and upgrades are fine for checking out new programs and features, but what happens when the software you already have has a bug and the company has not yet released a version that fixes that bug? This is where *patches* come in. A patch is a piece of object code (code that is produced by compiler) that copies over the offending code and fixes the bug. Software companies often will release patches when there are bugs in a released product and the company wants users to get a quick fix before the company can get the product upgrade on the market.

Jasc Software is one such company that employs patches. The makers of the useful Paint Shop Pro screen capture utility offers online maintenance upgrades to licensed users of its products. Users first obtain a registered version of the Paint Shop Pro software. Then, they can go to the Jasc Web site (`http://www.jasc.com`) to download a patch, and the site warns visitors that "these patches will only work on the registered versions of our products." Once the download is complete, users run the patch, and it modifies the original program.

Most patches work only on registered versions of software—this discourages unauthorized copying or pirating of software—but you may find an occasional patch that modifies unregistered software. Also, you should be aware that some software needs to be "patched" in steps. In our above example, Jasc users who have Paint Shop Pro 4.0 and want to upgrade to 4.14 need to first download and run the Paint Shop Pro 4.12 upgrade patch and then run the Paint Shop Pro 4.14 patch.

Driving Your Hardware

Not only can you upgrade your software over the Net, but also you can upgrade the software your hardware needs to communicate with your computer. These programs are called *device drivers*, and if you need to upgrade a hardware device, you also need to upgrade the hardware's driver. Most drivers come with your operating system, but if you buy a new device, you might need to load a new driver.

Not surprisingly, operating systems perform best when you have the correct drivers. You may not notice it, but updated drivers often lead to better performance or contain new features not available in the original versions. Therefore, it's a good idea to update your drivers whenever possible.

How does all this relate to the Internet? Plenty of information about drivers can be found online. Several notable Web sites, such as WinDrivers.com (`http://www.windrivers.com`), contain all you need to know about drivers. There are also all the company Web sites that offer drivers that can be downloaded.

A case in point is NEC, which recently released the Superscript 860 Laser Printer for Windows NT 4. Previously, the printer was compatible with other operating systems but not Windows NT, which is used by many corporations with internal networks. NEC announced the product availability with a press release on its Web site and also made the driver available via download at the site.

Browsing for Browsers

The Internet also is a great place to upgrade a certain piece of software all Net users have: the Web browser. Thanks to the Web browser marketplace war between Netscape Communications and Microsoft, and the minor skirmishes with other companies, both of the major Web browsers are being upgraded regularly. At one point, Netscape offered a standard version of Netscape Navigator 3.0, with upgrades to 3.01, 3.0 Gold, 3.01 Gold, as well as beta versions of 4.0. Microsoft also offers a variety of Microsoft Internet Explorer versions, the latest of which is version 4.*x*.

No matter which version you have, upgrading these two popular Web browsers is a snap. Under your browser's Help menu, you'll see a menu choice that reads either Software Updates (in Navigator) or Product Updates (in Explorer). Selecting this option will take you to the browser manufacturer's update page where you can get the latest upgrade to your browser.

One of the neat features of these "smart update" pages is they can remember which components you've installed and suggest new components to make your system work better for you. They also provide you with detailed information on how to configure your browser to perform the tasks you need it to do.

Where to Go

Now that you know what the Internet can do for you when you're ready to upgrade, you need to know where to look for software upgrades.

An obvious online place for upgrade information is the Web site of the manufacturer of the software you want to upgrade. Increasingly, companies are adding downloadable upgrades on their product pages. Just go to the company's home page and look for a button labeled Products or type **upgrade** or **update** in the Web site's search engine. You also may find information about upgrades in online press releases, which are usually found within the About Our Company sections. Web search engines, such as Yahoo! (`http://www.yahoo.com`) and MetaCrawler (`http://www.metacrawler.com`), also are good spots for finding upgrade information (although it is useful to search by product name when using them).

Online computer stores also are worthy sources of upgrade information. Superstores such as Egghead (`http://www.egghead.com`) often promote upgrades on their home pages. During a recent visit, Egghead featured the Windows 98 upgrade package. Some of these stores have upgrade sections where they either link you to company pages or actually sell the upgrades themselves. If they don't have specific update areas, however, you can still find useful information. You can learn about the latest version of the software and compare it to similar products on the market.

Another Internet source that is less well-known but certainly a prize is Versions!—a new, free service that is sure to take off when it becomes more widely known. Versions! sends you an e-mail message each time the developer of a product you have chosen releases an upgrade. With more than 63,000 listed products; a search engine that searches by keyword, product name, or developer; and optional notification of new products, Versions! (`http://www.versions.com`) is a must-see for those considering upgrading. Versions! also offers a premium service that lets users search for articles containing information about software upgrades.

Of course, the Internet isn't the only place for upgrades information. If your modem connection is down, or you just need to get out of the house, you can head down to your local computer store and compare software boxes. Most upgrades will prominently mention new features. Or, you can read the manual for telephone numbers and Web site information.

What to Do

You've located the upgrade you want, and you're ready to download and install it. Here's how.

First, make sure your system can handle the upgrade. If an upgrade offers cool, new features, it may gobble up more resources. Check those system requirements carefully. Also, be sure the upgrade works with your current version of the software.

Second, read the directions! Most Web sites have either a separate README.TXT file or Web page. We recommend you either memorize these directions or print them; during installation, you likely won't be able to read them.

Third, choose an appropriate place in which to save the upgrade. You might need access to the older version of the program; what if the upgrade has a bug in it and it crashes every time you run it? You'll likely be prompted to download the file to the directory where the current program sits. Instead, install the upgraded program to a new subdirectory (call it TEMP or a similar name) rather than to the subdirectory used by the version of the program you already have.

If its taking a long time to download the software, consider logging on at a less busy time. Immediately after an upgrade is announced is usually the worst time to try obtaining a copy, especially with popular software such as Web browsers. Another option is to order the installation CD-ROM online.

After you have installed the software, register it right away and pay if you are required to, before you have a chance to forget. Although some programs come with "nag" buttons ("This is your 480th day of a free 30-day trial"), others will simply quit working.

Let's look at a quick example. Quicken, the popular personal finance software from Intuit, regularly adds new features, and free upgrades are available to registered users. Head to the Quicken update site (`http://www.intuit.com/support/updates`) and choose the product you want to update. Here, you'll find details on cost (free updates are always available automatically online), update features, download time, and more.

What to Watch Out For

Although the Internet makes it easy to obtain software upgrades, thing can go wrong. Here are several trouble spots to avoid when downloading programs.

Viruses

You've probably heard it before, but it's worth repeating: Never, *ever* download something from the Internet without first checking it for a computer virus. These man-made pests can make copies of themselves over and over again, gobbling up all your memory and causing your system to crash. While reputable software companies ensure their upgrades are virus-free, it can't hurt to check them on your end, especially if you're downloading a file from a third party. You can't get a virus from the text of an e-mail message, but you can pick it up if a file comes through as an attachment to an e-mail message.

There are plenty of great antivirus programs on the market, such as VirusScan from Network Associates and Norton AntiVirus by Symantec. You can find great virus information at these Web sites, as well as at Antivirus Online, an online publication from IBM (`http://www.av.ibm.com/current/FrontPage`); NCSA Virus Lab (`http://www.ncsa.com/virus`); and Dr Solomon's computer virus information site (`http://www.drsolomon.com`).

Additional Upgrades

Software companies are constantly improving their offerings, and it's likely that you'll want to upgrade over and over again during the course of a few months or a year. When you buy new software, be sure to find out which upgrades (if any) will be available to you on the Net and how you will be notified. In addition, find out how upgrades to the rest of your system (are you upgrading from a Windows 95 version to a Windows 98 version?) will be taken care of. If you're going to upgrade your operating system, you'll want to know how much it will cost you to upgrade the rest of your software.

Cost

Watch out for hidden costs when you upgrade your software. This applies to both software you obtain from the Internet and software you get elsewhere. If you need to learn new features or train others to use the software, it may not make sense to upgrade each time a new version is released. In addition, you may find a particular upgrade is free at one site but costs you elsewhere, so look around for the best deal.

Encryption

Different Web browsers have different encryption capabilities. While we won't go into the security details of 40-bit encryption versus 128-bit encryption, suffice it to say many browsers are not very secure, but companies are beginning to require more secure browsers to visit their Web sites. If your browser doesn't let you onto a Web site to obtain software upgrades, your browser's encryption may be the culprit.

Technical Support

If you download upgrades via the Net, first determine which types of technical support will be available. When you buy boxed upgrades, you'll often receive detailed technical manuals; if you download the software, you may not receive the same material, especially if the downloaded programs are free. Find out what tech support is offered for people obtaining upgrades from Web sites. This is another motivation for registering your software; some companies won't provide tech support until you have done so.

TIP TIP TIP TIP TIP TIP TIP TIP TIP TIP TIP TIP TIP TIP TIP TIP TIP TIP TIP TIP TIP TIP TIP TIP TIP

The Internet is a wonderfully helpful community of individuals, so before you upgrade your system, talk to those who are in the know. Check out computer newsgroups such as `comp.os.ms-windows.win95.setup`**, Internet mailing lists such as the Great Lakes Windows NT Users Group, and message boards on various software company Web sites.**

Compatibility

While this situation is rare, you may find that an upgrade improves the program but hurts the performance of other software on your computer. Go online to read any information you can find about known incompatibilities regarding that particular software.

By exploring your online software upgrade options, you can get the latest versions of software easily—and all while keep those snowdrifts off your feet.

Upgrade Sources on the Web

To get more information about software upgrades, check out these handy sites on the World Wide Web.

BugNet What if you find a bug in that cool software, and you want to find out how to fix it? Or maybe you just want to know what to watch out for? BugNet has the answers. BugNet tracks PC bugs and fixes, and you can use this site to report glitches, learn about incompatibilities, and, most importantly, acquire upgrades that take care of those nasty headaches caused by computer bugs. The low-cost subscription may well be worth the money. `http://www.bugnet.com`

Download.com You're probably familiar with this site and its cousins Shareware.com and Freeware.com, but if you aren't, you'll thank yourself for visiting. Here, you'll be able to download the latest versions of popular and not-so-mainstream software packages, and you can try out much of the offerings. The weekly newsletter Download Dispatch will let you know what's new at the site. `http://download.com`

Frank Condron's World O'Windows If you need to update a device driver, you need to visit Frank Condron's World O'Windows Web site first. This up-to-date site is the place to be for information about drivers, and the Updates section is packed with facts on companies that have updated their drivers. Pick a company name, and you'll find a list of products and their latest version numbers, categorized by operating system. http://www.conitech.com/windows/index.asp

Ray's Windows 95 Upgrades Page This site lives up to its claim of being a wealth of resources for the Windows 95 user. You'll find dozens of links to software upgrades, updates, and patches. Especially helpful is the bulletin section at the top of the page, which alerts you to news stories related to upgrades. Then, scroll down to the links section for a directory of software upgrade categories, such as "free updates from Microsoft" and "Corel and WordPerfect support and updates." http://www2.gc.net/~rwclements/upgrades.html

continued

The PC Zone There are plenty of computer stores on the Web, but one that deserves mention for its availability of upgrades of software, hardware, and computer memory is The Zones Internet SuperStores. The PC Zone (there's also a Mac Zone) lets you browse through categories such as education, operating systems, and word processing. Although you won't find a separate section for upgrades, you can determine whether a software upgrade is available and compare versions of competing products. `http://www.zones.com/upgrades.htm`

Upgrading Your Operating System

This section will go through the steps of upgrading the most popular operating systems. Remember that you should not do anything before you back up your system!

Upgrading from DOS to Windows 95

There are two reasons to upgrade to Windows 95 from DOS: either you never had Windows on your computer, or you deleted everything and decided to install the new operating system from scratch. In either case, your equipment must fulfill these minimum system requirements: a 33 megahertz or higher 386DX processor (a 486 is preferred), 8MB of RAM, 50MB to 55MB of free hard drive space, and a Video Graphics Array (VGA) or higher resolution monitor and video adapter.

NOTE NOTE NOTE NOTE NOTE NOTE NOTE NOTE NOTE NOTE NOTE NOTE NOTE NOTE NOTE

DOS users who upgrade to Windows 95 have an advantage in that they don't have to relearn Windows, while users with Windows 3.*x* must prepare for a new interface.

Because you are upgrading from DOS and your computer is not loaded with a previous Windows version, buy the Windows 95 package that says For *PCs Without Windows!*, not the one marked *Upgrade*. It's available on CD-ROM or 3.5-inch disks.

Preparing Your System

Windows 95 installs its own system, including MS-DOS, so it doesn't matter which DOS version you currently have. If Windows has never been installed on your system, you probably are considering upgrading your current applications to their Windows counterparts. Before starting installation, make a complete backup of your data files. With a DOS-based computer, there is no benefit to backing up all of your application files unless you want to reuse them in Windows.

Because Windows 95 requires up to 55MB of free hard drive space, be sure your disk partition is large enough to support Windows and all its directories, especially if you are working with an MS-DOS version older than 4.0. Prior to 4.0, the partition size of DOS was limited to 32MB. In this situation, you must repartition your drive so you can install Windows 95.

Using the Boot Disk

The disk version of Windows 95 includes a boot disk containing an operating system and the files necessary to partition (FDISK.EXE) and format (FORMAT.EXE) your hard drive. If you are using a computer without an operating system, or the hard drive partitions are too small to install Windows 95 on, follow these steps.

WARNING WARNING WARNING WARNING WARNING WARNING WARNING WARNING

Changing hard drive partitions will cause data to be lost. Back up all important data before proceeding with these instructions.

1. With the boot disk in drive A:, reboot your computer.
2. When the command prompt appears, type **fdisk**, and press Enter.
3. From the FDISK screen, select Option 4. This screen displays the distribution of space on your hard drive. If your drive has more than one partition, each is displayed as EXT (extended) DOS under the Type heading. The heading Mbytes displays the size of the drive, and Usage indicates the percentage used by each Type.
4. After returning to the FDISK screen, select Option 3, Delete Partition Or Logical DOS Drive. If your hard drive is divided into logical drives, you must delete the logical drives in the extended DOS partition before deleting the primary DOS partition. After you delete all partitions, you may want to look at the partition information again (Option 4).

TIP TIP TIP TIP TIP TIP TIP TIP TIP TIP TIP TIP TIP TIP TIP TIP TIP TIP TIP TIP TIP TIP TIP TIP TIP TIP

Partition size depends on your hard drive capacity. To limit cluster size, make your partitions 128MB or less. It is best to divide the drive into smaller chunks for efficiency and performance. Setting aside a single drive partition to maintain your swap file limits fragmentation to a single location, which makes defragmentation easier and faster.

5. From the FDISK screen, set the active DOS partition (always drive C:). Next, using the FORMAT.EXE program, format each drive letter that the partitioning created. Remember to add the /S switch to the format command when formatting drive C:. This transfers the operating system so your computer will boot.

Installing on a 386

Installing Windows 95 from 3.5-inch disks on a 386 computer with 4MB of RAM will be extremely slow. To speed the process, you may copy the files on the disks to a temporary directory on your hard drive. Because these files (.CAB) are compressed, you will need to use the EXTRACT command located on Disk 1 to copy the WINDOWS 95_XX.CAB files to your hard drive and to copy files from Disks 2 through 12. The .CAB files are Microsoft Distribution Media Format (DMF), and MS-DOS commands such as COPY and XCOPY won't work on these disks.

To copy a .CAB file from a disk to your hard drive, use the following command:

```
extract /c a:win95_xx.cab c:\<tempdir>
```

with *<tempdir>* being the location of a temporary directory on your hard drive.

If possible, do not install Windows 95 or the Windows swap file on a compressed disk. Often, the free drive space reported by the utility is more than what is available. Also, using a compressed disk for the swap file may seriously degrade your system's performance.

Upgrading from Windows 3.*x* to Windows 95

Installing Windows 95 if you have Windows 3.1 is more than a mere upgrade. Windows 95 is a new operating system with new needs and features. Windows 95's ability to run existing applications is the only similarity between it and previous Windows versions. Once you look past the important backward-compatibility issue, however, the two programs chart their own courses.

Microsoft recommends a minimum of a 20MHz, 386DX processor and 4MB of RAM to run Windows 95. But to fully reach its operating potential, Windows 95 should be run on a 33MHz or faster 486DX microprocessor with a minimum of 8MB of RAM. 16MB is better. A typical installation requires 35MB to 40MB of hard drive space, and if you plan to access The Microsoft Network and Microsoft Exchange, you'll need another 20MB of hard drive space.

Finding Room

There are a couple of ways to regain some hard drive space to make room for Windows 95.

If your Windows 3.1 swap file is permanent, disabling it frees the space it now occupies on the hard drive. To change the virtual memory setting, go to the Control Panel, double-click the 386-Enhanced icon, then click on Virtual Memory to open the Virtual Memory dialog box. Windows 3.1 uses one of two methods to deal with its swap file—Permanent or Temporary. The other setting is None. Size displays the amount of drive space occupied by the swap file. If the Type is set on Permanent, that is the amount of drive space you will regain on the swap file's resident drive. If the Type is Permanent, select None from the Type list from under the New Settings area.

After making the change, your computer must restart Windows for the change to take effect. Deleting unnecessary files also clears hard drive space.

Protecting Your Data

It is important to back up all your important data files when upgrading to Windows 95. We recommend you also back up these files:

- All initialization (.INI) files in the Windows directory
- All Registry data (.DAT) files in the Windows directory
- All password (.PWL) files in the Windows directory
- CONFIG.SYS and AUTOEXEC.BAT files
- All critical Real mode drivers specified in the CONFIG.SYS and AUTOEXEC.BAT files
- Proprietary network configuration files and logon scripts
- All Program Manager group (.GRP) files in the Windows directory
- Any file crucial to the operation of any part of your system

Startup Files

Because of the nature of Windows 95, the AUTOEXEC.BAT and CONFIG.SYS files are no longer required in the startup process, except for drivers specifically used for certain hard drive controllers. If your CD-ROM drive and sound card are supported by Windows 95, you should delete any references to your 16-bit drivers in the CONFIG.SYS and AUTOEXEC.BAT files. Do not load any memory resident (TSR) programs unless it's absolutely necessary. Windows 95 uses VCACHE for disk caching, so make sure you are not loading SMARTDRV. You can remove the following commands from CONFIG.SYS:

```
stacks=
buffers=
files=
```

You also can remove MSCDEX from your AUTOEXEC.BAT file although Windows 95 should have already placed a REM command before it. You also can remove the `Set Temp=` line since Windows 95 will automatically set the `Set Temp=` line variable to the Temp directory it created in the Windows directory.

If you run memory resident programs, you will probably want to load them into upper memory. In this case, you must load a memory manager such as HIMEM.SYS from CONFIG.SYS.

If you are loading a video card refresh rate utility from the AUTOEXEC.BAT or CONFIG.SYS files, do not remove this command line. Windows 95 does not support ANSI.SYS, so if a program requires this driver, you will need to keep it active for loading from CONFIG.SYS.

Choosing a Setup Scenario

Windows 95 provides four installation options: Typical, Portable, Compact, and Custom. Each scenario installs a set of preselected files onto your system. Compact Setup installs the fewest files, while Custom Setup, according to your selections, can install the most. Custom Setup requires the most user input, so if you are uncomfortable providing your configuration information, don't select this scenario.

Our experience shows that the Typical Setup suits a large number of users and is the one to start with. It is easy to add or remove applications after installation.

Installing Windows 95 is more than an operating system upgrade. That is why Microsoft often uses the term *migration* to describe the move to Windows 95. It may take some getting used to, but you will find that Windows 95's features are worth the effort.

Upgrading from MS-DOS to Windows 98

Upgrading from MS-DOS to Windows 98 will arm you with a powerful 32-bit operating system that can take full advantage of a Pentium PC's 32-bit processing architecture.

Microsoft's new operating system, Windows 98, integrates the operating system with easier access to the Internet. The newly designed graphical user interface, or GUI—an interface that uses symbols, icons, and menus to carry out commands—features improved Dial-Up Networking integrated with the Internet Explorer Web browser to enable users to take full advantage of Internet resources.

During the installation processes you can choose to install the Active Desktop, which through an Internet connection will deliver the latest news, weather, stock prices, and even the latest updates for your system and application files directly to your desktop.

Other improvements with Windows 98 include direct support for hardware innovations such as universal serial bus (USB), Institute of Electrical and Electronic Engineers (IEEE) 1394 parallel port standards, and digital video disc, also known as digital versatile disc (DVD), drives. The new operating system also is easily maintained with a new System Information Utility containing system backup, cleanup, configuration, diagnostic, and automatic updating tools.

System Requirements

You need to make sure your system can handle the hefty hardware requirements of Windows 98. You need at least a 100MHz Pentium PC with 16MB of RAM and a CD-ROM drive. In addition, Windows 98 will take anywhere from 120MB to 300MB of hard drive space, depending upon the enhancements you choose to install.

Preparation

First things first, be sure to back up all your important data.

1. Check to make sure you have the latest Basic Input/Output System (BIOS) update. (The BIOS is firmware that controls how your PC operates.) If your PC was purchased before 1994, check with the vendor, and get an updated BIOS chip for your motherboard. If your PC is relatively new, it probably has a flash BIOS, in which case you may be able to download the BIOS upgrade from the PC vendor's Web site. You will need the latest BIOS update to be able to fully use Windows 98's features.

2. The next step is to create an MS-DOS boot disk. Place an empty disk in the disk drive (probably drive A:) and at the C:\> prompt, type **Format a: /s** and press Enter. Then, copy the FDISK.EXE, FORMAT.COM, and XCOPY.EXE files, located in the DOS directory (C:\DOS), to the disk. Simply type **copy c:/dos/fdisk.exe a:**, replacing the *fdisk.exe* portion with the file name of the file you are copying.

3. Restart your system with the MS-DOS boot disk in the disk drive. At the A:\> prompt (where A: is the letter of your disk drive), type **Fdisk** and press Enter. From the Fdisk Options menu, select Create DOS Partition or Logical DOS Drive. Then, choose to use the whole hard drive as the DOS partition and make it Active.

4. Once the partition is created, press Esc to exit Fdisk. At the A:\> prompt, type **Format c: /s** and press Enter. This will format and transfer the system to the hard drive. Finally, remove the disk from the drive and restart your PC.

5. Next, you will need to install the CD-ROM drive device drivers using the driver disk that came with the CD-ROM drive. Place the driver disk into the disk drive, then, at the A:\> prompt (where A: is the letter of your disk drive), type **Install** or **Setup**. The proper drivers will automatically install to your hard drive.

Installing Windows 98

Once all the prep work is taken care of, it's time to do the actual installation of Windows 98.

To install your new operating system, place the Windows 98 disc into the CD-ROM drive.

1. At the C:\> prompt, type the letter representing the CD-ROM drive (probably **D:**) and press Enter. At the D:\> prompt (where D: is the letter of your CD-ROM drive), type **cd\Win98** and press Enter. Then, type **Setup** and press Enter. Follow the instructions on the various Setup Wizard screens as the installation proceeds.

2. Although it's not necessary for Windows 98 to run, you may want to copy all the contents of the CD-ROM's Windows 98 directory (D:\WIN98) to the root directory (C:\) of your hard drive. This will enable you to install Windows 98 from your hard drive and refer to all the Windows 98 installation and .CAB files in the C:\WIN98 directory for future installations and updates as needed.

Once the installation is complete, you will be welcomed to a new world of colorful icons and pull-down menus. It's a far cry from the bland character-based DOS interface, and you will find that it's very easy to navigate.

Upgrading from Windows 3.1 to Windows 98

Upgrading from Windows 3.1 to Windows 98 will give your PC the full capability of a powerful 32-bit operating system while continuing to support your 16-bit DOS and Windows applications.

Windows 98, Microsoft's newest operating system, integrates the operating system with easier access to the Internet. The newly designed graphical user interface (GUI)—an interface that uses symbols, icons, and menus to carry out commands—includes improved Dial-Up Networking integrated with the Microsoft Internet Explorer 4 Web browser to enable users to take full advantage of Internet resources. The Active Desktop feature uses an Internet connection to deliver the latest news, weather, stock prices, and even the latest updates for your system and application files directly to your desktop.

Other improvements to Windows 98 include direct support for hardware innovations such as universal serial bus (USB), Institute of Electrical and Electronic Engineers (IEEE) 1394 parallel port standards, and digital video (versatile) disc (DVD) drives. And, the new operating system is easily maintained with a new System Information Utility containing system backup, cleanup, configuration, diagnostic, and automatic updating tools.

System Requirements

Before you begin the installation, make sure your system has the necessary hardware to support the new operating system. Your system should have at least a 100MHz Pentium processor, 16MB of RAM, and a CD-ROM drive. You also will need 120MB to 300MB of available hard drive space, depending on the enhancements you choose to install.

Preparation

First, make backup copies of all your important data. This will come in handy if something goes haywire during the installation.

Next, make sure you have the latest Basic Input/Output System (BIOS) update. (The BIOS is firmware that controls how your PC operates.) If you purchased your PC before 1994, check with the vendor, and get an updated BIOS chip for your motherboard. If your system is relatively new, it probably has a flash BIOS, in which case you may be able to download the BIOS upgrade from the PC vendor's Web site. You will need the latest BIOS update to be able to fully use Windows 98's features.

You also will need to deactivate any terminate-and-stay resident (TSR) programs or antivirus programs that are set to start when your PC is turned on. These types of programs can halt the Windows 98 upgrade procedure.

And, of course, it's always a good idea to create an emergency boot disk before upgrading anything on your system. Place an empty disk into the disk drive, and at the C:\> prompt, type **Format a: /s**. This will transfer the operating system to the disk.

Then, copy the AUTOEXEC.BAT and CONFIG.SYS files to the disk. You also will need to copy your CD-ROM drive device drivers that are referred to in the AUTOEXEC.BAT and CONFIG.SYS files. Use the Edit command in DOS to edit those files, referencing them to the A: drive location of the CD-ROM drive device drivers. When you're finished, restart your PC with this disk to ensure you can access your CD-ROM drive when booting from the A: drive.

Finally, take some time to clean up your hard drive before making the big switch. In Windows 3.*x*'s File Manager, use the Search utility (under the File menu) to locate any .TMP, .BAK, or .$$$ files. Choose Delete to remove them from your hard drive.

Then, check to see if Windows 3.1 has created a large permanent swap file. If so, you will need to remove it before the upgrade. Go to Control Panel in the Main desktop icon and select the 386 Enhanced icon. Click the Virtual Memory box and change your Type setup from Permanent to Temporary. Then, choose the recommended kilobytes of memory to be set up as a Temporary swap file. Exit Windows, restart your PC, then exit again. This process will make sure the large swap file is no longer taking up hard drive space. You will need to turn your computer back on before moving ahead with the installation.

Installation

Once you've gotten your system ready for the upgrade, place the Windows 98 disc into the CD-ROM drive and choose Run from the Program Manager File menu. In the Run dialog box, type **D:\Win98\Setup.exe**, where D: is the letter of your CD-ROM drive. Follow the instructions on the various Setup Wizard screens as the installation proceeds.

If you are not sure Windows 98 will work on your PC, use the option to save your current MS-DOS and Windows system files on your hard drive when it appears. This enables you to uninstall Windows 98 and restore your original

system files. You'll be able to delete this backup of your original system within Windows 98 once you are satisfied that the new operating system works properly.

When the installation is complete, copy all the contents of the D:\WIN98 directory to the root directory of your hard drive (C:\). This will enable you to install Windows 98 from your hard drive and refer to all the Windows 98 installation and .CAB files in the C:\WIN98 directory for future installations and updates as needed.

Upgrading from Windows 95 to Windows 98

If you're already running Windows 95 on your computer, you'll be amazed at how smooth and easy it is to upgrade to Microsoft's newest operating system, Windows 98. The upgrade process takes about an hour, but once you experience all the new features it has to offer, you will find that it was time well spent.

Before You Install

Windows 98 has some pretty hefty hardware requirements, so you will want to make sure your computer can handle the upgrade before you begin. Your system should have a Pentium processor and at least 16MB of RAM; 32MB of RAM is better. You also need to make sure you have enough free hard drive space. Windows 98 requires anywhere from 120MB to 300MB of space, depending on which enhancements you choose to install.

Once you've determined your system can handle Windows 98, you will want to check your hard drive for any problems. Run ScanDisk to find and repair any problems with files and directories. Click Start ➢ Programs ➢ Accessories ➢ System Tools ➢ ScanDisk. While you're at it, run your antivirus software to verify that there are no viruses on your system. You also need to make sure your hard drive has not been compressed. Installing Windows 98 on a compressed hard drive can cause serious problems. If you recently purchased your computer, chances are your drive is not compressed. To check, click Start ➢ Programs ➢ Accessories ➢ System Tools ➢ DriveSpace. From the menu, click Drive ➢ Properties. If the drive is compressed, click Uncompress. You may have to remove some files before DriveSpace can uncompress your drive.

Next, be sure to back up your important systems files, such as AUTOEXEC.BAT, CONFIG.SYS, WIN.INI, SYSTEM.INI, USER.DAT, and SYSTEM.DAT. Use Windows Explorer to copy these and any other important files to a disk. You also should make a new Windows 95 boot disk before performing the upgrade. Go to Start ➢ Settings ➢ Control Panel ➢ Add/Remove Programs. Click the Startup Disk tab and insert a disk into the disk drive, then, click the Create disk button.

Finally, be sure to turn off any monitoring programs, such as antivirus or crash protection software; they can damage Windows 98's installation. As an added precaution, use Windows Explorer to remove all applications from your Startup folder. You should not have any programs running during the installation. When you're finished, close Windows, power down the system, and restart the system to begin the installation.

Ready to Install

Insert the Windows 98 disc into your CD-ROM drive; the installation process should automatically start. If it doesn't, click Start, then Run. In the dialog box that appears, type **d:\win98\setup.exe** (where d: is the letter of your CD-ROM drive).

1. Windows 98's Welcome Setup will automatically scan and check your system. Click the Continue button to summon the Setup Wizard. When Microsoft's license agreement window appears, click "I accept," then, Next.
2. When prompted, type in the product registration code that came packaged with the disc and click Next. Then, you'll be asked to input some personal information.
3. Before the actual installation occurs, you will be asked if you want to save your old Windows 95 system files. If you have space available (approximately 50MB), click Yes. That way, if you decide you don't like Windows 98 or the installation crashes before completion, you can get Windows 95 back.
4. Next, you will be asked if you want to create a new Windows 98 Startup disk. Click Yes, but make sure you don't overwrite the Windows 95 Startup disk you just created.
5. Once the files start copying to your system, you will see a graph displaying the progress of the installation, as well as screens explaining the new features of Windows 98. Unlike Windows 95, you won't be asked to select an installation scenario. From the system scan performed earlier, Windows 98 determines whether you need a Typical, Portable, Compact, or Custom install.
6. Don't panic if your system shuts down and restarts several times; Windows 98 is simply using Plug-and-Play technology to determine which hardware and driver components it needs to install. When it's all finished, Windows 98 is ready to run.

Unfortunately, no installation is bulletproof. If you encounter a problem, hit Ctrl+Alt+Del key combination. If the Close Program window appears, highlight Setup and click End Task. If your system is completely frozen, turn off your PC.

In either case, your system should reboot back into Windows 95. Try installing Windows 98 again. If it still doesn't work, stop and call Microsoft's Technical Support.

The first time Windows 98 appears you'll see a Welcome To Windows 98 screen. Take a minute and click Maintain Your Computer. This launches a new Maintenance Wizard that deletes unnecessary files, checks your hard disk for errors, and can speed up your favorite applications.

Finally, if you have a connection to the Internet, click Start, then Windows Desktop Update. This feature will take you to the Microsoft Web site where you can download and install any new patches and updates for your new operating system.

Windows 98's Hardware Support

The Windows 98 Desktop doesn't look much different than Windows 95's; the major changes occur on the inside of the machine with the new hardware standards Microsoft's latest operating system supports. Microsoft says the result should be hardware that's easier to add and upgrade to PCs. Here are the hardware technologies Windows 98 is designed to support.

Universal Serial Bus (USB) Probably the most significant hardware innovation supported by Windows 98 is the Universal Serial Bus (USB). Designed to simplify hardware installation, USB allows users to immediately use USB-compliant components as soon as they are plugged in to the USB port. This will work with many kinds of *peripherals* (computer components that are on the outside of a computer) including mice, scanners, and modems. The maximum transfer rate for USB is an astonishing 12 megabits per second.

IEEE 1394 While it sounds more like a segment of the penal code than a computer technology, IEEE 1394 (also known by the FireWire trademark) has the potential to be a significant part of computer architecture for the future. Much like USB, IEEE 1394 is a high-speed standard designed to support peripherals. IEEE 1394 runs at a maximum 400Mbps, and the components are expected to be considerably more expensive than USB. You can expect to see IEEE 1394 used primarily in linking memory-hogging components such as video cameras and VCRs to computers.

continued

Digital Video Disc Support for Digital Video Disc (DVD) technologies will allow DVD-ROM players to eventually replace CD-ROM players in PCs. DVDs allow even more information to be put on small disc in addition to allowing full-length movies to be played on a PC from a single disc.

OnNow The OnNow power management technology will allow compatible computers to start up in just a few seconds rather than a minute or more. Also, computers with OnNow technology can be set up to receive data or do system chores when they appear to be off.

Enhanced monitor support Windows 98 will allow users to use multiple monitors on one PC simultaneously as well as offer enhanced support for TV tuner cards.

DirectX 5 This is the latest standard for entertainment software. DirectX allows manufacturers to design their software products (i.e., games) for Windows without having to worry about optimizing the software for every kind of PC hardware on the market. Therefore, in theory, games designed with DirectX 5 will be compatible with all PC hardware on the market.

Upgrading from Windows 95 to Windows NT 4

When it comes time to upgrade your desktop PC to a more stable and secure 32-bit operating system, a good choice is Windows NT 4 Workstation. The Workstation version works better for the desktop PC while still offering some of the networking capabilities of the more robust Windows NT 4 Server version, which is designed specifically for larger network environments.

Upgrading to Windows NT 4 Workstation from Windows 95 is not as simple as other operating system upgrades. These operating systems contain a system *Registry*, which is a hierarchical database that stores the information necessary to configure the system for one or more users, applications, and hardware devices. The upgrade path from Windows 95 to Windows NT is complicated by the difference in the Registry architectures, which results in applications and hardware registering themselves in different locations.

Support for hardware devices is another difference between Windows 95 and Windows NT 4 Workstation. Windows 95 has much broader support for hardware devices, especially in the area of multimedia devices. Windows NT does not currently have a mechanism to detect devices that it does not support. Therefore, you will run into problems when upgrading a Windows 95 system that includes a device that is not supported by Windows NT.

Microsoft plans to address this issue in the upcoming release of Windows NT 5 by making it more device-friendly and automating the upgrade path from Windows 95.

System Requirements

To install Window NT 4 Workstation, you will need a computer system with at least a 100MHz Pentium-class processor, 32MB of RAM, 120MB of available hard drive space, and a CD-ROM drive.

Preparation

Before you begin, check to see if all your Windows 95 devices are supported by Windows NT 4 Workstation by referring to the Hardware Compatibility List booklet that came packaged with Windows NT 4. You can get an up-to-date hardware compatibility list from Microsoft's Web site (`http://www.microsoft.com/hwtest/hcl`) and an application compatibility list at `http://www.microsoft.com/windows/thirdparty/winlogo/default.htm`.

WARNING WARNING WARNING WARNING WARNING WARNING WARNING WARNING

Laptop users be warned: Windows NT 4 does not support Plug and Play or power management. If you want to upgrade to Windows NT 4, you will need to add power management and PC Card support software or replace your laptop with a Windows NT laptop equipped with proprietary Plug-and-Play features.

As a safety net, Microsoft recommends you install Windows NT as a dual boot with Windows 95, rather than installing directly over Windows 95. When you are sure that Windows NT is working properly with all your applications, you can remove the Windows 95 portion. There are some considerations to be aware of, though, when setting up a dual-boot configuration.

The file allocation table (FAT) file system must be used on your hard drive when installing Windows NT because it is compatible with both Windows 95 and Windows NT 4. If you decide to delete Windows 95 later, you can convert your hard drive to use the more efficient NT File System (NTFS). If your version of Windows 95 is OSR2 and is using the FAT32 file system, you must convert the hard drive to FAT. See if you have the OSR2 version by going to Start ➢ Settings ➢ Control Panel ➢ System, and selecting the General tab. The version number for OSR2 is 4.00.950B.

To see if your hard drive is formatted with FAT32, go to My Computer, right-click the C: drive, and select Properties. The Type area will reveal your file system. To convert your hard drive to FAT, first, back up your hard drive. Then, from a Windows 95 boot disk with the FORMAT.COM file on it, format your hard drive using FAT instead of FAT32. Another option is to use a third-party utility, such as PowerQuest's PartitionMagic 3.0 (`http://www.powerquest.com`) to convert your FAT32 file system to FAT.

Once you have a FAT file system on your hard drive, insert the installation disc into the CD-ROM drive and follow the on-screen instructions. You also will want to have your installation booklet by your side. Remember, Windows NT files must be installed into a directory (C:\WINNT) other than the one where your Windows 95 files are located (C:\WINDOWS).

Re-Install Applications

Once the installation is complete, you will need to re-install your applications. With Windows NT running, re-install all applications into their same directories. This will allow you to use the applications in either Windows NT or Windows 95.

Removing Windows 95

After you have successfully tested all hardware and applications, you can regain nearly 100MB of hard drive space by manually deleting the Windows 95 directory (C:\WINDOWS). You will want to work with Windows NT 4.0 for a while before removing Windows 95.

Running Multiple Operating Systems on Your PC

If you need more than one operating system to run all the programs you use, then perhaps setting up your system to run multiple operating systems is the right option for you.

That's not to say you can just pop back and forth between operating systems the way you do with applications. Because you can have only one operating system running at a time, you will have to shut down and reboot your system each time you want to switch to a different operating system.

Popular choices in PC operating systems include MS-DOS, Windows 3.*x*, Windows 95, Windows 98, and Windows NT. Any or all of these operating systems can be installed on your PC's hard drive, however, there are specific procedures that must be carefully followed when installing these operating systems.

Before You Begin

First, back up your hard drive so you can restore your system if something should go wrong. In addition, you will want to create a bootable disk for your present operating system so you can boot from the disk if necessary. For instructions on bootable disks, see Skill 3.

With your backup and bootable disk in hand, you're ready to configure your operating systems.

DOS and Windows 95

The F8 function key will enable you to choose between DOS or Windows 95. When you see the Starting Windows 95 display in the upper-left corner of your monitor, pressing the F8 function key will reveal the Windows 95 startup menu, which will probably look like this:

1. Normal
2. Logged (\Boolog.txt)
3. Safe Mode
4. Step-by-step confirmation
5. Command prompt only
6. Safe mode command prompt only
7. Previous version of MS-DOS

The Command prompt only option will start your PC with a C:\> prompt in what is virtually MS-DOS 7.0. If you had an older version of MS-DOS in its original directory (C:\DOS) before you installed Windows 95, selecting Previous version of MS-DOS will revert your PC back to that version.

Windows 3.*x* and Windows 95

If you upgraded to Windows 95, using the original Windows 95 upgrade package from a Windows 3.*x* system *and* set up all the Windows 95 files in their own separate directory (C:\W95), you will be able to boot into Windows 3.*x* by pressing the F4 key when you see Starting Windows 95 appear in the upper-left corner of your monitor. However, the next time you start your PC it will start with Windows 95. This dual-boot option is only available if you have the original upgrade (Windows 95 version 4.00.950) and/or the Service Pack 1 (Windows version 4.00.950A) installed in their own directories and you have not deleted the files in the original Windows 3.*x* and DOS directories (C:\WINDOWS and C:\DOS).

If you have updated your Windows 95 system to the OSR2 (OEM Service Release 2) version, you will not be able to boot into Windows 3.*x*, even if it is still on your hard drive. Trying to do so will result in possibly booting into Windows 3.*x*, but the next time you start your computer, the operating system will not start, and you'll need to reinstall Windows 95. If you have Windows 95 OSR2, the only safe way to have the dual-boot option is to use one of the third-party multiboot utilities.

Windows 95 and Windows 98

Enabling your PC to boot into either Windows 95 or Windows 98 is a bit tricky and must be set up before you upgrade from Windows 95 to Windows 98. Before updating to Windows 98, with Windows 95 running, format a 3.5-inch 1.44MB disk. Right-click Start, click Explorer, right-click the A: drive icon (where A: is the letter of your disk drive) and select Format from the pop-up menu.

In the resulting dialog box, select Full and Copy System Files, then click the Start button. When the formatting of the disk is done, click Close and highlight the root directory (C:\) of your PC. Next, copy the MSDOS.SYS file from the root directory to the disk. Label this disk Windows 95 Boot Disk.

NOTE NOTE NOTE NOTE NOTE NOTE NOTE NOTE NOTE NOTE NOTE NOTE NOTE NOTE NOTE

Because MSDOS.SYS is a hidden file, you may need to go to the View menu on Windows Explorer's Menu bar, select Options, then, click Show All Files to make MSDOS.SYS visible.)

After you have created your Windows 95 boot disk, place your Windows 98 disc into the CD-ROM drive while holding down your Shift key (this disables the CD Autoplay feature). In Windows Explorer, highlight the \WIN98 folder on the disc and drag it to your C: drive. This will copy all the installation and .CAB files from the Windows 98 disc to your hard drive.

Now, go to Start ➢ Shutdown, then select Restart Computer In MS-DOS Mode. Click OK. Once your system has restarted in DOS, change to the Windows 98 directory (CD\WIN98) and type **Setup**. Follow the directions until you are asked to select the directory where you want to install Windows 98. Select Other Directory, click Next, then, type in a new directory name, such as C:\W98 or C:\WINDOWS98. The setup program will proceed to place all the necessary Windows 98 files in the newly named directory and rewrite the MSDOS.SYS file to note the new Windows directory location. When it is finished, your system will restart with the Windows 98 operating system. You will need to reinstall your programs for them to run in the new operating system.

If you want to boot into Windows 95, simply turn on your computer with the Windows 95 boot disk in the disk drive. The boot disk contains a copy of the original MSDOS.SYS file, which refers to Windows' being located in the original Windows 95 directories (C:\WINDOWS or C:\W95). Booting your system from this boot disk will send your system looking for Windows 95 in its original Windows 95 directories, thus starting your PC with the Windows 95 operating system.

Windows 3.*x*, Windows 95, and Windows NT 4

Placing the Windows 3.*x*, Windows 95, and Windows NT 4 operating systems on your hard drive is possible, provided you carefully follow installation procedures. To have the option of starting your PC with one of these operating systems, you'll need to make sure you have at least a 2GB hard drive formatted with the file allocation table (FAT) file system, as it is the only file system compatible between the three operating systems.

WARNING WARNING WARNING WARNING WARNING WARNING WARNING WARNING

You will not be able to take advantage of the more efficient FAT32 file system.

The best installation sequence is to install Windows 3.*x*, then Windows 95, and, finally, Windows NT 4. Make sure you install each into their own separate directories (C:\WIN31, C:\WIN95, and C:\WINNT, respectively).

WARNING WARNING WARNING WARNING WARNING WARNING WARNING WARNING

You will not be able to take advantage of the more efficient Windows NT 4 NT file system (NTFS).

Once all three operating systems are installed, the next time you power on your computer you will see the Windows NT boot loader menu from which you may select the operating system you would like to use. If you plan to use the same application in each of the operating systems, you will need to run the application's install program in each operating system. If an application has a different version available for each operating system, set up each application in its own directory with respect to the operating system, for example, C:*x*31, C:*x*95 and C:*x*NT (where *x* is the application's directory name). This will prevent conflicts between the application and the various operating systems.

Third-Party Products

Perhaps the easiest way to set up multiple operating systems is to use a third-party product, such as PartitionMagic or System Commander. PartitionMagic 3 and System Commander Deluxe allow you to reformat and/or partition your hard drive for the various operating systems without disturbing your existing applications and data. Then, when you turn on your computer, you will be able to choose which operating system you would like to use.

System Commander Deluxe is available from V Communications Inc. (`http://www.v-com.com`). Partition Magic 3 is available from PowerQuest Corp. (`http://www.powerquest.com`).

Are You Experienced?

Now you can...

- ☑ **download and install software from the Internet**
- ☑ **avoid common problems**
- ☑ **upgrade your operating system**
- ☑ **dual-boot more than one operating system**

SKILL 22

Upgrading the BIOS

- Understanding the BIOS
- Deciding whether you need an upgrade
- Finding the right upgrade
- Performing the installation
- Troubleshooting

How sweet it is when you turn on a computer and everything behaves as it should! And, considering how many glitches can occur, it sometimes seems amazing that a system starts up at all.

The purpose of a computer's *Basic Input/Output System* (BIOS, pronounced *bye-ose*) is much more significant than most users realize. The BIOS is a routine stored in read-only memory (ROM) that controls the communication between a PC and its hardware. When you turn on the "brain" of the computer, the central processing unit (CPU), the programming code stored in the BIOS takes an inventory of system hardware and prepares various installed components for work.

Without the BIOS, a CPU doesn't know how to control basic hardware operations, such as reading from, or writing to a disk, nor would it know how to manage interactions between the keyboard and the hard drive. Similarly, without BIOS code, the CPU can't communicate with the system clock or video board.

When adding a new device, such as a hard drive controller to your computer, you must upgrade the BIOS if the current one won't recognize it. Otherwise, the newly installed device will remain disabled. A BIOS upgrade also may make it possible for an older computer to take advantage of *Plug and Play*, a technology that simplifies the process of adding new hardware by enabling your system to immediately recognize peripherals once they are installed.

Understanding the BIOS

Typically, the term BIOS refers to the PC's main BIOS. But your computer may have other BIOSes in addition to the main BIOS, including a video BIOS to control the graphics display, a network BIOS to control the network adapter, and a Small Computer System Interface (SCSI) adapter BIOS to control all attached SCSI peripherals.

BIOS programs are typically stored in ROM chips located on the motherboard because information stored in conventional random access memory (RAM) disappears when you shut down the computer. ROM can be read, but not modified. RAM is a temporary storage area used to load program instructions and store files currently in use.

Several BIOS manufacturers, including Phoenix Technologies Ltd., American Megatrends International (AMI), and Award Software, have developed core BIOS code used on Intel motherboards. Intel, in turn, modifies this code before shipping its motherboards or chip sets to *original equipment manufacturers* (OEMs), such as the direct marketers Dell and Gateway. OEMs then tailor Intel's core code to their hardware.

Brian Zucker, manager of dimensions systems engineering at Dell Computer, explains, "Historically, the computer's memory timings used to be accessible in most BIOSes. Users could control memory speed and actually increase it beyond what it was designed to do. In some cases, these changes would work, but often users would wind up having failures. We turned off this feature in the BIOS to prevent customers from accidentally getting into trouble."

When Dell Computer releases a BIOS update, says Zucker, it's generally to add enhancements or fix problems reported in the field. "Several customers might report a problem a specific peripheral has with a piece of software. If we determine it to be a BIOS problem, we go in and fix it. Then we make that BIOS available to any customer who might encounter the problem," he said.

According to Zucker, if you're not running into any problems and you're able to get your work done, there's no need to change your BIOS. However, it's always good to see what's out there and to know what's changed, just in case you run into problems in the future. The good thing about BIOS updates is that they are fully backward compatible. "We do extensive testing on the BIOS before we release it," says Zucker, "to ensure that it works on current and all existing machines."

Starting Up with BIOS

The collection of BIOS programs stored in ROM determines how your computer starts. The BIOS performs the same set of routine operations every time. When you turn on a computer, programming code in the main system BIOS determines what hardware is installed. The built-in program checks if this hardware is working, then it searches for other BIOS-like programs that are installed on add-on boards in your system. If it recognizes any, it yields control of the system to those BIOS programs so that they can perform their initial inventory and tests.

When expansion board BIOSes have completed their startup routines, the main system BIOS continues with its tests, checking the computer's low-memory area and initializing the components it's designed to control.

Many BIOS operations occur very quickly, without users being aware of them. Sometimes, however, you may notice a particular stage in the BIOS *Power On Self Test* (POST). For example, since a video graphics array (VGA) controller adapter typically has its own BIOS chip, the software contained in video board ROM runs before the main system BIOS. As a result, the video board sign-on message may appear before the main system BIOS copyright notice, date, and version number.

Similarly, when the main system BIOS tests low memory, a memory test message appears. When it inventories the hard drive, disk drive, CD-ROM drive, and keyboard, lights flash on those devices.

Once preliminary tests are complete and everything checks out, the BIOS pulls up additional information by loading the operating system into memory. It does this by reading a series of small boot files (MSDOS.SYS, IO.SYS, CONFIG.SYS, and AUTOEXEC.BAT) from the active drive (usually drive C:, which is the hard drive). Operating system software and applications take over from there.

Determining Your BIOS Version

Users can determine which version of a particular BIOS they have when they boot up. The BIOS version number appears in a tag line on the very first screen. It might read, "AMIBIOS ©1992, American Megatrends, Inc., BIOS version 1.00.12.AX1T," or "AMIBIOS © 1992, American Megatrends, Inc., BIOS version A05." The version number (sometimes called the rev or revision number) refers to the OEM's customized BIOS.

When designing programs, software developers frequently use and build upon data stored in BIOS. If the BIOS in your computer has a bug or it lacks the ability to run a new peripheral, you may have to replace it. That's why the BIOS date and version number are so important.

A particular BIOS version can significantly affect PC performance. Two machines with identical hardware but different BIOS *firmware* (the software permanently stored in hardware chips), might behave differently. For example, in 1993, Gateway (formerly known as Gateway 2000) confirmed that some of its local bus systems with a particular BIOS had problems running certain memory-resident applications. (Bus refers to the electric connection used for the transfer of data among various computer system components.)

The BIOS in these faulty systems accessed an area of memory reserved for communication between applications. If users ran applications that occupied this part of memory, they were forced to reformat their hard drives. A corrected BIOS was eventually built into Gateway's newer models and the problem was resolved.

Flash BIOS

Many BIOS upgrades require replacing the old BIOS chip on your motherboard (the computer's main circuit board containing the CPU, RAM chips, and expansion slots) with a new one. Old 80286, 80386, and 80486 machines typically have two BIOS chips rather than one. A Pentium system, on the other hand, doesn't require a chip replacement. It stores BIOS on a special kind of memory chip, called *flash ROM* or *flash EPROM* (flash erasable, programmable read-only memory).

A BIOS that uses flash ROM chips is often called a flash BIOS. To upgrade flash BIOS, flash ROM chips simply run an update program and let the software perform the modifications. For example, in late 1995, Gateway posted flash BIOS updates on its electronic bulletin board. The updates were designed to integrate Plug-and-Play capabilities in its older Pentium computers (the P5-75 through P5-100 systems, and its P5-60 and 66, revision number 3 and 4 motherboards). Users who wanted to add improved Plug-and-Play capabilities simply ran this utility to update their system's BIOS program code.

To upgrade a flash BIOS, run the appropriate BIOS update program and let the software administer the appropriate changes. While updating doesn't require much skill, an incorrectly installed flash BIOS will prevent the computer from starting up, so pay close attention to update instructions.

Typically, computer manufacturers simplify the process by adding their own installation routines. All the user has to do is boot up using a disk containing the BIOS program and it will update the computer BIOS with minimal user involvement. The only word of advice, warns Zucker, is that users should not touch their machines while the disk is being accessed and the BIOS upgrade is taking place. "The last thing you want to do is power down your system during a BIOS upgrade because it will corrupt the existing BIOS and make your system unbootable," he says.

Finding the Right BIOS for Your System

When you purchase a computer, its BIOS firmware knows how to work closely with the system's installed components. To add new components, such as a 2GB Enhanced Integrated Drive Electronics (EIDE) hard drive, to a PC manufactured before 1995, you may have to upgrade your system BIOS so it can recognize drives with more than 1,024 cylinders (see Figure 21.1).

Computers manufactured in the early 1980s require a BIOS upgrade to use an enhanced graphics adapter (EGA) board, hard drive, local-area network (LAN) card, or any ROM-equipped expansion board. Older systems must upgrade the BIOS to take advantage of 1.44MB disks or 2.88MB disks, or to add support for 101-key Enhanced Keyboards, Novell networks, SVGA displays, password protection, additional serial ports, additional drives, and Plug and Play.

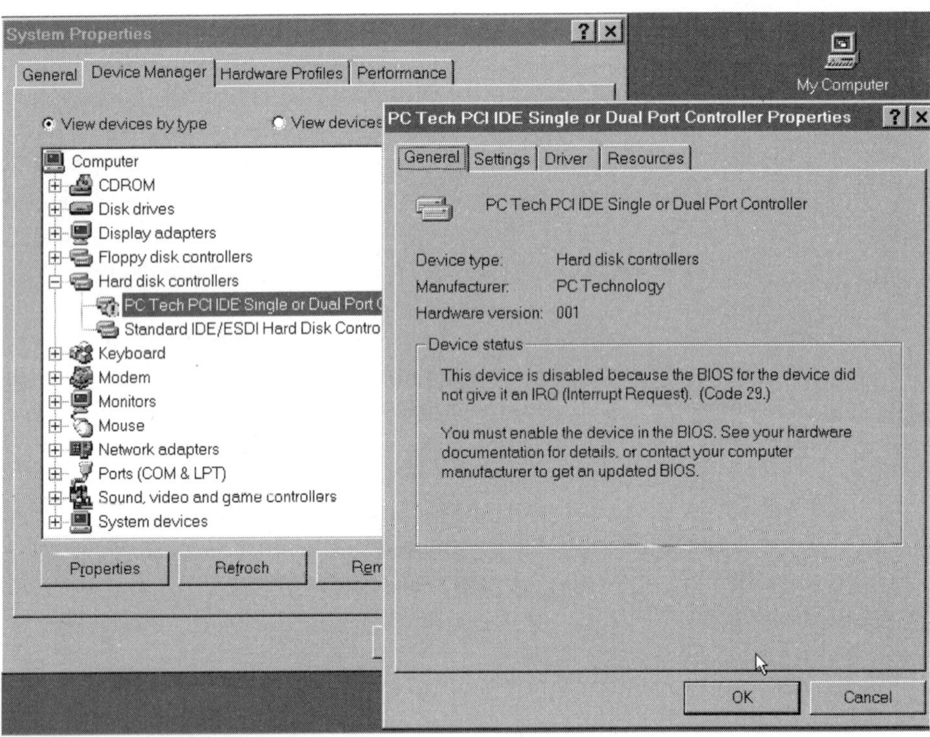

FIGURE 22.1: When adding a new device to your computer, consider upgrading your system BIOS if it doesn't recognize the new device.

Net Resources

Computer manufacturers often post BIOS updates on the Internet. You'll find these files on the Web in their respective support areas. For example, at the Gateway Web site (`http://www.gateway.com`):

1. Click the Technical Support link near the bottom of the home page.
2. Click the Hardware link in the Software Library area.
3. Click your type of system (such as Desktop/Tower, Portable, or Destination), and click the BIOS/Firmware Updates link.
4. Next, from the list of BIOS upgrade options, select the one that represents your computer motherboard model, and choose the appropriate BIOS from the list.

If you're unsure about which BIOS you need, reboot your system, then, note the BIOS information that displays. You also can call the technical support representatives at Gateway and ask which BIOS version your computer should be running. The technician will want to know which Pentium motherboard is installed in your computer. You'll find motherboard information on either the packing slip or the original invoice that came with your system.

Dell Computer also offers BIOS updates over the Internet (`http://www.dell.com`). Unlike Gateway, however, Dell simplifies the BIOS update process by tailoring it to your system needs. Thanks to a service document database of more than 35,000 pages, you merely click the Support link at the Web site, type in your System Service Tag or Express Service Code number, then, click the Submit button. A few seconds later, the personalized System Support Page for your system appears.

Next, click Flash BIOS–Recent Updates in the Drivers, Files, and Utilities section. The name, date, and size information for the most recent flash BIOS Update appears. Click the link to begin the download process. Save the file to your hard drive in a special folder created just for this purpose.

Before You Begin

Before updating any BIOS (whether it be for a Gateway, Dell, or other system), take the following precautionary steps. Reboot the machine and watch the screen for the message telling you how to enter your computer's Setup program. On a system with an AMI (American Megatrends Inc.) BIOS, you might have to press the DELETE or F1 key at startup. On a computer with a Phoenix BIOS, you may have to press Ctrl+Alt+Esc. Other computers use different methods to access their Setup programs.

Setup is that portion of your computer's BIOS that allows you to determine several of your system's basic characteristics. It tells the computer the bootup sequence it should follow (for example, the drives the system checks when it looks for the operating system), as well as the serial and parallel port addresses, and other important startup information. This vital configuration information is stored in a special *complementary metal-oxide semiconductor* (CMOS) chip. CMOS is generally used for RAM and switching applications, and operates at high speeds while using little power.

Also, because updating the BIOS might accidentally modify or erase current CMOS settings and render your system inoperable, one should be prepared for this possibility in advance. So, before upgrading, you should run the entire Setup program and write down all CMOS information, noting the settings for equipment installed in your system.

1. To run the Setup program for your computer, reboot as you normally would.
2. Almost immediately, a command such as: "Press Delete Key If You Want To Run Setup" appears on-screen. Follow this command to get to the Setup program. Write down everything you see. Pay special attention to phrases like "Page 1 of 2." You may have to issue a command, such as ALT+P, to see the settings stored on the next page. If another page is accessed, write down any additional settings on that page, as well.
3. When you are finished, on-screen instructions (typically at the bottom of the screen) will tell you how to reboot your system. If a problem occurs later on, you can re-enter the Setup program and use your notes to reconfigure the settings you recorded.

As an alternative, you may be able to document your computer's CMOS settings by moving through each CMOS on-screen display and pressing the Print Screen (or Prnt Scrn) key on your keyboard. Issuing a Print Screen command from the keyboard outputs a hard copy of the computer's current screen display. Be sure to print out the settings for all pages, as well as Standard (Main) and Advanced CMOS configurations, if available.

WARNING WARNING WARNING WARNING WARNING WARNING WARNING WARNING

Although Print Screen is a good option, it isn't always a viable one for all computer users. This function didn't always work properly on all computer systems we tested.

Getting Down to Business

Every BIOS upgrade is different. In the remainder of this skill, we describe BIOS upgrades for a Dell Dimension XPS M200s and a Gateway P5-90, both using the Windows 95 operating system. Exact commands and filenames depend upon the system being updated. Use our instructions as a general guide, but contact your computer manufacturer for BIOS upgrade specifics. This is especially true if you need to obtain a BIOS update on disk rather than over the Internet.

Getting BIOS Update Files

When you download a Dell BIOS upgrade from the Web, it appears as a self-extracting file containing both the BIOS update and a README.TXT file, with instructions for how to proceed. Those instructions should resemble the following. As Zucker says, "In general, BIOS upgrades are a safe thing to do. You should not feel uncomfortable about proceeding, just be careful to follow instructions."

1. After the download completes, click the downloaded file icon to extract its contents. After doing so, drag the original archive file from the download directory on your hard drive to the Recycle Bin. Right-click the Recycle Bin, then, choose Empty Recycle Bin to delete its contents.
2. Place a formatted system disk in drive A:, exit to a DOS prompt, then, type in the command specified in the instructions (such as **81619 a:**). This transfers the BIOS to a bootable disk. If you reboot with this disk in your drive, the BIOS update process begins automatically. It verifies your system configuration and asks you to press any key to continue.
3. Next, it asks you to press **Y** to replace the old BIOS (such as A05) with the new BIOS (such as A07). An alert screen notifies you that a BIOS upgrade is in progress and you should not reboot or power down your system until the update completes (typically 3 minutes).
4. When the job is done, the computer beeps twice, then, it informs you that the program was successful. You'll be asked to press any key to reboot. At Startup, a new BIOS revision number displays on the opening screen, reflecting the change you just implemented.

Creating a Bootable System Disk

Gateway, like Dell, provides BIOS upgrades free of charge. You must download Gateway's BIOS data to a bootable high-density system disk. Depending upon the BIOS revision number currently installed in your computer, you may even need to perform two BIOS updates. Prepare a bootable system disk as follows:

1. Place the disk to be formatted in the disk drive.
2. Double-click Windows 95's My Computer icon.
3. When the window opens, right-click the A: drive option (where A is the letter of your disk drive.)

4. Choose Format from the pop-up menu.
5. Select Full (from the Format Type section), then, check Copy System Files from the Other Options section.
6. Click Start.
7. Repeat the procedure to format a second disk. When you have two bootable disks, locate your original invoice. It will list the part number for your computer motherboard. You also can call Gateway technical support to verify the part number. As an alternative, reboot your system and note the BIOS revision number at the top of the screen. You'll be able to select the appropriate BIOS based on this BIOS revision number, because the same BIOS may be used on several different motherboards.

Updating the BIOS

Now, use your browser to access the Gateway Web site and navigate to the technical support area. Click the Documentation link called Motherboard Reference. Watch for a special reference table with links to BIOS revision numbers and motherboard part numbers. It will help you locate information about BIOS, memory, processor, hard drive, and controller upgrades for your system.

If you know either your BIOS revision number, or your motherboard part number, click one or the other. Gateway then displays the relevant information about your motherboard, with a link to the area where you can download the flash BIOS update.

For example, if you are running a Gateway P5-90 with a P54CMB Plato motherboard, clicking that link takes you to the appropriate information screens. You'll discover that the latest Gateway supported BIOS for this motherboard is 1.00.12.AX1T. However, in order to flash your system to 1.00.12.AX1T, your current P5 BIOS version number must be 1.00.09.AX1T. If it isn't, you must download P5AX1T.EXE, update to 1.00.09.AX1T, then download 1.00.12.AX1T to flash your BIOS once again.

Stage One

For a two-stage BIOS update, the first step will look something like this.

1. If your system has an 1.00.09.AX1 or lower revision number, click the P5AX1T.EXE link to download a self-extracting file containing the BIOS update AX1T for P5-90 systems. You'll be asked to save the file. Save it to its own folder. Write down the path to this folder so you can navigate there again after the download completes. Click the Save button.

2. After the download completes, open the folder containing the downloaded file, then double-click the file icon to extract the files. Read any README files for instructions. Print them for reference.
3. Insert a bootable disk in the disk drive. Copy all files from the download folder to the bootable disk. Do not copy the original compressed file or you'll run out of room. Also, don't copy the COMMAND.COM file.
4. Drag the original downloaded P5AX1T.EXE archive file from the download directory on your hard drive to the Recycle Bin.
5. Right-click the Recycle Bin, then, choose Empty Recycle Bin to delete its contents.
6. Reboot with the disk containing the BIOS files in your disk drive and follow the on-screen prompts. The system will display a Flash Memory Update Utility screen. Press Enter to continue.
7. Using the Down arrow key, highlight the Update Flash Memory Area from a File option. Press Enter.
8. Choose Update System BIOS if it's not already highlighted. Again, press Enter to continue.
9. Complete all steps. Eventually, you'll see a message prompting you to remove the flash disk from the drive, press Enter, and reboot. Follow these steps. A new BIOS copyright message will display on-screen at startup.

After flashing your system with P5AX1T.EXE, it's impossible to return to an earlier version. Run Setup to verify the CMOS settings are correct. The new BIOS may have reset your PC's Setup parameters to factory defaults, restoring the settings previously customized to their original state.

Stage Two

After flashing your BIOS to revision 1.00.09AXIT, you're ready to download the second file.

1. Return to the Tech Support area at the Gateway Web site and click the 1.00.12.AX1T link to initiate the download. Save the file to a new folder. After the download completes, double-click the compressed flash BIOS file to extract its contents. Remember to print out and read any README.TXT files for installation instructions.

2. Copy extracted files to a bootable disk.
3. Drag the original 12AX1T.EXE archive file from the download directory to the Recycle Bin, then, empty the bin to delete its contents.
4. Reboot with the disk containing the extracted BIOS files in your disk drive.
5. When the computer restarts with the second bootable flash BIOS disk in the disk drive, the Flash Memory Update Utility screen appears. Press Enter to continue.
6. After the Main Menu appears, use the Down arrow key to highlight the option labeled Update Flash Memory Area from a File. Press Enter to continue.
7. When the Update Flash Area window appears, Update System BIOS should be highlighted. If it isn't, use the Down arrow key to scroll to this option and highlight it. After it's highlighted, press Enter.
8. When the Enter Path/Filename window appears, use the Down arrow key to highlight 1012AX1T_.BIO in the Files box. Press Enter.
9. When the Verify Image window appears, make sure that Continue with Programming is highlighted, then press Enter.
10. Finally, after the Continue message appears, remove the bootable flash disk from the disk drive, then, press Enter. The system will reboot, displaying the message "BIOS Version 1.00.12.AX1T" on the startup screen.

To ensure that CMOS settings are correct, enter the CMOS configuration setup at startup and check the settings against your printed copy. If there are any discrepancies, modify the settings to match the printout. Be sure to save the changes when you exit.

Troubleshooting

If you inadvertently expand the archived BIOS upgrade files in the download directory, *do not*, under any circumstances, execute any BIOS program applications from your hard drive. If you do, you could corrupt your computer's CMOS settings, which must then be reconfigured manually from previously recorded notations.

In addition, you might trash a crucial operating system file, prompting a startup error message that reads "Bad or missing Sys file" or "Non-system disk."

If this message appears, insert the Windows 95 bootable disk in your disk drive, restart the computer, then, type **sys a: c:** at the C:\> prompt. The SYS command transfers IO.SYS and MSDOS.SYS (crucial DOS operating system files), plus the COMMAND.COM file to your hard drive without requiring reformatting. Once this transfer is complete, you can safely reboot. Everything should be back to normal.

The most serious problem with trashed CMOS settings is when your Disk Type setting has been trashed, as well. In this instance, you won't even get a C:\> prompt and the above repair method won't help. Hopefully, you previously made a record of your hard drive parameters so that you can manually re-enter them into the CMOS setup screen to remedy this problem. Without this information, you must call the computer manufacturer for technical support.

Thankfully, on many newer Plug-and-Play computers, the BIOS can automatically analyze your hard drive and put the correct hard drive settings into the CMOS setup on-the-fly.

Other Options

Even with a BIOS upgrade, your computer may not allow you to install hard drives larger than 2.1GB. The new BIOS also may not be compliant for the year 2000 (it may not allow your computer to roll the date over from December 31, 1999 to January 01, 2000). If your computer manufacturer does not provide the BIOS support you need, call the Oklahoma-based Micro Firmware company or visit its Web site (`http://www.firmware.com`) for information about BIOS upgrade options.

For example, while Gateway's BIOS upgrade for the P54C Intel motherboard provides for Plug-and-Play support under Windows 95, the new BIOS doesn't support processor upgrades, nor does it offer full support for IDE drives as large as 8GB. A Micro Firmware BIOS upgrade ($79, plus shipping) for the P54C motherboard does. It also promises faster bootup times, enhanced security, a smaller ROM footprint, plus backup and virus check reminders.

The first BIOS update you purchase from Micro Firmware arrives on disk as a self-contained Flash ROM Update utility. You cannot download this file from the Web. During the update process, the utility preserves your original BIOS settings, simplifying the installation so you don't have to bother with Setup.

In addition, it forces you to create a recovery disk, containing a backup copy of your computer's existing BIOS. Keep this emergency disk handy if you ever need to restore your original BIOS. And, once you purchase a BIOS upgrade from the company, you can freely download any further updates.

Hopefully, if your system BIOS update was successful, starting up your computer can once again be taken for granted.

Are You Experienced?

Now you can...

- ☑ **understand what the BIOS does and why you may need to upgrade**
- ☑ **know where to find BIOS upgrades**
- ☑ **install a new BIOS**
- ☑ **troubleshoot your installation**
- ☑ **explore other options**

SKILL 23

Troubleshooting

- Troubleshooting motherboards
- Troubleshooting RAM
- Troubleshooting BIOS
- Troubleshooting ports
- Troubleshooting hard drives
- Troubleshooting CD drives
- Troubleshooting disk drives
- Troubleshooting video cards
- Troubleshooting sound cards
- Troubleshooting mice and trackballs
- Troubleshooting inkjet printers
- Troubleshooting laser printers

Like flat tires and pimples, computer problems always strike at the most inopportune times. Generally, it's early in the morning the same day your report at work is due when you discover your printer is malfunctioning, your modem won't work, or—*gulp!*—your data is missing.

Computer gurus and techies may take such calamities in stride, but for those of us who expect our computers to work at least as reliably as our other electronic appliances, technical glitches can be devastating. They needn't be. Most problems that users run into can be solved fairly quickly without calling in the experts. You don't have to be a programmer or a certified technician to perform basic troubleshooting operations on your PC.

You can't expect to fix something, however, if you don't know where to start. For those of you who have PC experts for friends, have them spend time with you and give you some pointers. For the rest of you, consider this troubleshooting guide as your friend in the world of PC problems.

Our high-tech healing journey begins with an overview of what can—and can't—be fixed on a PC. We discuss some tried-and-true troubleshooting techniques so that you're not left in disarray when something goes awry. If you find you're having a problem with one piece or another of your computer equipment, page on over to the appropriate section, and let us take care of you!

Troubleshooting CPUs

Troubleshooting a malfunctioning central processing unit (CPU), otherwise known as a microprocessor, isn't exactly brain surgery, but it is one of the more consternating aspects of computer repair.

Microprocessors such as Intel 486 chips, Intel Pentium chips, or "clone" chips from companies such as Cyrix and AMD, are the brains of IBM-compatible personal computers. They handle the bulk of the actual computing that goes on in your computer. When they go bad, forget about using your PC until the problem is repaired. There is no work-around or quick fix for a bad processor.

Fortunately, microprocessors are probably the most reliable part of your computer, according to Christine Chartier, public relations manager at Intel Corp. "Nine times out of ten—no, I'd say 9.9 times out of ten—the problem is not your microprocessor, but something else in your system," says Chartier.

As Chartier rightly points out, something else is likely to go wrong with your PC before the microprocessor. But that's not to say CPUs never go bad. Mike Lederer, one of two PC repair technicians for more than 300 PCs at Nebraska Educational

Telecommunications in Lincoln, Nebraska, has seen some pretty amazing microprocessor failures in his day. "I've seen Pentiums melted down into puddles of plastic," says Lederer.

Few CPU failures are quite that drastic or easy to detect. (The smoke rising from your computer is a sure sign of *some* kind of meltdown.) More likely, your monitor will simply go blank or fail to boot if the microprocessor malfunctions. Of course, those are the same symptoms for other more mundane problems such as lose cables or bad SIMMs.

On those rare occasions when the CPU does go bad, you're going to have to eliminate nearly every other component in your PC before concluding that it's the CPU that is bad. Fortunately, your computer itself can give you some clues when a microprocessor is malfunctioning.

Microprocessor Diagnostics

Whenever you turn on your computer, it executes a *Power On Self Test*, or POST, which is essentially an inventory of all the PC's working components. If it detects that something is amiss, it generates error messages. While most error messages are indecipherable technical jargon, a few relate directly to the microprocessor.

Error Messages

A message reading "107 NMI Test Failed" is telling you a nonmaskable interrupt (NMI) test could not be performed. It may disappear if you reboot. If the problem persists, however, it may be a message that something is wrong with the CPU.

Some IBM computers (and a few clones) will generate an error message "115-System Board-CPU error" to let you know something is wrong with the microprocessor.

The error message "Internal Cache Test Failed—Cache Is Disabled" indicates a problem with the cache on either the motherboard or the cache built into 486 and Pentium microprocessors. Rebooting your computer may eliminate the problem. If it persists, use a diagnostic program such as Norton Utilities to see whether the problem rests with the CPU or with the motherboard.

Strange Beeps

Sometimes, problems with the microprocessor prevent the monitor from working. Beeps emitted by your PC during the POST can identify the problem. The meaning of these beeps differ according to the computer's Basic Input/Output System (BIOS), a type of program that lets the operating system software communicate with the microprocessor.

If you own a computer with American Megatrends (AMI) BIOS and hear five beeps in rapid succession, it signals a microprocessor failure. Turn off the computer, unplug it, open the case, and make certain that both the CPU and memory chips are properly inserted into their sockets. If reseating the CPU or chips doesn't solve the problem, the CPU may be bad.

If you hear seven beeps in rapid succession, it's a signal for the "Processor Exception Interrupt Error/Virtual Mode Exception Error." Again, you can try reseating the CPU or memory chips (SIMMs), but this message probably means the CPU is kaput.

PCs using the Phoenix BIOS use combinations of beeps similar to Morse code. Not only do these signals describe the problem, but they can tell you what to do to remedy it. Two single beeps followed by two sets of three beeps (1-1-3-3), for example, are telling you to initialize the CPU registers. Check your computer's documentation for instructions, particularly any documentation that refers to the BIOS.

Swapping Out

If error messages don't identify the problem and you're still convinced (after checking every other PC component) that the CPU is at fault, there's always the swap test. Find a computer identical to yours (right down to the version of the BIOS) and temporarily install the microprocessor in it. If that PC replicates the problems on your PC, then you've finally determined that there *is* something wrong with the CPU.

Now What?

Even if you've tracked a computer problem back to the microprocessor, it still doesn't necessarily mean that there's something wrong with the microprocessor. It could have simply become loose in its socket. If your computer has a Zero Insertion Force (ZIF) socket, make certain the lever on the side of the socket is pushed all the way down and clicks.

Loose SIMMs may imitate the symptoms of a faulty CPU. Make certain the SIMMs are properly inserted into their sockets on the motherboard. If the CPU is truly bad, then there's no real solution except to replace it. Check out Skill 5 for the details.

Replacement

CPUs are not cheap. In fact, they are among the most expensive components in your PC. Replacing them is not an option to be exercised haphazardly.

If you must replace the CPU, why not take the opportunity to upgrade your computer at the same time? Newer computers with ZIF sockets are designed to enable you to install a faster CPU, such as an Intel OverDrive chip. You can even upgrade some 486-class PCs to use a Pentium chip!

Upgrading is not always as easy as pulling one chip out and popping another chip into your PC. While some upgrades may be simple, others require changes to the BIOS and to your computer's clock (which is really a timer for coordinating the speed of the microprocessor and your PC's other components).

Whether you need to upgrade the BIOS depends on the model of your PC and the chip to which you are upgrading. Check your PC's manuals to see what BIOS it uses and read the instructions that come with the new chip. Changing your BIOS may require changing the read-only memory Basic Input/Output System (ROM-BIOS), which is another chip on your computer's motherboard. Newer computers allow you to upgrade your BIOS by uploading new BIOS software. Either way, you'll need to check with the company that manufactured your PC. Skill 22 deals with upgrading the BIOS.

Changing the clock will require making changes to either dip switches (small white switches) or jumpers (small plastic connectors between rows of pins) on the computer's motherboard. Again, you'll need to consult your computer's manuals or make a call to the manufacturer's technical support department.

It's a little more work than swapping out same-model microprocessors, but it's an extremely worthwhile operation. Besides, who said brain surgery would be easy? If you want to qualify yourself as a brain surgeon, you need to earn your credentials.

FAN-FARE

Along with static electricity, excessive heat poses one of the biggest hazards for your computer's microprocessor...and today's powerful microprocessors kick out lots of heat.

Every new processor manufactured is built with a heat sink, an assembly of fans designed to draw heat away from the CPU and dissipate it into the surrounding air. Most computers rely on the fan that cools the power supply to draw a sufficient volume of air through the PC and past the CPU's heat sink.

continued

Ironically, it's mostly older, less powerful microprocessors, such as double- and quadruple-speed 486-class chips, and the first generation of Pentiums that have the most problem with overheating. In fact, their heating problems led chip builders to incorporate heat sinks into the design of new chips.

Heat can be a problem whether you have an older CPU or a new CPU. Some poorly designed computers don't allow enough air to flow through the case. In some instances, expansion boards can interfere with air flow. Putting a PC in a cupboard, beneath a desk, or in another restricted location can also impede air flow.

If cooling is a concern, consider installing a combination heat sink/cooling fan for your microprocessor. They're available for as little as $13.95 although better and more reliable models sell for around $45. There are different models to fit different chips, so make certain you purchase the correct heat sink/cooling fan for your type of microprocessor.

Although designs vary, most simply clip to the top of the microprocessor. There is a double power cable leading from the fan. Find the power supply and remove the power cable that connects the power supply to the hard drive. Plug the cooling fan power cable into the power supply (only one plug will fit into the socket). Finally, connect the power cable from the hard drive to the second plug on the cooling fan cable. The double cable arrangement enables both the cooling fan and the hard drive to share a single socket on the power supply.

The one drawback to the add-on cooling fans is their reliability. If you rely on the fan to keep your CPU cool and the fan wears out, you and your processor are both likely to be hot under the collar.

Troubleshooting Motherboards

With improved sound, video, and three-dimensional effects making their way into many new software titles, computers need a boost to keep up with the times, and just adding more RAM may not be the answer. Upgrading may involve changing more complicated components, such as cache or a system's BIOS.

Confusing matters is the fact that there aren't any set rules for motherboard design. Not only are components in different locations on the motherboard, but some manufacturers allow components to be removed easily while others solder the components right onto the board. These soldered components dislodge only with a soldering iron.

Unless you look under the hood of a new computer, you take a gamble on what can be updated because the list of upgradeable features varies, depending upon the computer manufacturer and the type of motherboard.

The Mighty Microprocessor

When most computer manufacturers indicate that their PCs are upgradeable, the microprocessor is one of the first components on the upgrade list. Upgradeable chips usually reside in Zero Insertion Force (ZIF) sockets on the motherboard. These sockets include little levers that you use to quickly remove the old chips and insert the new ones. Without a ZIF socket, you may have to pry out the chip on your own. But most new computer owners don't have to worry about this; their new PCs should include ZIF sockets, which help prevent pins from breaking off the chips when removed. Very few systems actually solder the chip right onto the motherboard.

Just because you can remove your old chip doesn't mean you can replace it with a new Pentium processor, however. First of all, there are voltage issues to consider. When microprocessor manufacturers, such as Intel, improve chips and make them smaller, they often reduce the amount of volts the chips require to operate, says David Pistone, technical marketing manager at Intel. You can't replace a 486 microprocessor running on 5 volts with a Pentium processor operating at 3.3 volts. You need to use a chip replacement designed to overcome this hurdle, perhaps one equipped with a voltage regulator to take the 5 volts from the system and change it to the 3.3 volts the new chip can handle.

"If (consumers) try to do it another way, it may work for a few hours or days, but eventually, they'll burn up the processor," Pistone says.

Also, each microprocessor generation has its own pin configuration, so new chips simply may not fit into the older socket configurations. Intel has developed a replacement for its own chips. Intel's Pentium OverDrive processors can take care of all these problems for you, but the chips are limited as far as which processors you can upgrade. For instance, you can upgrade a 50MHz 486 processor with an OverDrive processor that will boost your system to a 63MHz Pentium. Or you can upgrade a 66MHz 486 to an 83MHz Pentium. But that's about as far back as Intel goes.

You also can upgrade newer Pentium processors with Intel's MMX technology. This technology lets PCs take advantage of redundancies when reproducing graphics and audio, increasing performance in multimedia applications. The chips are available only for Pentium processors, though. For instance, you can upgrade a 100MHz Pentium with an OverDrive chip to operate at 166MHz with MMX. According to Intel's Media Bench-mark, this would improve performance by approximately 150 percent when running audio, video, imaging, and 3-D software.

Boosting Your RAM

Another popular way to improve computer performance is to increase its horsepower by adding more random access memory, or RAM. Although many manufacturers solder RAM directly onto the motherboard, almost all motherboards also include slots so you can add more memory. Most memory modules are in the form of single in-line memory modules, or SIMMs.

Upgrading RAM, however, isn't as simple as it used to be. Advances in memory have widened the choices of RAM available. For instance, some RAM is now available as dual in-line memory modules, or DIMMs. DIMMs have a different pin configuration than SIMMs and won't fit into a SIMM's slot. Likewise, there is a higher-performance memory called Extended Data Out (EDO) RAM that may not be compatible with some motherboards and systems. Many 486 systems won't support this kind of memory, Pistone says.

Therefore, you have to check your computer's manual or call the manufacturer to find out which type of RAM will work with your system and if there are any limitations. (For information about upgrading RAM, see Skill 4.)

Caching In

Prepare for things to get sticky when you think about upgrading your cache. Adding more cache space, which holds in memory bits of data that are used often by the microprocessor, can speed up how quickly your computer operates, but it can be upgraded only in some forms on some systems.

Cache comes in two types. Level 1 (L1), also referred to as internal cache, usually is located in the microprocessor and normally isn't something you can tinker with. It's contained in small amounts, such as 8KB, 16KB, or 32KB. The other kind of cache, Level 2 (L2), is external cache and may be upgradeable. Common sizes of L2 cache are 256KB or 512KB.

On most motherboards, L2 cache is soldered onto the board, and you usually buy a system with a certain cache configuration. However, a few computer models actually put L2 cache into a socket on the motherboard. On those systems, upgrading cache would be similar to adding more RAM, Pistone says.

Changing Clocks

You should never consider upgrading the system clock. This clock, which coordinates all timing applications, is usually a crystal oscillator that's on the motherboard, and if you mess with it, Pistone says you can kiss your board goodbye. In the rare event your system clock does break down, you should take your computer to the manufacturer or a computer repair shop so it can be fixed by a professional. However, because computer repairs are so costly, it may be more economical to buy a new motherboard or even a new computer.

Keep in mind that system clock replacements won't necessarily speed up your system. To increase system performance, you should replace the microprocessor.

Altering the BIOS

Your computer's BIOS controls the start-up process of your computer, as well as other basic functions, such as working with the hard drive or monitor. Even though many people refer to the BIOS as software, it's actually firmware, a set of instructions encoded in the hardware's circuitry.

Ordinarily, you wouldn't worry about upgrading the BIOS from the motherboard. In newer systems, the BIOS is contained in flash chips, known as flash BIOS. Upgrading flash BIOS happens through software, meaning you can replace the old BIOS without having to physically tug a chip out of the computer. (See Skill 22.)

Adding More Ports, Slots, and Controllers

Occasionally, you need to upgrade—not to increase performance, but to add more capabilities to the system. Expanding your system internally by adding more expansion slots is really not an option, Pistone says, because the motherboard is only designed to accommodate a fixed number of slots. However, some expansion/adapter cards can plug SIMM sockets into the motherboard, so users can take advantage of older, lower-density memory rather than throwing it away and buying higher-density modules. This also could allow the user to access different size memory modules in the same system (i.e., a 30 pin in a 72-pin slot).

A few users may want to increase the types of components they can work with by adding another disk controller. The disk controller handles the operations of your disk drives and other storage drives. Although most users will never need to change their disk controller, some drive upgrades may require a new controller card, Pistone says.

Most consumer computers use Integrated Drive Electronics (IDE) controllers, unless they are high-end systems. IDE is capable of handling most hard drives and disk drives. But if you want to add a high-performance, SCSI hard drive, a high-speed CD-ROM drive, or another disk drive, you first may need to install a new SCSI controller card into an expansion slot.

The Sticky Stuff

Simply installing physical components can be difficult enough. However, there are additional considerations the average consumer should take into account. For instance, is the option you want to upgrade easy to get to? The processor may be positioned under other components you need to remove in order to replace the chip.

As technology advances, upgrading gets stickier. True, the industry has established standards over the years, so installing a new video card or sound card is painless. But, like everything else in the computer industry, there will always be exceptions.

Troubleshooting Random Access Memory

Sometimes, it really does get confusing: memory, hard drive, RAM, ROM. What it all boils down to is that there are two kinds of places your computer puts things: in permanent storage and in temporary, or volatile, storage.

Permanent storage is just what you'd expect; anything you put there will be there the next time you come back. A computer uses its hard drive for permanent storage. The hard drive is where you load your software and save your files. Barring an accident or a relatively unusual hardware failure, what you put there will stay there until you delete or modify it. By contrast, the computer uses volatile storage as a temporary place for whatever it is doing at the moment. Random access memory, or RAM, (often just called memory) is the main volatile storage area on your PC.

Like a well-organized cook, your computer wants to have all of the ingredients and utensils it needs right at its fingertips. This RAM area is where the computer gathers the tools it needs for a given task. It keeps them there while it's working in the program or performing the task that uses them. Some cooks clean up as soon as they're done; others leave their mess behind. Unlike a cook, RAM has an automatic clean-up contingency plan built-in so what's left behind gets automatically wiped out whenever the computer is turned off or rebooted.

This is, generally speaking, a good way to keep a clean house, but it can be frustrating if the computer was turned off due to a power outage, or if the reboot was necessitated by a program error. In those cases, whatever you were working on was wiped out of memory, along with any mess that was left behind by sloppy programs.

The Structure of Computer Memory

Computers are binary devices. This means all that they do is expressed internally with just two characters—zeros and ones—each of which is called a bit. The order and combination of these zeros and ones into 8-bit segments, called bytes, makes characters.

There are different classifications of memory, each of which is measured in multiples of these 8-bit bytes, called kilobytes (KB), and megabytes (MB). A kilobyte is equivalent to 1024 bytes. A megabyte is made up of 1024 kilobytes. Next in the progression is the gigabyte (GB), which is 1024 megabytes. PC memory hasn't moved into this size classification just yet, but PC processors from the 386 on can use (or address) memory into the gigabytes.

Conventional memory is the name for the first block of memory (0 to 1024KB). This memory area is further divided into system memory (0 to 640KB) and upper memory (640 to 1024KB). DOS uses the system memory area of conventional memory. Device drivers use the upper memory area of conventional memory.

When the first PCs were introduced in the early 1980s, nobody could imagine that more than 1MB of memory would ever be used. This much was, in fact, excessive. At that time, DOS needed just about 50KB of the 640KB that it knew how to use, and most PCs didn't even have a full 640KB installed. All personal computers, new and old, have some amount of system memory.

Extended memory describes memory beyond 1MB, so its precise size depends upon how much physical memory is installed on your computer. DOS was not designed to be able to use extended memory, but as programs grew and applications became more complicated, technicians figured out how to fool DOS into using some of it. DOS and its standard applications can use this part of memory with the help of an extender, such as HIMEM.SYS.

You can cheat a little bit, using the first 64KB of this part of memory, known as the *high memory area* (HMA) to store DOS. That leaves more conventional memory available for use by programs. Windows, with its voracious appetite for memory, is designed to take advantage of extended memory, as much as you'll feed it. It even uses something called virtual memory (described below) to make use of the computer's hard drive space when extended memory runs short.

Expanded memory is relevant only to DOS. Windows is able to use all memory beyond 1MB freely, but DOS has to be tricked into it. Expanded memory is one way DOS can be fooled into using memory beyond the 640KB system memory. DOS uses expanded memory only because it doesn't realize that it has moved out of conventional memory. An expanded memory manager handles this deception by swapping 64KB chunks of information, called pages, into and out of reach of the DOS application.

Virtual memory uses the computer's hard drive, which most of us think of just as a permanent storage device, for volatile storage (memory). If your computer has a 386 or better processor, along with Windows, it can use virtual memory to overcome RAM shortages. The computer just reserves a portion of the hard drive and writes information that would normally go into RAM into this space instead. This reserved area is called a *swap file*.

The swap file does a good job of increasing the memory available to applications. It lets you do more with your computer without buying and installing additional RAM chips, but it does have its limitations. It isn't as fast as real RAM and you can't use it on a drive that has been compressed (by Stacker or any other commercial drive compression utility). So, if you're running short of drive space and memory, it's time to add to one or the other.

RAM or the Hard Drive?

Less than 10 years ago, a nicely configured computer had a 20MB hard drive and just 640KB of RAM. At 32MB, today's nicely configured computer has more RAM than the 1988 model had in drive space (and you'd expect to see 2GB of drive space on that model). This massive change in both volatile and permanent storage has to do with the ever-expanding capabilities of PCs and the ways we use them.

Operating systems and applications have become more graphical and intuitive. This makes them easier to use, but it also means they take up more resources on your computer. The good news is that (with the exception of a period between 1993 and 1995 when supplies were strained) as the amount of memory that's required to keep up with the latest operating system and application program requirements goes up, the price of that memory has been going down.

Over time, the application programs that are available to PC users have improved significantly in two aspects: what they do, and how they look to the user (usability).

For example, word processing programs, which started out as editable typewriting tools, are now complex publishing programs. They offer a multitude of fonts, integrated graphics and charting, revision tracking, embedded color, and more. The latest even have features that link documents automatically to the Internet.

Using them has become easier, even as the output has become more complex. Embedded codes on a monotype, monochrome screen have been replaced by *What You See Is What You Get* (WYSIWYG) color views of documents, and icon-based interaction. Operating systems and operating environments have progressed similarly. With the introduction of Windows, PC users were given the option to interact with the computer via icons and pull-down menus, in place of typed commands. Luckily, with Windows' higher memory demands came programming that allows the PC to use memory beyond the DOS limit of 640KB. All of these advancements have led us to a greater and greater need for more and more PC memory.

Memory Errors and Performance Problems

Probably because of the fact that it is so vital to a PC's operation and performance, memory is the most common cause of frustration for PC users. Not enough memory will make you feel like programs are running at a snail's pace, if they run at all. Too many applications vying for the same precious piece of memory, no matter how much total memory there is to go around, will bring the computer to its knees.

The effect of RAM on overall system performance differs, depending upon what operating system or environment you use, and what applications you're running. Check the stated requirements for the operating system and applications that you use, keeping in mind the numbers they state are bare minimums because they're trying to sell software to the broadest market possible.

If you're running lots of highly sophisticated graphically oriented applications (such as three-dimensional games or full-motion video encyclopedias), then load up—the more RAM, the better. This is especially true for Windows 95/98, which is well-programmed to use whatever you can give it. DOS, on the other hand, can't use extra memory without the help of memory managers. Windows 3.*x* lies somewhere in between. Read on for specifics (organized according to operating environment) on errors you might encounter, what they're telling you, and what to do about them. You'll also find some optimization tips.

DOS

The greatest virtue of DOS is that it is small, efficient, and requires your computer to have just 512KB of memory (RAM). Plus, it uses very little space on your hard drive. If your computer is just running DOS, without Windows installed over it, it can't derive a lot of benefit from extended memory (memory beyond 1MB). If the computer's processor isn't a 286 or faster, you can't derive any benefit from extended memory. Some applications are specifically designed to use memory beyond 640KB, but the application itself and the things you are actively working on, still have to fit within DOS's 640KB allotment.

Minimum RAM Required	512KB
Recommended	1MB
Reality	depends upon applications

Bridging the gap between the 640KB that DOS can readily use, and even just 1MB, requires the services of a memory manager. The memory manager's job is to fool DOS into thinking that it's getting all of its memory from the conventional memory block. The latest versions of DOS, 6.0 and newer, include a memory management utility called MemMaker to help you get the most from your computer's memory. If you're using an older version of DOS, this is yet another good reason to consider an upgrade.

Checking Available Memory and Allocation in DOS If you're having performance problems, it's a good idea to take a look at how your PC's memory is being used. Memory, either the total amount or its allocation, could be the issue. There are two utilities available in DOS that can help you to see how much memory your PC has, and how it's using what it has.

You get the simplest view, and really, everything you should need for basic allocation diagnostics, by just typing **MEM** at the DOS C:\> prompt. It returns a screen that presents a simple report on how memory is being used on your PC: total, used, and free. It also gives you important information like whether or not DOS is loaded in high memory. After checking out how your memory is used, you may want to go directly to the sidebar entitled "Running MemMaker to Optimize Memory Use," to make some changes with the expert help of the MemMaker utility.

The second utility is the Microsoft Diagnostic program, and it is available under DOS version 6.0 and newer. To use this utility, type **MSD** at the DOS C:\> prompt. It returns a screen that gives you choices for checking on any component of your computer. Choose the box labeled Memory by typing **M**. It returns a more complicated memory map and the summary statistics similar to what you get from the MEM view. Stick with MEM for a basic view of what's going on, but if you need to know more, try MSD.

Running MemMaker to Optimize Memory Use

Windows 95/98 optimizes memory for you, unless you tell it you want to be in control, but why would you do that? Windows and DOS, however, can benefit from a little help. If DOS, revision 6.0 or later, is installed on your PC, then you have a tool to help you organize and optimize your computer's memory use. MemMaker is an easy-to-use utility program that reorganizes the information within your computer's memory for you, based upon the hardware available, and what operating systems and environments you use.

Before you run MemMaker, there are three things you need to do:

1. Back up your PC. At the very least, make copies of your AUTOEXEC.BAT and CONFIG.SYS files because MemMaker does make changes to these files in the process of optimizing the PC's memory. It's unlikely there will be a need to use the backed-up files, but if a problem does arise, these files will help get you back to where you started. To copy the files, just put a disk in the disk drive and type the following at the DOS C:\> prompt:

   COPY AUTOEXEC.BAT A:

   COPY CONFIG.SYS A:

2. Make sure you have DOS loading into the upper memory area. Type **MEM** at the DOS prompt. If the line MS-DOS Is Resident In The High Memory Area is included in the information that is returned, then move to step 3. If not, then you need to add the command DOS=HIGH to the CONFIG.SYS file. Open the CONFIG.SYS file in an editor, add DOS=HIGH on a new line, and then restart the computer.
3. Check your AUTOEXEC.BAT file for commands that automatically start programs. MemMaker restarts the computer multiple times during the process of doing its job, and if there is a line at the end of your AUTOEXEC.BAT file starting up Windows or the Word Processing program that you use, it will disrupt the process. At the DOS prompt, type **TYPE AUTOEXEC.BAT**, and press Enter. Look for any line ending in .EXE. If any are present, then open the AUTOEXEC.BAT file in an editor, and insert the word REM in front of any startup commands in the file. This just causes the command to be bypassed.

continued

Once the preparation work is done, you can run MemMaker from the DOS C:\> prompt:

1. Type **MEMMAKER**, then press Enter to start the program. MemMaker displays a screen that describes the program and then gives you the opportunity to Continue or Exit.
2. Press Enter to Continue to the next screen when prompted.
3. MemMaker asks if you want an Express or Custom setup. Press Enter for Express setup. For most users, Express setup is the best choice because it lets the program make decisions about the best changes to make, rather than asking you at each step of the way.
4. Next, the program asks if you have any programs that require expanded memory. Choose No, unless you know that you do require expanded memory. This step frees up more conventional memory. If you find later that you do need expanded memory, you can just run MemMaker again.
5. Press Enter. The computer restarts.
6. As the computer restarts, MemMaker evaluates drivers and programs, and how they're loaded, to determine what changes it can make to optimize memory usage. It makes those changes, then prompts you to press Enter again to restart once more. This time, MemMaker tells you to watch the screen for error messages.
7. The next screen prompts you to press Enter again if your system seems to be operating normally. If you didn't see error messages, press Enter.
8. The final screen shows you what changes were made, and how much memory of each type is available. Press Enter one last time to exit to DOS.

RAM Errors in DOS You may be encountering specific error messages rather than just performance problems. That's good news and bad news. The good news is that your PC is trying to tell you what the problem is. The bad news is that there definitely is a problem, but most can be resolved as described below. Following are some commonly encountered error messages that are related to RAM under DOS.

Error Message: Expanded Memory Unavailable

Cause: This message probably appeared when you tried to start up a program that required expanded memory, but your PC's memory usage is only optimized for a system that runs no programs that use expanded memory. This is a good way to set your computer up if, in fact, your programs don't use expanded memory because it frees up an extra 64KB of upper memory for DOS and applications to use. On the other hand, if you try to load a program that uses expanded memory, it will return this message.

Resolution: You just need to set up some expanded memory. MemMaker can do that for you. To run it, type **memmaker** at the DOS C:\> prompt. Follow the screen prompts, being sure to answer Yes when it asks whether or not you use programs that require expanded memory. (See the "Running MemMaker to Optimize Memory Use" sidebar and your DOS 6 manual for more information on MemMaker.)

Error Message: Not Enough Memory or Out Of Memory

Cause: This message may appear at the startup of an application program, or when you try to perform a function from within a program that's already running (such as printing or previewing a word processing file). It's especially discouraging to see this message still flashing up on the screen after you've added more memory to put an end to the problem once and for all. The problem is not total memory, but the DOS 640KB ceiling. This program is trying to squeeze what it needs out of the 640KB system memory segment of the conventional memory that DOS and its applications use.

Resolution: It's possible that running MemMaker, or a third-party memory manager, will clear some memory for you. Try it by following the directions in the "Running MemMaker to Optimize Memory Use" sidebar in this article. A memory manager will load as many things as possible into the upper memory block, possibly freeing up the system memory for you.

Error Message: EMM386 Exception Error #13...PRESS ENTER TO REBOOT

Cause: This means the microprocessor has encountered a general protection violation, meaning a program tried to access memory that it's not allowed to access. This error occurs when you try to install the EMM386.EXE device driver that's included with DOS on a less than 100 percent IBM-compatible computer.

Resolution: Remove EMM386 to see if the error goes away. If problems still occur, you'll need to find and correct them and then reinstall EMM386. Contact your PC's manufacturer and report the error. You may need a modified EMM386.SYS or EMM386.EXE device driver if there's the slightest incompatibility with the IBM PC standard. The corrected drivers that you get from the hardware manufacturer should fix it for you.

Windows 3.*x*

With Microsoft Windows, the base memory requirements are higher than for DOS, but the fact that it is not trying to squeeze all of its memory out of a 640KB block makes life with Windows a little bit easier than with DOS. Windows runs on any computer with a 286 or better processor, DOS, and 2MB of RAM. The reason that the memory requirements jump so sharply with Windows is that there's a lot going on: the multi-color graphical user interface, multiple opened windows, and all of the computing that a program does on top of that.

Miminum RAM Required	1 to 2MB (standard mode vs. 386 enhanced mode)
Recommended	4MB
Reality	8MB

Bits and Bytes

Knowing the terminology that's used to describe memory size can help you "get around" better as you sort things out.

Bit The smallest unit of measure for data and the space that holds it on your computer. This is the level at which all data is either a 1 or a 0.

Byte Made up of 8 bits, a byte is equivalent to a character. The order and combination of the eight ones and zeros (bits) defines a character.

Kilobyte (abbreviated as K or KB) 1024 bytes.

Megabyte (abbreviated as MB, M, or meg) 1024 kilobytes.

Gigabyte (abbreviated as GB, G, or gig) 1024 megabytes.

Checking Available Memory and Allocation in Windows 3.*x* Check to see how your PC is using memory. Sometimes a look at memory will point you towards the performance solution you need. When you're using Windows 3.*x*, you can check memory allocation directly, and in some detail, via the DOS utilities described earlier in this chapter. You can also use Windows to get a quick look at system resources. From Program Manager, click Help, and choose About Program Manager. At the bottom of the About Program Manager box, it tells you how much memory is free and what percentage of system resources are being used (see Figure 23.1). Windows gets sluggish if that percentage drops much below 50 percent. For more detail on how your memory is being used, try the DOS MEM command (described above in the "Checking Available Memory and Allocation in DOS" section).

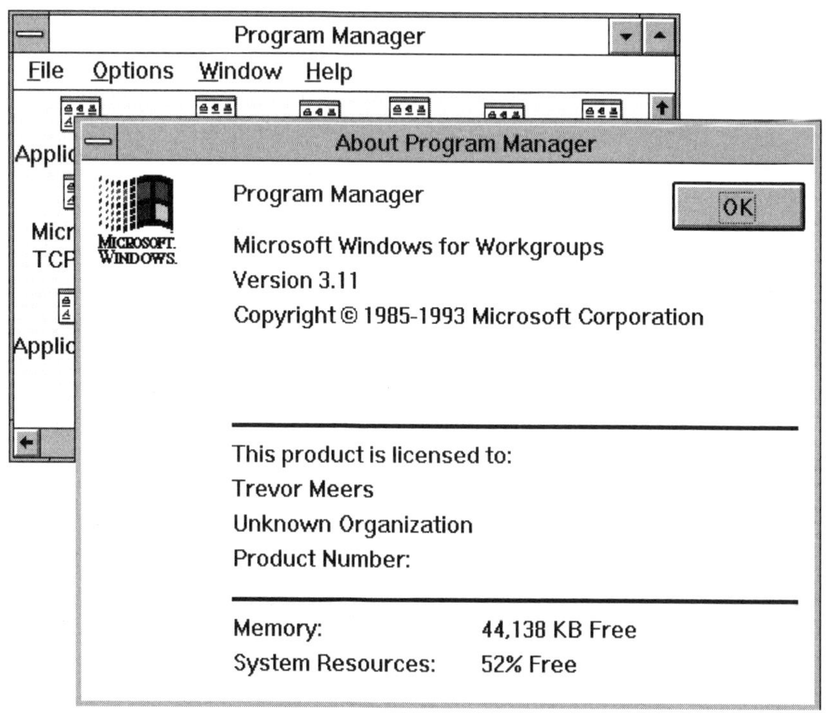

FIGURE 23.1: To check on the available memory in Windows 3.1 or Windows For Workgroups 3.11, access the About Program Manager window.

RAM Errors in Windows 3.*x* Error messages are your PC's way of telling you what's not working just right. If you are encountering specific error messages rather than just having performance problems, that's sometimes good because error messages point you in the direction of resolution. Following are some commonly encountered error messages that are related to RAM under Windows.

Error Message: General Protection Fault In Module...

Cause: A General Protection Fault (GPF) is a category of error messages as opposed to being a single error message. It usually results from conflict that arises when a program tries to access a restricted area in the computer's memory (RAM), and it usually causes the computer to lock up.

Resolution: When a GPF, or any other error, causes the computer to lock up, the only way to recover is to reboot (a.k.a. restart) by pressing the Ctrl+Alt+Del keys simultaneously. This restarts Windows and often clears out whatever caused the lock-up (but you will lose any unsaved files or data). Watch for clues in the GPF message itself, it will often cite the name of the file that triggered the fault. Try to catch that name and record it before the crash. That file name can lead you to the program or device driver that's setting off the GPF. Sometimes, reinstalling the offending program or replacing the driver can fix the problem.

If the problem persists, and it appears to have no relation to the application running, or the function you're accessing, then you'll have to consider the possibility that it's a hardware problem (maybe a faulty memory chip). See the "It Could Be the Chip" sidebar. For more tips and ideas on solving the mystery, get a copy of Microsoft's detailed GPF troubleshooting guide.

Error Message: Insufficient Conventional Memory To Run Windows; Reconfigure Your System To Increase Available Memory And Try Again.

Cause: It may be that you're trying to load Windows into the upper memory area (UMA), via a command such as LOADHIGH WIN or LH WIN, either by typing that command on the command line, or by its presence in your AUTOEXEC.BAT file.

Resolution: Load Windows into conventional memory using the simple command WIN, with no modifier, whether at the command line or in AUTOEXEC.BAT.

Error Message: Windows Will Not Use More Than The Virtual Memory Specified By The Recommended Size. Are You Sure You Want To Create A Larger Swap File?

Cause: If you set the permanent swap file size to more than the recommended size, this message displays, even if you haven't exceeded the maximum allowable size.

Resolution: It's not a problem. Windows will still increase the size of the swap file, and will use it, as long as you don't exceed the maximum size.

Error Message: Insufficient Memory For Application Requested Space, Decrease PIF KB Required And Try Again.

Cause: When you run Windows 3.1 in 386-enhanced mode on a PC with just 2MB of RAM, you can't run a 640KB DOS prompt.

Resolution: First, you really should consider adding RAM. This can't be the first time your 2MB memory has bitten you. While you're thinking about that, you can reduce the memory required to run the DOS prompt. The problem didn't exist in Windows 3.0 because it specified the memory *required* as 384KB, and memory *desired* as 640KB. Windows 3.1 just asks for 640KB. Use the PIF editor to edit the file DOSPRMPT.PIF, reducing the value for KB Required to 128 and set the value for KB Desired to 640KB. Alternatively, if your PC allows, create a permanent swap file of at least 1MB, and enable 32-bit drive access.

It Could Be the Chip

It is possible that the memory error you're getting is due to a broken, worn-out, or loose memory module. If the error repeats consistently, you should suspect a hardware problem. If you get any of the following messages at startup, they could be pointing to a problem with your memory modules:

- 2xx
- Parity Error
- Refresh Failure
- Timer Not Operational

continued

Try reseating the memory chips to ensure the connections are good. If the error still occurs, then you need to replace the bad memory module. Be sure to buy the exact same kind you pulled out. If you get this error after having just replaced or added RAM, it could be that you installed the wrong kind. Mismatched RAM on the motherboard, incorrect type of RAM (installation of parity RAM on a motherboard that requires non-parity RAM), non-proprietary RAM on a motherboard that requires proprietary RAM, or even the wrong speed of RAM can generate error conditions. When adding or replacing RAM, you should always install exactly what's already there.

Make More Memory When you run Windows 3.*x* in Standard Mode, it creates a temporary swap file for each DOS application you use and one for itself. These temporary swap files are hidden files whose locations are determined by the operating system. In 386-enhanced mode, just one temporary swap file is used, and it expands and contracts as needed, disappearing when the system is turned off or restarted. The creation and use of these files is automatic, you don't need to do anything to make it happen. If your computer is running in 386-enhanced mode, you also have the option of creating a permanent swap file.

A permanent swap file is the defined space of a fixed size on your hard drive, and it remains there until you change or delete it. The permanent swap file is faster than a temporary space because the system knows just where to go to find it, and its space is reserved, so it won't run out if the drive gets full. Of course, reserving space on your hard drive is a double-edged sword.

If you're running low on storage space, this swap file space is not available (even when it's not in use). Note that when it sets up a permanent swap file, Windows determines the recommended maximum size based upon what it finds on the drive in its search for a block of contiguous, free space. The swap file must be unfragmented. If you're finding that the size Windows recommends for the file is too small for the amount of free space you think you have, then run a drive defragmentation program before you set up the permanent swap file.

To create a permanent swap file on your computer's hard drive under Windows 3.*x*:

1. From Program Manager, open Control Panel.
2. Open 386 Enhanced.
3. Click the Virtual Memory button. The Virtual Memory dialog box appears, displaying current settings.
4. Select Change to change swap file parameters.
5. From the Drive list, choose the drive on which you want the swap file to reside.
6. From the Type list, choose Permanent.
7. In the New Size box, enter the size, in kilobytes, that you want the swap file to be, or press Enter to accept Windows' recommended size.

TIP TIP TIP TIP TIP TIP TIP TIP TIP TIP TIP TIP TIP TIP TIP TIP TIP TIP TIP TIP TIP TIP TIP TIP TIP

As a guideline for choosing size, the conventional wisdom is that the swap file should be equal to or somewhat larger than the physical RAM installed on your computer.

8. Select OK, then click the Restart Windows box to have the changes take effect.

Windows 95

Windows 95 continues the progression to a more sophisticated graphical user interface and more complex programming, and as a result, it requires more memory. It's hard to believe, but Microsoft says that 4MB is all that's required to run Windows 95, while 8MB is recommended.

Minimum RAM Required	4MB
Recommended	8MB
Reality	12–16MB (or more)

Even at 8MB, most users will be unhappy with Windows 95's performance. In reality, 12 to 16MB is what you're going to want in order to be comfortable, and more is even better. Windows 95's multitasking capabilities require a lot from your PC's memory, and also help to save you from memory errors (see Figure 23.2).

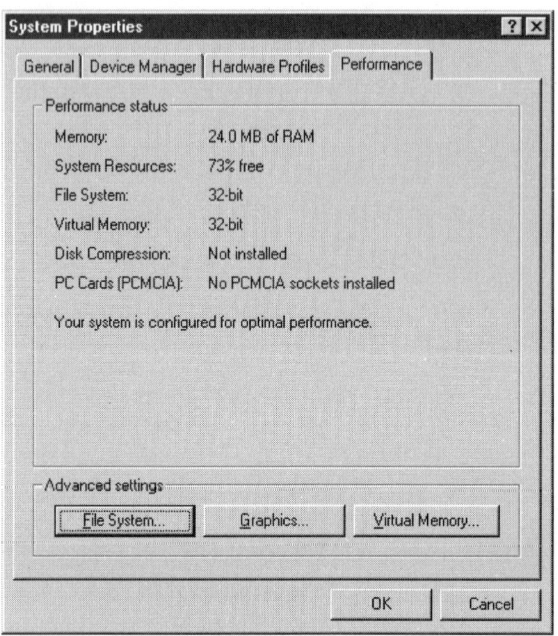

FIGURE 23.2: For Windows 95, System Properties is a valuable resource for viewing the performance status of your system.

Now, when you get one of those memory hiccups that used to boot you out of Windows 3.*x*, (or at least lock you up, necessitating a reboot to recover), you only get booted out of the program that's causing the hiccup. Windows 95 also added several other new features that enhance its memory handling and management, for example:

Dynamic caching As you add more memory, this feature puts it to use right away.

Background printing Windows 95 uses the PC's memory to print in the background, getting you back to work in your application faster.

Better support for DOS-based applications Windows 95 frees more conventional memory, thus DOS applications run better than they did under Windows 3.*x*. This also provides a means by which to run the greediest of DOS programs (those that required 100 percent of system resources, called single MS-DOS application mode).

Virtual memory Windows 95 has a sophisticated way of managing virtual memory that appears to give you the best of both worlds, from Windows 3.*x* to its dynamic swap file. This means you no longer have to decide whether to choose a permanent swap file (best for performance, but ties up drive space) or a temporary swap file (performance suffers, but the drive frees up). The Windows 95 swap file maintains a fixed location but shrinks and expands based upon need. Windows 95 pushes the least-frequently requested pages of memory out to the drive, keeping the most requested pages in the faster RAM.

Checking Available Memory and Allocation in Windows 95 You can get a quick look at memory usage via Help in Windows 95, just as you did in Windows 3.*x*. Click Start, then choose Help. Under Help Topics, select Memory and Check The Amount Of Memory. A small window appears. Click the arrow in the window, and another window pops up that shows how much RAM is installed and the percentage of system resources in use.

If you're having problems, try the Memory Troubleshooter utility that's included with Windows 95. The Memory Troubleshooter guides you through a series of steps to help you diagnose problems. You can access it through Help as well. Click the Start button, then choose Help ➢ Memory ➢ Troubleshooting. The Troubleshooter starts up, and prompts you with questions about the problems you're experiencing. It leads you to solutions, or even to programs included with Windows 95, that will run to help the problem (for example, ScanDisk).

Free It Up

Removing unnecessary memory hogs can help you go farther with less. Try the following solutions:

- If you're working in Windows, close some. When multiple application windows are open on the desktop, they are a drain on the system's memory resources. DOS windows especially eat up a lot of memory.
- Don't use complex pictures for wallpaper. Stick to those packaged with Windows. If the error occurred while you were trying to set up custom wallpaper, you might be using an invalid graphic file type (it must be a .BMP file). To test the file type, try opening up the graphic in Paintbrush. If it won't open in Paintbrush, it's not the right kind of file.

continued ➧

- Make sure you have free disk space for Windows to use as temporary storage (swap space). If you're using a permanent swap file, increase its size.
- Don't load more Windows fonts than you really need. They're pretty, but not critical.
- In Windows 3.*x* and Windows 95/98, minimize program groups and other icons that you're not using frequently.
- Don't use the screensaver. It's amusing, but not necessary.
- Reduce the number of colors specified for your video display. It doesn't make a terrific difference in appearance but does in memory usage.
- Turn EMM386 off if you're not running DOS applications. Delete the line from your CONFIG.SYS file that starts it up: DEVICE=C:\EMM386.EXE
- Restart Windows to clear out memory that might be reserved by the clipboard or by another application that neglected to release it.
- Run a utility to defragment your hard drive weekly, especially if you're using a temporary swap file.
- Set up a permanent swap file because its performance will be much better than with temporary swap files. Some programs require a permanent swap file be present before they'll even run.
- You may also simply not have enough physical memory, or RAM, on your computer. Windows 3.*x* requires a minimum of 2MB of RAM; Windows 95 specifies 4MB. That minimum is usually enough to squeak by with, but just barely. Remember, though, the application requirements may be higher, so verify that your system meets them. With memory, the axiom "more is better" really rings true. A 4MB minimum for Windows 3.*x* is more reasonable than the 2MB requirement that Microsoft cites, and 8MB would be even better. The same is true for Windows 95. You'll be very unhappy with less than 8MB, but 16MB is a reasonable goal.

RAM Errors in Windows 95 If you're getting error messages, then your PC is trying to tell you something. Here are some of the most common memory-related error messages encountered with Windows 95.

Error Message: This Program Has Performed An Illegal Operation And Will Be Shut Down.

Cause: This is similar to the General Protection Fault in prior versions of Windows. What it means is programs or drivers are in conflict over memory or are trying to access restricted areas of memory. The nice thing about Windows 95 is that, due to its multitasking capabilities, this error doesn't usually lock up or shut down the entire PC, just the offending program.

Resolution: If it locks you up, rather than shutting down the program as promised, then you need to press the Ctrl+Alt+Del keys simultaneously. Windows 95 will display "This Program Not Responding, Do You Want To Terminate?" Select Yes. If it persists, and appears to have no relation to the application running or the function you're accessing, then you'll have to consider the possibility that it's a hardware problem (maybe a faulty memory chip). Again, see the sidebar, "It Could Be the Chip."

Error Message: Fatal Exception Error

Cause: Windows 95 interacts with hardware differently than past versions of Windows, so you may get this error with Windows 95 when you run applications or drivers that never caused you any problems with prior Windows versions. If these errors occur randomly, that is, they're not associated with a specific repeatable action, then the most likely cause of this error is faulty RAM on the PC. Again, Windows 95 is accessing memory differently than Windows 3.*x* did. So, it may be placing frequently run program information in a faulty area on a memory chip (that didn't show signs of stress under Windows 3.*x* because it was storing infrequently used data there).

Resolution: You may need to replace the RAM chips. Follow the instructions below to use the RAM Drive to troubleshoot the memory. Also, see the sidebar, "It Could Be the Chip" for more information. For help with replacing RAM, consult your PC hardware documentation and refer to Skill 4.

Using RAM Drive to Troubleshoot Memory Problems in Windows 95 If Windows 95 seems to be acting strangely and is encountering problems and returning errors in places where everything was fine with earlier Windows versions, it could be a hardware problem. Strange as it may seem, even though prior Windows versions sailed smoothly on your PC, Windows 95 could be hanging itself on faulty physical memory that the others just weren't sensitive enough to find.

RAM Drive will help you test for faulty RAM. It's a program that lets you use your computer's memory as if it were drive space. By setting up memory as drive space, you may be able to detect and isolate a memory problem to a specific chip. Follow these directions:

1. Make a copy of your CONFIG.SYS file on a disk by typing the following command: **COPY C:\CONFIG.SYS A:**.
2. Restart your computer. When you see Starting Windows 95, press F8, then choose Command Prompt Only from the Startup menu.
3. Edit the CONFIG.SYS file to add the following line at the end of the file:

   ```
   DEVICE=<PATH>\RAMDRIVE.SYS <X> /E
   ```

4. See where *<PATH>* is? This is the location in which you should plug in where you want the RAMDRIVE.SYS file to be. See *<X>*? This is the total amount of RAM, in kilobytes, minus 4096 (that's for the 4MB you need to leave in order for Windows 95 to start up). An example line follows:

   ```
   DEVICE=C:\WINDOWS\RAMDRIVE.SYS 1288 /E
   ```

   This states that the file RAMDRIVE.SYS should be placed in the WINDOWS directory, and can use 1288KB of RAM (because we began with 16MB, and reserved 4MB for Windows 95).
5. Save the CONFIG.SYS file, and then restart the computer.
6. Work for a while to test the change. If the problems seem to be gone, then cut the amount of RAM allocated to the RAM Drive, via the CONFIG.SYS file, in half. Then, save the modified CONFIG.SYS file and restart the computer. Repeat until the problem occurs again. When it returns, you know that the segment of RAM that you just released from RAM Drive is the faulty segment. Replace it with exactly the same type of memory.

More Help: Finding the Answers

There are numerous resources you can tap into for additional help with memory issues and all sorts of other problems. Microsoft is a good starting point because they are the developers of all the operating systems and environments discussed here. Be sure you inquire about fees if you telephone their technical support staff because they do charge for phone support after an initial free period. There are other, less costly, ways to get information from Microsoft directly; their Knowledgebase technical support resource on the Internet is outstanding. There are numerous other good resources as well, including help forums and independent help resources available through the major online services and the Internet. Here is a list of resources that might have the tips you are looking for.

Microsoft Corporation

Internet: `http://www.microsoft.com`

BBS: MSDL/The Microsoft BBS: (425) 936-6735 (set your communications to 1200/2400/9600bps, no parity, 8 data bits, 1 stop bit)

The Microsoft Network: go to 'moli'

FAX Back: (800) 936-4200

Recorded Tips: (800) 936-4200

Technical Support Line: (800) 426-9400 for Microsoft Tech Support Phone Numbers—provides a listing of support numbers, by product. Select your product by name to retrieve its support number, or receive the full list by fax.

Corporate/Customer Service Line: (206) 882-8080

The Microsoft Knowledgebase: `http://www.microsoft.com`. This site is worthy of an independent entry due to its outstanding value as a troubleshooting, problem-solving, tip-gathering tool. This is the same database that Microsoft's own technical support staff uses to solve your problems, so why wait on hold?

continued

Find these key documents for help with memory issues. Keep in mind, however, that this is a very popular database so it may be difficult to access at times.

`http://www.microsoft.com/q66/4/20.asp`: Memory Management with Windows 3.0 and 3.1 (Article Q66420)

`http://www.microsoft.com/q95/5/05.asp`: Troubleshooting GP Faults (UAEs) (Article Q95505)

`http://www.microsoft.com/q91/0/88.asp`: HIMEM.SYS Memory Allocation Scheme (Article Q91088)

`http://www.microsoft.com/q76/9/22.asp`: ROM and RAM Error Codes Explained (Article Q76922)

There are lots of other Internet Web sites you can check, too. If you still haven't found what you need, try some of these:

- WinUser: `http://www.winuser.com`
- HelpMeNow: `http://www.helpmenow.com`
- PC Guide: `http://www.pcguide.com`
- Kingston Technology Corporation: `http://www.kingston.com`
- Samsung More Memory: `http://www.samsung.com`
- PC Webopaedia: `http://www.pcwebopaedia.com`

Troubleshooting the Basic Input/Output System

When your computer's Basic Input/Output System operates smoothly, it is virtually invisible. When it doesn't, it can make computing a nightmare. Why? To begin with, it controls a lot of functions that the user relies heavily upon. It is the firmware that determines what the PC can do without accessing software. In addition, it controls the boot sequence, security, keyboard, display, disk drives, serial communications, and many other functions.

Flash Updates

The BIOS resides on either a read-only memory (ROM) chip or a flash memory chip, known as Flash BIOS, so it will always be available, even if the hard drive fails. As a result, even with no drives in a system, you can still access the PC to add drives, a vital feature if your hard drive crashes. For at least the past six years, PCs have installed BIOS on flash memory chips. This makes updating BIOS as easy as downloading the most current version from the BIOS manufacturer.

To see whether your BIOS can be updated, check your manual. If the computer was purchased during the past six years or so, it probably can be updated this way. Otherwise, the manufacturer can provide a new physical BIOS chip. To find downloadable updates, either phone the manufacturer or search the Internet for the manufacturer's Web page. (Inference Find, at `http://www.inference.com/ifind`, is a good multi-search engine for this purpose because it is extensive and eliminates duplicate hits.)

BIOSs Are Not All Created Equal

BIOSs are divided into those that handle only DOS, those that also handle Plug-and-Play devices, and those that handle network applications. The Plug-and-Play variety are called PnP BIOSs or PnP-aware BIOSs, and always use flash memory. They have been used on most PCs since Microsoft introduced Plug-and-Play capabilities a few years ago with Windows 95. If you are upgrading to a PnP BIOS, the expansion board must also support Plug and Play. The Network Basic Input/Output System (NetBIOS) improves DOS BIOS by including functions for local-area networks (LANs). Special BIOSs for notebooks are also available that help extend battery life, thanks to advanced power-saving features.

BIOS manufacturers, even for the same category of BIOS, build significant differences into their products. And, over time, the differences in releases from the same manufacturer also can be truly amazing.

For example, American Megatrends' AMIBIOS 98 lets PCs boot from removable drives; works with Windows 98; increases the number of available sleep states; and fully supports the Universal Serial Bus standard, letting users quickly attach and reconfigure a wider range of peripheral devices (see Figure 23.3). AMI also allows remote setup capabilities; supports multiple languages including Chinese and Japanese; includes enhanced IDE support; offers multiprocessor support; and includes a host of services for original equipment manufacturers, allowing for further customization.

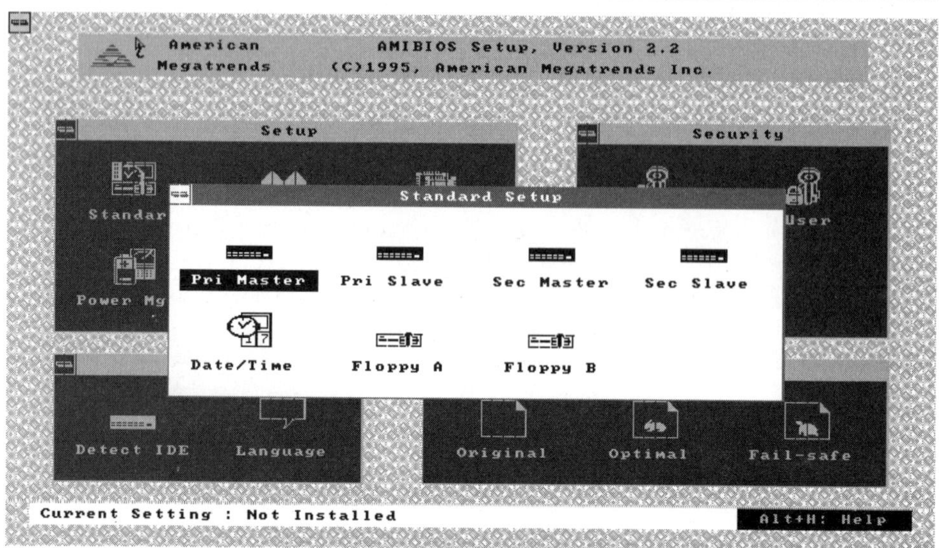

FIGURE 23.3: American Megatrends' AMIBIOS offers many options for individual customization.

PhoenixBIOS 4.0, from Phoenix Technologies Ltd., lets PCs boot from CD-ROM, a mixture of hard and disk drives, or from a LAN. It also supports up to four large hard disks and assigns complementary metal-oxide semiconductor (CMOS) bits as needed for maximum efficiency. In addition, it automatically detects the type of microprocessor your computer has, as well as its speed and memory capabilities; it detects bad single in-line memory modules (SIMMs); it complies with Plug-and-Play specifications; and it supports the Universal Serial Bus and Desktop Management Interface standards.

Support is another difference among manufacturers. A BIOS may be supported by the motherboard manufacturer rather than by the BIOS manufacturer. PC documentation, however, often doesn't identify that manufacturer. Instead, the BIOS manufacturer is listed. For example, American Megatrends (AMI) does not support or upgrade an AMIBIOS installed on third party motherboards, even though the board manufacturer is licensed by AMI. However, the motherboard manufacturer should support the BIOS and provide upgrades.

Altering BIOS

If you buy a PC and never add additional storage devices, you probably won't need to adjust BIOS settings. But, if you add a hard drive or another storage device, you can expect to adjust the BIOS. Sometimes this results in a frenzy of juggling addresses and interrupt request line (IRQ) settings that, at its worst, can compel you into CMOS to force the settings again, and again, and again.

To alter BIOS settings, you must enter the Setup menu while the PC boots. As the PC boots, the Power On Self Test (POST) is run, which diagnoses and initializes system components. A DOS message will appear that reads something like, "...Video RAM enabled…Shadowing enabled..." etc.

Before the POST completes and before the operating system is initialized, you have the opportunity to enter Setup, usually by hitting the Delete key. The message "Hit Delete to Enter Setup" will appear under the POST results. So, hit Delete, and then the Setup menu appears. Some of the various categories included in the menu are listed below.

System Setup Used to set the time, date, video system (EGA/VGA), as well as include system memory and extended memory, and list the disk drives.

Fixed Disk Used to list the drives and their master/slave status, and to allow changes based upon drive type. For example, the cylinder, heads, and sector/track data can be changed to match the present disk drive. And, the 32-bit I/O can be enabled or disabled, among other features.

Advanced System Setup Used for changing integrated peripherals, memory cache, memory shadowing, advanced chipset controls, PCI devices, and large disk access mode.

Boot Operations Used to specify the order in which the PC boots the drives, shows a summary screen during boot, and enables POST errors and disk checks.

Extended Features This may be as simple as Num Lock, toggled with Auto/On/Off.

Security and Antivirus Used to assign passwords for the supervisor, user, and startup, as well as for disk access. This also enables a virus check reminder and a system backup reminder.

Green PC Features Used to set power settings for doze, standby, and suspend, plus identify wakeup events (like using the keyboard).

Load Values from CMOS This loads the factory settings.

Save Values to CMOS This saves any changes.

To access information in this menu, hit either Enter or the Page Up/Page Down keys, depending upon whether details are needed, or whether they are on a toggle switch (such as enabled/disabled). Be aware different versions of BIOS and different manufacturers will list different features.

Warning to All Users

Before you make any changes to CMOS, copy your settings to paper (hit the Print Screen key for every possible BIOS setting) so they can be re-entered in the event of catastrophic failure. It's usually faster than searching through manuals for information that probably isn't listed.

Make changes in these settings one at a time, rebooting between each change. The safest advice is to start with something simple and forget any changes you're unsure of until you are absolutely, positively certain you know why you're making a change and how that change will affect your PC.

It's also a good idea to run performance benchmarks before and after changing BIOS settings so you will know whether any real improvements resulted from your changes. Benchmarks can be downloaded from the Internet, often from PC-related sites. They also can be found by doing a word search with a search engine.

Some BIOS changes are intuitive. For example, altering the Green PC settings can relieve minor annoyances, such as the PC going to sleep, but it won't foul up the system if you make a mistake. Enabling an internal cache, changing the date and time, and enabling virus check reminders also tend to be safe alterations. If you have the option of setting the wait states, set them low to maximize response speeds.

The Shadowing Effect

Shadowing speeds up the access to BIOS. It works by copying the BIOS information from the ROM chip to a faster random access memory (RAM) chip every time the PC is booted. This makes access about three times faster. For even faster performance, depending upon your system, you may be able to choose cacheable shadow RAM. That option caches the BIOS into main RAM and, on newer systems, accesses it using the L2 cache.

The L2 cache is an external memory setting that uses high-speed RAM to transfer information between the main RAM memory and the CPU. If you have the option of using an external cache, do so. Be aware, however, that it may switch itself off if the memory test fails during the POST. The internal memory is the L1 cache. It also should be enabled on 486 and faster CPUs. The internal memory is located on the processor itself. Depending on the BIOS manufacturer, external and internal cache may be listed separately or only as "Cache."

If your BIOS offers write-through or write-back cache options, you must determine which you value more: speed or safety. A write-through cache is somewhat faster, but offers none of the protection users need. A write-back cache saves data when the computer loses power unexpectedly. This occurs when the system locks up or when power outages occur.

Shadowing is more effective with DOS and Windows systems. But even with those systems, it is known for creating conflicts with hardware devices. To minimize conflicts, reboot the system after each change made to CMOS to ensure everything still works. It's much easier to undo one change by re-entering CMOS than to undo many.

The Hard Drive Ahead of You

Changing the hard drive specifications, and thus shutting your system down, is probably the most severe consequence of casual BIOS tweaking. It usually happens by changing a setting just to see what the other options are, and forgetting the original setting. Therefore, let the mistakes of others be a lesson to you; write down your settings before you even begin to look at options! If it happens anyway, your PC manual should list the specifications for the hard drive. If not, contact the manufacturer, write down the specifications, and re-enter them into BIOS. Afterwards, your system should recognize your hard drive. The alternative is to return to the default CMOS settings, as explained later in this article.

When installing an additional drive, a Plug-and-Play system should recognize it automatically. If not, make sure the new drive is physically installed properly (including master/slave settings) and that the cables are firmly in place. Reboot the system and, if the problem persists, enter Setup, choose Fixed Disk System, and check the specifications listed for the new drive.

PCs typically begin the boot sequence with A: and then C:—a disk drive and then the hard drive. This is where the PC looks for the operating system. You might save a wee bit of time by reversing the sequence. However, resist the temptation. If the operating system isn't found on C:, maybe because the drive failed or the operating system was erased, the PC may hang up, leaving users without an easy way to load the operating system or access the computer.

Some versions of BIOS include a turbo switch. Turning this switch off lets the PC's microprocessor slow down to the speeds of the early, 8 megahertz PCs to run very old software.

Pass It On

Passwords can be selected in the Security settings for the user and for the system administrator. You have the choice to enable, disable, or select passwords. Unless systems security is an issue, disable them. If you remember your password but can't access the system, the BIOS may have reverted to the default, factory password. Usually this will be the company name or a generic term such as BIOS, setup, or CMOS. Passwords are case-sensitive, so try several combinations.

If you forgot the password, you may need to reset either the CMOS itself, or the CMOS battery. First, try resetting CMOS. Check your PC manual for complete instructions. Some systems have password jumpers that can be set by moving the pins to the opposite position, for example, 2-3 rather than 1-2. The last option is to remove the battery from the motherboard (unless it's soldered to the board), and to replace it a few minutes later. Next, try the factory-set passwords again. If it still doesn't work, phone the BIOS manufacturer.

Error Messages

During POST you may get occasional error messages. The messages "Disk Drive A Error" and "Incorrect Drive A Type" (often accompanied with beeps) usually indicate a cable is loose. Turn off the PC. Remove the desktop computer case and make sure the cables to the offending drive are plugged in snugly. Reboot. If the problem still occurs, enter Setup and make sure the drives are listed and properly configured.

For keyboard errors, check for loose cables between the keyboard and the CPU. "Keyboard Error nn" means there is a stuck key. Clean your keyboard, then remove and clean the stuck key. "CMOS Checksum Error" indicates the battery is weak. Open the desktop computer case and replace the battery.

I/O addresses are the source of many conflicts, especially in Plug-and-Play environments that include non-PnP components. Because not all drivers and cards think in hexadecimal terms, they sometimes assign the same address to different components. Remember I/O addresses are given as ranges, such as 3B0-3DF. So, if two addresses fall within that range, assume they conflict.

Final Basics

If only the most basic BIOS settings are apparent, advanced settings may be hidden by the manufacturer. Dynamic RAM (DRAM) memory timing and cache static RAM (SRAM) timing may be among them, according to BIOS expert Scott Wainner (`http://www.sysopt.com`). To view hidden settings, Wainner recommends shareware utilities such as AMISetup and CTCHIPZ, that you can download and use to unlock these settings. CTCHIPZ instructions are written in German, but an English translation can be downloaded. (Links for these two programs are available from `http://www.sysopt.com/biosmod.html`)

If you experimented with BIOS settings and badly fouled up your system, reboot while holding down the key or keys used to enter Setup. This bypasses extended CMOS settings and is the first step in getting your PC up and running again. Once you get to the Setup menu, you can reload the original factory settings by choosing "Load Values from CMOS." Remember, however, any changes you have made to the BIOS since you bought the PC, such as adding storage devices, will not be reflected in these values.

BIOS Resources

For detailed help with BIOS, check the manufacturer's Web site as well as various newsgroups. Below are some other resources you can access.

Newsgroups

`Alt.comp.periphs.mainboard.asus`

`Intel.motherboards.pentium`

`comp.sys.ibm.pc.hardware.chips`

Web Sites

John Paul Rodrigue's BIOS Survival Guide v5.1 at `http://www.lemig.umontreal.ca/bios/bios_sg.htm`.

The BIOS Setup Information Guide at `http://www.sysopt.com/bios.html`.

Troubleshooting Ports

All communication between your computer and external devices is the result of properly configured ports. Through these doorways the printer can print, the scanner can scan, and the modem can dial. Without ports, your system isn't much more than a mute hunk of hardware.

This said, it's easy to see how pivotal ports are to the welfare and usability of your system. Ports are the connectors found on the back of the computer where all the hardware docks by way of the plug-in. In the internal scheme of things, the ports may connect directly to the motherboard, or they may be attached via a connecting card, depending on the system.

Docking Stations

On the back of almost every computer there are at least six standard ports. Usually, two are designated serial and one parallel. The others are for the keyboard, mouse, and monitor.

Typically, the keyboard and mouse ports are both round with six-pin connectors. The monitor will attach through either a 15-pin video port, or plug into a video card expansion port.

Serial ports use a 9-pin connector, and each pin has a specific purpose. Serial ports are used for peripherals such as modems, mice, and sometimes keyboards. They often are called communications (COM) ports, and the standard serial ports on the back of your computer generally will have built-in designations such as COM1 and COM2.

Parallel ports have a 25-pin connector, and are used primarily for devices that send or receive large amounts of data, such as printers and scanners. These ports often are called Line Printer (LPT) ports. The standard parallel port on the back of your system is customarily designated as the LPT1 port.

While serial ports only transmit one bit of data at a time along a single one-way wire, parallel ports allow attached devices to communicate to the computer by transmitting eight bits, or one byte, simultaneously, along the eight separate lines within the connecting cable. Both types of ports use bidirectional communication, meaning that both ends of the cable can transmit data. So when your printer is trying to print but is out of paper or ink, it can transmit this to your CPU, which commands an error message to pop up on the screen.

Too Few, Too Late

One of the most common port problems is simply not having enough of them. Many users find themselves in a bind when they don't plan ahead for additional peripherals and purchase a new external device, only to discover there's no place left to plug it in. Avoid this headache by mapping things out in advance.

You can increase the number of available ports on your computer by adding special expansion cards designed expressly for this function. Expansion cards fit into slots on the motherboard inside the computer or into empty slots on a horizontal riser board mounted to the motherboard.

Anytime you add new devices you can run into the most common port troubleshooting problem. The computer keeps track of where and when to send data by assigning every device, including ports, an input/output address (I/O address) and an interrupt request setting (IRQ). Addresses within your computer work in much the same way street addresses work; they give the computer destinations to which it can send data. IRQs give different devices priority over one another. For example, typically the keyboard is assigned IRQ 1, which means the computer will stop and listen to the keyboard before almost any other task.

When new devices are added to the system, they can accidentally be granted I/O addresses and IRQs already in use by other devices. As you can imagine, this leads to a bundle of problems in short order. Port troubleshooting often involves making sure the address and IRQ being used by the port is not being used by anything else.

For example, if you buy a serial port adapter card, hoping to increase the number of available ports, be sure it can be used with other interrupts besides IRQ4 and IRQ3. These interrupts will already be figured for use with COM1 and 2. If you need any additional ports, consider buying a multiport serial board. Multiport boards use up only one slot and one interrupt, but allow your system to collect and share data with several devices.

Using a Small Computer System Interface (SCSI) adapter is another way to increase the number of devices attached to your PC. SCSI devices can connect to each other in a daisy chain, meaning one device can plug into another, and another, and so on. You must check your PC's paperwork to see if you have an internal SCSI adapter. If you do, proceed carefully because you must follow specific steps to make this work.

Mouse and Keyboard

A familiar mistake that often occurs when a new computer is set up involves the keyboard and the mouse. Because these two connectors often look identical, people often plug them in the wrong ports. Two boot error messages will pop up if this happens, telling you the computer can't find the mouse and the keyboard. Switch them to their proper spots by looking for raised icons near the connectors on the back of the computer.

Once you plug in the mouse or keyboard to the appropriate port, you may have to reboot the computer before it will recognize the device.

Parallel Ports

Luckily, the only real problem with parallel ports is that you can't use very long cables between the system and the peripheral if you don't amplify the signal. Otherwise, errors may occur in the data. The longer the cable, the more likelihood for cross talk, a signal interference created by voltage leaking between the lines inside the cable.

The most frequently changed parallel port settings are accessed through software that comes with devices using the port. For example, if the printer is having difficulties, re-configure the settings by clicking on the Printers icon in the Control Panel. Right-click on the printer and choose Properties. All the port settings appear on the Details tab.

Click the Port Settings button and make sure the Check Port State Before Printing box is checked. This instructs Windows 95/98 to check the printer's status before it begins printing so that if any errors are detected and an error message is sent to the screen, you can correct the problem and retry printing.

The Spool settings box should only be used if you're using the printer for network printing. Otherwise, acquiesce to Windows default settings.

Serial Ports

Serial (COM) port problems are generally the most common of the port genre because they are the most frequently used for plugging in balky devices such as modems. Serial port conflicts typically arise when two or more COM ports use the same address or IRQ. This problem confuses the computer and can lead to even greater confusion for humans. Conflicts may cause system instability, device slowdowns, and other difficulties.

There are several things that should point to COM port address and/or IRQ conflicts. If the following things happen, either individually or together, you should look into the COM port and IRQ assignments:

- Nothing happens when the modem dials out
- The mouse is misbehaving
- The printer prints erratically or not at all (this is only a COM port issue if you're using a serial printer, rather than a parallel printer)

Help from Windows 95

In Windows 95, checking I/O address and IRQ details is less grueling than you might think. First off, if you're worried any of the ports are out of whack, you can always check their functionality in Windows 95. Choose System in the Control Panel found in My Computer. Click the Device Manager tab, select Ports, and then double-click the one you want to check. Windows 95 will tell you if the port is functioning properly.

Another Windows 95 helper for ironing out COM port conflicts is Plug-and-Play technology. Peripherals designated as Plug and Play should be a snap to add although this isn't always the case. The computer is supposed to automatically detect and configure the hardware, thus eliminating any IRQ conflicts. When a new device is recognized, the Plug-and-Play wizard goes to work, sorting out troubles so you don't have to.

To use Plug and Play, you must have Windows 95, a Basic Input/Output System (BIOS) that supports Plug and Play, and Plug-and-Play compatible hardware. If you have a computer system that did not arrive with Windows 95, or if you have recently upgraded to Windows 95, you will need to check to see whether your BIOS will support this feature. If Plug and Play doesn't work, you may receive a device conflict error message. Should this occur, you'll probably need to look at the IRQ assignments and do some arbitrating of your own.

Peruse the IRQ assignments by right-clicking the My Computer icon. Choose Properties, and then the System Properties window pops up. Click the Device Manager tab and then double-click Computer to open the Computer Properties menu. Choose the View Resources Tab and click on Interrupt Request, then all the IRQ device assignments should appear (see Figure 23.4).

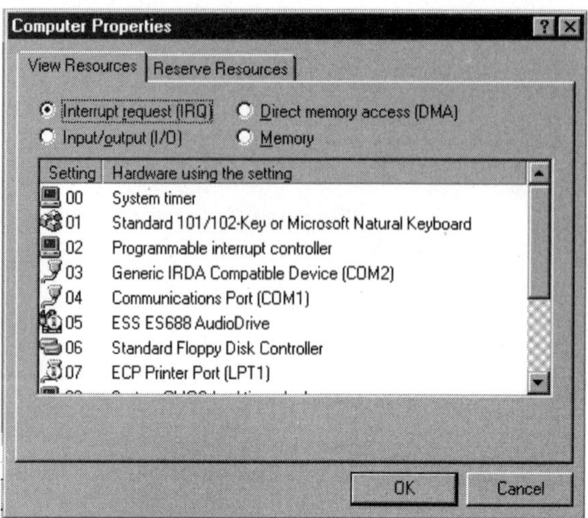

FIGURE 23.4: To help resolve COM port conflicts, view the IRQ assignments under Computer Properties and write down the related settings.

Take a closer look at this list. If there is a conflict, Windows 95 should already have identified it with a little yellow circle and an exclamation point. A red X next to the device indicates the device is not functioning at all. You can view the error information by double-clicking on the device name. Windows 95 should tell you which device is already using the interrupt request line.

This examination is usually much easier than fixing the problem. In some cases Windows 95 will help you sort out the difficulty. From the Start button, choose Help, then Troubleshooting, and double-click If You Have A Hardware Conflict. Follow the instructions on this troubleshooter first to see if the problem is an easy one that Windows 95 can guide you through.

Manual COM Port Configurations

Unfortunately, Windows 95's Help feature can't always solve the problems. If you need to do some investigation on your own, try keeping changes to a minimum in order to avoid further address conflicts. Write down each device and its current IRQ from the IRQ assignments list, so you can keep the designations straight as you're fiddling with things.

To change communications port configurations, right-click the My Computer icon and choose Properties. The System Properties box will appear with several tabbed sections. Pick the Device Manager Tab. A list of all devices presently installed on your system will be here.

Hit the plus sign next to the Ports icon. Another list appears underneath, cataloging all the communications ports assigned. Double-click the one that is giving you trouble. Another properties box appears, this one with four tabs.

The first tab, General, lists the device type, the device status, and the device usage (Figure 23.5). If you're having difficulties, it's likely the device status won't read "device working properly." The device usage area contains a box to check if you want to keep the original configuration.

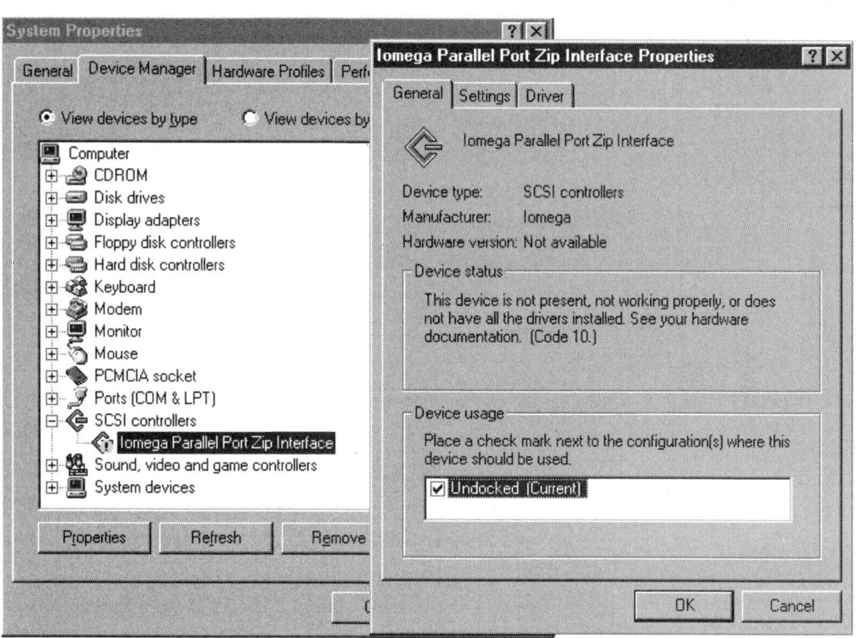

FIGURE 23.5: Investigate communication port settings and device status through System Properties in the Control Panel.

Port Settings is the next tab over. It lists five areas: bits per second, data bits, parity, stop bits, and flow control. This is the section where you can adjust more than simple address conflicts. Here the speed of the port can be investigated. Usually these settings should match the parameters of the installed modem.

Within this tab there is also a button marked Advanced Port Settings. Clicking it brings up a dialog window with a checkmark box labeled Use FIFO Buffers

(Requires 16550 Compatible UART). The universal asynchronous receiver-transmitter (UART) is the most common type of circuit used to connect modems and manage serial ports. It converts bytes into serial bits that can be transmitted and converts incoming data into parallel data so it can be received.

FIFO stands for first in, first out, which has to do with Windows 95's multitasking environment. With this box checked, which Windows 95 does automatically, the slider bars controlling the buffer settings may be adjusted. This will not work if you have an older UART.

The slider controls are for adjusting the receive buffer and the transmit buffer. These settings can be changed to correct connection and performance problems. Select lower settings to correct connection problems. For faster performance, however, select higher settings.

Back in the Communications Port box, the third tab over belongs to Driver settings. Included is a list of the driver files, and a button you can click to change drivers. There shouldn't be any need to spend time in this section.

Resources is the final tab. All the resource settings are shown, including the I/O address ranges and the IRQ setting for this COM port. There is a box to check for using automatic settings. It is possible for you to manually adjust the settings, but it is generally a much better idea to allow Windows 95 to manage them for you. If you've been experiencing difficulties with Plug-and-Play devices or other peripherals, go ahead and browse the configurations.

Click the list box labeled Setting Based On. You'll see a list of basic configurations. Go ahead and try each setting by clicking it to see if any of them will help you resolve the port conflict. Any new conflicts with registered devices will appear below in the Conflicting device list box. This allows you to record and change the driver settings on another conflicting device if necessary. If you hit on a combination that works, the words "No conflicts" will appear in that box.

WARNING WARNING WARNING WARNING WARNING WARNING WARNING WARNING

Keep in mind the more you fiddle around, the more likely it is that new conflicts will be introduced. If none of the suggested settings helps to resolve the conflict, reset all the settings you've changed back to the original configurations. If you've forgotten, refer to the notes you jotted down. If you found one that works, click OK to save the new settings. Then, make the settings active by shutting down the system and rebooting.

Due to the very nature of port conflicts, dealing with these difficulties can be frustrating and troublesome. Because settings and configurations may be different for each individual computer, there's no cut-and-dry answer. Part of the solution simply involves trying different combinations of settings until you hit upon the right one. Remember, most port conflicts can be resolved with a little patience and determination.

Troubleshooting Hard Drives

When it comes to a computer's internal organs, few are as vital to the system as the hard drive, and none is as valuable to the user.

Sure, you might lose the use of your computer temporarily if the processor goes kaput. But after a quick transplant, it's back to business as usual. But the problem isn't so easily solved when your hard drive dies. Lose your hard drive, and you'll lose millions of bytes of irreplaceable data. You can get a new hard drive, of course, but you still have to find a way to get by without the lost information. Ask anyone who's ever experienced the phenomenon known as a *hard drive crash*, and you'll quickly learn how frustrating it is to lose a hard drive.

Fortunately, most hard drive problems don't have such devastating results. With a little know-how, you can remedy the small problems before they become big ones. And with a little more know-how, you can prevent the small problems from ever occurring. But we'll discuss that a little later. The truth is, you can't do anything for your drive unless you know a little about it first.

Hard Drive Basics

A hard drive is a desktop or portable computer's primary means of data storage. The hard drive consists of five main components: a number of thin, rigid, circular disks, called platters, on which data is stored; the read/write heads that read data from and write data to the platters; an access arm that holds the read/write heads; a head actuator, which controls the movement of the access arm; and a spindle motor, which spins the platters at an extremely high rate of speed. These internal mechanisms typically are encased in a metal box that is connected to the computer's frame.

A personal computer sold today probably comes equipped with a hard drive that has a capacity of 1.6 to 4.8GB. A gigabyte is a unit of data measurement equal to a little more than one billion bytes. The average hard drive only a few years ago was capable of holding only a few hundred megabytes. And the first personal computers didn't have hard drives at all.

Undoubtedly, today's hard drives can hold substantially more data than their predecessors, but this also means that today's hard drives can cause substantially more problems to today's computer users. To avoid frustrating situations, computer users must be diligent in performing drive maintenance and must be aware of situations that could prove disastrous to a hard drive and the data stored on it.

We've divided our troubleshooting tips into two categories. The first category deals with problems that occur during or immediately following the installation of a hard drive. The second category concerns problems that occur anytime after that. Most of these latter problems have to do with the way data is stored on the drive.

The interesting thing about troubleshooting hard drives is that it's possible to avoid almost all the things that can go wrong with them. Except for manufacturer's flaws or egregious cases of drive abuse (shaking the hard drive, exposing the platters, putting it under an electrical magnet, etc.), the hard drive is a fairly stable component. Nevertheless, mistakes happen and things go wrong. We've come up with answers to some of the more common hard drive dilemmas.

Installation Problems

It's important to point out the majority of all hard drive problems occur during installation. If you can get the drive up and running, you'll have eliminated the source of most hard drive problems.

Every computer installation is fraught with peril. We've all heard the stories of systems that worked perfectly until new components were added. Of course, in some of these cases, the new component actually *was* the culprit. But most of the time, problems occur because the person performing the installation didn't read and follow all the directions, says Richard Haggan, technical support supervisor at Maxtor Corp.

"They tend to jump right in there and they forget some steps, whatever they may be," says Haggan. "Then we have to backtrack." It's always a good idea to read the directions completely before beginning an installation. That way, you'll be prepared for what comes next. And because you'll understand the entire process, you'll be less likely to skip a step you think is unimportant.

Of course, the installation instructions aren't always the easiest thing to understand and problems will crop up. Some of these are caused by human error.

For example, if the hard drive's power cable isn't connected correctly, then the drive won't work. One way to identify a problem with the power connection is to look at the tiny lights on the front of your computer. One of those lights is linked to the activity of the hard drive. When the hard drive is working, the light flashes. If that light doesn't come on when you turn your computer on, the hard drive probably isn't getting any power and you need to make sure the power cord is connected properly.

Another example of a problem caused by human error is an improperly connected data cable. If the hard drive indicator light flashes when you turn the computer on, yet you can't access the hard drive, then you can suspect this is the problem. This isn't the only reason for an inaccessible hard drive, but it's an easy one for you to fix. Besides, you don't want to waste your time calling technical support only to be told you didn't connect the hard drive to your system correctly.

To double-check the cable connections, remove the cover from your computer and locate the hard drive. It looks like a metal rectangular box and will be secured to the frame of the computer. The computer's user manual should tell you where it is if you can't find it.

After you locate it, see if it has two cables plugged into it. One cable actually consists of as many as four separate cords and probably has a plastic plug on one end. This is the power cable. The other cable looks like a wide ribbon. This is the data cable. Make sure the cables are connected securely to the drive. When you're certain they're connected properly, put the cover back on the computer and start it up. If the drive works, then it looks as if you've solved the problem.

But what if you've double-checked the cable connections and still can't get the drive to work? Here are many of the most common installation problems and their solutions.

Drive Doesn't Spin

In order for data to be read from or written to the drive, the platters on which the data is stored need to be spinning. As the platters spin, they make a soft humming noise. If you don't hear the humming noise and can't access the data on the drive, the first thing to do is check the power connection. If that checks out OK, then you might have a problem with the spin-up jumper.

A jumper is a tiny plastic box that has two holes in it. It slides over the tiny pins that are located on the back of the hard drive. These jumpers, which let you manually configure the settings for the drive, are on/off switches for the most basic drive functions.

A spin-up jumper is a jumper that lets you control the spin-up function. The spin-up jumper, like all the jumpers on a hard drive, needs to be configured correctly, prior to installation. Every drive is different, so you'll have to check the hard drive's instruction manual to find out how the spin-up jumpers should be set. If you get confused about how to set the spin-up jumper, contact the manufacturer of the drive or computer and ask for technical assistance.

No ROM Basic

This error message appears because the primary partition on the master (primary) hard drive isn't set to active.

What's a partition? Well, in simplest terms, it's an area on your hard drive that is treated as a complete storage unit. Each partition is divided into uniformly sized smaller compartments called sectors. Data is stored in groups of sectors, called clusters, and each cluster can store a maximum of one file. For more information about the storage areas of a hard drive, see the section, "Out of Disk Space," below.

Hard drives can be set to have more than one partition. Although this rarely happened with the smaller hard drives of yore, it happens quite regularly with today's multigig drives. Each partition is treated as a separate hard drive and has its own drive letter assigned to it.

If your drive is divided into multiple partitions, one of these partitions must be designated as the primary one; this is where the operating system is stored. If this partition isn't set as active, then you'll receive the No ROM Basic error message.

Setting the partition as active and solving the problem can be accomplished using FDISK, which is a DOS utility, or using the proprietary software that came with the hard drive. Which one you use will depend on which application you used to set the partitions originally. Because every manufacturer's software is unique, we'll show you how to set a partition as active using the universal FDISK.

NOTE NOTE NOTE NOTE NOTE NOTE NOTE NOTE NOTE NOTE NOTE NOTE NOTE NOTE NOTE

You'll need a bootable disk if you plan to use FDISK. You should have created one of these when you first installed your operating system. If you don't have one, you can contact your computer's manufacturer and ask for one.

Insert the bootable disk into the disk drive, then turn on the computer. When the DOS prompt appears, type **fdisk** and press Enter. At the resulting list of options, select the Set Active Partition option. Follow the on-screen directions for setting your main partition. You'll need to know the letter (probably C) assigned to the partition. The program will set the partition active and return you to the main menu. Press Esc to exit FDISK and return to the DOS prompt.

Master or Slave?

When you add a new drive to your system, there's one sure way to create drive identity problems: Don't configure the DS jumper correctly. This jumper must be set properly so your system can determine which drive is the master and which is the slave (the secondary drive).

Basically, if the DS jumper is present, the drive is designated as the master. If the DS jumper is absent, the drive is designated as the slave. Before you insert the drive, make sure the DS jumper is set properly. When they're shipped from the factory, most drives are set to be master drives. So if you're installing the drive as a master drive, you probably won't have to change the DS jumper. If you're setting the drive as a slave drive, you'll probably have to make a change.

NOTE

Every drive is different. The only way you'll be able to tell which jumper is the DS jumper is to read the user manual. If you're nervous about messing with the jumpers, call the drive manufacturer and a helpful technician will talk you through it.

Dual Drives, Single Boot

First of all, let us say adding a second hard drive to your system is one of the more dangerous upgrades you can perform. Advancements in storage technology have led to the introduction of other storage options, including high-capacity portable storage devices such as the Jaz drive, that are much easier to add to your PC. Before you add a second hard drive, give one of these other drives a long look. It might save you a few headaches down the road.

Now, if you've already installed a second hard drive on your computer, you may as well make the best of the situation. This means trying to fix all the little problems such a setup can create.

Here is one of those problems: You turn your computer on, and it only recognizes one of the hard drives. So you give the computer the three-finger thump (press Ctrl+Alt+Del simultaneously), and when it recovers, it recognizes both drives. Not a major problem, but it is an annoying inconvenience each time you use your computer. How can you avoid such frequent frustration? Three words: Reconfigure your BIOS.

The next time you turn your computer on, look for those magic words that grant entrance to the BIOS (software that controls the startup process of a computer). Usually, you'll see something such as Press F1 to enter Setup or Hit F2 for Setup. Follow the command. You have to be quick or the operating system will load and you'll have to reboot and try again. When you've done it correctly, the BIOS Setup screen should appear.

All you have to do now is follow our instructions, paying special attention to the Boot Options area of the BIOS. Disable both the Fast Boot Option and the Quick Power On Self Test options. Enable the Above 1MB option. If you see anything that mentions RAM Count, enable that, too. Set the Hard Disk Initialization Time Out option to 30. You may find all these settings in your BIOS. You may find only a few, or you may find none. Select the Exit And Save option when you're done.

Now that wasn't too hard, was it? Actually, the tricky part is that every system is different, so your BIOS might look quite different from any of the BIOSs we've seen. The BIOS is a very fragile part of your system, so if our solution doesn't seem to match your BIOS, don't touch anything; you could really foul up your computer. Instead, contact your computer's manufacturer, and tell someone in technical support you have a BIOS timing problem. If that person can't help you, you should receive the number of someone who can.

Usage Problems

After repeatedly writing and erasing data from the hard drive, the platters start to get a little dirty. We're not talking about dust and grime. Rather, we're talking about pollution of bytes and bits.

You see, when you write data to a hard drive, it is divided into sections (unless it's a small file, then it stays in one piece) and stored methodically on the drive. The location of the data is registered in the file allocation table (FAT; keeps a record of where data is stored on a drive) so the computer knows where it is when it wants it. Your hard drive becomes like a colossal warehouse, with thousands of crates of information stacked in neat piles. And if all you ever did was write data to a drive, these piles would always stay in the same place and you wouldn't have to worry about data integrity.

But you'll probably have to delete files from your PC, and that causes problems. You see, the file actually isn't deleted from the drive. Rather, reference to the file is deleted from the FAT. When new data is stored on the drive, it is recorded over the old data. And instead of storing the data in contiguous sections, it fills in the gaps left behind by deleted data.

Think of it in terms of our colossal warehouse. When you want to remove an object from the warehouse, the crate in which it's stored isn't removed. Rather, the object is removed from the case and the crate is marked as available in the warehouse foreman's register. When a new shipment of objects arrive, they don't get a new pile, or even new crate, to themselves. Instead, they're distributed among the many crates that are marked available in the warehouse foreman's register. As more objects leave, more arrive to take their places. Soon, similar items are stacked in various piles and the organization of the drive depends entirely on the warehouse foreman's register.

When this phenomenon of scattered data happens to your hard drive, it's called fragmenting. As you add and remove data from your drive, it becomes more fragmented. As it becomes more fragmented, it takes longer for your hard drive to locate files and execute programs. Performance may seem a bit sluggish. Some people may think this means the computer needs more RAM or a new hard drive. Actually, what it needs is a healthy defragmenting.

Defragmenting (or defragging as it's often called) is as easy as a few points and clicks in Windows 95/98. Open the Start menu, select Programs, and choose Accessories. Select System Tools from the list of options, then click Disk Defragmenter. Up pops a Select Drive window, asking you to choose the drive you want to defrag. Select the drive, then click OK. If your drive is in bad shape, the Disk Defragmenter immediately starts defragmenting the selected drive.

If your drive isn't in bad shape, however, you'll see a message indicating you don't need to defragment the drive right now. Because defragmentation takes a long time, especially if you have a high-capacity drive, we recommend you click the Exit button and wait to defragment your drive until you need to do so.

If your computer runs Windows 3.*x* or DOS, the process is basically the same. Exit Windows so you're looking at a DOS prompt, then type **defrag** and press Enter. This initializes DEFRAG, the DOS defragmenting utility. Select the drive you want to defragment from the list that appears on-screen, then press Enter. DEFRAG then analyzes the data stored on your hard drive and suggests a defragmentation option. We recommend heeding the suggestion.

And if your drive doesn't need to be fragmented, DEFRAG will tell you that. In that case, just select OK, press Enter, then select Exit, and press Enter again to exit DEFRAG and return to the DOS prompt.

When do you need to defragment your drive? Carl Salter, a senior technician with Maxtor Corp., says that depends on how you use your computer. If you install and uninstall lots of programs and files, you should defragment quite often, perhaps monthly, says Salter. But if you tend to use the same programs and don't add and remove files on a regular basis, you're probably safe defragging your drive every six months or so.

NOTE

The DOS and Windows defragmenting utility is meant to be used on uncompressed drives. Disk compression is a means of reducing the amount of disk space required to store a file; essentially data is squeezed so it fits into a smaller space on the drive. Most drive compression utilities have their own defragmenting applications; use those defragmenting tools.

File Not Available

Another typical problem of very active hard drives is data corruption. Yes, that means data is destroyed, and that's always a bad thing. But this isn't necessarily the end of the world for your hard drive. A little data corruption is to be expected when you give your computer a vigorous workout every day.

NOTE

We're talking about minor forms of data corruption. If the entire hard drive becomes corrupted or inaccessible, this indicates a bigger problem, probably a crash. The following solutions won't remedy a drive crash.

The three most common types of data corruption are file fragments (also called lost allocation units), cross-linked files, and bad sectors.

Maxtor's Salter describes file fragments as incomplete files or incomplete file entries. Essentially, that means the computer can't find all the data associated with the particular file. File fragments most often occur when an application is closed prematurely, before it had a chance to tell the system where it stored the data it was using.

For example, if you accidentally unplug your computer while you're in the middle of typing a document in your word processor, the portion of the document that has been typed since you last activated the Save command will end up as a file fragment.

The second type of data corruption is cross-linked files. This means there has been a mix-up on the hard drive and the FAT incorrectly recorded the location of some data. Think of it like this: Your friends live at 100 Main Street, but in your address book you incorrectly entered their address as 1000 Main Street. When you try to visit them, you're greeted by strangers because you knocked on the wrong door.

Similarly, when the computer looks for data that has become cross-linked, it won't be able to find the data because it won't be located where the computer thinks it's located. When this happens, you'll lose the data that has the incorrect FAT address. You might have cross-linked files if you can't access a file you've accessed previously.

Finally, we have bad sectors. But before we explain what a bad sector is, we need to explain what a good sector is. As we mentioned earlier, hard drives are divided into partitions, and these partitions are divided into sectors. A good sector is a place where data can be stored. A bad sector, on the other hand, is a place where data cannot be stored.

All of these problems have the same solution: ScanDisk (or Chkdsk as it's called in early versions of DOS). This utility diagnoses and repairs (or if a repair is impossible, it finds a workaround solution to) minor flaws, including file fragments, cross-linked files, and bad sectors, on a computer's drives.

To run ScanDisk in Windows 95/98, click the Start button, select Programs, and choose Accessories. Highlight System Tools and click ScanDisk. Choose a drive to scan, then click Start.

If your computer runs DOS or Windows 3.*x*, get to a DOS prompt (exit Windows if necessary) and type **scandisk**. (Type **chkdsk** if your computer runs DOS 6.1 or earlier.) As with Disk Defragmenter and DEFRAG, you select the drive you want to scan and let the program run itself.

If ScanDisk finds file fragments, it saves the fragment as a .CHK file. You then can view the file with a word processor. Just go to File Manager (in Windows 3.1) or My Computer (in Windows 95/98) and open the C: drive. Double-click a .CHK file, which should have a name such as File0001 or File0002. You'll be greeted by an Open With box, asking you to select a program with which to open the .CHK file. Highlight the Notepad option, then click OK. This brings the file up as a text document. Odds are you won't be able to make sense of what you find, but you might uncover a few usable fragments from a document you thought you lost.

ScanDisk also cleans up cross-linked files and marks bad sectors so the computer doesn't try to write data to these sections.

It's a good idea to run ScanDisk quite regularly. For active computers (those that are used on a daily basis), we recommend running ScanDisk every week. If you use the computer less often, you can run ScanDisk less often, but it's a good idea to run it at least once each month.

NOTE NOTE NOTE NOTE NOTE NOTE NOTE NOTE NOTE NOTE NOTE NOTE NOTE NOTE NOTE

Just a few warnings. Don't run ScanDisk on a network or from within a DOS shell application or Windows 3.*x*. Don't run ScanDisk on a compressed drive. Close all applications before running ScanDisk. And it's a good idea to back up your drive before using ScanDisk.

Can't Boot from Drive

Booting a computer isn't as violent as it sounds. A boot, when you're talking about computers, refers to a computer's process of executing the basic startup routine as dictated by the BIOS. During the process of booting up, the computer looks to a particular drive or drives (designated in the BIOS), where it can find the information it needs to get itself going.

If the computer looks to this drive and can't find this information, it will halt the setup and an error message will appear on-screen. If this happens to you, there are a number of possible reasons.

The first and most obvious reason is that you might have a disk in the disk drive. On most systems, the BIOS tells the computer to look first to the disk drive and then to the hard drive. Usually, the disk drive is empty and the computer, sensing that, proceeds to the hard drive.

But if a disk is inadvertently left in the disk drive, the computer will attempt to boot from it. The computer won't find the information it needs, and that causes the error message. If this happens, remove the disk and reboot (turn on again) the computer.

Another reason for the error message is not as innocent; you may have acquired a virus that has affected the *master boot record* (MBR; the instructions that tell the computer which drive to access during a bootup). This virus takes the place of the MBR when the computer is turned on, making it impossible for the computer to access the information it needs to boot correctly.

Such a virus creates a Catch-22 for the computer age: You need to run an antivirus program to remove the virus, but you can't access the antivirus program because the MBR is corrupt.

Fortunately, there is a solution, as long as you have a bootable disk. Stick the bootable disk in the disk drive, turn the computer off, and then turn it back on again. (Creating a bootable disk is covered in Skill 3.)

Remember when we said a disk in the disk drive could cause problems when the computer is turned on? Well, in this case, the disk will solve your problems. The bootable disk contains the operating system information for which the computer is looking. You won't receive an error message; you'll receive a DOS prompt instead. From there, run your antivirus program, making sure it checks for boot viruses.

A third reason for this error message is that the MBR may have become corrupt by the installation of more than one operating system on the hard drive. If you have reason to believe your system doesn't have a virus on it or the virus scan comes up clean and if you've installed more than one operating system on your hard drive, type **fdisk /mbr** at the DOS prompt. This will extricate the old corrupt MBR and replace it with a new clean one.

Out of Disk Space

This error message pertains to the way your hard drive is formatted to store data. As we mentioned earlier, a drive is divided into partitions. Each partition is divided into sectors, and a group of sectors is called a cluster. Data is broken down and stored in these clusters.

Every cluster in a partition is the same size. Files that contain more data than a single cluster can hold are broken down into pieces and divided among a number of clusters. But—and this is important to remember—a cluster can't hold more than one file.

This system of partitions, clusters, and sectors is great for keeping your hard drive organized, but it isn't very efficient. To illustrate this point, let's consider a hard drive that has 32KB clusters. If you choose to save an 89KB graphics file to this hard drive, the computer would divide the data into three parts and send the data to three separate clusters. Among these three clusters, there would be 7KB of unused storage space. That's not too bad.

But let's say you want to save an 8KB word processing file to this same hard drive. The computer stores the file in a single 32KB cluster. But that cluster alone will have 24KB of unused storage space. If you have lots of similarly sized files on your hard drive, you'll fill your drive when it reaches a quarter of its maximum capacity.

To solve this problem, you need to adjust the way your hard drive stores data. The FAT automatically determines the size of the clusters. It bases the size of the cluster on the size of the partition. If the partition is large, the FAT sets large clusters; if the partition is small, the FAT sets small clusters. The size of a cluster is determined by the size of the partition. Table 23.1 shows the typical cluster size and the number of sectors in a cluster for some standard partition sizes.

TABLE 23.1: Cluster and Partition Size

Partition Size (in megabytes)	Sectors per Cluster	Cluster Size (in kilobytes)
0 to 15	8	4
16 to 127	4	2
128 to 255	8	4
256 to 511	16	8
512 to 1023	32	16
1024 to 2145	64	32

Although you can't control the size of the clusters, you can control the size of the partitions. Just use FDISK or the proprietary software that came with the hard drive to set the size of the partitions.

Before partitioning a drive, we advise contacting the manufacturer of the hard drive. The manufacturer can tell you the easiest way to do it and tell you about the limitations of your drive. Use the software the manufacturer recommends and follow the directions exactly. Also, back up your data beforehand, just to be safe.

We'll use FDISK to set up a two-partition hard drive. Type **fdisk** at the DOS prompt, then press Enter From the resulting list of options, select the Create DOS Partition option, then press Enter.

You need to create a primary partition first; this is where you'll store the operating system. Choose the Create Primary DOS Partition option, then press Enter. Specify how much of the drive you want to allocate to the primary partition. We'll set the partition as 50 percent of the drive's entire capacity.

After you set the capacity of the primary partition, you'll return to the main menu, where you need to choose the Set Active Partition option. The on-screen directions will guide you through this process and return you to the main menu. Once again, choose the Create DOS Partition option and press Enter. From the resulting menu, choose Create Extended DOS Partition and press Enter. We chose to set this partition as the remaining portion (50 percent) of the drive.

When you return to the main menu, choose the Display Partition Information option. The resulting screen will tell you how the drives are configured. The primary partition probably will be listed as the C: drive. The extended partition probably will be listed as the D: drive. Take note of the drive letters.

Finally, you just need to format the partitions. Insert a system disk (a disk that contains basic operating system information so you can start your computer), type **format c: /s**, and press Enter. After the format is complete, remove the disk and reboot the computer. This time it should start without the help of the system disk. Format the D: drive by typing **format d:** at the DOS prompt. Now you're ready to reinstall the operating system and all your data.

It's best to create multiple partitions and set partition sizes when you first get a drive. Otherwise you'll have to reformat the drive, which entails erasing all the data from the drive. It's also important to think carefully about how many partitions you want and how large each partition should be. Too many partitions can be confusing; too few can be a waste of drive space.

Don't be frightened by the prospect of partitioning, though. It can be particularly useful on any hard drive that has a storage capacity of more than 1GB, and it's required for many drives that have capacities of more than 2.1GB.

A useful partition size is something close to 500MB. That's big enough to hold large programs and small enough to make a noticeable improvement in storage efficiency. But if you're afraid to make that decision by yourself, contact the drive's manufacturer for some advice.

NOTE

When you run FDISK, you might receive a Runtime Error message. This indicates there is damage to the hard drive or to the software that runs the hard drive. Contact the drive manufacturer for information about solving this problem.

Drive Crash

The last and worst problem that could happen to your drive is a crash. This means your drive has died. A crash can be caused by hardware (such as the read/write heads hitting the platters) or by software (such as a virus scrambling the FAT).

The symptoms of a drive that has crashed range from the drive making strange grinding noises to an Invalid Drive Specification error message. If you can't access your drive regardless of what troubleshooting solutions you try, odds are your drive has crashed.

At this point, if you've backed up your drive religiously, you're feeling mighty grateful that you have and you're mildly annoyed that you're going to have to buy a new drive. If you haven't backed up your drive, you're probably enduring one of the most horrifying experiences you've ever had.

Fortunately, there are some companies, such as DriveSavers (`www.drivesavers.com`) and Ontrack (`http://www.ontrack.com`), that can recover data from a crashed drive.

Before you call one of these places, however, you should do two things. First, call the drive manufacturer to find out if your drive is under warranty or if there's a way to save any of the data on the drive. Second, go buy a backup drive.

Safe and Secure

When you stop to think about all the data stored on your hard drive, it's mind-boggling that the drive can be efficiently organized at all. Thankfully, technology does most of the work. All you need to do is carry out a few drive maintenance tasks and periodically take note of how the drive is performing. Hopefully that's all it will take to keep your data safe and secure.

Troubleshooting Disk Drives

The encompassing phrase *disk drive* generally refers to any data storage device that uses a laser to write data to or read data from a storage medium. Within this category of high-capacity storage devices are the compact disk, read-only memory

(CD-ROM) drive; the compact disk, recordable (CD-R) drive; and the digital video disk (DVD; also referred to as a "digital versatile disk") drive.

From a practical standpoint, disk drives are one of the most important additions to the desktop PC in the past decade. From a troubleshooting standpoint, they're a nightmare. Why? Because disk drives were designed to bring large programs to the PC; they weren't designed to be fixed by amateurs.

If something goes wrong with a disk drive, says Mike Nguyen, product manager for the data storage products division at TEAC, it really goes wrong. "There isn't a whole lot of problems that you can fix yourself, with the exception of the common things," Nguyen says.

Fortunately, those common things aren't too tough to spot and fix. We'll help you recognize and solve some of the common problems that strike the most common of the disk drives: the CD-ROM drive. We'll also point out and explain some of the problems that demand professional service.

Installation Problems

Most new CD-ROM drives are of the Plug-and-Play variety, meaning they should be easy to install. And most of the time, they are. But *most* of the time isn't *all* of the time, and plenty of people can tell horror stories of Plug-and-Play installations gone awry.

Fortunately, Plug-and-Play technology has improved during the past two years, and many of the early problems with it have been remedied by now. That doesn't mean you'll never run into a problem when you're installing a CD-ROM drive. It simply means the problem more likely is caused by a user error or a mechanical malfunction than by the Plug-and-Play standard.

To minimize the chances of encountering an installation problem, read the instruction manual completely before starting. And when you start the installation, follow the directions exactly. If you must improvise, take careful notes so you can explain to a technical support technician what you did. Before you put the cover back on your PC, double-check the cable connections to make sure they're securely connected.

After you have the drive installed and have run the setup software, it's time for the moment of truth. Turn your computer off, then turn it on again. As it starts up, pay close attention to the small light on the front of the CD-ROM drive. It should flicker a bit while the operating system loads.

This light indicates when the drive is active. It flickers when you boot up (start the computer) because the computer checks the CD-ROM drive to make sure it's there. It also checks to see if a disk is inserted in the drive. If the light doesn't come on at all, you need to check the power cord and data cable connections.

Turn the computer off, remove the cover, and check the cable connections. After you replace the cover and turn the computer on again, the light should flicker. If it doesn't, you should reinstall the software. It's possible that something backfired during the first software installation, and you just need to run the setup again. After the software installation, restart the computer. If the lights still don't flicker after you reinstall the software, then you might have a faulty drive on your hands.

As one last safety check, push the eject button (the computer must be on) to see if the tray protracts from the drive. If it does, then the problem might just be a burnt-out light bulb. Contact the drive manufacturer for information about fixing the bulb or replacing the drive.

A Lost Drive

Once you've determined the drive has power coming into it, it's time to make sure the computer recognizes the drive. This is an easy thing to check in a Windows operating environment. Just open File Manager in Windows 3.1 or My Computer in Windows 95/98 and browse the group of drive icons listed on-screen.

You should see one icon representing the disk drive, one icon representing the hard drive, and one icon representing each of the other drives you have installed on your system, including one for your newly installed CD-ROM drive.

If you're using DOS, it's not quite as easy to determine if a newly installed CD-ROM drive has been recognized by the computer. Instead of looking for drive icons, you have to type the drive letter assigned to the drive and a colon (such as D:) at the DOS prompt. Press Enter.

If you receive in response a DOS prompt that bears the drive letter of your CD-ROM drive (such as D:\>), then you know the drive has been recognized by the computer. But if you receive an Invalid Drive Specification error message, then the drive hasn't been recognized by the system and you have some work to do.

Regardless of which operating system you use, the first thing to do if the drive isn't recognized is to run the installation software again. After the software installation is complete, restart your system and see if the CD-ROM drive has a corresponding icon in File Manager/My Computer or if the drive is accessible in DOS. If so, then the problem is solved. If not, keep reading.

Slave or Master?

Having ruled out a software problem, the probable cause of the unrecognized drive is a slave/master drive conflict. In other words, you forgot to set the jumpers correctly when you installed the drive in your computer.

Like a hard drive, a CD-ROM drive has jumpers on the back of it. A jumper, which is a tiny plastic box that has two holes in it, is an on/off switch for a basic drive function. In this case, the jumper determines whether a CD-ROM drive will be a master (primary) or slave (secondary) drive.

CD-ROM drives usually are installed as master drives so the default setting for the jumpers is the master setting. But if the CD-ROM drive is attached to the motherboard (the printed circuit board to which all the computer's components connect) via the hard drive's data cable, then the CD-ROM drive needs to be configured as a slave drive. And that means you need to reset the jumpers to the slave position.

NOTE NOTE NOTE NOTE NOTE NOTE NOTE NOTE NOTE NOTE NOTE NOTE NOTE NOTE NOTE

The data cable that connects the hard drive to the motherboard often has a second connector on it. This second connector can be used to connect any other drive to the motherboard and definitely comes in handy if all the motherboard's expansion ports are full. Instructions on how to connect a drive to this second connector are included with most CD-ROM drive upgrade kits.

Every drive is different, so you should refer to the drive's user manual to determine how to set the jumpers to the slave position. Because of its small size, you might need a pair of tweezers to help you slide the jumper off and on the pins. Contact the drive's manufacturer if you're unable to follow the user manual's instructions for repositioning the jumpers.

After resetting the jumpers to the slave position, double-check the data cable and power cord connections to make sure they're secure. Then put the cover back on the computer. Restart the machine and look in File Manager/My Computer or try to access the drive through DOS. You should see a drive icon or a DOS prompt that corresponds to the newly installed drive.

A Missing Driver

When you opened a hardware upgrade kit in the good old days of computing (that's anything prior to 1996), you were almost certain to find a few things inside. One of those things was a registration card, which cluttered up your desk until you had the courage to throw it away. Another was the user manual, which probably looked like it was written in Sanskrit. And finally, you received a disk that contained the component's device driver (a program that enables a peripheral to communicate with the rest of the computer system).

Fortunately, times have changed. Most products are registered via the Internet, so you can throw the registration card in the trash right away. Computer companies have realized the importance of user manuals and actually have begun to produce them in English. And the latest operating systems come equipped with built-in libraries of device drivers.

That's right; in many cases, the disks that held the device drivers just aren't necessary anymore. Although many CD-ROM drive manufacturers still include the drivers with every new drive they sell, some have stopped sending out disks as a way of cutting costs.

"But don't be scared by that," Nguyen of TEAC says. "If the box carries a Windows 95/98 or (Windows) NT certified logo, then it should be a Plug-and-Play drive, and the driver should be built into the operating system." Just run the setup software that came with the drive; it should locate the driver it needs and configure itself automatically (see Figure 23.6). If the operating system is unable to locate the driver for some reason, then you need to call the manufacturer and request that a driver be sent to you immediately.

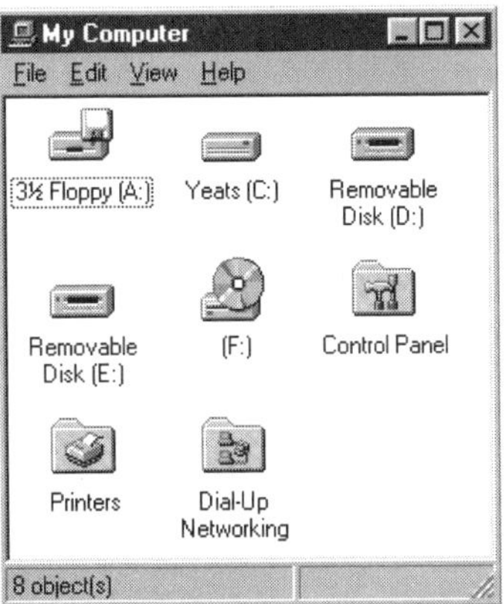

FIGURE 23.6: The manufacturer doesn't need to send a driver with your new CD-ROM drive; Windows 95 contains a built-in library of device drivers.

Operational Problems

Once the cables are secure, the jumpers set, the software installed, and the driver configured, then the CD-ROM drive should be good to go…unless you run into a snag. Here are a few of the more common problems you might encounter.

Audio CD Won't Play Automatically

Microsoft designed Windows 95/98 to maximize the entertainment value of the PC. For example, the operating system includes a built-in CD player application, which is appropriately called CD Player. When you insert an audio CD, the computer automatically opens CD Player and starts to play the CD. Or at least, that's what should happen.

If it doesn't, right-click the My Computer icon, then click the Properties option. Click the Device Manager tab in the System Properties window. Double-click the CD-ROM heading, then double-click the name of your CD-ROM drive when it appears. In the resulting window, click the Settings tab and make sure the Auto Insert Notification option is enabled (there should be a check in the box). If it isn't enabled, click the box so that a check appears in it (see Figure 23.7).

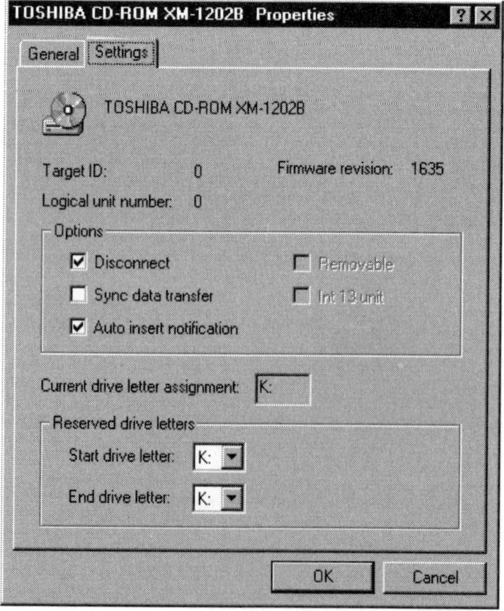

FIGURE 23.7: Audio CDs should start playing as soon as they're inserted in the CD-ROM drive. If not, you need to enable the Auto Insert Notification option in the drive's Properties window.

Restart your computer, then reinsert the audio CD in the CD-ROM drive. Music should start playing automatically. If it doesn't, make sure the speakers are plugged in and the volume is turned up.

Drive Can't Read

A CD-ROM drive should function flawlessly for a long time. But sooner or later a problem arises. Maybe the drive will spontaneously combust. Maybe the drive will be taken hostage by antitechnology terrorists. Or maybe you'll insert a disk in the drive, and a cruel error message will tell you the drive can't read the disk.

The first thing to do if the latter occurs is to eject the disk and reseat it in the tray or caddy. The CD-ROM should be positioned with the data side down and the label side up. Insert the caddy into the drive or press the eject button to retract the tray. Wait and see if you get an error message. If you don't, then you solved that problem.

But if you receive another error message, you may have a more serious problem on your hands. Before you curse the CD-ROM drive, however, make sure the problem isn't just a faulty disk. Take the CD-ROM to another computer and insert it in that machine's CD-ROM drive. If the disk doesn't work there, then the likely culprit is a bad disk.

How can a CD-ROM go bad? Well, it may have come off the assembly line that way, in which case you should return it to the software developer to get a new one. Or maybe the data surface has been damaged. Look for deep scratches or cracks on the surface of the CD-ROM. If that is the problem, then the only way you'll get a new one is by purchasing one yourself.

But if the surface of the disk is unblemished and you've tested it on another computer, then you're probably experiencing the effects of slippage. Essentially, slippage means the CD-ROM isn't spinning like it should.

To explain this a little better, we'll have to take a look inside the drive. At the center of a CD-ROM drive is a contraption that consists of a rubber ring and a magnet. When you insert a CD-ROM, the disk presses against the ring and is held in place by the magnet. When the PC tries to access the CD-ROM, the rubber ring spins. And the disk, which is attached to the ring, spins with it.

If the rubber ring gets dirty or dusty, then it can't get a tight grip on the disk. Consequently, as the rubber ring spins, the disk repeatedly falls off and reattaches itself. To the drive, this creates the illusion that the disk is slipping. To the user, it creates the reality that the drive doesn't work.

You can live with this problem at first. Work around it by removing the CD-ROM and reinserting it into the drive. Later, as the problem becomes more severe, your only solution is to have the drive serviced by a professional or send it to the manufacturer for a cleaning.

Tray Won't Eject

Here's a rule for you: Never force a tray or caddy into a CD-ROM drive after the computer has been shut down.

Let us explain. On many CD-ROM drives, the head carriage assembly (the contraption that holds the drive's laser) isn't locked in place when the computer is turned off. Consequently, when the tray or caddy is forced into the drive, the head carriage assembly is knocked out of whack.

Among the many negative effects this has on your drive is that it may prevent the drive from ejecting the tray or caddy. Another negative effect is the drive won't be able to read any CD-ROMs. The only solution to this problem is to send the drive to the drive manufacturer for service.

Disk Maintenance

To get the most from your CD-ROM drive, you only have to remember two things: Keep the drive clean, and keep the CD-ROMs clean.

The best way to keep the drive clean is to maintain a dust-free office or workstation. Don't open the windows in your office and keep the pets away from your PC. Also, don't leave the tray hanging out of the drive or prop the door open on the front of the drive. If you think your drive needs a good cleaning, take it to a computer shop or send it to the manufacturer. You shouldn't try to clean it yourself.

To keep the CD-ROMs in good shape, you should never touch the data surface of the disks. The best way to hold them is by the edges or with one finger in the hole in the middle of the disk. Store the CD-ROMs in their cases when they're not in use. If you need to clean a CD-ROM, use a soft dry cloth and wipe from the center out. Never wipe in a circular motion.

Treat It Right

If something goes wrong with your drive after you've installed it, odds are you won't be able to do anything about it. Fortunately, most of the problems that strike a CD-ROM drive can be prevented by keeping the drive and CD-ROMs clean and treating the drive with a little respect.

Troubleshooting Disk Drives

The disk drive is one of the stalwart components of the computer system. Before they came equipped with CD-ROM drives, sound cards, and hard drives, PCs were coming off the assembly line—or to put it more accurately, they were emerging from garages and basements—with at least one built-in disk drive.

And in the three decades since their invention, disk drives, and the disks that are inserted into them, have undergone few changes. In fact, they've changed in size only twice, when 8-inch disks were replaced by 5.25-inch disks and when 5.25-inch disks were replaced by 3.5-inch disks.

But longevity and a lack of change aren't the only reasons disk drives are such stable components of a computer system. Another reason is they're technologically simple. A disk drive basically has three parts: a spindle motor, which spins the disk when it is inserted into the drive; a stepper motor, which positions the head that reads data from and writes data to the disk; and a controller card, which contains the circuitry that controls the read and write processes of the drive.

When something goes wrong with your computer, you almost always can rule out the disk drive as the culprit. In fact, says Mike Nguyen, product manager for the data storage products division at TEAC, even when a computer malfunction seems to be caused by the disk drive, the problem probably lies elsewhere. The fault usually lies with the disk, the cables that connect the drive to the computer, the controller card, or the computer's Basic Input/Output System (BIOS; software that controls the computer's startup processes and the disk drive, among other things).

Incorrect BIOS Settings

According to Nguyen, the most common problem addressed by TEAC's technical support staff is an incorrect BIOS setting. The BIOS tells the computer where the disk drive is located and the capacity and size of the disk. If this setting is incorrect, the drive won't be able to read data from or write data to disks that are inserted into the drive.

This problem is recognized by error messages that appear on-screen when the user attempts to access a disk. The error messages, which may state Track Zero Bad or Disk Unusable, indicate the drive is unable to retrieve data from or record data to the disk.

NOTE NOTE NOTE NOTE NOTE NOTE NOTE NOTE NOTE NOTE NOTE NOTE NOTE NOTE NOTE

This problem usually occurs in conjunction with the installation of a disk drive. If you encounter one of these error messages when you attempt to access a drive that you've used for some time, it probably isn't a BIOS problem. Nevertheless, it's a good idea to check your BIOS settings before calling technical support.

If you encounter this problem, the first thing you should do is check your BIOS settings. To do this, shut down all programs, exit your operating system, and turn off the computer.

Turn the computer on again and watch the screen carefully. You should see an on-screen message describing how to enter the Setup mode. The message may state Press F1 to enter Setup, To enter Setup, press **U**, or something similar. This message appears for a second or two. You need to press the indicated key quickly, before the computer initializes the operating system.

If you don't get the key pressed in time, wait for the computer to finish setting up the operating system, then repeat the process of shutting down and turning off your computer. When you turn it back on again, be prepared to press the button that lets you enter Setup. The Setup area is a text-only interface and isn't the same setup area you use when installing a program or making changes to your operating system. You'll see a list of commands for navigating through the Setup area and a list of some of the system's basic components and settings. Using the navigation commands, you can move from component to component, changing the BIOS settings for each one. Although it's a good idea to explore this area if you've never seen it before, be *very* careful about making changes of any kind. Accidentally changing a setting may lead to problems that affect more than your disk drive.

Locate the settings for your disk drive. If you only have one disk drive, it should be labeled as the A: drive. If you have more than one disk drive, they should be labeled as the A: and B: drives. Locate the one that is causing you problems. If you don't know which one is causing you problems, you need to exit the Setup and become a little better acquainted with the computer and its user manual before you proceed.

After you've located the disk drive settings, make sure the drive is configured to support 3.5-inch, 1.44MB disks. That is, make sure it's configured to support those disks if that's what you use. If the drive is older and uses disks with a lower storage capacity or if the drive is designed to support 5.25-inch disks, make sure it's set to support that type of disk. If the disk drive is less than six years old, however, it most likely supports 3.5-inch, 1.44MB disks.

If the drive is configured to support the type of disks you use, then your problem lies elsewhere. Peruse the list of navigational commands to find the key or keys you need to press to exit the Setup area. You may receive a message indicating changes have been made and asking if you want to save the changes. If you didn't want to make any changes, select the No option. The Setup area will vanish, and soon the familiar interface of your operating system will appear on-screen.

If the drive isn't configured to support the type of disks you use, change it so that it is. Usually you can press the Spacebar or the Tab key to toggle among the setting options. After you've made the change, press the key or keys that lets you exit the Setup area. You may receive a message indicating changes have been made and asking if you want to save changes. Select the Yes option and your computer will save the changes and start to initialize the operating system. Soon you'll be back in familiar on-screen territory.

Check your drive by inserting a disk and trying to read data from it or write data to it. If it works, then you've fixed the problem. If it still doesn't work, check the rest of this section for more solution possibilities.

Head Out of Alignment

This problem sounds worse than an incorrect configuration setting, and it is. Think if your head were out of alignment, so that it laid sideways on your shoulder, your neck at a 90-degree angle. It would be tough to read books, street signs, or can labels on a store shelf.

Well, when your disk drive's read/write head is out of alignment, it too has a problem reading and writing data. If you receive an error message, such as Error Reading Drive A,when you attempt to access data from a disk, then the drive's read/write head probably is out of kilter.

Unfortunately, there's no way to fix this problem at home. But before you go through the arduous task of removing the drive from your system and sending it back to the manufacturer, perform this quick check to make sure the problem is with the head and not just with a disk gone bad.

Insert a disk into the drive and try to format the disk. To format a disk in Windows 95/98, double-click the My Computer icon, then right-click the A: drive icon. Select Format from the resulting pop-up menu and follow the on-screen instructions. In Windows 3.1, open File Manager, click the Disk menu, select the Format Disk command, and follow the on-screen instructions (see Figure 23.8). In DOS, type **format a:** at the DOS prompt.

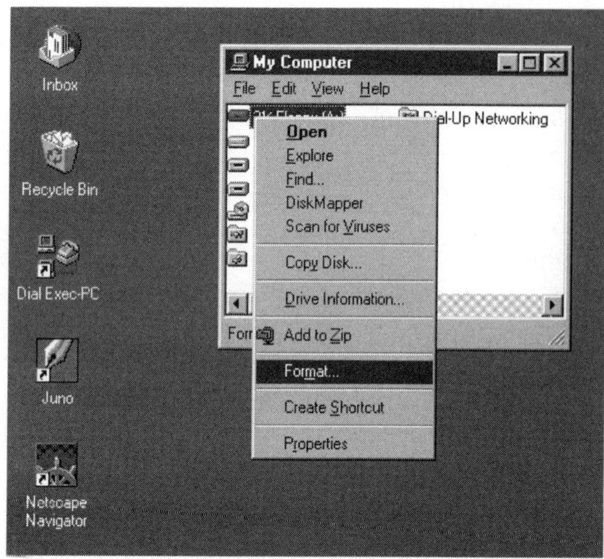

FIGURE 23.8: Formatting a disk prepares it for use in your drive. It also helps you determine if your drive's read/write head is out of alignment.

If the drive formats the disk without any problems, remove the disk and insert it in the disk drive of another computer and try to access it. If that computer can't recognize the disk or a pop-up error message asks if you would like to format the disk, then you're closer to a verdict.

But don't make a decision yet. Take the disk to yet another computer system and insert it in that drive. Try to access the disk. If the third computer can't recognize the disk or you receive a pop-up message asking if you would like to format the disk, then you can assume the drive's head is out of alignment.

Now it's time to remove the drive and send it to the manufacturer to be fixed. Consult the user manual or contact your computer's manufacturer for information about removing the drive.

Cables Inserted Incorrectly

Sometimes problems with a disk drive are due to human error. That's the case here. A cable that has been inserted incorrectly or not tightly enough can lead to drive failures. Whenever you have a problem with your disk drive, it's a good idea to check the cables before calling technical support.

The disk drive has two cables that connect it to the computer: The data cable, which looks like a wide ribbon; and the power cord, which is a four-slot plug with multicolored wires extending from it.

There's no trick to plugging them in correctly. Remove the cover from your computer and locate the disk drive. If you're not sure where that is, check the computer's user manual.

After locating the cords, examine them to make sure they're plugged in correctly. If they look loose, push them together firmly, but don't force the connection. There's only one correct way to plug the cables into the drive; if they don't fit together snuggly, then you're probably trying to insert them incorrectly. Remove the cable and make sure the pins and receptors line up with one another.

NOTE NOTE NOTE NOTE NOTE NOTE NOTE NOTE NOTE NOTE NOTE NOTE NOTE NOTE NOTE

Before working inside your computer, remove the plug from the wall. Also touch the metal frame of the computer to eliminate any static electricity you may have picked up.

There are a few tricks to knowing whether the problem lies with the cable connections. If the light-emitting diode (LED; a small red or green light on the face of the drive) never lights up, even when you insert a disk or turn the computer on, you probably have a problem with the power connection. Either that or the drive is completely dead, in which case you'll need to get a new one. Before buying a new drive, check the power cable connection and make sure it's inserted into the drive correctly.

If the LED is always lit, on the other hand, then the problem probably lies with the data cable. The cable's wide connector has a receptor that corresponds to a certain pin, called the 1 pin, on the drive. If the 1 pin isn't connected to the corresponding connector, then data can't travel between the drive and the computer.

Remove the data cable from the drive and locate the 1 pin on the back of the drive. In order to get a good view of the back of the drive, you may need to remove the screws that hold the drive to the frame of the computer. On the drive, the 1 pin is labeled with a small number "1" printed next to it. On the cable, the matching receptor usually is designated by a red strip that runs along one edge of the cable. When you insert the cable, make sure the red strip is closest to the 1 pin.

Put the cover back on the computer and plug it in to see if your problem is solved. If not, keep reading.

Spindle Motor Won't Spin

It's possible your drive won't work because the spindle motor won't spin. It's possible, but very unlikely, says Nguyen of TEAC. However, if your drive can't read any disks you insert into it—even disks you've checked on other computers—and if the LED lights up to indicate the drive is trying to read, write, or search for data, then this may be the problem.

The only solution is to get a new drive or send the broken one back to the manufacturer. Again, it's very unlikely this is the problem, but it's something you should know about in case you've tried every other troubleshooting solution with no success.

Disk Won't Eject

Sometimes you'll press the eject button on your drive and that pesky disk just won't come out. Then you'll get a great idea—the type of idea that separates the participants in life from the passersby. You'll get the idea to remove it with a bent paper clip. Or a knife. Or a pair of tweezers. Or a screwdriver. One way or other, you'll get that darn thing out.

Whoa, pardner. Don't start digging. You might lose your reputation as a man or woman of action, but you might be able to save the important data you have on that disk.

Sure, the disk may be caught on a bit of plastic. But it *might* be caught on a read/write head that came loose. If that's the case, you've already lost the drive. And if you yank the disk out, you'll yank the head across the exposed disk, literally shredding your data into bits and pieces. And then that will be lost, too.

If your disk won't come out, don't touch anything on your computer until you've contacted the drive manufacturer. The manufacturer can tell you how to retrieve the disk without losing your data.

Write-Protected Disk

Data cannot be recorded on a disk that is write-protected (see Figure 23.9). Fortunately, this is a very easy problem to fix. Simply remove the disk from the drive and look at the backside. In the upper-left corner is a small tab that slides up and down. If the tab is up, exposing a small hole, the disk is write-protected. Slide the tab down to remove the write-protection. Now you can record data on it.

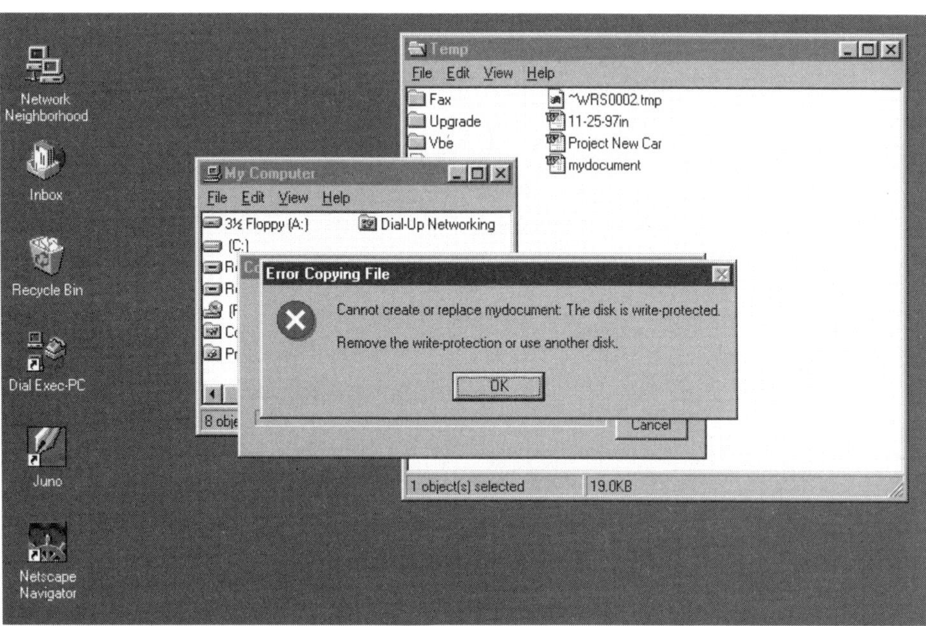

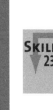

FIGURE 23.9: Write-protection prevents your computer from writing data to a storage medium. If you try to write data to a write-protected disk, you'll receive a message similar to this one.

Note that a disk usually is write-protected only if it contains important data or programs. Before you remove the write-protection from a disk, make sure you're not risking the loss of data you can't afford to lose. For more about disks, see the "Protecting Disks" sidebar.

Drive Maintenance

Just because the disk drive is virtually problem-free, doesn't mean you can abuse it or take it for granted. Here are a few things you should do to keep your drive in good working order.

The most important thing to do is keep it free of dust. Most disk drives have little trap doors that cover the openings of the drives when they're not occupied by disks. If your disk drive has one of these doors, make sure it snaps shut when you remove a disk. Don't try to rig it open permanently.

PROTECTING DISKS

Despite the popularity of high-capacity, portable storage mediums, such as Zip, Jaz, or LS-120 disks, the 1.44 megabyte (MB), 3.5-inch disk is still the most common method of moving data from one computer to another.

That means there's a lot of valuable data stored on those plastic platters. To keep your disks working well and your data safe, keep these maintenance tips in mind.

- Don't reformat a preformatted disk. Of course you'll occasionally need to reformat a disk, but the less you do it, the better, says Richard D'Ambrise, the engineering and technical support manager at Maxell Corp. of America. The reason has to do with the way a disk drive writes data to a disk. When a disk is formatted at a factory, it is formatted on computers that are optimized with a write current of 100 percent. Write current, explains D'Ambrise, is "the amount of energy needed to reorient the magnetic domain of a disk." Say what? Think of when you've recorded songs on an audio tape. If the tape has been used before, you might be able to hear, very faintly in the background, the old songs over which the new songs were recorded. The same happens with disks. If your drive isn't performing optimally, then it might not be able to write new data over the old data, diminishing the quality of the data stored on the disk.
- Keep the disk away from magnets. Everyone knows this. What everyone doesn't know is how many home and office devices have strong magnetic fields. A magnetic field emanates from coffee makers, copy machines, recording devices, basically anything that uses a lot of electrical current. When the disk isn't in your computer, keep it in a disk case, an empty drawer, or some other safe place. Note that X-ray machines in airports won't damage your disks. However, the wands that are used by airport security produce a strong magnetic field and will destroy the data stored on a disk.

continued ➧

- Use disks that have plastic shutters. Each time a metal shutter slides back and forth, small metal shards are deposited on the data-storing surface of a disk. Over time, this can damage the disk and make it impossible to recover data stored on it. Plastic shutters don't leave a residue on the surface. Also, don't open the shutter. This increases the amount of dust that gets on the surface.
- Avoid extreme temperatures. The recommended operating environment for a disk is quite liberal: temperatures between 32 and 140 degrees Fahrenheit, relative humidity between 8 percent and 80 percent (between 8 percent and 90 percent if you're storing the disks). Although disks can survive colder temperatures, let the disk adjust to the ambient temperature in your home or office before sticking it in your computer. This minimizes the chance of moisture accumulating on the surface. Similarly, disks can survive warmer temperatures, but don't store a disk in direct sunlight. Extreme heats can warp the plastic shell of the disk, rendering the disk useless.

If your disk drive doesn't have one of these doors, keep a disk inside the drive at all times. You don't have to push it all the way in; its presence in the mouth of the drive is enough to keep most of the dust from getting to the drive's head.

Try to keep the drive (and thus, the computer) in a dust-free area, if possible. Don't smoke around your computer, keep the windows shut and animals away, try to minimize humidity in the room, don't beat your rugs over the top of the computer, etc. This is good advice for general computer maintenance, but it's particularly important to the health of your disk drive.

If you think your heads might be dirty because you can't avoid smoking around your computer or the cat likes to sleep on it, you can purchase an inexpensive (less than $10) dry-type disk cleaner, which you insert into the drive. Wet-type disk cleaners are also available and may be slightly less expensive, but TEAC's Nguyen recommends that users go with the dry-type cleaners.

Something you don't need to do for disk drive maintenance is run ScanDisk or Defrag or any of the other system utilities built into the Windows and DOS operating systems. These tools are designed for use with your hard drive and won't do much good for your disk drive.

To sum it all up, you shouldn't have any problems with your disk drive. Don't stick a peanut butter and jelly sandwich into it. Don't kick it. Just keep popping those disks in and out, and the drive probably will outlive the computer.

Troubleshooting Video Cards

No one wants to be the bearer of bad news (especially when they're simply relaying someone else's problem) because they usually receive the brunt of the reaction.

For a computer user, the worst news possible occurs when the monitor goes blank or displays a string of error messages. But if your monitor could speak, it probably would say, "Don't blame the messenger!" Many problems related to the display may start elsewhere in your system, even though your monitor lets you know about the problems. Some of those problems originate with the video card.

A video card is a piece of hardware that controls the appearance of images and text on your computer's monitor. All data from the computer's microprocessor travels through the video card, which translates the signals and sends them to the monitor for display. Some video cards are expansion cards, while others are built into the motherboard, the PC's main circuit board. Video cards have several other names, including video controllers and video adapters. Some types of video cards, usually called graphics accelerators or video accelerators, contain additional chips that handle graphics computations, letting them work faster.

Common Problems

A correctly functioning display system requires three components to work—the video card, the monitor, and the video card driver, which is software that controls the card. Your display system can only be as powerful as the weakest link. If you have an ancient video card, using the newest monitor won't help your overall performance much. And a breakdown among any of the components will cause display problems, which you'll notice through the monitor. If you've determined the problem doesn't come from the monitor, try the following tips to get the video card working correctly.

No Image on the Monitor Screen

First, make sure the monitor is working properly; monitor problems are easier to correct than video card problems. If you can't correct the problem through the monitor, try these video card tips.

NOTE

If your display is completely malfunctioning and blank, try booting in Safe Mode as described in the sidebar.

- The video card's settings may be incorrect.
- Make sure the cables that connect to the video card or video controller inside the computer are tightly connected. To check them, you'll need to open the computer case. Be sure to disconnect the monitor and computer from all power sources before opening the computer case and ground yourself by touching some metal before reaching inside the case. While the case is open, make sure the video card is seated tightly into the expansion card slot. You should only be able to see a small portion of the top of the gold contacts on the card's lower tab. Check the physical state of the video card. On some older video cards, some of the chips occasionally work themselves loose from their sockets. If a chip is loose, gently push it back into its socket.
- Some monitors and video cards are incompatible. (This shouldn't be a problem unless you've changed the video card or monitor in your system after purchasing it.) If your display system is incompatible, you won't see any display, and you may hear some system beeps at startup that sound like error messages. Check your monitor and video card documentation to make sure the two are compatible. If you discover an incompatibility, you'll need to change one of the components, or you may be able to purchase a software or hardware patch that can correct the problem. Contact the manufacturers.
- If you recently added a video card, make sure the old video card is removed or disabled (unless you're planning to use both cards). Some computers ship with video controllers built directly into the motherboard. The original controller will have to be disabled; check your PC's documentation or check with the PC's manufacturer for instructions.
- You may have a corrupted or incompatible display driver. See the next problem for some tips on drivers.

The Display Driver Seems to Be Incompatible with My Video Card

If you've tried some of the other troubleshooting tips and can't seem to solve your display problem, you may have a driver problem. If you suspect the driver is corrupted, see the "Booting in Safe Mode" sidebar (if needed) and check below for information on reinstalling the driver from disk or from the Windows 95/98 CD. If the display doesn't work in normal booting mode but works properly in Safe Mode, the problem probably lies with your display driver.

An incompatible driver problem may occur if you've recently changed video cards or if you've upgraded from Windows 3.*x* to Windows 95. If you're using an old Windows 3.*x* display driver under Windows 95, you should upgrade as soon as possible because the older drivers don't support some Windows 95 display features. (See the next problem.) Your new video card should ship with its own driver on disk; install it using the techniques described below or in the video card's documentation.

You can check driver incompatibilities through the Control Panel. Double-click the System icon and then click the Device Manager tab. Under the Display Adapters icon, you'll see the current display driver. (Click the Display Adapters plus sign to see the available drivers.) If you see a yellow exclamation point over the driver's icon, the item is working incorrectly. Highlight the driver and click the Properties button to see its status. If you click the General tab in the selected driver's Properties window, Windows 95/98 will show whether the driver is working in the Device Status section in the middle of the window. Click the Resources tab to see the exact conflict that exists. If you want to change the driver, click the Driver tab.

In Windows 3.*x*, you can see your video settings by using the Microsoft Diagnostics Program. After exiting Windows, type **msd** at the DOS prompt and press Enter. Click the Video button. You'll see several pieces of information concerning your display.

To see which display driver Windows 3.*x* is using, open the SYSTEM.INI file using Notepad. The `Display.drv=` line in the [boot] section will show you the display driver currently in use.

Booting in Safe Mode

When you boot Windows 95 in Safe Mode, your system's startup files and device drivers will be bypassed, allowing Windows 95 to start up in a basic mode. If your display driver is causing your display problem, booting in Safe Mode will cause Windows 95 to use a generic display driver when booting.

continued

Turn on the computer and wait until you hear the Power On Self Test (POST) beep or see the Starting Windows 95 line, both of which should occur about 10–15 seconds into the boot process. After hearing the beep, press the F8 key. You should enter the Microsoft Windows 95 Startup Menu text menu. (If you don't see the menu, you probably pressed F8 at the wrong time. Reboot the computer and try again.) Highlight selection 3 (Safe Mode) and press the Enter key.

Windows 95 will start using the most basic configuration possible, bypassing any startup files you've set. You'll see Safe Mode in each of the desktop's four corners. You now can make changes to your display driver.

Windows 95 Display Features Aren't Available

You probably are attempting to use a Windows 3.*x* display driver, which can't support all of Windows 95's display features. To check your video driver, you need to open the SYSTEM.INI file with Notepad. Use caution when viewing this file; any inadvertent changes you make and save to SYSTEM.INI could cause your computer to work improperly.

To open Notepad, click the Start button. Then click the Programs ➢ Accessories ➢ Notepad. In Notepad, click the File menu and select the Open command. In the Look In box, find the Windows directory. Then type SYSTEM.INI in the File Name box and click the Open button. In the [boot] section of SYSTEM.INI, which should be at the top of the file, you should see a `display.drv=pnpdrvr.drv` line if you're using a Windows 95 display driver (see Figure 23.10). If you see anything else in the display line, you're probably using a Windows 3.*x* display driver. To close Notepad, click the File menu followed by the Exit command. If you made inadvertent changes to the file, Windows 95 will ask whether you want to save the changes. Click No.

If you upgraded your system from Windows 3.*x* to Windows 95, you probably won't have a Windows 95 display driver available for your particular video card. You'll need to contact your PC's manufacturer or your video card's manufacturer to find the updated driver. If one isn't available, you can use the standard VGA driver that ships with Windows 95. See below for instructions on changing your driver.

When you reach the Change Display Type window, click Change under Monitor Type. To use the generic Windows 95 driver, click Standard Monitor Types in the Manufacturers box. In the Models box, click Standard Display Adapter (VGA). Click the OK button, the Close button, and the Close button again.

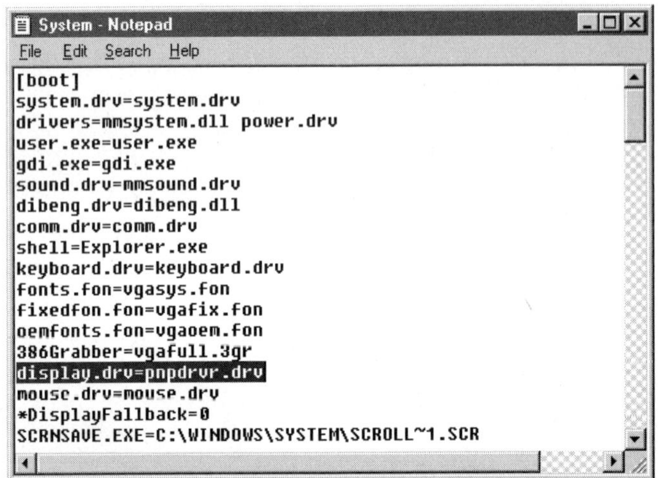

FIGURE 23.10: You can determine whether you're using a Windows 95 display driver by looking in your SYSTEM.INI file.

Distorted Images and Text

Try resetting the video card's settings. You especially will want to adjust the video card's resolution and refresh rate, the number of times per second the screen is redrawn. Some higher resolutions can cause display problems.

Disappearing Cursor

You may need to make an adjustment to the way Windows 95 handles your graphics hardware and video card. See the next problem for directions. Also make sure you have the newest driver for your video card.

If that doesn't solve the problem, you also can make the cursor bigger or add a shadow trail. In the Control Panel window, double-click the Mouse icon. In the Mouse Properties window, click the Pointers tab to choose a scheme using a larger cursor. Click the Motion tab to add a shadow trail.

To change your mouse settings in Windows 3.*x*, double-click the Control Panel icon in the Main program group. Then double-click the Mouse icon. In the Mouse window, you can adjust the speed of the mouse or add a shadow trail. Click OK once you've made the desired changes.

My Computer Frequently Locks Up

While this may be a problem with a certain program or with some other system settings, your video card may be causing the problem. If your video card can't handle some of the graphics requests from Windows and other programs, it may lock up. You can change the way Windows 95 uses your graphics hardware as a temporary solution for this problem.

In the Control Panel window, double-click the System icon. In the System Properties window, click the Performance tab. At the bottom of the window in the Advanced Settings section, click the Graphics button. In the Advanced Graphics Settings window, you'll see a slider bar and a pointer that signifies how Windows 95 accelerates your graphics hardware. The right side of the slider bar is Full, for the most acceleration, while the left side is None, for no acceleration.

For systems working well, Full is recommended. If you're having difficulty seeing the cursor at times, drag the pointer one setting to the left of Full (called Most). This should help make the cursor more visible, but you might notice a slight overall system performance dip (because of the lower graphics hardware acceleration).

If, however, you're having frequent system lockups and program errors, try moving the pointer two settings to the left of Full (the Basic setting). Click OK, followed by the Close button. Windows 95 then will ask you to click OK to restart the system.

WARNING WARNING WARNING WARNING WARNING WARNING WARNING WARNING

Be sure to close all programs and files prior to restarting Windows.

With less graphics hardware acceleration, hopefully your lockup problems will be alleviated. If you're still having problems, return to the Advanced Graphics Settings window and move the pointer left to None. Click the OK and Close buttons again, and Windows will again ask you to click OK to reboot.

If using any of these settings puts an end to the lockup problems, the video card is at the root of the problem. You can continue using your computer with the new setting, but you probably will notice Windows 95 and other programs working slower. Eventually you probably will want to replace your video card with a newer model to permanently fix the problem.

Display Settings in Windows 95

Many times, the settings of your video card are at the root of several display-related problems. We'll show you how to adjust various video card settings in Windows 95.

Before making any changes in the video card settings, be sure to check your monitor's documentation for its setting limitations. If you attempt to surpass the setting limits for your monitor, you could damage the monitor. Your monitor's user guide should contain a page listing its maximum settings.

With Windows 95, if you don't have your own video card driver (or display driver) you'll have two generic VGA drivers available. With Standard Graphics Adapter VGA, you can use a 640 × 480 resolution. With SuperVGA, which is more typical with newer computers and monitors, you'll have three resolutions, 640 × 480; 800 × 600; and 1,024 × 768. The lower resolution (640 × 480) supports 16; 256; 65,000; and 16.7 million colors, while the higher resolution supports only 16 and 256 colors. As you increase resolution, the greater demand placed on your video card reduces its ability to display colors.

NOTE NOTE NOTE NOTE NOTE NOTE NOTE NOTE NOTE NOTE NOTE NOTE NOTE NOTE NOTE

Your system's display driver and video card may be more powerful than what we've listed here and will have different colors and resolutions available.

To open the Display Properties window, click the Start button, followed by the Settings command and Control Panel. Then double-click the Display icon. Before making any changes to your display, close all other programs and save any files you have open.

Driver

Windows 95 usually finds your display driver, if one exists on your system, while it runs its hardware detection feature after installation. Otherwise, Windows 95 will use one of the generic drivers we discussed earlier. The display driver allows Windows 95 and the video card to interact.

If you want to change your display driver, double-click the Display icon in Control Panel, then the Settings tab in the Display Properties window. Click the Change Display Type button. In the Change window, the Adapter Type area shows the current display driver. If you want to change the driver, click the Change button. In the Select Device window, you'll see all of the drivers available (if the Show All Devices button is selected in the lower-left corner of the window). Click the proper manufacturer and model, and click the OK button. Windows 95 will prompt you for the driver disk or the Windows 95 CD. Then follow the installation instructions on the screen.

Resolution

You'll use the Display Properties window to set the video card's resolution, which defines the quality of the image on your screen. A higher resolution means your screen will display more pixels, yielding more space for images.

A 640 × 480 resolution is the minimum standard for most users. To see your current resolution, click the Settings tab in the Display Properties window. Along the right side of the window, you'll see a Desktop Area section with a slider bar. The lowest resolution is displayed when the slider is on the left side of the bar. You can increase the resolution by moving the slider to the right. As you move the slider, the sample display at the top of the window will change to reflect your selection.

NOTE

If you choose a resolution that your card can't support with the number of colors you've chosen, Windows 95 automatically will decrease the number of colors in the Color Palette area of the window.

After choosing the resolution you want, click OK. Windows 95 probably will display a warning box, telling you the screen will be redrawn with the new resolution, and you'll have to click OK. After a few seconds, you should see the new resolution. If Windows 95 can't display the new resolution because of limitations with your video card, your screen will remain blank for about 15 seconds. Windows 95 then should return you to your original resolution.

Higher resolutions will give you greater image quality, but it will cause the icons and items on your desktop to become smaller (see Figure 23.11). Many times the Desktop text will be too small to read at the highest resolutions. You can customize the screen to return the Desktop items to near their normal sizes using the higher resolution, though.

Underneath the slider bar in the Desktop Area section, click the Custom button. (When using some resolutions, the Custom button will be dimmed and unavailable.) You'll see a ruler, which you can click and drag to the right to increase the sizes of the Desktop items. At the top of the window, you'll see a box showing the percentage of all of the items that will increase or decrease in size. If you have a specific percentage in mind, you can type that number in the box.

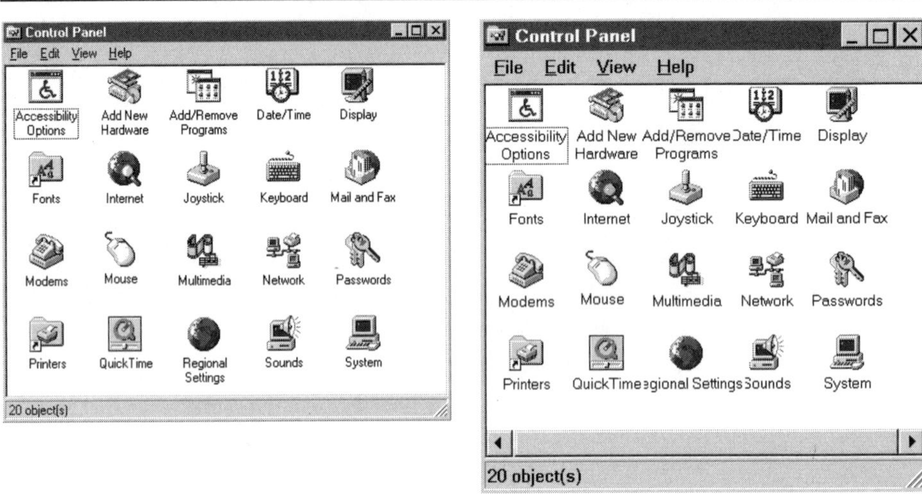

FIGURE 23.11: Different resolution settings will cause your display to look different, especially if you customize certain settings in a higher resolution. The higher resolution of these two is on the left.

Once you've made the change you want, click OK. Windows may warn you that some programs may not work correctly with the new settings. Click OK to continue. Then click OK again to restart Windows and activate the new settings. It's best to make changes in small percentage increments to avoid display problems.

Our programs all worked correctly with our customized settings, but they looked vastly different. Whether your customized settings work properly in your system depends on your video card and monitor. If you don't like the customized settings and new resolution and want to return to the original settings, simply move the slider bar in the Desktop Properties window to the original resolution setting and click OK. Windows may need to restart itself to reset.

After customizing some settings, the Display Properties window and other windows may be so large that the OK and Cancel buttons will no longer be visible on the screen. Remember, you usually can activate the OK button by pressing the Enter key. Move the slider bar to your original settings and hit the Enter key to return everything to its original setting.

Refresh Rates

Setting the correct refresh rate for your video card/monitor setup is extremely important. An incorrect refresh rate will cause a flickering screen and eyestrain.

In Windows 95, most users will be unable to directly set the refresh rate. Instead, Windows 95 and the display driver automatically determine the best refresh rate for your setup, based on the video card and monitor you have. However, the monitor type chosen during Windows 95 setup usually is a generic monitor, which probably won't be able to match the capabilities of your monitor in refresh rates, especially if you have a newer, top-of-the-line monitor.

The best method for setting refresh rates in Windows 95 is to make sure the operating system has the proper display hardware selected and the newest drivers for that hardware. In the Display Properties window, click the Settings tab. Next, click the Change Display Type button. You then can change the display driver (adapter) and the monitor, if needed, by clicking the Change button. Don't choose a monitor type that exceeds the capabilities of your monitor, which should be listed in your monitor's user guide. Exceeding the capabilities of your monitor could damage it. If you're in doubt, choose from the generic monitors, called Standard Monitor Types.

If you already have the correct hardware selected or if resetting the hardware doesn't help, try lowering the resolution. When most video cards run at higher resolutions, they lower the refresh rate, which may cause screen flickering and eyestrain.

Colors

Setting colors in Windows 95 is a fairly easy process. As we mentioned earlier, the number of colors you can display depends on the capabilities of your video card. Using higher resolutions often will limit the number of colors you can display.

In the Display Properties window, click the Settings tab. In the Color Palette section on the left side of the window, click the downward arrow to see the number of colors your video card supports. You may see 16 Color, 256 Color, High Color or 16-bit (which is 65,000 colors), and True Color or 24-bit (16.7 million). You will only see the number of colors listed that your video card will support. Click the number of colors you want. If you choose a number of colors that your card can't support under the current resolution, Windows 95 will automatically lower the resolution in the Desktop Area of the window.

As you increase the number of colors, you may notice a decrease in system performance for Windows 95, depending on the capabilities of your video card. For the average video card and the average user, 256 colors will provide the best mix of system performance and pleasing colors. For photos and other detailed graphics work, though, you may want 16- or 24-bit colors.

Troubleshooting Sound Cards

Computing is a naturally visual medium. When you're working with your computer on a word processing program or spreadsheet, you're concentrating on reading the computer screen. The only sounds you really encounter are the click of keyboard keys or an occasional system beep.

But when it's time for multimedia, sound takes center stage. Whether it's audio explanations in a business document or the roar of an airplane in a flight simulator, sound enriches your computing experience. The key to producing rich sound is a sound card, also called an audio card or a sound board.

A sound card is an expansion card that gives your computer the ability to produce audio. Programs that produce sound, other than basic system beeps, work best with a sound card. A sound card contains hardware that can convert computer language into sound and vice versa. Speakers or headphones let you hear the sound produced by the sound card. Nearly all new computers contain sound cards when they're sold.

Like any computer component, sound cards can malfunction. Most problems generated by sound cards can be corrected using Windows 95/98; sound cards rarely fail physically. If you're having any type of problem with your sound, you should make notes on the exact problem, the specific circumstances under which the problem occurs, and any error messages you see, says Lauren Haven, quality assurance engineer for Shark Multimedia, a leading manufacturer of sound cards.

"Then you know where the problem is," Haven says. "It really helps technicians when you can (narrow it)."

Common Problems

Before calling technical support, though, you can try several troubleshooting measures on your own. Here are some common sound card-related problems you may encounter and some potential solutions.

I Hear No Sound from the PC

This problem, unfortunately, has several potential causes, including a few that originate from your speakers. Let's start with the easiest to check.

- Make certain all cords are tightly connected. The connectors used to link sound cards with speakers can be knocked loose.
- Make certain the speakers are plugged into the correct jacks on the sound card; the jacks should be labeled. Some modem cards contain jacks that look

similar to jacks on sound cards. To avoid plugging speakers into the wrong card, make sure the speakers aren't plugged into a card that also contains telephone jacks.

NOTE

Some computers contain combination sound/modem cards, in which case you would want to plug everything into the same card. If you suspect your computer contains one of these combination cards, check your computer's documentation.

- Check the volume setting. Some sound cards have a volume wheel that you can access through the expansion card slot in the back of your computer. Most wheels have numbers that represent the volume; usually zero is no sound and nine is maximum sound. To test your sound, set the wheel at five. Often with newer computers, though, sound volume is controlled through Windows 95/98, which can override the volume wheel on a sound card. Most Windows 95/98 users will see a speaker icon in the lower-right corner of the Desktop, just to the left of the time. If a red circle with a line through it covers the speaker icon, your sound has been muted through the Volume Control window. If you double-click the speaker icon, you should open the Volume Control window. If you single click the speaker icon, you'll see a simple volume control bar, containing a sliding pointer that lets you adjust the volume or mute it. You also can access the Volume Control window by clicking the Start button in the lower-left corner of the Windows 95 Desktop. Click the Programs menu followed by Accessories, then Multimedia. Then click the Volume Control command to open its window. You control the volume through the vertical slide bar on the left side of the Volume Control window. Slide the pointer higher to increase volume; slide it to the bottom to shut off the sound. When you slide the pointer to the maximum volume, you probably will hear your speakers emit a humming sound. The Volume Control window also contains a Mute All box (see Figure 23.12). If this box contains a checkmark, you won't hear any sound no matter where you slide the volume control pointer. Click in the box to add or remove the checkmark. The Volume Control window should contain six areas: Volume Control, Line-In, Wave, Microphone, CD Audio, and Synthesizer. While you're testing the sound card, all of these areas should have their pointers set at medium level. If you don't see all of these areas, click the Options menu in the Volume Control window and click the Properties command. In the bottom half of the Properties window, place checkmarks in the box next to each option and click the OK button (see Figure 23.13).

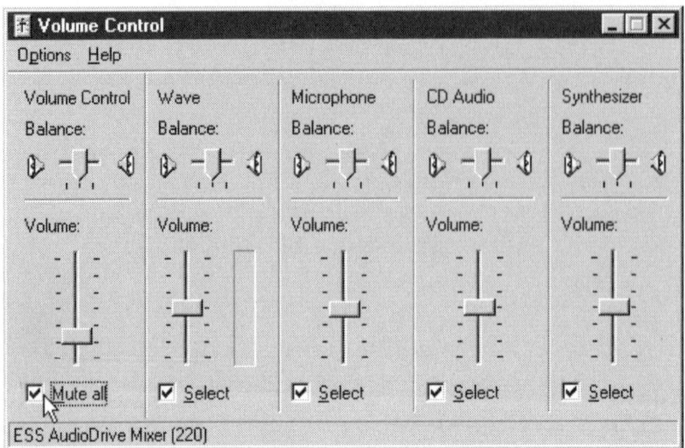

FIGURE 23.12: If the Mute All box is checked in the Volume Control window, you won't hear any sound.

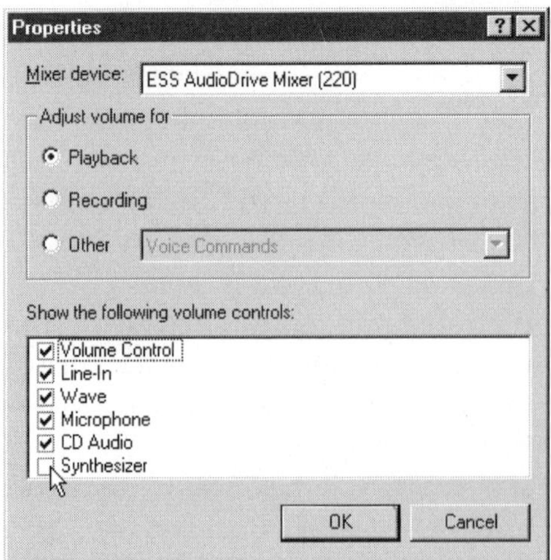

FIGURE 23.13: To have access to all audio options in the Volume Control window, use the Properties command under the Options menu.

NOTE NOTE NOTE NOTE NOTE NOTE NOTE NOTE NOTE NOTE NOTE NOTE NOTE NOTE NOTE

If you can't open Volume Control, skip ahead to the next problem.

Try plugging headphones into the jack on the back of the sound card. If you now hear sound, your problem lies with your speakers.

- Review whether you recently installed some new hardware or a new expansion card. The new hardware may be causing an interrupt request line (IRQ, communications routes between devices and the CPU) or *direct memory access* (DMA, a means of transferring data) conflict that interferes with your sound card. Try using Windows 95/98's Hardware Conflict Troubleshooter. (See "My Sound Skips or Is Scratchy and Unclear" at the end of this section.) If you're still having sound problems, try removing the new hardware and restarting the computer. If the sound now works, you'll need to contact the manufacturer of the new hardware to determine how to work around the conflict with the sound card.
- Make sure the sound card is inserted properly. If you recently installed some new hardware, you may have knocked the sound card loose (although this is fairly difficult to do), or you may have moved the sound card to make room and didn't reinsert it properly. Make sure the sound card is installed entirely into the expansion card slot; you should only be able to see a small portion of the top of the gold contacts on the card's tab. The back of the sound card, which is visible through the back of the computer case, should be aligned against the open slot.

If you've never opened your computer case, and the sound card has worked properly in the past, it's unlikely the card has come loose. If you suspect the card may have been knocked loose or inserted improperly, you may want to remove and reinsert the sound card.

Before attempting to reinsert the card, ground yourself by touching some metal on the computer case. While working with the card, touch only the metal back of the card whenever possible. If you must touch the card itself, touch only the edges of the green plastic because oil from your hands can damage the card's components. As you reinsert the card, you might find it easier to rock the card into the slot by placing a corner of the card in the slot first and then fitting the remainder of the tab into the slot. The card will be a tight fit, but you shouldn't have to push too hard.

I Don't Have a Volume Control Option

Depending on some choices you made when setting up Windows 95/98, you may not see a Volume Control command under the Multimedia menu. To add the Volume Control option, click the Start button on the Windows 95/98 Desktop. Then select the Settings command followed by Control Panel. Double-click the

Add/Remove Programs icon. Then click the Windows Setup tab at the top of the Add/Remove window (see Figure 23.14). In the Components box, scroll down until you find the Multimedia line and click it to highlight it. Then click the Details button. In the Multimedia window, scroll down until you see the Volume Control line. Place a checkmark in the Volume Control box and then click the OK button twice. You may be prompted for your Windows 95/98 CD at this time; if so, insert the CD and click OK. After copying the needed files, Windows 95/98 will automatically close the Add/Remove window.

FIGURE 23.14: If you don't have access to the Volume Control window, you'll need to use Windows 95/98's Add/Remove Programs feature.

I Have No Sound When Using the CD-ROM Drive

This problem has a few potential causes.

- The CD-ROM drive may be working incorrectly. Can you run programs from the CD-ROM drive? If not, you won't hear any sounds from it, even when attempting to play audio CDs. If the computer isn't recognizing the CD-ROM drive, you won't see an icon for the CD-ROM drive when you double-click the My Computer icon on the Windows 95/98 Desktop, and you'll need to reinstall the CD-ROM drive software.

- The CD you're attempting to use may not be in proper working order. Dirty or scratched CDs can work improperly. Try a different CD. Make sure the CD is aligned correctly in the drive.
- If the CD-ROM drive and CD are working properly, you'll need to check the CD-ROM drive's audio settings. Click the Start button on the Windows 95 Desktop, followed by the Settings command and Control Panel. Double-click the Multimedia icon. In the Multimedia Properties window, click the CD Music tab. Make sure the correct drive letter for your CD-ROM drive is listed (usually it's D:, unless you have multiple hard drives or multiple CD-ROM drives). Also make sure the headphones volume is set to High. Click OK.
- You may not have installed the CD Audio feature when installing Windows 95. Use the Windows 95 Add/Remove Programs feature described in the above problem to check. When you reach the Multimedia window, see whether the CD Player box contains a checkmark (meaning the feature has been installed). If it's not installed, click the CD Player box and click OK. You'll need your Windows 95 installation CD to complete the process.
- If all CD-ROM audio settings in Windows 95 appear to be correct, you're probably missing a cable that connects your CD-ROM drive with your sound card. This problem is most likely to occur if you've installed a new CD-ROM drive or sound card after purchasing the computer. The cables you need are probably included with your CD-ROM drive. Shark Multimedia's Haven says three types of connectors usually come with the cables. Most connectors are MPC-2 compatible (meaning they adhere to popular standards for multimedia PCs), with four-pin connectors on each end of a cable. Sony and Panasonic each make connectors as well, but these rarely are used. Haven says the Sony and Panasonic cables look similar and fit into the same connectors, but they are not interchangeable. Haven also says your CD-ROM drive manual should specify the type of connector you'll need. Many sound cards contain slots for each type of cable connector; make sure you place the cable connector into the correct slot on the sound card.

NOTE NOTE NOTE NOTE NOTE NOTE NOTE NOTE NOTE NOTE NOTE NOTE NOTE NOTE NOTE

If you install a new CD-ROM drive, use the cable that is included with it; don't try to use your old cable.

SKILL 23

I Can't Hear Music Created by Non–CD-ROM Computer Programs

Sound created by the sound card can't travel backward through the cable that connects the CD-ROM drive and sound card to the CD-ROM drive's headphone jack. Only sound generated from the CD-ROM drive can be heard through the CD-ROM drive's headphone jack. To hear sounds generated from the sound card, you should use the headphone jack on your sound card (look at the back of the card, which is visible through the back of the computer).

I Can't Play Certain Sound Files

The file may have become corrupted, and you may need to reinstall it. It's also possible that the type of sound file you want to use is incompatible with your sound card under its current configuration. You may need to find an add-on program that can help you play this type of file. Contact your sound card's manufacturer or search the Internet for shareware, low-cost software, that addresses the problem.

One Particular Program Has Sound Problems

You probably will need the program's user guide and installation disks to correct this problem.

- You may not have the correct sound card type selected in the program's audio settings. Some programs contain an Options command or a Properties command through which you can set the sound card. With most programs, though, you'll need to check the program's documentation for setting the sound card. If your particular brand of sound card isn't listed, first try setting the sound card type as SoundBlaster compatible (nearly all sound cards fit this description). If this doesn't work, you may need to contact the sound card's manufacturer.
- The program's input/output address, MIDI (Musical Instrument Digital Interface) address, or IRQ setting may be conflicting with other hardware devices. The required settings should be included with the user guide. If you can't find any specific settings, Haven says basic settings for most DOS games are Base Address: 220h, DMA: 1 or 5, IRQ: 5 or 10, and MIDI: 330. If you need to change the settings, see the last problem in this section for help.

- The program's sound files may be corrupted. You can attempt to reinstall these files from your program's installation disks.
- You may find that a particular program is simply incompatible with your particular sound card. Try contacting the program's manufacturer and the sound card's manufacturer to see whether any software patches are available to correct this conflict.

Recorded Sound Is Distorted or Doesn't Work

Sound cards not only replay sound, they let you record sound. But settings within Windows 95/98 determine the quality of the sound you create through a microphone. To change these settings, click the Start button followed by the Settings command and Control Panel. Then double-click the Multimedia icon. In the Multimedia Properties window, click the Audio tab. You now can set the volume and quality of your recordings and play backs. Louder settings may become distorted, depending on your speaker quality. If the volume for either setting is placed at Low, the setting will be muted.

Some Sound Files Don't Sound as Good as Others

Chances are some of the files you're using were created as 16-bit files, making them similar to CD quality, and some were created as 8-bit files, making them similar to radio quality. It's highly unlikely this problem is caused by your sound card or speakers. If, however, a single audio file sounds like it's fading in and out, it could signify a problem with a device conflict for your sound card (see the next problem).

My Sound Skips or Is Scratchy and Unclear

While this seems like a speaker problem, it may have roots in the sound card setup. The DMA channel or the IRQ line the sound card is trying to use may have more than one device attempting to use it, meaning the audio will be somewhat garbled.

NOTE NOTE NOTE NOTE NOTE NOTE NOTE NOTE NOTE NOTE NOTE NOTE NOTE NOTE NOTE

You may notice other hardware devices working improperly as well, especially in Windows 3.1 or DOS. In Windows 95/98, two or more devices attempting to use the same IRQ often are disabled by the operating system.

CARING FOR YOUR SOUND CARD

Taking physical care of your sound card is fairly easy. The less you have to handle it, the better. But there are times you must remove the card or handle it. Lauren Haven, a quality assurance engineer from Shark Multimedia, has a few tips for avoiding damage to your card when you must handle it:

- Ground yourself before handling the card by touching the metal computer case.
- Hold the sound card by its metal bracket; oil from your hands can damage the gold contacts on the card or any of the components contained on the card. If you must touch the card itself, only touch the edges.
- Dust usually won't hurt the card, but if you want to clean it, canned air is best. "I've never known a sound card to go bad from dust on it," Haven says.
- Don't use static spray or pencil erasers to try and clean the card (especially the gold contacts). If you spill something on the card, use rubbing alcohol sparingly on the plastic portion of the card and make sure it dries completely before reinstalling it.

Haven says sound cards rarely wear out. If you use the connectors on the back of the card frequently to change speakers, those connectors could deteriorate. It's more likely, however, that the sound card will become technologically inferior before any portion of it wears out.

Paying someone to repair a malfunctioning sound card usually is a bad idea economically. Chances are your sound card—if it's no longer under warranty—has been surpassed technologically by cards that cost about the sames as a repair bill.

"They're so cheap nowadays, I wouldn't advise going out and trying to fix it," Haven says. "It's not worth it, unless you have a special attachment to it."

You can try running Windows 95/98's Troubleshooting Wizard. Click the Start button and choose the Help command. Then click the Contents tab and double-click the book icon for Troubleshooting. You'll be able to choose from a list of several common computing problems; click the box of the problem you want to troubleshoot. In this case, we'll choose "If you have a hardware conflict" and double-click the question mark icon. In the Windows Help window, click the Start Troubleshooter box and follow the directions. This troubleshooter is extremely helpful in resetting a conflicting DMA or IRQ line.

To see your computer's various settings in Windows 3.*x* or DOS, use the Microsoft Diagnostic Program (MSD). Type **msd** at the DOS prompt and press Enter. The program will reveal the available lines and channels. Refer to your sound card's documentation to find alternate settings that may relieve the conflict.

To see the DMA or IRQ lines your sound card uses in Windows 95, click the Start button followed by the Settings command and the Control Panel command. Double-click the System icon. In the System Properties window, click the Device Manager tab and find your sound card driver, which should be marked with a multimedia icon. You may need to double-click the Sound, Video, and Game Controllers icon to see the sound card driver. Click and highlight the driver and then click the Properties button. In the Properties window, click the Resources tab. You'll see several settings for your sound card. Scroll through the Resource Settings box to see the DMA and IRQ settings (1 and 5 are common settings for the DMA; 5 and 10 are common for the IRQ). If conflicts exist, they'll be listed in a box at the bottom of the window, or you'll see a yellow exclamation point on top of the sound card driver's icon.

If you can't resolve the conflict through troubleshooting and you've determined it doesn't originate from your speakers, you may need to contact the sound card's manufacturer for help.

Troubleshooting Mice and Trackballs

Just 10 years ago, most PCs didn't even have a mouse. Today, the mouse is a standard component of every desktop system, although it can be replaced with an alternative input device such as a trackball, touch pad, digitizer, or pointing stick.

A mouse needs a spacious, flat desktop surface so the ball on its underside can move freely. You should use a mousepad underneath the mouse rather than trying to move it across a hard desktop. If your space is limited, or if you get tired of moving a mouse around, consider a trackball. Basically, a trackball is a stationary upside-down mouse that lets you move the ball directly with your fingers rather than across a flat surface.

Mice and trackballs don't need a lot of attention because they are relatively simple devices that rarely break down. When you think about the kinds of things that might cause problems, think of the Three D's: drivers, dirt, and design. Your mouse needs to be connected properly to your system, it needs to be kept clean, and its design and features play an important role in your comfort and satisfaction.

A Good Connection

Your mouse must be connected to your computer in order to work. Match the mouse's connector to an available serial or PS/2 port on your system, or make sure the mouse comes with an appropriate adapter. With your PC turned off, plug the device into the port, making sure it has a firm fit. If it doesn't seem to be attaching easily, make sure you have the pins and holes aligned properly. If you ever disconnect and reconnect your mouse while your computer is still running, it might not respond until you reboot your system.

Because Windows includes standard mouse drivers (programs that allow input devices such as mice to communicate with your computer), a simple mouse should work as soon as you connect it to your PC. More complex input devices come with their own software drivers that you install according to their directions.

If you share your PC with a left-handed user, have children who use a different device, or just get tired of using the same old mouse all the time, you can double up on your input device choices. Attaching one device to your serial port and one to your PS/2 port lets you switch between trackball and mouse, or left- and right-handed devices, without unplugging and replugging. Both devices need to support the same drivers, or you'll have to switch drivers when switching devices. To change drivers in Windows 95/98, double-click Mouse in the Control Panel and then click the General tab. Click the Change button and select the appropriate mouse and driver.

A bad cable can cause your mouse to act strangely, so make sure the cable leading from your mouse to the computer is free of obstructions and heavy objects that might damage it. If the cable is sharply bent, it could develop creases or breaks over time. If you experience sporadic cursor movement when you move the cable, the cable is probably worn and you need a new mouse.

A Clean Mouse Is a Happy Mouse

Although the furry little creatures by the same name tend to run around erratically, this is not good behavior for your computer mouse. A cursor that dances around the screen or won't respond correctly to your clicks and movements is a clear indication your mouse needs to be cleaned.

There are many different mechanisms used to detect mouse movement. Although many manufacturers still use mechanical systems, others have moved to optical-mechanical, optical, and digital-optical technologies. In a mechanical mouse, there is a ball inside the mouse casing that is in contact with a pair of rollers that detect horizontal and vertical movement. The rollers are connected to small slotted wheels that rotate and alternately block and unblock light from a diode (a device or circuit that allows electronic currents to travel in one direction).

The computer calculates the rate of the blinking light, determines how fast the mouse is moving in each direction, and adjusts the cursor movement on-screen. Mechanically, it is much the same for many trackballs, except you directly manipulate the ball with your fingers to guide the cursor.

Cleaning Your Mouse

As the ball moves over a mousepad or is guided by your fingers, it picks up dust and grime. After enough dirt accumulates, you begin to lose control of the cursor. You should clean your mouse or trackball on a regular basis, rather than waiting for erratic behavior to occur. If you have been using your mouse for a while without ever cleaning it, you might be surprised at how much grime has accumulated inside. For a mechanically operated mouse, follow these instructions:

- Turn off your PC.
- Turn the mouse upside down. There will be a plastic circle with a hole in its middle. The ball pokes through this hole.
- Press lightly with your fingers and rotate the plastic circle counterclockwise to loosen it.
- Remove the plastic collar and ball.
- Wash the ball in lukewarm water. Do not use any cleansers; the chemicals might damage the mouse. Wipe the ball dry with a lint-free cloth or let it air dry.
- Using a swab and rubbing alcohol, wipe any grime from the plastic collar and inside the hollow cavity where the ball was. Inside the cavity, you will see tiny wheels or rollers; be sure to clean these as well.
- When you are done cleaning, put the ball back into the cavity and replace the plastic collar. Turn the collar clockwise to tighten it.

Ergonomic Comfort

Although mice require only small finger motions to click the buttons and short wrist movements to guide the cursor around the screen, these movements can cause muscle strain from an overly tight grip or from repetitive arm movements. Trackballs require less desk area but a lot of finger movement and wrist support. More than ever, input devices are designed with the user in mind, which means an emphasis on ergonomics, injury prevention, and intended use. The design of your mouse or trackball will determine how comfortable you are using it and whether you develop injuries such as carpal tunnel syndrome from lengthy use.

Your mouse or trackball should fit your hand comfortably. You should be able to move the mouse smoothly across the mousepad and click the buttons easily. Some mice have subtle indentations, grips, or texturing that might improve your grip. The placement of buttons on a trackball and the size and placement of the ball should allow for a comfortable hand position. If the buttons are too close to the ball, you will be forced to hold your hand at an angle from your forearm (rather than relatively straight), which can cause strain.

The market is full of various sizes, shapes, and designs of mice and trackballs, so you don't have to settle for the basic one that came with your system. If possible, try a unit before buying it to see if it responds well and is comfortable for you. Use multiple devices for several minutes each, simulating your normal activity, before you make your purchasing decision. In addition to comfort and durability, look for a tracking resolution of 400 dots per inch (dpi) or more, a one-year or longer warranty, and (with the exception of cordless models) a long cable.

Location is everything, and that applies to mice as well as a business or home. Try to place your mouse so your arms and hands are in a comfortable, relaxed position. You shouldn't have to stretch to use the unit. Your forearms should be parallel to the floor and your wrists and hands should be in line with your forearms. The best height for your mouse is 26.5 inches above the floor, rather than the 29 inches of the traditional desktop, so you might want to attach a mouse tray on the underside of your desk.

Mousepads are available in a wide array of sizes, colors, and styles. Look for one with a natural rubber base to avoid skids. Either cloth or plastic pads work well; it's a matter of personal taste. If you choose a cloth pad, look for one that is decorated with a permanent dye process rather than a raised silk screen that can wear off. A plastic pad should be slightly textured so it's not too slick.

Add a wrist rest to your mousepad to help avoid carpal tunnel syndrome. A pad that is separate from the mousepad will let you adjust the pad and the rest independently for the best fit. Be careful of wrist rests with a prominent front edge because that can compress sensitive nerves.

TIP

Be sure to take breaks from using your mouse. No matter how many precautions you have taken regarding design and location, you can still cause stress injuries by prolonged use of an input device.

Changing Mouse Settings

A mouse or trackball's design is just one aspect of customizing your input device to fit your needs. Software settings allow you to fine-tune your input device to make it easier and more convenient to use. For example, you can adjust a mouse for left-handed use, change to larger mouse pointers that are easier to see, and reduce mouse actions such as double-clicking to a single click. Some software is available through your Windows Control Panel and is outlined here. Other programs come bundled with input devices or are available as shareware or in retail outlets. These programs, combined with mice and trackballs that feature multiple programmable buttons, can turn your mouse into a mighty mouse.

Left-Handed?

In the Windows 95 Control Panel, double-click Mouse to display the Mouse Properties box (see Figure 23.15). The Buttons tab lets lefties switch buttons on the mouse by choosing Left in the button configuration box. When the buttons are switched, the right-mouse button (under your index finger) becomes the primary button used to click and the left mouse button becomes the secondary button. Remember when instructions say to right-click you will actually be left-clicking. This might sound confusing, but for southpaws, use of the switched buttons will come naturally.

Double-Click Speed

At the bottom of the Buttons tab is an adjustment area for your double-click speed. By setting it slower or faster, you will change the length of time that can pass between clicks of your primary mouse button when you are double-clicking an object. If you are an inexperienced mouse user or are having difficulty getting double-click to work, try moving the slider to the left to lengthen the interval needed between clicks. Use the test area in the window to test the double-click speed. If the jack-in-the-box appears or disappears, your double-click action has been recognized.

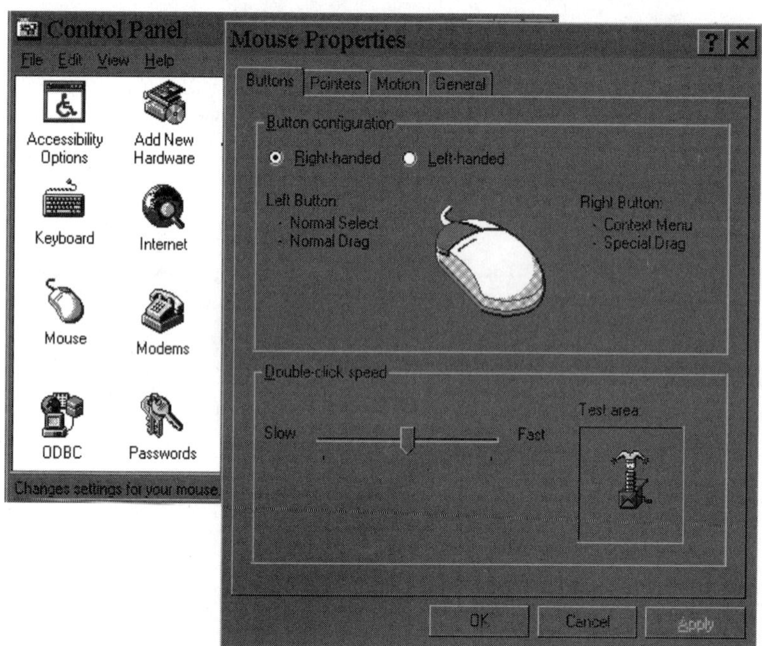

FIGURE 23.15: You can customize your mouse using Windows software settings.

Some Pointers on Pointers

As you work on your computer, the pointer shape provides a visual clue as to what the system is doing or which action you can perform next. It might appear as an hourglass, a pointer, crosshairs, or another design, and it can be stationary or animated. Click the Pointers tab to change the design scheme of your mouse pointer and then select a pointer scheme from the drop-down list to display the pointers associated with that scheme. To change the appearance of a pointer, select Browse and double-click the filename of a different pointer.

When you click Browse, a list of available Windows cursors should appear. If they do not, click Add/Remove Programs in the Control Panel and select the Windows Setup tab. Then click Accessories and Details to see if a checkmark appears next to Mouse Pointers. If not, select it and click OK twice to add the files. These cursor schemes include large and extra large cursors for easier viewing. Animated cursors will have a file extension of .ANI, static cursors will have a

.CUR extension. Many shareware and retail programs are available that provide a wide variety of pointers.

Cursor Movement

To adjust the speed at which your cursor moves on-screen, click the Motion tab. Use the slider to make the movement slower or faster. Adding a trail makes your cursor look like several arrows in a row when you drag it across the screen. This makes it easier to see, particularly on LCD screens. To enable this option, select Show Pointer Trails and use the slider to adjust the length of the trail.

Use Your Keyboard as a Mouse

Windows 95/98 comes with some options designed to make it more accessible to users with physical impairments, although they are useful to anyone. One option, MouseKeys, lets you use your numeric keypad to move your mouse pointer. This is a convenient feature if you're recovering from a repetitive stress injury or if you have a notebook computer on which you don't want to install a mouse.

To access these accessibility features in Windows 95/98, double-click the Accessibility Options icon in the Control Panel. If this component is not available, click Add/Remove Programs in the Control Panel, select the Windows Setup tab, click Accessibility Options, and click OK to install. To enable MouseKeys, click the Mouse tab in the Accessibility Options box and check the Use MouseKeys box.

A Better Mouse

Manufacturers are offering a wide array of improved mice and trackballs in addition to other input devices. The leading mouse manufacturers are Kensington, Logitech, and Microsoft but many others are in the market, each with their own combination of ergonomic comfort, buttons, and software features. No longer confined to a basic point-and-click mechanical mouse, you can opt for an optical mouse, a cordless one, or even one you operate with your feet. Many are sealed units that do not require any special maintenance or cleaning. Software features let you adjust mouse properties, simplify mouse-related functions such as dragging and double-clicking, or program mouse buttons to enable operations such as File Open, Delete, or Page Up or Down.

All these variations of the basic mouse let you choose what works best for your type of computer setting and usage. Mice don't make us scream now, they make us dream, and those dreams of comfort, low maintenance, and performance are coming true.

Troubleshooting Inkjet Printers

Inkjet printers, the best value in color printing, have taken the market by storm. Now available for less than $200, inkjets revolutionized the home printer market by making high-quality printing available to all users, regardless of budget. But no printer retains its quality unless it's well-maintained. We give you some simple tips you can follow to keep your inkjet printer in top condition. And, should your printer ever have problems, we list some possible fixes so you can avoid a trip to the repair shop.

NOTE

Although the steps we discuss below are suitable for most printers, you should always check with your printer's documentation before trying to fix any problems. Specifically, you should review your printer's documentation to make sure there aren't warnings against certain actions. If the documentation instructs you to do things differently than we do, follow the printer's documentation. In addition, always turn your printer off before you open it. If your printer is still under warranty (even though none of the actions we discuss in this article should void the warranty) you should check the warranty regulations to ensure you don't violate any rules.

Keep Your Printer Happy

Maintaining your printer means keeping good habits and using common sense. First, you need to keep your printer clean by using a dust cover. Although some manufacturers market special covers for their printers, a towel will usually do just as well. You will want to make sure you don't cover the printer when it's running or when it's still warm from use because excess heat can damage electrical components. To keep your printer clean, you'll also want to keep pets, unsupervised young children, and food and liquids away from your printer.

You should clean your printer regularly because dust and debris can hinder your printer's operation. Check your printer's manual to see how often you should clean the printer. There will almost certainly be special instructions on how to clean it and what you should use. Following these instructions will help you avoid damaging your printer.

In general, though, cleaning your printer shouldn't be a big production. First, unplug your printer's power cord. Get a clean, lint-free cloth and wipe all surfaces on the outside of your printer. If you find dirt that doesn't want to come off, you can use a mild detergent, such as dish soap, as long as you make sure none gets into the printer itself.

After you have cleaned the outside of the printer, it's time to turn your attention to the inside. Open your printer and remove the paper and the paper tray. Make sure you wipe off the paper trays before you reinsert them. Use the clean, lint-free cloth, but make sure it's *dry*; you don't want to short out your printer. Don't take the cartridge out unless you know it needs cleaning.

Before we proceed, locate the rod or track that your printer's carriage runs on. The carriage is the chassis that holds the print cartridge. Don't clean this track unless your documentation instructs you to because this can damage your printer.

For the rest of the interior, except the print head, the print cartridge, and the rod or track that they run on, use your cloth to pick up paper bits and dust. Don't worry about ink that has fallen to the bottom of your printer. Again, make sure you don't clean any moving parts unless your documentation specifically instructs you to do so. For instructions about how to clean your printer's paper rollers, consult your documentation for instructions.

NOTE

Some stores still sell printer cleaning kits. They are not a must-have. You may find miniature vacuums come in handy for removing hard-to-reach dust particles, but they aren't necessary. A decent, lint-free cloth will do the trick.

No More Ink Blots

Inkjet printers work much like dot matrix printers; both create a series of small dots on the page to create letters and images. The difference lies in the printing mechanism.

While the traditional dot matrix uses a ribbon much like an old-fashioned typewriter, the inkjet printer uses a cartridge that supplies the ink. Instead of physically pressing a ribbon to the paper, the printer's *inkjets* (which give the printer its name) shoot ink onto the page. This mechanism is efficient and can produce high-quality print unless the inkjets become clogged with excess ink. Fortunately, the ink can be easily removed with proper cleaning.

If you know your printer is having a problem with ink buildup, (you will see streaks on printed pages or faulty type) the problem could be with your cartridge, your print head, or both.

If it's the print head, there is probably a buildup of ink in the nozzles where the ink comes out. Consult your documentation for instructions about how to clean your printer's print nozzles and ink cartridge. Often, particularly with new printers, you can use your printer's device driver (a program that allows a peripheral device to communicate with the computer) to clean the nozzles. The driver will instruct your printer to shoot a powerful stream of ink that will unclog the nozzles.

If you're using Windows 95/98, you can access your printer's driver by clicking the Start button and selecting Printers from the Settings menu. In the window that appears, right-click the icon that corresponds to your printer and select Properties from the context menu that appears. Consult your documentation for more information.

Sometimes, there will be a utility or some software included with your printer to handle the cleaning of the nozzle. Consult your documentation for instructions. In some cases, you might have to clean the nozzle manually. Do not proceed without consulting your documentation; if you mess up, you could damage your printer. If you are in doubt or feel uncomfortable about cleaning your nozzles, consult a computer technician.

In contrast to the nozzles, cleaning the cartridge is straightforward. First, check your documentation for specific instructions so you don't ruin your cartridge. Then shut off, unplug, and open your computer. You might have to press a release lever before popping the cartridge from the carriage. Look at the cartridge and identify where the ink comes out. Take a cloth dampened lightly with distilled water and wipe the excess ink from the cartridge. When the ink is obviously loose, put the cartridge back in the printer, close it, and plug it in.

Reload, Don't Rebuild

To replace an empty cartridge, you can follow the steps listed above for removing a cartridge. Before you insert your new cartridge, however, make sure you remove the tape from the ribbon. That tape prevents ink leaks, but unless you remove the tape, it also can prevent your printer from getting the ink it needs to print. To make sure your ink cartridge performs at its best, keep the cartridge in its wrapper until you are ready to use it; this will prevent the ink from drying out and clogging the nozzle.

If you have a printer that requires you to change cartridges to switch between printing in color or in black, make sure you store your idle cartridges in the storage containers that came with your printer. If you don't have these containers, use a zip-up plastic bag.

After you're done changing cartridges, you might have to notify your printer's device driver because many drivers monitor the ink level in the cartridge. You might need to adjust their settings when the cartridge is replaced. Refer to your documentation for more instructions.

In Case of Emergency

No matter how carefully you maintain your printer, there will come a time when your printer won't work. The solution to your problem might be simple.

WARNING WARNING WARNING WARNING WARNING WARNING WARNING WARNING

You should never try to fix any mechanical malfunction unless you feel completely comfortable with the steps you're taking. Obviously, you don't want to do more damage than is already present; getting the printer repaired by a professional is much cheaper than buying a new printer. Also, remember to never do anything that violates your printer's warranty.

When your printer isn't working correctly, the first step in diagnosis is observing the symptoms. Do your printer's lights come on when you turn it on? If not, see the "More Power to You" section below. If your printer comes on, but it doesn't print anything, see the "Restoring the Connection" section. If your printer has trouble printing pages with lots of graphics and multiple fonts, see the "Thanks for the Memory" section. If you can print, but you're getting text in the wrong place, garbage, or poor quality text, see the "Sorting Out the Mess" section.

More Power to You

If your printer's lights aren't on, make sure the printer is actually on. Press the power switch to make sure it's in the right position. If this doesn't do the trick, turn the switch off and check the power cord. Is it connected firmly to the wall outlet? Is the other end of the cord squarely inserted in the printer's power cord outlet? If either of these are loose, tighten the connections and try to turn on your printer again.

If the steps mentioned above don't remedy the problem, your printer's power supply or fuse is probably broken. If the power supply is on the outside of the printer, you can replace it yourself. However, if there isn't an easy way to detach the power supply, you will have to take your printer in for service.

Restoring the Connection

If your printer is on but doesn't print anything, make sure your printer is online, meaning that it expects to receive data from the computer. Generally, printers have a light that comes on when the printer is online. If you don't know which light is which, check your documentation.

If you hear unusual grinding noises, your print carriage (the assembly that holds the ink cartridge) might be stuck. Turn off your printer, unplug it, then open it. If the carriage is stuck, you will see it is on one side of the printer and will not move easily. Check your documentation for advice on how to solve this problem. If the documentation isn't helpful or you cannot loosen the print head easily, take the printer in for service.

Make sure the paper is fed correctly into your printer. If there is a paper tray, make sure it is inserted all the way. Also, make sure you don't overload the paper tray and that the paper is aligned properly before you insert it.

A corollary paper problem is the paper jam. If paper has partially entered or exited the printer, this is almost certainly the problem. Also, if you can't get your printer to come back online, it's probably due to a paper jam. You know the drill: turn off, unplug, and open your printer. Then look to see if there is any ripped paper inside your printer. Follow your printer's documentation to get the paper out. Remove your paper and reload it according to your manual's instructions. Never overfill the paper tray or allow the paper eject tray (which is where the paper comes out of the printer) to overflow.

If your printer is online and has paper inserted correctly, you should check the cable next. Turn off your computer and printer. After they're both off, check to make sure the cable connecting the computer and printer isn't loose. If it is loose, push it in firmly and try again. You might find you have to use clasps or miniature screws to fasten the cable into place; use these tools, they're not there simply for decoration.

Another thing you should check is to make sure your program is printing to the right printer. If you're using a Windows operating system, most applications allow you to choose a printer in the Print window.

After you open the Print window (by giving the Print command), make sure your application is using the printer you want it to use (see Figure 23.16). If there isn't any listing for your printer in the window, you will need to install the driver. If you don't have a driver for your printer, and one isn't available in your operating system, see the "Finding a Lost Printer Driver" sidebar.

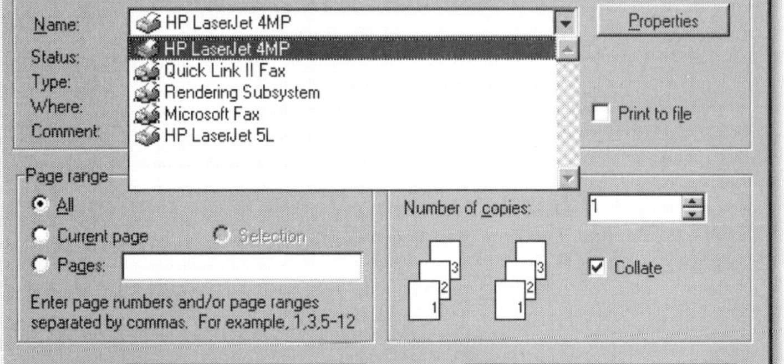

FIGURE 23.16: Make sure you always specify the printer you want to print to or your document could end up going to the fax driver or some other inhospitable place.

FINDING A LOST PRINTER DRIVER

Windows provides many printer device drivers—programs that let a computer and its peripherals communicate—within the operating system. But no company, not even Microsoft, can build in support for every printer that has ever been created. For any number of reasons, you may find yourself without the software that you need to get Windows 95 to recognize your printer. Here are some ideas to try if you find yourself without a device driver.

The Internet Many manufacturers keep archives of their driver software on their World Wide Web sites. If you don't know the company's Web address, first check the Printer Manufacturers and Drivers page at `http://www.printgrc.com/template/pdrivers.cfm`. If it isn't there, you can try to find the site through a Web search engine such as Yahoo! (`http://www.yahoo.com`).

continued

Vendor The store or outlet that you bought your printer from might have drivers if you have lost the disks. They may or may not let you have them for free.

Manufacturer You can always call your manufacturer directly. If they have the driver, the company will tell you where you can get it or how you can send away for it. If you request disks be sent to you in the mail, the manufacturer will probably charge you.

Comparable drivers If your manufacturer is unwilling or unable to help you, and Microsoft has not produced a driver for your printer, your next option may be to try to use a comparable driver from the list of drivers that Windows 95/98 provides you. This is never the best option, but it can give you reasonably good printing or even printing that satisfies all the potential of the printer. If you find yourself forced into this avenue, check with your vendor or manufacturer to see if there is a comparable printer to yours that is supported. A printer that is virtually identical to yours might be supported, but the printer might be produced under a different name or even under a different brand. If you can't find anyone to help you and you really want to try to this method, which we have to stress again is never the best solution, search the list of available drivers for a model that is fairly comparable to your printer. For instance, Hewlett-Packard printers are common, so some companies model their products after the established HP product line. Finding and testing comparable drivers is often much more trouble than it is worth. Remember, if your printer driver is unattainable, it is probably because you own an older printer. You can always upgrade to a newer printer, as these are now selling for less than $200 in many places. If your printer doesn't work with Windows 95/98, it may be a clue that you should upgrade.

If you still can't print, try to print with another application or print a test page if your printer driver allows it. Refer to your documentation for more instructions on this. (In Windows 95/98, you can get to your printer driver through the Start button's Settings menu. Select Printers, then in the Printers window, right-click your printer's icon, then select Properties from the context menu that appears.

You should be able to print a test page from one of the driver's menus.) If the test page prints, it means you need to check the printing options within your applications or that your printer cannot handle the load you're giving it. See the next section on what to do if your printer can't handle your print jobs.

You might want to check out your operating system's printer control mechanism (the window or the control box that allows you to control your printer). In Windows 3.*x*, the Print Manager appears when you try to print something. If the Print Manager doesn't appear or doesn't have any printing jobs listed when you open it, then your applications are not working right. Check your applications' print options.

In Windows 95, the equivalent to the Print Manager is the Printer Control Window, which can be accessed from the Start menu by selecting Settings ➢ Printers. Double-click the printer icon to see the listing of printing tasks, or you can right-click the icon to make sure the printer is not paused (see Figure 23.17). (It's paused if there is a checkmark next to the phrase Pause Printing. To restart a paused printer, click the Pause Printing listing.)

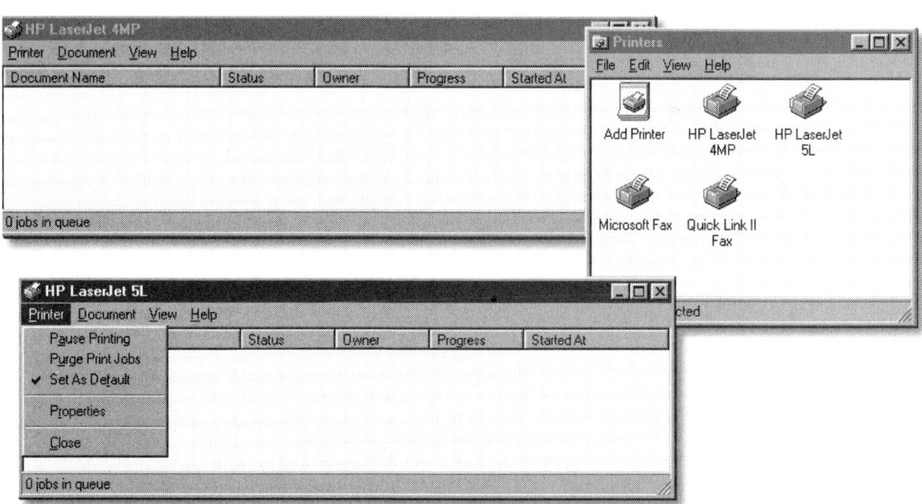

FIGURE 23.17: You can get to these Print control windows in Windows 95/98 by double-clicking the printer icon in your Printers window. Note the printer listed in the bottom window is paused but can be easily restarted using the Printer menu.

You can control most of your printer's operations from this window, including purging bad print jobs. By purging, we mean deleting a print task. Click the listing of the job you want to delete, then press Delete on your keyboard. The listing should disappear.

If you still can't isolate the problem, there is a slight possibility your cable might be bad. If you have another cable on hand, substitute it. Again, make sure your printer and computer are both off before you change the cord. Refer to your documentation for more assistance.

Thanks for the Memory

If your printer takes a long time to print graphics- and font-heavy documents, your printer and computer probably don't have enough power between them to handle the work. You will know for sure if your printer can more easily print small graphics or plain-text documents that use only one font.

You can generally make your printer print faster if you decrease the printing resolution, for instance, from 600 dots per inch (dpi) to 300dpi. Because the printer doesn't have to worry about as many dots, it can print much more easily.

In Windows 95/98, you can generally set your printer's resolution by altering its driver's settings. Click the Start button and select Printers from the Settings menu. Right-click your printer's icon and select Properties. Click through the tabs at the top of the box to find the resolution controls. Set your printer's resolution to a lower number, if possible, then click OK (see Figure 23.18).

Changing the resolution in Windows 3.*x* is just as easy. First, open your Control Panel group by double-clicking it. Then, double-click the Printers icon. This will bring up the Printers window. Click the listing of the printer for which you would like to change the settings, then click the Setup button on the right side of the window.

Within the Setup window that appears, you will probably see the resolution controls; if so, reset the resolution, then click OK or Close to continue and then close the Printers box. If you don't see the resolution settings when you open the Setup window, you should try the different buttons in the box; the resolution controls are probably hidden in a subordinate dialog box. If you run into trouble, refer to your documentation.

Of course, printing at high resolutions is more fun, not to mention much more useful. To enable your printer to print at high resolutions, your computer needs to have sufficient memory and disk space. Why does your computer need the additional disk space? Because most current operating systems use virtual memory, which is a technique in which the operating system uses the hard drive to store necessary information that won't fit in random access memory (RAM).

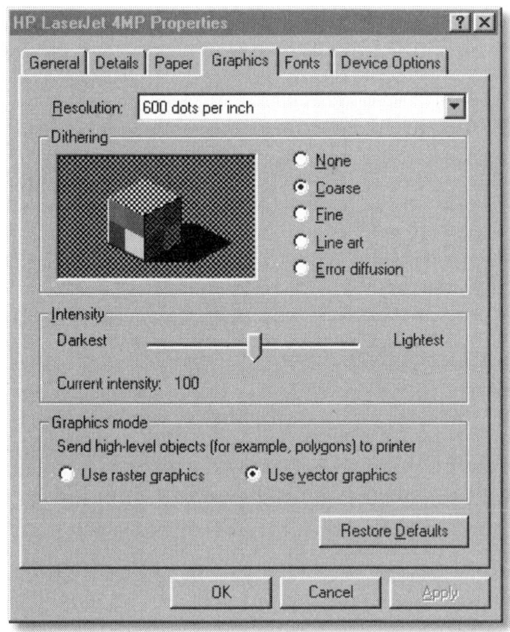

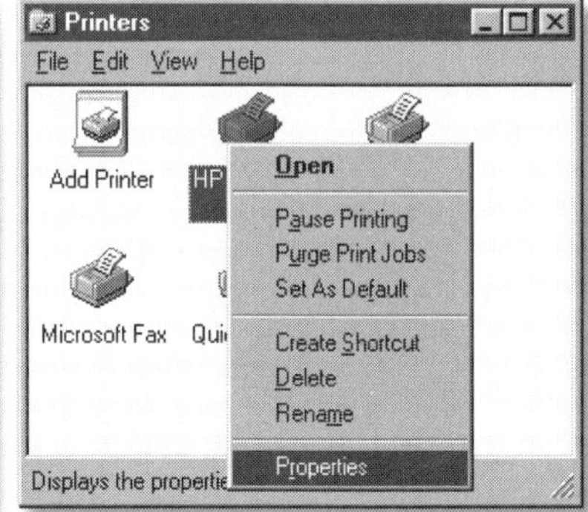

FIGURE 23.18: Right-click your printer icon in Windows 95/98 and select Properties to get to your printer driver. Note that right-clicking gives you all kinds of options when working with your printer.

Make sure your operating system has at least 50MB of virtual memory. Or even better, allow it to control its own virtual memory settings. Of course, to use 50MB of disk space, your computer must have 50MB available on the hard drive. If you have less than 50MB of free space, the time has come to archive some files to disks, add a new hard drive, or remove some programs that you don't use very often. Also, you can erase temporary files and Internet downloads that you no longer need.

As for memory, make sure that, if you're using Windows 95/98, you have at least 8MB of memory, though many programs won't run well with less than 16MB. Even more memory is even better. If you're using Windows 3.*x*, you need at least 4MB, but for graphics, you should really have 8MB or more. Adding memory is generally the most cost-effective way to improve performance on a computer that isn't obsolete.

Sorting Out the Mess

If your printer is printing poorly or with the wrong format, there are several possible culprits. First, if the print quality is too light, the problem is probably your ink cartridge. (Again, check your documentation to make sure you don't do anything to harm your printer.) Turn off your printer, open it, and remove your cartridge. Has the cartridge expired, that is, no ink is flowing? If the cartridge is clogged, you'll have to clean it. More likely, it has expired, so you'll need to change it. See our instructions earlier in this article.

If the text is clear but garbled or in the wrong position on the paper, you'll want to make sure your applications are using the correct driver. Check the destination printer in the application's print window (the one that opens when you give the print command). Does the listing match your printer's name exactly? If it doesn't, you should install the proper driver. If you don't have a driver for your printer and one isn't available in your operating system, check our "Finding a Lost Printer Driver" sidebar for help on where to find the appropriate driver.

If the printer output is good, but it's in the wrong place on the page, make sure your paper is in the printer correctly. Take the paper out, fan it by flicking the ends between your thumb and forefinger, then reinsert it into the paper tray according to your documentation.

If your printer is printing successfully, but you're not satisfied with the printing output, check the quality of the paper that you're using. Some kinds of paper do not work well with inkjet printers due to the way the fibers absorb ink. Try some specially made inkjet paper to see if that improves the quality of the output. If it does, you know to stop printing with the paper you previously had been using.

Finally, if you're experiencing sloppy output, your printer may simply not be clean enough. Use our cleaning instructions above to ensure dirt isn't your problem. Make sure to check that your nozzles and print cartridge are clean.

Find a Designated Driver

Printers require the correct driver to run in a Windows environment. You might find that your printer doesn't have the appropriate driver installed and that your version of Windows doesn't make the correct driver available. If you have the disks that came with your printer, the driver is probably on one of them; follow the documentation instructions on installing it.

To install your printer's drivers, see if there are special instructions in the documentation before you proceed. Manufacturers such as Hewlett-Packard and Epson like to throw in extra features and administrative tools that need special installation.

The actual installation of the drivers will depend upon your operating system. Check its documentation or your printer's documentation for more assistance. If your operating system comes with multiple drivers and your driver isn't listed (and you don't have a driver disk), see our sidebar for suggestions.

Troubleshooting Laser Printers

Laser printers produce the fastest and highest-quality print of any printer on the market, and now they are finally priced so home consumers can afford them. For those of us who have used laser printers at work for years, we can only say "it's about time."

But for all their convenience and power, laser printers don't retain their high reliability and print quality if you don't properly maintain them. This section will help you make sure your laser printer stays in the best possible condition. Our tips hopefully will prevent a trip to the repair shop should your printer experience trouble.

Understand the Mechanics

Before we get started, let's take a look at how laser printers work. The *laser* we keep referring to is a beam of energy the printer shoots onto its drum, which is a moving cylinder inside the printer used to transfer images to paper. This energy heats the drum so it can pick up toner, which is a powdery form of ink used by laser printers and copy machines. The toner is then applied to the paper that moves through the printer.

All this happens extraordinarily quickly as the paper passes underneath the drum picking up the ink that forms letters and graphic images. Because we are talking about laser beams, the internal parts of the printer get extremely hot, so you should always use caution when trying to open and fix your printer after it has been running. Always let it cool before you work on it.

WARNING WARNING WARNING WARNING WARNING WARNING WARNING WARNING

Even though the instructions we detail below will work for many printers, you should always check with your printer's documentation before you try to fix any problems. Review your printer's manual to make sure there aren't particular warnings against certain actions before following our instructions. If the documentation gives you instructions that differ from ours, then follow the printer's documentation. In particular, you should check the manual's instructions on cleaning; many manufacturers do not want users cleaning the mechanical components of the printer.

If your printer is under warranty, check the warranty regulations to ensure you don't break any rules, even though none of the actions we discuss in this article should violate the warranty agreement.

For the Long Haul

To keep your printer in top condition, use common sense and keep good maintenance habits. Obviously, you need to keep your printer clean; using a dust cover is an excellent way to do this. Although some printer manufacturers market special covers made especially for their printers, a towel or cloth will usually do just as well. Because the internal components get so hot, you'll want to make sure you don't cover the printer when it's running or when it's still warm from use because excess heat can damage electrical components. To keep your printer clean, you'll also want to keep pets, unsupervised young children, and food and liquids away from your printer.

As for cleaning your printer, you should check your printer's manual for information about how often you should clean it. If there is no advice about cleaning your printer, make sure the manufacturer recommends cleaning it all; some companies advise consumers never to clean their own printers. If your printer's documentation does allow for you to clean the printer, but it doesn't offer a recommendation on how often, try cleaning it every three to six months. This should be often enough to clear out the dust and debris that can hinder your printer's operation.

Follow your manual's instructions about how to clean the printer to avoid damaging your printer. In particular, some printers have special brushes and cleaning tools for you to use. Make sure you use these tools and follow the instructions explicitly. If you ever feel uncomfortable cleaning your printer, take it to a professional.

In general, though, cleaning your printer shouldn't be a big production. Before you start cleaning, make sure you consult your documentation to see if there are any parts of the printer you should never clean or touch. Then, unplug your printer's power cord and let it cool. Get a clean, lint-free cloth and wipe down all surfaces on the outside of your printer.

After you're done with the outside of the printer, it's time to turn your attention to the inside. Open your printer and remove the paper. If your printer has a paper tray, remove it and wipe it off thoroughly before you reinsert it. Use the clean, lint-free cloth, but make sure it's *dry*; you don't want to short out your printer. You want to run your cloth along the inside of the printer (for those parts that you're allowed to clean) to pick up bits of paper, dust, and toner particles.

Check your printer manufacturer's site on the World Wide Web to see if there are any cleaning utilities that can be downloaded. These special programs send special instructions to your printer to burn off toner particles that may be clogging your printer. If you don't know the Web address of your manufacturer, check out the GRC Quality Imaging Supplies Printer Manufacturers and Drivers Web page at `http://www.printgrc.com/template/pdrivers.cfm`.

Some stores still sell printer cleaning kits. For older printers, these might be helpful, particularly if you've lost the original cleaning tools. You might find that miniature vacuums are handy for removing hard-to-reach dust particles, but they aren't necessary. A clean, lint-free cloth will do the trick.

NOTE

As for additional maintenance requirements for you printer, check your documentation. A regular cleaning is the only maintenance most companies suggest.

Get the Toner You Need

It should be fairly apparent when your cartridge runs out of toner because the print will become lighter. To replace a depleted cartridge, you should refer to the printer's documentation; always turn off your printer and make sure it has had a chance to cool. Before you insert your new cartridge, remove the tape from the ribbon. The tape prevents toner leaks, and unless you remove the tape, it also can prevent your printer from getting the toner it needs to print. To make sure your toner cartridge performs properly, don't let the cartridge sit out of its wrapper for any longer than necessary, and make sure it doesn't get excessively hot or cold.

Before you resort to changing your cartridge, you should try shaking it first to redistribute the remaining toner in the cartridge. This often will extend the life of the cartridge. Be careful when you do this; make sure you aren't standing on good carpet or anything else that can be easily damaged. Hold the cartridge with one hand on each end. You want to hold the cartridge so the toner output part of the cartridge is pointing up. Now, gently raise the left end of the cartridge and lower the right end. Now, raise the right end and lower the left end. Repeat for 30 seconds. This can put off the replacement of the print cartridge for weeks or months, depending upon how much you use your printer.

You might have to notify your printer's driver software after you're done changing cartridges because some printer drivers monitor the toner level in the cartridge and must adjust their settings when the cartridge is replaced. A driver is a program that controls and enables the computer to work with a peripheral, in this case, a printer. Refer to your documentation for more information.

Some Days Are Better than Others

Even if you maintain your printer perfectly, even if you're careful never to hurt it, eventually there will come a time when your printer won't work. The solution for your problem could be relatively simple. However, if your printer's problems turn out to be mechanical, you should never attempt to fix any mechanical malfunction unless you feel comfortable with the steps you're taking. Obviously, you don't want to damage the printer any more that it already is; getting the printer repaired by a professional is often much cheaper than buying a new printer.

When your printer has problems, you must first determine the symptoms. Do your printer's lights come on when you turn on the printer? If not, read the "Power for the Beam" section of this article. If your printer comes on, but it doesn't print anything, turn to the "Communing with the Computer" section. If your printer has trouble printing pages with lots of graphics, multiple fonts, or both, see the "Printing Amnesia" section. Finally, if you can print, but you're getting text in the wrong place, garbage, or poor-quality text, read the "Wading through Blotches" section.

Power for the Beam

If your printer's lights aren't on, make sure the printer is actually on or plugged in. Press the power switch on and off to make sure the switch is in the right position. If this doesn't do the trick, turn the switch off position and check the power cord. Is it connected firmly to the wall outlet? Is the other end of the cord squarely inserted in the printer's power cord outlet? If either of these are loose, tighten the connections and try to turn on your printer again.

Some newer printers don't have power switches because they are on continuously, though most of the time they are in power-saving mode. If you have one of these printers, there should be a printer reset button that you can press to see if your printer's power is on.

If the steps mentioned above don't fix the problem, your printer's power supply or fuse is probably broken. If the power supply is on the outside of the printer, you can replace it yourself. However, if there isn't an easy way to detach the power supply, you will have to take your printer in for service.

Communing with the Computer

When your printer has power but can't print, first check that your printer is online, meaning that it expects to receive data from the computer. Generally, printers have a light that signals when the printer is online. If you don't know which light is which, check your documentation.

Make sure the paper is fed correctly into your printer. If there is a paper tray, make sure it is properly inserted. Also, make sure the paper tray isn't overloaded and that the paper is aligned properly before you insert it.

A related paper problem is the paper jam. If paper has partially entered or exited the printer, this is almost certainly the problem. Also, if you can't get your printer to come back online, it's probably due to a paper jam. You know the drill: turn off the printer, unplug it, give it time to cool, and open your printer. Now, look to see if there is any ripped paper inside your printer. Follow your printer's documentation to remove the paper out. Remove your paper and reload it according to your manual's instructions. Never overfill the paper tray or allow the paper eject tray (where the paper comes out of the printer) to overflow.

Remember to use high-quality laser paper. Other kinds of paper can jam more frequently. Spending more money for better paper will save you headaches in the long run.

If your printer is online and has paper, you should next check the cable. Turn off your computer and printer. After they're both off, check to make sure the cable connecting the computer and printer isn't loose. If it is loose, push it in firmly and try again. You might find you have to use clasps or miniature screws to fasten the cable into place; use these tools. They're not there simply for decoration.

Many applications allow you to choose a printer for its output; make sure your program is printing to the right printer. If you're using a Windows operating system, most applications allow you to choose a printer in the Print window. After you open the Print window (by using the Print command), make sure your application is using the printer you want it to use. If your printer isn't listed in the window, you will need to install the driver. If you don't have a driver for your printer, and one isn't available in your operating system, see our "Finding a Lost Printer Driver" sidebar in the "Troubleshooting Inkjet Printers" section for help on where to find a driver.

If none of these suggestions resolves the problem, try to print with another application or print a test page if your printer driver allows it. Refer to your documentation for more help.

If you use Windows 95/98, you can access your printer driver from the Start menu by selecting Settings ➢ Printers (see Figure 23.19). In the Printers window, right-click your printer's icon, then select Properties from the context menu that appears. You should be able to print a test page from one of the driver's menus. If the test page is printed, it means you need to check the printing options within your applications or that your printer cannot handle the load you're giving it. See the next section on what to do if your printer can't handle your print jobs.

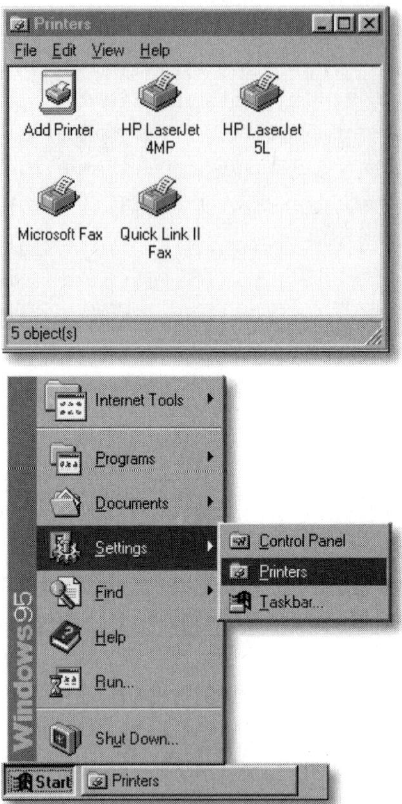

FIGURE 23.19: Use your Start button to get to the Printers window in Windows 95/98. This gives the user more control over installed printers.

It's also a good idea to check out your operating system's printer control mechanism, which is the window or the control box that allows you to control your printer. Under Windows 3.*x*, the mechanism is the Print Manager that appears when you try to print a document. If the Print Manager doesn't appear or doesn't have any printing jobs listed in it when you open it, then your applications are not working correctly. Check your applications' print options.

For Windows 95/98 users, the equivalent to the Print Manager is the Printer Control window, which can be accessed by from the Start menu by selecting Settings then Printers. Double-click the printer icon to see its listings of printing tasks, or you can right-click the icon to make sure the printer is not paused. The printer is paused if there is a checkmark next to Pause Printing. To restart a paused printer, click the Pause Printing listing. You can control most of your printer's operations from this window, including purging (deleting a print task) bad print jobs. Click the listing of the job you want to delete, then press Delete. The listing should disappear.

When the above suggestions don't help matters, there is a small probability that your cable might be bad. If you have another cable on hand, substitute it. Again, make sure your printer and computer are both off before you change the cord. Refer to your documentation for more assistance.

Printing Amnesia

If your printer takes a long time to print graphics and font-heavy documents, you could have a memory problem; your printer and computer probably don't have enough memory capacity between them to handle the work. You will know for sure if your printer can more easily print small graphics or plain text documents that use only one font.

To make your printer print fast, you can reduce the printing resolution, for instance, from 600 dots per inch (dpi) to 300dpi. Decrease the printer's resolution settings like this allow the printer to produce output much more easily.

In Windows 95/98, you usually can set your printer's resolution by altering its driver's settings. Click the Start button and select Printers from the Settings menu. Right-click your printer's icon and select Properties. Click through the tabs at the top of the window to find the resolution controls. Set your printer's resolution to a lower number, if possible, then click OK.

Changing the resolution in Windows 3.*x* is just as easy. First, open your Control Panel group by double-clicking it. Then, double-click the Printers icon. This will bring up the Printers window. Click the listing of the printer for which you would like to change the settings; then click the Setup button on the right side of the window. At this point, within the Setup window that appears, you will probably see the resolution controls; if this is the case, reset the resolution, then click OK or Close to continue and, after that, close the Printers box.

If you don't see the resolution settings when you open the Setup window, you should try the different buttons in the box; the resolution controls are probably hidden in one of the subordinate dialog boxes. If you run into trouble, refer to your documentation.

To enable your printer to print at high resolutions, your computer must have sufficient memory and disk space because most present operating systems use virtual memory, which is a technique in which the operating system uses the hard drive to store necessary information that won't fit in random access memory (RAM), which is the main type of memory that is read from and written to by the microprocessor and hardware.

Typically, the more RAM a computer has, the more information it can handle at one time, and it handles that information faster. When printing at high resolutions in Windows 3.*x*, you need at least 4MB of RAM, but 8MB or more is preferred. In Windows 95/98, you need at least 8MB, but 16MB or more is best.

Make sure your operating system has at least 50MB of virtual memory. Even better, allow it to control its own virtual memory settings. Of course, to use 50MB of disk space, your computer must have 50MB available on the hard drive. If you've fallen to less than 50MB of free space, transfer some files to disks, add a new hard drive, or remove some programs you don't use very often. Also, you can erase temporary files and Internet downloads that you no longer need.

How much memory your computer needs depends upon your operating system. If you're using Windows 95, you need at least 8MB of memory, though many programs won't run well with less than 16MB. Even more memory is even better. If you're using Windows 3.*x*, you need at least 4MB, but for graphics, you should really have 8MB or more. Adding memory is generally the most cost-effective way to improve performance on a computer that isn't obsolete. (By *obsolete*, we mean any computer with a processor that is slower than a 486-class system. If you're still using a 386-class or older processor, consider upgrading because you can't take full advantage of any Windows operating system.)

Another step you can take is to expand the memory in your printer. Many users don't realize most graphics-capable printers have memory inside, much like a PC. This memory comes in cartridge or card form and gives your printer the power it needs to take on difficult jobs without relying on the PC to handle all of the memory-intensive processing. Generally, printers come with enough memory to do basic jobs such as text and limited graphics. Of course, printers designed especially for graphics will come with a lot of memory, to allow for very demanding jobs. Most of the time, laser printers have space for additional memory to allow users to boost their printing power.

Expanding your printer's memory is a relatively easy undertaking. Obviously, refer to your documentation before you proceed. First, open your printer's memory compartment to ascertain that there is room for more memory. (The compartment is probably in the back of your printer. You will probably have to take out some screws to remove the compartment cover.)

You don't want to buy more memory for your printer before you're sure there is room, even if the documentation says there is plenty. Second, you will need to purchase the memory cartridges or cards for your printer. Before you buy anything, make sure you know which kind of memory works with your printer. Cartridges and memory cards are not necessarily interchangeable; check with your printer's vendor and your documentation to make sure you're getting the right kind of memory.

Finally, you just slide the memory into the printer, making sure you follow the instructions in the documentation explicitly. If you ever feel uncomfortable in the process, it might be wise to have a professional perform the installation for you.

If your printer doesn't have any more room for additional memory, sometimes you can take out the existing memory cards and replace them with higher-capacity cards. It may seem like a waste to dump perfectly good memory, but sometimes this is your best option for expanding your printer's capacity. Check with your vendor for more information.

Wading through Blotches

If your printer is printing poorly or with the wrong format, there are many possible culprits. If the quality of print is too light, the problem is probably your toner cartridge. (Again, check your documentation to make sure you don't do anything to harm your printer.) Turn off your printer, open it, and remove your cartridge. More likely, it is running low, so you'll need to shake it or change it. See our instructions earlier in this article.

Sometimes drivers aren't particularly well-made when they are released by the manufacturer. If you're experiencing problems with your printer, it might be worth checking with your computer's manufacturer to see if there is a more current driver, particularly if your printer is part of a new line.

If the text is clear but garbled or in the wrong position on the page, you'll want to make sure your applications are using the correct driver. Check the destination printer in the application's print window (the one that opens when you give the print command). Does the listing match your printer's name exactly? If it doesn't, you should install the proper driver. If you don't have a driver for your printer and one isn't available in your operating system, see the "Finding a Lost Printer Driver" sidebar in the "Troubleshooting Inkjet Printers" section.

If you're not satisfied with the printing output, and the output basically matches what you see on your computer screen, evaluate the paper you're using. Some kinds of paper do not work well with laser printers because of the intense heat the printers produce. You can tell this is particularly true if the paper smells burnt or is curled when it exits the printer. Try higher quality laser or photocopy paper to see if that improves the quality of the output. If it does, you know to stop printing with the paper you previously had been using.

Finally, if your output includes blotches or streaks, your printer might not be clean. Refer to your printer's documentation. You might need to change your cartridge, or you might need to have your computer professionally repaired.

Your Software Chauffeur

All printers require the correct driver to run in a Windows environment. You might find that your printer doesn't have the appropriate driver installed and that your version of Windows doesn't make the correct driver available. If you have the disks that came with your printer, the driver is probably on one of them; follow the documentation instructions on installing it.

In any event, installation of a driver depends upon your operating system and your printer's documentation. Most laser printer manufacturers include special tools to go with their printers. Of course, these require special installation. Check your printer's documentation (and your operating system's documentation) for more assistance. If your operating system comes with multiple drivers, and your driver isn't listed, and you don't have a driver disk, see the "Finding a Lost Printer Driver" sidebar in the "Troubleshooting Inkjet Printers" section.

For single-color graphics and text, the laser printer cannot be beaten. If your printer comes from a decent manufacturer, it should provide you with the printing capabilities that you need for many years. Just keep it clean and be smart, and you should avoid trips to the repair shop.

Are You Experienced?

Now you can...

☑ **troubleshoot just about anything!**

SKILL 24

Tips and Tricks

- Tips on systems
- Tips on input devices
- Tips on scanners
- Tips on storage devices
- Tips on audio and video components
- Tips on printers
- Tips on modems
- Tips on working online

This section is not only for the computing users who want to learn anything and everything about hardware, inside and out, it's also for those of you who don't want to waste any more time dealing with their computing hardware than they have to. For those of you in the latter category, and you know who you are, we included our top tips about everything from preventative maintenance to getting the maximum fuel efficiency out of your long hardware miles. For the enthusiastic computing users out there, we made sure we included several enlightening tips to make your computing experience even more enjoyable than it already is, as well as a few extra tips you can add to your list of trivia questions.

Systems

Some of these are pretty intuitive, and some will be new to you—and will save you money in the long run!

- **Give your case some space.** Fresh air needs to flow through your computer's case to dissipate the heat generated by your microprocessor, motherboard, power supply, and the other devices it contains. Place your case in a spot where it can get plenty of fresh, cool room air. Avoid putting it in spots where it will recirculate the warm exhaust air.
- **Adopt an open door policy.** Specially designed computer desks and work stations feature compartments for the computer case. These compartments are great for keeping dust out of your computer when it's not in use, plus it helps to keep your work area looking neat and professional. But make sure that fresh air can flow in and out of the space so the case doesn't recirculate warm exhaust air. If necessary, open the door to the cubbyhole when you use the PC so fresh air can enter and warm exhaust air can exit.
- **Dust off that dust cover.** If your computer case sits on the floor, a table top, or in some other open space, invest a few dollars in a dust cover. The cover will keep dust and other contaminants (such as spilled coffee, hair spray, or animal hair) out of the case when the computer is not in use. Be certain, however, to remove the dust cover when using the computer.
- **Keep your expansion slots covered.** Computers are designed to draw air in to their cases to cool their components and then to expel the used air. So air can flow through the case the way the designer intended, make certain that the expansion slots on the back of your PC are always covered (by either an expansion card or a slot cover).

- **Dust your case regularly.** Dust your computer case and monitor at least once a month; do it even more often if your work area is particularly prone to dust build-up. Dust attracts more dust and it all can eventually find its way inside your computer case. Don't use furniture polish on your electronics, though. Use a dusting product designed especially for electronics, such as Endust for Electronics or STATX, and a clean soft cloth. Do *not* use these products on the interior of your computer case, however.
- **Clean inside your case, too.** Open up your computer case every two or three months and give it a good blast of compressed air to remove dust build-up from the motherboard, single in-line memory modules (SIMMs), and other hardware components.
- **No static, please.** Even the smallest jolt of static electricity can ruin a microprocessor, SIMM, or other essential piece of computer circuitry. Before opening your computer case for any reason, ground yourself to remove any static charge built up on your body. You can discharge the static electricity using specially designed grounding strips, or simply by touching something else before touching your computer.
- **Beware of winter static build-up.** The same warm, dry air that causes your skin to dry up and crack during winter, also promotes static electricity. Be especially careful to discharge the built-up static charges when working on your PC during cold weather months.
- **Unplug before uncovering your case.** Before removing the case to work on a computer, always unplug the power socket from the source—either the wall outlet, the power strip, or the surge protector. And make certain all of the devices attached to the computer (including the monitor, printer, and external modem) are also unplugged. Don't rely on simply turning off the power strip or surge protector.
- **Don't plug devices into the computer when its power is on.** Never plug in a mouse or keyboard into a computer when it is turned on. It could fry your computer's motherboard.
- **Let your PC cool down before repairs.** Wait at least five minutes after unplugging a computer before opening the case. That will give the microprocessor, power supply, and other components time to cool down.

- **Give your PC a firm foundation.** PCs aren't nearly as delicate as you might think. Nevertheless, it's a good idea to place them on a solid, steady surface where they're not likely to get bumped or jolted while in use. And once you turn on a PC, never move it—not even a fraction of an inch. Moving an operating PC can damage the hard drive.
- **Give your cables plenty of room.** Give your PC case plenty of clearance in the back for the electrical cable, monitor cable, keyboard cable, printer cable, and so on. If you have to bend the cables severely to fit between the socket and the wall, you're causing unnecessary wear and tear on the sockets and cords.
- **Good connections all around.** Take extra care and go the extra step by using the screws or thumbscrews on the cables to attach the plugs into the sockets, it'll assure a better connection and minimize wear.
- **What is your PC setup?** How much do you *really* know about your computer's hardware and software? Do you know what version of Basic Input/Output System (BIOS) software it uses? And how much random access memory (RAM) does it have? This is really important stuff to know when you call for technical support or install new hardware. Ironically, you may not find this information in the documentation that came with your computer because manufacturers continue to make minor changes to PCs, long after the manuals have been printed. But the operators' manual will tell you how to use a utility program that will list all of your computer's hardware and key software, including the operating system version. Launch this setup utility and make a word-for-word record of all of the PC's settings for later reference. (See Figure 24.1.)
- **How to set up your setup.** Find out from your computer's operating manual how to launch the setup utility. Some PCs require you to punch a specific key (F10) during a specific instance during the Power On Self Test (POST). Others allow you to enter the setup from your C:\ prompt using a combination of keystrokes, such as pressing the Ctrl+Alt+Esc keys simultaneously.
- **Reinstalling your PC's setup.** Your computer's setup is stored in a memory chip called a complementary metal-oxide semiconductor (CMOS), which is powered by its battery. If the battery dies, the computer won't boot up without the setup information from the CMOS. If you have a record of the setup, however, you can use the setup utility to manually type in the setup information and boot up the PC yourself.

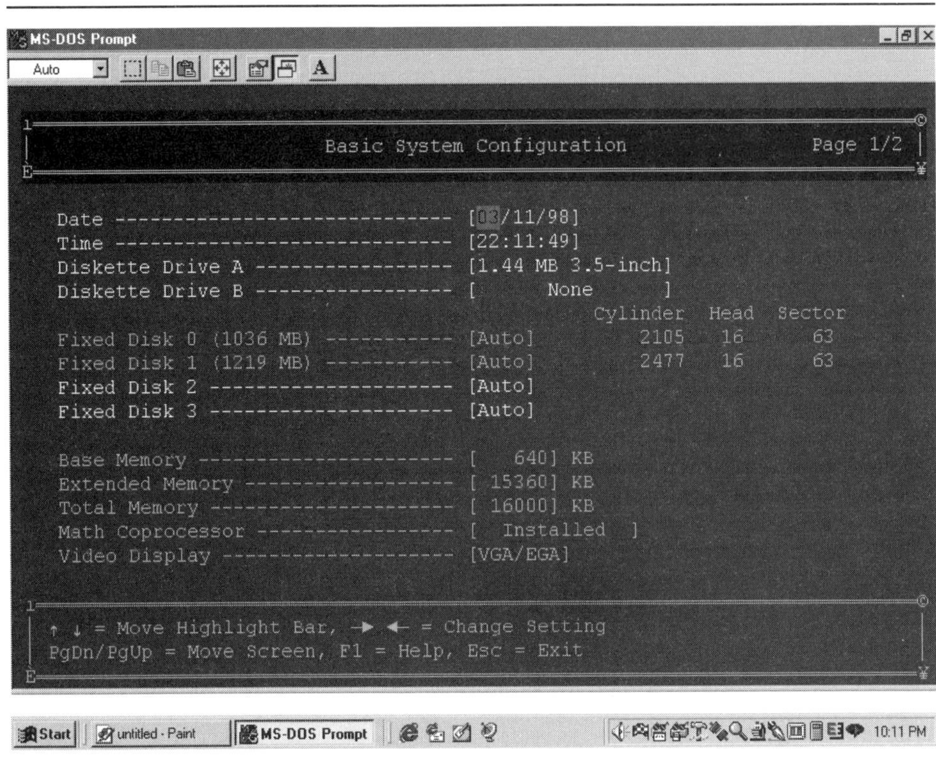

FIGURE 24.1: The BIOS will give you helpful information about your system.

- **Know your PC's interrupt request settings.** Many computer components communicate directly with the microprocessor chip. If they all communicated at once, though, the signals would collide and the computer would freeze up. To avoid this, the computer uses interrupt request lines (IRQs) to assign priorities to messages from different pieces of hardware. Windows 95 and new Plug-and-Play peripherals automatically assign IRQs to avoid conflicts, but older operating systems and peripherals sometimes use the same IRQ at the same time and crash the computer. Make a list of your IRQ assignments to check for potential conflicts and to avoid conflicts when installing new hardware. You can find a list of your computer's devices and the IRQs assigned to them by opening the Control Panel, then accessing the System utility in the Windows 3.*x* operating system. In Windows 95, click the Start button, then access Settings ➢ Control Panel ➢ System ➢ Device Manager. (See Figure 24.2.)

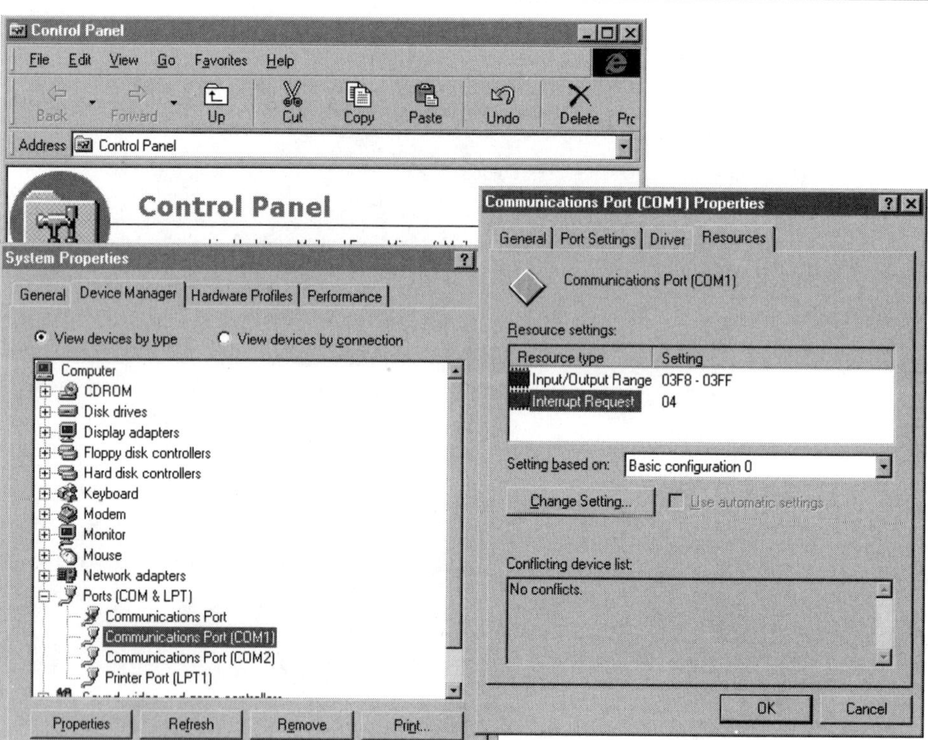

FIGURE 24.2: Check IRQ settings in the Device Manager.

- **Know how to share IRQs.** Sometimes, your computer just doesn't have enough IRQs to go around. If you must use one IRQ for two devices, make certain they are two devices that aren't likely to access the microprocessor at the same time. For example, a scanner and a modem might peacefully coexist on the same IRQ as long as you don't use both at the same time.
- **Update your ROM-BIOS.** The BIOS controls communications between your microprocessor and all other computer components, from the keyboard to the hard drive. As new and improved components are created, computer manufacturers create new and improved BIOS software to work with them. Upgrading the BIOS will improve the way your computer works and also fix many bugs that were discovered after your computer was built! Older computers stored the BIOS on a read-only memory (ROM) chip (called ROM-BIOS) that

can't be upgraded. These chips have to be replaced with new ROM-BIOS chips. Newer PCs, though, use a flash ROM that can be upgraded with software available from the computer manufacturer. This type of software can usually be downloaded for free from the manufacturer's site on the World Wide Web, which will also provide detailed instructions on installing the new BIOS.

- **RAM up your PC's speed.** Probably the quickest, easiest, and cheapest way to boost your computer's performance is to increase its RAM by adding SIMMs. SIMMs are small circuit boards that contain RAM chips that plug into special slots on the motherboard. SIMMs store information on microchips and can access the information more quickly than a hard drive. All the information on a SIMM is erased when the computer is turned off, however. How much RAM you need depends on your operating system and the kinds of programs you use. A computer with Windows 3.*x* that is used primarily for word processing will probably operate just fine with 8MB of RAM. A computer with Windows 95 that is used for desktop publishing or database management probably needs a minimum of 32MB. All software packages describe exactly how much RAM the program needs to operate.

- **Wait just a nanosecond.** The speed of SIMMs is calculated by the time it takes to retrieve information measured in nanoseconds, or one-billionth of a second. Typical SIMMs are available in speeds of 60, 70, or 80 nanoseconds. The lower the number, the faster the SIMM.
- **Know your RAM.** Before adding SIMMs to your computer, see what kind of RAM your computer uses. Older PCs use Fast Page Mode (FPM) RAM. Newer PCs are capable of using the faster Extended Data Output (EDO) RAM or burst EDO RAM. The newest computers are equipped with synchronous DRAM (for dynamic RAM, also called synchDRAM), which is faster yet. Don't confuse any of these, however, video RAM (VRAM), a special type of RAM chip designed to work with your computer's video controller.
- **Mix and match SIMMs.** SIMMs are typically available in capacities of 8MB, 16MB, and 32MB with different speeds. You can install SIMMs of different capacities. For example, you could install two 8MB SIMMs and one 16MB SIMM for a total of 32MB of RAM.
- **Use memory banks to segregate and mix SIMMs.** How much RAM you can add to your computer depends on the number of SIMM slots on the

computer's motherboard. Moreover, computers group slots in banks. A typical computer might have two SIMM banks, each with two SIMM slots—enough slots for four SIMMs. Use the banks to segregate different types of SIMMs. For example, you can put ordinary FPM SIMMs in one bank and EDO SIMMs in the other. Or you can put 8MB SIMMs in one bank and 16MB SIMMs in the other. Consult your computer's documentation for detailed information on how to mix and match SIMMs.

- **Open up a branch memory bank.** You can increase the number of SIMM slots on your computer by using a SIMM doubler, a smaller circuit board that fits into a SIMM slot and has connections for two more SIMMs. SIMM doublers (such as the SIMM 72 Plus 4) are available through specialized computer catalogs and on the Web.
- **Recycle old SIMMs.** Newer PCs use SIMMs and SIMM slots with 72 connectors, while older PCs use SIMMs and slots with just 30 connectors (or "pins"). Normally, you can't use older 30-pin SIMMs in 72-pin SIMM slots. You can, however, buy a device that allows you to plug 2, 4, or 8, 30-pin SIMMs into a small circuit board and then insert that into a 72-pin SIMM slot. Again, these devices (such as the SimmStack) are available through specialized computer catalogs and on the Web.
- **Don't bother to upgrade onboard RAM.** Really, really old personal computers didn't use SIMMs, but instead soldered the RAM chips onto the computer's motherboard. Forget about replacing or upgrading the RAM on these dinosaurs unless you're really handy with a soldering iron, and even then we doubt it would be worth your trouble.
- **Add video RAM to accelerate monitor performance.** Older personal computers used the same RAM to process data that they used to process video images displayed on the PC's monitor. For several years now, PCs have used separate and distinct RAM to process video. This video RAM or VRAM can be installed on chips within your computer's motherboard, or on the video controller itself. Many computer delays occur because of the time it takes for the video controller to process data into a video image, especially for video-intensive programs such as desktop publishing or 3-D graphics. Adding VRAM—usually by swapping a low capacity 1MB VRAM chip with a high capacity 2MB or 4MB VRAM chip—will eliminate or minimize these video processing delays. And it will cost just a fraction of the price of buying a new video controller.

- **Disable onboard controllers to add faster plug-in controllers.** Some manufacturers build video controllers (which convert data into the video images displayed on monitors), audio controllers (also known as sound cards or audio boards), fax/modems, and other devices right into the motherboard. Other manufacturers use devices that plug into the computer's expansion bus. Devices built into the motherboard (onboard controllers) keep down the cost of computers, but have inherent limitations. You can disable onboard devices by changing jumper switches on the motherboard. Once the device is disabled, you can replace it by plugging a new controller into the computer's expansion bus. If the documentation that came with your PC doesn't explain how to disable an onboard controller, contact the manufacturer's technical support operation.

- **Replace the onboard video controller.** If your computer is more than a year old and you make extensive use of graphics-intensive programs (such as full-motion video or graphics programs), consider disabling the onboard video controller and installing an accelerated video controller.

- **Replace the onboard fax/modem.** If you use your computer to surf the Web, consider disabling the onboard fax/modem and installing a faster internal modem or a faster external modem.

- **Push your bus to the speed limit.** When you upgrade your computer by installing expansion cards (also known as expansion boards) in your expansion bus, purchase devices that make maximum use of the bus speed. Newer computers are equipped with Video Electronics Standards Association buses (also known as VL buses or a VESA local bus) and the newest computers are equipped with Peripheral Component Interconnect (PCI) buses. Both VL and PCI computers transfer data faster than the older Industry Standard Architecture (ISA) buses. An expansion card designed to fit into the slots on an ISA expansion bus will work on a computer's VL or PCI bus, but it won't work any faster. To get the true benefits of the VL or PCI buses, you'll need to install VL or PCI cards. A VL or PCI expansion card won't fit into an ISA expansion slot. A PCI computer may include both ISA and PCI expansion slots. (Ditto for a computer with a VL bus.) If you want to replace onboard controllers with expansion cards, use the high speed slots (PCI or VL) for the video controller or hard disk drive controller. Consult your computer's documentation for more information.

- **Speedier serial connections.** Computers use the serial port (also known as a communications port) to communicate in 2-bit chunks of data with devices including external modems. Computers use a universal asynchronous receiver/transmitter (UART) chip to convert 8-bit, 16-bit, and 32-bit chunks of data into 2-bit chunks that can be transmitted through the serial port. If your computer uses an older 8250 or 16450 UART chip, you can speed up the serial connection by replacing it with a newer 16550 or 16550A UART chip. Your computer manual should include a diagram of the motherboard and a description of a UART.

- **Install a high speed serial communications card.** Some computers' UART chips are soldered to the motherboard. Other computers combine the UART function into a *chipset* (a single chip designed to do the work of two or more chips), which can't be replaced without affecting a whole range of functions. In these instances, you can speed up your serial port by installing a high speed serial communications card in a slot on the expansion bus. These high speed serial cards bypass the UART and are available through most computer stores, computer catalogs, and various Web sites for $25 to $100.
- **Use an internal fax/modem.** If your serial port is causing a bottleneck between your computer and your high-speed external modem, consider installing an internal modem in a slot on the computer's expansion board. Just like a high speed serial communications card, an internal modem bypasses the UART and enables the fax/modem to operate at its full capacity.
- **The SCSI option.** The Small Computer System Interface (SCSI, pronounced *scuzzy*) enables a computer to connect up to 16 peripherals (such as external modems, scanners, or storage devices) to a single port. Most IBM-compatible personal computers aren't equipped with SCSI ports, but you can install a SCSI adapter card in your computer's expansion bus. Not only do SCSI ports transfer data faster than conventional parallel or serial ports, but SCSI peripherals are, in general, easier to set up and run than conventional peripherals. (Unfortunately, they also tend to be more expensive.)
- **Install a PC card drive.** If you own both a desktop computer and a laptop computer—and if your laptop is equipped with a PC card slot—consider installing a PC card drive on your desktop computer. PC slots are sockets designed to accept small devices (ranging from modems to network interface cards to hard drives) about the size and shape of a credit card. Installing a PC card slot on your desktop will allow both your desktop and laptop computers to share peripherals.
- **Purchase peripherals with pass-through ports.** With external hard drives, external modems, scanners, printers, and other peripherals, sometimes there are just too many plugs and not enough ports. If your PC is running out of

ports, look for peripherals equipped with pass-through ports. A pass-through port is actually a plug with a port built into its backside. You can piggyback a second plug on a first plug, letting both plugs share the same socket. It's a good solution when two devices aren't likely to access the port simultaneously, such as a scanner (an input device) and a printer (an output device).

- **Pay attention to your power supply.** Your computer uses a transformer, or power supply, to convert 110 volts of alternating current (AC) from your wall socket into 5 or 12 volts of direct current (DC) used by the microprocessor, the hard drive, SIMMs, and the rest of your PC's components. Problems with the power supply can manifest themselves in all kinds of problems with your computer. One strong indication of a malfunctioning or poorly functioning power supply is a loss of your computer's setup information, which is stored in the CMOS chip. The CMOS operates 24 hours a day, 365 days a year, and is powered by a battery that is recharged by the power supply. If the power supply doesn't generate enough power, the CMOS battery will lose its charge and the CMOS will ultimately forget your PC's setup!

- **The grating noise of a power problem.** Another tip-off to a power supply problem is a grinding noise that occurs when the computer starts up, but stops after the computer has warmed up. Although you may suspect a problem with your hard drive, the grinding noise may be coming from the fan that cools the power supply. If the fan isn't working right, the power supply may overheat and burn out. The fan is built into the power supply, so you'll need to replace the entire power supply.
- **Gibberish and a faulty power supply.** Gibberish in the middle of a saved file (caused by a power fluctuation while data was being written to the hard drive) or inexplicable computer crashes are other possible symptoms of a problem with your power supply.
- **Test your power supply with a multimeter.** You can test your power supply using a device called a multimeter, which is available at electronics dealers such as Radio Shack. If your PC's operating manual doesn't explain how to test the power supply, contact the manufacturer's technical support service for instructions.
- **How much power is enough?** Power supplies are rated in terms of the total direct current voltage they can produce, starting at about 150 volts. Each device you install inside your PC's case draws more power. For example,

adding 16MB of RAM can draw an extra 80 volts! A plain PC with a CD-ROM drive, sound capabilities, and 16 MB of RAM needs about 200 volts. Add 5 volts for each additional megabyte of RAM, 15 watts for every additional expansion card, and 30 watts for every additional hard drive. External devices (such as scanners) draw their power directly from the wall socket, however.

- **Impure power problems.** The electricity coming out of your wall socket should provide 110 to 120 volts of AC, but fluctuations in that supply aren't at all uncommon and they can damage your PC. Power surges (also called spikes) can ruin a microprocessor or a modem. Lower-than-optimum power can force your power supply to overwork itself and go bad. If you're concerned about your power supply, check it with a voltmeter (available from Radio Shack and similar stores), or have an electrician check it out.
- **Why PCs and appliances don't mix.** Refrigerators, air conditioners, and other household appliances can draw large amounts of power when they start up. Even smaller appliances such as mixers and vacuum cleaners can affect electrical power. Avoid plugging your computer system into circuits shared by devices that draw large amounts of electricity or that generate electrical interference.
- **Are you grounded?** Like any expensive electrical device, your computer has a power supply chord with a three-prong plug: two for power and one for the ground. But just because your wall socket has three holes doesn't mean that it's properly grounded. If you don't know for a fact that an outlet is properly grounded, have an electrician check it out.
- **Invest in a line conditioner.** If you have problems with your electrical supply, consider purchasing a device called a *line conditioner*. A line conditioner doubles as a surge protector, but also assures a steady, even flow of electricity from the wall socket to your computer system. For the ultimate in protection, invest in a combination line conditioner/universal power supply.
- **Ground your modem.** Modems are as susceptible to power spikes as any other part of your computer system, and can be damaged by even slight electrical surges transmitted through phone lines. Make certain your surge protector includes a phone jack to protect your modem.
- **Inkjets and surge protectors.** Many inkjet printers have a special cleaning cycle that removes ink from the printing heads when the power switch is turned off. But if you plug your inkjet printer into a surge protector—and

use the surge protector to turn the printer on and off—the printer can't complete the cleaning cycle. Instead, turn off your printer and give it a few seconds to complete the cleaning cycle before you turn off the surge protector.

- **A big fan for your microprocessor.** Some computers use a small fan to blow air over the microprocessor and keep it cool. If the fan malfunctions, though, you may not discover the problem until the microprocessor burns out. Check the fan on a periodic basis to make certain it's running properly. If not, replace it with a new fan or a heat sink—a kind of radiator that draws heat away from the microprocessor.
- **Replace the onboard hard disk drive controller.** Another common bottleneck on many computer systems is the device that controls communication between the computer and the hard disk drive. Installing a high-speed disk drive controller can reduce some of the wait, particularly with data-intensive programs such as spreadsheets and databases. (See Figure 24.3.)

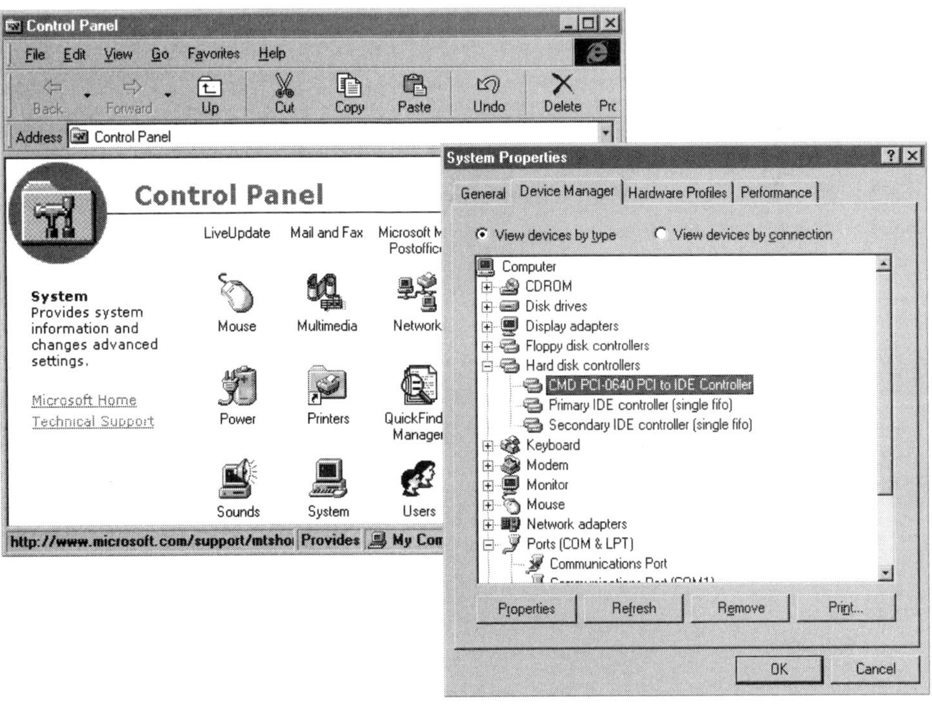

FIGURE 24.3: A new hard disk drive controller can improve speed.

- **The ultimate upgrade: microprocessor transplant.** Just as a heart transplant can breath new life into a heart patient, installing a new, faster microprocessor can breath new life into a sluggish computer. But upgrading the microprocessor may require a host of other changes, including changing the voltage by moving jumper switches on your PC's motherboard; changing the motherboard bus speed by moving jumpers; moving expansion cards; and upgrading the BIOS. You may find it easier and more cost effective to add more RAM, a faster hard drive controller, and a faster, more powerful video controller.

Input Devices

There are a lot of things that can go wrong with input devices, and ergonomics is a big concern these days; our bodies just weren't made for some of this technology! But unless you decide to head for the woods, this is an issue that must be resolved.

Getting Started

These tips should keep you sane.

- **Check your keyboard.** If you're a typing machine, you want maximum comfort and response from your keyboard. To achieve this, make sure the keys are firmly attached and don't require too much force when you're typing.
- **Keep it sturdy.** When purchasing a keyboard, keep in mind that a heavier one is generally sturdier and will be less likely to move around the desk while you are typing.
- **Keyboard placement.** Although many people put their keyboards on their desk in front of their monitor, this may not be the most comfortable position, especially if the height of your desk and/or chair cannot be adjusted. You can purchase a keyboard drawer for around $25 that attaches to the underside of the desk. It might be worth some extra money to purchase a fully adjustable keyboard tray that can swivel, tilt, lift, or lower for maximum comfort. In addition, a keyboard tray keeps your keyboard from getting a damaging knock off your desk.
- **Tip your keyboard.** A slanted keyboard is easier to type on than one lying flat on your desk. Most keyboards have adjustable legs on the underside that can be pulled into place so one end of the keyboard is higher.

- **Consider a split keyboard.** Although it may be challenging to use at first, an ergonomic keyboard, which divides the key layout in two, may give you relief from carpal tunnel syndrome by keeping your elbows a natural distance apart and your wrists straight.
- **Mouse placement.** Try to place your mouse so your arms and hands are in a comfortable, relaxed position. You shouldn't have to stretch to use it. Your forearms should be parallel to the floor and your wrists and hands should be in line with your forearms. The best height for your mouse is 26.5 inches, rather than the 29 inches of the traditional desktop, so you might want to attach a mouse tray on the underside of your desk.
- **External mouse for portables.** A poorly designed pointing device can increase hand and wrist strain. If you will be doing a lot of data entry on the road, bring an external mouse.
- **Pick your mouse carefully.** The market is full of various sizes, shapes, and designs of mice and trackballs. Your mouse or trackball should fit your hand comfortably. Some mice have subtle indentations or texturing that might improve your grip. The placement of buttons on a trackball and the size of the ball are important because if the buttons are too close to the ball, you will be forced to hold your hand at an angle from your forearm, rather than relatively straight, which can cause strain. If possible, try out the mouse or trackball before purchase to check its response and comfort.
- **Move mouse pointer without the mouse.** If you are recovering from a repetitive strain injury caused by the overuse of your mouse, or you want to use your computer without a mouse, you can move the mouse pointer with the numeric keypad on your keyboard. Double-click the Accessibility Options icon in the Control Panel. Click the Mouse tab and select Use MouseKeys.

General Use

These tips will help you in your day-to-day work.

- **Get comfortable with your mouse.** If you're using a mouse for the first time, it will take some time before it feels comfortable. To hasten that process, use the Solitaire card game included with Windows to practice your clicks, double-clicks, and dragging skills.
- **Give your mouse a tail.** Normally, the cursor travels without leaving a trail. To make the cursor more visible as it moves across the screen, double-click

the Mouse icon in the Control Panel and choose the Motion tab. Select Show Pointer Trails and specify the tail length.

- **Keep your finger on your mouse.** Have you ever been in the middle of clicking and dragging an object across the screen when your mouse ran out of maneuvering room? Don't take your finger off the mouse and start over. As long as you keep pressing down with your finger, you can pick the mouse up and move it to a new location to continue your drag-and-drop operation.
- **Keep that joystick stuck, plus other helpful tips.** Desk stability is important. You don't want your joystick to bounce around on your desk in the heat of action. If you want your joystick to adhere to your desk, try using double-sided sticky tape or Velcro on your desk surface and joystick bottom. To become more comfortable with your joystick if you're a first-time user, check out the information available at `http://www.chproducts.com/FAQ4WEB/CHFAQ.html`.
- **Put your mouse in a pocket.** Are you concerned about where your mouse sleeps when it's not in use? For around $5 you can buy a mouse pocket that attaches to the side of your monitor or other surface.
- **Untangle the mouse cord.** If you've ever wrestled with a tangled mouse cord, you might appreciate a mouse cord holder that provides smoother movement and greater control. Office supply companies sell clips that attach to your mouse pad and mouse pads that include a cord holder.
- **Clip cords together.** If all the cords from your input devices look like a tangled mess behind your desk, organize them with cord clips sold in computer supply stores.
- **Get rid of cords altogether.** Wireless infrared technology lets you point and click without being attached to the system with a cord. A variety of infrared input devices are available and offer freedom of movement and a cord-free environment.
- **Disconnect yourself.** When you are making a presentation, disconnect yourself from the projector by using a wireless mouse or other remote-control pointing device. It will add flexibility and professionalism.
- **Press Esc to cancel a command.** The Esc key, located in the upper-left corner of your keyboard, lets you cancel commands and stop tasks that are underway.

- **Use Windows 95 keys.** The keyboards on newer computers have two keys to the right of the spacebar and one to the left that are used with Microsoft's Windows 95. Pressing one of the keys that looks like the Microsoft Windows logo is like clicking the on-screen Start button. The other key has an icon of a tiny pull-down menu. When you press it, you will open the menu for the current program. As always, press Esc to exit out of a task.
- **Switch between open programs.** Use Alt+Tab to switch between open programs. Hold the Alt key down while pressing Tab. Each time you press Tab, a box will appear displaying the names of the open programs. When you see the one you want, release both keys.
- **Close an open window without a mouse.** You can close an active window by pressing Alt+F4. Once all open windows have been closed, pressing Alt+F4 again will give you the opportunity to shut down your computer.
- **Use the mouse to speed up scroll bars.** In Windows applications, rather than clicking the Up and Down arrows on the scroll bar to move up and down in small increments, click and drag the little box in the middle of the scroll bar. It will move you around the window a lot faster!
- **Perform tasks faster with Ctrl key.** If you are working in a program in Windows, you can often use the Ctrl key with directional arrows to perform tasks faster. For example, in a word processing program, pressing the right arrow (→) alone will move you one character to the right, but pressing Ctrl+right arrow will move you one word to the right.
- **Use keyboard for screen captures.** Take a snapshot of the screen by pressing Print Screen. The image will be copied onto the Windows Clipboard. Copy only the active window by pressing Alt+Print Screen.
- **Try a triple-click.** You've single-clicked. You've double-clicked. But have you triple-clicked? If you have ever needed to select an entire paragraph in a document you should know this little trick. Rather than click and drag, position your cursor in the middle of the paragraph and triple-click.
- **Right-click powers with and without the mouse.** If you are new to Windows 95, pay attention to what right-clicking your mouse can do. Right-clicking an object displays a context-sensitive drop-down menu, so making changes is a breeze! To emulate a right-click from the keyboard and select a right-click menu of commands without using your mouse, press Shift+F10.

- **Using Windows 95 without a mouse.** Sometimes you just don't feel like reaching for your mouse or it simply isn't working properly. In any case, you can press Ctrl+Esc to open the Start menu. Press Alt+spacebar to display the System menu. To switch between buttons on the Taskbar, press Alt+Esc. Press Enter when the button you want is highlighted.

Customizing

There are many ways to customize your setup. Hopefully these tips will get you started.

- **Kids' stuff.** If you have younger children using your computer system, consider purchasing a keyboard, mouse, and/or trackball designed just for smaller hands.
- **Change keyboard sensitivity for children.** Young children may not press hard enough on keys, or they might press too long, resulting in inaccurate and confusing entries. Adjust the keyboard sensitivity by double-clicking the Accessibilities icon in the Control Panel and selecting the Keyboard tab. Click Use FilterKeys and then select Settings. Under Filter Options, select Ignore Quick Keystrokes And Slow Down The Repeat Rate, and click Settings. In the Slackest section, adjust the amount of time that a key must be pressed in order for it to be recognized, anywhere from zero to two seconds. Have your child type into the test area and click OK when the desired rate is obtained. This setting will override any settings in the Keyboard's control panel. (See Figure 24.4.)
- **A toddler's keyboard.** Your toddler doesn't have to understand function keys or the alphabet to use your computer if you use keyboards designed especially for toddlers. For example, the Comfy Activity Center introduces toddlers to computers with brightly colored buttons, color and music keys, a roller and telephone, and interactive children's software. If you don't want to switch between keyboards, their EasyKeys plastic overlays fit over a regular keyboard. For those just learning their ABCs, Kidtech offers My First Keyboard. It's a colorful board with oversized keys in alphabetical order on a flat membrane surface so it is easy to wipe clean.
- **A less confusing keyboard for children.** To a child, the alphabetical keys on a regular keyboard can be lost in an array of function keys and special buttons. Keyboards designed for children, such as kidBoard from KidBoard Inc., use color-coded keys for numbers and letters to help them learn letter and number placement. Different colors for the left- and right-handed keys also encourage them to use both hands while typing.

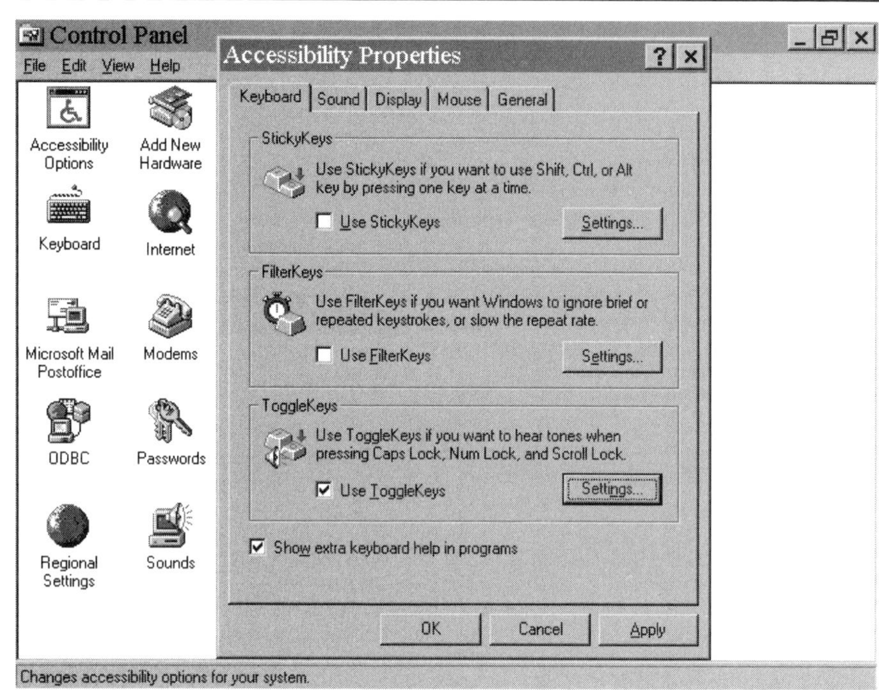

FIGURE 24.4: The FilterKeys setting adjusts the sensitivity of your keyboard.

- **Children may not like mice.** Just because you are comfortable with a mouse doesn't mean young children will be. A trackball might work better for them. Microsoft's EasyBall is a bright yellow, baseball-sized trackball nestled above a large blue button. Designed for children ages 2 to 6, its stationary design separates navigation from button pressing, making it less likely your child will accidentally move the mouse cursor while trying to click an object.
- **Adjust mouse wheel sensitivity.** If your mouse has a wheel, adjust the wheel's sensitivity by clicking the Mouse icon in the Control Panel. Select the Wheel tab and enter a value. For a more sensitive wheel, increase the value to 5; for less sensitivity, enter a 1 or 2.
- **Adjust repeat character delay.** To adjust how much time elapses before a key begins repeating while being held down, double-click the Keyboard icon in the Control Panel. Select the Speed tab and drag the Repeat Delay slider. Test the delay setting by clicking in the box below the slider and holding down a key.

- **Adjust repeat character rate.** To adjust how quickly characters repeat as you hold down a key, double-click the Keyboard icon in the Control Panel. Select the Speed tab and drag the Repeat Rate slider. Test the rate setting by clicking in the box below the slider and holding down a key. (See Figure 24.5.)

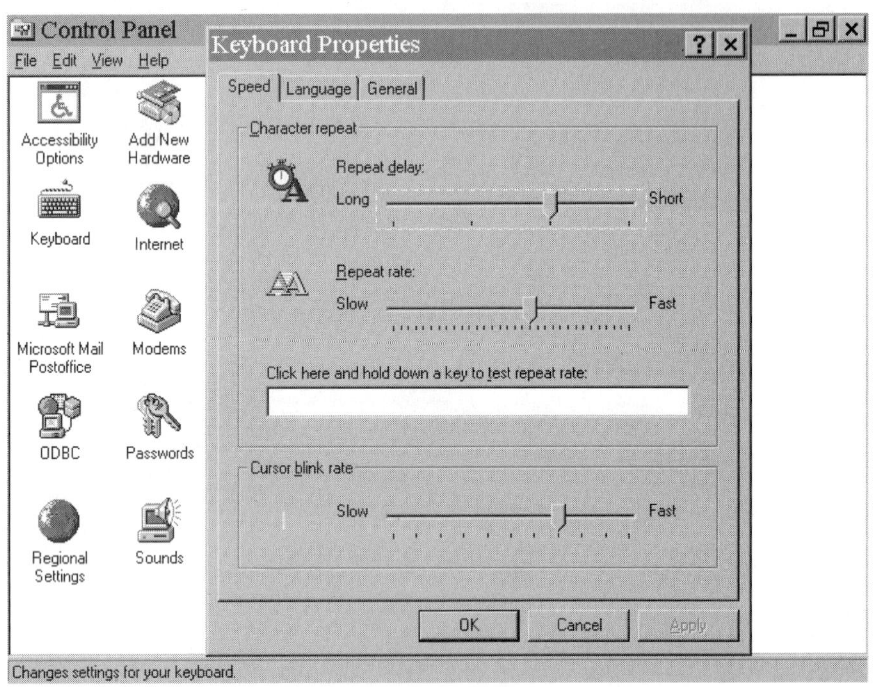

FIGURE 24.5: The slider will adjust character repetition.

- **Change the cursor blink rate.** To change the rate at which the cursor blinks, double-click the Keyboard icon in the Control Panel. Select the Speed tab and use the slider to adjust the cursor blink rate.
- **Change the order of your keys.** You don't have to use the standard QWERTY keyboard layout. A Dvorak keyboard, said to allow faster typing once you become familiar with it, places all vowels and punctuation marks on the left side and all consonants to the right. As an alternative to purchasing this type of keyboard, or if you want different key placements to avoid accidentally pressing certain keys, you can rearrange your keyboard. Pry the keycaps off

with a small flat-bladed screwdriver and put them back on in any order you want. It is essential that you use a remapping program, however, to let your computer know the new arrangement.

- **Adjust mouse double-click speed.** In the Control Panel, double click Mouse to display the Mouse Properties dialog box. Click the Buttons tab; at the bottom is an adjustment area for your double-click speed. By setting it slower or faster, you will change the amount of time that can pass between clicks when you are double-clicking an object.
- **Set up a left-handed mouse.** In the Control Panel, double-click Mouse to display the Mouse Properties dialog box. The Buttons tab lets lefties switch buttons on the mouse by choosing Left-handed in the Button Configuration section. When the buttons are switched, the right-mouse button becomes the primary button used to "click" and the left-mouse button becomes the secondary button. (See Figure 24.6.)

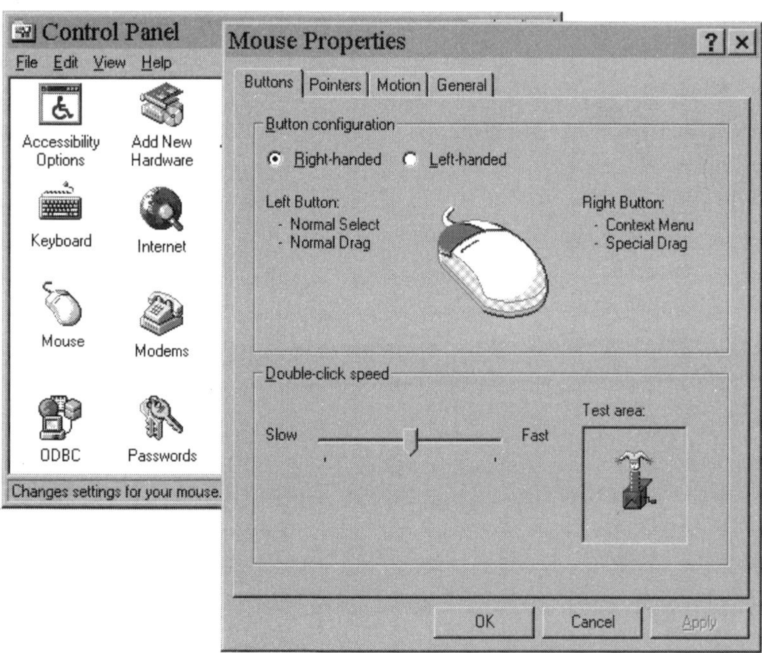

FIGURE 24.6: Lefties can change their mouse configuration to work in a more natural fashion.

- **Change your mouse pointer.** Double-click Mouse in the Control Panel. Select the Pointers tab, and then choose a pointer scheme from the drop-down list under Scheme.
- **Change cursor movement speed.** To adjust the speed at which your cursor moves on the screen, double-click the Mouse icon in the Control Panel. Select the Motion tab. Use the slider under Pointer Speed to make the movement slower or faster.
- **Make the cursor easier to see.** Add a pointer trail to make your cursor easier to see. Double-click the Mouse icon in the Control Panel. Choose the Motion tab and select Show Pointer Trails. Use the slider to adjust the length of the trail.
- **Use a language other than English.** In Windows 95, double-click the Keyboard icon in the Control Panel and then click the Language tab. Select the language you want to use or click Add to add another language to the list. You may have to use the setup disk to load the necessary files. Certain languages may require you to install multilanguage support; open the Add/Remove dialog box and make sure a checkmark appears beside the language you want to use.
- **Use the Accessibility options.** To take advantage of the input device options designed for people with physical impairments, double-click the Accessibility Options icon in the Control Panel. If this component is not available, click Add/Remove Programs in the Control Panel, select the Windows Setup tab, click Accessibility Options, then click OK to install. In the Accessibility Options dialog box, click the Keyboard tab to display the available options and select the ones you want to enable.
- **Type with StickyKeys.** Customize Windows to recognize key combinations, such as Ctrl+P, even when the keys aren't pressed simultaneously. Double-click the Accessibility Options icon in the Control Panel. Click the Keyboard tab and check the StickyKeys setting box.
- **Slow the repeat rate.** Use FilterKeys to ignore brief or repeated keystrokes, or to slow down the repeat rate. Double-click the Accessibility Options icon in the Control Panel. Click the Keyboard tab and check the FilterKeys setting box.

- **Audible notice of locked keys.** If you make typing mistakes because you press the Caps Lock key instead of the Shift key, use ToggleKeys to emit a tone when Caps Lock, Num Lock, or Scroll Lock are pressed. Double-click the Accessibility Options icon in the Control Panel. Click the Keyboard tab and check the ToggleKeys setting box.
- **Create hot keys**. You can assign hot keys so you can switch between open programs and documents by pressing a key combination. Right-click the program's shortcut and choose Properties. Click the Shortcut tab and in the key line, press the keys you want to use, such as Ctrl+Shift, and click OK. To test it, open the program, minimize it, and press the key combination to open it back up again.
- **More intelligent mice.** Look beyond the basic mouse that came with your system. It's not representative of what's on the market. Mice come in many designs with multiple, programmable buttons and numerous features that make operations, such as surfing the World Wide Web, much easier.
- **Take it slow during software calibration.** Some games will request joystick calibration before you begin to play. Read and follow the instructions that came with that particular game because some are specific as to what buttons you must press, and in which order.
- **Go digital.** Tired of joystick calibration routines? Take a look at the digital joysticks entering the market. They use a different technology than analog joysticks and some digital models have eliminated the need for recalibration.
- **Select the right gaming device.** When playing games, some problems are caused by choosing the wrong joystick. One of your first considerations should be the type of games you want to play and whether you are a casual or competitive game player. This will determine the features you need on your joystick, such as programmable buttons. Check the product boxes of both gaming devices and game software to see of there are compatibility lists to help guide you.
- **Simultaneous play by multiple players.** If you want to have multiple players on a system, be aware that analog technology does not allow for simultaneous play by more than two players, and if two analog joysticks are used on one system, one of the sticks has limited functionality. Digital technology provides opportunities for simultaneous play by multiple players, however, not all game ports will support digital controllers so you may have to purchase a separate game card.

Fixing Problems

Here's the meat of the matter: What to do when something goes wrong?

- **Check your keyboard's connection.** As simple as it may seem, a common cause of an unresponsive keyboard is an improper connection. There are two connections, one directly into your keyboard and another into your computer. Do *not* plug or unplug any input device while your computer is running. Doing so could temporarily disable the device or damage its circuitry or connector.
- **Free up sticking keys.** To make sure all of your keys are responding properly and are not sticking, turn your system off and disconnect your keyboard. Then press and gently wiggle each key to make sure it is moving freely. If you need to remove any keycaps, do so by carefully prying them off with a small screwdriver or similar tool; reattach them by setting each in place and pressing down firmly.
- **Unlock your keys.** If your keyboard is working but doing strange things, check to see if you have inadvertently pressed a key such as Caps Lock or Num Lock. On many keyboards, this is indicated by a green light on the corner of the keyboard.
- **Text insert problems.** If you seem to be typing over text instead of inserting new text, you may have pressed the Insert key. To deactivate Insert, simply press it again.
- **Unresponsive numeric keypad.** If the numeric keypad isn't responding, you probably just need to engage the Num Lock key so the keypad enters numbers rather than cursor movements.
- **New keys for old PCs.** Older keyboards generally used a different connector than those found on newer ones. If you have purchased a newer keyboard for use on an older system and the connector doesn't match your older PC, you can buy an adapter for around $10 at a computer supply store.
- **Give your mouse a pad.** A mouse needs a spacious, flat desktop surface so the ball on its underside can move freely. Look for a mouse pad with a natural rubber base to avoid skids. A plastic pad should be slightly textured so it's not too slick.

- **Check the mouse cable.** A bad cable can cause your mouse to act strangely, so make sure the cable leading from your mouse to the computer is free of obstructions and damaging, heavy objects. If the cable is sharply bent, it could develop creases or breaks over time.
- **Don't be irked by IRQs.** If you are installing input devices, their Interrupt Request (IRQ) setting must be set to one that is not already in use. This helps to avoid conflicts with other hardware devices. If you are not sure what IRQs are in use, click the System icon in your Control Panel, and then choose the Device Manager tab to display a list of devices connected to your system. Click the Print button to print a list of all devices and the system summary. Included in this list will be an IRQ Summary.
- **Adding a joystick to your system.** For a joystick to work properly, your system must recognize it is there. If you do not see a Joystick icon in the Control Panel, you need to add your PC game port as new hardware. In the Control Panel, click the Add New Hardware icon to open the Add New Hardware Wizard. Follow its instructions to add the game port or new game card as a device. When it is finished, you will need to shut down and restart your computer.
- **Calibrate your joystick.** Calibration is a process used to adjust the mechanical and electrical alignment of the joystick itself. In the Control Panel, double-click the Joystick icon to display the Joystick Properties dialog box. Under Current Joystick, select the appropriate number. Click the down arrow under Joystick Selection, scroll through the list, and select the appropriate driver for your joystick. If your joystick has trim dials, physically center the notch on each. Click the Calibrate button and carefully follow each step of the on-screen instructions for calibrating your joystick. Click the Test button to test the joystick's calibration. If they are not responding properly, recalibrate. (See Figure 24.7.)
- **Is your joystick not connected properly?** If you get a message that your joystick is not connected properly, you may have selected a joystick with more axes than Windows can correctly detect. Double-check your Joystick Selection in the Joystick Properties dialog box. Also, make sure your Gameport Joystick setting is enabled and it does not have an Input/Output conflict. (See Figure 24.8.)

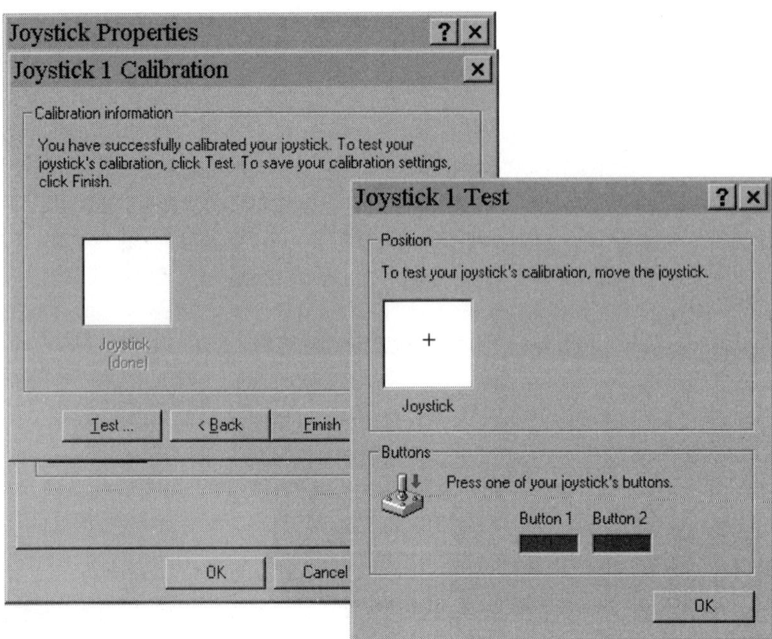

FIGURE 24.7: The Joystick Properties dialog box contains the controls for your joystick.

- **Control joystick drift.** Drifting or rolling indicates a loss of joystick input control. To determine if the drifting is caused by a certain game, try another game to see if the problem is consistent. If your joystick is erratic only in certain games, check each game's manual for information relating to joystick setup and game cards. You might have to run each of the game's software calibration or joystick setup program again.
- **Joystick annoyances.** In addition to joystick features, pay close attention to your comfort level, especially during long hours of play. Check to see if movement is rough as you rotate the stick, or if the rubber boot is noisy, or if there are other minor annoyances. Problems that seem minor at the time of purchase can become very annoying in the midst of an intense game.

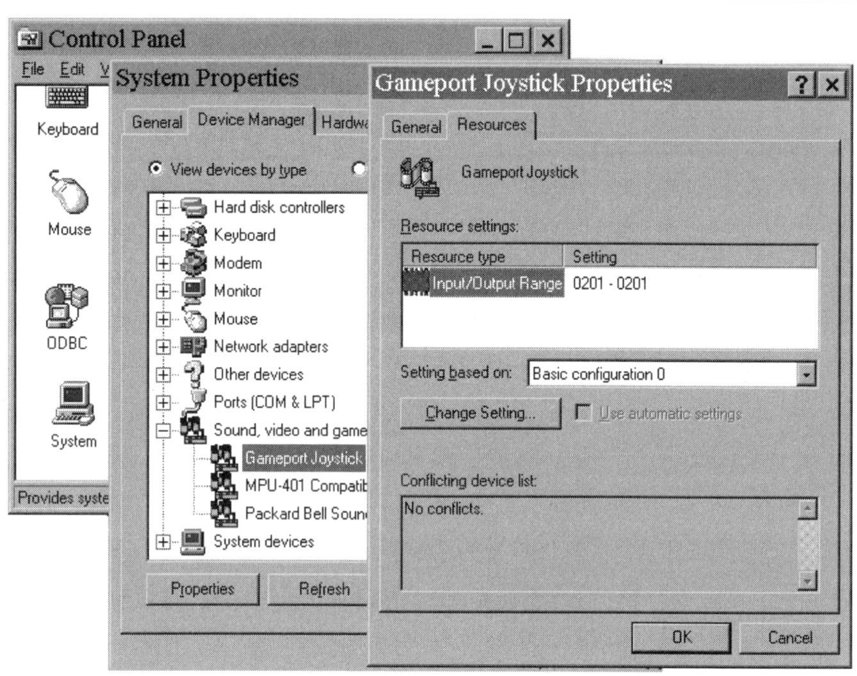

FIGURE 24.8: Check your joystick setup in the Device Manager.

- **An unresponsive joystick.** If you aren't getting any response from the joystick, your game might be using the default setting and is using the mouse or keyboard as the control device. Locate an option within the game that allows you to select the correct input device. Look for a configuration menu, an installation or setup program, or check the game's documentation.
- **Speed-adjustable game cards.** Some joystick problems might indicate the need for a dedicated speed-adjustable game card. Values determined from a calibration routine are generated by the computer, sent through the game card, and then to the joystick. If you run your joystick off of a nonspeed-adjustable game card, such as a combination sound/game card, the values expressed by that card are determined by the speed of a computer. Plugging the same card into a 75MHz computer and a 233MHz computer would result in significantly different speed values. On the flip side, some games do not like speed-compensating game ports and you may need to disable the speed compensation or use a normal game port.

- **Joystick woes.** DOS-based games usually try to communicate directly with the hardware to run sound and use input devices such as joysticks. Most DOS-based games won't work under Windows NT because that operating system doesn't allow applications (even games) to communicate directly with the hardware. Check the game manufacturer's Web site or other Web sources such as newsgroups to find out if someone has figured out a way to run the game on Windows NT. You can also configure your system to dual-boot, letting you load either DOS or Windows NT when you start your system.
- **Check before and after adding an extension cable.** If you add an extension cable to a mouse or trackball, test the input device, both before and after adding the cable. If problems develop, this will allow you to identify the source.
- **Use the correct mouse software.** The software drivers that came with your mouse may not work on all operating systems, for example, Windows 95 and Windows NT. Make sure you are using the correct software when installing a mouse on your system.

Maintenance

Keys sticking? Mouse jumping? You may need to clean your work area up a bit.

- **Don't eat at the keyboard.** Eating or drinking while working at your computer can cause crumbs or liquids to spill onto your keyboard. This can result in keyboard response problems. If you can't resist the urge to eat and drink while spending long hours at the computer, keep refreshments as far away from your computer and its peripherals as possible. Make it a point to periodically check if any crumbs, grime, or liquids have spilled and clean them up right away.
- **Cleaning up liquid spills.** If you accidentally spill a liquid on your keyboard, quickly disconnect the keyboard and turn it over to drain as much liquid out as possible. Liquids such as soda, juice, or coffee are more serious than water because they contain sugars and acids that can be corrosive to the inside of your keyboard. Letting them dry on your keyboard will result in some stickiness, so try to clean those spills with a slightly damp cloth. Use a towel to dry what you can and let the keyboard air dry for a day or longer depending upon how much was spilled. If you experience problems such as sticking keys, pry the keycaps off, clean with a slightly damp cloth, and let dry before reattaching the keycaps. If you still experience problems, we'd suggest buying a new keyboard.

- **Liquids and laptops don't mix.** The keyboard on a laptop computer is more sensitive to liquid spills because the liquid can seep past the keyboard and directly zap drive circuitry, the power supply, memory chips, and/or the motherboard. If a spill happens, carefully remove the keys and clean the contact points. Be sure to use a barely damp cloth and give your laptop a couple of days to dry. Better yet, don't drink around your laptop at all; unlike a desktop unit, you can't just buy a new keyboard.
- **Clean your keyboard periodically.** Even if you keep food and drink away from your computer, your keyboard will still need to be cleaned occasionally. Be sure to turn off your computer and disconnect the keyboard before doing so. Computer accessory outlets carry a variety of cleaning items. They include surface cleaning solutions, absorbent cloths, antistatic wipes, swabs, cans of compressed air that blow dirt particles out of hard-to-reach areas, and small hand-held vacuums. Keyboard cleaner kits include tools specifically designed to reach into the spaces in between keys. You can also use denatured alcohol (99 percent isopropyl alcohol) or a general purpose household cleaning product to wipe your keyboard clean. Foam eye shadow applicators work well for reaching in between keys.
- **Find those dust bunnies!** Although a good surface cleaning will help your keyboard, you may want to periodically pry the keys off and clean the dirt out from underneath the keys. Avoid prying off the large keys like the spacebar, as they usually have springs underneath that might be difficult to get back in place. Be sure to put the keys back on in the correct order.
- **Keep your mouse clean.** As dust and grime accumulate on the mouse ball, you'll begin to lose control of the cursor. You should clean your mouse or trackball on a regular basis, rather than waiting for erratic behavior to occur. To clean your mouse, turn off your PC and remove the ball. Rinse the ball in lukewarm water and wipe it with a lint-free cloth, or just let it air dry. Clean the ball cage with rubbing alcohol on a swab, making sure to remove the grime from the mechanism inside. You can use compressed air to blow out any dust, and use a toothpick or small screwdriver to scrape off any sticky buildup.
- **Cover things up.** To protect your keyboard and monitor from dust and spills, purchase removable covers for them. These antistatic, water-repellent covers are generally made of vinyl or slightly more expensive and durable nylon. The $6 it costs for a cover is a wise investment, particularly if you work in a dusty environment.

- **Put a skin on your keyboard.** If your environment is particularly dirt prone, such as a mechanic's shop where data entry will be made with greasy fingers, a keyboard skin is essential. This cover fits tightly over the keys to protect it while you work.
- **If it's broke, don't fix it.** If a keyboard, mouse, or other input device is knocked to the floor or suffers other rough treatment, damage could occur to its internal components or circuitry. Other than removing or reattaching keycaps, do *not* attempt to take a keyboard apart and fix it because there are no serviceable parts inside. Some computer repair businesses will attempt to fix most input devices, but our advice is to obtain a repair estimate first. You may be better off just buying a new one.

Scanners

What kind of scanner is best for you? How can you get the most out of your scanner? Read on.

- **Why to choose a flatbed scanner.** Flatbed scanners can scan single-sheet pictures, text, and books. Mid-range to high-end models are even more flexible, with optional transparency adapters that allow the scanning of slides and negatives, plus sheet feeders that allow the high-volume scanning of pictures and text. Because their moving parts are behind glass, they're accurate and won't damage your originals. They're bulky, though, so measure your desk space first to see if you have room for one.
- **When sheetfed scanners are best.** Sheetfed scanners use less desk space than flatbed scanners. Their built-in sheet feeders give you an edge in speed when you must scan many originals. Also, some models allow the scanning head to be removed to allow you to scan originals that can't go through the feed slot, such as books and oversized sheets. You may want to evaluate multifunction units that combine a scanner with fax and printer features just to make sure they aren't trying to offer too much and not doing any of it well.
- **Are transparency scanners worth the money?** A competent flatbed scanner often sells for under $400. A scanner made to scan 35mm negatives and slides can cost 2 to 4 times as much. Buy the transparency scanner if you have a large collection of slides or negatives to scan because flatbed scanners handle small slides poorly and with limited resolution. However, if most of your scanning will consist of other items, save your money and go with a less expensive scanner.

- **The quickest connections to set up.** There are three major ways scanners connect to your computer. Most hand scanners and some early flatbed models use proprietary interface cards that use up an expansion slot and are hard to set up. Most low-cost scanners plug into your printer (parallel) port, and most mid-range to high-end scanners use a Small Computer System Interface (SCSI) card. Your parallel port allows you to connect a scanner in just a few minutes.
- **When SCSI isn't SCSI.** Mid-range and high-end scanners typically use SCSI adapter cards, which have several advantages. A true SCSI card can support up to seven devices "daisy-chained" from a single cable, and each device can be used simultaneously. If your scanner comes with a SCSI card, check to see if it's a standard model. If it's built especially for that scanner, you may not be able to connect anything else to it.
- **Testing your scanner, part 1.** Your scanner may come with a special test program, if not, here are some ways to see if it's working correctly. First, does it scan? With a sheetfed scanner, you should see the photo move through the scanner. With a flatbed scanner, you should see a moving bar of light beneath the scanner lid (similar to what you see when a copier scans a sheet of paper) as the scan takes place. In either case, you should see a facsimile of your page show up on-screen.
- **Testing your scanner, part 2.** If you get a picture that looks very distorted, check the scanner software settings. In most cases, you must tell the scanner what type of image you're scanning. If you're scanning a color photo and have Line Art or OCR selected, you'll get a distorted image. Set your image type before you start your scan. If you selected the wrong type, cancel the scan and try again after selecting the correct type.
- **What sheetfed scanners do best.** Use a sheetfed scanner to save space and to take advantage of built-in automatic sheet feeding. Keep in mind that books, slides, negatives, and oversized originals are off-limits.
- **What flatbed scanners do best.** Flatbed scanners offer a wider range of possibilities. With a transparency adapter, you can scan negatives or slides, although a dedicated transparency scanner is better. Books are no problem either. Whenever possible while scanning pictures, choose a picture that's similar in size to the final image. While you can scale the scanned image to a different size, starting with the same size can make things a lot easier.

- **What hand scanners do best.** Often regarded as being "toy scanners" and notorious for being hard to hold steady, hand scanners do have one virtue: they're often the only way to scan fragile old books without destroying the spine that holds the pages in place.
- **TWAIN and your scanner.** Most scanners use a technology called TWAIN to link the scanner with a photo-editor or other application. The TWAIN (Technology Without An Interesting Name, really!) software is customized to each scanner, but provides a standard interface between that scanner and programs like Adobe Photoshop, Corel Photo-Paint, and others.
- **Which program should you use to scan?** It's best to use your full-featured image program to scan your pictures. To set it up, look for a menu option like Import or Acquire Image. Select this, and you should see a list of TWAIN-compatible devices, including your scanner. Pick your scanner from the list, and your image-editing program will use the scanner's TWAIN program to scan the picture and transfer it to the editor.
- **Choosing the correct scanning options.** Depending upon the scanner, the TWAIN program used for scanning may describe images either by their type or by the "target" (where the image is ultimately destined). Select the correct type of image for what you want to scan. The Color Photos setting will optimize the scan for millions of colors and the Line Art setting will scan the image as black and white. If your TWAIN program mentions a target, this affects the resolution of the scan, as well as some other options. (See Figure 24.9.)
- **Scanning for the screen.** Will the image be used for printing or for on-screen viewing? On-screen viewing is done at resolutions around 72dpi (dots per inch). If your original is the same size as what you want the final result to be, just scan it at 72dpi and you'll have a perfectly-sized screen image.
- **Scanning for print.** If your scanning software doesn't list targets with automatic settings, use other options before you scan. For line art, scan at 300–720dpi, depending upon the printer resolution you'll use. For color photos transferred to a color printer, scan at about 150–180dpi. If you plan to enlarge a wallet photo or slide to a 5×7 (or larger sizes), scan it at 300–360dpi.
- **From text to text.** A scanner is just half of what you need if you're planning to scan documents and reconvert them into editable text. Optical character recognition (OCR) software from Xerox (TextBridge), Caere (OmniPage), and others provide the missing link you need. Before you buy an OCR program, make sure your scanner is supported by the program.

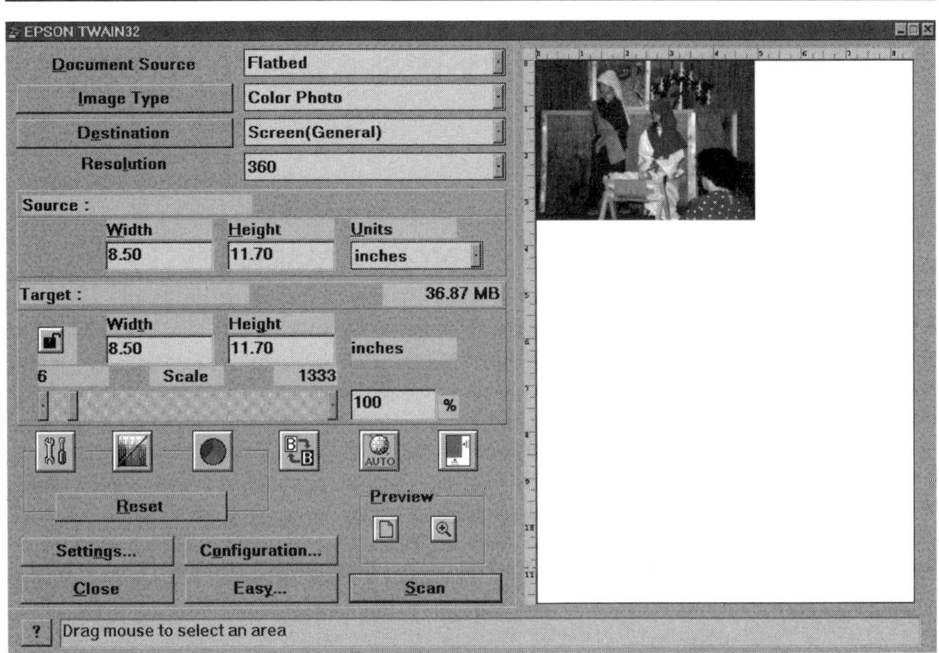

FIGURE 24.9: If something looks awry, you may have the wrong scanning options set.

- **Scanning for OCR.** Some OCR (text-recognition) programs provide extra enhancements over the traditional black-and-white line-art scan option. Caere's OmniPage Professional, for example, can run the scanner in a dot-matrix mode to better recognize text from inexpensive printers. Many programs also offer a fax-optimized mode that tries to compensate for the low resolution of fax printouts.

- **Using preview mode.** Preview, or "pre-scan" mode, runs the scanner over your document or photo in a special high-speed mode to allow you to zero in on what part of the image you want in your final scan. Use this mode to make sure your document is straight and that you have the correct image type selected before you scan.

- **Perfecting your scanning passes.** Early flatbed color scanners had to use three passes (one for each primary color) to create the final color image. But, as in color newspaper and magazine printing, multiple scans can allow the page to slip out of register due to vibration, causing a fuzzy final image. Whenever possible, do your scanning with a single pass.
- **Creating a better original.** Many TWAIN programs allow you to adjust exposure and other advanced settings during the scan itself. You can also adjust the image after the scan if you're using photo-editing software such as Abode's Photo Deluxe or Photoshop, or Corel's Photo-Paint, to name just a few. If your photo-editing software offers features like Equalization and Auto Levels, you'll find it easier to correct your pictures after scanning with default settings.
- **Avoiding mistakes you can't undo.** Photo-editing software can be so powerful that it's easy to mess up a scanned photo in no time flat. So, save your scan as soon as you can. Enable the Undo feature if your software has it. Take advantage of features like Snapshot and Checkpoint that allow your program to recall a version of your photo before your last fatal change.
- **Using automatic enhancements.** Several photo-editing programs offer automatic picture enhancements these days. Try them and see how well they work to fix common problems with your pictures. They'll commonly try to straighten crooked pictures, fix color problems, and adjust pictures that are too dark or too light. Make sure you save your scan before fixing the picture because some enhancements can actually make the picture worse.
- **When doing adjustments manually works better.** Since automatic image enhancements often create a "homogenized" image, consider making your own image adjustments in the following cases: an image that's deliberately "high-key" (mostly light tones) or "low-key" (mostly dark tones); an image that's taken at sunrise or sunset, when color shifts are part of the beauty of the picture; and an image that's taken at an odd angle.
- **The best of both worlds.** Some high-end image-editing programs like Adobe Photoshop and Corel Photo-Paint offer a way to create a series of image-editing commands you can replay as desired. Photoshop's version is called Actions. Once an action is created, Photoshop inserts each menu or keyboard command you give it into the action file. You can play back all of an action or just a single command. (See Figure 24.10.)

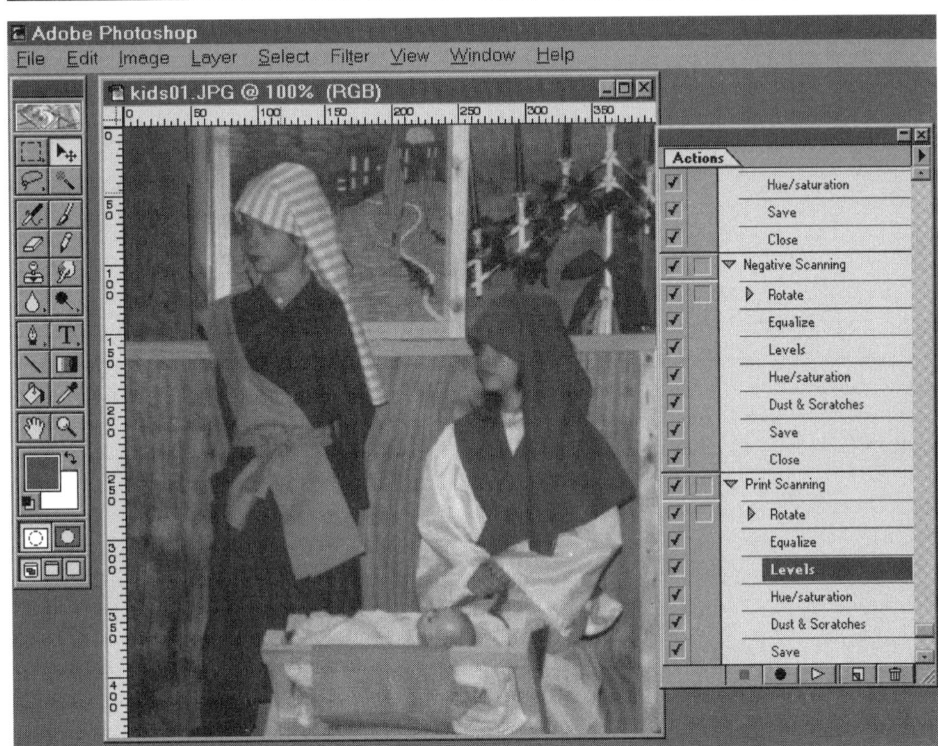

FIGURE 24.10: Photoshop allows more sophisticated manipulation of images.

- **Obtain a better photo by using Equalize and Levels.** These common commands help improve picture quality. Equalize broadens the brightness/darkness range in the image, which eliminates the muddiness in underexposed pictures, or the faded colors in overexposed pictures. Next, to fine-tune the picture, use the Levels feature, which allows you to adjust the brightness and contrast in the mid-tones of your image (the shades between black and white).
- **More about Levels and contrast/brightness.** Levels also allows you to adjust the bright and dark tones. To improve the impact of both black-and-white and color images, adjust the contrast and brightness, which affects the entire range of tones or colors in a picture. Usually, only minor adjustments are necessary if you've already used Equalize and Levels.

- **Fixing photos with problems.** If your photos are less-than-perfect, try the following features that are found in many popular photo editors. The Dust And Scratches feature removes visible damage, while Jaggy Despeckle and Despeckle work to help minimize the grainy look of small snapshots from cheap cameras. Keep in mind that all of these slightly reduce image sharpness.
- **Scanning several photos at once.** If you have several snapshots, save time and effort by placing them all on the scanning area of your flatbed scanner. With many TWAIN drivers, you can perform a single preview scan, then scan each picture individually to apply the image-enhancement options listed above. Once all of the pictures are scanned, remove them and add more while you process the first batch.
- **Scan horizontals vertically.** You can get about four 3.5″×5″ or 4″×5″ prints on a typical flatbed scanner glass. What if some of them are horizontal? No problem. Lay them sideways on the glass, and correct their orientation with the Rotate feature in the photo-editing software.
- **Use the right equipment to scan negatives and slides.** 35mm negatives and slides ideally should be scanned with a desktop or internal slide scanner equipped with a filmstrip adapter (normally supplied with the scanner). Flatbed scanners are less desirable (due to lower maximum optical resolution), but will work when equipped with a transparency adapter (which shines light through the negative or slide).
- **Flatter is better.** A slide scanner with a filmstrip adapter will hold the strip of negatives in place to give it a great scan quality. A flatbed scanner is likely to have problems with negatives, because even negative holders won't hold the film flat enough. The best move? Get an 8″×10″ piece of high-quality glass with beveled or taped edges—keep it clean and scratch-free—and put it over the negatives to flatten them. Be sure it's thin enough to allow the transparency adapter to be in proper position.
- **Scanning negatives as positives.** Depending upon the scanner's TWAIN driver, you'll often have the option to scan negatives as negative or positive. Obviously, your end result needs to be a positive (looking like a scanned print). But, often the scanner's negative-positive conversion is a lot slower than scanning a negative as if it's a positive. If you do this, just use the Invert command in your photo editor to create the positive image you need. This works well with black-and-white negatives only. Unfortunately, color negatives have an orange cast!

- **The dreaded foul color cast.** Many color images more than 20 years old are deteriorating, causing your vacation and family memories to become, literally, off-color. Digital scanning can give you back natural color, and sometimes your scanner can do it for you automatically.
- **Restoring natural color yourself.** If you must use a photo editor to fix the colors, look for a Color Balance command in the menus. This option works best if you have a good eye for color, because it requires you to decide what adjustments to make. Slider controls that show color opposites and real-time previewing (sometimes requiring you to push a button) help you restore natural color. The color pairings are cyan-red, magenta-green, and yellow-blue. (See Figure 24.11.)

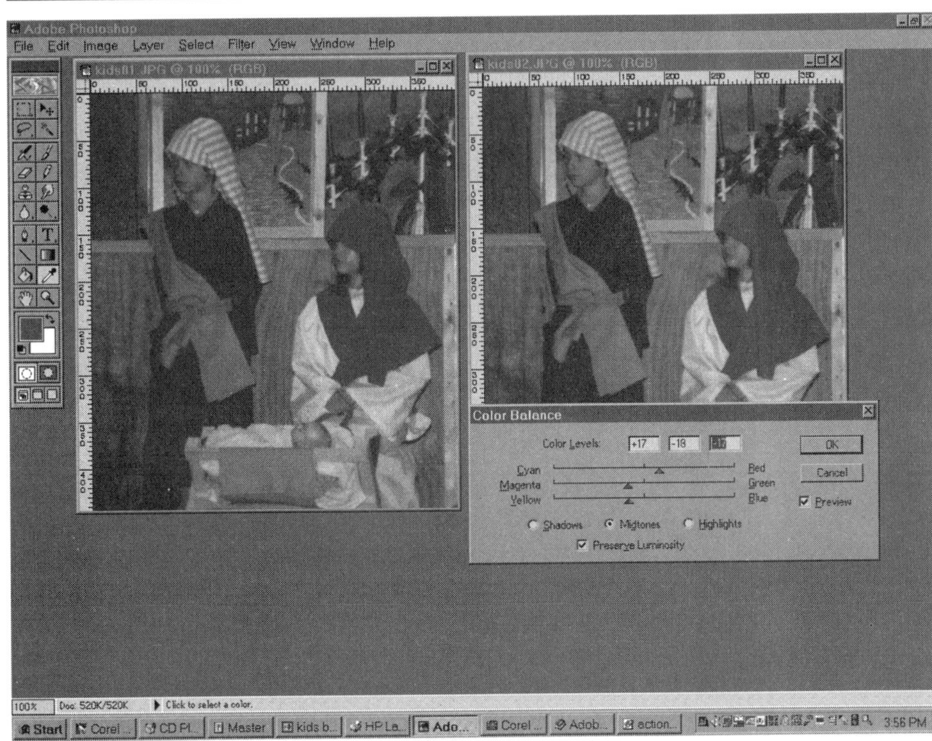

FIGURE 24.11: Use the Color Balance feature to adjust color.

- **When your image is reversed.** This problem happens a lot if you scan slides or negatives; you reverse left and right, or scan the image in upside down. No problem! Just look for an Image Flip command (sometimes it's an option under Image Rotate). Flip horizontally to make signs read correctly again, and flip vertically to keep Uncle Joe from standing on his head.
- **Fixing a crooked picture.** Some photo-editing programs offer the automatic "de-skewing" of a crooked original. Often these features don't work as advertised. To fix a crooked picture by hand, first make sure the picture was put into the scanner straight. On a flatbed scanner, you could try compensating for skewing by how you place the print. A better option is to use the Rotate feature, which lets you select a percentage and direction. Try selecting 1 to 2 percent for a slightly skewed picture, and save your picture before each rotation.
- **About the JPEG option.** JPEG (.JPG) images offer great compression ratios, and they're a great choice for photographic storage or Web site display. How does the image get so small? JPEG compression "throws away" some image information. But if it throws away too much, your image looks bad. Maximum quality still provides an image 60 percent smaller than the original.
- **Other choices to consider.** Want to put that picture on your Windows Desktop? Save it as a bitmap (.BMP) file. If your photo is destined for PageMaker and a future publication, consider using TIFF (.TIF). What about the popular CompuServe GIF (.GIF) format? At only 256 colors, it's actually better for logos than photos. If you're scanning line art, we'd suggest the venerable PC Paintbrush (.PCX) format. It tends to make small files and is widely supported (except by Microsoft's Paint application).

Storage Devices

Memorize these tips. You will be tested later.

- **The cable connection.** Make sure all the cables that link your storage drive to your PC are connected properly. You shouldn't need to force a cable connection; the cable's plug should fit snugly and securely into the appropriate socket.

- **Don't let a ribbon get in the way.** If you need to look inside your computer, make sure you fold all the cords and cables out of the way before you replace the cover. A cable pressing against an expansion card could damage the card or knock it out of place.
- **Power on.** Connect your internal drive to your system's power supply. And don't forget to connect the multicolored power cord to your PC when you install a drive.
- **Portrait of a drive.** Before replacing a drive, it's a good idea to pull out your drawing utensils. Diagram the current position of the old drive and the position of the cables that connect to the drive. The new drive will probably fit in your system the same way, and the diagram will help you double-check your work once that old drive is gone.
- **Knock on metal.** During a drive installation, touch the metal frame of your PC as often as you can to discharge any static electricity. One zap of static electricity is all it takes to destroy a computer's exposed circuitry. Better yet, stay away from carpets and rugs any time you open your computer.
- **A big drive in a little bay.** Storage drives traditionally come in two sizes: 3.5-inch and 5.25-inch. If you upgrade or replace a drive, make sure you have a bay to accommodate your drive. With special brackets, you can fit a 3.5-inch drive into a 5.25-inch bay, but no amount of prying and pushing will get a 5.25-inch drive into a 3.5-inch bay.
- **Ex-SCSI me.** Unless you're with a business or just like to spend money, skip the Small Computer System Interface (SCSI) drives. SCSI drives provide better performance—they're faster and provide better data integrity—than the more common Integrated Drive Electronics (IDE) or AT Attachment Packet Interface (ATAPI) drives, but they cost more and the performance difference is negligible to the average computer user.
- **Horizontal and vertical drive bays.** Internal hard drives, disk drives, and most removable storage drives can be installed in either vertical or horizontal drive bays. Similarly, most external drives can be positioned horizontally or vertically on your desk. Disk drives, including CD-ROM and DVD drives, are the major exception and need to be installed in horizontal drive bays.
- **The software dilemma of installation.** In most cases, the hardware portion of a drive installation is the easy part. It's the software portion of a drive installation that can wreak havoc with your computer system. Back up all important data and read the directions thoroughly before installing a drive.

- **No smoking please.** For the health of your storage device, keep your office clean. Dust, animal hair, smoke particles, and other microscopic contaminants all put your data at risk. Take your system to a local computer shop for a thorough cleaning if you think it is particularly dirty.
- **Stop the spread.** If you copy data from one storage medium to another, make sure the source drive or medium is virus-free. If you let a virus get beyond its source, it's almost impossible to eradicate it completely.
- **Don't give up.** Whether your hard drive crashes, a magnet ravishes your disk, you smash your CD-ROM underfoot, or your dog eats your tape cartridge, you may be able to recover the data if you're willing to fork over the cash. Contact DriveSavers or Ontrack to learn about their extensive data recovery services.
- **Keep it steady.** Position your external storage device someplace where it won't get knocked around or accidentally bumped off your desk. Also, don't move your external storage device while it's working. You risk corrupting the data and potentially damaging the drive.
- **Can your PC handle it?** Not every computer can handle an additional drive. Make sure your PC has an available drive bay, serial port, parallel port, SCSI port, or whatever it needs to accommodate an extra drive. If you're not sure about your system's limitations, call the computer manufacturer for details.
- **Choosing drivers.** One of Windows 95's coolest tricks is an automatic-detection feature that recognizes and locates new hardware when it's added to the system. When the hardware is detected, Windows 95 searches its library of drivers and automatically supplies one. This works out great when you don't have a driver on disk, but you shouldn't use it if you have a special installation disk that contains a driver. When the hardware setup screen asks if it should use the Windows 95 default driver, insert the drive's installation disk and click the Have Disk button to avoid future troubles.

Hard Drives

The hard drive may be your most precious possession. Treat it well.

- **PCs built before 1995.** Before upgrading a hard drive, read the user manual and contact your PC's manufacturer to learn about your system's limitations. If you have a computer built before 1995, it probably doesn't support the newest hard drives on the market. That means you won't be able to add that new multigigabyte hard drive without doing some finagling.

- **Partition parturition.** For the most efficient use of a high-capacity drive, you should format a new drive into multiple partitions. Use the FDISK command or the partitioning software that came with your new drive to create as many as 23 drive partitions. A useful partition size is something around 500MB.
- **Designate master or slave drives.** When adding a second hard drive to your system, you must designate one as the master (primary) drive and one as the slave (secondary) drive. The easiest option is to designate the new drive as the slave drive.
- **Pick your system.** You can use a second hard drive to run a second operating system on your PC. This is a good option for users who like to run specialized graphics or gaming applications in a native DOS environment but prefer the easier-to-use Windows 95 for basic computing functions.
- **The need for speed.** If the only thing you care about is getting data from a drive to your processor as quickly as possible, get a hard drive. Hard drives have faster data transfer rates—as fast as 66MB per second—than any other storage device. A primary reason is because the drive mechanics are all internal; other drive types are slowed down by their removable storage mediums.
- **Looking for info.** As with data transfer rates, hard drives sport the fastest seek times of all data storage devices. The seek time measures how long it takes a drive to find data on a data medium. When you're looking for a new drive, check the specifications for its average seek time. Fast CD-ROM drives have an average seek time of 85ms; average hard drives have seek times of less than 10ms.
- **Never enough.** Can't imagine how you'd ever fill a gigabyte of storage data? Well, just load Windows 95, Office 97, and Microsoft Internet Explorer on your computer and see how much room you have left. If you need to upgrade your hard drive, think of a drive capacity that is bigger than you would ever need—then buy a drive that has a capacity twice as big.
- **Got a light?** When you access your hard drive or turn on your PC, an indicator light on the front of the computer should light up. If it doesn't light up but you can access your hard drive, then the light bulb probably is burned out. If you can't access your hard drive and the light doesn't light up when you turn on your PC, however, then the hard drive probably isn't getting any power. You need to check the power connections to the drive.

- **No crowding.** Always keep at least 10 percent of the drive empty. If your hard drive has a total capacity of 2.4GB, for example, you should consider the drive full when you have 240MB of free space left. (See Figure 24.12.)

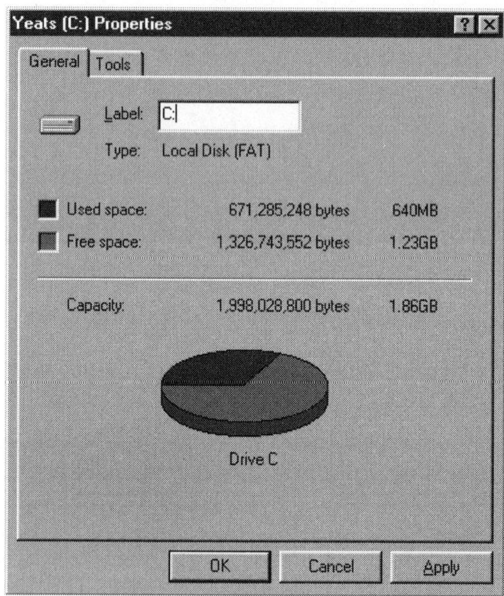

FIGURE 24.12: The properties page of your hard drive will show you how much resources you have available.

- **The weekly cleaning.** One of the best things you can do for your hard drive is to regularly run the ScanDisk utility. In Windows 95, open the Start menu, select Programs ➢ Accessories ➢ System Tools ➢ ScanDisk from the resulting list of options. In DOS, just type **scandisk** at the C:\> prompt.
- **Don't forget to defrag.** Defragmentation is the process of reorganizing the data stored on your hard drive and should be performed at least once every six months. In Windows 95, open the Start menu, select Programs ➢ Accessories ➢ System Tools, and click Disk Defragmenter from the resulting list of options. In DOS, just type **defrag** at the C:\> prompt.
- **Compression stress.** You can use a compression program to double the storage capacity of your hard drive. Be forewarned, however, that disk compression may lead to hard drive problems down the road. In Windows 95,

open the Start menu, select Programs ➢ Accessories ➢ System Tools, and click DriveSpace from the resulting list of options. In DOS 6.2 or newer, type **drvspace** at the C:\> prompt.

- **Backup decisions.** It's imperative to back up your data files. But if you installed a program from a CD-ROM or disk, you probably don't need to back up those program files. If your system crashes, just re-install the programs and restore the data files.

Disk Drives

See Skill 7 for more on disk drives.

- **Making the 5.25-inch disk transfer.** Although there are plenty of people still using the 5.25-inch disks to store valuable data, this predecessor to the 3.5-inch disk is, for all practical purposes, obsolete. It's a good idea to transfer the data on your 5.25-inch disks to 3.5-inch disks before it's too late. If you don't have the resources to do it, ask your local copy shop or computer store if they'll do it for you.
- **Write protection.** The easiest way to protect data stored on 3.5-inch disks is through write protection. Sound tricky? It's not. Look at the back of a disk. In the upper-left corner you'll notice a small tab that moves up and down. Make sure the tab is pushed up so the small hole is exposed. Now you won't be able to record data to or delete data from the disk.
- **One size doesn't fit all.** A disk drive is designed to use disks of a particular size only. For example, a 3.5-inch disk drive only reads data from and writes data to 3.5-inch disks. No matter how you fold it, a 3.5-inch disk drive won't be able to read data from or write data to a 5.25-inch disk.
- **Don't store disks in drive.** Eject and remove a disk from a drive when you're done using it. If there's a disk in the drive when you turn on your computer, the PC won't start and you'll transmit any viruses that were on the disk to the hard drive.
- **Removing disks from drives.** Pressing the eject button is the only method you should use to remove a disk from a drive. Don't try to use a screwdriver, a knife, a paper clip, or any other contraption to remove a disk; you could do serious damage to the drive and the disk. If the drive won't eject the disk when you press the eject button, immediately contact the drive manufacturer.

- **No peeking.** Although it may be tempting, don't slide a disk's shutter open to look inside. A piece of dust, pet hair, or something similar may blow into the disk and contaminate the surface. Consequently, you'll lose the data stored on that disk.
- **Close the trap door.** Most disk drives have trap doors that cover the openings of the drives when they're not in use. If your drive has one of these doors, make sure it snaps shut each time you remove a disk. Don't try to rig it open permanently.
- **No formatting needed.** Before you use a preformatted disk, don't reformat it. Every time you format a disk, it diminishes the disk's ability to store data. You may occasionally need to format a disk, but the less you do it, the healthier your disk will be.
- **Magnetic distraction.** A magnet can corrupt or erase the data on a disk. Keep your disks away from magnets as well as coffee makers, copy machines, and recording devices—anything that has a strong magnetic field. Keep your disks in a disk case, an empty drawer, or some other safe place when they're not in use.
- **Plastic, please.** Use disks that have plastic shutters. Metal shutters discard small metal shards every time they slide back and forth. Over time, these shards build up into a residue on the data surface, rendering the disk useless for data storage.
- **Temperature and humidity recommendations.** The recommended operating environment temperature for a disk is between 32 and 140 degrees Fahrenheit. Similarly, the recommended relative humidity is between 8 percent and 80 percent. Keep these factors in mind when you're storing and using your disks. And never store a disk in direct sunlight.
- **Warm that disk up.** If you accidentally leave a disk in an extremely cold place for an extended period of time, such as inside your car in the middle of winter, use only after the disk has returned to room temperature. When a disk is warming up, tiny drops of water may build up on the disk surface. Condensation of this sort won't damage the data, but it may damage your drive if you stick a damp disk in your drive. Before you use a cold disk, let it warm up at least 24 hours.
- **No need to stuff.** You shouldn't use a disk compression utility to compress the data stored on your disks. A disk has such a small capacity that it just isn't worth the bother. For a buck and a half, you can buy another disk.

- **Too tiny to organize.** Don't worry about using a defragmentation utility, such as Disk Defragmenter, or an error-checking utility, such as ScanDisk, on your small-capacity disks. Trying to clean and organize the data stored on a small-capacity disk is like trying to organize two nuts in a peanut shell.

Compact Disk Drives

- **Drive speed.** The most important factor in disk drive performance is the drive speed, which measures how quickly data is transferred between the drive and the processor. The first disk drives had a data transfer rate of 150Kbps; that's one-speed or 1×. Subsequent drives were measured in relation to that. A drive speed of 8× is eight times faster (1200Kbps) than the speed of the first disk drives; a drive speed of 24× is 24 times faster (3600Kbps) than the speed of the first disk drives.
- **Jumper settings.** Before installing your internal disk drive, make sure its jumpers are set correctly. The default factory settings are correct for most computers, but it's a good idea to double-check them before you get the drive installed and put the cover back on the computer. Check the user manual for details.
- **Multimedia woes.** Because CD-ROM and DVD drives rely so heavily on your system's audio and video capabilities, it's important you know a little something about your computer's sound and video cards before you install a disk drive. Get out the user manual for these components and read the technical specifications before starting the disk drive installation.
- **Faster going downhill.** The listed drive speed for the latest disk drives is a maximum drive speed. The data transfer rate varies according to whether data is stored closer to the inside or outside track on the disc. For example, the drive speed for a 32× drive may range from 13× to 32×.
- **To DVD or not DVD?** DVD has earned a lot of attention in the media recently, but it has yet to capture much shelf space in the retail markets. Before you jump into the long-anticipated realm of DVD media, make sure you can rent DVD movies at your local video store or buy DVD-ROM applications from your local computer store.
- **But I want it!** Ever wonder what the super-fast CD-ROM drives have that your 2× or 4× drives don't have? Well, with a slower disk drive you may have

to wait a little longer to install an application from a disk and video playback may stutter occasionally. That's about it. Unless you're into high-end multimedia applications, you can probably get by with that slower drive.

- **Follow that driver.** The performance of a disk drive depends on whether you have the proper device driver (a program that enables a peripheral to communicate with the computer system). If your drive is experiencing performance problems, check the drive manufacturer's World Wide Web site to see if you need to download a new driver.
- **I can't hear you.** Make sure your computer speakers are plugged in correctly and turned on before you try to play an audio CD or a multimedia CD-ROM.
- **No prying.** Pressing the eject button is the only method you should use to open a disk drive. If the drive won't eject the disk when you press the eject button, contact the drive manufacturer immediately. Using a screwdriver or some similar tool to pry the disk out of the drive could do serious damage to your drive.
- **Don't leave fingerprints.** The best way to hold a disk is by the edges or with one finger in the hole in the middle of the disc. Never touch the disc's data surface. If you have to clean the disc, use a soft dry cloth and wipe from the center out. Never wipe the disk in a circular motion.
- **Say no to cracks.** Never insert a cracked or broken disk into a disk drive. A small crack in the disk surface has the potential to damage the drive. And even if that doesn't happen, the drive won't be able to read data from the disk anyway.
- **Don't push it.** Never push a disk tray closed when the computer is turned off. In fact, it's never a good idea to push a disk tray into the drive when you have an eject button that will retract the drive for you. Forcing the tray into the drive may damage the drive.

NOTE NOTE NOTE NOTE NOTE NOTE NOTE NOTE NOTE NOTE NOTE NOTE NOTE NOTE NOTE

Drives that use a disk caddy instead of a tray generally require you to push the caddy into the drive. Because these drives have no other method of caddy retraction, it's OK to push a disk caddy into the drive.

- **It's not a cup holder.** Don't use an extended disk tray to hold anything other than a compact disc. Reports of users mistaking the disk tray for a cup holder are probably untrue, but there are people who use the tray as a holder for paper, pencils, scissors, or just about anything that might show up on a desk. Not only can this bend or break the tray, but it also increases the amount of dust that could contaminate the drive.

Other Drives

High-capacity storage drives allow you to keep a vast amount of data on hand. Here are some tips for keeping things straight.

- **Tape or disk.** In general, tape drives have the largest data capacity of all storage devices. They're also the slowest. If you need to perform a daily backup of 50GB of network data and you have all night to do it, use a tape drive. If you're backing up the data files on a personal computer and you want to do it while you check your e-mail, use a disk-based back-up storage device, such as a Zip or Jaz drive.
- **Backup variety.** There are three types of backup: full, selective, and incremental. Full backup saves all the data on a drive; selective backup saves only selected files; and incremental backup saves only the data modified since the last backup. A successful backup plan employs all three backup types.
- **One size fits all.** If you want to add a high-capacity portable storage device to your PC, but you don't have any empty drive bays and your parallel and serial ports are full, consider replacing your disk drive with an LS-120 drive. This drive can read data from and write data to standard 1.44MB disks as well as special 120MB disks.
- **Tapes and printers don't match.** If you're looking for a backup storage device and you have a printer connected to your computer, you might want to consider something other than an external tape drive. Many external tape drives connect to the parallel port; so do most printers. To avoid the conflict, look for a tape drive or some other storage device that doesn't connect to the parallel port.
- **A little spring cleaning never hurt.** To keep your tape drive's read/write head clean, give it an occasional dose of alcohol—isopropyl alcohol, that is. Dip a cotton swab in the alcohol and rub the head gently. Let the head dry

completely before using the drive. This is also a good way to keep your audio tape player running properly, too.

- **Protect your data.** Hardware is easily replaceable; data is not. Keep removable disks and tape cartridges safely stored in their cases and away from magnets, extreme heat, and extreme cold. If you're archiving extremely important data, it's a good idea to keep the archived copies at a location away from your computer system.
- **Keep data clean.** As with hard drives, high-capacity portable storage devices, such as a Jaz or LS-120 drive, need to be cleaned and organized once in a while. Use the ScanDisk and Disk Defragmenter utilities (see tips in the "Hard Drives" section) to clean and organize your drives as often as necessary. You don't need to run these utilities on small-capacity disks (disks with a capacity of 2.88MB or less) and tape drives.
- **Archive efficiently.** If you copy data to a tape drive, make sure the source drive is clean and well organized. A poorly organized source drive will transmit poorly organized data to a tape drive, which results in inefficient archiving. Use the ScanDisk and Defrag commands on your source drive as often as necessary.
- **Like with like.** You'll never get a tape drive to read a Jaz disk. Nor will a Zip drive read a tape cartridge. You must use the appropriate storage media with the corresponding storage device. Also, never insert anything other than the appropriate storage media into a storage device.
- **Prevent an accident.** Write-protect your data when it's stored on a portable storage medium. As with disk drives, you can write-protect data stored on most storage media. Check the user manual for details.
- **Write it down.** Clearly label every disk or cartridge with its contents. Not only does that help you remember what is contained on the storage medium, but it also tells other people that the disk contains important data—at least, it was important enough that you cared to label it—and shouldn't be erased.
- **Compression stress.** You can use DriveSpace or a third-party compression utility to maximize the amount of storage space on a high-capacity portable storage medium. Unless you're using the data for archiving purposes only, however, we recommend skipping the compression; spend the money to buy another disk or cartridge.

- **What do you need?** Decide what your storage needs are and how much you can afford to spend before you purchase an alternative storage device. Don't let a salesperson or an obnoxious ad affect your purchasing decision. The right storage device for your situations is out there.
- **Get out.** When you're done using a disk or cartridge, remove it from the drive. Your data is safer if the medium on which it is stored is kept away from the drive. This is an easy way to prevent accidental deletions.

Audio Components

The following tips will have you rocking out as you work.

- **Check the sound card status.** To check the status of your sound card, use Windows 95's Device Manager. Click Start ➢ Settings ➢ Control Panel. In the Control Panel window, double-click the System icon, and click the Device Manager tab. Look for the Sound, Video, And Game Controllers listing and click its plus sign icon. Click your sound card's listing and click the Properties button. The Device Status area of the Properties window should tell you whether the audio card is working properly.
- **Change sound card drivers.** To manually change sound card drivers in Windows 95, follow the directions above to open your sound card's Properties window. Click the Driver tab and the Change Driver button. Click the Show All Devices button. Choose the manufacturer and model of your new sound card. Then click the OK button. Insert any disks that Windows 95 requests. Once the new driver is installed, you'll need to restart Windows.
- **Automatically install drivers.** To have Windows 95 automatically install a new sound card driver, double-click the Add New Hardware icon in the Control Panel window. Click the Next button in the next three windows. Windows 95 then will find the sound card and prompt you to insert the necessary disks. After the driver is installed, click the Finish button. You'll then need to restart Windows.
- **Sound card volume wheels.** While it's preferable to make volume-level adjustments through Windows 95, some sound cards contain a volume wheel that allows you to manually adjust volume levels. Most volume wheels are available through the back of the card.

- **Check sound card jacks.** Sound cards typically have several jacks available on the back of the card. If you experience some audio problems, check the sound card to make sure you've plugged each component into the correct jack.
- **Avoid touching sound card components.** When installing or handling a sound card, only touch the metal back of the card whenever possible. Oil and dirt from your hands could damage the components on the card.
- **Changing the default sound card.** By default, Windows 95 uses the default sound card for recording and playing back sounds. You can select any audio device to perform these tasks, though. In the Control Panel window, double-click the Multimedia icon. Next, click the Audio tab, then select the device you want to use for recording and playing back sounds.
- **Update programs for new sound card.** If, after installing a new sound card, you experience problems with sound from the programs that worked fine with the old sound card, chances are you need to update the programs' settings to recognize the new card. With some programs, you may need to reinstall them so they can use the new sound card.
- **Connect CD-ROM drive to sound card.** In some multiple-hard-drive systems, you may run out of IDE (Integrated Drive Electronics) ports on your motherboard, leaving you without a home for your CD-ROM drive. But, with the correct hardware, you can plug an ATAPI CD-ROM drive into your sound card, if it contains an IDE- or ATAPI-compatible port.
- **Choose sound schemes.** Choose a sound scheme for Windows 95 events through the Sounds icon in the Control Panel. When the Sounds Properties window opens, you can select a different sound scheme for each of the different Windows functions listed under Events. (See Figure 24.13.)
- **Temporarily stop the audio CD auto play.** Windows 95 automatically plays audio CDs when they're inserted in the CD-ROM drive. You can prevent this from happening with the current CD by holding down the Shift key as you close the CD-ROM drive.
- **Permanently stop the audio CD auto play.** If you want to disable audio CDs from playing automatically each time you insert them, double-click the My Computer icon. Select the Folder Options command from the View menu. Click the File Types tab and the AudioCD listing, then click the Edit button. In the Actions box, click and highlight the Play listing, then click the Set Default button. To finish, click the Close button twice.

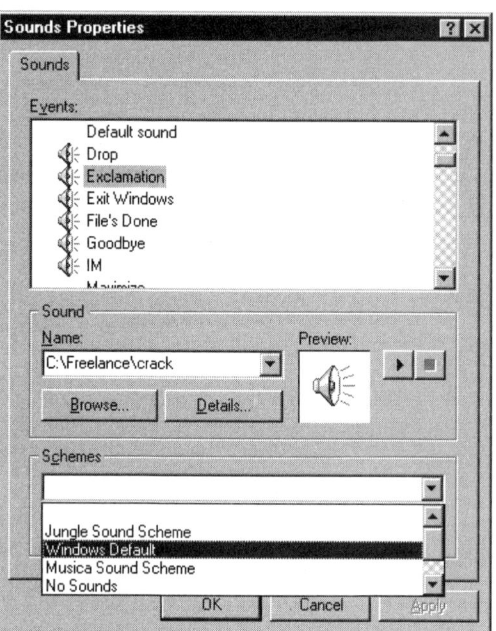

FIGURE 24.13: The Sounds Properties dialog box allows you to choose which sounds you want associated with which actions.

- **Playing an audio CD.** You can start the CD Player program by clicking Start ➢ Programs ➢ Accessories ➢ Multimedia ➢ CD Player. Then click the Play button.
- **Set audio CD play order.** When playing audio CDs, you can choose the order in which the songs on the CD will be played. Insert an audio CD and open CD Player. Click the Disk menu and the Edit Play List command. Then pick and choose the order for the songs.
- **Playing audio CDs with a new file.** You can use a file other than CDPLAYER .EXE to play audio CDs inserted in your CD-ROM drive. Double-click the My Computer icon. In the My Computer window, click the View menu and the Folder Options command. Then click the File Types tab. In the list, click AudioCD and the Edit button. In the Actions box, click Play, followed by the Edit button. In the Application Used To Perform Action text box, type the path and filename of the program you want to use.

- **Selecting audio quality levels for recordings.** At the bottom of the Multimedia Properties window, choose the level of audio quality desired under the Preferred Quality section. Remember that high-quality recordings will require far more storage space than low-quality recordings. (See Figure 24.14.)

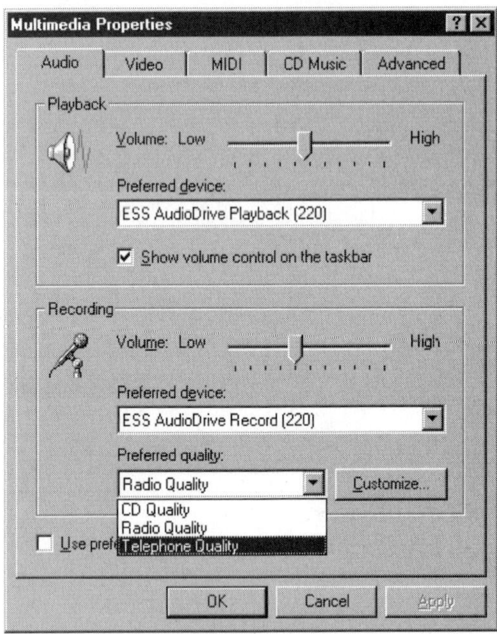

FIGURE 24.14: Change the audio quality in the Multimedia Properties dialog box.

- **Fixing CD-ROM audio problems.** If you're experiencing problems hearing audio from CD-ROM programs, you can test the CD-ROM drive by playing an audio CD and plugging headphones into the jack on the front of the drive. If you can hear the sound through the headphones, the CD-ROM drive is producing sound properly; the problem is with your sound card or speakers. Now plug the headphones into the jack on the back of the sound card. If you can't hear the sound through the headphones, the problem may lie with the connection between the CD-ROM drive and the sound card.
- **Don't use CD-ROM discs in stereos.** Never play a CD-ROM disc—even one that contains audio tracks—in your stereo's CD player. You could damage your stereo's speakers.

- **Don't use stereo speakers with your PC.** Using speakers from your stereo with your computer is usually a bad idea. Speakers designed for computers are magnetically shielded, meaning they won't cause interference with your monitor. Also, because a sound card produces a relatively weak signal when compared to a stereo, many stereo speakers can't reproduce computer sound.
- **Choose speakers based on your audio usage.** Some PC speakers will sound better with certain types of audio files. For instance, some reproduce MIDI (musical instrument digital interface) files better than .WAV (wavetable synthesis) files; others reproduce audio CDs extremely well. Decide what type of audio you use most often, and then test the speakers you plan to buy with that type of audio file.
- **Fixing silent speakers.** If you don't hear any sound from a set of new speakers, try these troubleshooting tips. Check Windows 95's sound settings to make sure they aren't muted. Make sure the speakers are plugged into the correct jack on your sound card. Some speakers require electrical power (either from batteries or an AC adapter) to function. Check your sound card for a volume wheel; set it at the middle setting. Check the volume control on the speakers themselves. Plug headphones into the speaker jack on the sound card. If you now hear sound, your speakers probably are malfunctioning.
- **Clean speakers carefully.** Never clean the front of a speaker with an overly damp cloth; if water enters the front of the speaker, it could damage the components. You can, however, wipe the speaker case with a slightly damp cloth. Never open a speaker's case; the inside should never need cleaning.
- **Avoid using splitters.** When connecting speakers to the sound card jack, don't use a Y-splitter to attach another component to the same jack. The signals for the speakers will be weakened by a Y-splitter, possibly to the point where the speakers won't work correctly.
- **Limit RF interference.** Computer speakers sometimes experience radio frequency (RF) interference. Often times, the cable that connects the sound card to the speakers is the cause of the RF interference. Try shortening the cables as much as possible to reduce interference. You also can try repositioning the speakers to reduce outside interference or purchase some RF interference blocking devices.

- **Use external speakers with portable PCs.** When using a portable computer for presentations, there's little you can do to improve the sound from the portable's built-in speaker. Bring along an external pair of speakers or a good pair of headphones for presentations.
- **Headphones vs. speakers.** When listening to a recording you made on your PC, the audio file usually will sound better through headphones than through the speakers.
- **Adjusting headphone volume.** You can adjust the volume of headphones connected to your CD-ROM drive by double-clicking the Multimedia icon in the Control Panel window. Click the CD Music tab and the Multimedia Properties window. The Headphone slider controls the volume and balance.
- **Using built-in speaker for .WAV files.** If you don't have a sound card installed, you can play .WAV files through the PC's built-in speaker. While the PC's speaker won't produce high-quality sound, it's better than no sound at all. Instead of using Media Player to play .WAV files through the built-in speaker, use Sound Recorder.
- **Use basic settings to test speakers.** When testing a new speaker system, be sure to set the software and speakers to use the most basic settings. Test the balance and volume levels to make sure the speakers are accepting input properly. Then enact the special effects, such as surround sound and equalization, one at a time and make sure the speakers have responded properly each time.
- **Improve subwoofer's bass.** For maximum bass sound from your subwoofer (if your PC's speaker system contains a subwoofer), try placing the subwoofer in the corner of the room, with two walls and the floor surrounding it. That will force the sound back into the room. If you can't find a suitable corner, just place the subwoofer on the floor with a wall at its back.
- **Create a makeshift microphone.** If you don't have a microphone connected to your sound card, you can create a makeshift microphone by using headphones that are compatible with a Sony Walkman portable radio. Plug the headphones into the sound card's microphone jack and speak into them.
- **New microphones need electricity.** If you purchase a new microphone for use with your computer system, chances are it will require some electrical current to work properly. Some older sound cards don't provide enough current to support newer microphones. You may need to upgrade your sound card or install a battery in the microphone.

- **Silence microphone feedback.** If you have a microphone connected to your system and you occasionally hear feedback, perform two preventative measures. First, move the microphone as far away from the speakers as possible. Second, turn down the recording volume when the microphone is not is use. Double-click the speaker icon in the Taskbar. In the Volume Control window, click the Options menu and the Properties command. Next, click the Recording button. Place a checkmark in the Microphone box (if needed) and click OK. Drag the slider down in the Microphone area to lower the volume.
- **Install MIDI sequencer device.** To play MIDI sounds, you must have the MIDI Sequencer Device installed. To see whether this device is installed, double-click the Multimedia icon in the Windows 95 Control Panel window. Click the Advanced tab and double-click Media Control Devices. If you see a MIDI Sequencer Device listing, click it and then click the Properties button. If the Use This Media Control Device button is selected, you should be able to play MIDI sounds. If you need to install the MIDI device, use Windows 95's Add New Hardware Wizard.
- **Add a new MIDI instrument.** When adding an external MIDI instrument in Windows 95, double-click the Multimedia icon in the Control Panel window. Then click the MIDI tab and the Add New Instrument button to start step-by-step instructions.
- **Installing multimedia components.** If you don't see Media Player or Sound Recorder in your Windows 95 configuration, the components may not have been installed during your initial Windows 95 setup (such is the case with a Compact setup). Use the Windows 95 Add/Remove Hardware feature to add these features.
- **Using sound recorder.** The Sound Recorder program contained in Windows allows you to record, play, and edit sound files. To open Sound Recorder, click Start ➢ Programs ➢ Accessories ➢ Multimedia ➢ Sound Recorder. To use Sound Recorder, you need a sound card, speakers, and a microphone.
- **Making special-effect changes.** Click the Effects menu in the Sound Recorder window to make special-effect changes to your audio files. (See Figure 24.15.)

FIGURE 24.15: Effects such as volume, speed, echo, and reverse can be made under the Effects menu.

- **Change the default recording device.** In Windows 95, you can change your default playback and recording device through the Control Panel window. Double-click the Multimedia icon and then click the Audio tab. In the Preferred Device area, select the audio device you want from the drop-down lists for Playback and Recording.
- **Mix two sound files.** In Sound Recorder, you can mix two sound files together. Open one of the files you want to mix. Move the slider to the area in the file where you want the second file to begin. Click the Edit menu and the Mix With File command. Type the name of the second file that you want to mix with the first file and click OK. Click the Save As command under the File menu to save the mix as a new file. Click the Insert File command under the Edit menu if you simply want to insert one sound file within another.
- **Add sound to an existing file.** Adding sound to an already created sound file is easy in Windows 95. Open the sound file you want to alter. Move the slider to the point where you want to add sound (if the slider is located anywhere other than the end of the file, your recorded sound will overwrite the file's sound). Click the Record button to begin adding your sound through your microphone. Click Stop to end the recording. Then click the Save As command under the File menu.
- **Remove sound file editing.** Prior to saving an edited sound file, you can return to the file's original configuration. In the Sound Recorder window, click the Revert command under the File menu. Then click the Yes button. Once you've saved the file with its changes, though, you can't undo them.

- **Convert audio file quality.** If you've recorded low-quality sounds in the past and want to convert them to high-quality, first open the sound file you want to convert in Sound Recorder. Then click the File menu, followed by the Properties command. Choose the format you now want in the Format Conversion area of the window. Click the Convert Now button, click the format and attributes you want, and then click the OK button.
- **Set correct compression formats.** Some .WAV files will not play in Windows 95 unless you have the correct compression formats installed. Double-click the Add/Remove Programs icon in the Control Panel window. Click the Windows Setup tab. Then click the Multimedia listing in the Components area and click Details. Make sure the Audio Compression box has a check mark in it; if not, click the box and the OK button. Then insert the Windows 95 CD-ROM as instructed.
- **Inserting sound into documents.** Many types of documents can have sound files included in them. Using Sound Recorder, open the sound file you want to insert. Click the Copy command from the Edit menu. Then open the document you want to add the sound to, and within the document, click at the position where you want to add the file. Click the Edit menu and the Paste command to insert the sound file. With some programs, you'll need to click the Insert menu and choose to insert the sound file.
- **Copy audio file segments into documents.** You can copy and paste any portion of an audio clip into another file. Open the audio file into the Media Player program. Move the slider to the point of the audio clip that you want to begin copying. Now click the Edit menu and the Selection command, then click the From button. The current position of the slider is represented by the number (in minutes and seconds) in the From box. Now type the ending position of the selection in the To field. Click the OK button. The selection you've created will appear as a blue line on the slider bar. Click the Edit menu and the Copy Object command. The portion of the file you selected is copied to the Clipboard. Open the file into which you want to copy the audio clip, place the cursor where you want the audio clip to appear, and click the Paste command from the Edit menu.
- **Adding sound to Windows 95 events.** You can add any sound saved on your hard drive to a particular Windows 95 system event. Double-click the Sounds icon in the Control Panel window. In the Events area of the Sounds Properties window, click the event to which you want to add a sound. Then select the sound file you want to link to the event (click Browse to search through your hard drive for the file). Click OK.

- **RealAudio needs fast connection.** When using RealAudio to listen to audio clips and radio broadcasts over the World Wide Web, the clips will sound choppy and will skip unless you have at least a 14.4Kbps connection to the Web.
- **No sound? Check the mute setting.** If you don't hear any sounds on your computer, first check to make sure they aren't muted. When the computer is muted, the speaker icon on the right side of the Taskbar will be covered by a red circle with a slash through it. To regain sound, click the speaker icon and remove the checkmark from the Mute box.
- **Silence your PC.** Put a checkmark in the Mute All box under the first column in the Volume Control window to silence your PC. (See Figure 24.16.)

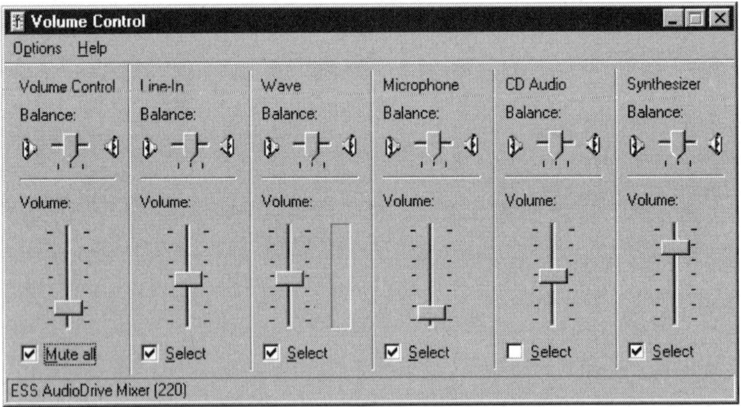

FIGURE 24.16: Your computer will lie silent if you click in the Mute All box.

- **Choose a new volume.** Adjusting the volume level in Windows 95 is an easy process. Click the speaker icon on the right side of the Taskbar. Move the slider bar up for increased volume and down for decreased volume. You can gain greater control over audio functions through the Volume Control window. Either double-click the speaker icon to open Volume Control or click the Start button, the Programs menu, the Accessories submenu, the Multimedia submenu, and the Volume Control command.
- **Improve audio performance.** If you experience problems with audio not matching the actions on-screen in certain programs, especially games, your computer's resources probably are being pushed to the maximum. Try closing all other programs to allow the current program to have all the resources it needs.

- **Improve scratchy audio.** If your sound card sometimes makes scratchy sounds when replaying certain sound files, check your sound card's documentation to make sure you're using the correct DMA (direct memory access) settings. Also make sure you're not trying to play a 16-bit sound file on an 8-bit sound card.
- **Use PC as speaker phone.** If you want to use your computer as a speaker phone, you'll need to purchase a telephony card, which combines the features of a sound card with a modem. After installation, the new telephony card will replace your current sound card and modem card. You'll be able to plug speakers and a microphone into the telephony card. Software included with the telephony card should provide your PC with speaker phone capabilities.
- **Reduce .WAV file storage space.** If you're trying to copy .WAV files from your desktop PC to a handheld PC running Windows CE, you need to reduce the files' storage size before copying them. First, place a copy of the .WAV file in a temporary folder on your desktop PC's hard drive. Open the copied file in Sound Recorder. Now click the File menu and the Save As command. Then click the Change button. In the Sound Selection window, click the Name drop-down menu and select Telephone Quality. The lower-quality sound file will require far less storage space, and, on the handheld PC's small speaker, you probably won't notice the difference in quality. Click the OK button and the Save button. Now copy the file to your handheld PC.
- **Changing Windows CE's sound settings.** You can use .WAV sounds on your handheld computer through Windows CE. To make changes to Windows CE's sound settings, click the Volume And Sounds icon in the Windows CE Settings window. You can change the alarm clock sounds in the Windows CE Calendar program through the Edit menu and the Reminder Defaults command.

Video Components

Multimedia can make your life much more colorful. Pay attention to these steps to maximize your usage.

- **Find the latest video drivers.** If you're using video drivers not made for your video card, you may see some error messages when trying to access the properties of the video card in Windows 95's Display Manager window, even though your system may seem to be working correctly. This probably means Windows 95 has defaulted to a VGA driver, allowing the display to work, but your video card's full capabilities aren't being utilized. It's a good idea to find the latest driver for your video card from your card's manufacturer.

- **Check your video driver version number.** If you aren't sure whether your video card driver is made for Windows 95, double-click the System icon in the Control Panel window. Click the Device Manager tab, then click the plus icon next to the listing of display adapters. Next, double-click your video card's listing and click the Drivers tab. If the driver's version number isn't a 4.*x*, it's an older driver. Contact your video card's manufacturer for an upgrade.
- **VGA: better than nothing.** If your video card manufacturer doesn't offer a Windows 95 upgrade for your display driver, you should replace the Windows 3.*x* driver with a standard VGA driver, available on the Windows 95 CD-ROM. In the Control Panel window, double-click the Display icon, then click the Settings tab, and the Change Display Type button. In the Adapter Type section, click the Change button. Click Show All Devices and click Standard Display Types in the Manufacturers box. Now click Standard Display Adapter (VGA) in the Models box and click OK. Insert the Windows 95 CD-ROM when directed.
- **Don't use the Wizard for video driver installation.** Don't run the Add New Hardware Wizard to replace an older video driver with an upgraded one; you'll probably run into a hardware conflict.
- **Start Windows 95 safely.** If you experience video driver problems when attempting to load Windows 95, you can start the operating system (OS) in Safe Mode to bypass some problems you may be having, allowing Windows 95 to load. When you see the "Starting Windows 95" message appear on-screen, press the F8 key. Then choose Safe Mode from the Startup menu.
- **Disabling the built-in video card.** Many computers have video cards built directly into the motherboard. If you ever want to install a new video card, you'll need to disable the original video card and rework your Setup files to recognize the new card, both of which can be difficult processes. If you experience problems running Windows 95 after installing the new card and its drivers, use DOS to return to VGA mode, which will allow you to at least open Windows 95, where you then can make the changes to reflect your new video card.
- **Check your hardware status.** Sometimes in Windows 95, hardware devices can experience conflicts that you may not know about. It's a good idea to

check the status of your devices a few times a year, especially the display driver. Double-click the System icon in the Control Panel window and then click the Device Manager tab. If you see any devices marked with a yellow exclamation point icon, click the device and click the Properties button to see the exact conflict. If you can't fix the conflict, click the Remove button to delete the device, then restart Windows. If the hardware is needed, Windows 95 should help you set up the device after restarting.

- **Multimedia performance.** Lower settings for the color palette and less-detailed resolutions will improve your PC's multimedia performance. (See Figure 24.17.)

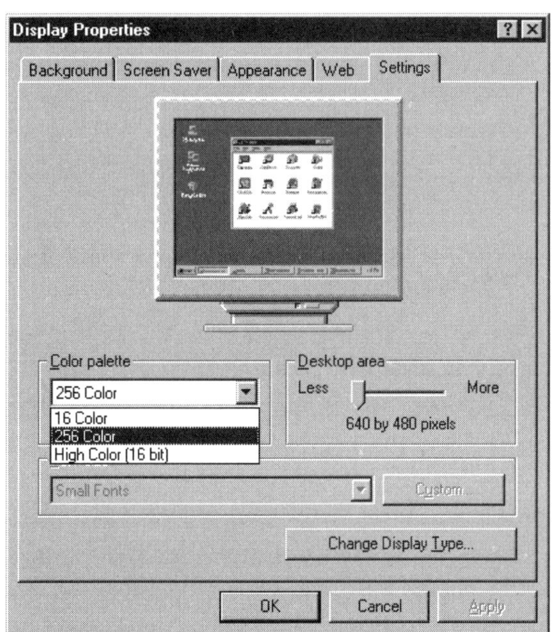

FIGURE 24.17: Your computer will run quicker if you don't make it work too hard on the multimedia front.

- **The more video RAM, the better.** The amount of video random access memory (RAM) contained on your video card goes a long way towards determining the type of work you can do. If you want to run 24-bit color at a high resolution, you'll need a minimum of 4MB of video RAM.

- **Know your monitor limitations.** Use caution when setting up your type of monitor in Windows 95. If you choose a monitor setting that exceeds the capabilities of your monitor, you could damage the monitor. To check your monitor type, double-click the Display icon in the Control Panel window, and click the Settings tab, followed by the Change Display Type button. Next, click the Change button in the Monitor Type section and click Show All Devices. Choose your monitor's manufacturer and model.
- **Windows 98 will allow two monitors.** Windows 95 cannot support more than one video card. However, Windows 98 (whenever it is available) is supposed to include support for two video cards, thereby allowing two monitors.
- **Never, never open a monitor case.** Never open your monitor's case because if you do, you'll not only ruin the unit, you could actually electrocute yourself. All monitors contain interior power sources that hold significant electrical charges, even when they aren't plugged in.
- **Be wary of monitor noises.** Popping noises coming from your monitor usually signal a serious problem. Try cleaning dust off the monitor screen and replacing the monitor's power cord. If the popping noises continue, take the monitor to a repair shop.
- **Use degaussing cautiously.** If your monitor contains a degauss control, use it cautiously. The control is designed to remove magnetization from the monitor and help return the monitor's natural colors. However, each time you use the control, the cathode-ray tube (CRT) becomes more susceptible to overheating.
- **Shield your monitor from interference.** If your monitor's image appears scrambled or wavy at times, make sure no devices near the monitor, such as a motor or fan, are causing magnetic interference. If your monitor is plugged into a power strip, it may be receiving interference through the strip. Try plugging the monitor directly into the wall outlet.
- **Watch out for interference from your monitor.** Computer monitors yield electromagnetic rays as they create the images you see on your screen. Most monitors are shielded to prevent these rays from leaking outside their cases. However, if your monitor doesn't have the proper shielding, you may notice interference from the electromagnetic rays by observing nearby radios or televisions. For a quick fix, move the radio or TV farther from the monitor; for a long-term (and much safer) fix, you need to have the monitor fixed or replaced.

- **Set monitor at eye level.** When setting up your monitor, make sure the top of the screen is either at eye level or just below eye level. It should be 18 to 24 inches away from your face.
- **Prevent eye strain.** If you're experiencing eye strain during computer sessions, try taking short breaks twice an hour to give your eyes a chance to refocus and rest. Remove glare on the screen either through a screen filter or by removing lights that shine directly on the monitor.
- **More monitor controls are better.** When choosing a monitor, look for one that allows plenty of control on your part. Most newer monitors contain several controls that allow you to clear up fuzzy images or improve color registration.
- **Monitor shadowing is normal.** When displaying an all-white background, some monitors may show some shadowing on the background (where portions of the screen look off-white or light gray). Many monitors have this quirk and it doesn't signal any serious problems.
- **Set brightness control correctly.** Colors on a monitor may appear washed out if your brightness control is turned up too high. The best method for adjusting your brightness is to open to an all-black background, such as any screen within DOS. Now turn the brightness control to maximum, which should change the black background to a dark gray. Then turn the brightness back down, stopping once the background returns to black. This is your optimum brightness setting.
- **Waking up your monitor.** When using Windows 95's energy-saving sleep mode, your computer's display should return as soon as you hit a key or move the mouse. However, if your computer locks up after going into sleep mode, you probably have a monitor or video card that doesn't support sleep mode. Check the documentation to see if both devices meet the EPA's Energy Star standard.
- **Energy-saving features.** Newer monitors allow you to set their energy-saving features through the Display Properties window. (See Figure 24.18.)
- **Shortcut to Display Properties.** To open the Display Properties window quickly, right-click any blank space on the Desktop, and then click the Properties command in the pop-up menu.
- **Stop your screen saver.** To prevent a screen saver from kicking in and ruining a download session you're performing, click the Start button and leave the Start menu open on the screen.

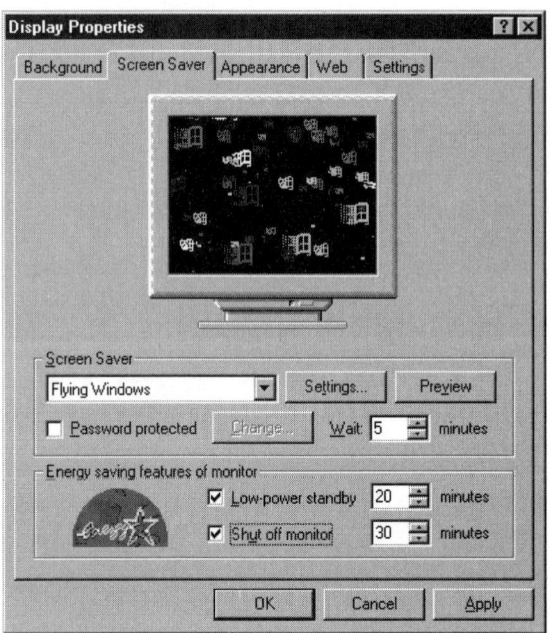

FIGURE 24.18: You can switch your monitor to low-power standby or to switch off altogether after a certain time period.

- **Clean lenses give clear views.** Dusty monitor screens, dirty digital camera lenses, and smeared scanner glass and lenses all will affect the quality of the images you see. You can clean all of the glass surfaces for such hardware products with a slightly moistened, lint-free cloth.
- **Digital camera key components.** Remember your PC capabilities when purchasing a digital camera and keep an eye on two factors. One, make sure the camera either stores images in .JPEG format or can convert images to .JPEG, otherwise you may not be able to send the images to other people. Also, make sure the camera allows removable storage devices (flash cards), otherwise you'll need to have a computer handy when the camera's internal storage device is full.
- **LCD screen woes.** If your digital camera uses an LCD screen to aid you in aiming the camera, you may have problems seeing the screen in bright sunlight. In fact, you may need to purchase an eyepiece viewer for use in sunny conditions.

- **Storage space vs. quality.** Many digital cameras offer various quality and compression settings. Obviously, the highest resolution and lowest compression settings will produce the best quality of images, but they'll also require the most hard drive storage space—space you may not have. Try combining the various settings to find the quality level you can live with while economizing your hard drive space.
- **Digital camera download options.** When transferring files from a digital camera to your computer, you have several options, including a serial port, a parallel port, a PCMCIA (Personal Computer Memory Card International Association) slot, an infrared connection, and a disk drive. However, the fastest transfers occur through the SCSI (Small Computer System Interface) port, with transfer speeds ranging from 5MB to 20MB per second.
- **Downloading drains battery power.** When downloading images from your digital camera to your computer, be sure to use the camera's AC adapter. The download process will quickly drain the batteries of the camera.
- **Digital video cameras make setup easy.** When setting up a video conference, you can choose either a specialized digital video camera (more expensive) or an off-the-shelf video camera (less expensive). However, setting up an off-the-shelf video camera probably will require a connection through a video-conference board, which can be a difficult process. Digital video cameras often easily connect to the computer's parallel port.
- **A no-brainer: remove the lens cap.** Make certain the lens cap is off your digital camera before using it. Yes, this sounds like a no-brainer, but because many digital cameras don't connect their view finders with the lenses, you won't notice the lens cap by looking through the view finder.
- **Avoid bright reflections.** When using a digital camera, you have to watch out for many of the same potential lighting problems you find when using a traditional 35mm camera. Bright reflections are especially troublesome for digital cameras, causing areas that appear as white blotches.
- **Scan oversized images.** Scanners aren't limited to what they can scan by their physical size. When scanning an oversized image, first make sure the image's length or width is no more than 28 inches (on an 8½- by 14-inch scanner). Make marks every 8 inches on the long edge of the image to allow for overlapping. Then determine the final size of the output you want. Now align the right corner of the image with the scanner. Make sure you're

scanning the entire area and you've set the scaling based on the final size you want. Next, move to the next 8-inch mark and scan again until you've completed the upper half of the image. Repeat the process for the lower half. Then use image-editing software to put together the various pieces and create the large image.

- **Scan 3-D images.** You can scan three-dimensional objects with relative ease. The objects can't be any larger than the scanner's size, and you probably won't want to scan heavy objects in order to avoid damaging the scanner. When scanning a 3-D object, just place it on the scanner and darken any lights above the scanner. If you can, remove the scanner's lid to avoid reflective glare; otherwise place dark paper over the propped lid.
- **Scanners vs. system resources.** When choosing a scanner, you need to consider your computer system's resources. Scanned files take up a lot of hard drive space on your computer, and the scanner will need to occupy some of your computer's RAM. You'll also need to set your computer to display 24-bit color (16.7 million colors), which will make the display match what you'll see on the scanned image.
- **Improve your original's quality.** With scanned images, the quality of the original greatly determines the quality of the scanned image. You can help improve the quality sometimes, though. If you're attempting to scan an image from thin paper, place construction paper or thin cardboard behind the paper to limit the amount of light that penetrates the paper.
- **Scan in grayscale to save hard drive space.** To limit the size of a scanned black-and-white file on your hard drive, make sure to scan the image in grayscale instead of color. Also, if you scan an image at a lower resolution, it will occupy less hard drive space than a high-resolution image.
- **Use 24-bit color for TV images.** When using a TV Tuner card, which allows you to capture still images from a television broadcast as .BMP files, you need to work with at least a SVGA video driver. If you try to display TV Tuner images at 256 colors or lower, the images will be greatly distorted, with colors often appearing reversed. To properly display television images, you'll probably want 24-bit color.
- **Adjusting video clip size.** You can choose the size of video clips through the Multimedia Properties window. (See Figure 24.19.)

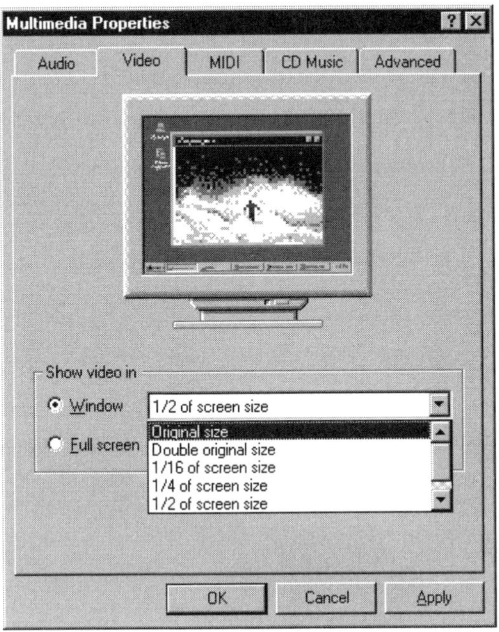

FIGURE 24.19: Video clips can be almost any size on your monitor.

- **Upgrade to Windows 95 versions.** If you are running the Windows 3.1 or DOS versions of multimedia programs under Windows 95, you'll almost certainly find improved performance and benefits if you upgrade to the Windows 95 version of the software. While the older versions run adequately under Windows 95, they don't take full advantage of Windows 95's multimedia strengths.
- **Large CD-ROM cache improves video.** When running video clips from a CD-ROM drive, you can improve the quality and smoothness of the clip by increasing the size of the CD-ROM cache. Double-click the System icon in the Control Panel window and click the Device Manager tab. If you see a CD-ROM listing, then you have protected-mode CD-ROM drive caching. If you have no CD-ROM listing, you have real-mode caching. Click the Performance tab ➢ File System, and select the CD-ROM tab. For protected-mode caching, make sure the pointer for Supplemental Cache Size is at the far right (Large). For real-mode caching, click the No Read Ahead command in the Optimize Access Pattern For drop-down list.

- **Test CD-ROM drive speed.** Test your CD-ROM drive's speed by playing an .AVI file. Check the motion of the graphics and see how they match with the sound. Then copy the .AVI file to your hard drive and again play the file. If the match between the graphics and the sound is significantly better, your CD-ROM drive isn't powerful enough to handle today's multimedia.
- **Improve .AVI file performance.** *Don't* run the files over a network, increase the size of the CD-ROM cache, or load SMARTDrive in the AUTOEXEC.BAT file.
- **Paste video clips into files.** You can copy and paste any portion of a video clip into another file. Open the video file into the Media Player program. Move the slider to the point of the video clip that you want to begin copying. Click the Edit menu and the Selection command. The current position of the slider is represented by the number (in minutes and seconds) in the From box. Type the ending position of the selection in the To box, click the radio button next to the From box, and click OK. The selection you've created will be marked by a blue line on the slider bar. Click Edit ➢ Copy Object. The portion of the file you selected is copied to the Clipboard. Open the file into which you want to copy the video clip, place the cursor where you want the video clip to appear, and click the Paste command from the Edit menu.
- **Media player and .MPEG don't mix.** If you want to view .MPEG files in Windows 95, you'll need to install a third-party software program. The Media Player program cannot play .MPEG files.
- **Fixing animation problems.** If you experience problems while running animated sequences, you may have an incorrect listing in your SYSTEM.INI file. Open the SYSTEM.INI file in Notepad. Scroll through the SYSTEM.INI file until you find a [mci] section. You should see the line `avivideo=mciavi.drv` somewhere in this section. If not, add the line and exit Notepad before restarting Windows 95.
- **Fixing QuickTime conflicts.** QuickTime for Windows, versions 1.1 and 2, may cause problems while running .MOV files in Windows 95 when your video card uses the S3 chip set. When this problem occurs, you may find .MOV files are interrupted when you move the mouse, or a white line may appear through the middle of the video clip. Use Notebook to open the QTW.INI file in the Windows directory. In the [Video] section of the file, add **Optimize=Driver** on a separate line. (You may need to add the [Video] section as well.)

- **QuickTime, watch double installations.** When playing files in QuickTime, it's especially important to make sure you have only one version of QuickTime installed on your computer; many software programs install versions of QuickTime throughout your hard drive. Click the Start button, the Find menu, and the Files Or Folders command to search for QuickTime files (QTW.*).
- **Play video files at lower resolutions.** When playing video files and graphic animations in Windows 95, to save system resources, don't play the files at any greater resolution than 800×600. With lower resolutions, your video card will be able to maintain the speed of the file.
- **Getting the most out of your graphics hardware.** The Full setting in the Advanced Graphics Setting window allows for maximum video card functions. (See Figure 24.20.)

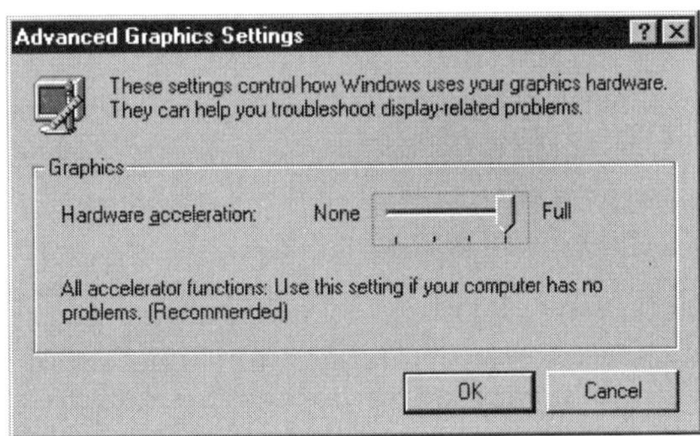

FIGURE 24.20: Allow your hardware Full acceleration for best performance.

- **Watch the 1,000-font limit.** Windows 95 can only contain about 1,000 fonts in its Fonts folder. Some programs, including CorelDRAW, attempt to install several hundred fonts into the Fonts folder, which may exceed the limit and cause your Windows 95 Desktop to change appearance.
- **Customize startup and shutdown screens.** Windows 95's startup and shutdown screens are customizable .BMP files. You can create your own .BMP file to display in these areas using Paint. The file must be created in 256 colors at 320×400 resolution. The boot screen is LOGO.SYS (the .SYS extension is used to help hide the file), the initial shutdown screen is LOGOW.SYS, and the final shutdown screen is LOGOS.SYS. Simply rename the .BMP file you want to use as one of the logo files. Copy the logo file you're replacing to disk in case

you want to use it later. (Sometimes your system won't have all of these logo files.) You also can edit the logo files using Paint.

- **Make more Desktop room.** To make additional room on your Windows 95 Desktop, you can shrink the shortcut icons. Right-click anywhere on the Desktop, then click the Properties command in the pop-up menu. Click the Appearance tab, then the Icon command in the drop-down menu, and in the Size area, select 16. Click the Apply button to see how the icons will appear. Note that long names under these icons may be difficult to read now. Try another size if 16 is unacceptable, or return the size to 32. Click OK to save the current configuration.
- **Return color to Windows 3.*x* icons.** Windows 3.*x* users occasionally will experience video problems with their icons in Program Manager. If a particular program group contains too many icons for its memory allotment to handle, the icons sometimes appear black. You can move some of the icons to a new program group or reduce your display settings to 256 colors to help alleviate the problem.

Printers

Printers are one of those little perks that can give you beautiful output. Treat it right!

- **Before you buy.** If you can't figure out how to remove a jammed piece of paper and replace the toner cartridge in the store, don't bring it home. If you use special paper or forms, bring samples into the store and make sure the printer you're about to buy can handle them.
- **Test your printer controls.** Make sure you understand all controls and indicators before you leave the store. More importantly, make sure you can reach the on/off switch. Many printers place their controls in awkward places, forcing you to reach in back of the machine.
- **Printer speed.** For desktop laser printers, look for engine speeds of 4 pages per minute (PPM) to 8PPM. In color inkjets and network color laser printers, look for 1PPM in color printing. For network use, look for monochrome models that can do 12PPM.
- **Real printer speed.** Most printers do not live up to their speed specifications, although inkjet printers have statistics that are closer to the truth than what

laser printers claim. Testing is conducted under optimum conditions using the latest technology and rarely is multitasking considered. Before buying any printer, test it with your own documents, and never use their demo page—they've tweaked it for faster delivery.

- **Print smaller fonts to test detail.** To really see distinctions between the output quality of different laser printers, print documents and graphics in smaller point sizes. At 6 points and below, you'll see whether your top printer choice can handle detailed images.
- **Analyze printing costs.** While inkjet printers are initially much cheaper than laser printers—by around 25 to 50 percent—in the long run they can be much more expensive. Depending on the amount of ink required, the real cost of printing a full-page graphic can cost as much as 30 to 50 cents per page on an inkjet printer vs. 2 to 3 cents per page for a laser printer. Laser printers will also last longer and require less maintenance and daily care.
- **Speed demons.** Printing graphics and colors slow down any inkjet printer, however, even in monochrome, color inkjet printers pale before the blazing speed of all laser printers, including the low-end models. In addition to the complexity of what you're printing, printer performance is also affected by your PC's speed and random access memory, the type of operating system you have, and the application you're using.
- **Restocking fees.** Return policies have changed. Many 30-day money-back guarantees are shrinking to 15-day policies and, in every case, you'll need a receipt. Beware, many retailers charge a 15 percent restocking fee if you lose the box or return damaged goods. If you're returning a laser or inkjet printer with an opened cartridge, they will charge you for the cartridge. Ask about restocking policies before you buy.
- **Extended warranties.** Whenever possible, pay by credit card because many will back you if there's a dispute. Some credit cards carry automatic extended one- to two-year warranty protection plans. In other cases, an extra $100 extends the manufacturer's warranty for four years.
- **Don't overlook the Web.** Ready to buy a new or used printer? Companies like Onsale (`http://www.onsale.com`) and Cyberswap (`http://www.cyberswap.com`) literally auction off everything from Pentium PCs to color printers. Customers typically save 20 to 30 percent off the original equipment price, although delivery can take several weeks.

- **Juice problems.** For laser printers in the home, make sure your electrical outlet has enough juice to power your printer, plus whatever else is plugged in (PC, modem, fax, etc.). If the lights on your printer dim when it's printing, plug your printer into another outlet.
- **Make printer cartridges a perfect fit.** Laser and inkjet printer cartridges are not interchangeable. Make sure the cartridge you buy fits your printer. For best results, buy toner cartridges from the manufacturer that made your printer. Generic-brand cartridges are usually cheaper, but because they are designed to work with different printers, they're not optimized for any specific manufacturer's printer. Also, if defective, they can void your printer's warranty. Factor in the price of a replacement cartridge before you buy a printer.
- **Extend paper trays.** If work space is crucial, measure the printer with paper input and output trays completely extended. Keep in mind, a manufacturer's measurement of a printer is usually with all input and output trays collapsed. Also, if your printer inexplicably stops working, make sure all trays are seated properly.
- **Cable connection.** New printers get better performance using a new bidirectional IEEE 1284 compliant cable (about $15). Older cables can cause poor-quality output, freezes, and other problems because they're not built to handle the complexity of today's data.
- **Record the important numbers.** Record your new printer serial number and model number. Should you call for technical support, be prepared to tell the technician if your printer is hooked up to a network, what software you're using, and whether or not you're using any special font cartridges or software fonts.
- **Choose your inkjet printer carefully.** Many three-color inkjet printers, known as *CMY* printers because of the colors they use—cyan, magenta, and yellow—swap between various colors and combine for black ink images. Output is not only slow, but it blurs easily. These printers generally have small ink cartridges. The smaller the ink tank, the higher the per page cost. You'll save money (and aggravation) with a four color (*CMYK*) printer (the *K* stands for black).
- **Separate ink cartridges.** If you're shopping for an inkjet printer, buy one that uses separate color cartridges. That way, you don't have to throw out the entire cartridge just because you've run out of one color.

- **Update your drivers.** Chances are whatever driver came with your laser or inkjet printer has already been replaced. (A *driver* is like a universal translator that helps your PC talk to your printer.) New printer drivers fix known incompatibilities, improve speed, and print quality. Generally, they're updated quarterly. The fastest way to get a driver is to go online and download it from the manufacturers' Web site, bulletin board, or online forum. If you're not connected online, check your user manual and call the company. They should send the new driver for a minimal shipping charge.
- **Check on your printer's drivers.** To see what version of printer driver you're using, click the Start button in Windows 95, select Settings ➢ Printers, then right-click the printer in question and select Properties. On Hewlett-Packard laser printers, select the Paper tab, then click the About button. Keep in mind that other printers may install proprietary printer software and the About button will be located under a different tab. In all NEC SuperScript models, for example, the About button is located under the Setup tab. (See Figure 24.21.)

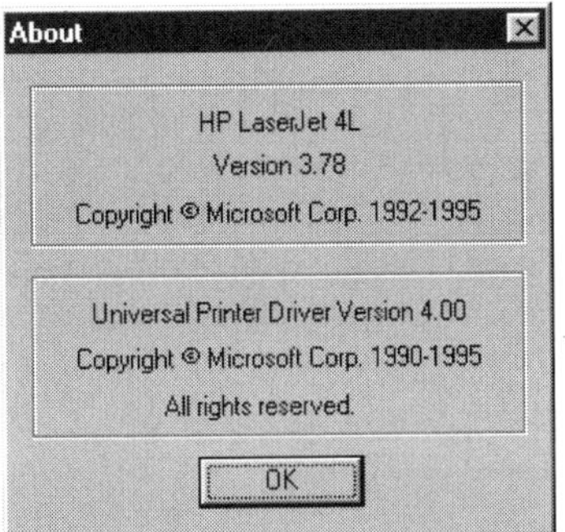

FIGURE 24.21: The About dialog box gives you essential information about your printer.

- **Bookmark important manufacturers.** If you're connected to the Web, visit and bookmark important Web sites critical to your PC's performance. This list should include manufacturers for printers, modems, monitors, CD-ROM driver browsers, ISPs, etc. These sites are a tremendous resource for free downloads, product updates, technical support, troubleshooting tips, customization tricks, FAQs, and newsgroups.

- **Update drivers automatically.** Another way to make sure you have the latest printer driver is to get CyberMedia's indispensable Oil Change (`http://www.cybermedia.com`). Once installed, Oil Change scans your hard drive and notes the products you're using. Then it scours the Web and displays a list of available updates, new products, shareware, patches, drivers, and even games. Each item comes with a description, including any problems it repairs.
- **Corrupted printer drivers.** Printer drivers are just like any other file and can get corrupted, especially if you've had to restart Windows without properly shutting it down. If your printer has suddenly started printing fragmented documents or printing in the wrong typeface—after making sure all cables are connected, and then rebooting both your PC and printer—try reinstalling the printer driver. In Windows 95, click Start ➢ Settings ➢ Printers, double-click the Add Printer Wizard, and follow the on-screen instructions.
- **Keep the installation CD-ROM or disks.** We can't stress this point enough—keep your original installation package. You never know when you might have to reinstall a printer driver. If you've misplaced your CD-ROM or disk, don't panic. Simply install a printer driver for a earlier model. A driver for a Hewlett-Packard LaserJet 4 will also work on a LaserJet 5 and LaserJet 6, even though it may not access all the new features.
- **Less graphics, longer life.** Printing graphics not only takes a lot of time but eats toner. The fewer graphics you print, the longer you can expect your cartridge to last.
- **Use fewer dots per inch.** The lower the dpi (dots per inch) resolution, the less toner is used. Conversely, the higher the print density the more toner gets used. To save money, turn down toner settings. In a laser printer, switching from 300 or 600dpi to draft mode can save as much as 25 percent more toner! 300dpi is plenty for regular text letters. The dpi settings are generally listed under Properties. New laser printers, like NEC's Superscript 860, have a software-controlled toner-saver feature.
- **Turn color off.** If it's not a final draft, always print in draft or monochrome mode. Color increases the per page cost by two or three times. This is especially important if the printer is being used by children who can quickly run through a color cartridge.
- **Addressing envelopes.** Don't buy cheap envelopes. Poor construction causes paper jams and wrinkled edges. Avoid envelopes with metal claps, windows, Tyvec, or other synthetic materials. Be careful with envelopes that

come with pull-off adhesive strips that could come off inside the printer. Also, even though slots that let you feed in envelopes and stationery (without removing the standard paper supply) are common in laser printers, you may not find them in all inkjets. Make sure you know how well (or not) your inkjet prints envelopes before you buy it.

- **Difficulty switching gears.** Most laser printers let you switch between a default paper tray—where the printer feeds the paper automatically—to a manual feed. Others direct documents to the main output tray or straight through to the rear slot. The "straight through" path is recommended for heavier paper, envelopes, and transparencies to avoid paper jams. Switching trays in some printers is as easy as pushing a lever to direct traffic. Others, like the NEC 1260, use software to control the paper flow—which means you have to access the software and change the configuration.

- **Create a second printer driver.** Instead of switching back and forth between trays or paper paths, a smarter solution is to create a second copy of the printer driver and set it up as a default to manual feed or print to rear slot. That way, when you want to print a document or an envelope, you can keyboard Ctrl+P, and when the Print dialog box appears, select the second driver from the drop-down menu. To switch back, use your mouse to click and select the original driver. (See Figure 24.22.)

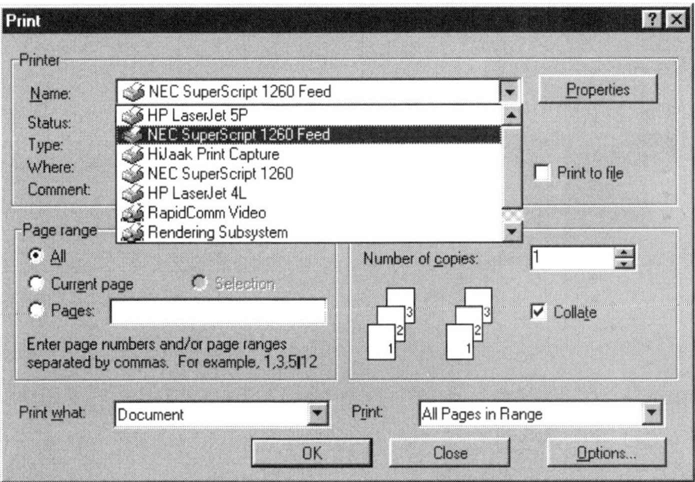

FIGURE 24.22: Make it easier to print by manual feed by creating a second printer driver.

- **How to create a second driver.** To create a second driver, click Start ➢ Settings ➢ Printers, then double-click Add Printer. Follow the Wizard to install a second printer driver exactly the same as the original. Be sure to give it a name you'll remember like "NEC Envelopes" or "Manual Feed."
- **Printer Desktop shortcut.** If you're using Windows 95 and your applications support drag-and-drop print, you can print documents on the fly, without first opening the application that created them. To start, you'll need to create a shortcut for your printer and plunk it on your Desktop. The easiest way is to click Start ➢ Settings ➢ Printers, and when the printer folder opens, right-click your printer icon and select Create Shortcut. A Windows 95 shortcut display will ask you if you want to place the shortcut on your Desktop. Click Yes. Now, using Windows Explorer or Internet Explorer 4.*x*, locate the document you want to print, then use your mouse to drag and drop it on the printer icon. The application used to create the document will magically open, then send the file to the printer, and close.
- **Print multiple copies.** Using the same drag-and-drop operation listed above, you can print multiple documents from different applications. Just select them and drop them on the printer icon.
- **Print documents from the Start menu.** To quickly print a file listed in Documents within the Start menu, simply right-click the file and select Print. This opens the application used to create the document, sends the file to the printer, then closes the application. Selecting the Quick Print option sends the file to your default printer.
- **Printing scanned photos.** When printing scanned high-quality photos on an inkjet printer, you don't need to have a dpi higher than 240 to produce the best results. A higher dpi of the image will only result in a much larger file requiring additional processing time without any improvement in output.
- **Spool printer jobs.** Speed up printing by activating the spooling feature in Windows 95. This passes data to your printer only when it's ready to receive it so you can get back to work because you're not waiting for the document to print. Go to Control Panel, open the Printers folder, right-click your printer icon, select Properties ➢ Details ➢ Spool Settings. Make sure the following radio buttons are clicked on: Spool Print Jobs So The Program Finishes Printing Faster and Start Printing After First Page Is Spooled. Spool Data Format should be EMF. If you have a new IEEE 1284 cable, make sure the Enable Bi-Directional Support for this printer button is also turned on. When you're finished, click the OK button, then click the OK button again.

- **Print to a file.** Sometimes you want to look at a document before you print it. To print a document to a file instead of to your printer, from the menu of most word processors you can click File ➢ Print (or Ctrl+P), and when the Print dialog box appears, check the box next to Print To File.
- **Compare your fonts.** Too many fonts rob system resources and slow down Windows, so it's a good idea to trim your font list. Keep only what you need. To compare fonts, click the View menu, then select List Fonts By Similarity. To remove a font, right-click it and select Delete. Be sure not to erase base fonts like Times New Roman, Arial, Courier, and others required by Windows 95. Programs like Quarterdeck's CleanSweep (`http://www.quarterdeck.com`) can safely uninstall unused or unwanted fonts.
- **Use TrueType fonts.** Different laser printers use different fonts, which is why a document printed on one laser printer looks different when it's printed on another. The only way to create documents that look the same on any printer is to use TrueType fonts. To see a list of TrueType fonts installed on your PC, click Start ➢ Settings ➢ Control Panel, and double-click the Fonts icon. TrueType fonts have *TT* in the icon, standard fonts have an *A*. (See Figure 24.23.)

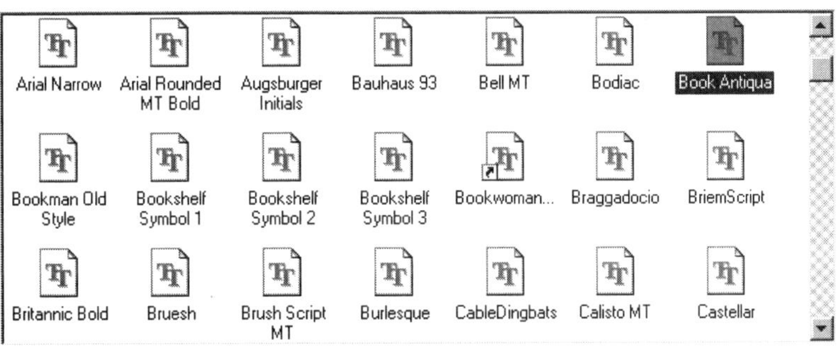

FIGURE 24.23: These TrueType fonts are identifiable by their icon.

- **Preview your fonts.** If you'd like to see what a font looks like, either on-screen or on the page before printing a document, Windows 95 users can sneak a peek using a font preview feature. Click Start ➢ Settings ➢ Control Panel, and double-click Fonts. Double-clicking the font's icon (or name) opens a window that shows you how the font scaled in comparison to a number of different sizes. Click Print to print out a copy.

- **Test page countdown.** To see how many pages your cartridge really prints—or to compare brands or even a remanufactured cartridge against a new cartridge—print out a test page when you install a new toner cartridge. When you're ready to replace it, print out another test page and subtract the older page count from the current total.
- **The gang's all here.** For printing drafts, consider ganging up pages. Blue Squirrel's ClickBook For Windows (`http://www.bluesquirrel.com/clickbook`) saves time, paper, and toner by squeezing two, four, or eight printed pages on a single sheet. It also handles double-sided printing.
- **Printer life expectancy.** While life expectancy varies from printer to printer, how the printer was used can shorten or extend its useful lifetime. Don't buy a printer that's produced more than half a million pages already.
- **Recycle paper.** Instead of throwing away draft copies created on an inkjet, put papers on a flat desktop tray and use the back side. Be sure to clean your inkjet regularly. Do not, however, do the same thing with drafts from a laser printer. The heat can melt the ink and leave it inside your printer, clogging up rollers and causing damage.
- **Recycle ink cartridges.** Consider finding a local service that refills old ink cartridges or buys used ones. Check your telephone business directory pages or call around to different computer department stores to find out who they recommend in your area.
- **Hewlett-Packard can help you recycle cartridges.** While you won't get any money, Hewlett-Packard's Toner Cartridge Recycling Program will dispose of empty cartridges for free. Simply repack your old cartridge in an empty toner box, slap the enclosed pre-packaged UPS shipping label on it, and call UPS for a pickup. If you don't have the UPS label, call Hewlett-Packard and ask for one.
- **Refill kits.** Steer clear of do-it-yourself inkjet refill kits. Not only is the ink quality poor, they tend to leak. You're better off with an ink replacement cartridge like those sold by MVM Products (`http://www.ink-jet.com`).
- **Too good to be true.** If you see a toner cartridge sale that seems too good to be true, check the expiration date on the toner box before you buy. Older cartridges can dry up and the result is poorly produced pages. If you do stock up on toner cartridges, don't buy so many that you run the risk of some going bad before you use them. Toner cartridges have about a two-year shelf life.

- **Unclog your nozzle.** Inkjet nozzles can be as small as 30 microns (that's about the width of a human hair), so any dust that gets into the cartridge will eventually clog your print heads. Be very careful when replacing cartridges.
- **Prevent clogging.** If you're not going to use your inkjet printer for a prolonged period—for example, you're going on a business trip or vacation—remove the cartridge from the printer and place a piece of tape over the printhead to prevent drippage and ink evaporation. This also prevents the head from clogging. Also, unplug and cover the printer.
- **Repeat performance.** Dust in inkjet printers manifests itself as *microbanding*—these are lines or blank spaces that appear in the output. Every inkjet has different instructions on how to clean its printer heads. Check your user manual and keep in mind that you may have to repeat the procedure several times.
- **Paper jam culprits.** Avoid offset, pre-printed forms, glossy or colored paper, multi-part forms, or pre-punched paper *unless* it is specifically designed for an inkjet, laser, or dot-matrix printer. The heat from a laser printer can melt the ink on preprinted forms. Glossy paper can tend to flake after printing, while multi-part forms are usually too thick to pass through a laser printer. Check pre-punched paper for small paper bits or holes that can get caught inside the printer and cause jams. When jams are in the fuser area, check for dirt or toner that might have leaked into the fuser assembly. If jams happen frequently, try changing paper. Bond paper with a high cotton content can cause dirt inside the printer.
- **Picking paper.** While the growing trend is towards multi-purpose paper—paper that can be used in a laser printer, inkjet printer, copier, and fax machine—before you buy, make sure. Hewlett-Packard sells special paper for laser jets and inkjets. Other companies sell recycled paper specially designed for inkjet and laser printers. To save money, buy paper by the case instead of one packet at time. For best results use 20lb paper with a brightness factor in the 90s. All this information is listed on the label. The lower the weight, the thinner the paper.
- **Getting paper out of a jam.** Open the hood and remove the paper. In older printers, you have to return the printer to an online state, usually by pressing the online button. You also have to wait for the printer to reset itself. If the printer still won't print, chances are you missed a piece of paper. Carefully recheck the gears, rollers, and all along the paper path. It only takes a small

piece, like a paper-hole from punched paper, to create a printer jam. If the printer is still jamming, try changing paper, reseating the paper cartridge, reseating the toner cartridge, and as a last resort, changing the toner cartridge.

- **Character dropouts.** If the page prints, but characters or words are missing or fuzzy, chances are the photosensitive drum in the toner cartridge is damaged. Replace it and see if the problem disappears. In some printers, when you change the toner, you may accidentally put a thumb print on the drum and ruin the cartridge. Read instructions carefully.
- **Black holes.** Large black areas on your paper can be caused by bad paper, a dirty fuser area, or a bad or damaged toner cartridge. Try installing a new toner cartridge, changing paper, and cleaning the inside of your printer. The best rule of thumb regarding any image defect on the output is to clean up, change the toner cartridge first, and see if that clears up the problem.
- **Sticky situations.** Be sure pre-packaged labels are designed for the heat of a laser printer. Don't reuse partial label pages by resending them though your laser printer. You run the risk of allowing the adhesive from the label page (or a label itself) to stick to the printer roller. Saving a few cents by reusing labels could cost $100 or more in printer repair and replacement costs.
- **Terminate toner trouble.** If your laser printer says your toner is running low or isn't printing with even darkness across the page, try this trick: Remove the toner cartridge and rock it gently from side to side to redistribute the toner powder.
- **Moisture causes paper jams.** Paper with too much moisture can cause paper jams or come out curled. Even if it prints out perfectly, moist paper can also cause blurring and fuzzy letters or graphics. Store paper in an unopened box and never place it directly on the floor. Keep paper elevated and stacked horizontally, not vertically.
- **Controlling the vertical lines.** Generally, vertical lines on the page are caused by a particle caked on the corona wire. Try cleaning the wire with a swab stick dipped in alcohol, but be careful not to break it. Check the manual for specific instructions. If that doesn't work, change the toner cartridge.
- **Printing from the Internet.** If you're not in a rush, you can use the Web to create and print business cards, stationery, labels, and any other custom-printed materials. Check out PrintLink@CopyMax (`http://www.iprint.com/officemax.html`).

- **Browser printing.** Just like your word processor, Netscape Navigator 4.*x* has a print preview feature that lets you peek at a Web page before printing. From the menu, click File, then Print Preview to determine a document's length, its page breaks, and select which pages to print.
- **Removing the URL and date.** When printing pages off the Internet, if you don't want the Web address or date stamp printed on the Web page, you can remove them. In Netscape Navigator 4.*x*, click File ➢ Page Setup, and under Header And Footer uncheck whatever you don't want printed. When you're finished, click OK. It's a bit harder to do this in Internet Explorer 4.*x*. Click File ➢ Page Setup, and delete the codes under Header And Footer. If you want to reinstate the Header And Footer, you'll have to type in the same code, so it's a good idea to write them down or copy them to a file before permanently deleting them.
- **Print the entire Web page.** If you have problems printing or saving a document in your browser, it's usually because the document hasn't finished loading. Click Refresh or Reload, wait until the page is finished downloading, then click Print or Save As.
- **Fan your paper.** For laser and inkjet printers, you can prevent paper jams by fanning paper and envelopes with your thumb to loosen up individual sheets.
- **Self-diagnostic test.** Every printer can print out a one-page test without being connected to a PC. Check your manual and run a self-diagnostic test. A printer that can't run a self-diagnostic test requires professional attention. If a printer can print out a test, that's a sign that your problem is computer- or software-related. Remember to reset the printer and put it back online before trying to print.
- **Thanks for the memory.** Printers, like people, sometimes get confused when presented with too much information. Try turning your printer and PC off, wait for 15 seconds, then restart them. This will clear whatever is jamming up the memory. If that doesn't work, turn everything off again, then restart your computer first, wait until it goes through its entire setup routine, and then turn on your printer. If your printer works after trying this last suggestion, then your PC is probably sending confusing signals to your printer at startup.

- **Turn everything on.** Is your printer turned on? Sure it sounds simple, but when your printer suddenly stops working and you need your documents *now*, it's easy to overlook the obvious. Make sure your printer is plugged in and turned on. Check the outlet, make sure it's working. If your printer is plugged into a surge protector (as it should be), make sure the surge protector is also on. A sudden power surge may have tripped the unit and automatically shut it down.
- **Online/offline.** Is your printer online? Many printers have an online and offline button on the front panel and you have press a button until the light clicks on, indicating that the printer is online. In the offline position, the printer is technically on, however, it can neither accept information from your PC, nor print it.
- **Check your software.** If you're having a problem printing, make sure your software is installed properly (paying careful attention to printer setup). Is the software configured to run with your printer? Do you have the right printer driver? If you share a computer, make sure someone didn't change a setting or print a fax and forget to put your default printer driver back the way you set it up.
- **Memory problems.** Older laser printers come with less memory. They can work great for straight text—depending on the software—but you may have a hard time printing out complex graphics. Even when you can add more memory, many older machines just can't do the job.
- **Special effects.** Both Word for Windows and WordPerfect provide similar special printing features plus watermarks, white on black lettering, and more. New NEC SuperScript models come with print manager software that allows two-sided, booklet printing, and other options. (See Figure 24.24.)
- **Cleaning the outside.** Clean the outside of your printer at least once a week. Wipe away dust, dirt, animal hair, and other contaminants using a damp, lint-free cloth dipped in water or rubbing alcohol. Beware: stronger cleaners can damage the printer case.
- **Cleaning the inside.** Pop the hood and remove the toner cartridge. Clean all the gears, rollers, and all along the paper path. To clean the rollers, use rubbing alcohol or Bestine (a solvent available at many art stores).

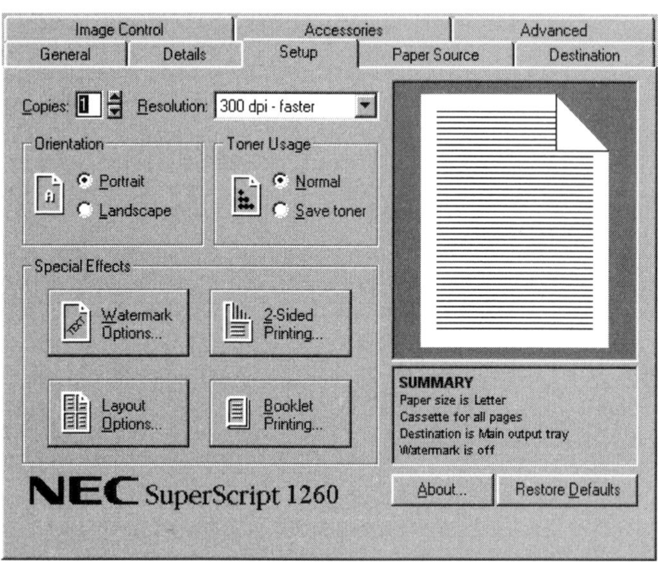

FIGURE 24.24: The latest printers can put out some fancy footwork.

- **Print a blank page.** Run a clean page through your printer. This will pick up lint, dust, and stray toner. In some printers, you'll have to take the printer offline and then press the form feed button. Or, open your word processor to a blank page and select the print command. If it won't print a blank page, type any character, and then select print.
- **Cover it up.** Dust, dirt, pet hair, and other environmental factors can damage a printer. Covers keep your printer safe and clean when not in use. Make it a habit to turn off the power and cover up your printer at the end of each work session.
- **Don't use air blowers.** Don't use a compressed air blower to clean out your laser or inkjet printer. You risk blasting dirt and dust back into the printer. Instead, buy a small portable vacuum. (You can also use it on your keyboard.) Be sure to check your manual for instructions on cleaning your printer.
- **Can't take the heat.** Toner cartridges are sensitive to heat, light, and humidity. Leaving it in your car trunk on a hot day can damage the cartridge. Store cartridges horizontal, not vertical, and in a sensible temperature range between 32 to 95 degrees. Otherwise, you risk toner clumping.

- **Making adjustments.** Filling a paper tray to the brim or adjusting the paper guides too tightly can cause paper jams. Always leave a dab of room.
- **Zero in on the cartridge.** In most printers, the fastest way to fix a problem—or even diagnose its source—is to change the toner cartridge. Generally, this will solve 80 percent of all printer problems.
- **Loud noises.** Inkjet and laser printers are relatively quiet machines but they do make noises. A whirring noise is probably indicating that the printer is rotating the fuser and stirring the toner to prevent damage from the roller blade staying in the same position for too long. Load grinding noises, however, are a warning sign. Try changing the toner cartridge. If the noise persists, your printer needs professional help.
- **Dot-matrix printers.** Dot-matrix printers, also called impact printers, are still your best choice for printing large volumes of output when cost is an issue and print quality is not a primary concern. These printers offer the lowest cost per page value and are virtually maintenance free.
- **Dot-matrix paper handling.** Newer impact printers, like those from Epson, let you "cue" up to four different types of paper. This feature helps because you no longer have to switch between printing continuous form checks, invoices, labels, and a single page letter.

Modems

These days, your modem is one of your best accessories.

- **Avoid downtime; use a fast modem.** The most important factor in modem performance is the modem's data transmission speed. Measured in terms of *kilobits per second* (Kbps), the data transmission speed determines how quickly data is transported between the sender and the receiver. Average modem transmission speeds vary between 14.4Kbps on the slow end and 56Kbps on the fast end. The faster the transmission speed, the less time you spend waiting for data.
- **Before upgrading, evaluate connection choices.** Before you upgrade your modem, look into the other Internet connection possibilities, such as cable modems, satellite modems, and *xDSL modems*. These devices generally offer faster data transmission speeds than typical modems, but they also tend to cost more money. Weigh the benefits with the costs to decide which connection

option is best for you. (The term xDSL stands for *digital subscriber lines*. The descriptive acronym xDSL refers to all DSL-type modem transmission technologies, which use advanced modulation arrangements to compress data onto copper wires.)

- **Internal or external modems?** When you upgrade your modem, you'll have to decide whether to use an internal or external model. Generally, if you want to save money and you aren't afraid to take a look under your PC's hood, go with an internal modem. If you want an easy installation and don't mind paying a little more, go with an external modem.
- **External modems' on and off switch.** One of the benefits of having an external modem is you can turn it on and off without restarting your PC. Just flip the switch, shut down your Internet software, wait a few seconds, then turn the modem back on, and restart the Internet software. This is the first thing you should do if you experience a connection error or just think your modem isn't running properly.
- **When IRQ conflicts arise.** Interrupt request line (IRQ) conflicts can stop your online journey before it begins. If you have problems with your modem and you use Windows 95, right-click the My Computer icon, select Properties from the drop-down menu, and click the Device Manager tab. Double-click the Computer option to open the Computer Properties window. Click the Interrupt Request (IRQ) option and make sure the IRQ setting for your modem's communications (COM) port doesn't have any other listed responsibilities. If it does, consult the modem's user manual for instructions on configuring the modem's IRQ setting.
- **Turn off that noise.** If you can't stand the screeches and squawks your modem makes when it connects to the Internet, use the modem volume control to get some online peace and quiet. In Windows 95, right-click My Computer and select Properties from the resulting pop-up menu. In the System Properties window, click the Device Manager tab. Make sure you activate the View Device By Type setting and double-click the Modems option. Double-click the name of your modem, and click the Modem tab in the resulting window. Slide the speaker volume to Off, then click OK.

NOTE NOTE NOTE NOTE NOTE NOTE NOTE NOTE NOTE NOTE NOTE NOTE NOTE NOTE NOTE

The method for hushing a modem varies with each operating system and software package. Consult your user manual for details.

- **Busy signals, part 1.** As the number of people using the Internet has increased, it has become quite common for users to receive busy signals in response to attempted dial-ups. To minimize the odds of receiving a busy signal, use the Internet during off-peak times. The Internet tends to be busiest on weekday evenings; mornings and weekends tend to be the least busy.
- **Busy signals, part 2.** Another way to combat busy signals is to switch *Internet service providers* (ISPs). There are lots of ISPs out there that just don't have the facilities to meet customer demand. If your ISP can't satisfy your Internet needs, find one that can. Check with your long-distance service provider or a local computer store for connection alternatives in your area.
- **Resolve connection problems.** If you're experiencing connection problems but aren't sure whether the problem lies with the modem or your ISP, use a phone dialer application to call a friend. In Windows 95, for instance, click the Start button, select Programs, open the Accessories group, and click Phone Dialer. In the resulting window, enter the telephone number of a friend. If the call rings through, then the problem most likely lies with the ISP and you should report it immediately. If the call doesn't ring through, the problem probably lies with the modem. Make sure you configured it correctly before calling the manufacturer.
- **Red modem lights mean stop.** Most external modems sport a row of red lights that light up when the modem is active. If you try to make a call while the modem is active, you'll disconnect your Internet connection and get an earful of whistles and squawks. Before you pick up your phone to make a call, make sure these lights are off.
- **A second phone line.** If you use the Internet a lot, consider purchasing a second phone line for your home. Designate one line for phone calls and another for Internet use. That way, you'll always have access to the Internet and you still can receive calls. Plus, if you use the Internet for business purposes, you may be able to deduct the second line on your taxes.
- **Don't expect your modem to reach full speed.** A modem's data transmission speed is a measurement of the modem's maximum transmission speed. That means you'll rarely, if ever, transmit data as quickly as your modem claims it can.
- **Understanding upload speed limits.** It's important to note that a 56Kbps modem can transmit data at that speed in only one direction—from the Internet to your PC. Because of data encoding limitations, you can't upload data to the Internet any faster than 33.6Kbps.

- **Phone and modem lines.** On the back of every modem—internal or external—are two jacks. Usually, one is marked Phone and the other is marked Line. To use the modem, you must plug an active telephone cord (one that is plugged into a standard wall jack) into the Line jack on the back of the modem. If you want to use the telephone line for phone calls when you're not using the modem, plug a telephone into the Phone jack on the back of the modem.
- **Set the switches.** Most modems have jumpers or *dual inline package* (DIP) switches that need to be configured for each system. Before you install the modem, read the manual to determine how to set these switches. Contact the modem manufacturer if you run into any problems configuring these hardware settings.
- **Make sure you plug it in.** If your modem suddenly stops working or doesn't work after you install it, carefully double-check all the connections. It only takes one loose plug or cord to render the modem useless.
- **Get a modem cable.** An external modem connects to a serial port, but that doesn't mean you can use any old serial cable to connect the modem to your PC. You need to go to the store and buy a $10 modem cable if you want that modem to function properly.
- **A COMmon problem.** COM port conflicts are a common cause of connection consternation. One way to avoid COM port problems is to make sure your external modem is connected to the appropriate serial port. In general, COM port 1 corresponds to serial port A and COM port 2 corresponds to serial port B. If you're not sure which serial port is A and which one is B, check your computer manual.
- **Expansion slot slip.** An internal modem should fit snugly into an expansion slot. If you're having problems with a recently installed internal modem, double-check the expansion slot connection. The top of the modem card should run parallel to the top of your desk. If the card is slanted or otherwise installed improperly, remove it and insert it correctly into the slot.
- **Tone or pulse telephones.** A phone system uses one of two dialing methods: tone or pulse. When you configure your Internet connection, you need to know which dialing method your phone uses. Basically, if your phone allows for touch-tone dialing, set your modem software for tone dialing; if your phone allows for rotary dialing, set your modem software for pulse dialing. If you're uncertain about which dialing type to buy, call your local telephone company for information.

- **UART conflict.** Because of potential conflicts with your computer's *Universal Asynchronous Receiver/Transmitter* (UART; the device that manages the flow of data between a modem and the communications software), you should choose an internal modem if you plan to upgrade the modem on an older (486 or older) computer. Unlike external modems, internal modems contain built-in UARTs that override the UART on your system's motherboard.
- **Phone cord extensions.** If you want to use your modem, you need access to a phone line. Unfortunately, the architects may not have considered that point when they designed your house. Use a phone cord extension—available at most electronics stores—to solve this problem without moving your furniture or drilling holes in the wall.
- **Turn external modems on.** If you upgrade from an internal modem to an external modem, don't forget to turn on your modem. Unlike internal modems that run on your computer's power supply, external modems have their own power source and power switch.
- **Faxing fun.** A fax modem extends the capabilities of your PC, but only if you turn the modem on. If you want to receive a fax, you either need to keep your computer on and your communications software open at all times, or you need to ask the sender to call you before transmitting the fax so you can get your system ready.

Working Online

You and your modem can get you a plethora of information, if you know how to access it online.

- **Find the right dial-up speed.** When dialing up the Internet, it's best to communicate with a modem on the other end that's running at the same speed because the speed at which data is sent depends upon the speed of the slower modem. First, make sure your Internet service provider (ISP) can support your modem speed. Then, set your dial-up speed to one setting faster than your modem speed. If you're using a 28.8Kbps modem, for example, select 38000 (which is equivalent to 38.4Kbps) when configuring your modem.
- **Stop tying up the phone line unnecessarily.** Does your ISP charge by the hour and do the kids often forget to log off? You can set your connection to automatically disconnect you after a long period of idleness. To do so in Windows 95, go to Dial-Up Networking, right-click the ISP icon, choose

Properties ➢ Configure, open the Connection tab, and check the radio button for Disconnect A Call If Idle For More Than *x* Minutes.

- **Trade in glitz for substance.** If pages are taking a long time to download to your browser, the culprit is often hefty graphic files. Almost all Web browsers allow you to turn off all graphics; look for some sort of auto-load graphics command that you can turn off and on.
- **Clean up your cache.** Your cache stores Web pages you visit in a temporary file. While this saves you time surfing because your browser will check to see if a page has been cached, and, if so, it will load it first, this can eventually clog up your hard drive. Clean it out regularly, or after particularly long sessions online.
- **Learn to reload.** Did a Web site suddenly hiccup and stop loading? It might be just a temporary glitch. To find out, hit the Reload (or Refresh) button on your browser and see if the entire page appears this time.
- **Watch your cookies.** Some Web pages will send cookies to your browser. *Cookies* are tokens or messages that can identify your particular Web browser and alert the Web server that you (the individual user) have accessed the Web site. If you don't like the feeling that Big Brother is watching you, take advantage of a feature most browsers have; they can be configured to alert you when a cookie is being sent and let you stop accessing that page.
- **Streamline that URL.** If you're tired of typing an entire universal resource locator (URL, a Web address) such as `http://www.nameofsite.com` every time you go to a new site, save yourself some effort. Most Web browsers default to `http://`, so you rarely need to type that in. Even better, the later versions of most browsers default to adding `www` for you before a name and `.com` afterward, so usually you can simply type **nameofsite** in your browser's Address Bar to get to `http://www.nameofsite.com`.
- **Do more at once.** Are you downloading software from one site and checking out sports scores on another? Pop open two browser windows at once (usually done by a command in the File menu called something such as New Browser). You can then toggle back and forth between the two browser windows.
- **Minimize your wait.** Certain sites will load faster at certain times of the day. For example, a stock market site may be extremely busy just after the market closes, while a sports site may be slow to access late at night. Choose the

time of day you access a site wisely, you'll have better luck when others are less likely to be clogging it.

- **Ship 'em and share 'em.** Have you come across a great Web page that you want your friend or colleague to see? Rather than opening a mail reader, typing in the URL and sending the e-mail message, most browsers let you send a page directly. Look in the File menu on your Web browser for a Mail Page or Send Page command.
- **Keep your money safe.** Online transactions are becoming more commonplace, but that doesn't mean you should ignore safety. Most browsers can be set to notify you if the information you are sending across the Internet is insecure. Also, be sure to look on the Web site for security information, such as the name of the encryption software being used for consumer protection.
- **There's no place like home.** Most people find themselves visiting one particular site over and over, whether it's their company home page or their favorite search engine. Instead of bookmarking that page, make it your home page. You can usually find this option under the Edit or View menus. Once you have your favorite Web site set up, all you have to do is click the Home button on your browser desktop to access it.
- **Organize your online life.** Bookmarks are fantastic tools for locating information, but if you've been online for any amount of time, you may find that scrolling through all of them is almost as bad as using a search engine to find them each time. Just as e-mail messages can be organized into folders and subfolders, so can bookmarks. Try separating them into Work, Fun, Computer, Friends, etc.
- **Learn your search engine features.** Different search engines have different features. For instance, Yahoo! lets you choose how recent Web pages must be, and LycosPro differs between sites, page titles, and URLs. A minute spent learning how to use them now will save you hours looking through the results in the long run.
- **Become familiar with Boolean commands.** Most search engines, such as Excite, include Boolean commands that can eliminate pages of unnecessary results. Suppose you're looking for information on John Denver, and you don't want to turn up every page that mentions Denver (the Broncos, Denver International Airport, etc.). Using *John AND Denver* will turn up only those pages that contain both names.

- **Do more than search with search engines.** Search engines do more than return pages; many of them also categorize the results. Say you're looking for four-wheel drive cars, but the only ones you can think of are Audis. A search engine such as Yahoo! will show you which categories Audi falls under, and you can then go to the category to find similar automobiles.
- **Use your resources.** Search engines aren't the only Web sites that gather related information; the Web is packed with specialty online databases. Take a look at Dow-Jones Interactive (plenty of news), WESTLAW (legal resources), and GaleNet (academic and literary sources).
- **Keep your logins straight.** Are you registering at dozens of sites, and you can't remember all your logins and passwords? Choose the same login name and password for every Web site, but use ones that are different from the login ID and password to your ISP (for security reasons).
- **Sample, sample, sample.** There is plenty of free stuff on the Internet, especially software, so try before you buy. Go to a site such as `http://www.shareware.com` that lets you download and try out all kinds of programs on a trial basis. Don't assume that if one company is selling it, another company's free offering won't also do the trick for you.
- **Learn to right-click.** Have you come across a great graphic on a Web site and decided that you want to save it as wallpaper for your Desktop? With the cursor on the image, right-click and you'll see a variety of options, including saving the image to your hard drive, viewing the HTML code, sending the link to others, and more.
- **Know what you're downloading.** When you download a file from the Internet, you take the risk of also downloading a virus. Protect yourself by reading the site or visiting a neutral site for virus information. (The Anti-Virus page at `http://www.geocities.com/SiliconValley/1710` is a good bet, or you can also install virus-combating software.)
- **Take advantage of e-mail alerts.** The Web is chock-full of useful information, but finding it can be tough. So, some clever Webmasters have created e-mail alerts, which are messages sent out via e-mail that let you know what's new on their Web sites, almost like a table of contents to new material. Subscribing to these can save you time if you are interested in a particular topic.

- **Subscribe to an e-mail news service.** Want to read your daily horoscope, check your stocks, or get the latest headlines? Rather than going to the Web, you can have the information sent to your e-mail box using a service such as InfoBeat (`http://www.infobeat.com`).
- **Spam, be gone.** Telemarketers calling during dinner are bad enough, but now the problem of junk phone calls and junk mail has moved to the Internet. If you're receiving e-mail from people trying to sell you things you don't want, you're not alone. Spamming happens when salespeople send bulk unsolicited e-mail. Spoil the spammers by telling your ISP; they have more resources than you do and they want to keep you happy by helping you fight spammers.
- **Use mailing lists wisely.** Mailing lists are collections of people who get together to discuss particular topics, and they don't take to newcomers' off-topic postings. "Listen" for a few days before posting your comments. Also, avoid flames by contacting the mailing list's owner/moderator and get approval before posting a slightly off-topic post.
- **Find the blind CC function.** Have an e-mail you want to send to dozens of people? Rather than listing all of their names in the CC line, use the blind CC function in your mail reader. This will save your recipients from scrolling through all those names to get to the meat of your message.
- **Don't forget newsgroups.** When you hear the word "Internet," the first thing that probably comes to your mind is the Web. But the Internet is more than just the Web; newsgroups can be valuable sources of information. Taking a trip to San Francisco? A newsgroup for its locals can be a great place to ask questions.
- **Find newsgroups via the Web.** Newsgroups are great resources, but finding them can be tough. Deja News (`http://www.dejanews.com`) is a wonderful and useful tool. You can search by topic or category, browse by top level, or follow one of its other options.

Extras

These are all the little things that you may not think of, but it's best to cover all the bases!

Travel

Traveling with a computer is more and more popular these days. It's getting so that you can't escape it.

- **Secure your laptop computer while traveling.** Laptop computers are among the most often stolen items for business travelers. An electronic alarm, set to sound when your laptop is farther than 10 to 20 feet away from you, clips on easily. When choosing alarms, look for an adjustable distance setting, a battery self-test, a small size, and an LED (light-emitting diode) that flashes when the alarm is turned on.
- **A laptop carrying case spreads the load.** For truly rugged use, choose a steel case that can withstand being dropped and is amply padded to protect the computer. For routine use, an over-the-shoulder case should be well-padded, organized with separate compartments for the laptop, disks, battery pack, input device(s), cables, files, pens, and business cards. The strap should have a wide leather section to disperse weight properly.
- **Spare your muscles with a PC backpack.** A PC backpack can free your hands and distribute weight more evenly than a traditional briefcase can. Choose a waterproof backpack with adjustable straps and separate compartments for a laptop computer, battery pack, cables, disks, and input device(s), along with an expanding gusset for notebooks. An external compartment for pens, paper clips, and other supplies is also a good idea.
- **Acoustic coupler for modem use on the road.** Some hotels still don't offer data ports. An acoustic coupler lets you connect your modem through the phone in your room. Look for the fastest transmission speed possible, an international phone adapter, and a power adapter.
- **International converters increase options.** Traveling abroad? Your laptop computer probably won't run on the international electric current standard, or even have a plug that fits into international outlets. Buy an international converter with at least an 80-watt, power-up capacity, and a thermal fuse to protect your laptop from a power overload. Converters are available at many electronics or office supply stores.
- **Modem savers identify digital lines.** Identify digital lines with a modem saver before they fry your analog modem. Look for a modem saver with an adapter for international phone jacks. It must have the ability to change phone line polarity to adjust for conditions in different phone systems, even within the United States.

- **Power inverter increases laptop computer mobility.** Turn your car's cigarette lighter into two AC outlets with a power inverter. Look for one that protects against car battery drainage and offers at least an 80-watt capacity, plus power-up capabilities.

Security Options

Having a computer opens you up to any number of security problems. Follow these guidelines to keep yourself safe.

- **Increase monitor privacy.** Slipping on a monitor privacy screen limits readability to only those who aren't directly in front of the monitor. From an angle, the screen is translucent. Look for a privacy screen that slips on and off easily, just in case you need to change your monitor's angle, as well as one that simultaneously reduces glare, static, and dust build-up.
- **Lock your disk drive.** If security is an issue, lock your disk drive to prevent unauthorized data downloading. Look for locks that do not void your PC or drive warranties, as well as ones that install without special tools.
- **Lock your desktop.** A desktop lock prevents unauthorized access to your PC. Look for a locking system that secures your computer case or one that includes a coated cable and a secure padlock that cannot easily be broken into.

Inside Your PC

Remember: Safety first!

- **PC tool kit needed for internal work.** Look for demagnetized heads and tools in both metric and English versions. Socket wrenches should have thin heads to reach into tight spaces. Make sure your tool kit also has a chip puller, so you can remove microprocessor chips easily, without bending their prongs.
- **Cool your Pentium chip.** Dissipate the extra heat generated by a Pentium microprocessor. Look for PC fans that operate only when they're needed, typically at 25 degrees Celsius (77 degrees Fahrenheit) or higher. Installation should be simple, either by snapping the fan onto the chip or by exposing an adhesive backing and placing it on the Pentium chip.
- **Ground yourself for internal work.** When you remove the computer case cover, ground yourself to the PC with a "grounding strap" to avoid discharging static electricity into the PC itself or the components you are handling.

The strap slips onto your wrist and clips to the PC, dispersing any static to a broader area, and eliminating possible damage to your computer's internal components.

- **Eliminate static.** Special computer chairmats can be used in your office to drain static charges and then disperse them into the atmosphere before they can harm your PC. Look for a cordless chairmat to avoid possible tripping, and one that has ramped edges so chairs can roll on and off easily. Ensure that it grips the flooring firmly to eliminate gradual slippage.

Electrical Components

Electricity powers your computer. Make sure it's safe and efficient.

- **Dealing with power outages.** Uninterruptible power supplies (UPSs) provide power for only a short time, allowing a system to be powered-down safely. Ideally, choose a network-grade power generator that automatically saves data and shuts down your system during power failures—vital if you leave your computer on continually. Look for one with multiple power outlets, noise filtration, multi-step surge protection, and a total equipment protection guarantee.
- **Add surge protectors.** If you don't have a UPS with surge protection, add a designated surge protector. Make sure your peripherals, like a printer, modem, and scanner, are also protected by plugging them into the surge protector. While you can buy surge protectors for $20 or less, steer clear from cheaper models that fall short when it comes to the level of protection and the warranty. Some come in the form of power strips, but the best surge protectors will include a static "stopper" and noise protector from electromagnetic and radio frequency devices. A good surge protector costs about $50 and has a UL 1449 surge protection rating of 330 volts stamped on the product or box. Look for a model with a fax outlet, a long cord, and a continuously powered outlet so it can't be accidentally switched off.
- **Share peripherals easily.** This auto bi-directional data switch from Linksys lets two users share a printer or other peripherals, automatically. Use one from Linksys that has an electronic data switch so the machine(s) will switch automatically and you'll never have to leave your desk to manually operate a switch yourself. The switch should also queue print jobs. A two-way switch lets your PC receive data from the peripheral. Check out the Linksys Web site for more information (`http://www.linksys.com`).

- **Power strips light the way.** Power strips help minimize the *outlet octopus* syndrome. Look for strips with a lighted on/off switch and a built-in circuit breaker to protect your equipment from power surges. Some even have space for the extra wide plugs that are so common among computer peripherals, like speakers. If you have children, look for power strips with safety covers.
- **Printer energy saver.** Put your printer to sleep and save electricity. A printer energy saver powers the printer down when it is idle, using only 1.5 watts, and cutting its electricity usage in half. When purchasing a printer energy saver, look for one with built-in buffers to capture the incoming data you may be sending to the printer while it is still warming up.
- **Strip away static.** Antistatic PC pads and strips minimize the risk of discharging static from your body to your computer. Antistatic strips adhere to the keyboard and should be touched before typing or doing anything else with your PC. Antistatic pads are also available for this same purpose and are about the size of a mouse pad.
- **Phone outlet adapters increase outlet space.** Avoid the cost and frustration of installing multiple phone jacks by adding two- or three-plug phone jack line adapters. To maximize their potential, buy two in different widths and install them so one is on top of the other. This combination lets up to three lines plug into a one-line phone jack without noticeably degrading transmissions. This is particularly useful for a phone, fax, and modem combination.
- **Flat plugs help you use outlets in tight spots.** Flat plugs (on extension cords) that are about 1/4 to 1/2 inch thick, let you plug in multiple normal-sized plugs, and are useful when trying to use those hard-to-reach outlets behind furniture or in tight corners.
- **Organize your cables.** Between the PC and the wall, cable ties or heat-activated shrink tubes are not only useful, but safer. For open areas, choose either cable organizers or rug strips, depending upon the number of cables you are running. Before buying, gather the measurements of your bundled cables (in diameter) so you will know how much space you need in whichever organizer you decide to use.

Cleaning

It's these little things that will extend the life of your computer and peripherals.

- **Protect keyboards from spills.** Keyboard skins—molded, plastic keyboard covers—slip snugly over keyboards to allow typing and data input, while still protecting the keyboard from spills, dust, and smoke. Look for a snug fit and a flexible, transparent, tear-resistant "fabric." Make sure the keyboard skin allows users to type easily, without affecting adjacent keys or key response time. Hundreds of different skins are made to fit virtually any keyboard.
- **Dust protection.** Dust is one of your PC's greatest enemies. After you power down, slip a dust cover over the monitor, computer case, and keyboard. This is especially important if you open any windows near your PC. For maximum protection, look for waterproof, heat dissipating covers, with an antistatic, cotton-backed vinyl to eliminate the static discharge that may occur when removing vinyl covers.
- **Keyboard vacuums eliminate static.** Vacuuming the dust from your keyboard is a great idea, but only if you avoid discharging static electricity. Choose a keyboard vacuum specifically designed for PCs. It should include toner pickup capabilities, a crevice attachment, and a filtration system to prevent redistributing the dust.
- **Clean impossible-to-reach places.** Dusting gas removes dust and dirt particles, including microscopic contaminates and metallic oxide deposits inside your computer case. Add an extension tube to reach tight spots. Combine this procedure with a regular and thorough external cleaning of the PC and your office. Use dusting gas only in a well-ventilated area. (Dusting gas does not harm the ozone layer.)
- **Repel dirt with screen cleaners.** Static attracts dirt. So, when you clean your monitor's screen, choose a multipurpose, antistatic cleaner to remove dirt and static. Be careful though, some cleaners can harm antiglare or laptop computer screens. Antistatic products are available in spray cans, sheets, and wipes. For more economical cleaning, buy a computer cleaning kit that includes a surface cleaner, glass cleaner, cleaning swabs, and lint-free cloths.
- **Filter the air.** Remove up to 99.97 percent of the airborne dust, pollen, and smoke from your office with a portable air cleaner. Choose a model that fits your room and has a quiet, variable-speed fan and an effective filter (that is also easy to change).

On the Surface

Maximize your space with these tips.

- **Hide your keyboard.** A good keyboard drawer has several functions. It should include a built-in wrist rest, fit most standard keyboard models, lock firmly in the extended position, and offer adjustable heights. Additionally, it should have organization space for pens, paper clips, etc. Choose one with a table-top or under-desk mount.
- **Multipurpose monitor stand.** Modular monitor riser systems let you elevate your monitor to the desired height, and include a side-mount copyholder, speaker trays, a media storage rack, and a sliding storage drawer. Look for speaker trays that hold several different sizes of speakers.
- **Monitor platform that adds flexibility.** Look for an adjustable monitor platform with a 360-degree rotation, that can hold 60lbs. securely—even during earthquakes. Look for secure pivot points that will ensure that the monitor arm maintains the position you chose, plus rubber traction pads to keep the monitor from slipping off its stand.
- **Adjustable mouse tray reduces strain.** Look for a mouse tray that swivels out of sight and lets you adjust both the horizontal and vertical positions. It should have a smooth surface and sturdy construction. And, it should have at least a 180-degree swivel feature and, ideally, a palm rest.
- **Add a mouse drawer.** If you need a keyboard drawer, a mouse drawer probably is also a good idea and a way to save even more desktop space. The drawer attaches underneath the work surface and should include wrist and palm rests, as well as the ability to slide out smoothly and lock firmly into place to provide a stable surface.
- **Computer case stand increases desk space.** Computer case stands let you turn desktop computer cases sideways, like towers, thereby increasing desk space. Look for a stand that fits your computer case snugly and is wide enough to prevent the computer case from tipping over. Foam pads or rubberized grippers hold the computer case securely in place and avoid scratching it or the desktop surface.
- **Swing the phone out of the way.** Maximize useable desk space with a rotating phone stand that lets you put the phone exactly where you want it, without taking up desk space. Look for a retractable arm with 360 degrees of swivel mobility and about 20 degrees of tilt. The phone stand should also have a rubber surface to prevent the phone from sliding off.

- **Speaker stands hold speakers firmly.** Speaker stands can elevate your speakers and place them adjacent to your monitor. But if your monitor is tilted, the speakers may be knocked off easily. Look for stands that fit your monitor and hold the speakers firmly in place, regardless of the monitor's tilt or swivel position.
- **Paper holders reduce neck strain.** Look for a paper holder that handles several sheets of letter or legal size paper and displays the paper at your eye level. It should also work equally well on either side of your PC. Extended arm paper holders should tilt and swivel, as well as have a guide that adjusts so it even holds one loose sheet of paper securely. If the paper holder is metallic, it should have an antistatic surface.
- **Use a paper holder for your laptop computer.** A laptop computer paper holder removes the strain of looking down constantly when entering data into a laptop. Look for one that clips on easily, folds away neatly when not in use, and holds papers firmly. Some models fit desktop computer monitors also. Ensure that one can be reattached and removed easily, time after time.
- **Fabric clips replace pins.** For cubicle dwellers, clips specially designed for fabric office panels keep notes handy, without damaging the fabric panels. One note of warning, however, they're hard to find. The brand we finally found at an office supply store was called Future Klip.
- **Reduce monitor glare.** A monitor filter should reduce 99 percent of the glare and 99.9 percent of the ELF and VLF radiation. The filter should also include antistatic parts, as well as tinted glass. Filters can snap on or be mounted with Velcro or other adhesive accessories.
- **Add lighting.** Choose a desk lamp with at least two lighting levels, plus height and swivel adjustments, and an adjustable lamp head. A shade will diffuse light over a wider area than a lamp with a bare bulb. Ensure that the lamp has a heavy base or that it clamps securely to a surface.

Media Storage

Organization cannot be underestimated.

- **Organize disks logically.** Hounded by disks? Disk filing sheets let you organize disks logically in a three-ring binder and allow you to add new sheets according to application name or version number. In addition, look for filing sheets with write-on labels.

- **CD carrying cases eliminate the need for jewel cases.** Discard bulky jewel cases. Instead, use special CD cases that require a fraction of the space of jewel cases, but still effectively protect CDs. Wetsuit-style cases are rugged, washable, and padded with slip-resistant surfaces. Most can store about 24 CDs safely.
- **Lift-out trays maximize filing space.** Create a second level within your deep file drawers by inserting a lift-out disk storage tray. Expect one 4.75″ × 13″ × 4.5″ tray to hold about 80 disks. Look for a tray with a divider and numerous slots to hold items neatly.
- **Modular filing system grows gradually.** Flip-top boxes are fine for a few disks or CDs, but they can be quickly outgrown. Pull-out drawers snap together thereby letting your media filing system grow one drawer at a time. Some drawers can also be combined into one system that stores disks, tapes, and CDs.

Ergonomics

Keep your office environment safe.

- **Design your office efficiently.** For a permanent office, consider a wrap-around desk with two work surfaces—one for your PC and another for your paperwork. Make sure you can position papers on either side of the PC so that you have extra room to spread out your work. Ideally, it should also have a keyboard drawer and built-in file drawers.
- **Workstation desks hold it all.** If space is cramped, consider one fairly large desk for your PC, printer, and related supplies. Make sure it has plenty of leg room when you're seated, plus a sturdy keyboard drawer that glides out smoothly into the extended position. Another thing to consider is finding a workstation desk that has the ability to place the monitor on either the left or right side of the desk. If you opt for an ergonomic view-down monitor position, ensure that there is enough space to see the monitor easily between the keyboard and other items, such as shelves.
- **Rest that aching back.** Add a lumbar support to a standard office chair to relieve some of the strain of lengthy computing work. Look for an adjustable back rest that seems to mold to your back size for maximum support, as well as one that is sized according to the type of office chair you're using. Ideally, a fabric back rest should be machine washable for easy cleaning.

- **Adjust your sitting position with a footrest.** Using a footrest will automatically cause you to change your sitting position, relieving tired muscles from the strain of sitting improperly. If you feet often are cold, look for a heated footrest. Any footrest you buy should also be examined to make sure it is easily adjustable with your height and holds itself into position firmly (without the hazard of sliding out from under you).
- **Force yourself to sit up straight.** A hot item with chiropractors in the 1980s, the back chair—a seat with a knee rest, but no back support—forces users to place their weight on their knees and their hips, relieving pressure from their spine. Look for a chair with an adjustable height and seat, as well as plenty of padding. Check its padding to ensure that bolts cannot be felt when sitting. For occasional use, choose a folding model.
- **Use an adjustable task chair.** A good computer chair should have high-density foam and include a swivel seat and casters. Everything about the chair should be adjustable: its built-in lumbar support, the height and tilt of the seat, and the back height and tilt. Even the arm height should be adjustable so that the chair can be fitted perfectly to match anyone's individual needs. Seat adjustments should have a pneumatic jack for making smooth adjustments.
- **Get a massage.** Some companies offer a 15-minute massage as a benefit. Really! If your company doesn't offer this benefit, check out Panasonic's Web site (`http://www.panasonic.com`) and look at their Shiatsu Massage Lounger as another possible alternative. It's a reclining chair with a full foot rest for leg massage, along with fingertip controls and different types of massage motions. The Shiatsu Massage Lounger also includes tapping, rolling, and kneading—even more attractive for those with chronic back pain. Some chairs such as this even come with timers. After a day of PC troubleshooting, this is just what the doctor ordered.
- **Home automation is simple.** Look for a home automation system that is expandable and includes a universal remote and keychain remote, controls for specific hours as well as dusk to dawn controls, and a battery backup system to restore programmed events after power outages. Ensure that additional timers for any device you wish to automate are readily available and that the system can accommodate at least 100 devices.

- **Decrease noise with a printer sound cover.** If the clatter of a printer annoys you, decrease it with a sound cover. Look for a cover that promises at least a 90 to 95 percent sound reduction and includes a built-in cooling fan. Many models also hold spare paper, toner cartridges, and other consumables. Floor models and desktop stands are also available.

Fight Carpal Tunnel

An especially large concern these days, carpal tunnel syndrome can be a painful affliction. Avoid it at all costs.

- **Wrist rests combat carpal tunnel syndrome.** For maximum comfort, choose a padded, adjustable wrist rest that slips easily under the keyboard. Rigid, padded, and waved foam designs are available, as well as special rests for laptop computer users.
- **Hand and wrist exercisers relieve tension.** Latex or gel-filled exercisers relieve tension as you squeeze them by increasing blood flow into the fingers, hands, wrists, and forearms. Look for an exerciser that fits your hand comfortably, feels good to your touch, and holds your interest. Keep it by your phone for spontaneous use and stress relief.
- **Mouse cradle cuts fatigue.** Like wrist supports, mouse cradles reduce the stress that causes repetitive motion injuries. Look for a mouse cradle with a smooth surface and adjustable heights.

Are You Experienced?

Now you can...

☑ **Maximize your work and play potential with hundreds of cost-saving, time-saving, fun-exploiting tips!**

APPENDIX A

Manufacturer Index

In the course of this book we've talked about how to upgrade just about every part of a computer. Before you dive into an upgrade you'll want to check the prices and features of the components and peripherals you're considering buying. For example, you may want to contact some of the manufacturers on this list to find out about purchasing a new motherboard or the cost of upgrading your RAM.

NOTE NOTE NOTE NOTE NOTE NOTE NOTE NOTE NOTE NOTE NOTE NOTE NOTE NOTE NOTE

Keep in mind that the computer marketplace changes constantly—some of the information on this list may have changed since we contacted these vendors.

CD-ROM Drives

Matsushita Electric Corp.

1 Panasonic Way
Secaucus, NJ 07094
(800) 726-2797
(201) 348-7000
Fax: (201) 392-6007
`http://www.panasonic.com`

NEC Computer Systems Division

1414 Massachusetts Ave.
Boxborough, MA 01719
(800) 632-4636
(508) 264-8000
Fax: (508) 635-4666
`http://www.nec.com`

Pioneer New Media Technologies Inc.

2265 E. 220th St.
Long Beach, CA 90810
(800) 444-6784
(310) 952-2111
Faxback: (310) 952-2309
`http://www.pioneerusa.com`

Plextor Inc.

4255 Burton Drive
Santa Clara, CA 95054
(800) 886-3935
(408) 980-1838
Fax: (408) 986-1010
`http://www.plextor.com`

Sony Electronics Inc.

3300 Zanker Road
San Jose, CA 95134
(800) 352-7669
(408) 432-1600
Faxback: (800) 766-9022
`http://www.sel.sony.com/sel`

CPUs

Cyrix Corp.

P.O. Box 850118
Richardson, TX 75085
(800) 340-7501
(972) 968-8387
Faxback: (972) 968-8609
`http://www.cyrix.com`

Evergreen Technologies

806 N.W. Buchanan
Corvallis, OR 97330
(800) 733-0934
(541) 757-0934
Faxback: (541) 757-7350
`http://www.evertech.com`

IBM

Route 100
Somers, NY 10589
(800) 426-2968
(914) 766-1900
Faxback: (800) 426-4329
`http://www.ibm.com`

Intel Corp.

2111 N.E. 25th St.
Hillsboro, OR 97124
(800) 321-4044; (503) 696-8080
Faxback: (800) 525-3019
`http://www.intel.com`

Kingston Technology Corp.

17600 Newhope St.
Fountain Valley, CA 92708
(800) 835-6575
(714) 435-2600
Fax: (800) 435-0056
`http://www.kingston.com`

Hard Drives

Conner Peripherals

See *Seagate*.

Insight Enterprises Inc.

6820 South Harl Avenue
Tempe, AZ 75283
(800) 927-2931
(602) 902-1000; (602) 333-3000
Fax: (602) 902-1153
`http://www.insight.com`

Iomega Corp.

1821 W. Iomega Way
Roy, UT 84067
(800) 697-8833
(801) 770-2028
Faxback: (801) 778-5763
`http://www.iomega.com`

Maxtor Corp.

510 Cottonwood Drive
Milpitas, CA 95035
(800) 262-9867
(408) 435-7884
Faxback: (800) 262-9867
`http://www.maxtor.com`

O.R. Technologies Inc.

42 W. Campbell Ave.
Campbell, CA 95008
(408) 886-3000
Faxback: (888) 286-6422
`http://www.ortechnology.com`

Quantum

500 McCarthy Blvd.
Milpitas, CA 95035
(800) 624-5545
(408) 894-4000
Faxback: (800) 434-7532
`http://www.quantum.com`

Seagate

3081 Zanker Road
San Jose, CA 95134
(800) 732-4283 (automated)
(408) 456-4500
Faxback: (408) 456-4501
`http://www.seagate.com`

Western Digital

8105 Irvine Center Drive
Irvine, CA 92618
(800) 832-4778
(714) 932-5000
Faxback: (714) 932-4300
`http://www.wdc.com`

Memory

Hewlett-Packard

3000 Hanover St.
Palo Alto, CA 94304
(800) 752-0900
(415) 857-1501
Faxback: (800) 333-1917
`http://www.hp.com`

Intel Corp.

2200 Mission College Blvd.
P.O. Box 58119
Santa Clara, CA 95052-8119
(800) 628-8686
(408) 765-8080
Faxback: (800) 525-3019
`http://www.intel.com`

Toshiba America Information Systems Inc.

9740 Irvine Blvd.
P.O. Box 19724
Irvine, CA 92618
(800) 334-3445
(714) 583-3000
Faxback: (800) 457-7777
http://www.toshiba.com

Motherboards

American Megatrends Inc.

6145-F Northbelt Parkway
Norcross, GA 30071-2976
(800) 828-9264
(770) 246-8600
Faxback: (770) 246-8787
http://www.megatrends.com

Micronics Computers & Orchid Technologies

4565 Northport Loop West
Fremont, CA 94538
(800) 577-0977
(510) 651-2300
Faxback: (510) 661-3199
http://www.micronics.com

RAM

First Source International

7 Journey
Aliso Viejo, CA 92656
(800) 761-9866
(714) 448-7750
Fax: (714) 448-7760
http://www.firstsource.com

Ingram Micro Inc.

1759 Wehrle Drive
Williamsville, NY 14221
(800) 456-8000
(716) 633-3600
Faxback: (714) 566-1900
`http://www.ingrammicro.com`

Kingston Technology

17600 Newhope St.
Fountain Valley, CA 92708
(800) 337-8410
(714) 435-2600
Faxback: (800) 435-0056
`http://www.kingston.com`

PNY Electronics

299 Webro Rd.
Parsippany, NJ 07054
(800) 234-4597
(201) 438-6300
Faxback: (800) 234-4597
`http://www.pny.com`

Multimedia Kits

ATI Technologies Inc.

33 Commerce Valley Drive E.
Thornhill, Ontario, Canada
L3T 7N6
(905) 882-2626
Faxback: (905)882-2600
`http://www.atitech.com`

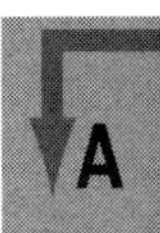

Aztech Labs

45645 Northport Loop West
Fremont, CA 94538
(800) 886-8859
(510) 623-8988
Faxback: (510) 623-8989
`http://www.aztechca.com`

Creative Labs Inc.

1901 McCarthy Blvd.
Milpitas, CA 95035
(800) 998-1000
(408) 428-6600
Fax: (405) 742-6611
`http://www.creaf.com`

Diamond Multimedia Systems Inc.

2880 Junction Ave.
San Jose, CA 95134
(800) 468-5846
(408) 325-7000
Faxback: (800) 380-0030
`http://www.diamondmm.com`

Graphics Cards

ATI Technologies

33 Commerce Valley Drive E.

Thornhill, Ontario, Canada
L3T 7N6
(905) 882-2626
Faxback: (905)882-2600
`http://www.atitech.com`

Boca Research

1377 Clint Moore Road
Boca Raton, FL 33487
(561) 997-6227
Faxback: (591) 994-5848
`http://www.bocaresearch.com/`

Diamond Multimedia Systems, Inc.

2880 Junction Ave.
San Jose, CA 95134
(800) 468-5846
(408) 325-7000
Faxback: (800) 380-0030
`http://www.diamondmm.com`

Orchid Technology

See *Micronics Computers Inc.*

VideoLogic Inc.

1001 Bay Hill Drive, Suite 310
San Bruno, CA 94066
(800) 578-5644
(415) 875-4167
Faxback: (800) 203-8587
`http://www.videologic.com`

Sound Cards

Aztech Labs Inc.

45645 Northport Loop East
Fremont, CA 94538
(800) 886-8859
(510) 623-8989
Faxback: (510) 353-4325
`http://www.aztechca.com`

Creative Labs Inc.

1901 McCarthy Blvd.
Milpitas, CA 95035
(800) 998-1000
(408) 428-6600
Fax: (405) 742-6611
`http://www.creaf.com`

Logitech Inc.

6505 Kaiser Drive
Fremont, CA 94555
(800) 231-7717
(510) 795-8500
Faxback: (800) 245-0000
`http://www.logitech.com`

Turtle Beach Systems

5 Odell Plaza
Yonkers, NY 10701-1406
(914) 966-0600
Faxback: (914) 966-0600
`http://www.tbeach.com`

Operating Systems

IBM

Route 100
Somers, NY 10589
(800) 426-2968
(914) 766-1900
Faxback: (800) 426-4329
`http://www.ibm.com`

Microsoft Corp.

One Microsoft Way
Redmond, WA 98052
(800) 426-9400
(206) 882-8080
Faxback: (800) 936-4100
`http://www.microsoft.com`

Index

Note to the Reader: First level entries are in **bold**. Page numbers in **bold** indicate the principal discussion of a topic or the definition of a term. Page numbers in *italic* indicate illustrations.

Numbers

A

B

C

D

E

F

G

H

I

J

K

L

M

N

P

Q

R

S

T

U

V

W

Z